Teaching
Foreign-Language Skills

Kristin Lems

Wilga M. Rivers

Teaching
Foreign-Language Skills

Second Edition

The University of Chicago Press

Chicago and London

THE UNIVERSITY OF CHICAGO PRESS, CHICAGO 60637
THE UNIVERSITY OF CHICAGO PRESS, LTD., LONDON
© 1968, 1981 by The University of Chicago
All rights reserved
Published 1968. Second Edition 1981
Printed in the United States of America
85 84 83 82 81   1 2 3 4 5

WILGA M. RIVERS is Professor of Romance Languages and Coordinator of Language Instruction, Harvard University. Among her many publications are *The Psychologist and the Foreign-Language Teacher* (University of Chicago Press, 1964) and a series, *Practical Guides to the Teaching of French/German/Spanish* (and other languages).

Library of Congress Cataloging in Publication Data

Rivers, Wilga M
   Teaching foreign-language skills.

   Bibliography: p.
   Includes index.
   1. Languages, Modern—Study and teaching.   I. Title.
PB35.R43   1981   407   80-24993
ISBN 0-226-72907-7
    0-226-72098-5 (cloth)

Contents

Contents

Contents

Preface:
For Students and Teachers

This book has been written for all who are interested in lively and effective language teaching—those following a course of preparation for future language teaching and those, more experienced, who would like to improve their teaching by drawing from more recent thinking in the field. Some will be foreign-language teachers in the sense that the language they teach is not generally used in the community from which their students come; for their students the work of learning is for the most part a formal one. Others will be teachers of a second language—one which is in general use for communication in the community but is not the native language of the students. In this case, what is learned through instruction and individual study will be reinforced and supplemented by hearing and using the language outside of the formal setting of the school or college. It has not been possible within the scope of this book to deal in detail with the specific problems of bilingual classes, although much of the material in this book will be useful in any language-learning situation. There are references in the Bibliography for those with a special interest in bilingual schooling, and these will supplement what is provided in the text.

Some of you will expect a book of this type to tell you exactly what techniques to use to present any particular aspect of the language you are teaching to students at a specific level. You may be surprised to read instead a theoretical discussion of the linguistic and pedagogical background to the teaching of each language skill. This book is intended to prepare you for a teaching career, not for the lessons you may have to give in your first few weeks in the classroom, although there is much information for this period of your career as well. You will find a great deal of information on specific techniques for classroom teaching, but the desirability of employing these techniques will, in each case, be discussed in the light of what is known about the way people learn languages and the nature of the skill to be taught, as well as their suitability for the achievement of the objectives the students have in mind when enrolling in the course.

During your teaching career you will be faced from time to time with changes in emphases and recommendations from various quarters for the adoption of new procedures. Your studies in methodology should give you an understanding of the foundations of foreign- and second-language pedagogy, so that you may be able to read about and intelligently assess new trends as they develop, with sufficient flexibility to adjust to changing circumstances. You will then be well prepared to think out for yourselves new ways of presenting language material which are consistent with the aims you have set yourself but which are also valid procedures from a theoretical point of view. It is the opportunity to innovate in this way with confidence which will keep your interest in your chosen vocation at a high level.

It is intended that this book be used in association with regular visits to classrooms to watch experienced teachers coping with the types of problems discussed in these pages. Such visits will make the material in each chapter more real to you and will be a source of ideas on how to approach specific problems which will arise during a language lesson. Practical hints of this type have little place in a method textbook, partly because the particular needs of readers in this area are unpredictable, and partly because original ways of presenting some structure, or varying the classroom presentation at some specific point, are best acquired from discussion with teachers whom you have watched at work. During your student-teacher training you should begin to make notes of interesting and potentially useful ideas gathered while you have been observing other teachers' classes.

Many of you may wonder why no examples in any particular language are given in this book. There are several reasons for this decision on the part of the author. First of all, the theoretical and practical discussion is intended to guide teachers of many different languages. It would not be feasible to include examples from more than four or five of these languages (and even these would make the book inordinately long); yet even then the examples given might not be the ones you really needed. To make up for this deficiency, the author has produced, with collaborators, a series of *Practical Guides to the Teaching of French/German/Spanish/English as a Second or Foreign Language** (with Hebrew in preparation). That companion series does not duplicate the information in this book, but is intended to complement it with illustrative examples and discussions of problems of particular languages. The instructor in the methods class will also work on the practical application of the ideas expounded in the text to the specific languages which will be taught to the students. Further material important for teachers of certain languages is given in the Annotated Reading Lists near the end of each chapter, in the Bibliography, and in the footnotes.

*New York and Oxford: Oxford University Press, 1975–78. (The *Guides* are abbreviated here as *PG*'s.)

This second edition is a complete reworking of the 1968 edition. The general division of the material into chapters and the order of progression from theory to practice have been retained. Faithful users of the book will find that much they have valued in the past is still available to them. However, much water has flowed under the bridge since the sixties. Views of language learning and language teaching have evolved, as have theories of linguistics and psychology. Students' needs and interests are no longer the same. New circumstances have required new responses from language teachers. It is hoped that this revised edition will meet the needs of the new generation of teachers coming into the profession and help seasoned and enthusiastic professionals to keep in touch with new trends, while retaining a firm grip on what has proved effectual in their past experience.

Some may object that most students are not in classes which are homogeneous units, advancing in planned sequence, as much of this book seems to presuppose. The writer, an experienced teacher of languages, is well aware of this fact, and hopes that informed theoretical, as well as practical, discussion will help the teacher to see what kinds of adaptations existing realities impose.

There are some changes in format. Provocative questions have been inserted, in boldface type, in the text of each chapter. These are intended to enliven class discussion, while giving the lone reader a feeling of involvement in the developing theme. At the end of the chapters, Research and Discussion sections propose more substantial projects, which may serve as term assignments or small research projects for individual teachers who would like to find out more on their own. (A Research and Discussion project or a suggested reading preceded by an asterisk involves material not discussed in the body of the chapter.)

Naturally, some teachers will wish to present the material in an order different from that in the book. This applies particularly to some sections of chapter 14 (Early Language Learning; The Textbook; Vocabulary Learning; Language for Specific Purposes; Planning the Language Lesson; and Classroom Management). These topics will be studied independently at the moment when they are most needed by the students.

This book is, then, only part of a course in methods of language teaching. It is intended as a source of ideas for discussion in and out of class, and as a guide to further study for all who read it. Reading and discussion are, of course, not enough. It is the author's earnest hope that these will be followed by enlightened experimentation in the classroom to see how the ideas in the book work out in practice.

Preface

May all my readers enjoy, as much as I have, long careers as teachers of languages.

Finally, my sincere thanks are due to Jane Bourque, Phyllis Dragonas, Anne Huguenard, Gladys Lipton, Helene Loew, Marlies Mueller, and David Stern, who willingly gave suggestions for improving certain sections of the book; and to Tobie Kranitz, Pat Giersz, Betsy Levitas, and Ann Boruvka for unflagging support in the onerous task of preparing the manuscript.

WILGA M. RIVERS

Harvard University,
Cambridge, Massachusetts
September 1980

1· Objectives of Language Teaching

International understanding, intellectual training, cultural enrichment, interpersonal communication, language for practical use, a feeling for language (our own and those of others): amid a welter of such
slogans, trainee teachers approach their foreign-language or second-
language teaching careers with some understandable uncertainty.
What, they ask themselves, is the role of language learning in the
educational program, and in what ways should they present a new
language to their students to make it most useful and interesting to
them?

As a part of initial training, trainees are usually sent into several
classrooms to see the way experienced teachers are approaching their
task. Let us join some trainees in an inconspicuous place at the back
of the room.

Classroom A
In the first room, our trainee teachers take a seat out of the view of
the students and open notepads. The students, seated in rows, are
opening their language textbooks and preparing for the day's lesson.
They are about to begin a new section. Before them on the page is
a *reading selection* with, above it, two or three long columns of new
vocabulary items with native-language equivalents. These the students have been asked to learn by heart the night before. As this
memorization is a rather boring chore, some of the students are hastily
babbling over to themselves some of the words they have not yet
learned. The lesson begins with a quick written test of these new
words. Students, when asked to give their answers, spell out the
words letter by letter in their native language, because they feel shy
and uncertain about attempting strange sounds in front of their classmates. (They have evidently not been taught the names of the letters
in the new language, so they cannot use those.) The teacher is not
very satisfied with the result of this quiz, but the work for the day
must be covered, so the lesson moves on. The students are asked to
read out in the new language the selection in the book before them.
One after another they stumble through the sentences. After a while
this reading around the class is omitted because the procedure is too
painful for the teacher and too embarrassing for the students. For a
few sentences the teacher reads the passage aloud to the class instead.

1

Then the students are asked to look over the rest of the passage silently, because the reading-aloud process seems rather wasteful of class time for the little it achieves.

Then begins the process of *translation*. One after another, students translate the sentences of the passage into their native language, with occasional help from the teacher. Things are progressing well: the teacher can now pass on to what is clearly the real business of the day. On the chalkboard there is a lucid outline of the use of the past tense, examples of which have been artificially and cunningly worked into the reading passage. Warming to the task, the teacher explains in great detail in the native language the traditional *rules* for the use of this particular tense in all the logically possible situations. Where these explanations involve terminology with which the students are presumed not to be familiar, some time is taken to teach this terminology as it applies to the grammar of the native language, and it is then applied to the new language. The students copy into their books various rules, examples, and what seem to them to be even more numerous exceptions.

The teacher asks a few questions. When the students appear to have grasped the point of the grammatical exposition, they settle down to spend the rest of the lesson on the not-too-demanding task of writing out *paradigms* and filling in blanks in *grammatical exercises,* or they translate—from their native language into the language they are learning—sentences in which the past tense is required. For this latter exercise the students are presented with sentences which have been artificially constructed to include all possible aspects of the rules being studied. Many of these sentences are very unlikely to be of real use to the students, who frequently distort the original meaning as they try to construct their own version of this strange language. Exercises the students have not finished in class and the learning of the rules and paradigms are assigned for home study, with the extra spice of a few irregular verbs and some more vocabulary items for the next day's reading selection.

As our would-be teachers move on to the next classroom, their minds go back over what they have just observed. On reflection, it occurs to them that they heard very little of the target language during the lesson—a little reading aloud at the beginning of the lesson and a few isolated words and phrases from time to time. Most of what they did hear in that language was halting and badly pronounced. "Perhaps time and further study will bring improvement," one trainee says to the others—but they wonder.

Classroom B

In the classroom down the passage, an energetic teacher comes into the room and greets the class in the language being learned. The students reply in the same language and wait expectantly. The teacher continues to *talk in the language* about objects in the classroom, to ask questions, and to give orders. As the students obey the orders they are given, they tell the class in the new language what they have been doing, and the class tells the teacher what has been performed. The lesson then develops around a picture which illustrates an *area of vocabulary* and certain activities associated with the situation depicted. In this lesson, the picture shows some people shopping. The teacher describes in the language what the students can see in the picture, demonstrating the meaning of new relational or action words by miming until the class looks enlightened. The students repeat the new words and phrases and, in response to questions, try to *form their own sentences* in the language on the model they have heard. They do this with a greater or lesser degree of accuracy according to the individual student's grasp of what has been said.

When the students appear to have understood and assimilated the area of vocabulary or usage to which they have been introduced and have shown evidence of being able to use it orally, they *read* a passage of similar content aloud from their books, reading after the teacher at first and then individually. The passage is *not translated* by the teacher or the students, but the teacher asks questions about it in the new language, to which the students reply in that language. Where further difficulties of vocabulary or structure occur, these are explained exclusively in the language being learned, and students make notes on these explanations, again in the new language. The lesson ends with a song in which the students join with gusto. Throughout the lesson there has been a great deal of *activity* by teacher and students alike. Not surprisingly the teacher, having conducted several lessons of this type during the morning, is very glad to sit down in the staff common room for a quiet cup of coffee with our observers.

On their way to classroom C, our trainee teachers begin to wonder whether the two teachers they have observed so far may be considered to be engaged in the same activity. There are more surprises in store for them upstairs.

Classroom C

Arriving a little late in the classroom on the second floor, our observers see books again very much in evidence. This time the students are using small *readers* rather than large textbooks. On looking into the reader that the teacher has given them to peruse, the trainee teachers notice that it contains a continuous reading text of some twenty pages, written in a simple style in the target language within the limits of a frequency word count.[1] As words occur in the text for the first time, they are explained in the target language at the foot of the page. The story seems to be interesting and amusing. Since this reader is new to the class, the teacher is endeavoring to interest the students in its contents. With the help of some pictures, she describes in simple sentences in the new language the setting of the story, which is in the country where the language is spoken. She talks very briefly about the main characters, writing their names on the chalkboard. To interest the students still further in the story, she reads the first section of it aloud in the language in as interesting a way as possible, with the students following the text in their books. She asks in the native language a few *questions* about what she has been reading and then tells the students to reread the section silently, looking for answers to certain questions which they were unable to answer. When they have reread this part of the text, she asks them more questions, this time in the language they are learning; the students find the answers in the text, framing their replies in the target language.

For the second half of the lesson, the students form working pairs, or choose to work on their own. They settle down to read as much of the story as they can during the remainder of the lesson. A quiet murmur is heard from various parts of the room as the students concentrate on their task. As difficulties arise, they seek the teacher's help. As they reach the end of certain divisions of the reader, they take the book to the teacher, who asks them questions in the native language about what they have just read. Sometimes she gives them a short true-false test in the language being learned to see whether they have understood the details of the story. As the lesson draws to a close, the teacher asks how many pages the various pairs or individuals have read, and congratulates those who have read the most. For home study, the students are asked to write short answers in the target language to questions on the section they have been reading.

Classroom D
From the classroom across the way comes the sound of voices. The lesson has already begun. As our observers settle down, they hear the class repeating sentences in the new language in chorus, imitating the pronunciation and intonation of the teacher. They are learning the

1. For a discussion of frequency word counts for different languages, see *PG's*, chap. 6.

various utterances in a *dialogue* based on an everyday incident in the life of a student in the country where the language is spoken. Some sketches illustrating the meaning of the sentences the students are repeating have been drawn on the chalkboard. The students are not looking at these clues, but are intent on watching the lip movements and expressions of the teacher. From time to time, however, individual students will glance at the sketches as if to reassure themselves that they really understand the meaning of what they are saying. The students' textbooks are closed.

When a pair of sentences is being repeated well in chorus, the teacher asks halves of the class to repeat this section, one in response to the other. When these smaller groups are repeating well, he asks the students to repeat the sentences by rows. Since the sentences seem now to be well memorized, the teacher calls on individuals to repeat the new sentences, sometimes in association with sentences learned the preceding day. If the individuals falter, the teacher returns to interchanges between small groups or reverts to choral repetition until the difficult part has been mastered. After a certain amount of material has been learned in this fashion, students act out the conversational interchange in pairs. When the dialogue sentences are well learned, the students open their books and practice reading together after the teacher what they have just been repeating.

The time has now come for closer study of parts of the dialogue sentences, so the teacher moves on to the *drilling of structural patterns*. The class repeats several times after the teacher a pattern sentence containing a structural element which the students will need to be able to use quite flexibly in new utterances. The students then repeat several other sentences of identical structure but with minimal changes of vocabulary. At a word cue from the teacher, the class constructs a slightly different sentence on the same structural pattern. At another cue, the structure is again produced with a further slight variation of lexical content. Seven or eight changes of this type are effected by the class in chorus as they continue their practice. At one stage the class appears to hesitate, and some students look puzzled. At this point the teacher makes a short comment on the sentences being constructed, drawing attention to what they have in common. The practice then continues with greater assurance on the part of the students. When the choral repetition is ringing out clearly and confidently, the teacher gives the cues to small groups, and finally to individuals, to make sure that all have assimilated the uses of the structure being drilled.

As a consolidating activity, the students perform a chain drill. One student asks his neighbor on the right a question similar to one in the dialogue. She replies using a structure from a dialogue learned earlier in the week. She then turns to her neighbor on the right and asks him a question which she has based on something they have been learning. This chaining activity continues until one student falters. The class laughs good-naturedly, and the teacher starts a new chain in another part of the class. For home study, the students take away cassettes on which the dialogue they have been learning has been recorded. They will play this material over to help them memorize the dialogue sentences thoroughly. The teacher also asks them to transcribe several times certain words and phrases from their textbook which will present difficulties for them in writing.

As our observers make their way back to the teachers' common room, they reflect on what they have seen during the day. Why, they ask each other, have all these language teachers been conducting their lessons so differently when they must surely be moving toward a common goal? Over coffee they endeavor to find out what the four teachers have been trying to achieve.

Teacher A seems a little disconcerted when asked about her long-range objectives in teaching a new language. "It is tremendously important that the students know their grammar," she says, "and they'll never pass their examinations if they cannot write a good, accurate translation." Beyond this, she seems to think that the aims of her lessons are self-evident: "They must know their past tense," she adds, in a way which precludes further discussion.

Teacher B says: "I want them to be able to speak the language and understand it, and I want them to know something about the people who speak the language. I don't want them to translate. I want them to think in the new language as they do in their own, whether they are engaged in conversation, reading, or writing."

"But our students will rarely have the opportunity to speak the language," interrupts teacher C. "When they leave my classes, I want them to be able to pick up a book or a magazine in the language and read it without having to stop and translate every phrase or look up every second word in a bilingual dictionary. This is the most important thing for them to learn in their language class."

"I want them to be able to do all these things," says Teacher D quietly. "I want to train them carefully in all the language skills: in listening and speaking as well as in reading and writing. I want to lay solid foundations for these skills by giving them confidence in the active use of the structural patterns of the language. I try to train them in each skill in succession in relation to any section of the work, so that what has been learned in one skill area acts as a foundation for learning in the next. And I am most anxious for them to understand the cultural patterns and ways of thinking of the speakers of the language," he adds. "I believe they become conscious of this as they learn to think in the patterns of another language, but I work it into the dialogues too."

"Perhaps you've all got something there that you can share with each other," says the department head thoughtfully as she gathers her books for the next lesson.

- **Analyze a class you watched recently. Does it match any of the models described? In what ways? If not, write a description, like those above, of what went on in the classroom.**

AIMS AND OBJECTIVES

Our observers feel bewildered. They have watched the work of four experienced teachers and have found that each of these teachers has a different combination and priority of objectives in mind. They have seen widely differing techniques for achieving these objectives even when the objectives, as stated, seemed to coincide. Where does the trainee teacher begin? At least one fact emerges clearly from the situation described: it is the teacher's objectives that determine the way the language lesson is organized.

It is objectives, then, that trainee teachers must consider first. Many teachers whose classes they will observe have never really thought through their objectives in relation to the situation in which they are teaching and to the goals of the students in their classes. Their teaching techniques consequently are diverse and imitative, drawn from many different sources. Frequently such teachers teach as they were taught by teachers who taught as they were taught, and techniques appropriate to another era, which had different objectives, are perpetuated. From time to time such teachers add a few techniques that they have seen demonstrated at a meeting, or of which they have read, but their approach to their lessons remains fundamentally unchanged. Their students may not find the lessons particularly interesting or exciting, but if they pass the examinations set by the department, their teachers are satisfied.

Such teachers continue to conduct their classes as they have always conducted them, unaware of the fact that objectives in language teaching may be changing around them and that their teaching may have become anachronistic and irrelevant to the young people who pass through their classes. With the passing of time, new situations arise for a nation and its people, or for a district and its schools, and these establish priorities of objectives for the teachers of other languages, who must be continually aware of such changes if their teaching is to be appropriate to the generation of students before them.

It is a useful exercise for teachers or trainee teachers to set down in some order of priority their long-range objectives in teaching another language. On analysis, the answers of any substantial group of teachers will usually be seen to fall into seven categories. The priorities ascribed to these categories of objectives will vary from country to country, from period to period, and from situation to situation, but each of the seven will appear, either in implicit or in explicit form, among those listed.

The seven classes of objectives are as follows:
- to develop the students' intellectual powers through the study of another language;
- to increase the students' personal culture through the study of the great literature and philosophy to which the new language is the key;
- to increase the students' understanding of how language functions and to bring them, through the study of another language, to a greater awareness of the functioning of their own language;
- to teach students to read another language with comprehension so that they may keep abreast of modern writing, research, and information;
- to give students the experience of expressing themselves within another framework, linguistically, kinesically, and culturally;
- to bring students to a greater understanding of people across national barriers, by giving them a sympathetic insight into the ways of life and ways of thinking of the people who speak the language they are learning;
- to provide students with the skills that will enable them to communicate orally, and to some degree in writing, in personal or career contexts, with the speakers of another language and with people of other nationalities who have also learned this language.

Each of these objectives has at some time or in some place predominated in the stated aims of language teachers.

The Past
It is not proposed here to set out in detail the history of language teaching. Teachers should, however, be familiar with the leading personalities and movements which have determined many of the features of the major teaching methods. They will then be able to reexamine the appropriateness of certain techniques in their own situation in full cognizance of the aims of those who first advocated them. The references in the Annotated Reading Lists at the end of

chapters 1 and 2 should be studied with close attention. The reader should note where and when a particular article or book was first published, in order to view it in perspective. From this reading it will be evident that each of the well-known language-teaching methods has derived from an educational philosophy or a pedagogical theory which has satisfied certain demands or requirements either of the period in which it flourished or of the peculiar situation of the people who adopted it.

The first aim listed, *the development of the student's intellectual powers,* was emphasized at the time when modern language teachers were trying to justify their area of study as of equal value with the study of the classical languages. As a result, modern language teaching took on many of the traditional features of the teaching of Greek and Latin. Since, at that period, faculty psychology[2] formed the basis for educational theory, it is not surprising that language teachers justified the inclusion of their subject in the educational system by asserting its value for training in memory and in the application of logical processes. In conformity with this aim, class lessons were devoted to the learning of rules and the presumably logical application of these rules in the translation of sentences which were carefully constructed to force the student to think about details of the structure and vocabulary of the new language. There was much memorizing of paradigms and lengthy vocabulary lists. As with the classical languages, pronunciation was considered of minor concern. This is what the teacher in classroom A had in mind.

The distinctive contribution of language learning to such intellectual development, in a form which other disciplines do not provide, is difficult to identify, particularly since approaches to language learning and teaching have radically changed and, in actual practice, are most diverse. Intellectual, or cognitive, development is a legitimate aim of all education, but that it is furthered specifically by the techniques described is unproven.

At a time when high school and university-level education was the province of an intellectual and social elite and career needs were less pressing for the average student, it was feasible to regard the learning

2. The mind was considered to have certain faculties (such as those of concentration, reasoning, analyzing, and remembering) which could be better trained through the study of certain subjects than others. Classical studies, philosophy, and mathematics were considered to be particularly appropriate for such mind-training. See R. F. Butts and L. A. Cremin, *A History of Education in American Culture* (New York: Henry Holt, 1953), pp. 176–79, and R. S. Woodworth, *Contemporary Schools of Psychology,* rev. ed. (New York: Ronald Press, 1948), pp. 12–13. Despite intensive research in recent years, psychologists now realize that they know very little about how the mind operates.

of another language primarily as the *key to the great literature and philosophy of another culture*. Many students in modern language courses at the advanced level had already spent a number of years in close study of the language and had studied in some detail the literature and philosophy of their own culture. With the increasing availability of advanced education for an ever-increasing proportion of the population, the great expansion in subjects available to the student for study at the high school level and beyond, and increasing competition for admission to advanced professional preparation, this situation no longer holds. Students today have much less time in which to acquire knowledge of another language as one small part of their education, yet the literature and philosophy of many cultures, quite alien from their own, interest and attract them. These they will approach through reliable translations, since it is not feasible for them to attempt to learn all the languages involved.

Although literature, in its broadest sense, will always provide interesting and thought-provoking material for language classes, this aim has become less appropriate as the principal objective for all students at other levels. Literature, in the native language and in other languages, will continue to be an important element in the general education of students, who should be encouraged to explore beyond their own language. For the full value of another literature and philosophy to be experienced in the original language, however, an advanced level of comprehension needs to have been attained, a level not all students who are interested in the language will reach while studying with us. The specialized study of the literature in another language, as distinguished from the enjoyment of what it has to offer to the general reader, will remain an important objective for those students whose special interests lie in this direction.

The Present

As we shall see, the last five of the aims listed above would appear to be the most relevant for the vast majority of the students in our language programs today. Of recent years there has been a rising interest in research into language as such, into the acquisition of language and its use by individuals, and into the way language functions within societies. This intense interest has led to a continuing reexamination of language-teaching methods. We have seen also the development of rapid communications, and the proliferation of international contacts on the group and individual level which require that citizens of today's world be able to communicate with one another. There has been a growing emphasis in many countries on the right of minority groups within societies to the use of their mother tongue in their contacts within the wider society and in the education of their children. With these changes has come a realization of the need to be able to communicate readily with people who speak other languages and to understand, sympathetically as well as intellectually, their ways of thinking and reacting. With rapid advances in all branches of knowledge, it has also become imperative for many people to be able to read some of the enormous quantity of specialized information being poured out by printing presses and computers all over the world, while, at a more modest level, one should be able to read at least instructions, directions, and the daily newspaper in the language of one's neighbors.

Since schools reflect the pressures and needs of society, each of these objectives should be kept in mind in developing a language program. The selection of objectives and the order of priority assigned to them will be determined by geographical situation, national demands, and the interests and aspirations of the types of students in our classes. These may well vary for specific courses within a program.

From one point of view, we may regard all five of these objectives as intertwined and interdependent. An understanding of the nature and uses of language is basic to a methodology which develops effective communication skills. Effective communication is impeded by lack of understanding of the culture of the speakers of the language and by personal diffidence in expressing oneself through a new medium. Fluency in reading with direct comprehension derives from the ability to think in the language, which is facilitated by active control of the communication skills of listening and speaking. For many types of reading material, mere comprehension of the printed words is valueless without the ability to interpret what one is reading in the light of cultural patterns and attitudes.

- **What are the factors in your local situation which will help you decide the principal objectives of your language teaching?**

STUDENT ATTITUDES AND INTERESTS

So far, the major emphasis of this chapter may appear to have been on the objectives of language courses as perceived by the teacher or the profession. What about the students? In the preceding discussion they have not been ignored. There have been several references to their interests and aspirations. How can we know what these are? One straightforward approach is to ask the students themselves. Rivers 1976 and in NEC 1979, Reinert 1970, and Jakobovits in NEC 1970 describe how this may be done.

We are interested in a number of things about our students.

1. Who are they? What is their background? What are their career interests? their scholastic preferences? their leisure-time occupations? their ethnic heritage? their experiences with people from different backgrounds?
2. What are their attitudes toward learning another language? Why are they learning this language at this particular time? What are their attitudes toward people who speak other languages? toward people who speak this language?[3]
3. What do they want to get from the study of this particular language at this time? Are they merely fulfilling a requirement of some kind? Are they fulfilling a requirement but hoping to get something further from the effort expended? Are they mostly interested in being able to communicate orally with speakers of the language? in reading newspapers and magazines; novels, plays, or poetry; or specialized material of some kind? in understanding films or television and radio programs? in being able to sing in the language? in understanding how people who speak the language feel about things and do things? in some other use for the language?
4. How do they prefer to learn another language? orally or through written material? through explanation or practice? on their own or with other students in small or large groups? intensively or over a longer period? with carefully structured materials and regular correction or through attempts at immediate use with little explanation or correction? with or without technological aids (cassettes, computer programs, slides)?

After we have found out who our students are and how they feel about language learning and language courses, we are in a much better position to decide appropriate objectives in a particular teaching situation, select a methodology, and design courses which provide what our students are seeking.

- **Establish a profile of yourself by answering the questions asked in this section. Discuss your attitudes and interests with others in your teacher-training class to sensitize yourself to the range of personal preferences represented.**

SOCIETAL PRESSURES

As well as the expressed interests and needs of students, and influencing these, there are societal pressures to be considered which are shaping the entire school program. These pressures reflect the demands of the community as represented by its citizens, many of whom

---

3. See also Gardner and Lambert 1972; John H. Schumann, "Social Distance as a Factor in Second Language Acquisition," *LL* 26, 1 (1976): 135–43; and Schumann 1978.

are the parents of our students. The language program, as a part of the educational enterprise, must be equally responsive to these pressures as are other areas of study. Because of the many interests and views in a modern pluralist society, some of these pressures may, in the short term, seem contradictory. Yet response there must be if the program is to survive and prosper.

Societal pressures will vary in different places at different moments in time. The thoughtful teacher will recognize a particular need which has become apparent and will adapt the program so that language study remains in step with and contributing to the type of education the community desires. In this latter part of the twentieth century, we may identify *ten educational pressures* which are being generally felt, although not all necessarily in one school or district. There have been and will be others.

For purposes of discussion, these ten trends will be divided into two categories, depending on whether they emphasize the pragmatic and utilitarian value of education or its role in the development of humane individuals able to live with each other and share in a common life in a small world. Studying and discussing the list will make trainee language teachers more aware of the complexity of their involvement in the educational process.

A. What can the students do with what they are learning in practical domains?

    1. Accountability, competency-based education, minimal competency testing, thorough teaching of the basics.[4]

    2. Career education.[5]

    3. Equality of educational opportunity and mainstreaming.[6]

    4. Lifelong learning and community education.[7]

B. What can this area of study do for the individual student as a person and as a citizen?

    5. Self-actualization, personality development, self-enhancement, humanistic education.[8]

---

4. NEC 1975; F. Steiner, *Performing with Objectives* (Rowley, Mass.: Newbury House, 1975); Valette and Disick 1972.

5. K. A. Lester and T. Tamarkin, "Career Education," in Jarvis 1974, pp. 161–87; "Career Education," in NEC 1974, pp. 127–43, 151.

6. "Foreign Languages for All Students," in NEC 1970; C. Hosenfeld, "The New Student Role: Individual Differences and Implications for Instruction," in Jarvis 1975, pp. 129–66. "Mainstreaming" refers to the educating of children with various disabilities in regular classrooms.

7. F. L. Coppedge, "Lifelong Learning," in Jarvis 1976, pp. 9–35.

8. B. Galyean, "Humanistic Education: A Mosaic Just Begun," in Jarvis 1976, pp. 201–43; Moskowitz 1978.

13

6. Interpersonal relations and communication.[9]
7. Multicultural education, values clarification, understanding and appreciation of one's own cultural heritage and that of others.[10]
8. Development of an international or global perspective.[11]
9. Developing the full potential of the gifted.[12]
10. Revived emphasis on the value of a liberal education and the role of the humanities.[13]

• **Discuss with your fellow students the part that language learning can play in relation to each of these trends and how the language course must be adapted in order to do so effectively.**[14]

Areas of Controversy

Can the learning of another language be justified as part of the general school curriculum?
In the twentieth century there are many demands on the curriculum. The rapid development of new fields of knowledge and the overwhelming increase of information in established areas of study require foundational knowledge of many kinds to be imparted at an early stage, yet only a certain number of hours are available for courses in any educational institution. The curriculum must be continually reviewed in the light of present and future needs. Traditional acceptance can no longer justify the inclusion of any subject in the program. Each must justify its place in the face of the claims made for others.

9. Wardhaugh 1976; G. A. Miller, "Nonverbal Communication," in Miller 1973, pp. 231–41; W. M. Rivers, "The Natural and the Normal in Language Teaching: Where's the Difference?" in Schulz 1977, pp. 101–8.

10. F. M. Grittner, "Pluralism in Foreign Language Education: A Reason for Being," and G. Morain, "Cultural Pluralism," in Lange 1971, pp. 9–95.

11. L. A. Strasheim, "An Issue on the Horizon: The Role of Foreign Languages in Global Education," *FLA* 12 (1979): 29–34; R. L. Hayden, "Relating Language to International Education: Some Do's and Don'ts," in *Profession 77* (New York: MLA, 1977), pp. 38–43, also in *ADFL Bulletin* 8 (1977): 16–21.

12. Naiman, Fröhlich, and Stern 1978; G. Lacy, "Developing Defensible Differentiated Programs for the Gifted," and "The Social and Emotional Development of the Gifted/Talented," with extensive bibliography (New York, New York State Education Department, n.d.).

13. E. J. Delattre, "The Humanities can Irrigate Deserts," *FLA* 11 (1978): 7–8; J. Moravcsik and A. Juilland, "The Place of Foreign Languages in a Curriculum for Liberal Education," *ADFL Bulletin* 8 (1977): 10–12.

14. The contribution of language study to each of these educational trends is discussed in detail by Rivers, in NEC 1979, pp. 20–34.

We may first ask whether the learning of second and third languages can be justified on the grounds of utility. Will the study of a particular language prove useful to students after they have left school? In a society where the language taught is either the national language which is not the native language of the student, a second language in widespread use, or the language of a neighboring country with which there is close and constant contact, the answer to this question will clearly be affirmative. In societies where this is not the case, it is very difficult to judge which of a number of languages will be of practical use to particular students during their lifetime. It is undeniable that knowledge of one or more of the commonly used languages of international communication can be of use in many careers in trade, commerce, international and national agencies, diplomacy, journalism, certain areas of science and engineering, librarianship, and of course teaching. Moving beyond the personal level, however, it is important for most countries in the modern age that they have available a body of people able to communicate with persons of other nations in their own language. The geographical position, international relations, commercial exchanges, and cultural associations of each country will determine the most useful languages for its citizens to learn.

To justify the place of languages in the curriculum, we need a more cogent argument than that of utility. There are very few subjects beyond the basics that can be irrefutably justified on the grounds of their ultimate usefulness to individual students, and there is even disagreement on which subjects constitute the basics. We must ask ourselves whether the study of another language contributes anything to the total educational experience of the learners which such study alone can provide or which it can provide more effectively than any other subject in the curriculum.

There is obvious value in being able to communicate directly with people who speak another language (both those who speak the language as natives and the great number who have also learned the language as a foreign or second language). What is more, the experience of learning a language by a conscious process and endeavoring to communicate in it gives students a deeper understanding of the nature and role of language, the forms and nuances of their own language, and the problems of communication. As they penetrate beyond the mere combining of language elements to the meanings which native speakers encode in their language, they come to understand more intimately the ways of thinking and reacting of persons of another culture. These deeper meanings are often lost or disguised in translation of speech or writing. As students act out the role of speakers of a particular language, trying to use the language as those speakers would use it, to see things as they would see them, and to read what they would read, they are able to identify with speakers of the language in ways which are not possible in a course in social studies or literature in translation. This experience fosters greater appreciation of another culture and a wider tolerance of different ideas and patterns of behavior.

Other advantages which devolve from knowledge of another language are more frequently cited: the knowledge of a language provides ready access to its heritage of literature and thought; it introduces students to activities which can prove enjoyable and profitable to them in their leisure time (a factor increasing in importance as hours or days of work decrease in many occupations); it increases their interest in and enjoyment of travel; it enables them to correspond freely, by letter or tape, with persons in other countries for business or pleasure; it opens up to them sources of information for their occupational or leisure-time interests; properly presented, it gives them experience in language learning which will enable them to learn third or fourth languages more efficiently, should this necessity arise in later life.

The arguments in favor of the learning of a new language which are set out above are valid only if the language is taught in such a way that these advantages do in fact accrue: if the language is so presented that the students do in fact learn to communicate and to apprehend meaning directly in reading; if they are in fact guided into an understanding of the culture of the speakers of the language; and if they are taught how to learn a language efficiently. In many language classes this is not the case. Students often acquire quite erroneous notions of what is involved in an act of communication. They come to look upon the new language as a code to be transformed in tedious fashion into their own code, and they learn to view the other culture as peculiar, somewhat ridiculous, and obviously inferior to their own. In such cases the learning of another language is hard to justify as an essential part of anyone's education.

Who should learn another language?
The attitude one takes to this question derives from one's philosophy of education. If the program of education for the individual child is designed from a utilitarian standpoint (that is, in order to provide students with skills that will enable them to fill useful roles in society), then the study of another language will be limited to those most likely to reach the stage of mastery where the new language can become an efficient tool in business, in diplomatic relations, or as a key to

sources of information. Since research has shown a high degree of success in language study in school situations to be related to overall scholastic ability,[15] the study of a language would in this case be limited to an elite group.

If the basic aim of the educational program is to provide all students with the opportunity to develop every aspect of their personality and talents to the fullest, then each student should have some experience in learning another language. Through acting out the role of a person from another culture, the student may come to realize that all people do not think and act alike and that "difference" does not necessarily mean inferiority or lack of moral principle. All students should be given some insight into the achievements and problems of groups of people other than those of their own society. They should also have the opportunity to examine with closer attention the tool of language which they use every day, in order to understand more fully its nature and function.

The school curriculum should provide students with an organized introduction to the many avenues of human knowledge and experience: showing them the possibilities which lie before them, giving them some experience of what these avenues promise, and providing them with some of the elementary skills they will require to enter into these avenues. Since language learning is one such avenue, all students should have the opportunity to savor what it offers. Taught by active methods, where the language is used and enjoyed and the people who speak the language are sympathetically presented, a language studied at the elementary level is accessible to all, although all do not assimilate it to the same degree or at the same pace. Of course, many students will not continue studying the language to a level of mastery, because their major interests lie elsewhere. They will, however, have derived substantial educational benefit from this language experience, which should not be limited to those for whom the use and study of languages will become a lifetime concern.

The utilitarian aspect of education will acquire real importance for most students only at the advanced level of study, when they are preparing for a career and must therefore devote their time more exclusively to skills that will serve their future purposes. At this stage, some students will choose the study of other languages as their main focus of attention, while their fellows will continue to study a language only as an auxiliary to their main career interest or as a potential source of future enjoyment.

---

15. P. Pimsleur, "Testing in Foreign Language Teaching," in Valdman 1966, pp. 176–77.

17

- **Study the following statements (A, B, and C) about the educational value of studying another language. Which one seems to you to be the most defensible for discussions with administrators, curriculum committees, parents or teachers of other subjects? Try to draw up a statement of your own which is realistic in the situation in which you teach.**

A. *Values of Foreign Language Study*[16]

The study of a foreign language, like that of most other basic disciplines, is both a progressive *experience* and a progressive acquisition of a *skill*. At no point can the experience be considered complete, or the skill perfect. Many pupils study a foreign language only two years; longer time is of course needed to approach mastery. At *any* point, however, the progress made in a language, when properly taught, will have positive value and lay a foundation upon which further progress can be built. It is evident therefore that the expectancy of values to be derived from language study must be relative to the amount of time and effort devoted to it.

The study of a foreign language, skillfully taught under proper conditions, provides a *new experience,* progressively enlarging the pupil's horizon through the introduction to a new medium of communication and a new culture pattern, and progressively adding to his sense of pleasurable achievement. This experience involves:

1. The acquisition of a set of *skills,* which can become real mastery for professional use when practiced long enough. The international contacts and responsibilities of the United States make the possession of these skills by more and more Americans a matter of national urgency. These skills include:

   a. The increasing ability to *understand* a foreign language when spoken, making possible greater profit and enjoyment in such steadily expanding activities as foreign travel, business abroad, foreign language movies and broadcasts.

   b. The increasing ability to *speak* a foreign language in direct communication with people of another culture, either for business or for pleasure.

   c. The ability to *read* the foreign language with progressively greater ease and enjoyment, making possible the broadening effects of direct acquaintance with the recorded thoughts of another people, or making possible study for vocational or professional (e.g., scientific or journalistic) purposes.

16. The following subsection is reprinted from the Foreign Language Program Policy of the Modern Language Association of America in *PMLA*, pt. 2, September 1956.

2. A new understanding of *language,* progressively revealing to the pupil the *structure* of language and giving him a new perspective on English, as well as an increased vocabulary and greater effectiveness in expression.
3. A gradually expanding and deepening knowledge of a foreign country—its geography, history, social organization, literature, and culture—and, as a consequence, a better perspective on American culture and a more enlightened Americanism through adjustment to the concept of differences between cultures.

Progress in any one of these experiences is relative to the emphasis given it in the instructional program and to the interests and aptitude of the learner. Language *skills,* like all practical skills, may never be perfected, and may be later forgotten, yet the enlarging and enriching results of the *cultural experience* endure throughout life.

B. *The Unique Contribution of Foreign Language Study*[17]

The unique contribution of foreign language study, which is truly educational in the sense that it expands our students' personal experience of their environment and truly humanistic in that it adds a new dimension to their thinking, is the opportunity it provides for breaking through monolingual and monocultural bonds, revealing to the students that there are other ways of saying things, other values and attitudes than those to which their native language and culture have habituated them. Through this experience, they may develop new attitudes to ideas and peoples which will reduce their bondage to the familiar and the local and increase their sympathy for persons of other cultures and languages. The new generation of students in our schools is internationalist and interculturalist in its aspirations; it is also brutally direct in demanding the rationale of what we are doing and of what we are asking the members of that generation to do. This basic contribution which foreign language can make to their development is one which they would welcome: but they must see that what we do in our classrooms really achieves such a purpose or they will drop out as soon as they conveniently may. If "the first task of education . . . is to raise the level of awareness and response to *all* ideas, events, people and objects," then foreign language taught with this end firmly in view can still claim that it has a rightful place in the overall educational program of the school.

17. The following subsection is slightly adapted from Rivers 1976, pp. 226–27. Quotation is from H. Taylor, as cited by A. E. Lean in *And Merely Teach* (Carbondale: Southern Illinois Press, 1968), p. 58.

C. *Language Study in Higher Education*[18]

From the earliest days of civilization—and until quite recently—it went without saying that the principal business of education was to ensure that an educated person had a mastery of language. What makes human culture and civilization possible is that the products of imagination and inquiry can be accumulated and transmitted; and a main instrument of this accumulation and transmission is written language. The traditional curriculum of American higher education recognized this central position of language through its insistence on training in the reading and writing of English, and through the requirement that students learn to read and speak at least one foreign language. In recent years, however, there has been a well-documented decline in the capacity of college students to use their own language and a widespread abandonment of the requirement that students learn a foreign language. We believe that this trend is alarming and that its consequences could be extremely dangerous.

Language study is not a polite elegance left over from the education of a leisure class; it is a profound inquiry into the meaning structure by which we interpret the world to ourselves and to others. A theoretical understanding and practical experience of language *as language*—as a signifying system—underlie many intellectual disciplines that try to meet the complex problems of contemporary society. It is only through mastery of languages—at the minimum, one's own and one that isn't one's own—that we can begin to understand the importance of language as system, code, tool, and model for further understanding.

On the one hand, language is the best available model for understanding the structures of human expression. On the other hand, a full and useful understanding of the role of language is linked to the cultural contexts in which language arises: to the values implicit in a society's culture. It is one of the most profound truths about human languages that each colors the whole mode of apprehension of those who speak it. This truth cannot be grasped from within any one language, but only by the formulation of some set of ideas in two languages so that the contrast can be experienced in that case and understood, by analogy, in other cases. The acquaintance with a second culture through its language effects a transformation of our own understanding of the content of human beliefs and practices.

---

18. The following subsection is a statement prepared by the MLA Committee on Language Study in Higher Education. Reprinted by permission of the Modern Language Association of America from the *MLA Newsletter* 9, no. 1 (1977), p. 8. © 1977 by The Modern Language Association of America.

The study of English and foreign languages continues to be of imperative significance in American higher education. Those who are not accurate and fluent in the major language of their society are crippled in their careers by an inability to express themselves. They are unable to cope with the distortions of language imposed by bureaucratic or technical jargon, or to engage in the kind of authentic dialogue that is needed among individuals and groups in our society. A lack of training in foreign languages creates linguistic barriers between us and the rest of the world and, more and more, isolates us from the thoughts and aspirations of existing and evolving world culture. America ought surely to be the leader in recognizing linguistic pluralism and in providing the means to the only real communication among cultures: knowledge of one another's languages.

To a society threatened by uncontrolled technological development and political fragmentation, the theoretical and practical understanding of language continues to offer a means of knowledge, a mode of communication, and an instrument of judgment and growth.

Annotated Reading List

HISTORY OF LANGUAGE TEACHING

Kelly, Louis, G. *25 Centuries of Language Teaching*. Rowley, Mass.: Newbury House, 1969. Historical perspective on methods and materials used today. Full of surprises.

Grittner, F. M. "The Historical Roots of Foreign Language Teaching in America." Chapter 1 of Grittner, 1977, pp. 1–24.

Chastain, Kenneth D. "Second-Language Study: Historical Background and Current Status." In Grittner 1980, pp. 1–25.

WHY STUDY ANOTHER LANGUAGE

Alter, Maria P. *A Modern Case for German*. Philadelphia: American Association of Teachers of German, 1970. Gives a rationale which applies to all languages.

Dodge, James W., ed. *The Case for Foreign Language Study*. New York: Northeast Conference and MLA/ACTFL, 1971. A collection of readings discussing the reasons for including foreign languages in the curriculum and the pros and cons of a foreign language requirement.

Lippmann, Jane N. "Rationale for Language Study." In Jarvis 1974b. Discusses traditional arguments for language study, distinguishing between learner reasons and teacher reasons. Extensive bibliography.

WHO SHOULD LEARN ANOTHER LANGUAGE?
"Foreign Languages for All Students?" Report of Working Committee III. In NEC 1970, pp. 105–33. Discusses the implications for the teaching program of encouraging all students to study another language.

OBJECTIVES IN LANGUAGE LEARNING AND TEACHING
Rivers, Wilga M. "Educational Goals: The Foreign Language Teacher's Response." In NEC 1979, pp. 19–51. Discusses the potential contribution of language study to ten emphases in general education; reports on objectives in fifty countries and fifty states for various languages; and provides a questionnaire with suggestions for its use in establishing local objectives.

STUDENTS' ATTITUDES AND INTERESTS
Jakobovits, Leon. "Foreign Language Attitude Questionnaire." In NEC 1970, pp. 9–30. Also in L. A. Jakobovits, *Foreign Language Learning: A Psycholinguistic Analysis of the Issues,* pp. 294–317. Rowley, Mass.: Newbury House, 1970.
Reinert, Harry. "Student Attitudes Toward Foreign Language—No Sale!" *MLJ* 54 (1970): 107–15.
Rivers, Wilga M. "The Non-Major: Tailoring the Course to Fit the Person—Not the Image," and "University of Illinois Questionnaire on Interests in Foreign Languages." In *Speaking in Many Tongues* (hereafter cited as *SMT*), exp. 2d ed., pp. 169–223. Rowley, Mass.: Newbury House, 1976.

*MOTIVATION
"Motivation in Foreign Language Learning." Report of Working Committee II. In NEC 1970, pp. 31–104. Discusses the importance of instructional, learner, and sociocultural factors in student motivation.
Grittner, Frank M., ed. *Student Motivation and the Foreign Language Teacher: A Guide for Building the Modern Curriculum.* CSC 1973. Skokie, Ill.: National Textbook Co., 1974. Considers the role of the teacher in motivating students. Contains recommendations concerning the content, nature, and scope of the foreign language program.
Rivers, Wilga M. "Motivating through Classroom Techniques," and "Motivation in Bilingual Programs." In *SMT,* pp. 88–99, 100–108.

* An asterisk indicates an item that has not been dealt with in depth in the chapter in which the item appears.

Schumann, John H. "Social and Psychological Factors in Second Language Acquisition." In Richards 1978, pp. 163–67.

TEACHING OF SPECIFIC LANGUAGES
"Classics in America." In NEC 1976, pp. 101–28.
Alatis, James E. "TESOL: Teaching English to Speakers of Other Languages." In Grittner 1980, pp. 88–103.
Watts, George B. "The Teaching of French in the United States: A History." *French Review* 37, no. 1 (October 1963): 9–165.
Zeydel, Edwin H. "The Teaching of German in the United States from Colonial Times to the Present." In *Reports of Surveys and Studies in the Teaching of Modern Foreign Languages,* ed. J. W. Childers, Donald D. Walsh, and G. Winchester Stone, Jr., pp. 285–308. New York: Modern Language Association of America, 1961.
Ellison, Fred P. "The Teaching of Portuguese in the Past Fifty Years"; and Ellison, Fred P., and Andrews, Norwood, Jr., "Portuguese in the High Schools." In Walsh 1969, pp. 235–64.
Parry, Albert. *America Learns Russian.* Syracuse, N.Y.: Syracuse University Press, 1967.
Leavitt, Sturgis E. "A History of the Teaching of Spanish in the United States." In Walsh 1969, pp. 222–34.
Chomsky, William. "Hebrew in America." Chapter 13 of *Hebrew: The Eternal Language,* pp. 245–69. Philadelphia: The Jewish Publication Society, 1969. (Originally published 1957.)

Research and Discussion

1. Ask the teachers in the school where you are teaching or observing to write down what they consider to be their primary objectives in language teaching. Assign the responses to major categories and compare the emphases which emerge with a similar tally of the objectives of the trainee teachers in your methods class. Discuss any trends you can discern. Do teachers from different neighborhoods show distinct differences in objectives? How are these related to their teaching situations? (Compare your survey with the results of the Rivers survey in Rivers 1979.)

2. What are your views on a foreign language requirement? Is it justified? Give the pros and cons. If you consider it justifiable, at what level should it be established? Should any other subjects be a required part of the curriculum? At what level?

3. As a language teacher, how do you view the "back to basics" movement? In what ways, if any, is your subject involved?

4. In the school where you are teaching or observing, or in a neighborhood school, study the attrition rate for the language you are teaching (that is, the drop in enrollments from the beginning class to the highest-level class). Make a similar study for another subject (e.g., mathematics). What conclusions can you draw from your data?

5. Prepare for a parent-teacher association meeting, a school board meeting, or the local newspaper, a statement of the reasons why second or foreign languages should be encouraged in the schools in your district. Include a discussion of which languages are appropriate and the level at which study should begin. (See Alter 1970; Dodge 1971; and Rivers 1979.)

*6. Motivation has been studied by psychologists for many years. What insights can such studies bring to the teacher of a second or third language? How do these insights affect the teacher's decisions on objectives in a specific teaching situation? (See references in the Annotated Reading List.)

7. Find out the attitudes toward language study and the objectives of the students in your language class or the class you are observing. What do the results of your enquiry suggest for the modification or development of the language courses in the school? (See *SMT,* chapters 13 and 14; Reinert 1970; and Rivers 1979.)

8. What does the term "liberal education" convey to you? (Read around in the library and find out what this term has meant at other times and in other places.) Does the study of another language have any place in a liberal education? Explain the reasons for your answer. (See Rivers 1979.)

9. In the district in which you teach or intend to teach, should all students be given the opportunity to study another language? Discuss the pros and cons for different types of students. (See *SMT,* chapter 15.)

10. What should the schools in your area do to increase public awareness of the importance of the study of languages and to encourage increased support for language programs? Draw up a detailed proposal.

2· Language Teaching Methods

As we read the story of language teaching over several centuries and analyze the theoretical positions basic to various approaches, we can distinguish two main streams of thought, each developing an integrated system of techniques devolving from its fundamental premises. For convenience, we shall term representatives of these two groups the formalists and the activists. Emphases in language teaching tend to swing from a preference for one approach to a growing attraction to the other, as successive generations of teachers seek to correct any imbalance which may have developed from the particular preoccupations of their predecessors. Obviously many classroom teachers take a position between these extremes, applying formalist techniques for some sections of the work, or for some levels of instruction, and activist techniques for others.

Language Analysis or Language Use?

Formalist and activist tendencies may be discerned in the early teaching of the classical languages. When Latin was required for oral communication among scholars and as the medium of instruction, it was taught through active use of the language by the student. Gradually a more formalist approach became general, with emphasis on the study of forms (e.g., parts of speech and their paradigms). The learning of rules and their application in every detail became the chief occupation of numbers of students. This approach was later adopted by many teachers of modern languages. Voices were continually raised, however, urging the presentation of the language in its most useful form, and the gradual acquisition of language forms through using them frequently in realistic language situations. The de-emphasis or re-emphasis of one or the other of these approaches is basic to many of the controversies, switches, and changes which sweep through the language-teaching profession from year to year.

Deduction or Induction?

Formalists have relied mostly on a deductive form of teaching (moving from the statement of the rule to its application in the example). Activists have advocated the apprehension by the students themselves of the way the language is working. They prefer students to develop a rule or generalization themselves after they have heard (or seen) certain forms and used them in a number of ways; this is a process of *inductive* learning (moving from examples to a rule).

Details of Grammar or Functional Grammar?

Formalists with a commendable regard for thoroughness have sometimes become too preoccupied with the pedantic elaboration of fine details of grammar. Activists have consistently urged a functional approach to structure. The student is first taught what is most useful and most generally applicable and is left to discover at later stages the less frequent or exceptional. As a result, formalist teaching has often been based on artificial exercises and has led to a stilted use of language, in which the student incorporates, in attempts at speech, features of the written language encountered in literary works. Activist teaching, on the other hand, has sought to familiarize the student first with the forms of the language used for general communication in speech and in less formal writing, teaching the more literary or formal use of the language at an advanced level only. The formalist lays great stress on accuracy in the application of grammar rules; the activist is more patient with student errors, believing that confidence and success in communicating meaning in the language are of greater importance than a sterile perfection of form.

Passive or Active Classroom?

In actual classroom procedures, a strictly formalist approach has favored a passive student situation, where the student receives instruction and applies it as directed. An activist approach, to be effective, requires ready participation by the student in the learning activities. Discovery of the facts of language by the student and active use of the language for the expression of personal meaning are encouraged. In other words, the formalist emphasizes *teaching* of the language, while the activist is more interested in providing opportunities for the student to *learn* the language.

Priority of Writing or Speech?

These divergent attitudes toward various aspects of language learning have led to a very different order of priorities in the teaching of the four skills of listening, speaking, reading, and writing. The formalist tends to place high value on skill in reading and accurate writing (often as demonstrated by the ability to translate). The activist lays emphasis on the spoken language and considers practice in oral communication to be a necessary accompaniment to fluent reading and original writing.

Languages have been taught to students down the centuries by *a variety of methods,* and with competent teachers students learn what their teachers feel it is important for them to learn. No matter what method is in vogue or is officially advocated, teachers who are professionally alert will adapt its techniques to their purposes, to their own personality, and to what they feel is appropriate for the particular classes they are teaching, always keeping in mind the age level of the students and their educational needs in the situation in which they find themselves. Any method ceases to be efficient when it is applied inflexibly, according to set procedures, in every situation.

As we study the evolution of language-teaching methods, we see what is most effective in each method being taken up again at a later date, elaborated and refashioned, so that the best of the past is not lost but serves the purposes of the present. Consequently, one observes rather infrequently any particular method in use in its pure form, unless it has suddenly returned to fashion and favor, often under a new name. Much more frequently one will meet modifications and combinations, as teachers adapt the method that is in vogue to suit their own teaching style in their particular situation.

- **By temperament and previous experience, would you consider yourself a formalist or an activist? How were you taught a language? How do you prefer to teach a language yourself?**

Evaluating Language Teaching Methods
As a prelude to the study of techniques for teaching the various language skills, we shall examine some of the major methods which have held sway in the past century: the grammar-translation method, the direct method, the reading method, and the audio-lingual or aural-oral method. We shall relate these to recent studies in linguistics and cognition and show where new trends are leading.

In evaluating the effectiveness of any method, trainee teachers should keep certain questions in mind. They should ask themselves what are the objectives of the method under discussion and whether these objectives are appropriate for their present teaching situation or the types of students they will teach. They should then consider whether the techniques advocated by the proponents of the method achieve the stated objectives in the most economical way (that is, whether they provide the most direct route to these objectives). Since techniques may be economical in the attainment of objectives but intensely boring, inhibiting, or overdemanding for the students, they should next ask whether these techniques maintain the interest and enthusiasm of the learners, and at what level of instruction. In view of the great variation in abilities and interests within today's student body, they will wish to consider also whether these techniques are appropriate for all types of students and whether they can be easily adapted. Finally, they will keep in mind a question which is often overlooked: whether the demands these techniques make on teachers are such that they can carry a full teaching load. Some methods are excellent for a one-hour demonstration class but demand so much preparation or expenditure of effort by the teacher that they have to be modified in a normal teaching situation.

With these five questions in mind, we shall now consider the objectives and techniques of the four methods we have listed.

THE GRAMMAR-TRANSLATION METHOD

In classroom A, we saw a grammar-translation class in action. Such classes will be found in schools all over the world. This method cannot be traced back to the tenets of any particular master teacher, but it is clearly rooted in the formal teaching of Latin and Greek which prevailed in Europe in the nineteenth century. In the latter part of the century, these formal techniques were adapted to the teaching of modern languages by Plötz in Germany. Plötz's ideas rapidly spread to other countries.[1]

When Latin was no longer being learned as a language for communication among scholars, its primacy as a matter for study could not be justified on utilitarian grounds. Indeed, utility was considered at that time an inappropriate criterion to be applied to any area of advanced study. The learning of Latin and Greek was justified as an intellectual discipline. The mind was trained, it was asserted, by the logical analysis of the language, much memorization of complicated rules and paradigms, and the application of these in translation exercises. Latin and Greek were further justified as the key to the thought and literature of a great and ancient civilization. The reading and translation of texts was considered of great importance, as were written exercises in imitation of these texts. Modern languages were accepted as reputable areas of study only after much controversy and opposition from the supporters of classical studies. They had to prove themselves to be of equal value for the training of the mind and as the key to a great literature and civilization. It was inevitable, then, that modern-language teaching methods should be modeled at this stage on the methods already employed for the teaching of an ancient language which was no longer in use for communication and of which even the original pronunciation was in doubt.

1. For the history of the grammar-translation method, see Kelly 1969, pp. 51–54, 175–76; and Titone 1968, pp. 27–29.

The classical method has persisted in many areas, despite attempts to introduce methods more appropriate to the teaching of a living language with a contemporary literature to students whose range of interests and abilities is very wide. Certain nineteenth-century textbooks which continued to be used and imitated well into the twentieth century were notable for the meticulous detail of their descriptions of the grammar of the language (based on the traditional expectations of Latin and Greek grammar), their preoccupation with written exercises, especially translation exercises, and their lengthy bilingual vocabulary lists. They usually contained long extracts from great writers, chosen for their intellectual content rather than for the level of difficulty of the language or their intrinsic interest for the modern student. Such textbooks dominate the work of the teacher whose immediate aim becomes the completion of all the exercises in the unit and the covering of all the units in the book in a given period of time.

Teachers who were themselves taught by this method and who have not had sufficient exposure to other possible approaches to teaching a language continue this tradition. New textbooks modeled on the old tend to imitate the grammatical descriptions and exercises of their predecessors with the result that archaic structures and obsolete vocabulary and phrases continue to be taught to successive generations of students. Teachers who wish to adopt active methods, but are forced to use such textbooks, try to introduce some practice in communication into their classes. They are, however, frustrated by the academic and inappropriate forms of language and the enormous range of vocabulary the books contain, while their students are bored by the repetitive nature of the innumerable written exercises.

Classroom Application

The grammar-translation method aims at inculcating an understanding of the grammar of the language, and training the student to write the new language accurately by regular practice in translating from the native language. It aims at providing the student with a wide literary vocabulary, often of an unnecessarily detailed nature. It aims at training the student to extract the meaning from texts in the new language by translation into the native language and, at advanced stages, to appreciate the literary significance and value of these texts. These aims are achieved in the classroom by detailed grammatical explanations in the native language, followed by practice on the part of the students in writing paradigms, in applying the rules they have learned to the construction of sentences in the target language, and in translating consecutive passages of prose from the native to the target language. Texts in the target language are translated into the native language orally and in writing. Ideally, their literary and cultural significance is also discussed, although in many classes, because of the limited time available, this may be done very perfunctorily, if at all.

Students are expected to know the rules for the correct association of sounds with the graphic symbols in the foreign writing system. They are given little opportunity to practice these associations, however, except through reading aloud from time to time in class and through writing, from dictation, passages that are usually of a literary character. The target language is not used extensively in class, although the teacher may ask questions about the subject matter of a reading passage, which the students will usually answer with sentences drawn directly from the text. Often these questions are given to the students in writing and answered in writing. Students taught by the grammar-translation method are frequently confused when addressed in the language they are learning because they have had little practice in listening to it. They may also be very embarrassed when asked to pronounce anything themselves.

Critique

What, then, can be said in favor of the grammar-translation method? Applying our five questions, we find that it sets itself limited objectives, and that its techniques do achieve its objectives where the students in the class are highly intellectual and interested in abstract reasoning. Such students try to understand the logic of the grammar as it is presented; they learn the rules and exceptions and memorize the paradigms and vocabulary lists. They become reasonably adept at taking dictation and translating foreign-language texts into the native language. Their translation of native-language texts into the foreign language may not produce versions which sound natural to a native speaker, but the best of them are accurate and comprehensible, with careful attention to the many rules the students have been taught. After several years, the best students know many words in the new language and have an intellectual grasp of structure, which can become active if they have the opportunity to live for a period of time in an area where the language is spoken.

The grammar-translation method is not successful, however, with the less intellectual students, who muddle through, making many mistakes over and over again, thus building up cumulative habits of inaccuracy which are difficult to eradicate at a more advanced stage. These less gifted students find language study very tedious and usually drop out of the class as soon as they possibly can.

The method is not too demanding on the teachers; when they are tired, they can always set the class a written exercise. The techniques described in this section can be used with large groups who listen, copy rules, and write out exercises. Much of the correction can be done by the students themselves in class, as the teacher discusses the correct version of an exercise, dictation, or translation which has been written on the board. It is easy to make tests which are similar to the work that has been done in class and to assign grades for these. Teachers do not need to show much imagination in planning or teaching their lessons, since they usually follow the textbook page by page and exercise by exercise.

The main defects of the method were pointed out as it was described. Little stress is laid on accurate pronunciation and intonation. Communication skills are neglected. There is much stress on knowing rules and exceptions, but little training in using the language actively to express one's own meaning, even in writing. In an endeavor to practice the application of rules and the use of exceptional forms, the student is often trained in artificial forms of language, some of which are rare, others old-fashioned, many of little practical use. The language learned is usually of a literary type, and the vocabulary is detailed and sometimes esoteric. Average students have to work hard at what they consider laborious and monotonous chores—vocabulary learning, translation, and endless written exercises—without much feeling of progress in the mastery of the language and with very little opportunity to express themselves through it. Their role in the classroom is, for the greater part of the time, a passive one—they absorb and then reconstitute what they have absorbed to satisfy the teacher.

THE DIRECT METHOD

Advocates of active classroom methods continued to make themselves heard in various countries throughout the nineteenth century,[2] and by the end of the century some of them had had considerable influence on modern-language teachers. These theorists shared a common belief that students learn to understand a language by listening to a great deal of it and that they learn to speak it by speaking it— associating speech with appropriate action. This, they observed, was the way children learned their native language, and this was the way

2. See P. Hagboldt, "The Teaching of Languages from the Middle Ages to the Present," in Newmark 1948, pp. 5–9; and E. A. Méras, *A Language Teacher's Guide,* 2d ed. (New York: Harper, 1962), pp. 35–45. We associate with the nineteenth-century direct-method movement such names as Viëtor, Passy, Berlitz, and Jespersen.

children who had been transferred to a different linguistic environment acquired a second language, apparently without great difficulty.

The various "oral" and "natural" methods which developed at that time can be grouped together as forms of the direct method, in that they advocated learning a new language through direct association of words and phrases with objects and actions, without the use of the native language by teacher or student. Speech preceded reading, but even in reading students were encouraged to forge a direct bond between the printed word and their understanding of it, without passing through an intermediate stage of translation into the native language. The ultimate aim was to develop the ability to think in the language, whether one was conversing, reading, or writing.

Classroom Application

This renewed emphasis on the target language as the medium of instruction in the classroom meant that correct pronunciation became an important consideration. Since the study of phonetics had developed during the second half of the nineteenth century, teachers were able to make use of its findings on the mechanics of sound production and to adopt its newly developed system of notation.[3] Direct-method teachers frequently began a language course with an introductory period during which students were taught the new sound system. Often, for several months, the only representation students saw of the sounds and expressions they were learning to produce and discriminate was a phonetic notation. In this way, it was argued, they were able to develop correct pronunciation without being influenced by a script which they already associated with native-language sounds. This emphasis on acquiring an acceptable pronunciation from the beginning remains a feature of direct-method teaching today.

A direct-method class provides a clear contrast with a grammar-translation class, just as the activities in classroom B, in chapter 1, contrast with those in classroom A. The course begins with the learning of target-language words and phrases for objects in the classroom and for actions which can be performed by the students. When these expressions can be used readily and appropriately, the learning moves to the common situations and settings of everyday life. With this in view, the lesson often develops around specially constructed pictures of life in a country where the language is spoken. Where the meaning of words cannot be made clear by concrete representation, the teacher resorts to miming, sketching, manipulating objects, or giving expla-

---

3. The notation referred to is the International Phonetic Alphabet (I.P.A.), the first version of which was published in 1888.

nations in the language being learned, but never supplies native-language translations, except as a last resort. From the beginning, the students are accustomed to hear complete, meaningful sentences which form part of a simple discourse, often in the form of a question-answer exchange or an anecdote recounted by the teacher.

Grammar is not taught explicitly and deductively as in a grammar-translation class, but is learned largely through practice. Students are encouraged to form their own generalizations about grammatical structure by an inductive process through reflecting on what they have been learning. In this way, the study of grammar is kept at a functional level, being confined to those areas which are continually being used in speech. When grammar is taught more systematically, it is taught in the target language with the use of target-language terminology.

When students are introduced to reading material, they read about things they have already discussed orally, the teacher having prepared the students for the reading selections through an oral presentation of new words and situations. Texts are read aloud by teacher and students, and the students are encouraged to seek direct comprehension by inferring meanings of unknown elements from the context, rather than by seeking equivalents in a bilingual vocabulary list. Where the meaning cannot be discovered in this way, the teacher gives explanations in the language being learned, using pictures and gestures where necessary. Students are never asked to translate passages into their native language; instead, their apprehension of the meaning is tested by questioning and discussion in the target language. They learn to write the language first of all by transcription, then by composing summaries of what they have been reading or writing simple accounts of what has been discussed orally. They gradually move to creative compositions. The classroom is continually filled with the sounds of the new language, since all activity is closely linked with the use of the language in speech and writing.

Critique

At its best, the direct method provides an exciting and interesting way of learning a language through activity. It has proved to be successful in releasing students from the inhibitions all too often associated with speaking another tongue, particularly at the early stages. If care is not taken by the teacher, however, students who are plunged too soon into expressing themselves freely in the new language in a relatively unstructured situation can develop a glib but inaccurate fluency, clothing native-language structures in foreign-language vocabulary. This "school pidgin" is often difficult to eradicate later, when grammatical structure and vocabulary are being more systematically studied, because it has been accepted and encouraged for so long.

It is unrealistic to believe that the conditions of native-language learning can be recreated in the classroom with adolescent students. Unlike the infant learner, adolescent or adult students already possess well-established native-language speech habits. These will inevitably influence the forms in which they express themselves in their early attempts at spontaneous communication, unless they have been given some systematic practice in the structures they need to express these ideas. This kind of transfer and adaptation of preceding knowledge will be most noticeable at first at those points where the target language diverges significantly from what the native language has led the student to expect, especially if students are trying to express themselves at their normal level of sophistication, which at this early stage is far beyond the simple target-language means at their disposal. In unplanned discourse which arises from a situation created in the classroom, all kinds of structures may be heard, or needed, by the speaker. It is very difficult to restrict their occurrence or to ensure that they will recur with sufficient frequency for the student to be able to assimilate them. In the pure form of the direct method, insufficient provision is made for systematic practice and repractice of structures in a coherent sequence. As a result, students often lack a clear idea of what they are trying to do, and many make haphazard progress.[4]

Since students are required at all times to make a direct association between foreign phrase and situation, it is the highly intelligent student with well-developed powers of induction who profits most from this method, which can become discouraging and bewildering for the less talented. As a result, the members of an average class soon diverge considerably from each other in degree of language acquisition. The method makes great demands on the energy of teachers. They have of necessity to be fluent in the language and very resourceful, in order to make meaning clear in a variety of ways without resorting at any time to the use of the native language. The greatest success with this method is achieved in situations where the student can hear and practice the language outside the classroom. (Its principal tenet, that only the target language must be used at all times by teacher and student, has to be observed in classes where the students come from a number of different language backgrounds.) For these

4. In some forms of the direct method, like the Berlitz method, a careful sequence of structural development was followed.

reasons many teachers who enjoy the direct method approach now use it with various modifications.

The Modified Direct Method

The direct method continues to flourish in its modified form in many areas. To counteract the tendency toward inaccuracy and vagueness, teachers have reintroduced some grammatical explanations of a strictly functional kind, given in the native language, while retaining the inductive approach wherever possible. They also add more practice in grammatical structures, sometimes with the use of substitution tables,[5] the forerunners of pattern drills. Where it is difficult to make the meaning of words and phrases clear by sketch or gesture, they give a brief explanation in the native language. They have also reintroduced occasional translation of words and phrases as a check on comprehension of precise details in reading.

These modifications of the direct method reflect the tendency of practical teachers to be eclectic. (The eclectic approach is discussed at the end of this chapter.)

THE READING METHOD

After the publication in 1929 of the Coleman report as part of the *Modern Foreign Language Study* in the United States, it became clear that the majority of American students studied a foreign language for a period of two years only. Since the acquisition of any serious level of competence in all four language skills requires much more than two years in the usual nonintensive school situation, the report maintained that the only reasonable objective for such a short period of study was the development of reading ability. In Coleman's own words, the objective of two-year courses should be to develop "the ability to read the foreign language with moderate ease and with enjoyment for recreative and for vocational purposes" (Coleman 1929, p. 107). Because teachers in other countries were reexamining their objectives in school language study too, this report had considerable influence. As a result of the Coleman recommendations, teachers began to seek the most effective ways of developing the reading skill, so that the graduate of a language course of limited duration would be capable of independent reading after formal study of the language had ended.

In the reading method, students were to be taught to read the new language with direct apprehension of meaning, without a conscious effort to translate what they were reading. A distinction was made

5. Examples of substitution tables are given in *PG*'s, chaps. 4 and 8.

between intensive and extensive reading (see chapter 9), and emphasis was placed on developing autonomous silent reading and increasing individual reading rate. Frequency word counts were developed and used as the basis for graded readers written to conform to certain levels of word frequency. In these readers, introduction of new vocabulary was carefully controlled. Since the systematic building of knowledge of vocabulary was considered important, students studied basic word lists based on these frequency levels. To make these lists more palatable to students, the words were often grouped around themes or centers of interest.

Teachers who followed Palmer's lead (Palmer and Redman 1932, pp. 65–73, 105) felt that facility in reading could not be developed unless the students were trained in correct pronunciation, comprehension of uncomplicated spoken language, and the use of simple speech patterns. The students could then read aloud to help them with comprehension, and "hear" the text mentally as they were reading silently. This oral approach to reading was more in tune with the convictions and practice of direct-method teachers and made the new reading courses more acceptable to them.

Writing was to be limited to exercises which would help the student remember vocabulary and structures essential to the comprehension of the text. The study of grammar was to be specially geared to the needs of the reader, for whom quick recognition of certain verb forms, tenses, negations, and other modifications was important, but for whom active reproduction of such features was unnecessary. In other words, only the minimum essentials of grammar were to be incorporated into the course at this stage.

∴ recognition not production

Classroom Application

Where the reading method is adopted, the study of the language usually begins with an oral phase. In the first weeks, students are thoroughly initiated into the sound system of the language and become accustomed to listening to and speaking in simple phrases. It is maintained that the auditory image of the language that they are acquiring will assist them later when they turn to the reading of a text. After the introduction of reading there continues to be oral practice in association with the text. This usually takes the form of reading aloud by the teacher or a student, followed by questions and answers on the text.

The main part of the course is then divided into intensive and extensive reading. Intensive reading, under the teacher's supervision, is more analytic and provides material for grammatical study, for the acquisition of vocabulary, and for training in reading complete sentences for comprehension. Students are not asked to translate but are encouraged to infer the meaning of unknown words from the context or from cognates in their own or other languages. During this intensive reading, the teacher is able to check in detail the degree of comprehension achieved by each student. For extensive reading, students work entirely on their own, reading many pages of connected discourse graded to their personal level of achievement. Special readers have been published with adapted texts which conform to specific levels of word-frequency and idiom counts and introduce new vocabulary at a predetermined rate. In this way the students are guided by the teacher from level to level as their reading ability develops. They acquire a large passive vocabulary, or recognition vocabulary, which varies according to the material each has been reading.

The students' comprehension of what they have read is tested by questions on the content of the reading material, not by translation. So that the students may read with greater appreciation of cultural differences, class projects are undertaken on the background of the country where the language is spoken and on the ways of life and customs of the people. These projects often entail further reading in the new language as the students gather the necessary information.

Critique

The reading method increases the ability of the better students to read in another language. Because of the quantity of reading required, however, it can be frustrating for students who have reading difficulties in their native language. The system of extensive reading gives students the opportunity to progress at their own rate; students within the same class can work with readers at different levels of difficulty. The method also arouses the students' interest in the people who speak the language and a curiosity about their way of life.

If not sufficiently controlled, the system of extensive reading can lead to satisfaction with quantity rather than quality—number of pages perused rather than degree of comprehension. Some students are content if they can pick out the main line of development of the thought, even if they are unable to answer questions of detail, particularly details dependent on structural elements rather than on lexical items. The system of graded readers, while valuable from the pedagogical point of view, can give a false impression of the level of reading achieved. It is doubtful whether more than a small minority of students can read ungraded material with ease and direct comprehension at the end of a short reading course. When average students encounter ungraded material too soon, they are usually forced back into deciphering with the aid of a dictionary, and valuable training in the reading skill is wasted.

As a justification for short, nonspecialized language courses, the reading aim is thus spurious. (Courses where students learn to read specialized or technical material for career purposes are another question.)[6] Language courses which are not long enough to ensure a reasonable level of language mastery may be justified as providing an educational experience which gives some insight into the ways of thinking of another people, some understanding of how language works, and some realization of the problems of communication; but the degree to which language learned during such short courses will provide useful skills for students in later life must not be exaggerated. Success will depend on students' continuing perseverance and individual effort as they develop later confidence in approaching unadapted texts in areas of personal interest.

The reading method in the period following the Coleman Report produced students who were unable to comprehend and speak the language beyond the very simplest of exchanges. World War II and the increasingly closer contacts between nations in the succeeding years made it apparent that the reading skill alone was not enough if language study was to serve purposes beyond the most restricted, personal ones. National interests and those of increasingly mobile populations demanded a reemphasis on oral communication as a basic objective of the language course. Consequently, a new approach was developed in response to new needs.

THE AUDIO-LINGUAL METHOD

In the early years of World War II, American military authorities discovered the degree to which the study of languages had been neglected in the United States when they were faced with a totally inadequate supply of interpreters for communication with their allies and with enemy contacts. In an attempt to rectify this situation as quickly as possible, they called for the help of the American Council of Learned Societies, whose members had already been at work analyzing lesser-known languages and developing intensive language-teaching programs in certain universities.

In this wartime setting, understanding a native speaker and speaking a language with near-native accent were first priorities. With high motivation, small classes, explanations of structure by linguistic experts, and long hours of drilling and active practice with native in-

---

6. Specialized reading courses are discussed in detail in the *PG*'s, chap. 6, subsection "Reading for Information," and in chap. 14 below.

formants, using graded materials based on this analysis of structure, selected members of the armed forces acquired a high degree of aural-oral skill for specific purposes and situations.

The origins of the intensive language-teaching methods developed in the 1940s and 1950s may be found in the work of the American structural linguists and cultural anthropologists who were working in the same climate of opinion as the behaviorist psychologists. In the twenties and thirties, the call had been sounding for a strictly scientific and objective investigation of human behavior. In linguistics, this investigation took the form of a descriptive approach to the study of language. Structural linguists tried to describe the sound patterns and word combinations of each language as they observed them in a corpus, without attempting to fit them into a preconceived framework based on the structures of Greek and Latin, or the traditional grammar of English. The descriptive approach was particularly appropriate, since a number of these linguists were interested in the description of American Indian languages and other little-known non-European languages, which they found to be very different from the languages to which they were accustomed.

The descriptive approach led to research into what people really do say in their mother tongue, in contradistinction to what traditional grammarians may maintain they ought to say. (For most of the linguists in this American context, the mother tongue was English.) Fries, for instance, examined mechanically recorded conversations and a large number of letters by ordinary people to identify the characteristics of modern American English.[7] This nonprescriptive attitude toward language caused much heated debate, like that which later followed the publication of the *Webster's Third New International Dictionary*. This edition gives place in its columns to the words people use, even though their acceptability may be questioned by purists.[8] The structural linguists were also interested in levels of language appropriate for different social situations (see Joos 1961).

At this period, much research was being carried out by anthropologists into patterns of human behavior in a culture. To them, language was clearly an activity learned in the social life of a people, just as were other culturally determined acts. Language use was a set of habits, established, as later behaviorist research in psychology was to suggest, by reinforcement or reward in the social situation.

7. The Fries project is described in H. A. Gleason, Jr., *Linguistics and English Grammar* (New York: Holt, Rinehart & Winston, 1965), pp. 17–20; and C. C. Fries, *The Structure of English* (London: Longmans Green, 1952), p. 3.

8. An indication is given, however, of their level of acceptability (e.g., some words are marked "substandard").

The native language as learned behavior was acquired by the infant in spoken form first, and this led to the assumption that students will acquire a second language more easily if it is presented in the spoken form before the written form. This notion seemed even more self-evident to the early structural linguists because many of the languages they were studying did not exist in written form, or possessed very little written literature.

In the 1950s, teachers of languages in schools and universities became interested in the techniques developed by the army, and also in those used extensively for teaching English to foreign students studying in the United States.[9] New teaching materials for high school and undergraduate study of the commonly taught languages (Spanish, French, German, and later Russian and Portuguese) were prepared by experienced teachers with the advice of linguists who had made descriptive analyses of the languages, and these teaching materials were tried out in schools. After successive revisions, the earliest materials of this type came on the American market in the late fifties.

The new emphasis on being able to communicate in another language led to the coining of the term "aural-oral" for a method which aimed at developing listening and speaking skills first, as the foundation on which to build the skills of reading and writing. As "aural-oral" was found to be confusing and difficult to pronounce, Brooks suggested the term "audio-lingual" for this method (Brooks 1964, p. 263). Both terms are still in use.

In 1958, American concern about the language-learning situation in schools found expression in the National Defense Education Act (NDEA). This act provided funds for research in language teaching and learning, and for intensive training courses (for practicing teachers) in listening and speaking skills, in the understanding of linguistic principles, and in the use of audio-lingual techniques in the classroom.

New aids for teaching, in the form of magnetic tape and language laboratory equipment, were becoming available, and these were found to be very useful for practice in listening and sound production as well as practice with grammatical structure. Matching funds were also made available by the U.S. government for installing such equipment in schools and colleges.

9. The most notable research center for methods and materials for teaching English to foreign students in American universities was the English Language Institute of the University of Michigan. See C. C. Fries 1945. It should be noted that most of the basic ideas on which audio-lingual or aural-oral teaching is based had been already put forward by H. E. Palmer (1921).

The Audio-Lingual Method

Five Slogans

Five "slogans of the day"[10] guided teachers in applying the results of research in structural linguistics to the preparation of teaching materials and to classroom techniques.

1. Language is speech, not writing

As we normally learn our mother tongue in spoken form before being introduced to its representation by graphic symbols, and as speech, or sound communication, is the form in which all natural languages first developed, proponents of the audio-lingual method laid stress on learning to understand and speak at least some of the language before learning to read and write it. This order of presentation (listening and speaking before reading and writing) was accompanied by great emphasis on correct pronunciation and intonation. The early introduction of the written form of the language was regarded as a potential threat to mastery of the sound system and to the development of a near-native accent, because the symbols used in writing or printing, at least with European languages, already had associations with native-language pronunciations. A time lag was advocated between the introduction of new material orally and its presentation in graphic form. This time lag might occur within one lesson or last as long as several weeks.

Emphasis on spoken language led to a radical change in the type of material selected as a basis for teaching in the early stages. Complete utterances were learned from the first lesson and these utterances were expressed in colloquial forms of speech which would be used in a country where the language was spoken by a person of age and situation similar to that of the learner. Such utterances contrasted with the stilted, literary style of language often presented in elementary textbooks of an earlier period. Students were encouraged to listen to and repeat these utterances at normal native speed with the usual elisions and liaisons of the native speaker.

This first slogan did not mean that the written form of the language was neglected. After an aural-oral introduction, reading and writing activities were developed and continued to an advanced level.

2. A language is a set of habits

Just as other social habits are acquired by children growing up in a particular culture, so is the language of their group. How such habits are acquired was the basic question. Early audio-lingual exponents were strongly influenced by the operant conditioning theories of

10. For a discussion of these five slogans, see W. Moulton, "Linguistics and Language Teaching in the United States 1940–1960," in Mohrmann, Sommerfelt, and Whatmough 1961, pp. 86–89.

B. F. Skinner, who holds that habits are established when reward or reinforcement follow immediately on the occurrence of an act. Skinner considers that the origin of the act, the understanding of the act by the actor, and the attitude of the actor to the act are not factors which can be objectively studied and are therefore not to be taken into account in the consideration of habit formation.

The application of this concept in audio-lingual techniques took the form of mimicry-memorization (usually of dialogue material) and structural pattern drilling (whereby students learned to manipulate structures to a point of automatic response to a language stimulus). When we are using our native language, we are not conscious of the structures we are using to convey our meaning. Audio-lingual techniques aimed to provide the student with a similarly automatic control of the framework of the new language. Unimpeded by attention to forms, the speaker could then concentrate on how to express the message.

3. Teach the language and not about the language
This slogan reflects the revolt of the early audio-lingual teachers against the excessive classroom discussion of grammar rules of the grammar-translation method. The audio-lingual teacher believed that students should spend their classroom time on active oral practice of the language. A detailed analysis of structure was regarded as an advanced study for the linguistically inclined, but not essential for the student whose main aim was to be able to use the language in communication.

4. A language is what its native speakers say, not what someone thinks they ought to say
The materials students learned audio-lingually contained structures in common use in the countries where the language was spoken. Contemporary colloquial clichés of conversation were taught in the dialogues. Careful attention was paid, however, to levels of language, to ensure that the colloquial speech learned was of a type which native speakers would find acceptable in the mouths of students. Situations in the dialogues were carefully described so that students would be conscious of the emotional effect of the language they were using, whether formal or informal, respectful or condescending, friendly or hostile, subservient or gently teasing. At advanced levels, attention was also paid to regional differences of pronunciation and expression.

5. *Languages are different*

Structural linguists rejected the notion of a universal grammatical system which can serve as a framework for the organization of the facts of all languages. They analyzed each language according to its unique interrelationships. Early audio-lingual proponents believed that the major difficulties for the language learner were to be found at those points where the structural or pronunciation requirements of the new language contrasted with the native-language habits of the student. Audio-lingual materials were designed, wherever possible, to present the problems of a specific foreign language to students who spoke another specific language, so that contrastive difficulties might be anticipated and practice provided at just such problem points. The most useful structures and those most easily confused were presented first, with continual drilling and review to ensure mastery.

Contrary to direct-method practice, many audio-lingual textbooks provided native-language versions of the dialogues, not with word-for-word glosses but with idiomatic expressions which conveyed the same ideas as the foreign-language expressions in the dialogues. Students were encouraged to try to use the expressions from the dialogues in situations approximating those of the foreign culture.

Traditional translation exercises were regarded by audio-lingualists as a dangerous occupation in the early stages of learning another language because of the tendency of students to look for exact equivalents of individual words. On the other hand, students might be asked to transpose rapidly short stimulus sentences from the native language to the foreign language in translation drills. In this case the native-language stimulus, a simple, uncomplicated utterance, provided a valuable aid for eliciting utterances in the target language. Prolonged and detailed translation was kept for advanced stages, when it was to be taught as a skill with its own techniques.

Classroom Application

The audio-lingual method aims at teaching the language skills in the order of listening, speaking, reading, and writing. Material is presented in spoken form, and the emphasis in the early years is on the language as it is spoken in everyday situations; reading and writing at this stage play supportive roles. At advanced levels, when the last two skills receive increasing emphasis, students are introduced to more literary forms of expression. At all stages, however, the listening and speaking skills are kept at a high level by continual practice.

At the first level of instruction, learning is based on dialogues containing commonly used everyday expressions and basic structures of high frequency. The vocabulary content is kept to a useful minimum so that the student may concentrate on establishing a firm control of structure. The dialogues are learned by a process of mimicry-memorization, as in classroom D. Students learn the dialogue sentences by heart, one by one. First they listen carefully to the teacher, or to a native model on tape, until they can distinguish the sounds and intonation of the phrase to be learned. Then they repeat the phrase after the model until they are repeating it accurately and fluently. When most students can repeat it acceptably on their own, further phrases are learned. This learning process is at first a group activity. Students repeat the phrase together in chorus, then in smaller and smaller groups (i.e., halves of the class, then rows), and finally as individuals. If a group falters, the class returns to choral response; if the individual falters, the teacher returns to small-group response. This choral response becomes dialogue when several phrases are already learned: question and answer are now exchanged by halves of the class, rows, or teacher and class, with frequent reversal of roles so that all students can have practice in both asking questions and answering them.

After a dialogue has been learned, adaptations of the dialogue, with a more personal application to the student's own situation, provide further consolidation of learning and give opportunity for more flexible use of the material. These are acted out by the students.

When the dialogue sentences are very familiar, pattern drills based on the structures in the dialogues usually become the main activity. (The various types of structural pattern drills are discussed in chapter 4 below.) Some authors of audio-lingual texts prefer to develop drills on structures different from those in the dialogues, believing that in this way they can provide a more logical development of basic language requirements. They maintain that dialogues should be used solely for familiarizing students with the common expressions that make for a natural conversational exchange in everyday situations, and that dialogues become artificial when they are written to contain specific structures for later drilling.[11] Even where the structures to be drilled are drawn directly from the dialogue material, pattern drills develop the potential of the structures beyond their function in a particular dialogue, giving the students practice in using them in wider contexts.

Structural pattern drills are first practiced orally, with a classroom technique similar to that for dialogues. Choral response is followed by small-group practice and then individual response, with a return

11. A distinction is drawn between *conversation-facilitation* dialogues and *grammar-demonstration* dialogues in chapter 7 below.

to the larger group when the smaller group or the individual falters. Some teachers give an explanation of the structure before drilling the students in its use. Others wait until the students have achieved some facility in manipulating a particular structure before giving the rule for the structural changes observable in the drill. Coming at this stage, the rule is not a prescription telling the students what they should do, but a generalization setting out in organized form what the students have been doing in the drill.

After some sections of the work have been learned entirely orally without recourse to the textbook, the student is systematically introduced to the reading of the printed script. For some languages there are particular difficulties at this point, because of a different script or because there is no easily predictable relationship between the sounds and the symbols. With languages which use the Roman or Cyrillic script, seemingly familiar symbols can lead to incorrect pronunciations. To obviate such mistakes, the students, in the audio-lingual approach, first read what they have memorized and practiced orally in class, and their attention is drawn by the teacher to the relationships between sounds and symbols. Even after they have been allowed access to the printed page, they are always taught new material orally and given oral practice with the script before being allowed to work with it on their own. It is not until they have a firm grip of most basic structures that they are presented with material to read which is not an adaptation or recombination of what they have already learned orally.

In the beginning stages, writing is imitative, consisting of transcriptions of words and dialogue sentences from the book. Students may also be given the opportunity to write out variations of structural pattern-drill items, just as they have constructed variants orally in class sessions. After they have acquired a small stock of useful expressions and some confidence in manipulating basic structures, they will be encouraged to express themselves more independently on certain topics by giving oral reports to the class and by writing these down in the form of short compositions. These first efforts at recombining what has been learned in order to make comments of a more personal nature are controlled in content so that students will not fall into linguistic traps of which they are quite ignorant. The student may be asked to answer a series of questions or to follow a basic framework set out in the target language. At the elementary level of instruction, all oral and written practice of this type is kept within the limits of what has been learned thoroughly. The emphasis is on structuring the situation so that the student will not make mistakes, or at least will make very few.

45

At more advanced levels, attention turns more and more to reading materials. Well-written passages, carefully chosen for the level of difficulty of the language and for the authentic picture they convey of the culture of the people who speak that language, are read in the target language. Even at this stage, however, listening and speaking are not neglected: texts are discussed orally, and sometimes students listen to recordings of them. Written composition provides students with further opportunities to use the material they have learned in a more individual fashion. When students have learned to read fluently in the new language, they are encouraged to embark on wider reading of their own choice.

Critique

The stated objectives of the audio-lingual method are the development of mastery, at various levels of competency, in all four language skills—beginning with listening and speaking, and using these as a basis for the teaching of reading and writing. Paralleling this linguistic aim is the endeavor to develop understanding of the culture of other peoples through experience with their language.

By the techniques we have described, audio-lingualists do achieve success in developing comprehension and fluency in speaking the target language, within a limited body of language material, very early in the students' learning experience. From the beginning, students learn segments of language which can be of immediate use for communication, and are trained to understand and produce utterances in the new language with recognizable and acceptable sound patterns and at a normal speed of delivery. With much practice in listening, students are trained in auditory memory and in making fine discriminations among sounds.

Structural patterns are systematically introduced and repracticed, and students are given very thorough drilling in the production and variation of structural elements which they must learn to use eventually without conscious attention to their systematic features. Reading and writing are not neglected; nor are they left to develop haphazardly. Materials in these areas are based on the student's growing knowledge of the structure of the language.

Students in audio-lingual classes experience very early in their studies a sense of achievement in being able to use what they have learned. The techniques advocated permit of active participation by all students for most of the time, yet in circumstances (e.g., choral and group response and drill) which protect them from the embarrassment that students in more traditional classes feel on hearing themselves uttering strange sounds and phrases in front of their classmates. The type of practice advocated is well suited for individual work with recorders or in a language laboratory.

There are, however, certain dangers in this method of teaching which can be avoided if the teacher is aware of them and takes steps to counteract them.

If audio-lingual training is given in a mechanical way, students may progress like well-trained parrots—able to repeat whole utterances perfectly when given a certain stimulus, but uncertain of the meaning of what they are saying and unable to use memorized materials in contexts other than those in which they have learned them. Students must be trained from the first lesson to apply what they have memorized or practiced in drills in communication situations contrived within the classroom group.

Techniques of memorization and drilling can become tedious and boring, causing fatigue and distaste on the part of the student. A successful application of the audio-lingual method requires inventiveness and resourcefulness on the part of the teacher, who must be continually alert for opportunities to vary the presentation of material and to force the students into interesting situations where they will feel a spontaneous desire to express themselves through what they have learned.

If students are trained to make variations on language patterns without being given a very clear idea of what they are supposed to be doing in the process, they may not understand the possibilities and limitations of the operations they are performing. As a result, they may have difficulty in using these structural patterns for expressing their own meanings. With a well-structured sequence of dialogues and drills, there will be little need for lengthy explanations of structural relationships. Students will become aware of these through the way in which material is being used in communication activities. Where these relationships are not clear, the teacher will need to draw the attention of the students to the crucial element in a series of drills, so that they may realize the significance of variations they are making and thus absorb the structural meaning.

Whether the audio-lingual method is appropriate for all types of students and for students of all ages is another controversial subject. Experience has shown the method to be appropriate for younger children, who love to mimic and act out roles and to learn through activity rather than through explanations and the learning of facts. The less gifted student also seems to profit from this method. These students find it hard to cope with the abstractions of grammar and are often left behind by students of higher intelligence in the direct method, where they must acquire the meanings of words and the functioning of structural patterns inductively. In the audio-lingual method they are carried along by the work with the group; they learn to mimic, repeat utterances, and manipulate structures with relative ease, and so they feel they are making progress. They enjoy learning the language while they are with the class, usually dropping out before they fall too far behind to be able to cope with more autonomous activities. The most gifted students sometimes become bored long before other students have had enough structured practice to develop firm control of morphological and syntactic associations. The teacher must help these rapid learners to understand their own need for systematic practice, beyond mere intellectual understanding. They should not, however, be kept at practice they do not need, when they could be using the time for personal expression in the language. They should be encouraged to seek contacts with native speakers to practice using the language actively. Where this is not possible, they should read a wide range of contemporary material personally selected. The use of take-home cassettes for individual practice enables students to spend more or less time on structured practice, depending on their individual needs.

The audio-lingual method makes considerable demands upon the teacher. It requires near-native articulation and intonation in modeling utterances for students. Teachers lacking in this area must learn to use recorded models and work along with the class in making up their deficiencies. The method calls for considerable energy if the teacher is to keep oral practice moving smartly, and imagination and enterprise in using persons and situations in the classroom if the text material is to acquire reality and relevance. It is difficult for a teacher to teach a number of parallel classes during the day by this method without becoming weary of the material and physically and emotionally exhausted. Teachers who are in this situation may need to introduce more reading and writing activities than they might have wished if they are to maintain the same level of energy in classes throughout the day.

RESTORING THE COGNITIVE ELEMENT

In the sixties, a number of criticisms of the then dominant audio-lingual method were voiced,[12] reflecting certain problems teachers had experienced in their classes. Beliefs about the nature of language and language learning were also evolving, with the development of

12. The most detailed critique of the audio-lingual method, and one of the earliest, was Wilga M. Rivers 1964, which contains a chapter (13) of recommendations for improving audio-lingual teaching.

transformational-generative grammar and cognitive psychology. (These are discussed more fully in chapter 3.)

In 1965, Carroll had reviewed recent developments in linguistics and psychology. He concluded that the "audiolingual habit theory" was "ripe for major revision, particularly in the direction of joining with it some of the better elements of the cognitive code-learning theory," which he defined as "a modified up-to-date grammar-translation theory." Neither of these theories, he maintained, was closely linked to any contemporary psychological theory of learning, and both could be improved by taking into consideration the appreciable body of knowledge that had accumulated in the area of verbal learning. He advocated constant alternation among varied patterns in drilling, emphasis on meaningfulness, proper attention to visual-symbol systems in student learning, conscious attention to and understanding of critical features of what one is learning, and making as many kinds of associations as possible, whether auditory, visual, or kinesthetic, to ensure better learning and retention.[13]

Cognitive-Code Learning

Carroll's proposals led to a plethora of recommendations for a "cognitive code-learning" method of teaching languages. This was much discussed but ill defined and consequently never gained the status of what one might call a method.[14] Chastain tried to pin it down in 1971. He took as "one basic tenet of the cognitive approach" that "students never be expected to meet new structures prior to the explanation of those forms. The term 'cognition'," he continued "implies proceeding from mental understanding and awareness to practice; from studying a structure to seeing it used in context. In other words, the term 'cognition' implies a conscious acquisition of 'competence' followed by a conscious application of the 'competence' in the conscious development of 'performance' skills."[15] (Whether this is in fact what cognition implies will be discussed in chapter 3.)

Chastain's is, of course, a deductive approach. In discussing "cognitive" materials, Chastain states that "a cognitive book would not

---

13. J. B. Carroll, "The Contributions of Psychological Theory and Educational Research to the Teaching of Foreign Languages," *MLJ* 49 (1965): 273–81.

14. E. M. Anthony, "Approach, Method, and Technique," in H. B. Allen and R. N. Campbell 1972, describes *"method"* as "an overall plan for the orderly presentation of language material, no part of which contradicts, and all of which is based upon, the selected *approach*. An approach is axiomatic, a *method* is procedural." An attempt was made to develop a cognitive-code method, based on a cognitive approach.

15. K. Chastain, *The Development of Modern Language Skills: Theory to Practice* (Philadelphia: The Center for Curriculum Development, 1971), p. 48. For an explanation of the terms "competence" and "performance," see chapter 3 below.

proceed in an inductive fashion. . . . A cognitive book would proceed from focus on structural forms and functions, to exercises, to reading."[16] The class is structured so that "each day the students have some new material, some exercises, and some application activities" (1971, p. 51; 1976, p. 156). All four skills are taught at once. "The materials are so arranged that the learner is first exposed to the parts to be learned and then to the total communicative picture" which is presented through reading and listening materials (1976, pp. 150, 157). Chastain proposed the following order of learning—step 1: comprehension of new grammatical concepts which are presented deductively; step 2: practice in selection of linguistic forms to fit the context in exercises; step 3: the study of reading and listening materials, with some opportunity provided for students to produce messages intended to communicate their thoughts to someone else (1976, pp. 156–57).

Critique
No distinctively new activities are proposed for this form of "cognitive" teaching, but rather a return to the traditional order which moves from deductive explanations of rules to exercises in the use of those rules, followed by demonstration of the rules in action, in stretches of discourse, or application of the rules in contriving messages in the language.

Here we may refer to the first section of this chapter, "Formalists and Activists." If induction-deduction is regarded as a main axis, we have the direct method at one end of a continuum, the inductive end, and the grammar-translation method at the other, or deductive, end. A desire to systematize or structure the material to be taught brought a transition from direct method to modified direct method,[17] and eventually to the audio-lingual method. The procedural order and associated activities proposed by Chastain swing his recommendations to the deductive end of the continuum. They emphasize other formalist characteristics also, such as a preference for language anal-

16. Chastain, *The Development*, p. 48. These sentences do not reappear in the second edition of the book (Chastain 1976), but the remaining quotations from Chastain in this and the following subsection do (the 1976 page references are given for these). The deductive approach and procedures outlined in this section remain unchanged in the 1976 book (pp. 147 ff.).

17. The French *méthode audio-visuelle* in *Voix et Images de France* (Paris: Didier, 1962) may be viewed as a more structured form of the *méthode directe*. It was designed for use with small groups of students of mixed language backgrounds, learning French in a French-speaking environment. It kept, therefore, to the direct method principles of an inductive approach and the keeping of all learning materials and activities in the target language in order to stimulate the formation of direct links between concepts and target-language words.

ysis before language use and the type of learning situation where students are receiving instruction and applying it as directed.[18]

Cognitive Habit-Formation Theory

In 1971, Carroll drew attention to much misapplication of the ideas he had expressed in 1965. "Our field," he said "has been afflicted with many false dichotomies, irrelevant oppositions, weak conceptualizations, and neglect of the really critical issues and variables."[19] In particular, he deplored the tendency to oppose "rule-governed behavior" and "habits" as incompatible concepts in language learning.

To Carroll, a habit is "any learned disposition to perceive, behave, or perform in a certain manner under specified circumstances. To the extent that an individual's language behavior conforms to the habits of the speech community of which he is a member, we can say that his behavior is 'rule-governed.' "[20] The rules of the linguist, he explains, are "statements of [some] of the conditions under which certain language habits manifest themselves in a given speech community."[21] A rule is an abstraction, but a habit is what has actually been learned; in other words, "the notion of 'habit' is much more fundamental, psychologically, than the notion of 'rule.' "[22]

Carroll, therefore, sees a place for habit formation as well as rule learning in language teaching. He proposes a meaningful synthesis between habit-formation theory and cognitive-code learning theory, since people learn languages by the conscious acquisition of knowledge about the language that with time and appropriate experience is converted into habits. As for an inductive versus a deductive presentation, Carroll points out that research thus far has shown that "neither alone is adequate; for effective teaching there must be considerable alternation between rules and examples. It hardly matters whether one starts with the rule or the example as long as this alternation exists."[23]

The real problem, according to Carroll, is that an overemphasis on linguistic rules and grammaticality may lead to an underemphasis on

18. Chastain says, "The students proceed through the book in its arranged order, studying the structural presentations, the exercises, and then the application activities" (*The Development*, p. 50; Chastain 1976, p. 156). See also Appendix II, "Discipline," in *The Development*, pp. 369–73.

19. J. B. Carroll, "Current Issues in Psycholinguistics and Second Language Teaching," *TQ* 5 (1971): 102.

20. Ibid., p. 103. For a discussion of rule-governed behavior, see chapter 3 below.

21. Carroll, "Current Issues," p. 103.

22. Ibid., pp. 103–4.

23. Ibid., p. 112.

the meanings associated with the communicative situation, meanings that derive from the perceptions and intentions of speaker and hearer.[24] Great attention should be paid to the formation of truly functional habits—the habits of actual language behavior.[25] It is to the provision of many opportunities for such practice that the teacher's attention should be directed.

"NATURAL" LANGUAGE LEARNING

An approach to language teaching that constantly recurs through the centuries is the attempt to achieve a language-learning situation which resembles as closely as possible the way children learn their first language. The experience of little children seems to us so effortless, so enjoyable, and so successful in contrast to most classroom language learning that the possibility of reproducing it with adolescents or adults acquires an irresistible fascination.

Basically the natural approach involves setting up informal situations where students communicate with each other and their teacher and, through communicating, acquire the new language. (This is the goal of most language camps.) To be successful, this type of teaching has to be conducted with a deep concern for the student as a human being who has emotional needs to be satisfied as well as intellectual and physical ones. There must exist a relationship of acceptance and equality between student and teacher and between student and student if any genuine interaction is to take place. Trust and confidence are the key words.[26] Since the student is not taught explicitly but learns through experience with the language, this is an active, inductive approach.

The nineteenth-century proponents of the "natural method" rejected all use of books in their teaching and taught students to rely only on their ear, thus "picking up the language" as an immigrant might do when acquiring the language informally in a new country.

24. Ibid., p. 106.
25. Ibid., p. 111.
26. For a discussion of the type of relationship which should exist, see Wilga M. Rivers, "The Natural and the Normal in Language Learning" in H. D. Brown 1976, pp. 1–8; and "The Natural and the Normal in Language Teaching: Where's the Difference?" in Schulz 1977, pp. 101–8. For a description of natural language learning, see Tracy D. Terrell, "A Natural Approach to Second Language Acquisition and Learning," *MLJ* 61 (1977): 325–37. The most wide-ranging research into informal group learning of foreign languages has been conducted by Curran in implementing the Counseling-Learning Model (Community Language Learning). C-L/CLL is described in Curran 1976. Chap. 2: "Learning: A Counseling Model," pp. 19–43, which describes the emotional evolution during counseling-learning sessions, is valuable reading for all who are interested in their students as persons and individual learners.

This perfect opportunity for the immigrant to acquire a language in an environment where that language is spoken is often idealized. Sweet, in 1899, in discussing the claims for the natural method of his day, remarked that "the results of picking up a language entirely by ear from the beginning may be seen in uneducated adults who come among a population speaking a strange language: after years of residence in the country they are often unable to utter anything but a few words and phrases" (Sweet 1899, p. 76). The natural method, he maintained, "almost necessarily implies a residence in the country where the language is spoken" (ibid., p. 75). Even then, he advocated systematic study to offset the problems of what one has misheard or confused. Studies by Krashen and Seliger of foreign students learning English in the United States support Sweet's contention. They have found that formal instruction plays an important role in language proficiency. When students were matched for active practice, those with more instruction were more proficient.[27]

Recent researchers in second-language acquisition have become interested in the differences between what is learned in an informal environment where the language is spoken and what is learned through systematic study. Krashen has proposed that the first be termed *acquisition* of a language and the second *learning*. In language acquisition, in an informal situation, he believes, "linguistic abilities are internalized 'naturally,' that is, without conscious focusing on linguistic forms. It appears to require, minimally, participation in natural communication situations." Language learning, on the other hand, is "a conscious process, and is the result of either a formal language learning situation or a self study program."[28] (The problem in applying this distinction too rigorously is that data are often not available on the degree to which the apparently "natural acquirer" who is successful is actually consciously self-teaching. See Naiman et al. 1978.)

What is missing from the conventional structured language-teaching situation, in this view, is the opportunity to acquire natural language in a subconscious manner from hearing and using it[29]—an element considered to be essential to complement what is learned in systematic study. The present approach to natural language learning, then,

27. S. D. Krashen, "The Critical Period for Language Acquisition and its Possible Bases," in Aaronson and Rieber 1975, pp. 214–17.
28. S. D. Krashen, "The Monitor Model for Adult Second Language Performance," in M. Burt, H. Dulay, and M. Finocchiaro, eds., *Viewpoints on English as a Second Language* (New York: Regents Publishing Co., 1977), pp. 152–53.
29. An approach which specifically emphasizes subconscious assimilation of language material is G. Lozanov's Suggestopedia. For references, see note 42 below.

seeks the best of both worlds. Students study the language system-atically on their own or in the language laboratory (computer-assisted instruction fits in well here) and class sessions are devoted entirely to natural interaction.[30] These sessions provide opportunities for the students to create new utterances[31] from a basis of linguistic knowl-edge. To facilitate comprehension and expression of one's own mes-sage, emphasis for these communication sessions is on the acquisition and use of a wide vocabulary, rather than on the complexities of grammar. (The problems of learning how to communicate freely in a classroom setting are discussed more fully in chapter 8.)

THE ECLECTIC APPROACH

Teachers faced with the daily task of helping students to learn a new language cannot afford the luxury of complete dedication to each new method or approach that comes into vogue. They need techniques that work in their particular situation with the specific objectives that are meaningful for the kinds of students they have in their classes. On the other hand, teachers need the stimulation of a new approach from time to time to encourage them in reading, discussions with colleagues, and classroom experimentation. Trying out new ideas in class is exciting and challenging. It is for these reasons that many experienced teachers are eclectic in their teaching: they like to retain what they know from experience to be effective, while experimenting with novel techniques and activities which hold promise for even more successful teaching.

This eclectic approach has an honorable ancestry, which includes such highly esteemed giants of the language-teaching profession as Henry Sweet and Harold Palmer.

Sweet believed that "a good method must, before all, be compre-hensive and eclectic. It must be based on a thorough knowledge of the science of language. . . . In utilizing this knowledge it must be constantly guided by . . . psychological laws" (Sweet 1899, p. 3). Sweet sought "a mean between unyielding conservatism on the one hand and reckless radicalism on the other" (ibid., p. vii). His search was for general principles on which language teaching should be based, rather than the "one absolutely invariable method" (ibid., p.

---

30. Lambert Sauveur, the leading proponent of the Natural Method in the United States in the nineteenth century, had also proposed that students study the textbook at home as preparation for active use of the language in class. See Kelly 1969, p. 261.

31. H. Dulay and M. Burt call this process "creative construction." See "Creative Construction in Second Language Learning and Teaching," in H. D. Brown 1976, pp. 65–79, and in Burt and Dulay 1975, pp. 21–32.

82). These general principles were to be supplemented by special principles concerning the teaching of specific languages.

In *The Principles of Language-Study,* published in 1921, Palmer speaks of "accepting any two or more rival expedients and . . . embodying them boldly as separate items in the programme, in order that each may fulfil its function in a well-proportioned and well-organized whole" (Palmer 1921, p. 141). He calls this the *multiple line of approach.* "We use," he says, "each and every method, process, exercise, drill, or device which may further us in our immediate purpose and bring us nearer to our ultimate goal; we adopt every good idea and leave the door open for all future developments; we reject nothing except useless and harmful forms of work. The multiple line of approach embodies the eclectic principle . . . , for it enjoins us to select judiciously and without prejudice all that is likely to help us in our work" (ibid.).

Eclecticists try, then, to absorb the best techniques of all the well-known language-teaching methods into their classroom procedures, using them for the purposes for which they are most appropriate. True eclecticists, as distinguished from drifters who adopt new techniques cumulatively and purposelessly, seek the balanced development of all four skills at all stages, while retaining an emphasis on the early development of aural-oral skills, where this is appropriate to the objectives of their courses. They adapt their methods to the changing objectives of the day and to the types of students who pass through their classes. They gradually evolve a method which suits their personality. To be successful, an eclectic teacher needs to be imaginative, energetic, and willing to experiment. With so much to draw from, no eclecticist need lack for ideas for keeping lessons varied and interesting.

Areas of Controversy

Should foreign-language skills be learned in the order in which children learn their native language?

The order recommended by audio-lingualists for the learning of foreign-language skills (listening, speaking, reading, writing) is sometimes justified by the argument that it is the order in which children learn their native language. The situation of the child learning a first language and that of the adolescent or adult student learning a second or third language are, however, dissimilar in many ways.

Children are exploring their environment, forming concepts, and acquiring language at the same time. They are surrounded by the speech of their family group for most of their waking hours and soon learn the sound combinations that can get them what they want and need. Their smallest, most incorrect attempts at imitating this language are rewarded by approval and interest, and gradually they find themselves able to communicate their needs and excitements by this new means. All these factors encourage them to greater efforts at mastery.

Our students already possess an effective means of communication. To learn another, which is not essential for their basic needs, they must limit themselves and embarrass themselves by their obvious incapacity to express their real meaning. Their incorrect efforts often bring more disapproval than would a discreet silence on their part. Sounds which their social group has previously approved are now not considered adequate. For many of them, all this language-learning business is merely a classroom activity which ceases at the end of the hour.

Adolescent or adult students have been trained to study with books and pen. Now they may be denied these aids and asked to depend on their auditory memory. They may also be asked to produce strange sounds which make them feel rather ridiculous. Their minds are full of their first language, many of the concepts of which do not appear to parallel those of this new language. It is obvious that they have neither the motivation nor the unique situational opportunity of the languageless infant.

This order of learning language skills cannot be justified, then, merely by analogy with native-language learning. It may seem, however, a logical order in communication-oriented classes. Since a language is an arbitrary code associated with the behavior of a certain group of people, it must, if it is to be understood, be pronounced and phrased as this group has habitually pronounced and phrased it. After students have heard the correct spoken form of the language, they can attempt to reproduce it themselves. Until they have learned the accepted pronunciation, phrasing, and intonation, they cannot read it as it would be read by a native speaker. Unless they have read over a script demonstrating the way speakers of the language consider it should be written, they cannot attempt to write it themselves.

The basic question for the teacher is not one of nature or logic but of the best order of presentation from the pedagogical point of view. Are languages learned more efficiently if the skills are ordered in some way for presentation of language material? In the middle of the nineteenth century, Marcel proposed for introductory study the order:

reading, listening, speaking, writing.[32] Gouin, at the end of the century, proposed that one begin with speaking accompanied by physical activity, to be supported later by writing.[33] Postovsky has proposed listening and writing, with no speaking for the initial period,[34] while Asher has advocated listening with physical action as the only response.[35] The Silent Way requires the teacher to say as little as possible so that students' speaking is the principal activity.[36] The grammar-translation method begins with reading and writing. One can make a case for concurrent listening and reading for introductory study.[37] Many textbooks begin with reading and speaking about what one has read (in this case, even the questions to which the student is responding may be printed in the book). Many different combinations of skills seem to have been successful in introducing the student to the language. It is what is done with the learned material to extend it as early as possible to active use that is crucial.

Decisions on ordering of skills will depend on the aims of the course. Where communication skills are the main objective, listening and speaking seem the obvious place to begin, and, of these, recent research tends to favor listening as the more important initially until the student has acquired some feeling for the intonation and phrasing of the language. If reading is the primary objective, texts may be tackled directly through deciphering techniques.[38] Motivationally speaking, the aural-oral skills are a good starting point for any general course because most students come to their first language class with the notion that language is something one hears and speaks. Should we disillusion them so soon?

An aural-oral beginning also lends itself to much activity and participation by the students—an approach much more likely to gain and keep their interest than another hour plunged in a book. It is this

32. C. Marcel, writing in the heyday of the Natural Method, opposed the confusion of the order of learning the mother tongue with that of learning a second language. See Kelly 1969, p. 216.

33. For a detailed description of Gouin's approach, see Titone, 1968, pp. 33–37; and *PG's*, chap. 1.

34. V. A. Postovsky, "Effects of Delay in Oral Practice at the Beginning of Second Language Learning," *MLJ* 58 (1974): 229–39; and "Why not Start Speaking Later?" in Burt, Dulay, and Finocchiaro 1977, pp. 17–26. See also discussion on pp. 177–78.

35. J. J. Asher, "The Learning Strategy of the Total Physical Response: A Review," *MLJ* 50 (1966): 79–84; and *PG's*, chap. 1. Other references in chap. 6, note 25, below.

36. Gattegno 1972; C. Dominice, "The Silent Way: A Student looks at Teaching," *ADFL* 5 (1973–74): 23–24; Stevick 1980, pp. 37–82; and *PG's*, chap. 1.

37. W. M. Rivers, "Linguistic and Psychological Factors in Speech Perception and Their Implications for Teaching Materials," *SMT*, pp. 142–43, discusses concurrent listening and reading.

38. See "Reading for Information," in *PG's*, chap. 6.

aural-oral emphasis that makes the language class so different from the general run of school subjects, and this in itself can be an attraction.

Should the written form of the language be withheld from the students until they are able to use the material orally?
Early audio-lingual proponents required that students work with all material until they had a good control of it. This did not mean, of course, that the student had to know the language thoroughly before learning to read or write it. It meant that in the early stages all language learning and practice were to be in the aural-oral mode, the students being introduced to the graphic symbols (the written form of the language) only after they had demonstrated mastery of a certain body of material. Then they would learn to read and write what they had learned orally. Even after the introduction of a script, all new material was to be presented and practiced orally before being read or written. Some audio-lingual experimenters suggested periods of as long as twenty-four weeks before students saw anything in graphic form,[39] although periods of from six to ten weeks were more common. It was believed that this time lag reduced the amount of interference from native-language habits of pronunciation associated with the printed symbols, where these were similar for the two languages, and that it forced the students to concentrate their attention on accurate and thorough learning of the new material.

Many experienced teachers have objected to this particular aspect of the audio-lingual approach. They have found that some students feel very insecure when they are forced to depend on the ear alone, partly because they find it hard to remember all they hear in a situation where so many of the sound clues are unfamiliar to them, and partly because all through school they have been trained to work with books. Such students can develop emotional reactions to purely aural-oral work which hinder them in the learning of the language. Still other teachers have found that students from whom all graphic representation of the foreign language is withheld will make their own imperfect notes surreptitiously and thus learn incorrectly.[40] They believe it is better for students to see the correct, accepted version of the written language at an earlier stage and learn to use it as a help and support for learning and practice.

Students who have immediate access to a graphic representation of what they are learning will often depend on it too much and not

---

39. See F. Marty's description of the Middlebury College experiment in *Language Laboratory Learning* (Wellesley, Mass.: Audio-Visual Publications, 1960), p. 75.
40. Ibid., p. 76.

give sufficient time to practicing until the work is assimilated and internalized. It seems a reasonable approach to present all new material first in oral form, especially in the elementary sections of the course; to give students practice in working with this material orally until they can handle it with ease; then to train them with the script, which they can then use as a help for clarification and assimilation. This sequence can take place within one lesson. Neither teacher nor student should feel, however, that once the material is presented in graphic form the time for practice is over. After students have received some help from the printed version, they should be given opportunities to practice the material orally until they can demonstrate that they have learned it thoroughly and are able to apply it to situations of their own devising.

Annotated Reading List

HISTORY OF LANGUAGE TEACHING

Newmark, Maxim, ed. *Twentieth Century Modern Language Teaching: Sources and Readings,* pp. 1–86. New York: Philosophical Library, 1948. Articles on leading movements and personalities in modern-language teaching from the Middle Ages to the present day.

Titone, Renzo. *Teaching Foreign Languages: An Historical Sketch.* Washington, D.C.: Georgetown University Press, 1968. Useful summaries of the approach to language teaching of many leading exponents through the centuries.

METHODS OF LANGUAGE TEACHING

Direct Method (with modifications)

Sweet, Henry. *The Practical Study of Languages.* London: Oxford University Press, 1964. A reprint of the 1899 text (Dent).

Jespersen, Otto. *How to Teach a Foreign Language.* London: George Allen & Unwin, 1904. Reissued 1961.

Reading Method

West, Michael. *Learning to Read a Foreign Language and Other Essays on Language-Teaching.* London: Longmans, 1941.

Bond, O. F. "A Reading Technique in Elementary Foreign Language Instruction: [I] Structure; [II] Results and Implications." *MLJ* 14 (1930): 363–74, 532–44. Coleman, A. "A New Approach to Practice in Reading a Modern Language." *MLJ* 15 (1930): 101–18.

Audio-lingual Method

Brooks, Nelson. *Language and Language Learning: Theory and Practice.* 2d ed. New York: Harcourt, Brace & World, 1964. Lado, Robert. *Language Teaching: A Scientific Approach* New York: McGraw-Hill, 1964.
Both Brooks and Lado give a clear exposition of the methodology and techniques of the audio-lingual method.

Rivers, Wilga M. *The Psychologist and the Foreign-Language Teacher.* Chicago: University of Chicago Press, 1964. A description and critique of the audio-lingual method with an analysis of the psychological assumptions on which it is based. Gives recommendations for improving its effectiveness.

Cognitive Approach

Carroll, John. B. "The Contributions of Psychological Theory and Educational Research to the Teaching of Foreign Languages." In Valdman 1966. Original article proposing that some elements of "cognitive code-learning theory" should be combined with the prevailing "audiolingual habit theory."

———. "Current Issues in Psycholinguistics and Second Language Teaching." *TQ* 5 (1971): 101–14. States that there is no real conflict between "audiolingual habit" and "cognitive-code learning" theories, nor between rule-governed behavior and language habits and that both are necessary in language learning.

Chastain, Kenneth. *Developing Second-Language Skills: Theory to Practice.* 2d ed. Chicago: Rand McNally, 1976. Discusses audio-lingual and cognitive theory and proposes language-learning activities which he considers to be "cognitive."

Rivers, Wilga M. "The Foreign Language Teacher and Cognitive Psychology or Where do We Go from Here?" In *SMT,* pp. 109–30. Discusses areas of cognitive psychology and their implications for language learning and teaching.

Natural Language Learning

Terrell, T. D. "A Natural Approach to Second Language Acquisition and Learning." *MLJ* 61 (1977): 325–37.

Eclectic Method

Palmer, Harold E. *The Principles of Language-Study.* London: Oxford University Press, 1964. A reprint of the 1921 text (Harrap).

Rivers, Wilga M., et al. *Practical Guides to the Teaching of French/German/Spanish/English as a Second or Foreign Language* (New York and London: Oxford University Press, 1975–78).

————. "The View from the Top—A Wider Perspective." In NEC 1979, pp. 11–18. Gives a detailed rationale for an eclectic approach to meet the needs of different kinds of students.

Research and Discussion

1. (a) Watch a language class (or a videotape of your own teaching) and note the techniques used in the lesson. (b) Take your description and classify the types of activities you have observed. (c) Beside each type, set down the assumptions about language learning on which it is based. (d) Did the lesson reflect a consistent methodology (that is, were the techniques employed part of an overall plan of instruction based on a coherent set of assumptions about language learning)? Discuss inconsistencies in practice that you have detected. (Were these inconsistencies warranted by some aspect of the classroom situation?)

2. (a) Set down what you yourself believe about language and language learning. (b) List the types of activities you think are important in a language-learning class. (c) Beside each of the class activities you have listed, set down the assumption about language or language learning it seems to imply. (d) Compare this list with your own statement of beliefs. How can you make your classroom practice reflect more precisely what you believe about language and language learning?

3. (a) Write down two headings: *habit-formation approach* and *cognitive approach*. Then make lists of techniques which seem to you to exemplify each of these approaches. (b) Consider the usefulness or otherwise of each of the techniques you have listed (for which aspect of language learning? for which type of student? for which level of instruction? in which kind of learning situation?).

4. Curran and Lozanov are both psychotherapists interested in the language-learning process who have made proposals for language-teaching situations. Describe Curran's Community Language Learning[41] and Lozanov's Suggestopedia.[42] Can you identify elements

41. For Community Language Learning (CLL), see Curran 1976; review of Curran's approach by E. Stevick, *LL* 23 (1973): 259–71; articles on CLL by H. D. Brown, P. G. LaForge, and J. Rardin in *TQ* 11, 4 (December 1977): 365–87; Stevick 1976, pp. 125–33; and Stevick 1980, pp. 85–226.

42. For Suggestopedia, see W. J. Bancroft, "The Lozanov Language Class," ERIC Documents on Foreign Language Teaching and Linguistics, 1975, 53 pp. ED 108 475; "Suggestology and Suggestopedia: The Theory of the Lozanov Method," 1977, 56 pp., ED 132 857; and "The Lozanov Method and its American Adaptations," *MLJ* 62 (1978): 167–75; G. L. Racle, "Can Suggestopaedia Revolutionize Language Teaching?" *FLA* 12 (1979): 39–49; R. W. Bushman and H. S. Madsen, "A Description and Eval-

common to both approaches? How would they fit into the program in which you are or will be teaching? (Compare your findings with those of Rivers in Yorio, Perkins, and Schachter 1979.)

5. Find out what you can about the Dartmouth Method.[43] Compare it with audio-lingual and direct methods. What similarities do you find and what differences?

6. Does the Silent Way[44] teach communication? Compare it with the direct method.

7. Gouin based his method on action-chains. Compare and contrast his techniques with the "total physical response."[45]

8. Find a Cleveland Plan textbook (the direct method approach of De Sauzé)[46] and a rationalist direct method or verbal-active[47] textbook. Compare and contrast the approach of the authors of these books to materials development and classroom techniques.

9. Study recent journals of the professional association for the particular language you teach. What type of methodology seems to be advocated at the moment by the leaders in your language area? From your experience as a learner and as an observer, how does this conform with the way this language is actually being taught at the present time?

*10. Krashen and Seliger propose a feature analysis for differentiation of and comparative research in the efficacy of various language teaching methods for adult learners.[48] Analyze according to this technique four methods of your choice.

uation of Suggestopedia—A New Teaching Methodology," in Fanselow and Crymes 1976, pp. 29–39; and Stevick 1980, pp. 229–59.

43. For the Dartmouth method, see J. A. Rassias, "New Dimensions in Language Training: The Dartmouth College Experiment," *ADFL* 3 (1971): 23–27, and "Why We Must Change," *ADFL* 3 (1972): 9–13; S. Luxenberg, "All the Class a Stage," *Change* 10, 1 (1978), special issue, Report on Teaching 5: 30–33.

44. For the Silent Way, see n. 36 above.

45. See nn. 33 and 35 above.

46. For de Sauzé, see K. C. Diller, *Generative Grammar, Structural Linguistics, and Language Teaching* (Rowley, Mass.: Newbury House, 1971), chapter 7. The second edition of this book is titled *The Language Teaching Controversy* (see Diller 1978).

47. See R. Hester, ed., *Teaching a Living Language* (New York: Harper and Row, 1970); and *PG*'s, chap. 1.

48. S. Krashen and H. Seliger, "The Essential Contributions of Formal Instruction in Adult Second Language Learning," *TQ* 9 (1975): 173–83.

3· Theories of Language and Language Learning

To many people—former students in our schools—learning another language is essentially a question of grammar. We hear the complaint: "I was never any good at learning languages because I could never remember the grammar." In the description in chapter 1 of foreign-language teaching in four classrooms, we saw that some of the variation stemmed from the attitudes of the teachers toward grammar. "It is tremendously important that the students know their grammar," said teacher A, while teacher D spoke of giving the students "confidence in the active use of the structural patterns of the language"— surely another way of speaking about grammar. Some teachers, on the other hand, maintain that we can speak and write our native language with ease and assurance "without knowing any grammar," and that a knowledge of grammar should therefore not be required of the person learning another language. Yet others maintain that our students cannot use their native language properly, in speech and writing, because they were never "taught grammar." So the controversy goes on. As soon as the fundamental question of the role of grammar is raised in language-teaching circles, the discussion becomes animated, even heated, and, before the discussion has finished, at least some of the participants are likely to have taken up rigid and uncompromising positions.

WHAT IS GRAMMAR?
To most people, grammar is the rules of a language set out in a terminology which is hard to remember, with many exceptions appended to each rule. Few people stop to think of the origin of these "rules" or of their validity; still fewer ask themselves why there are so many exceptions. Most people have been taught "grammar rules" at school and are convinced that these rules have existed since schools began; they may not be questioned; they tell us what is right and what is wrong in what people write and say. They seem immutable despite the fact that the language we hear and read every day does not necessarily conform to the standard established in the rules.

It is because of this almost superstitious regard for the "rules of grammar" that scholars who have dared to rewrite the grammar of an established language have sometimes been treated as iconoclasts and dangerous heretics. They have rejected time-honored injunctions and prohibitions in order to bring the "rules" into conformity with actual usage, and have thus appeared to some to be threatening the very foundations of the established order.[1] In attempting to describe in a new way the operation of the language, they have cast doubt on the validity of accepted categories and proposed new ones, thus continuing a long tradition of linguistic research.

GRAMMATICAL ANALYSIS AND DESCRIPTION

Few teachers, let alone students, are aware that such basic and apparently "natural" categories as "parts of speech" have evolved through the discussions of grammarians over the centuries. Lyons points out that for Plato the category "verb" encompassed what we call adjectives as well as verbs, since it represented words that express the action or quality in the predicate (Lyons 1968, pp. 10–11; this view has been resurrected by some contemporary linguists). Aristotle established three classes of words: nouns, verbs, and "conjunctions," the latter class containing all words not considered nouns and verbs (in Plato's sense of the word; ibid., p. 11). The Stoics classed the adjective with the noun. It was not until the late second century B.C. that the adverb, pronoun, and preposition were categorized, (p. 12), while the adjective had to wait until medieval times (p. 11).

The writing of a grammar is basically an attempt at systematization and codification of a mass of data which may at first sight appear amorphous but within which recurrent regularities can be discerned. The way in which this systematization is approached will depend on the convictions of the grammarian about the nature of language.

There is nothing sacrosanct about the grammatical categories one linguistic system may establish. Nor do we have any assurance that the categories established for words at the surface level of one language will necessarily be valid for another, quite different language, although for convenience in language teaching we may sometimes use the same category labels for some approximately equivalent functions. Some familiar categories may not be apparent in the new language, as for instance in Japanese, where there are no segments equivalent to our definite articles or relative pronouns. One of the advantages of learning a new language is the opportunity it affords to observe the different forms and categories speakers of different languages have evolved for communicating their experiences, in both the outer world of physical reality and the inner world of emotion and

---

1. An example of this emotional reaction can be seen in the title of a book opposing C. C. Fries's approach to English grammar: *Who Killed Grammar?* by H. Warfel (Gainesville, Fla., 1952).

thought. These may be reflected in a completely different surface-level "grammar."

Linguists have taken many different approaches to the analysis and description of languages, each approach bringing us some new insights into what we are doing when we are communicating. Some linguists have analyzed utterances into constituents which occupy specific positions in the structure of an utterance (although they may be rearranged to vary meaning), as in structural grammar. Others have preferred to identify segments of utterances which fulfill certain functions in conveying meaning, as in case grammar, which uses such categories as agent, patient, instrument, or locative. Still others, as in transformational-generative grammar, seek to analyze an utterance logically. The latter is an approach with a long history in linguistics. The initial division of all sentences in transformational-generative grammar into noun phrase (NP) and verb phrase (VP) reverts to the Platonic classification, which identified the subject of a proposition and what was said about it (or the predicate). Subject and predicate approximate the *topic* and *comment* of Hockett and the *theme* and *rheme* of the Prague School of linguistics, with the difference that both of these sets of terms distinguish functional rather than logical categories (Hockett 1958, p. 201; Vacheck 1966, p. 18). The topic of a sentence may actually be the grammatical subject or it may be in the predicate, and stress or word order will often determine the distinction of topic from comment. "Theme" designates the old information or given, supplied by the context, whereas the "rheme" refers to the new information about the theme. Again the rheme may be the predicate of the utterance or it may be expressed by the grammatical subject.

In the European tradition, grammatical analyses have come down to us from the scholars of ancient Greece, and the basic divergence in approach which existed among grammarians at that time is still reflected in the differing viewpoints we hear today. For some grammarians, language reflects a reality which exists beyond language itself, whether categories of logic derived from man's innate neural organization, or relationships observable in the physical world; for others, a language is a purely arbitrary set of associations among which systematic relationships can be discerned and described and for which categories can be established in terms of the unique system of the particular language being studied. For those who hold the first of these views, the categories of grammar are the same for all languages, because the external reality they represent is the same for all men; for those holding the second view, each language must be described in terms of its own coherent system.

The Greeks originally described their language in terms of observed form and function (that is, relationships among elements of the language); but to the formal categories they had established they also attached concepts which related this system of classification to the external environment. Later, Greek language description passed, by way of Latin, to other languages, European and non-European, for which this particular description of forms and relationships was no longer necessarily valid. As a definition of the established categories according to forms of the Greek language was now meaningless, it was the conceptual interpretation which was transformed to the new situation. These conceptual interpretations (e.g., nouns as names of people, places, and things; verbs as a class of words denoting actions or states) were vague and inexact in their application to the various categories, even in the Greek language. Referring as they did to features of an environment familiar to all men, they were, however, readily adopted by grammarians of other languages, who, despite obvious discrepancies, proceeded to tailor the descriptions of their own languages to what they accepted as being categories of universal application.

In the thirties and forties, structuralists raised objections to the practice of describing any and every language with the same set of conceptual terms. They considered these hindered the precise identification of elements of structure and their interrelationships in a wide variety of language systems, many of which were very different from the well-studied Romance and Germanic languages. From this ferment emerged different ways of describing languages. The grammarian looked for recurrent features and arrangements of words and morphemes without having recourse to meaning as the basis for making distinctions. Taking grammatical form as the criterion, form-classes were established which could be grammatically defined. As Gleason put it: "If our understanding of structure is based on meaning, and our understanding of meaning on structure, we are in a most vicious circle. . . . In order to make the study of meaning as effective as possible, we must first have an objective understanding of structure" (Gleason, 1961, pp. 94–95). The commonly accepted parts of speech (such as nouns, verbs, adjectives, prepositions), regarded as form-classes, were now considered to be language-specific, to be defined for a particular language, according to the structure of that language, and this definition would not necessarily be applicable to any other language.

When these methods were applied to the description of little-known languages which had never before been closely studied, they passed unnoticed except by scholars in the field. When they were applied to languages for which there were well-established and widely accepted grammatical analyses of the traditional kind, these innovations caused considerable bewilderment and sometimes aroused active resistance.

The intense interest in transformational-generative grammar in the fifties and sixties revived the notion of universal categories applicable to all languages, although these were now considered features of an abstract deep structure from which surface forms developed after the operation of a series of transformations. Despite this underlying identity as categories, they might take quite different forms in the tremendous diversity of surface structure of the world's languages. No matter what the language, the basic sentence could be broken down into such categories as noun phrase (NP) and verb phrase (VP). These could then be subdivided into more restrictive categories for which familiar terms like determiner, noun, verb, and adverb (or adverbial) were used, although their definitions did not always conform strictly to the usage of traditional grammar.

Clearly, there are many ways of looking at languages. Language teachers need to develop flexibility in their thinking in this regard, so that they may be able to see, and present to their students, the structure of a new language as it is, and not as an imperfect reflection of their own language. Students need to learn that there is more than one way of codifying thought and meaning. Thus the introduction to a new language becomes an exciting exploration. Understanding a diversity of cultures begins with an appreciation of the infinite potential for linguistic diversity.

Spoken or Written Language?

Further discussion and controversy were provoked by a shift of emphasis in grammatical study from the structural patterns of written language to those of spoken language. Although some grammarians down the centuries had always maintained that speech is the fundamental model from which written forms have been derived, written language data were, until recently, more readily available in a permanent form than records of speech.[2] For a long time, then, written language was the traditional basis for grammatical study. With the development of recording equipment, modern linguists have had greater opportunities than their predecessors to examine in depth the characteristics of spoken language. Their analyses of speech data have shown the degree to which the patterns used in oral communication diverge from the accepted patterns for writing a language.

2. The Sanskrit grammarian Pānini, writing between 350 and 250 B.C., discusses speech and pronunciation, presenting the sounds in an involved, but very precise, phonemic system.

67

Since written language represents the production of literate and educated persons who often edit their original output, taking pride in their ability to produce a polished product, it evolves less rapidly than spoken language, conserving many forms which are no longer heard. On the other hand, examination of what people actually say has revealed that many forms which grammarians have declared to be incorrect and unacceptable are current in the everyday speech even of educated persons. Grammars derived from speech data may therefore be expected to diverge to some extent from grammars of written language if they are faithful to the recorded corpus. To many people who have been trained from childhood to believe in a standard of "correct speech," to which in actual practice nobody conforms in every detail but which is enshrined in grammar books, the inclusion in new grammars of the patterns of spoken language has seemed to give so-called "nonstandard" forms a stamp of official acceptance. Purists have revolted against such permissiveness. The concept of a grammar as a description of all the observed phenomena in a language as it is spoken and written, rather than as a prescriptive manual to which they can turn for guidance, is an idea which many have found hard to accept.

Parole and Langue

Since the time of the Swiss linguistic scientist Ferdinand de Saussure (1857–1913) it has become customary to distinguish between two aspects of language: *parole* and *langue*. What people say in a language is *parole,* and this varies to some extent from individual to individual and from situation to situation. *Parole* is affected by the purposes of speakers, their emotions at the time when they are expressing themselves, or the circumstances of the utterance. A speaker may, for instance, be tired, or preoccupied, or in great haste. The individual memory and attention span of the speaker play a role. Speakers are also affected by the developing content and the reaction of their listeners. As a result an utterance may be begun in one conventional form and finished in quite another. An individual piece of writing also falls into the category of *parole* and is similarly affected by many contingencies.

Because of the variety of factors which may affect the form of a specific utterance or piece of writing, it is difficult to study *parole* systematically. From samples of *parole* (spoken and written) can be abstracted the system of language habits of a whole social group, "the social side of speech, outside the individual who can never create nor modify it by himself" (Saussure 1959, p. 14); this is what de Saussure terms *langue*. It is this systematic patterning underlying individual utterances which makes it possible for one person to understand or be understood by another. Native speakers acquire this language system through their experiences in the cultural group, and the system can be discerned, however imperfectly, in everything they say or write. A grammar is not a description of *parole,* with its infinite and unpredictable possibilities of variation, but of the coherent system of patterning in *langue.*

When we say that a grammar describes spoken forms of language, it is the abstraction, the average drawn from the individual utterances of many speakers, to which we are referring, and not to particular utterances, which may be "ungrammatical" in that they do not conform in certain details to the language conventions of the group. These individual lapses and idiosyncrasies are different from the "common errors" listed in school textbooks. "Common errors" have a distribution far beyond the individual; they are a part of *langue.* Often they provide evidence of evolution in the language; they are the growing edge of change. At other times they represent forms and patterns in common use which prescriptive grammarians have ignored or rejected, either because they did not fit neatly into the system they had elaborated or because they were used by members of a social group which the grammarians considered inferior. As living patterns they have flourished despite all efforts through the schools to bring about their extinction. Modern linguists attempt to account for these phenomena in their grammars, as well as for those already covered in traditional grammars.

- **Look at the textbook you are using at present, or one you intend to use. How is the language handled in this book? (Spoken or written forms? formal or informal? prescriptive or descriptive approach? appropriate for oral communication or reading? generally useful or specialized?)**

ASPECTS OF LANGUAGE

There are various ways of approaching the description of a corpus of language data. Some grammarians begin with phonology and move on to morphology, syntax, and semantics, describing each as a separate system while showing points of interaction among them. Others consider these four traditional areas of analysis to be so closely interwoven in the expression of meaning that they must be dealt with as manifestations of one basic structural system which is not apparent in surface phenomena but must be sought by analysis in depth. Some linguists have ignored semantics as being too diffuse to describe as a formal system, others have dealt with it separately from syntax, while still others have considered it central to all linguistic description.

Language description and analysis has aroused keen interest during the last fifty years. The exponents of traditional grammar have continued to refine the categories and rules of the predecessors. The proliferation of nontraditional approaches, however, has left the non-linguist bewildered by their diversity, with no obvious criterion for selection among them. We have had the immediate-constituent or structural grammar of Bloomfield, which held sway until the end of the fifties. Then came the transformational-generative grammar of Chomsky (the *Syntactic Structures* model in 1957 and the *Aspects* model in 1965). In the form of Extended Standard Theory, Chomsky's approach still flourishes. The tagmemics of Pike, the stratificational grammar of Lamb, and British systemic linguistics, exemplified by Halliday, continued on their way, despite the closing of ranks behind Chomsky. Recently there has been revived interest in the functionalism of the Prague school. In the generative mode, Fillmore developed his case grammar; Ross, Lakoff, and McCawley their generative semantics; and Chafe his meaning-structure grammar. Each has been very influential in its own sphere. We now hear of the relational grammar of Perlmutter and Postal, the daughter-dependency grammar of Hudson and Schachter, and Montague grammar, to name but a few of the leading contenders for the attention of linguists.[3]

If linguistics has something to say to language teachers (and Chomsky, at least, was not sure that what it had to say was obvious),[4] where does the language teacher begin? A basic understanding of how the proponents of two influential schools of linguistic thought

3. References for immediate-constituent grammar and transformational-generative grammar are given in later footnotes to this chapter. For tagmemics, see R. E. Longacre, *Grammar Discovery Procedures* (The Hague: Mouton, 1964); for stratificational grammar, S. M. Lamb, *Outline of Stratificational Grammar* (Washington, D.C.: Georgetown University Press, 1966); for systemic grammar, M. A. K. Halliday, *Explorations in the Functions of Language* (London: Edward Arnold, 1973), and *Language as Social Semiotic: The Social Interpretation of Language and Meaning* (London: Edward Arnold, 1978); for Prague School, see Vacheck 1966; for case grammar, C. J. Fillmore, "The Case for Case," in *Universals in Linguistic Theory*, ed. E. Bach and R. T. Harms (New York: Holt, Rinehart and Winston, 1968); for generative semantics, G. Lakoff, "On Generative Semantics," in Steinberg and Jakobovits 1971; for meaning-structure grammar, W. L. Chafe, *Meaning and the Structure of Language* (Chicago: University of Chicago Press, 1970); for relational grammar, D. Johnson, "On the Role of Grammatical Relations in Linguistic Theory," in *Papers from the Tenth Regional Meeting of the Chicago Linguistic Society*, ed. M. La Galy, R. A. Fox, and A. Bruck (Chicago: University of Chicago, 1974); for daughter-dependency grammar, R. Hudson, *Arguments for a Non-Transformational Grammar* (Chicago: University of Chicago Press, 1976); for Montague grammar, B. H. Partee, ed., *Montague Grammar* (New York: Academic Press, 1976).
4. N. Chomsky, "Linguistic Theory," in NEC 1966, pp. 45, 49.

have viewed language will help to loosen up the ideas of the language teacher and make the viewpoint of linguistically-oriented books and articles more comprehensible. At the same time we will discuss what some theorists of language teaching and learning have been able to draw from ongoing linguistic research.

IMMEDIATE-CONSTITUENT OR PHRASE-STRUCTURE GRAMMAR

The approach to grammar associated with the names of such linguistic scientists as Bloomfield, Fries, Bloch, and Hockett,[5] is called immediate-constituent or sometimes phrase-structure grammar. It differs from traditional grammar in its concentration on structural meaning in the sense in which Fries uses this term. For Fries there are three types or "modes" of meaning in language: lexical, structural, and social-cultural.[6] *Lexical meaning* is what we commonly consider the "dictionary meaning" of words; it is not regarded by structuralists as a part of grammar, being an area of study in its own right. *Social-cultural meaning* refers to the special significance which language elements acquire for persons living in a particular culture and is related to the values, customs, and interests of the social group; this again is considered by Fries to be outside the realm of grammar. There remains *structural meaning,* which is conveyed by the relationships among the elements in an utterance. As Fries expresses it: structural meanings are "specifically signaled by a complex system of contrastive patterns.[7] In traditional grammar, as found in school textbooks, structural meaning has been expressed in conceptual terms. As a result, the function of one element in relation to other elements within a segment of discourse has frequently been confused with the functioning of these elements in a contextual situation (that is, in the expression of an idea or message). Structural grammar attempts to explain grammatical relationships solely in terms of the formal features observable within the language corpus.

In language analysis as practiced by structuralists, structural meaning is established at several levels. Syntactic relationships are identified first (that is, relationships between sections of a sentence, between phrases such as a noun phrase and a verb phrase, or between words within phrases). Larger entities are gradually broken down by

---

5. L. Bloomfield, *Language* (New York: Holt, Rinehart and Winston, 1933); C. C. Fries, *American English Grammar* (New York: Appleton-Century-Crofts, 1940); B. Bloch and G. Trager, *Outline of Linguistic Analysis* (Baltimore: Linguistic Society of America, 1942); and Hockett 1958.

6. "Meaning and Linguistic Analysis," in Allen 1964, pp. 107–9 (reprinted from *Language* 30 [January–March, 1954]: 57–68).

7. Ibid., p. 108.

a process of binary division into smaller and smaller constituents, until ultimate constituents which can undergo no further division are identified. The constituents at a particular level under consideration are called immediate constituents. At the level of the word, constituents are grouped into categories according to function, these functional categories being signaled by formal features. Thus *word-class* membership indicates identity of relationship with other elements in the structure and is not, as in traditional grammar, conceptually based. These functional categories are more rigorously related to the particular system of the language being analyzed than the presumably universal categories of traditional grammar. Below the word level, segments of words are identified as *morphemes*, that is, the smallest elements which convey meaning, and therefore the ultimate constituents in morphology. Since stress and intonation signal relationships between the segments, or constituents, at any one level they are termed *suprasegmentals*. Phonology is studied separately from morphology and syntax, the stream of sound being reduced in a similar fashion to its ultimate constituents, the *phonemes*, which are the smallest elements of sound conveying distinctions in meaning. The hierarchy of binary combinations in phrase structure is usually represented by a tree diagram that clearly indicates the relationships between groupings of constituents at higher and lower levels.

Structural Principles in the Classroom

Structural grammar had considerable influence on the preparing of materials for language teaching. The emphasis on structural rather than lexical or situational meaning was basic to the development of pattern or structure drill. In pattern drills, certain formal or functional features are isolated, and students are taught to create new utterances in response to formal cues rather than as an expression of personal meaning.

Pattern drills were developed as a technique for building habits in the new language. Talking about the operation of the foreign language in conceptual terms or in terms applicable to the system of another language was discouraged. This change of approach did not mean the abandonment of grammar, but made the active practice of grammatical structures the core of the language program. The structuralist influence also led to the teaching of phonemic distinctions in the sound system of the language rather than phonetic differences. Suprasegmentals (stress, intonation, elisions, juncture) were also emphasized as essential to meaning.

TRANSFORMATIONAL-GENERATIVE GRAMMAR

Transformational-generative grammar sprang primarily from the research of Harris, Chomsky, and Halle.[8] Its exponents concentrated their research in the areas of syntax and phonology, with some work in semantics, particularly by Katz.[9] (They considered that most morphological properties could be more conveniently studied in association with the lexicon.) Unlike some immediate-constituent grammarians, transformationalists saw no need to discard the categories of traditional grammar, while recognizing that their boundaries needed to be redefined for different languages.

Competence and Performance

Basic to transformational-generative theory is the distinction between competence and performance (Chomsky 1965, pp. 3–9). The *competence* of speaker-hearers is their intuitive knowledge of the complex system of rules of their language. Evidence of the existence of this underlying competence is provided by the intuitive recognition by native speakers of the degree of grammaticalness of any utterance in their language and by their ability to produce grammatical utterances, although they may not in fact always do so. *Performance* is the term used for their production of utterances in actual situations. As with *parole,* performance is very variable and may not conform at all times with the speaker-hearer's competence. Language competence is established in the first place from a study of sentences which are samples of performance, but once a theory of competence is elaborated it can be used in the study of the more complex aspects of performance.

According to Chomsky's formulation, the native speaker has internalized a complex "system of rules that relate signals to semantic interpretations of these signals"[10] and which can generate all the grammatical sentences of the language. The speaker-hearer is not conscious of this system; nevertheless, it determines the form of all utterances. Transformational-generative grammarians seek to ascer-

---

8. Z. Harris, "Discourse Analysis," *Language* 28 (1952): 1–30, and "Co-occurrence and Transformation in Linguistic Structure," *Language* 33 (1957): 283–340; also M. Halle, "Phonology in a Generative Grammar," *Word* 18 (1962): 54–72. These three articles are reprinted in *The Structure of Language,* ed. J. Fodor and J. Katz (Englewood Cliffs, N.J., Prentice-Hall, 1964). See also M. Halle, *The Sound Pattern of Russian* (The Hague: Mouton, 1959); Chomsky 1957, 1965, and 1972b; N. Chomsky and M. Halle, *The Sound Pattern of English* (New York, Harper and Row, 1968).

9. See J. J. Katz and J. A. Fodor, "The Structure of a Semantic Theory," *Language* 39 (1963): 170–210; J. J. Katz, *The Philosophy of Language* (New York: Harper and Row, 1966), and *Semantic Theory* (New York: Harper and Row, 1971).

10. N. Chomsky, *Topics in the Theory of Generative Grammar* (The Hague: Mouton, 1966), p. 10.

tain these rules from a study of overt performance. They delve beneath the surface structure of utterances to the deep structures that have generated these utterances by a series of transformational rules from basic strings of structural formatives, which are the product of abstract universal principles.

For the transformational-generative linguist, every utterance can be analyzed through successive transformations (processes such as replacement, addition, deletion, changes of position) until its base structure is revealed. Where base structures are particularly simple, they are very like what have been called kernel sentences. The base structures, containing only obligatory transformations such as agreement, conform to the abstract systems of grammatical relations which can be discovered in the deep structures of all languages. According to Chomsky, these universal abstract systems are not learned by children in the process of acquiring their native language but correspond to the structure of their innate neural organization. As examples of such universals, Chomsky cites the subject-predicate relationship, and the noun-verb distinction, which appears in all languages even though the boundaries between what is considered a noun and what is considered a verb may vary. According to Chomsky and Halle, phonological structure is derived by rule from the syntactic structure and is, therefore, equally derivative from the deep structure of the language, with both the syntactic and the phonological systems contributing to the semantic interpretation of an utterance.

Grammar, then, is a system of transformational and rewrite rules which can predict all possible sentences of the language, but none which the native speaker will consider unacceptable. Generative grammar can deal with ambiguities which surface phrase-structure grammar would not elucidate: it provides a method for uncovering the variation in deep structure of two utterances which would appear identical in an immediate-constituent analysis. It can also uncover basic sentences which have become embedded or nested in other sentences. In these ways it is more powerful than immediate-constituent grammar.

- **Think for a moment about the sentence, "Flying planes can be dangerous." This sentence, out of context, is ambiguous, since two interpretations are possible. How would you paraphrase these two interpretations so that the surface structure of your paraphrases would reveal the differences in meaning? In analyzing them, can you detect more than one base structure?**

CHANGING VIEWS OF HOW LANGUAGE IS ACQUIRED

In the behaviorist theory of stimulus-response learning, particularly the operant conditioning model of Skinner,[11] all learning is regarded as the establishment of habits as the result of reinforcement or reward. According to this theory, infants acquire their native-language habits in the following fashion. At some stage during random babbling, infants make some sound which resembles the appropriate word for some person or object nearby. For this, the infant is rewarded by approving noises or smiles, and so the probability that the same grouping of sounds will be emitted in a similar situation is increased. With repeated reinforcement a habit is established, and the child continues to name this person or object in the same way. As children continue to imitate sounds, more combinations are reinforced. When they name something imperiously, it is brought to them. In this way, they learn to use words with sentence intention as mands, and later to combine words to convey more complexity of meaning. As they acquire more of the syntactic and morphological variations of the language, they create new combinations by generalization or analogy, sometimes making mistakes by producing analogies which are not permissible in that language. By a trial-and-error process, in which acceptable utterances are reinforced by comprehension and approval and unacceptable utterances are inhibited by lack of reward, they gradually learn to make finer and finer discriminations, until their utterances begin to resemble more and more the speech of the community in which they are growing up.

The behaviorist view of native-language learning was rejected by a number of theorists, notably Chomsky and Lenneberg. These writers maintained that certain aspects of native-language learning made it impossible to accept the habit-formation-by-reinforcement theory.[12] Lenneberg drew attention to the fact that all children, with the rare exception of children with certain physical disabilities, learn a language to a similar degree of mastery of basic structures, despite great differences in cultural environment and amount of parental attention. All children learn the language of their community at about the same age, irrespective of the degree of structural complexity, and all children seem to pass through the same stages of development in acquiring it. Lenneberg pointed out that child language learning does not appear to be a process of pure imitation, but seems to involve

11. B. F. Skinner, *Verbal Behavior* (New York: Appleton-Century-Crofts, 1957).

12. N. Chomsky, "Linguistic Theory," in NEC 1966, p. 44; and E. Lenneberg, "The Capacity for Language Acquisition," in *The Structure of Language,* ed. Fodor and Katz, pp. 579–603 (revised and expanded version of "Language, Evolution and Purposive Behavior" [1960]).

active selection from what is heard and personal construction of forms, according to the child's developing system. Combining of words in meaningful sequences seems to develop at a stage when the infant realizes that sounds and objects or situations have some relationship. The available evidence, he felt, supported the view that this realization is a matter of maturation.

Lenneberg considered that speech is a species-specific ability which is peculiar to man. He maintained, with Chomsky, that man has certain innate propensities for acquiring a language, and for acquiring a language with a complicated grammar. He drew attention to the fact that children add endings to nonsense words in a way which they have never heard around them, and that, as they master various aspects of syntax, they produce utterances they have certainly never heard before. Chomsky, with his interest in the hierarchical operation of syntax, was struck with the way children seem quite rapidly to internalize a highly complicated system of grammar, so that they are able to recognize and produce at will any number of novel utterances. To him, it was manifestly impossible for the child to acquire this system of grammar by some vague process of imitation and generalization.

Chomsky theorized that the innate logical structure of the child's nervous system (the child's *faculté de langage*) conforms with the abstract universal categories and organization underlying language. Consequently, children identify the basic syntactic system of the language to which they are attending, and mastery of the language develops from this identification, rather than being built in through repetition and reinforcement.

As Lenneberg puts it: "Obviously, children are not given rules which they can apply. They are merely exposed to a great number of examples of how the syntax works, and from these examples they completely automatically acquire principles with which new sentences can be formed that will conform to the universally recognized rules of the game. . . . Words are neither randomly arranged nor confined to unchangeable, stereotyped sequences. At every stage there is a characteristic structure. . . . The appearance of language may be thought to be due to an innately mapped-in *program* for behavior, the exact realization of the program being dependent upon the peculiarities of the (speech) environment."[13]

13. Lenneberg, "Capacity," pp. 599–600.

THE IMPACT OF TRANSFORMATIONAL-GENERATIVE THEORY ON LANGUAGE TEACHING

Surface Structure and Meaning

Transformational-generative linguists made it clear by their analyses that apparent similarity of surface forms of a language may camouflage important differences in meaning. Chomsky's classic example of this fact was the juxtaposition of the two sentences, *John is eager to please* and *John is easy to please*. In the former, John does the pleasing; in the latter, someone else pleases John. It became clear that intensive drilling of indiscriminately selected surface features which appeared to represent the same "pattern" of item arrangement could lead to error when the student attempted to develop new sentences by analogy with the forms practiced. Teachers and materials writers began to look much more carefully at the items to be used in drills to ensure that the "patterns" were really analogous at the deep-structure level.

Creative Aspect of Language Use

As we have noted, Chomsky hypothesized that language was not acquired by children through a form of conditioning dependent on reinforcement or reward. He maintained that human beings come into the world with innate language-learning abilities in the form of a language acquisition device (LAD) which proceeds by hypothesis testing. Children make hypotheses and compare these with their innate knowledge of possible grammars based on the principles of universal grammar. In this way, the individual's competence, or internalized knowledge of the grammar of the language, is built up, and this competence makes language use, or performance, possible. Language use is thus rule-governed behavior which enables speakers to *create new utterances* which conform to the rules they have internalized.[14]

This "creative aspect of normal language use"[15] caught the attention of language teachers as well as linguists: at any moment, a speaker may produce an utterance which has never been heard before in that identical form, and this utterance will be understood by other speakers of the language who have never before heard an identical utterance. To Chomsky, this "stimulus-free and innovative"[16] property of language is what cannot be explained in terms of stimulus-and-response habit formation and generalization. It can be explained in terms of an internalized system of rules that can generate an infinite

14. Chomsky 1965, pp. 25–26, and "Linguistic Theory," pp. 43–49.
15. Chomsky, *Topics,* p. 11.
16. Chomsky, "Linguistic Theory," p. 46.

number of grammatical sentences that will be comprehensible and acceptable when uttered with the appropriate lexical items in a communication situation.

Affirmations such as these caused teachers to take another look at the popular technique of requiring students to memorize long dialogue sentences and to practice using them in the precise form memorized. Materials writers looked carefully at their dialogues and concentrated on producing much shorter exchanges, containing useful building blocks of language that students could adapt to express their meaning in their own way. This viewpoint also led to a reemphasis on teaching students to understand the operations of the grammatical system, so that they could use it effectively to generate new utterances. It highlighted the necessity to encourage students from the beginning stages to experiment creatively with the small amount of language they had acquired, thus learning to form new combinations to meet new circumstances rather than merely practicing material they had memorized. Teachers began to provide many more opportunities in their classes for spontaneous discussion and for impromptu activities that simulated actual situations in which the students might find themselves in the foreign culture.

- **How much provision does your textbook make for the creative use of language?**

Rule-Governed Behavior

The words "rule-governed" applied to language use appealed to those teachers who had worried about the fact that grammar rules were not systematically presented, explained, and learned in the inductive procedures of the audio-lingual approach. They proposed a return to explaining grammar rules first, thus involving students' reasoning processes in language learning, in contrast to what some called the "mindless" drilling in audio-lingual classes. This emphasis on explanations of grammatical functioning was a major feature of what came to be known as cognitive-code learning (see chapter 2).

That a deductive instructional approach of this type is more "cognitive" than the inductive, discovery approach to grammar of audio-lingual methodology is by no means evident, since induction requires cognitive processing just as much as deduction does. It is extremely doubtful that Chomsky was preaching the superiority of deductive over inductive processes. Transformational-generative grammarians arrive at their linguistic rules by a process of induction, as does Chomsky's hypothesis-testing first-language learner (see p. 77). Furthermore, the "rules" to which Chomsky was referring were not pedagogical explanations of language functioning but rules "of great abstractness and intricacy," inherent in the structure of a language, which, according to Chomsky, there is no reason to suppose can be brought to conscious awareness.[17] Chomsky's views did not, therefore, provide justification for reintroducing into the classroom the unreliable ad hoc grammar rules of traditional textbooks, authored often by persons with little knowledge of linguistic theory. Textbook rules had been criticized earlier by British linguists of the systemic school for their "unclear categories, heterogeneous criteria, fictions, conceptual formulations and value judgments, . . . inaccurate phonetics and confusion of media" (Halliday, McIntosh, and Strevens 1964, p. 157).

Chomsky distinguishes between two types of grammars. "A grammar in the traditional view," he says, "is an account of competence. It describes and attempts to account for the ability of a speaker to understand an arbitrary sentence of his language and to produce an appropriate sentence on a given occasion. If it is a pedagogic grammar, it attempts to provide the student with this ability; if a linguistic grammar, it aims to discover and exhibit the mechanisms that make this achievement possible."[18] Acceptable performance is not possible while competence is defective. Practice in performance in the classroom is practice in generating new utterances, according to the rule system as one has experienced it, not in parroting utterances produced by the teacher. This innovative ability will, according to Chomsky, exist only to the degree that underlying competence exists (that is, to the degree that the rule system has been internalized).

Students who have merely constructed utterances according to a pattern set by the teacher, without a realization of the way the new structural system is operating in these utterances, will be at a loss when they need to construct novel utterances to convey their own message. They must move beyond the stage of producing utterances by analogy with other utterances to the stage where they are constructing utterances in conformity with the grammatical system of the new language, but without that conscious preoccupation with the rules which causes the speaker to falter. In other words, they need to have "internalized" the rules so that these can be applied rapidly and effortlessly to express the nuances of their meaning.[19]

17. Chomsky, *Topics*, p. 10. For a more detailed discussion of Chomsky's viewpoint, see Wilga M. Rivers, "Rules, Patterns, and Creativity," in *SMT*, pp. 9–20.

18. Chomsky, *Topics*, p. 10.

19. Bahlsen, who was a student of Plötz, the nineteenth-century proponent of the grammar-translation method, recalls that having to write a letter or speak in the foreign language would raise before his mind "a veritable forest of paragraphs" and "an impenetrable thicket of grammatical rules." Quoted in Titone 1968, p. 28.

How the rules are to be "internalized" so that they work for the speaker-hearer in this way is the eternal problem of language teaching. The way they operate may be practiced intensively, with attention to the crucial element of the drill, but the rules must then be applied by the students in sentences of their own devising. Alternatively, they may be explained concisely and clearly, in relation to their role in the total language system, and then practiced to achieve a facility of application (for a shorter or longer time, depending on their complexity), with plenty of opportunity provided for spontaneous production. Only through active attempts at expressing meaning does the student become confident in using the rules to express personal messages. However the problem is tackled, the three elements of understanding, some form of practice, and use to express personal meaning are essential if students are to use the language effortlessly, as native speakers do.

- **How are rules introduced into the lessons in your textbook? Inductively, deductively, or both? Before, after, or during practice exercises? Through verbal description or in schemas? Exhaustively or functionally? How do you evaluate the quality of these rules?**

Hypothesis Testing

The theory of an innate language acquisition device that proceeds by hypothesis testing had considerable influence for a while on studies of the acquisition of a first language by children. This led researchers interested in the acquisition of second and third languages to investigate whether a later language was acquired in the same fashion as the first, drawing in some way on the same innate language-acquisition faculty.

A number of early studies in second-language acquisition tried to find a parallelism between the order of acquisition of a limited number of grammatical morphemes of English by first-language (L_1) and second-language (L_2) learners.[20] This, they felt, would demonstrate that the L_1 and L_2 learners were following a similar developmental path and using comparable strategies in language acquisition. The order of acquisition of these morphemes was found to be significantly different for L_1 and L_2 learners, although the same morphemes did seem to be among the first acquired by both groups of learners. The acquisition order of morphemes reported for L_2 was considered by some to be an artifact of the measuring instrument. Others found that the order of acquisition reported for L_1 correlated highly with the fre-

20. The particular morphemes involved in these studies are listed in N. Bailey, C. Madden, and S. Krashen, "Is There a 'Natural Sequence' in Adult Second Language Learning?" *LL* 24 (1974): 236.

quency of occurrence of these morphemes in native-speaker speech. Researchers then became interested in the speech L_2 learners were hearing from other children and the adults with whom they were in contact. This reintroduced the question of the role of imitation versus that of innate developmental strategies in L_2 acquisition. For classroom learning, the type of speech heard from the teacher or taped material was clearly of interest in this regard, as was its general usefulness for active communication.

Most of this early L_2 research concentrated on the acquisition of a second language by young children (and some adults) in informal settings or bilingual classes.[21] More studies of older learners in formal instructional settings are needed if the results are to be useful to the foreign-language classroom teacher. Research is continuing in this direction.[22]

First-language acquisition researchers with a strong interest in syntax observed that young children seemed to pass through a series of *interim grammars*, of increasing degrees of complexity, as they tested hypotheses about the form of the languages they were learning. These interim grammars were described and studied synchronically (that is, at a particular point in time) as discrete syntactic systems. This approach interested those concerned with the acquisition of second or foreign languages. The term "interlanguage"[23] came into use to describe the kind of language a particular second-language learner was using at a given time, that is, the learner's version of the new language, which deviated in certain ways from that of a native speaker. This interlanguage was considered to be the product of hypotheses the second-language learner was testing about the form of the grammar of the new language. Lack of comprehension on the part of the hearer, or inability to draw coherent meaning from a text, would, it seemed, lead the learner to reject one hypothesis and develop another, thus modifying the interim grammar which had produced the aberrant utterance or interpretation. There has been much controversy as to the degree of interference, or negative transfer, from the first language

21. For a useful summary and assessment of developments in this area, see K. Hakuta and H. Cancino, "Trends in Second Language Acquisition Research," *Harvard Educational Review* 47 (1977): 294–316. Original studies are reprinted in Hatch 1978.

22. See, for example, S. D. Krashen and H. W. Seliger, "The Essential Contributions of Formal Instruction in Adult Second Language Learning," *TQ* 9 (1975): 173–83; H. Seliger, "Does Practice Make Perfect?: A Study of Interaction Patterns and L_2 Competence," *LL* 27 (1977): 263–78; J. Schachter, "An Error in Error Analysis," *LL* 24 (1974): 205–14; and J. Schachter, A. F. Tyson, and F. J. Diffley, "Learner Intuitions of Grammaticality," *LL* 26 (1976): 67–76.

23. L. Selinker, "Interlanguage," *IRAL* 10 (1972): 219–31.

that can be detected in the student's interlanguage[24] and the degree to which the student's deviations from authentic second-language forms represent developmental errors of a universal character (that is, deviant forms similar to those observable in children learning this language as a first language).

Some L_2 researchers have rather vehemently discounted the notion of interference, or negative transfer, from first-language use, because they see it as support for a habit-formation view of language acquisition. (Positive transfer where the two languages operate in similar fashion is more difficult to distinguish from new learning.) Later L_2 acquisition studies of single individuals over a protracted period of time have, however, brought to light instances of what looks very like negative transfer of L_1 features, or at least of L_1 concepts, in L_2 use, although the nature and degree of such transfer has still not been determined.[25] It has been suggested that these instances of what looks like interference represent hypothesis testing, in the sense that L_2 learners are testing the hypothesis that L_2 structure = L_1 structure. It may also represent the very natural process of falling back on what one knows and adapting it when faced with a situation for which one does not have the L_2 linguistic means.

Whatever the final issue of this controversy, foreign-language classroom teachers were rather bewildered to be told that negative transfer from L_1 was practically nonexistent, since they had regularly observed instances of something which looked very much like it in the speech and writing of their previously monolingual L_2 learners. Clearly, interference from previous learning does not always come from L_1. When students are learning third and fourth languages, it seems more commonly to come from a more recently learned language, or at least from the non-native language over which the language learner has the weakest control. This may be L_2, L_3, or L_4 (see Appendix B).

The hypothesis-testing and interlanguage theories slowly began to affect classroom practice. Teachers who had been trained to structure classroom situations so that students would not make errors, or hear errors from others, were now urged to accept errors in second-language production as indicators of progress through interim grammars and as guides to the incorrect hypotheses their students had formed.

24. For a discussion of the contrastive analysis versus error analysis controversy, see S. N. Sridhar, "Contrastive Analysis, Error Analysis, and Interlanguage: Three Phases of One Goal?" in *Studies in Language Learning* 1 (1975): 60–94, also in *Indian Linguistics* 37 (1976): 258–81; and B. Spolsky, "Contrastive Analysis, Error Analysis, Interlanguage, and Other Useful Fads," *MLJ* 63 (1979): 250–57.

25. See studies by H. Wode, K. Hakuta, and R. Ravem in Hatch (1978).

Others pointed out that a study of the errors made by individual students would reveal to the teacher the strategies these students were employing in trying to learn the language.[26] Attention was also drawn to the problem of fossilized forms, that is, incorrect forms which remain in the speech and writing of student learners, even though they have been taught and appear to understand the rules.[27] Research is needed into this phenomenon. At present we do not understand why some forms become fossilized and not others, and especially what teachers can do to avoid or remedy a problem which has long been the bane of teachers and students at the intermediate and advanced levels.

The convergence of the emphases just discussed has led to a new realization of the active role of the language learner, as opposed to the teacher, in the language class. Whether students study the grammar of the language in class with the help of the teacher, or out of class (as programmed or individual preparation based on the textbook, or through language laboratory practice), much more time is now devoted than formerly to communicative interaction among students as an indispendable element in learning to use a language. This means moving beyond skill-getting to skill-using,[28] frequently in small group activities. In this way, the innate capacities to acquire a language that all individuals are considered to possess are tapped; students have ample opportunities to test their hypotheses about the nature of the new language; their interim grammars are accepted and tolerated while they refine their hypotheses through continued study, and they have the opportunity for much practice in creating new utterances in actual communication.

- **Discuss certain fossilized errors you have observed in your teaching or in your own learning of a language. What do you think are the reasons for this fossilization? As a teacher, what can you do to help students overcome these tendencies?**

THE INFLUENCE OF SOCIOLINGUISTICS

The field of sociolinguistics, or sociology of language, grew rapidly during the 1960s and 1970s. This branch of linguistics concerns itself particularly with language as it is used for communication within the social group. It employs the concepts and research techniques of sociology and social psychology, as well as linguistics. It brings to

26. See C. Hosenfeld, "Cindy: A Learner in Today's Foreign Language Classroom," in NEC 1979, pp. 53–75.

27. Selinker, "Interlanguage," p. 215.

28. These terms, and the model of language-teaching processes associated with them, are explained in the *PG*'s, p. 4, and *SMT*, p. 23.

light interesting information about language in organized communicative interaction within a community, about domains of language use, speech varieties within a community, the language behavior of ethnic groups, bilingualism and multilingualism, and language planning at a national level. Clearly, these are subjects of great concern to the language teacher.

Hymes elaborated a concept of *communicative competence* which soon began to affect the language-teaching community. To Hymes, the most novel and important aspect of sociolinguistic research was to establish "what a speaker needs to know to communicate effectively in culturally significant settings."[29] Although the term "communicative competence" was often loosely used as though it were no different from "creative language use," Hymes's concepts soon began to have considerable effect. Materials writers and classroom teachers realized that students needed to know more than how to express ideas in correct grammatical patterns (or in incorrect patterns as they struggled to express ideas and concepts for which they did not yet have the linguistic means). Students needed also to know the culturally acceptable ways of interacting orally with others—appropriate levels of language to use in different situations; conversational gambits; what gestures and other body language were appropriate; when one might intervene in conversation and when one should wait for others; which questions and comments might be made and which would offend. They also needed to understand the message content of stress and intonation. (For further discussion, see chapter 7 below.)

The British systemic linguists had earlier emphasized differences in grammar and lexis appropriate for a variety of situations. For these they used the term "registers." Certain types of language, they maintained, are acceptable in the community, even expected, for certain situations and for special purposes. Registers differ according to field of discourse (for instance, the language may be for technical or nontechnical purposes); mode of discourse (there are notable differences in most languages between spoken language and literary text); and style of discourse (this depending on the relationship between the speaker and hearer, colloquial speech differing considerably from formal speech).[30] Persons who are not native speakers of a language can easily cause offense and give wrong impressions by mixing elements from several registers in speech and writing. Students in foreign-language classes should be made conscious of this problem of

29. Gumperz and Hymes 1972, p. vii; and Dell Hymes, "The Ethnography of Speaking," in Fishman 1968, pp. 99–138.

30. The matter of "registers" is discussed in full in Halliday, McIntosh, and Strevens 1964, pp. 87–98.

registers and taught to recognize differences, so that they may not only choose the right register for a particular purpose but be able to keep a section of discourse within the one register. They should also be sensitive to the register being used by persons who are speaking to them, since this is often an important cue as to the level of language within which they are expected to continue the communicative interchange.[31]

The study of the culture in which the second language is embedded is an important aspect of foreign-language teaching. If any degree of cultural competence of the type Hymes discusses is to be acquired, students need opportunities to interact with native speakers in natural settings. This kind of interaction is provided in exchange and study abroad programs. Where these are not feasible for all students, ethnic festivals and language camps can provide social contexts where authentic communicative interaction may take place, particularly if any available native speakers living in or visiting the area are invited to attend. Where it is appropriate, students should be encouraged to mingle with the local community of speakers of the language they are learning and help them in any way they can. Teaching aides and paraprofessionals may also be recruited from the local community to add authenticity to the classroom experience.

- **Discuss errors you yourself have made in mixing levels of language or registers. What do you do, or can you do, to help students develop a feeling for appropriate language use in different situations?**

SEMANTICS AND PRAGMATICS

Meanwhile, the theoretical linguists had been exploring new areas. The case grammar of Fillmore, the generative semantics of Ross, Lakoff, and McCawley, and the meaning-structure grammar of Chafe all declared semantics (or meaning) to be basic to any theoretical model of language. With the emphasis on semantics, pragmatics (that is, the rules of language in use) rose in importance, since meaning was seen to be dependent to a large degree on the situations in which speech acts occurred.

These approaches influenced work on first-language acquisition. Researchers like Roger Brown and Schlesinger found the early utterances of young children to be more readily explicable in semantic terms, such as agent, action, instrument, patient, experiencer (or what Brown called "semantic roles") (see Brown 1973; Schlesinger 1977). Others preferred to emphasize functions. "Use," Bruner

31. For examples of five levels of language in use, see *PG*'s, chap. 1, C5.

found, "is a powerful determinant of rule structure,"[32] and Halliday analyzed his child's initial utterances in terms of distinct functions: instrumental, regulatory, interactional, personal, heuristic, imaginative, representational, and ritual (Halliday 1973 and 1975). (These are discussed in chapter 7 below.)

Language teachers found the functional approach of more value for application than some of the more abstract linguistic models of the preceding decade.[33] There was a growing emphasis on designing classroom activities, so that the language use elicited would reflect normal purposes of language in interactional contexts. Teachers began to recognize the artificiality of many language exercises and adapt them so that they reflected more authentic uses of language.[34] For instance, "practicing the interrogative" would be replaced by students asking each other or the teacher questions of some relevance to their daily life and activities, or going out of class to ask a native speaker questions about his or her life and work. Materials writers began to pay more attention to the communicative act and the levels of language within which the students needed to operate in order to respond appropriately with different interlocutors in different circumstances.

MENTALISM, PSYCHOLINGUISTICS, AND COGNITIVE RESEARCH

As we have noted, the structural linguists had absorbed many of the ideas of their contemporaries in psychology—the behaviorists. In the early sixties, many psychologists were turning away from habit-formation studies to the areas of perception, thought processes, the encoding and expression of meaning, information processing, memory, and the acquisition of concepts and language by children. Since they were becoming more and more interested in problems which involved language, these cognitive psychologists naturally found compatible the contemporary theory of transformational-generative grammar, with its interest in what goes on in the mind of the speaker-hearer and in the nature of the innate mechanism which, in Chomsky's view, made the acquisition of a human language possible. Chomsky considered linguistics to be a branch of human psychology with much to contribute to a "theory of acquisition of knowledge that gives due

32. Jerome S. Bruner, "From Communication to Language—A Psychological Perspective," *Cognition* 3 (1974–75): 283.

33. For an application of Halliday's functions to language teaching, see Wilga M. Rivers, "The Natural and the Normal in Language Teaching: Where's the Difference?" in Schulz 1977, pp. 101–8.

34. See Wilga M. Rivers, "Talking off the Tops of their Heads," in *SMT;* and the *PG's.*

place to intrinsic mental activity."[35] The cognitive psychologists, who were feeling the need for a theory of language on which to base their research, were ready and willing to accept the collaboration the transformational-generative grammarians were offering them.

It was inevitable, then, that the interlocking interests of linguists and cognitive psychologists should lead to a gradual merging of theoretical positions and research projects. Many studies using transformational-generative theory as a framework were reported in the areas of sentence processing, speech perception, and the acquisition of a first language by children. As we have seen, these first-language studies had considerable influence on early second-language acquisition research. Gradually psycholinguistics became established as a discipline in its own right.

Early in the 1970s, however, some cognitive psychologists who were interested in language acquisition, production, and comprehension began to find the abstract theoretical models of transformational-generative linguists too constricting in their research (see, e.g., Slobin 1971, p. 24). From trying to show experimentally that models proposed by the linguists had psychological reality, they returned to developing their own models from their empirical findings. Other psychologists devoted their energies to the promising and burgeoning areas of perception and computer simulation of cognitive processing. It seemed to many that what might be innate was not a specific capacity to acquire languages, but rather general cognitive and perceptual processes which were basic to other areas of human learning as well. Thus it became easier to align psychological studies of language acquisition and use with the findings of Piaget on the stages of cognitive development from infancy to maturity (Inhelder and Piaget 1958).

Just as much new information was becoming available on perceptual processes, sections of the language-teaching profession were turning their attention to listening and reading. Postovsky advocated an initial period of listening to a new language, with writing as a supporting activity, before students attempted to produce anything orally. He considered this a more efficient approach than practicing structures and memorizing sentences of the language. In his experiments, students were not expected to begin to produce sentences themselves for some time, unless they felt like doing so.[36] Whether teachers accepted this view or not, they began to pay much more

35. N. Chomsky, *Language and Mind* (New York: Harcourt, Brace & World, 1968), pp. 76, 84.
36. Valerian Postovsky, "Why Not Start Speaking Later?" in Burt, Dulay, and Finocchiaro 1977, pp. 17–26.

attention to developing the listening skill as a most important area of language learning. To develop ability to understand native speakers, it was realized, students needed much practice in listening to authentic materials recorded in natural situations, rather than to artificial materials concocted for school purposes (see *PG*'s, chap. 3). Reading again achieved prominence as an important area of language learning, and much attention was paid to new information on the reading process as "a psycholinguistic guessing game."[37]

Research into cognitive processes is an area which teachers will watch with interest as they look for guidance in improving the teaching and learning of languages. As teachers of second or foreign languages, we are interested in how human beings perceive messages (in speech or writing) and how they process and interpret them. We are interested in the way new information is transformed by receivers as they relate it to information already stored; how what they receive is recoded and organized for storage, not as atomic items but within complex semantic networks; how recoded information moves from short-term to long-term storage; and how it is retrieved. We are interested in forgetting, which is intricately involved with the concept of memory as an active process rather than a repository of inert items. This leads us to what will be remembered. Here we are at one of the interfaces between cognitive and dynamic psychology, because what we process from what we perceive is related to individual motivation and meaningfulness. We can also learn much from studies of concept development, particularly cross-cultural conceptualization; and if we are to teach about another culture, we need to understand the formation and retention of stereotypes and how these may be adapted and changed.

THE AFFECTIVE ELEMENT
Sensitive teachers have always recognized the determining role that the affective component plays in interpersonal communication. Students who do not feel at ease with their teacher and their fellow students are reluctant to attempt to express themselves in another language—an experience which involves not only stripping oneself of the protective devices refined use of a well-known language provides, but also returning to a much less mature level of expression, which can make the adolescent or adult learner feel both foolish and vulnerable. Once language learning becomes more than the study of rules and paradigms, and their exemplification and demonstration in

37. Kenneth S. Goodman, "Reading: A Psycholinguistic Guessing Game," *Journal of the Reading Specialist* 4 (1967): 126–35; and Smith 1973.

reading and writing, and moves toward real communication of ideas, emotions, and aspirations, dynamic and personality psychology have a contribution to make. For these reasons affective-based approaches to learning began to have an impact on foreign-language teaching in the 1970s, in particular humanistic psychology, as elaborated by Maslow (1970), Carl Rogers (1969), and G. I. Brown (1971).

Maslow maintained that the individual has a hierarchy of needs to be satisfied: at base level, there are physiological needs; then, in ascending order, needs for security, belongingness, esteem for self and for others, and finally self-realization, which cannot be achieved while the lower-level needs remain unsatisfied (Maslow 1970, chap. 4). These needs lead to complex interrelationships within a group, the individuals of which are in need of support and fulfillment at different levels of the hierarchy at any one time. Since any genuine communication requires that one feel at ease in the situation, these interrelationships among students and between teacher and student affect the success of the communicative interaction, even apart from differing levels of language control. Affective factors also determine what is meaningful and relevant for the students at any particular stage. Brown's confluent education emphasizes the importance of working with both feelings and intellect at the same time in both individual and group learning.

In practice, the humanistic approach has resulted in the inclusion in language-learning materials of vocabulary and activities for expressing one's feelings, for sharing one's values and viewpoints with others, and for developing a better understanding of others' feelings and needs.[38] A language class is a particularly suitable environment for meeting affective needs, because much of the activity can take the form of role playing, simulation games, and small-group discussions. Masks and puppets help the more inhibited to express themselves with less risk. The expressive arts (impromptu drama, music, and song) allow for free flow of imagination and self-expression. Yet all of these activities require the student to seek the most appropriate forms in the new language to express nuances of meaning.

With this reemphasis on individual worth and difference, language teachers became conscious of the fact that individual students prefer different modalities of learning: some learn best through the ear, some through the eye. They also learn at different rates and employ quite different strategies for understanding and retaining the material to be learned. With this new understanding, teachers were no longer satisfied with a monolithic "what is good for one is good for all" ap-

---

38. For applications of this approach, see Moskowitz 1978.

proach. The 1970s saw a flowering of experimentation with individualized learning programs, diversified content, and courses of differing lengths and intensity.

• **Invent some activities for an elementary class that will enable the students to find out about themselves and each other in an unthreatening way. (Make sure that the activities involve language material the students know and can use.)**

THE TEACHER'S CHOICE

The many new directions opened up by research in linguistics and psychology have provided teachers with many ideas for program development and teaching approaches. By their very diversity they have liberated teachers to plan and adapt their programs with due attention to the objectives of their students and the needs of the district in which they are teaching.[39] Teachers now feel free to develop the style of teaching with which they themselves feel most at ease, for it is only by feeling at ease themselves that they can set their students at ease in the potentially anxiety-creating environment of the active second-language class. They will continue to learn more about language from the linguists and about language-learning processes from the psychologists, but it is only the classroom teacher, experiencing daily the interaction of these two, who can finally decide on the most appropriate approach to teaching and course content in the local situation. Foreign-language teachers must make their own decisions as informed professionals, if study of another language is to provide the mind-expanding, humanistic experience that comes from insight into other ways of thinking and behaving, as well as the career skills which modern students have a right to expect as a product of their years of schooling.

Annotated Reading List

LINGUISTICS

Bolinger, Dwight. *Aspects of Language.* 2d ed. New York: Harcourt Brace Jovanovich, 1975. A readable introduction to the areas studied by linguists, with many examples and self-testing questions.

Pearson, Bruce L. *Introduction to Linguistic Concepts.* New York: Alfred A. Knopf, 1977. A refresher course in linguistic theory,

---

39. For a discussion of how teachers can adapt their language teaching to the needs of their students and the community, see Wilga M. Rivers et al., "Language Learners as Individuals: Discovering their Needs, Wants, and Learning Styles," in Alatis et al. 1981.

ranging from nineteenth-century historical grammar to Lakoff and Chafe.

Allen, J. P. B., and Corder, S. Pit, eds. *Readings for Applied Linguistics*. Vol. 1 of the Edinburgh Course in Applied Linguistics. London: Oxford University Press, 1973. Contains original articles by a number of scholars of language, including structuralists, transformational-generativists, functionalists, and sociolinguists.

LINGUISTICS AND LANGUAGE TEACHING

Roulet, Eddy. *Linguistic Theory, Linguistic Description, and Language Teaching*. Trans. C. N. Candlin. London: Longman, 1975. A useful description of competing linguistic theories and their potential for application to the problems of language teaching.

Wilkins, D. A. *Linguistics in Language Teaching*. Cambridge, Mass.: MIT Press, 1972. Attempts to create a bridge between linguistics and methodology of language teaching by investigating how legitimately knowledge of linguistics contributes to the taking of decisions about language teaching. Deals with linguistic attitudes to language, phonology, grammar, vocabulary, sociolinguistics, psycholinguistics, and error analysis.

Wardhaugh, Ronald. *The Contexts of Language*. Rowley, Mass.: Newbury House, 1976. A study of the contexts in which language is used and how these contexts affect and are affected by language. Includes the biological, psychological, personal, functional, and social contexts.

SECOND LANGUAGE ACQUISITION

Richards, Jack C., ed. *Understanding Second and Foreign Language Learning: Issues and Approaches*. Rowley, Mass.: Newbury House, 1978. A series of articles by leading scholars on second-language acquisition research and its relevance for language teaching.

Hatch, Evelyn. *Second Language Acquisition: A Book of Readings*. Rowley, Mass.: Newbury House, 1978. Full details of a number of case studies and experimental studies of second-language acquisition by young children and adults, demonstrating the variability of speed of acquisition and learning strategies.

*LEARNING THEORY

Carroll, John B. "Learning Theory for the Classroom Teacher." In Jarvis 1974b, pp. 113–49. Gives a model of school learning. Discusses theories of language acquisition, cognitive psychology, memory, forgetting, and transfer. Extensive bibliography.

AFFECTIVE OR HUMANISTIC EDUCATION

Disick, Renée S., and Barbanel, Laura. "Affective Education and Foreign Language Learning." In Jarvis 1974b, pp. 185–222. Discusses the interrelationship of thinking and feeling, motivation, classroom characteristics that facilitate affective growth, and affective techniques for foreign language teaching. Bibliographical references.

Galyean, Beverley. "Humanistic Education: A Mosaic Just Begun." In Jarvis 1976, pp. 201–43. Discusses psychological, moral, affective, transpersonal, and confluent education, demonstrating how to use self-reflective language for target-language practice.

Moskowitz, Gertrude. *Caring and Sharing in the Foreign Language Class: A Sourcebook on Humanistic Techniques.* Rowley, Mass.: Newbury House, 1978. Discusses affective models of teaching and gives 120 humanistic, affective, or awareness exercises, with appropriate vocabulary in seven languages, and the levels and structures for which the exercises are appropriate.

Research and Discussion

1. Watch an elementary-level language lesson where students try to develop personal questions from material they have memorized in a dialogue and practiced in a pattern drill. Make notes of the kinds of errors they make. How do these relate to the material they memorized and the practice drills? What proposals would you make for improving the teaching sequence?

2. What types of "common errors" were you taught to avoid in your native language in school? Do you use any of these forms or structures in informal speech? Do you hear them used by others? By whom and in what circumstances? Listen carefully to some radio or television talk shows. Were any of these forms used? What have you learned about your own language from this exercise? What structures do you hear in the language you are teaching which do not appear in class textbooks?

3. Examine a series of pattern drills. Do the "patterns" being practiced really form a set of items which operate structurally in an identical fashion, or is surface-structure similarity masking differences in the underlying meaning? Make proposals for the improvement of these sets of drills.

4. Reflect on the "creative aspect of normal language use." Is it true that each sentence we utter (apart from formulae like greetings and cocktail party clichés) is a completely new creation that has never been heard in that form before? If this is so, what makes it

possible for us to understand each other? Listen to people around you. Do you consider their utterances to be "stimulus-free"? What implications do your conclusions have for language teaching? (See also W. M. Rivers, "Rules, Patterns, and Creativity," in *SMT* 1972 or 1976).

5. How do you consider the rules of grammar can be internalized? Draw on your own experience of language learning. What were your strategies? Discuss and share these with others in the class.

6. If you are not a native speaker of the language you are teaching, make a tape of an unprepared oral presentation (recount an anecdote, describe yourself and your particular problems at the moment, or give a lively account of the story of a film or book you have just enjoyed). Analyze, or get a friend to analyze, your production to see what fossilized errors you consistently make. Have you been aware of these before? Can you state the rules you are not observing? Have you tried to correct these errors in the past? To what do you attribute these fossilizations? Discuss your problems and your theories about them with others in your class.

7. Observe your conversational behavior during one day and keep a diary of the levels of language and registers of discourse you have used in different situations. Would you be able to make appropriate adjustments of this type in the language you are teaching? Are the students in your class (or the class you are observing) being made aware of these types of distinctions? What could be done to improve their ability to function in different types of situations and relationships?

8. Think back over your own language-learning experience. What emotional problems did you experience in learning the language? Inhibitions? Embarrassment? Shyness? Disgust with yourself? Unwillingness to try to communicate in the language with particular persons? Inexplicable errors at crucial moments? Tension? (See also Appendix B.) What do you propose for overcoming such problems for students in a language class? Or when trying to communicate out of class with native speakers?

*9. What are the particular affective problems of students in bilingual classes? What light does Maslow's hierarchy of needs throw on these particular problems? (See also W. M. Rivers, "Motivation in Bilingual Programs," in *SMT* 1976).

*10. Read some experimental studies on student errors (from *LL, TQ, IRAL, MLJ, FLA, AL* or *RELC;* see also notes 21 and 22). Reconsider the errors you observed in your own speech (Q. 2) or those you have noted during a class observation. Have you any theory on their origin? (See Sridhar in note 24.)

4· Structured Practice

In many foreign-language classrooms in the early part of the twentieth century, emphasis was placed on the intellectual aspect of language learning. There was much talk about details of the grammatical system and the meanings of words, followed by practice in constructing written phrases and sentences according to the rules. Communication skills were expected to develop after the systematic study of the written language, if at all. This approach produced students who could construct well-formed sentences slowly and carefully, after running through the many rules they had learned and after editing and reediting what they had written down. They usually had difficulty, however, in comprehending normal speech and in constructing utterances at a satisfactory rate which would enable them to participate comfortably in real communication.

In a revolution of language teaching methods, the major emphasis swung to the early cultivation of the speaking skill. Students were to be taught from the beginning to use quite complicated segments of the new language (which they had learned by imitation and memorization) in the production of meaningful utterances by analogy and variation. They would thus be able to construct many useful sentences orally before they had a clear understanding of the systematic operation of the language. This approach was considered to be consistent with native-language use, where speakers seem to use language, in all its complexity, without conscious effort and without being able to verbalize the rules to which their language production is conforming.

At one extreme we have had students able to recite rules and paradigms and concoct artificial samples of the foreign language without being able to communicate effectively. At the other extreme we have had students who were very fluent in the production of set phrases, and in recombining these to form pseudo-communicative utterances, but who were often unable to create new utterances at will to convey their personal message.

Since neither of these approaches seemed to produce fluent language users, it has seemed to some that languages cannot be taught, only acquired individually through constant exposure to a full range of authentic speech which activates innate language-learning capacities. Some advocates of this position have recommended that we abandon organized teaching through structured materials, and look to communicative interaction by itself to develop communicators. Applied inexpertly, this approach can produce foreign-language users who are very glib in putting together reduced forms of the language unsystematically, and frequently incomprehensibly. Competent use of another language is more than any of these. We may identify *two levels of language use* for which our students must be prepared. At the first level is the manipulation of language elements which occur in fixed relationships in clearly defined closed systems (that is, relationships which will vary within very narrow limits). We need facility in correctly combining and varying these elements, in order to express our meaning comprehensibly according to the demands of the language system. At the second level is the expression of personal meaning, for which possible variations are infinite, depending on such factors as the type of message to be conveyed, the situation in which the utterance takes place, the relationship between speaker and hearer or hearers, and the degree of intensity with which the message is to be conveyed. At the second level we have an intention to express, for which we select appropriate means, within our knowledge of the potentialities of the new language system; and through this selection we call into play the necessary first-level elements.

It is clear, then, that one type of learning situation will not be sufficient for the task. A place must be found for practice in putting together systematic elements of the language in meaningful ways, as well as for understanding and drawing from a complex system with its infinite possibilities of expression. These together provide the foundation for attempts at real communication in the new language. Since the role of the systematic elements in combination in formulating communicative messages will be apprehended only as the student attempts to communicate, practice in real communication among persons must be engineered as early as possible, so that students are using what they know in situational contexts.

In this chapter, we shall consider suitable materials for practice at the first level of language use, while continually bearing in mind that items for practice at this level should always come as close as possible to authentic utterances which might be used in communication. The second level will be discussed in more detail in chapters 6 and 7.

GRAMMATICAL EXERCISES FOR CLASSROOM AND LABORATORY

What types of teaching materials do we find in language classrooms? Frequently the class text reflects the way some enthusiastic and successful teacher has organized the language material for students over a period of some years. Close analysis and tabulation of the contents will usually reveal undue emphasis at certain points and inexplicable superficiality at others. The basis of choice of material and of sequencing in such texts is empirical rather than deriving from any scientific study of the way the language is structured. Nor does the writer seem to have any clear notion of what students are expected to be able to do with the language at the end of the course. The exercises provided for the student also reflect the teacher-writer's preferences and prejudices. If the author is a talented teacher, the exercises may be interesting and varied, but, as a general rule, they follow well-defined patterns which are repeated from unit to unit. There is often a multiplicity of exercises, and it is left to the teacher to decide whether to use them all as they are set out or to present the same material in a different way. Most teachers find it less arduous to take the first course.

Traditional Types of Exercises
Let us look, then, at some of these traditional types of exercises. They often follow an explanation of a grammatical feature which has been introduced, rather artificially, into a preceding reading passage or dialogue. In the exercise, students may be asked to write out paradigms, or to construct forms in the foreign language according to a traditional grammatical description (e.g., the instruction may read: "Write the 3d person plural, future, interrogative, negative" of some verb). Often the exercises require the changing of unnaturally complicated sentences from singular to plural, from affirmative to negative, from declarative form to interrogative, or from one tense to another. Students may be asked to combine sentences in specific ways, to add some elements to sentences, or to fill in blanks with words which change form according to structural environment. They may be asked to translate involved sentences from the native language to the target language.

Less desirable features of exercises found in some traditional textbooks are as follows:
1. Vocabulary used in the exercises varies considerably from item to item. It may favor words with peculiar spellings or irregularities that students readily forget. In this way the attention of students is easily diverted from the grammatical purpose of the exercise, and they may make slips which do not reflect basic misunderstanding of the grammatical point at issue.
2. Items often involve the simultaneous manipulation of several grammatical features in complicated interrelationships. This makes a testing rather than a learning activity of each item. Stu-

dents easily make mistakes in some aspects of the item while concentrating on others, so that it becomes difficult to decide what they do and do not know.

3. Items often consist of a mixture of target-language and native-language forms, the students being asked to find equivalents for the native-language forms to complete the target-language sentences. This may appear to be an innocent enough procedure, but, used indiscriminately, it can give the unfortunate impression that there is a one-to-one equivalence between forms in different languages which it is the student's task to discover. This develops a "translation mentality" in the students at an early stage, which hinders them from seeing interrelationships within the new language that may differ from the interrelationships of discrete parts in the native language.

4. The exercises are usually designed to be read, analyzed, and then written. As written exercises they can be edited and reedited in the search for an acceptable answer. Exercises designed for written practice are usually unsuitable for oral practice. Before attempting to use such exercises for oral work, the teacher should personally try items out orally to see whether the vocabulary load and complications of structure make it difficult to hold the complete sentence in immediate memory in order to make the required changes.

5. Exercises usually move rather rapidly from one aspect of a grammatical feature to another, trying to include in a short sequence of sentences every possible facet of the feature under study. In this way, they are designed to test whether the student has understood the reasoning behind the grammatical explanation which preceded the exercises. Here again, the difference between testing and learning exercises has not been understood. If the performance of the students at this stage seems to show that they have not assimilated all that was explained, the teacher will usually expound still further on the grammatical feature, repeating explanations in different words with perhaps some further examples, and then send the students back to the exercise to demonstrate their intellectual understanding of the point at issue. If more graduated practice is provided in the first place, before a testing item is given, students will not normally require repetitious explanations, and more time can be devoted to actual practice.

6. There are seldom enough learning exercises which help students to understand aspects of a grammatical rule, from which they can build up a picture of the whole. As soon as students can complete the testing exercise more or less accurately, teachers usually

move on with the textbook to the next unit and expound on, and test, new grammatical rules in the same cursory fashion.

7. Succeeding units rarely give practice in the work of preceding units. Often they fail to reuse grammatical features (or even vocabulary) just studied. Not surprisingly, teachers find after some months, even weeks or days, that the students' "intellectual understanding" of preceding units has dimmed, or even faded away, and the students themselves wonder why they continue to misapply rules they thought they knew so well.

Systematic Practice of Grammatical Features

Although exercises of the type described have been in use for many years, they have not proved outstandingly successful in developing lasting facility in the expressive use of grammatical features. As a result, scholars and teachers have devoted much time and effort to devising more effective ways of ensuring that students will be able to apply readily what they have studied. Types of exercises have been designed which give students opportunities for systematic practice of particular features in naturally phrased and easily remembered target-language utterances. Lexical items are limited in variety in order to concentrate attention on the grammatical features under study. In this way, understanding of structural interrelationships (that is, of structural meaning) grows through use of structure, and not merely through intellectual apprehension. Intensive practice exercises of this type are often called structural pattern drills. They are based on the assumption that to learn a language effectively students need to develop habits of intralanguage association. Thus, when they attempt to express themselves in a new language, they will not be preoccupied with the functioning of those language elements which vary only within restricted systems.

There has been much controversy on whether, in using a language, we operate according to rules we have internalized or habits we have acquired. Much of this discussion has been at cross-purposes. Understanding of grammatical rules and practice of rules with changes in lexical content and in different combinations and variations are both essential if the language user is to operate freely and effortlessly in the expression of meaning. Carroll has defined a habit as "any learned disposition to perceive, behave, or perform in a certain manner under specified circumstances. To the extent that an individual's language behavior conforms to the habits of the speech community of which he is a member," he says, "we can say that his behavior is 'rule-governed.' "[1]

From the point of view of effective teaching, we need to realize that habits of language use can only be effective when students understand the conditions under which such speech habits are appropriate. We need techniques that help students "internalize the rules" so that the results of this rule acquisition are evident in their language production. Mere explanation of rules has not proved effective in this regard. Neither has systematic practice without understanding of the rules. When due attention is paid to both, students learn how to operate within the system with confidence and flexibility.

In this chapter, the term "structure" will be reserved for the underlying system of principles which determine the observable interrelationships of language elements. These overt interrelationships will be called "structural patterns." Through practice in the use of these structural patterns, the student comes to understand more fully how the structural system functions for a native speaker in the expression of a multiplicity of meanings.

A structural pattern is, then, a typical combination of interrelationships. Formed by various arrangements of lexical items, it conveys a meaning beyond the lexical content of these items themselves. To learn to use for their own purposes the meaning conveyed by the pattern (that is, its structural meaning), within the limitations imposed by the context of the utterance, language learners must be able to reproduce the pattern without hesitation, no matter what lexical items may be involved. In the simplest form of drill, they do this by substituting lexical items within the same pattern framework.

Hill has stated that "every occurrence of language is a substitution frame,"[2] an assertion that would be challenged by Chomsky.[3] It is true that flexible use of language involves more than lexical substitution, that it involves choice of direction within the system, but this choice, once made, forces the speaker into the use of certain structural patterns. It is within the limited range of permissible variations of each specific pattern that the student of a new language must learn to operate. The real problem is in identifying the types of patterns or

1. J. B. Carroll, "Current Issues in Psycholinguistics and Second Language Teaching," *TQ* 5 (1971): 103.
2. A. A. Hill, *Introduction to Linguistic Structures: From Sound to Sentence* (New York: Harcourt, Brace & World, 1958), p. 5.
3. N. Chomsky, in "Linguistic Theory" (NEC 1966, p. 44), says: "Linguists have had their share in perpetuating the myth that linguistic behavior is 'habitual' and that a fixed stock of 'patterns' is acquired through practice and used as the basis for 'analogy.' These views could be maintained only as long as grammatical description was sufficiently vague and imprecise."

frames which students will find most useful for structuring their meaning. Surface patterning can be misleading and disguise divergent meanings at a deeper level. Language patterns which provide effective practice share a semantic organization which underlies lexical variations.

Variation practice of regular structural patterns of this type can be useful if not prolonged unduly. It familiarizes students with morphological variations, word order changes, agreements of various elements of an utterance (e.g., subjects and verbs, number and gender of nouns, pronouns, or adjectives); or with insertion, deletion, or rearrangement of elements for specific types of utterances (e.g., interrogation or negation). It is also useful for review or remedial purposes when students are finding certain forms or arrangements difficult to remember and use appropriately. The practice must not become an aim in itself. It is much easier to conduct organized practice of grammatical forms than it is to encourage communicative exchanges of real messages, which is the ultimate objective of the language class.

TYPES OF STRUCTURAL PATTERN DRILLS

Moulton suggests that the three main classes of structural pattern drills reflect three basic approaches to the analysis of syntax: tagmemics or slot-and-filler theory, the theory of immediate constituents, and transformational grammar.[4] Although the drills may not be derived directly from any or all of these three theories, they are built on characteristics of language structure which these theories attempt to elucidate.

Slot-and-Filler Drills

In *tagmemics,* an utterance is regarded as a type of frame, consisting of slots into which words which fulfill a similar structural function may be inserted. Once a particular type of frame has been identified as a consistent pattern, students may be given practice in substituting in the slots a variety of fillers, provided that each filler, or lexical variant, performs the same function in the frame as the original item for which it is being substituted (e.g., "a boy" may substitute for

4. W. G. Moulton, "What Is Structural Drill?" in *Structural Drill and the Language Laboratory* ed. F. W. Gravit and A. Valdman, pp. 11–14. (The Hague: Mouton, 1963). Tagmemic theory is described in Kenneth L. Pike, *Language in Relation to a Unified Theory of the Structure of Human Behavior,* 2d ed. rev. (The Hague: Mouton, 1967), and in Eastman 1978, where its similarities to case grammar are discussed (pp. 96–106, 145–46). References for other theories of syntax are given in notes to chapter 3 (the theory of immediate constituents in note 5; transformational grammar in note 8).

"a teacher" in the "subject as actor" slot). As in Fillmore's *case grammar,* a noun phrase filling a subject slot may have a number of semantic interpretations or functions: agent, instrument, goal, location, and so on.

In the slot-and-filler mode, students are able to practice the construction of innumerable sentences of very different meanings while retaining the basic structural pattern. This type of drill is appropriate so long as no changes in word order are required when substitutions are made. Sometimes the insertion of a new item in one slot will involve a morphological change for an item in another slot (as with singular-plural, masculine-feminine adjustments in some languages, changes of person or case in relation to the verb, or adjustments devolving from a change of preposition); at other times, substitution in one slot will automatically lead to substitution in another slot in order to maintain some type of grammatical consistency.

The purpose of the drill is to concentrate the attention of the students on one structural problem at a time and to provide them with steady practice in handling this problem in various lexical contexts, without requiring them to focus attention on other details of the sequence. To ensure this type of practice, care must be taken to keep to a minimum the number of changes to be made in one operation. In some drills, this is achieved by maintaining one section of the original utterance intact, while making consistent changes in a dependent section. This is sometimes called a "fixed increment drill."

In order to keep the student working entirely in the foreign language, cue words or expressions in the language are given to trigger the desired change in the next step of the drill; these cues may indicate the word to be substituted, or they may form a question which forces out an answer containing the intended formal change. If drills of this preliminary type are to be effective, students must be kept alert to the meaning of the sentences they are uttering. This can be achieved by encouraging students to suggest cue items, after an initial period of familiarization practice.

Immediate Constituent Drills

The preoccupation of the *theory of immediate constituents* with the hierarchical nature of language structure is reflected in expansion, contraction, and combination drills. Students are shown how to expand, contract, or combine sentences in specific ways and are then given practice in these operations, with attention to any resulting modifications. For instance, they may learn to add expressions of time, place, or manner; to reduce clauses to phrases or to single words without changing meaning; or to combine sentences or phrases in different ways.

Transformation or Conversion Drills

Even before the development of the theory of syntax as a series of transformations from deep structures, language teachers recognized the value of asking students to transform or convert sentence patterns from declarative to interrogative, from positive to negative, from active to passive, from past to present or future, and so on. Directed dialogue is a form of transformation drill, as is much of the traditional question-answer practice.

Transformations may often be cued by a single word which sets the tone for a different syntactic requirement (e.g., *Today is Thursday. Yesterday? Yesterday was Wednesday*); by the asking of a question (e.g., *He writes poetry. Do you? Yes, I write poetry, too*); or even by the supplying of an answer for which a question must be created (e.g., *I am late. Why are you late?*).

Transformational-generative grammar has not had a marked effect on the development of practice exercises. It has, however, restored respect for many older types of conversion exercises which have long been in use. It has also aroused interest in the different ways in which the same meanings can be encoded (e.g., *Will you come with me? Coming too?*). Recent studies in sociolinguistics have emphasized the importance for students to learn the appropriate circumstances in which to use such variants if genuine communicative ability is to be developed.[5]

CHARACTERISTICS OF A STRUCTURAL PATTERN DRILL

With the emergence of a certain vogue for pattern drilling, accelerated by the need for taped materials suitable for use in language laboratories, many commercial publishers hastily reset exercises in existing textbooks in some kind of pattern-drill format. Similarly, authors with little training in the technique tried their hand at the new form of exercise. As a result, teachers found these inexpertly created drills very difficult and frustrating for their classes or else so simple that students were bored by the lack of challenge. Despite changes of approach and unresolved controversy, many textbooks and most laboratory tapes still contain pattern drills, possibly because teachers and students have found they have their uses. Some writers of materials have heeded the criticisms that have been voiced and have

5. More detailed descriptions of the different types of structural pattern drills and intensive practice exercises, with examples in various languages, will be found in the *PG*'s, chap. 4.

been able to construct more effective and interesting drills. The quality of drills in both commercial and teacher-prepared materials, however, is still very variable.

It is important for teachers in training to be able to recognize well-constructed drills. They should also understand the direction in which they might try to modify them to make them more effective as learning devices which will help, not hinder, the development of communicative ability in the language. Trying to construct a series of drills themselves will help teachers to recognize when drills in textbooks or on tapes are well designed for student practice. They should then record their series and work through it themselves orally (without a script) to see whether there are any faults which will frustrate or irritate student learners.

The following observations will serve as an evaluative checklist.

1. A drill series is designed to help the students learn how to manipulate grammatical structures, *not to test* what students already know. The series should therefore provide sufficient practice in the use of each element to develop student confidence in its use before moving on to the presentation of another structural pattern.

2. Each drill is normally devoted to *one specific structural pattern.* The students are thus able to concentrate on one language problem at a time. Novice drill-constructors will need to pay very careful attention as they develop each drill or they will find that they have unwittingly allowed a feature from another pattern to creep into the sequence.

3. The structural feature to be drilled will have been *encountered already* by the students in recent study material—in a dialogue which has been studied, in a reading passage, a conversation, or a series of example sentences with a grammatical explanation.

4. The pattern will be drilled consistently through a series of *six to eight cue-response items* in order to give the students time to assimilate the structural pattern, or the pattern change, before they are asked to make more complicated variations.

5. *Changes* made between one cue-response item and the next will be *minimal,* involving usually one lexical change with, at most, an associated adjustment (or short series of interrelated adjustments) of a formal nature. As the students move into the next drill in a series, the pattern will be varied to a minor degree. This is in accordance with the principle of programmed instruction: that the sequence should be so designed that the students will produce the correct response on practically every occasion.

6. Each utterance in a series will be *short,* so that the students will have no difficulty keeping each sentence in their minds as they try to construct variants according to the cues given.

7. Each item will be a *complete utterance* of a type which could conceivably occur in a conversational exchange. In this way the students will be acquiring intralanguage associations in useful segments of language.

8. The drill will be designed in such a way that the cue will provoke *only the desired response* and not other feasible responses. Since the response is to be followed by immediate confirmation (in the form of the correct response, given for purposes of comparison and imitation by the teacher or the voice on the tape) there must be *no ambiguity.* Any cause for hesitation can only be bewildering to the students, interrupting the smooth flow of the drill exercise.

9. In a structural pattern drill, variety of *vocabulary will be kept to a minimum.* Only very familiar words will be used, so that the attention of students is not distracted from the structural feature which they are learning to manipulate. (Vocabulary itself may be the subject of a drill, in which case the students will be learning many new words, usually in semantic sets.)

10. Both cue and response items will usually be *in the foreign language.* With a certain amount of ingenuity and imagination it is possible to construct cues which will evoke most of the structural features which need to be drilled. Where this is not possible, a translation drill will be used. A translation drill differs from the traditional translation exercise in that it conforms to all the preceding recommendations (consistency of pattern in the series, concentration on structural pattern, restriction of vocabulary range, probable complete utterances, and so on).

11. Drills will be *conducted orally* until the students are responding readily and accurately to the cues. For variety, shortened segments of the drills may sometimes be used as reading or writing exercises, but not to the exclusion of oral practice. Drills are designed primarily for training with ear and tongue, rather than for visual scanning. Because of their format, they can become very tedious when not performed orally.

12. Drills will *not be purely imitative,* although some imitative drills are necessary as introductory devices when students are being familiarized with a structural pattern. After an initial repetition drill, drills should be designed to require thought on the part of the students, with attention focused on the point of teaching; in other words, extraneous complications should be eliminated.

13. Drills will be *varied* in type to alleviate the boredom engendered by one kind of activity.

14. The teaching phase of a series of drills will be followed by a *testing phase*. This may be accomplished by re-presenting in random order material which has been drilled in a programmed sequence, in order to see whether students can still select the required response on hearing a particular type of cue.

15. Alternatively, a logical progression of drills may work up to a testing drill, where *multiple substitutions* require full concentration from the students and distract their attention from the grammatical feature they have been practicing. If the students are still able to manipulate accurately and effortlessly the feature they have been practicing, while concentrating their attention on other elements of the utterance, they may be presumed to have acquired a firm control over it.

16. Some provision will be made for students to *apply what they have learned* in the drill series in a communication situation within the class group—by questions and answers of a personal nature, through some form of game, or in brief oral reports. Students will move more freely toward this type of language use if they have been encouraged to add segments of their own to the drill sentences.

FROM INTENSIVE PRACTICE TO SELF-EXPRESSION

If drills are to fulfill their ultimate purpose, which is to enable students to express their own meanings in the new language, then the drills students perform must all be moving in this direction. It is certainly easier for teacher and students if all the thought content of exercises is already supplied; yet students trained merely to manipulate materials are usually at a loss for words when expected to make up their own utterances.

With real communication in mind from the first, drills and exercises should be designed so that they require students to supply a segment of their own choosing. In simple substitutions like the following: Teacher: *I have a knife;* teacher-supplied cue: *fork:* student response: *I have a fork;* student speech is completely under direction. Let us call these type A exercises. They are useful only for presenting the form of a new structure. A small change of procedure can move this substitution in the direction of autonomous communication or toward a type B exercise: e.g., teacher: *I have a knife. Mary, what do you have?* Mary's response: *I have a nail file. Tom, what do you have?* Tom's response: *I have a pencil.* The students are performing the same operation on a structure as in a type A exercise, but they are passing the structure through their own meaning system in order to form a sentence of their own. (If Mary volunteers the segment *Tom, what do you have?* the exercise passes from a completely teacher-dominated activity to a student-directed activity, and this is a further step toward autonomous activity.)[6]

Paulston classifies drills as *mechanical, meaningful,* and *communicative.*[7] A mechanical drill can be detected, according to Paulston, by substituting a nonsense word. If the student can still produce the correct answer, the drill is mechanical, e.g., teacher: *I have a knife;* teacher-supplied cue: *cong;* student response: *I have a cong.* This is a type A activity. In a meaningful drill, the student must understand the teacher's contribution to be able to respond, e.g., teacher: *She's outside;* student 1: *Where is she?* student 2: *She's outside;* teacher: *She's eating;* student 1: *What's she doing?* student 2: *She's eating.*[8] In a communicative drill, the student remains within the structure being practiced, but "adds new information about the real world[9] (e.g., teacher: *Is that your book?* student 1: *No, it's Jill's;* teacher: *Is that her book too?* student 2: *No, it's Peter's*). This is a type B exercise.

- **Examine some drills from a textbook or lab manual.**
  a. Are they type A or type B exercises?
  b. Are they mechanical, meaningful, or communicative drills?
  c. Allowing for some type A items for presentation of structure, how would you go about changing the other type A drills in the series to meaningful or communicative (type B) drills?

CLASSROOM PRESENTATION OF STRUCTURAL PATTERN DRILLS

Like other teaching procedures, structural pattern drilling may be performed well or badly. The fact that the drilling is ineffective is not always apparent to the inexperienced observer. An energetic teacher who is not very sensitive to student reaction may conduct a series of drills at a smart tempo, receiving a prompt response from students right through to the end of the series, without being conscious of the fact that the students' minds are not on their task and that they are merely parroting what has been suggested to them by the programming of the exercise. The students from such a class are at a loss

6. See W. M. Rivers, "From Linguistic Competence to Communicative Competence," in *SMT,* p. 43; and *PG*'s, chap. 4.

7. See Paulston and Bruder 1976, pp. 3–10; or C. B. Paulston, "The Sequencing of Structural Pattern Drills," *TQ* 5 (1971): 197–208; or C. B. Paulston, "Structural Pattern Drills: A Classification", *FLA* 4 (1970): 187–93.

8. Paulston and Bruder 1976, p. 7.

9. Ibid., p. 9.

when asked to apply what they have been learning because they do not have a clear concept of the meaning of what they have been repeating, nor of the significance of structural changes they have been making. No lasting value will come from intensive activity which bypasses meaning.

The following suggestions for the stages of presentation of a series of drills are designed to avoid mindless repetition.

1. Students should *encounter a certain structural pattern several times* in authentic stretches of foreign-language discourse (that is, in context: in dialogue, reading passage, or conversation) before practicing it in drills. In this way they will be able to observe its relationship to other structural elements in the language system. If students have doubts as to its function, this should be explained to them quite clearly; otherwise, much of the drilling will be a waste of time.

2. Before being asked to produce the structural pattern orally, students should *hear it a certain number of times,* so that they are able to recognize it aurally. If the pattern is embedded in a dialogue, they will be hearing it repeatedly as the class works with the dialogue. It may also be heard a number of times in classroom performance of actions, question-answer sequences, or through preliminary listening exercises. At this initial stage, the students are becoming familiar with the pattern, not with some rule about the pattern, and they begin the process of assimilating it as a whole.

3. As the drill period begins, students are presented aurally with several examples of the structural pattern grouped together in a *repetition drill,* which is a presentation type of drill. As they respond to these early drills, they begin to discern a certain consistency of structure in the various utterances, and form a concept of the type of manipulation they will be expected to perform in later segments. In this repetition series, only a limited number of well-known lexical items will occur, so that the attention of the students is not distracted from the structural pattern they are to learn to use.

4. Each item in the series is presented to the students, and they asked to repeat it, at a *normal speed* of production and with a *natural intonation.* This does not mean that the speech must be rapid; it may be at a moderate speed of delivery, but it must not be distorted in a way which would strike a native speaker as unnatural.

5. At this point, the responses of the students are *imitative;* they are not asked to produce anything which has not first been mod-

eled by the teacher or a voice on tape, and they try to capture intonation and stress as they repeat the sentence.

6. At the next stage, the students are asked to produce variants of the pattern with some *difference in lexical content* in response to a cue. The variations in lexical content will usually entail modifications of the structural pattern (e.g., some morphological change, some form of agreement for number or gender). Students receive confirmation of the acceptability of their responses as they compare them with the correct version supplied by teacher or tape.

7. As students work through this drill, with its variations of the basic structural pattern, they begin to recognize the regularity underlying the changes. Because of their natural tendency to organize what they wish to remember, they start to evolve for themselves a *generalization* which will account for the consistencies they have observed. If the drill is well planned and the feature of grammatical structure is uncomplicated, the generalizations of most of the students will be valid.

8. At this stage, the teacher will observe the students' responses carefully. If it is clear that the students are a little uncertain of the *crucial feature* of the pattern they are varying, a brief comment will elucidate the point at issue. All that is generally required is a few words to guide the students to a correct interpretation of what they are trying to do. (If the drill is poorly constructed, or the structural pattern seems particularly strange to the students, a longer explanation may be necessary. Very complicated structures are not usually practiced in this type of drill.)

9. When it is clear that the students understand what is involved, they will continue to practice the structural pattern with further *variations,* thus constructing new utterances by analogy with preceding utterances, and in full cognizance of what they are doing.

10. When the teacher judges by the alert and ready response of the class that the structural pattern has been assimilated, the students will be presented with a *mixed drill,* or a multiple-substitution drill, to see whether the response is still prompt and accurate when the student is not guided to the correct answer by the logic of the programming.

11. The teacher will not consider the structural pattern to be thoroughly learned until students are able to use it in the wider context of *conversational exchanges* in the classroom. If this evidence is not forthcoming, the teacher will provide further practice with the pattern in a subsequent lesson.

12. Even when the structural pattern appears to be thoroughly assimilated, the teacher will give the students *further oral practice* with it before many lessons have passed, so that they will not forget how to use it. Students will be encouraged to use the structural pattern to say something which concerns them personally.
13. The *review* of the pattern may be through reading material in which variations of the structure appear in a meaningful context. If the review takes a written form, the students will be encouraged to use the pattern in sentences of their own creation.
14. Structural pattern drills are essentially oral practice in the manipulation of grammatical features. They should, for the most part, be conducted *without the visual support of a script,* so that students may concentrate their attention on active formulation of utterances. This does not preclude a brief glance at the drill in the textbook early in the session, to help fix certain features in the minds of the students, always provided that the students then strive for confident and fluent response without further support from the text. If the students are allowed to follow drills in their books throughout the practice session, they will feel they know the work before they have really assimilated it. Having made a mental note of what is involved, they may become bored with what seems to be overinsistence on such a simple feature, without realizing that they cannot use it actively. The teacher also may be misled by the ready response. Oral drills without a script are very challenging in that they require the students to process the material actively as they respond.

Variation in Drill Presentation

There is a danger with structural pattern drilling that a zealous but unimaginative teacher, believing that the more students repeat the patterns the sooner they will be able to speak the language spontaneously, will keep the students at useful but uninteresting drills for far too long. Such drilling becomes very tedious for students, who may either seek escape in absentminded vocal participation or grow to loathe the language lesson or the laboratory session. Too much intensive drilling of a structural pattern to a point of automatic response can develop in students an inflexibility which prevents them from producing the appropriate grammatical formation in contexts where the cue is not identical to that of the drill.

This danger can be avoided if the teacher finds ways of ensuring a certain amount of repetition and response to cues without always following the same drill procedure. Sometimes the introduction of the drill material may be so designed as to provide practice in aural recognition and comprehension. At other times, the desired variations of the structural patterns may be cued by the presentation of pictures or objects as a change from aural cues. This demands constant attention from students and is an antidote to absentminded participation. A cue which leads to a humorous or unexpected response relaxes the students and renews their interest in the activity, keeping them alert for what is coming next. Group and row participation in drills can be given a competitive element which retains the attention of the students. Many drills may be given the appearance of a game, or of elementary communication, by provoking the students into asking the teacher a series of questions in response to cues; or the items of a drill may develop a series of comments about the activities and interests of teacher and students.

Certainly *game techniques* should be employed to provoke the students into using structural patterns in natural situations after a period of intensive drilling. With a little thought, the teacher will find that many well-known parlor and television games, and children's guessing and repetition games, are easily converted into extensions of pattern drills.[10] The more simple and familiar the game the better, because complicated new games demand so much concentration from the students that they distract their attention from the language forms they are supposed to be using. The more students are interested in an activity in the target language, the more they feel the desire to communicate in the language, and this is the first and most vital step in learning to use language forms spontaneously.

Although this section has concentrated on structural pattern drills, it must be borne in mind that drill techniques are also appropriate for learning the sound system of the language, increasing knowledge of vocabulary items and their appropriate use in context, and improving skill in writing. Drills, carefully designed, are a useful technique for training at the lower level of manipulation of language elements; they concentrate attention on specific points of difficulty until these are mastered. They are, however, merely a step on the way, as we shall see in chapters 7 and 8. The ultimate aim is confident and spontaneous use of the language, which involves the integration in complicated ways of the separate elements which have been drilled. Perfection at the pattern-drill level, no matter how impressive to the observer, cannot be an end in itself. It is a fruitless activity unless care is taken

---

10. Many games are described in the *PG*'s. They may be located through the index rubric, "Games."

to see that the result of all this effort is the ability to use the language to express some message of one's own.

PROGRAMMED INSTRUCTION

Programmed instruction has had its ups and downs since the early days of experimentation with teaching machines and programmed textbooks in the fifties. Its adaptation to language teaching became a subject of intense investigation and experimentation in the sixties. At this time, tape recorders and language laboratories were expected to take over most of the intensive practice in grammar and sound production. The development of these aids seemed to promise more freedom for teachers to use their classroom time in the active practice of communication.

The emphasis in the seventies on individualized instruction (often with teacher-prepared materials) and on computer-assisted instruction (CAI) revived interest in the most effective ways to program learning for self-instruction. Some textbooks of this period committed the study of grammar to programmed materials which students were to prepare before coming to class. Class time was then devoted to active use of what had been learned. Recent advocates of natural language learning seem to support this approach. Programming, therefore, still holds some interest, and the principles for programming language-learning materials which are still widely in use should be understood by teachers.

Programming has been applied at different times to the learning of the sound system of a language, to morphology and syntax, to the development of reading and writing skills, and to the learning of writing systems. In this chapter we shall concentrate on its applications for the learning of grammar rules and practice in their use.

Early Programming

Mention has been made in chapter 2 of the influence on foreign-language teaching techniques of the psychological theory of B. F. Skinner. Skinner himself applied his theory, derived from his experiments with rats and pigeons, to a method of teaching factual material to human subjects.[11] Although he was not the first person to devise materials for self-instruction,[12] it is from his work that we can date the widespread interest in programmed instructional materials. His famous article "The Science of Learning and the Art of Teaching"

11. For Skinner's views on human learning, see Skinner 1972.
12. Sidney Pressey was experimenting with programs for "teaching machines" as early as 1924. For articles by the leading figures in the early programming movement, see Lumsdaine and Glaser 1960.

(1954) has been studied, quoted, and reprinted constantly.[13] It should be read as a background to any study of programmed instruction.

Skinner's principles for changing behavior (reinforcement of correct responses in a series involving minimal changes) were already being used extensively by some foreign-language teachers in the fifties. These principles were basic to the pattern practice techniques which were advocated by early leaders of English as a foreign language in the United States (Fries 1945) and which were much in evidence in intensive language programs during World War II. The programming movement encouraged the writers of language-teaching materials to examine more closely the sequencing and development of their drills and exercises.

Theoretical Considerations

How students learn is a vital question for all teachers. Psychological insights into learning processes can make teaching more efficient and productive. Naturally, there are numerous psychological approaches to human learning, and research findings are continually changing the perspective for teachers. Since Skinner was a pioneer in the area of programmed instruction, it is important to understand his theoretical position when considering this subject.

For Skinner, learning is demonstrated by a change in behavior. His operant conditioning experiments have led him to believe that changes in behavior can be induced as follows: a behavioral response is made to occur through control of the environment in which the subject is placed; a reinforcing or rewarding stimulus which follows this response makes the response more likely to recur; if this rewarding state of affairs consistently follows the selected response, the response becomes conditioned as a habit. If the response is undesirable, it is left unrewarded and soon becomes extinguished. An experimenter wishing to induce a certain pattern of response, even something quite different from the subject's typical behavior, waits until a response occurs which resembles in some way the desired behavior. This response is then rewarded and not others. Methodically the experimenter continues to reward responses which approximate more and more closely the desired behavior, and not to reward others, until through a series of "successive approximations" the behavior is shaped to a preconceived pattern. In this fashion, subjects can be induced to make very fine discriminations among similar stimuli, and to follow through a complex series of well-defined responses.

13. *Harvard Educational Review* 24 (1954): 86–97. This article has been reprinted in Lumsdaine and Glaser 1960, pp. 99–113, and as chapter 2 of Skinner 1968.

How Programming Works
The programming movement adopted the Skinnerian paradigm of learning and applied it as follows: programmers draw up very careful specifications of the *terminal behavior* they wish to induce in the learner; they also analyze the initial or existent behavior of the learner; they then establish a program (that is, a sequence of learning steps) by which the learner's responses will be shaped until the desired behavior is demonstrated. This program controls the learning environment of the students. Sometimes it is presented in a programmed textbook, sometimes in some type of teaching machine or by computer. Through a series of *frames* which the students must study, the amount of attention to be given to any one element of the sequence and the order in which these elements are to be studied are under the control of the programmer, who can therefore prescribe as much practice as is deemed necessary at any one point. The programmer prompts or provokes responses to the frames. These responses are given immediate *reinforcement,* in that the students receive confirmation of the acceptability of their responses without delay, by seeing or hearing the correct version with which they may compare their own. The aim of the programmer is to present the material for learning in such a sequence and in such easily digested segments, or *minimal steps* that the student will not make mistakes but, constantly reinforced by success, will develop habitual behavior of the kind desired by the programmer.

Where a *computer* is used, students have ready access to a repeated display of the rules whenever they feel they need to review them. With a request to the computer they may rework any steps as often as they please with immediate correction. Many computer programmers incorporate reinforcement through expressions like "Good, Jane," or "Bravo" when answers are correct. Computer programs also keep track of successes and failures, so that at any point students or instructor may find out how well the learning is proceeding. They can also provide the student with further practice in the types of items which have been causing trouble, without the student having to riffle through material he or she already understands and can use. Printouts of each student's work may be studied by the instructor and the programmer to see what extra steps or helps should be included in the program, which steps could be omitted, and where instructions and explanations have not been clear.

There are certain ways in which programmed self-instruction is theoretically (that is, with ideal conditions and first-class programs) considered superior to the usual classroom instruction. It provides for active participation by the student throughout the learning session.

Structured Practice

Each student is able to make far more individual responses in the same period of time than as a member of a class group. If students learn what the programmer has intended them to learn, they proceed to new work; if they have not succeeded in learning it, they may remain at the same point in the instructional material until they have had sufficient practice. At times they may be directed back to earlier material for further study. In this way, programmed materials are considered to be *self-pacing,* providing for individual differences in rates of learning which cannot be accommodated in the classroom. With no time limit set for the completion of any section of the program, the faster-learning student is not held back and the slow-learning student is not harassed and bewildered. A program which is seriously planned is revised according to the errors made in trial runs by the students. Many aspects of the program sequence are thus determined by representatives of the group for whom the program is intended, rather than by some theoretician detached from the learning situation.

Where the program is integrated with tapes or cassettes, or where the computer terminal has an audio component,[14] programmed work need not be entirely in printed and written form. Much of the practice may be oral, with the correct responses provided by the audio component, as in regular language laboratory work.

Programmers emphasize the fact that the program does not replace the classroom teacher. Students left to work on their own for long periods with programmed materials miss the stimulation they receive from their interaction with a person interested in their progress.[15] The program does, however, free the teacher from constant attention to the needs of a large group of students, so that personal attention and tuition may be given to those students who most need help, at the moment when they need it.

In individualized situations where programmed materials are in use, it is essential for the teacher to move around from student to student helping and encouraging. To avoid the feeling of isolation, students may also be encouraged to work through the materials in pairs, or to meet in small groups at regular points in the program to help each other, test each other, and display their knowledge. The points in the program where they come to the teacher for evaluation of their progress should not be too far apart, so that they constantly feel there is interest in what they are doing and how they are doing it.

14. For an account of computer systems for foreign language learning, see James W. Dodge, "Educational Technology," in NEC 1980.

15. F. Marty, *Programing a Basic Foreign Language Course* (Hollins College, Va.: Audio-Visual Publications, 1962), pp. 16–17.

Programmed Instruction

Students working with carefully constructed computer programs do not seem to experience the feeling of isolation and depersonalization that some expect. The programmer has tried to anticipate as many of their problems as possible, and the individual corrections and comments on students' specific weaknesses and misunderstandings create the feeling of a dialogue with someone intensely interested in them personally. Students do not feel embarrassed to ask the computer the same question for the sixth time. The computer never pressures students, for it never moves on to further practice or new work until the student requests it. Some students have commented that "the computer is so kind." Certainly its patience is inexhaustible.

Types of Programs

Two types of programs have been advocated by researchers. The first type, the Skinnerian program, is *linear* in the sense that students work their way step by step through the whole sequence. The second type, *intrinsic* programming as advocated by Crowder,[16] provides by branching techniques for fast-learning students to skip parts of the program and for slow-learning students to be directed to supplementary sets of frames of a remedial nature.

Linear programs require constructed responses, often the filling in of a blank in a frame. The acceptable answer is then given for comparison. Each correct response prepares the way for the next step in the program, with each step being indispensable for the comprehension of the succeeding step. It is this careful arrangement of steps which shapes the student's learning, in accordance with Skinner's theory, toward the desired terminal outcome. Sometimes responses are imitative or echoic of earlier material; sometimes they are elicited by the logic of the progression of steps; sometimes they are prompted by the provision of some elements of the required response which help students to find the rest. Where some parts of the response are supplied, these may be faded out gradually in succeeding frames until the student is able to make the response without prompting.

The aim of a linear program is for the student to pass through it from beginning to end making the minimum of errors that is consistent with occasional inattention and distraction. For its success in promoting learning it is therefore very dependent on the size of the step

---

16. N. A. Crowder, "On the Differences between Linear and Intrinsic Programming," in de Grazia and Sohn 1964, pp. 77–99.

from frame to frame.[17] If the step is very small, an error-free passage is possible for most students. Such a program, however, may bore or irritate many students because the answers, being too obvious, do not require alertness and careful thought on their part. In this case the advantages of immediate confirmation of correct response are dissipated, since there is no great feeling of success in comparing unmistakeable answers in this time-wasting way. Step size may also be too great, not only forcing some students into error but discouraging others from pursuing the task to the end; it is at these points that programmers, in revising their work, must devise intermediate steps to help the students.

Intrinsic programming is characterized by the provision of multiple-choice answers for selection of response. These multiple-choice answers are constructed so that all the choices except the correct one reflect possible errors due to misunderstanding of the learning material. According to their choices of answer, learners are either directed to new material or branched off into a series of remedial frames, which explain why the choice was inappropriate and reteach what was not understood. Where a programmed textbook is used, the various segments of the program may be "scrambled" so that student users cannot ignore branching directions and proceed directly with the program. They must know the correct responses in order to determine the position in the book of the next section of new material. Intrinsic programming is based on the premise that learning takes place through a trial-and-error process—that students can learn from their mistakes. It is considered by its proponents to be more sensitive to individual differences in learning than linear programming because it provides shorter programs for faster learners and more detailed study, or practice, for slower learners.

Intrinsic programming was not much used, initially, for language teaching. It was considered inadvisable for students of a new language to be presented with incorrect alternatives which they might well "learn" from the program in the place of the correct responses. Furthermore, allowing students to skip sections seemed to some to be a concession to those who easily acquired an intellectual understanding of the logic of a sequence of ideas and did not feel the need for extensive elaboration or practice.

With the growing use of computers, however, the value of teaching through student errors has been exploited. When students make

17. For Skinner's own views on linear programming, see B. F. Skinner, "Some Implications of Making Education More Efficient," *Behavior Modification in Education,* ed. C. E. Thoresen, 77th Yearbook of the National Society for the Study of Education (Chicago: University of Chicago Press, 1973), p. 452.

wrong choices, the computer program explains why the particular response seemed right to the student, and corrects misapprehensions. It then directs the learner back to the original question to try to make a more enlightened selection from among the choices given, or directs them to remedial work before presenting further questions of a similar nature from a bank of possible items.

In teaching cultural concepts (see chapter 11), the approach of teaching through choices, some of which are correct and some not, enables the programmer to explain what are not concepts of the culture and why, as well as what the authentic concepts are.

Some linear programmers have attempted to make greater provision for individual rate of progress without resorting to intrinsic methods. Carroll[18] has experimented with the introduction into the program of "loops," which enable the students to rework material a number of times, eliminating mistakes on successive passages through the loop. In this way all students are given what seems to the programmer to be sufficient practice, yet students who need to do so are able to repractice the material as often as they wish before proceeding to a new section.

Programming and Language Learning

In this book the important question to be asked about programmed instruction is: Is it appropriate for the special requirements of learning a language? Careful programming of the types described above is useful in the development of sound discrimination and production, aural and reading comprehension, skill in the manipulation of language elements in closed systems, ability to write the language accurately at the nonspontaneous level, and the learning of writing systems. It can also be used in teaching the factual aspects of cultural studies. For language learning, the teaching machine, programmed textbook, or computer display needs to be accompanied by sound and recording facilities. Some visual element (films, filmstrips, videotapes, slides, cartoons, or other pictures) can facilitate the learning. These can easily be synchronized with the computer program. They can be supplied in a learning carrel, along with the sound facilities, for use with programmed textbooks.

With a purely self-instructional language course, there is always the danger that students will learn very thoroughly the form and possible combinations of elements in certain contexts, without gaining facility and confidence in using these at the level of active commu-

18. J. B. Carroll, "A Primer of Programmed Instruction in Foreign Language Teaching," *IRAL* 1, no. 2 (1963): 129.

nication. Spolsky, in discussing this type of inflexibility, makes a distinction between "knowing a language" and "language-like behavior." He asserts that being able to recite a number of sentences in another language is *language-like behavior,* while *knowing a language* "involves the ability to produce an indefinite number of utterances in response to an indefinite number of stimuli."[19]

Both Marty and Valdman advocate, in association with periods of self-instruction, sessions in small groups,[20] where students can practice using what they have learned in actual communication with an instructor and with each other. In such sessions the students are able to display what they know and to receive the reinforcement of comprehension and approval from their fellows and their teacher. This encourages them to persevere in the self-instructional part of the course. Such opportunities for interaction are absolutely essential if students are to develop uninhibited facility in using the language as it is used in the real world: for communication of information and emotions or for sharing experiences and pleasures. (This subject is discussed fully in chapter 8.)

Problems of Programmed Instruction
One of the major problems in the programming of language courses is the elaboration of detailed specifications of the desired terminal behavior. Since the students will learn what the program teaches them, this preliminary work must be very well thought out if the students are to develop all-round skill in language use. Authors of programs must decide what type of language mastery they wish to develop, setting out some practical and well-defined criteria of attainment; they must establish what skills are involved in this terminal behavior, and what elements are essential to the exercise of these skills; and finally they must establish pedagogically useful groupings for the great number of elements thus identified. In order to establish these essential basic elements, they will need to draw on the most thorough linguistic descriptions of the language available to them. In some cases they may find a contrastive study of the foreign and native languages useful to pinpoint possible problem areas for the students. An analysis of errors commonly made by students learning this language is also a valuable guide to the author of the program, indicating which elements need special emphasis and, with intrinsic program-

19. Bernard Spolsky, "A Psycholinguistic Critique of Programmed Foreign Language Instruction," *IRAL* 4, no. 2 (1966): 124.
20. F. Marty, *Programing,* p. 21; and A. Valdman, "Toward Self-Instruction in Foreign Language Learning," *IRAL* 2, no. 1 (1964): 7.

ming, which choices will provide the most self-teaching for the learner.

Having made a detailed analysis of elements to be learned, the author then needs to discover the most effective order for introducing these elements into the program. The educational level of the students and their reasons for studying a language will need to be taken into consideration at this point. Frequently the most effective progression for learning will be discovered, not by logical forethought, but by trying draft materials out on groups of students. Their experience will then reveal where adjustments or reordering of presentation is advisable.

Descriptions and analyses of terminal behavior in language learning, that is, the breaking down of language as it is used into discrete elements, can lead to a preoccupation with the teaching of innumerable details about the language. Important as these elements are, they can distract attention from the real "terminal behavior," that is, the whole of language as it operates in an act of communication, whether in speech or writing. The author of the program must be continually aware of this danger and make every effort to see that whatever has been studied in isolation is immediately repracticed in a natural context, so that the continuous fabric of the language is respected and recognized.

It is clear, then, that programming for self-instruction in foreign languages is a task for a team of experts, not for the individual classroom teacher, who will have neither the basic training, time, nor money to undertake such a demanding project. Our discussion of what is involved in a good program will, however, assist teachers in evaluating programmed courses and adapting them for the use of their students.

Experimentation with programmed courses is long and very costly, requiring much revision after trial use with students. The cost of complete courses is likely to remain high until a much greater volume of sales is assured. The use of full programs of self-instruction in language learning also involves the provision of recording-playback equipment for each student and, preferably, of take-home cassettes for home study. In order to justify the expense involved, schools need to ascertain that the programs they are introducing will be much more effective than the regular classroom and laboratory teaching. Such programs are, of course, essential for languages not commonly taught in educational institutions, the cost of the materials then being covered, for the most part, by special funding.

Even where full-length programmed courses are out of the question, many schools find short self-instructional courses for specific purposes a help in their teaching. Such courses usually provide for individual learning of certain circumscribed areas of particular difficulty (e.g., the use of a new alphabet, sound discriminations and production in the new language, or the practice of certain structural features). Short remedial courses in such areas are very useful to the teacher who wishes to provide extra practice for the slow learner, the absentee, or the transfer student. Carefully designed short courses are also useful for accelerating the learning of gifted students for whom the pace of normal classroom instruction may be tedious. Students of this type enjoy the freedom to progress which individualized programs provide.

Without attempting to create a completely self-instructional program, teachers may learn from a study of programming theory many things that will improve their approach to the organization of their teaching and help them adapt textbooks for individualization of instruction. Teachers attempting to write short self-instructional programs for some purpose should keep in mind the following facts:

- Vague definitions of the desired terminal behavior will lead to the creation of a confused and aimless program.
- Students will learn what the program teaches and will arrive at specific behavior only if the program is designed to lead them to it.
- Optimal step size is usually smaller than the inexperienced programmer realizes. This is the way in which programmed instruction differs from the usual textbook presentation.
- The sequence of a program should not be haphazard; it must follow a very careful development. For this reason programs cannot be written hastily, following a progression the teacher has used in a classroom presentation. In class the teacher can immediately remedy deficiencies in the materials by re-presenting sections in a new way as soon as it becomes evident that the students have not understood. This is not possible with programmed self-instruction.
- Immediate confirmation of learning should be built into the program in some way.
- The program must provide sufficient challenge to keep the students alert and interested.
- Students will be encouraged to persevere if the material leads them at certain intervals to subgoals which give them a sense of progress and achievement on the long road to the final goal to which the program is directing them. These stages are usually marked by short, self-correcting tests which enable the students to gauge their progress and identify their weaknesses.

Programmed Instruction

While teachers are waiting for easily available programs, well designed and well constructed, which are appropriate for the level of the students they are teaching, they should concentrate on seeing that the drills and exercises they use in classroom and laboratory are as well organized and as helpful to the students as the best programmed self-instructional materials.

- **Work through a unit of a programmed textbook for a subject which is not well known to you. Write down your impressions of the experience.**

Individualized Instruction and Programming

One of the tenets of individualized instruction is that students should be able to work their way through materials at their own rate of learning. To achieve this end, assignments or learning packets, contracts, performance objectives,[21] and variable credit have been proposed.[22] Sometimes the learning packets are constructed on programming principles, sometimes not.

Individualized instruction, however, implies much more than working through structured materials at one's own pace. Since it is based on meeting the learning needs of individuals, it also implies attention to preferred modes of learning and to individual goals. Many students like to work in pairs or small groups, or even in large groups, with help from other students or the teacher. Where oral communication is a major objective, working individually with programmed materials, even those with an audio component, is insufficient. Practice in communication with others is essential.

Individualized instruction should not, therefore, be identified with independent study with programmed materials. The latter has its place as has the former. Teachers wishing to use either of these approaches will examine the needs of individual students and help them to choose the type of learning experience most appropriate to their personality, aptitude, and goals.

---

21. *Specification of terminal behavior* is the basis of *behavioral* or *performance objectives*. A performance objective sets out the behavior a student will be able to demonstrate after learning, the purpose for requiring this behavior, the conditions under which the behavior will occur, and the criterion by which the teacher will be able to judge whether the expected behavior has been acquired. For a discussion of performance objectives in language teaching and the problems associated with them, see W. M. Rivers, "Individualized Instruction and Cooperative Learning: Some Theoretical Considerations," in *SMT*, pp. 245–48.

22. See books and articles on Individualized Instruction in the Annotated Reading List.

Annotated Reading List

STRUCTURAL PATTERN DRILLS

Stack, E. M. *The Language Laboratory and Modern Language Teaching*, pp. 117–83. 3d ed. New York: Oxford University Press, 1971. The chapters "Audiolingual Exercises" and "Pattern Drills" should be very carefully studied. Examples of suggested forms of drills and exercises are given in English, French, German, Italian, Russian, and Spanish.

Rivers, Wilga M., et al. *Practical Guides*. Chapter 4, "Oral Practice for the Learning of Grammar," discusses six types of oral practice exercises (repetition, substitution, conversion, sentence modification, response, and translation exercises). Discusses effective construction and possible pitfalls. Examples are given of type A and type B exercises.

Grittner, F. M. *Teaching Foreign Languages*. 2d ed. New York, 1977. Chapter 8, "The Pattern Drill," discusses what pattern drills are and are not, with examples in English, French, German, and Spanish.

Rivers, W. M. *The Psychologist and the Foreign-Language Teacher*. Chicago: University of Chicago Press, 1964. Chapter 8, "The Right Response," and chapter 13, "Practical Recommendations," discuss problems of classroom and laboratory presentation of structural pattern drills.

Contrastive Structure Series. Charles A. Ferguson, General Editor. Chicago: University of Chicago Press. This series is a guide to areas of major difficulty for students working with these pairs of languages:

Kufner, H. L. *The Grammatical Structures of English and German*. 1962.

Agard, Frederick B., and Di Pietro, Robert J. *The Grammatical Structures of English and Italian*. 1965.

Stockwell, Robert P.; Bowen, J. Donald; and Martin, John W. *The Grammatical Structures of English and Spanish*. 1965.

PROGRAMMED INSTRUCTION

Carroll, J. B. "A Primer of Programmed Instruction in Foreign Language Teaching." *IRAL* 1/2 (1963): 115–41. A thorough study of the principles and practical requirements of programming for foreign-language study. Selected bibliography on programmed instruction. Essential reading.

Howatt, A. "Programmed Instruction." In J. P. B. Allen and Corder 1974, pp. 232–54. Gives examples of a linear and a branching program in an invented language, Novish. Discusses how to design a program with its essential features of *objective* and *plan,* which must be in accordance with a *general strategy* of language teaching. Concludes with a sample program for teaching the use of *since* and *for* in English.

Valdman, A. "Programmed Instruction and Foreign Language Teaching." In Valdman 1966, pp. 133–58. Shows how the theory of programming works in practice, with examples from programs for French, English, and Italian.

Northeast Conference. "A New Look at Learning." In NEC 1962, pp. 19–60. Practical problems of programming are discussed, with examples in Latin and Spanish. Outlines ways in which principles of programming can be applied by teachers who are not using teaching machines or programmed textbooks.

*INDIVIDUALIZED INSTRUCTION

Rivers, Wilga M. "Individualized Instruction and Cooperative Learning: Some Theoretical Considerations." In *SMT,* pp. 236–55. A rationale for individualized instruction, with a critique of performance objectives.

Grittner, F. M., and LaLeike, F. H. *Individualized Foreign Language Instruction.* Skokie, Ill.: National Textbook, Co., 1973. How to individualize instruction explained in detail.

Logan, G. E. *Individualized Foreign Language Learning: An Organic Process.* Rowley, Mass.: Newbury House. 1973. The process and problems of individualizing instruction described in detail by one of the most experienced practitioners in the field.

PERFORMANCE OBJECTIVES

Valette, R. M., and Disick, R. S. *Modern Language Performance Objectives and Individualization. A Handbook.* New York: Harcourt Brace Jovanovich, 1972. Shows how to establish and write performance objectives for all aspects of language teaching, with examples in English, French, German, and Spanish.

Research and Discussion

    1. Look at grammar exercises in one unit of a textbook from which you studied the language you will teach. What are the strengths and weakness of these exercises? Look at another unit further on in the book. Are the exercises different in type? What improvements would you propose for a revised edition of the book?

    2. Examine recent textbooks and select the one you would like to adopt for your own classes. What features of the presentation

and practice of grammar appealed to you? In what ways will you need to modify or supplement the textbook in order to have interesting classes?

3. Examine some structural pattern drills from a language learning laboratory manual. How do they tally with the structural pattern drill checklist (pp. 000–000)? What other qualities do they have?

4. Take a traditional type of grammar exercise designed to be read and recited or written out. Try to make an oral drill from it. Tape the cues and see if you could perform the drill orally yourself without the help of a script.

5. How did you learn to use grammatical features yourself? Write a critique of the way you were taught. How do you intend to teach students to be able to use grammatical features?

6. Take a grammar rule from a traditional textbook. Examine the examples given to illustrate the rule and the examples in the exercises based on the rule. Is the rule as given sufficiently explicit to cover all of these examples? Can you think of unacceptable sentences which could be created by applying the rule exactly as it is stated?

7. Select a set of drills from a lesson or unit and propose and describe (a) some games which could be used to achieve the same purposes and (b) some games which could be used to practice what had been learned in the drill in the more natural atmosphere of competition.

8. Write a programmed unit, for the language you intend to teach, for the study of the agreement of the adjective with the noun, or the morphology of the present tense, or the position of the adverb.

*9. What progressive steps would you take to individualize the instruction in the class to which you have been assigned?

*10. How was individualization of instruction viewed in earlier efforts like the Winnetka and Dalton Plans? How did these plans begin, develop, and wane? (Useful references may be found in Grittner 1977.)

5· Teaching Sounds

We have all had the experience, when listening to foreigners speaking our language, of having great difficulty in understanding what they are trying to say, not because of their lack of knowledge of vocabulary and language structure but because the sounds they produced seemed peculiar and the voice rose and fell in unexpected places. Even immigrants who have lived in the country for twenty years may have a "foreign accent" which makes them difficult to understand. Since language is a means of communication, it is not enough for our students to learn words, phrases, grammatical features, if they are not able to produce these in a way which makes their utterances comprehensible to a native speaker of the language.

Helping students to acquire an articulation and intonation which are comprehensible and acceptable to native speakers poses one of the most difficult problems for teachers of languages. The seriousness of the problem depends on the degree of difference and the nature of the differences between the sound systems of the first and the second languages. Some oriental and African languages have a system of tones to which many learners of these languages are not accustomed and thus find difficult. Similarly, speakers of tone languages experience difficulty in learning correct production of nontonal languages. The carryover of a different stress or intonation system is also a frequent cause of incomprehensibility.

Even with cognate European languages, pronunciation problems may be greater than students realize. English and French, for instance, show extreme differences in their phonological systems, and speakers of either of these languages have considerable difficulty in speaking the language of the other without a marked "foreign accent." Before teachers can overcome these inherent difficulties with any degree of efficiency, they must have a clear understanding of the nature of the problem.

As Stockwell and Bowen have pointed out, "Our problem as teachers of a second language is to build into the nervous system of each learner a new set of choices and restrictions. It is our impression that it is in the nature of nervous systems that they reject conflict, that they seek unification, orderliness, coherence, and simplicity. In introducing a distinct and separate linguistic organization into a nervous

system where one such organization is already comfortably established, we must necessarily encounter stubborn resistance and energetic efforts to amalgamate the new with the old'' (Stockwell and
Bowen 1965, p. 3). As a result, students tend to assimilate the sound
system of a new language to that of their native language, or to that
of another foreign language they have learned. In the latter case, it
is usually the most recent or weakest of the other languages the
student knows which causes the most interference, as though the
subconscious mind were saying: "This is 'foreign.' Try this" (see
Appendix B).

ACOUSTIC AND ARTICULATORY PHONETICS

The extensive study linguists in the present century have made of
many languages has made it abundantly clear that each language has
a sound system in which all the elements are interrelated, so that
incorrect production of one sound can seriously affect production of
others. It is very rare indeed to find two languages with identical
sound systems. Since these differences in sound systems have a physiological basis—for example, variations in the position of the speech
organs or in breath control—teachers must understand the physical
aspects of sound production. They will not necessarily teach these
facts, but knowledge of them will help teachers to identify the physical
reasons for inaccurate approximations of new sounds by their students. They will then be able to give their students useful guidance
in correcting faulty production.

Sounds are differentiated by their timbre (which is caused by the
different degrees of resonance resulting from the shape and size of
the cavities, or resonating chambers, formed in the mouth and nose),
and by variations in the frequency and amplitude of the waves on
which they are carried (these variations creating differences in pitch
and loudness). The study of the fine distinctions in pitch, loudness,
timbre, and duration of sounds of different languages and dialects
constitutes the field of acoustic phonetics. Articulatory phonetics
studies such aspects as the opening and closing of the vocal cords
and of the nasal passage, and the varying positions of the tongue and
lips which alter the shape and size of the resonating chambers in the
mouth and determine the differences in vowel sounds, at times imped-
ing the free flow of air from the lungs to form consonants. The subject
matter of acoustic phonetics is very technical and needs to be interpreted for the classroom teacher. Every language teacher should,
however, understand the principles of articulatory phonetics as they
apply both to the native language of the students and to the language
they are learning. In this way, the particular difficulties of the tran-

sition from one language to another can be explained. Contrastive studies of the phonology of various pairs of languages have appeared, and teachers should study publications of this nature as an essential part of their professional preparation. Some available studies are indicated in the Annotated Reading List to this chapter.

A "foreign accent" is inevitable if students attempt to produce the sounds of a new language while keeping their mouths shaped and their tongues placed as for similar sounds in their native language. The position of the tongue (against the teeth, the gums, or the palate); the height of the highest part of the tongue (front or back of the tongue, high, at mid-level, or low in the mouth); the lips rounded or unrounded—all these elements combine to alter the shape of the front and back resonating chambers in the mouth and thus alter the timbre of the sound produced. The ways in which the airflow is impeded (by tongue tip raised and pressed against the gums, for instance, or tongue tip turned down and pressed against the teeth; by lips held closed and released suddenly; or by air accumulated before release and released slowly) result in distinctly different consonantal sounds. The vocal cords enter into play and, by allowing air to pass freely at times, may add another dimension, called voicing, to the consonant sound. The airflow for the vowel or for the consonant may pass through the mouth only or through the mouth and the nasal cavities, the result being a distinct difference in timbre.

Since so many elements are involved in sound production, the number of possibilities is enormous. A given sound can be reproduced accurately by an appropriate conjunction of these various elements, even though a different combination will sometimes achieve the same effect. The teacher needs to understand how the students are using their speech organs in producing native-language sounds and what they should be doing to reproduce the sounds of the new language acceptably, in order to help them beyond a certain stage of earnest but inaccurate imitation.

Each language has its characteristic and interrelated mouth positions. Teachers often concentrate on teaching mouth positions for those sounds which do not exist in the native language, while allowing students to produce native-language near-equivalents for the rest. This produces the undesirable situation where a student has to make, in midword, mouth adjustments which are almost impossible physically or at least difficult and awkward, thus deforming the neighboring sounds, which would otherwise have been correctly articulated. The student must be made aware of the overall pattern of the integrated phonological system of the new language and of the fact that incorrectly articulated consonants will affect the production of vowels, as

127

vowels will affect consonants. Adopting a new system of articulatory positions requires steady practice and muscle training. The student has to develop not only an auditory but also a kinesthetic image of the correct sound, and to develop facility in transferring impulses from brain to correct speech muscles.

- **Which sounds in the language you are teaching are the most difficult for your students to produce? Which ones are they most likely to assimilate to sounds which exist in their native language?**

SOUND VARIATION AND COMPREHENSION

As well as articulatory differences among sounds, the language teacher should understand the concept of the *phoneme*.[1] A phoneme is the smallest element of sound in a language which is recognized by a native speaker as making a distinction between language units. Each vowel or consonant in the sound system of a language can be produced in a number of slightly varying forms, within a certain band of tolerance, before it ceases to be recognizable to another native speaker in its normal context of accompanying sounds. These slightly varying forms are called allophones of the phoneme. Differences of an allophonic kind are phonetic and may be indicative of the social level of the speaker, of some group membership, or of a personal idiosyncrasy.

What seems to be a very small phonetic difference may, while being merely allophonic in one language, signal a distinct difference of meaning in some other language. The difference between [f] and [v] does not result from a change in position of tongue and lips, but is purely a matter of voicing (the opening of the vocal cords); yet for a speaker of English this distinction is very important because it brings about a change in meaning (e.g., from "fear" to "veer"; from "feel" to "veal"). In a language where such a change in voicing does not alter the meaning, the difference between [f] and [v] will continue to be a phonetic difference but will not constitute a phonemic differ-ence. A study of the phonemic system of the language to be taught will enable the teacher to emphasize those phonetic differences which will make what the student says intelligible or unintelligible to a native speaker.

Understanding of phonemic distinctions becomes most important at those points where the phonemic systems of the first language and the second language do not coincide. Students listening to a new language in the early stages will "hear" the phonemes of their own

1. The phoneme was a concept of structuralist linguistics. Its validity has been challenged by generative phonologists. The concept is, however, a useful one for language teaching.

language, that is, they will automatically classify new sounds as variants of familiar native-language phonemes. Students in whose language the distinction between /ü/ and /u/[2] does not determine differences of meaning will not at first notice this distinction. It is at such points of divergence that students will have to be taught by aural discrimination exercises to "hear" differences of which they have never before been conscious. Until they can perceive these differences readily, they will have difficulty in producing acceptable imitations of these sounds.

GENERATIVE PHONOLOGY

Structural linguists studied items (distinct units or phonemes) and their arrangement or distribution. Generative phonologists concentrate on *process rules*. Certain variants in pronunciation of morphemes occur systematically in certain sound environments. In the generative approach, a basic variant is selected as the underlying form of a morpheme; and rules of sound variation, which apply throughout the language, are established. When these rules are applied in a certain order, they modify the underlying form to produce the variants we see in the language. Native speakers know how these rules apply in their language and produce the required variants without conscious awareness of the changes they are making. Learners of a new language have to learn these rules consciously and apply them in appropriate contexts until they have acquired a feeling for the process involved.

Traditional language materials have usually presented variants of this type as exceptions, or have developed ad hoc rules to cover several groups of exceptions where similarities of process were apparent. Generative phonology brings to light the systematic nature of the process of variation, so that language learners can apply similar rules to the variant behavior of a number of different morphemes. This should lead to economy in learning. To date, very few language-teaching materials have included exercises based on generative rules, although some articles have appeared describing how such rules may be used in teaching.[3]

2. In I.P.A. notation this distinction would be inscribed [y] and [u]. For a discussion of the conventions used for notation of phonetic and phonemic distinctions, see p. 144.

3. W. B. Dickerson, "The Wh Question of Pronunciation: An Answer from Spelling and Generative Phonology," *TQ* 9 (1975): 299–309; "Generative Theory in TESL Practice," *MLJ* 61 (1977): 179–87. For the theory, see Sanford A. Schane, *Generative Phonology* (Englewood Cliffs, N.J.: Prentice-Hall, 1973).

PROSODIC FEATURES

Frequently neglected by language teachers are the indispensable elements of *syllabification* (internal juncture), *stress,* and *intonation* (variations in pitch). In a situation where we do not hear clearly in the native language it is these features that assist us in piecing together the import of what we have heard. We have all had the experience of completely misinterpreting the utterances of a foreigner who stressed the wrong syllables when speaking our language and superimposed the intonation of his native language. Stress and intonation may also change considerably the emotional impact of what we hear and make the subtle difference between a polite request and a brusque demand. With incorrect intonation a question in some languages may be interpreted as a statement of fact, with resultant breakdown in communication. The teacher should, therefore, emphasize these prosodic elements from the beginning, making clear their important role in comprehensible speech. Teachers should watch carefully to see that students develop and retain acceptable habits in these areas as well as in the correct production of sounds.

Unfortunately, it is often in the area of stress and intonation that language teachers who are not native speakers have the most difficulty themselves. It is essential for them to keep their control of these aspects of the language at a high level, through deliberate study of stress and intonation patterns; through constant ear-training by listening to recordings, radio, and films; and by as frequent association as possible with native speakers. Teachers need to keep in mind, however, that native speakers who have been away from their native land for a considerable period cease to provide reliable intonation models.

The Teacher's Pronunciation

Unless tapes or records of the production of native speakers are being used extensively, students cannot advance in articulation and intonation beyond the stage their teacher has reached. As students imitate, teachers will hear their own weaknesses chorused back at them in all their undisguised inaccuracy, frequently exaggerated at the most difficult points. Continually hearing inaccurate approximations in the classroom will gradually make teachers less conscious of their own defects, and their accent will inevitably deteriorate over a period of years. It is essential, then, that teachers work at the improvement of their own pronunciation. This is not as difficult now as it used to be because teachers have access to tapes and records of native speech with which they can practice very profitably, even if they do not wish to use such aids in class.

It must be emphasized, however, that in areas where students cannot readily meet native speakers of the language or travel to a country where the language is spoken, tapes and records should be incorporated in the work of the class as often as possible so that students may imitate authentic speech, rather than even a good approximation of it. There are always students who, given such opportunities, can readily acquire a more nearly native pronunciation than that of the non-native teacher.

INTRODUCING THE PHONOLOGY OF THE NEW LANGUAGE

The student's first contact with the sound patterns of the new language may occur at elementary school, junior high school, senior high school, or college. The *differences in age and maturity* at these various levels will involve different techniques and emphases.

Preadolescent Students

Younger children enjoy mimicry and may frequently be engaged in activities which are largely repetitive. Older students like to understand what they are doing and why. Younger children are less self-conscious about making strange sounds and behaving in ways which are different from those of their fellows and of the community around them. They are still living in a child world, where make-believe comes naturally. Adolescents are striving to make themselves acceptable in the adult world as well as to impress their peers. They are anxious to behave in a way which distinguishes them from "silly children."

At elementary and junior high school level, the sound patterns of the language may be taught in the context of language material used actively over and over or memorized. Students repeat after the teacher the various sounds as they encounter them in context. The material for these early lessons should not be artificially constructed to include only certain sounds and not others. It should consist of utterances selected because they are natural and usable. Although the teacher will choose only specific sounds for closer attention and practice during a particular lesson, the student's ear will at the same time gradually become accustomed to the whole phonological system with its distinctive articulatory features and its stress and intonation patterns. Much of the work of the class will be acting out roles, participating in games and competitions, and singing songs. The students will be making their first efforts at producing sounds which the teacher will not be taking up individually until later, but they will be slowly acquiring them in a natural context and in their normal interrelationships.

131

Even younger students will identify the sounds of the new language as variants of familiar native-language phonemes. It will be necessary to instruct the children briefly and succinctly in correct articulation and to insist on attentive imitation of phrases and sentences until this correct articulation becomes habitual. In this way the whole phonological system of the language will be covered as part of an ongoing learning process, rather than as a separate activity only relevant during "pronunciation practice."

It is at this stage that choral repetition is of great value. It gives each student ample opportunity to practice making sounds, thus giving essential exercise in new muscle movements and time to develop an auditory memory of the sound patterns. In choral practice, shy children are hidden in the crowd and acquire confidence in articulating strange sounds, while children with less aptitude for faithful imitation are carried along and must articulate faster than they would on their own. Students who acquire the pronunciation of a new language rapidly are given ample opportunity for expression and are imitating the correct model at all times. This contrasts with a one-by-one classroom situation, where students often have very few opportunities to practice aloud and are condemned to long periods of listening to the incorrect efforts of their less gifted fellows.

Even at the preadolescent stage, however, children possess powers of mimicry to a greater or lesser degree, and their imitation of sounds may be startlingly inaccurate. The teacher who listens only to chorus repetition may be under the illusion that all is well. The inevitable errors of a number of the children (confusion of vowel sounds, incorrect articulation of consonants) will be masked by the torrent of sound. If the class has regular access to a language laboratory, this will provide the students with the same advantages as choral repetition: maximum opportunity for individual imitation of a correct model, protection from the embarrassment of recitation before critical peers, the on-moving lesson, which draws from the student a faster participation. Furthermore, the teacher will be able to hear and analyze individual difficulties, and give help where needed, without interrupting the work of others who do not have the same difficulties. (At this level of instruction, more profit will be gained from the laboratory if it is used for short periods at frequent intervals.)

Adolescent and Adult Learners

For students beginning a language at senior high school or college level, the introductory lessons may well include some direct instruction in the differences between the phonological systems of the native language and of the target language. This may be for short periods at the beginning of successive lessons, as long as such theoretical instruction is always accompanied by the learning of some authentic language material that is usable in class activities. In this way, the students feel they are really getting to grips with the language from the beginning, while having the opportunity to apply what they have just learned about sounds in a practical context.

If correct articulation, stress, and intonation are to become habitual, students must not be expected in the early stages to pronounce, or read on their own, or act out anything which has not been practiced orally with the teacher or a model. Teachers who take the easy way of allowing their students to work for long periods from books when their acquisition of the sound system is still at a delicate and uncertain stage will be repaid by hearing a rapid deterioration in articulation and intonation, as their students try to produce sounds to match the familiar and unfamiliar combinations of letters before them. Native-language sounds will creep back in, and remedial practice will have to be instituted.

Aural Discrimination and Production

In order to overcome the the the natural tendency of the student to "hear" in the categories made familiar by the native language, the teacher will need to give aural discrimination exercises in which the differences between apparently similar sounds in the native and foreign languages are clearly demonstrated and in which near equivalents within the foreign language are distinctly differentiated.

For discrimination purposes, a sound should not be presented in isolation, since it then differs from the way in which it is perceived in association with other sounds. In normal utterances, sounds very rarely occur in isolation except for occasional exclamations like *Oh!* and *Ah!* If words are contrasted in which the vowels or consonants to be discriminated are in different environments (as in s*i*ng/s*ee*p, or *d*aily/pe*t*al), factors like consonant anticipation, assimilation, vowel reduction, or consonant loss may come into play. It then becomes difficult to demonstrate the essential auditory differences. For these reasons, minimal pairs are often used for training in aural discrimination. These are pairs of words which differ only in pronunciation of the sounds being practiced. Examples of minimal pairs for aural discrimination of English sounds would be *sheep/ship* or *fat/vat;* and for French *rue/roue.* Even minimal pairs, however, after a preliminary exercise, should be heard in a larger context, as they would be in normal language use *(It's a sheep; it's a ship).*

- **Work out some minimal pairs for problem sound distinctions in the language you will teach. Then put them in a short context. What**

is the effect of the context? Is it possible to maintain a minimal contrast in a larger context than one or two syllables in this language? If not, why not?

After some practice with aural discrimination of minimal pairs, students should have the opportunity to produce a specific sound themselves, first in simple phrases and then in longer sentences. These sentences should be naturally phrased utterances which the student might well encounter in conversation in the new language. Teaching the student to say artificially constructed tongue twisters, in which a particular sound is repeated a number of times, may have its place as an amusing diversion, relaxing the tension of concentrated learning. These tongue twisters sometimes act as mnemonic devices for rule reference. There is, however, no guarantee that skill acquired in such manipulations will transfer to a real communication situation. For such transfer to take place, practice must involve useful phrases that the student is likely to use on some future occasion.

After students have practiced particular sounds in longer utterances, the teacher should listen attentively to their rendering of them in the normal language work of the day. If the students still retain correct articulation while concentrating on other aspects of the language, then it is clear that they need no further drilling in the production of these sounds in artificial exercises.

A teacher who has to take over an advanced class which has been poorly trained in pronunciation may need to give instruction and practice, in the sequence outlined, as a regular feature of the lessons for some time. In this case, aural discrimination of correctly and incorrectly articulated sounds will need to precede direct practice, because the students will have developed the habit of identifying what they are saying with what they are hearing. They will at first think correct pronunciation of foreign-language speech is artificial and even amusing.

Dictation

Where spelling complications do not make it inadvisable (that is, when certain groupings of letters always represent certain sounds), *dictation* can be a useful technique for verifying whether students have learned to make certain discriminations among sounds. In the early stages, material dictated should be essentially a recombination of what has already been used orally or for reading practice. At advanced levels, the dictation usually serves a triple purpose: as an exercise in aural comprehension and discrimination; as a test of the student's knowledge of combinations of letters which traditionally represent specific sounds; and as a test of knowledge of structural elements, particularly those of a morphological nature. If the dictation is to be used solely as a check on aural discrimination, it must be very carefully constructed so as to exclude other complications.[4]

In classes where students have been taught a phonetic or phonemic script (see p. 144), dictation of sounds which students write down in this script will be used as verification of discrimination of sounds. Reading back the phonetic or phonemic script can then be used as a check on the students' production of these sounds.

Rhymes, Poems, and Songs
Not to be overlooked as a device for pronunciation practice is the learning by heart of rhymes and poems. These must be carefully chosen so that the vocabulary, thought content, and structures are appropriate to the level the students have reached. Rhymes and poems for early stages should preferably be narrative or descriptive, with short lines, uncomplicated ideas, and a certain amount of repetition. For younger children, many nursery rhymes and counting rhymes are suitable. Counting rhymes are frequently nonsensical, in a whimsical way, with a certain charm because of their rhythm, vowel music, or alliteration. Because of their lack of meaning, they lend themselves readily to repetition purely for pronunciation purposes. Rhymes and poems learned by heart can be repeated in chorus or by individuals many times over, becoming more attractive with familiarity, whereas dialogue sentences or prose passages which were repeated as frequently would long since have become tedious and boring.

Some sounds are more easily produced by a foreigner on a musical scale; this applies particularly to vowel sounds, which, because of the way they are formed, can vary in pitch. Frequent singing of simple songs can establish good production of these sounds, so long as slurring is immediately checked and attention is paid to clear articulation. Many folk songs have repetitive choruses which provide excellent practice in the production of basic vowels.

Tape Practice
The development of good pronunciation is undoubtedly an area in which the tape recorder and the language laboratory can play a very effective role. The tape can provide an authentic model for imitation, an untiring and unvarying model which is clearly heard by every student. It enables students far from the country where the language is spoken to saturate themselves, if they so desire, in the phonological

4. Eight different ways of giving dictation are proposed in the *PG*'s, chap. 8.

atmosphere of the language. With the availability of cassette recorders, students can take the language with them wherever they wish to go, and listen and practice in complete isolation and anonymity. If this is to happen, however, the teacher must provide material more interesting than minimal pair exercises.

With full recording-playback facilities in a laboratory, the students are able to compare their production with that of the unchanging model and rerecord until they are satisfied with their approximation of each utterance. Just as obviously, the laboratory can confirm the students in bad habits practiced with great zeal and earnestness, and students who are not properly prepared by their teachers to monitor their own production may listen to quite inaccurate efforts with considerable satisfaction.

If the laboratory is to be effective in the developing of acceptable articulation and intonation, the way in which it is to be used must be carefully studied. Students must be given instruction and practice under supervision in the difficult task of detecting their own weaknesses, and also in methods of remedying the weaknesses of which they become aware. This is a task which requires a certain maturity. Younger students should not be left to work on pronunciation unmonitored in the laboratory, although older students may be encouraged to use it on a library basis, if clear self-instructional assignments are available.

Monitoring students in a laboratory is not an easy task. Students interrupted too frequently or for too long find it difficult to take up the thread of their work. Monitors have only a brief interval in which to assess the major weaknesses to which they wish to draw the student's attention. At some stage a tape should be made of each student's oral production. This may consist of the reading of a text constructed to contain the major pronunciation difficulties the student will encounter in the new language. Each student's pronunciation should then be analyzed and strengths and weaknesses noted on a pronunciation checklist. While monitoring, teachers should have a checklist for each student available, so that they may concentrate on the improvement of the areas of weakness of a particular student and consult notes on what they have already drawn to this student's attention during previous sessions. Such a list will enable them to give useful advice in a precise and succinct fashion which makes each interruption as short and as immediately useful as possible. If the students have similar checklists they can mark the weaknesses drawn to their notice and thus work more purposefully toward improvement.

Even in schools *where no laboratory is available,* the teacher should have a checklist of particular problems of pronunciation against which to note each student's progress. The teacher keeps such a checklist in his or her textbook and marks down observations about particular students at odd moments during oral and reading lessons. A systematic approach to pronunciation problems will achieve much more satisfactory results than a hit-or-miss assessment based on the most glaring mistake that strikes the teacher's ear in one particular lesson.

EVALUATING PRONUNCIATION

The evaluation of pronunciation has been made considerably easier by the advent of the tape recorder. Judging the level of acceptability of each student's pronunciation as he or she reads or recites is a chancy process since sound is fleeting. Some aspects of the pronunciation or intonation may elude the listener whose attention is caught at that moment by some other element in the utterance. When a tape is made of each student's production, the teacher is able not only to listen several times to one section before deciding on the grading, but also to listen again to the work of other students and make immediate cross-comparisons of level of proficiency.

Various approaches to the evaluation of pronunciation and intonation have been proposed.

1. The teacher may make a subjective global assessment such as: this is excellent; it's very good; it's good; it's weak; it's lamentable. (This approximates a five-point scale of ABCDE.) Such an approach may be useful when performed by an experienced teacher, and it has its place as a rough sieve through which to sort a large number of students in a placement procedure. Any mistakes in placement are then corrected by instructors during the early sessions.

2. A detailed marking scheme may be followed where points are allotted for particular features (e.g., for grouping of words; particular difficulties of vowel or consonant; word linking and other forms of juncture; syllabification, stress, and intonation; and the general fluency and comprehensibility of the rendition). A methodical tabulation of this type makes the final grade an expression of something concrete.

3. Higgins considers the "sound quality" of vowels and consonants to be the primary sources of information to the listener and the vowel length, juncture, rhythm, and intonation to be the secondary sources of information. He proposes a four-point scale for measuring student performance as follows: Unintelligible (U), Intelligible (I), Acceptable (A), and Near Native (NN).

- The *unintelligible* level provides too little information for the listener. "The student makes less than the full range of primary distinctions . . . , and does not consistently make any of the secondary distinctions."
- The *intelligible* level provides the listener with enough information for analysis, but it is a strain to comprehend. "The student makes all primary distinctions but very few secondary ones. The secondary information . . . may clash with the primary information."
- At the *acceptable* level, the listener can analyze the information and understand. "The student makes all primary distinctions and some secondary ones; none of the secondary information clashes with the primary information."
- At the *near native* level, the student will always be understood and may sometimes be taken for a native. "The student makes all primary and secondary distinctions" (Higgins 1969, pp. 127–28).

Higgins uses this system to distinguish beginning, intermediate, and advanced stages of learning. Beginners, naturally, are U at all times, but work toward "A or I in known items or situations," "I or U in new items." By the end of the intermediate stage they are "A in known items and situations," "I in new items." The aim of advanced students is to be "A at all times," "NN perhaps in well practised situations" (ibid., pp. 128–29).

- **Do you agree with Higgins's targets for the different stages of learning? How do they tally with your teaching or learning experience? Can you suggest any other systems for evaluating pronunciation?**

PHYSICAL AND PSYCHOLOGICAL PROBLEMS OF TEACHING SOUNDS

In the language class where oral work plays a prominent role, certain problems of a physical or emotional character are encountered—problems of a kind which do not assume the same importance in the teaching of book-oriented subjects. The teacher must be conscious of the bases of these problems and alert to detect when poor performance has causes other than inattention, poor study habits, or lack of interest in the subject.

Occasionally the teacher will find in the class a student, often eager and attentive, who seems quite unable to reproduce sounds with any degree of accuracy and has difficulty with any form of aural comprehension. As time passes, this student develops an emotional block with respect to all oral work, is embarrassed when asked to participate orally, and is nervous and tense when dictation or testing of oral work takes place. A quiet individual conference frequently reveals that such a student has some difficulty in distinguishing between different vowel sounds (which have distinctive qualities of pitch and timbre) and in retaining patterns of intonation (this requiring a similar ability to that of retaining a musical phrase). Such a student may be to some degree tone-deaf or deficient in tonal memory.[5]

Students with difficulties of this type are capable of achieving great fluency and accuracy in reading and writing the language, and a thorough knowledge of structure. They feel relaxed in such activities. They may also learn to express themselves fluently in the language, even if their articulation and intonation are faulty. They should be encouraged, when listening to utterances in the new language, to relax and concentrate on interpreting, from the elements they do distinguish, the full import of the utterance. All languages are redundant, in that more elements are included in the utterance than are essential for comprehension (see p. 153). It is for this reason that we are able to follow dialogue across a crowded room, over a noisy telephone line, or from the worn soundtrack of an old film. Experimentation has shown that speech can suffer all kinds of distortion before it becomes unintelligible, and students with a tonal problem must learn to piece together the message from the limited spectrum of sound they are receiving. They can be helped with intonation or with tone patterns by the use of visual outlines. Properly guided, students with hearing difficulties which are not physically extreme can, with practice, become reasonably proficient, with occasional lapses, in conversational exchanges.

Unless teachers are conscious of the problems facing the student who has difficulty in relying on the ear alone, they may become tense and anxious themselves as they attempt to "reach" such students. Their tension compounds the tension the student is already experiencing and causes a feeling of panic in which the student ceases to hear anything distinctly in a blur of sound. This stage is detectable in the language laboratory when the student is working without a

---

5. Experiments concerning the value of tests of ability to distinguish musical elements such as pitch, loudness, rhythm, time, timbre, and tonal memory in the prediction of the degree of success in foreign-language learning have shown tests of tonal memory to have some predictive value. The comments in this section apply to the occasional student with real deficiencies in some of these areas, and not to the majority of our students who have normal capacities to varying degrees of adequacy in this regard. For reports of experiments, see: P. Pimsleur, L. Mosberg, and A. Morrison, "Student Factors in Foreign Language Learning" (section on Pitch Discrimination), *MLJ* 46 (1962): 163–64; R. Leutenegger and T. Mueller, "Auditory Factors and the Acquisition of French Language Mastery," *MLJ* 48 (1964): 141–46; and R. Leutenegger, T. Mueller, and I. Wershow, "Auditory Factors in Foreign Language Acquisition," *MLJ* 49 (1965): 22–31.

script. The student mumbles, makes a few sounds which do not make words in the language, and frequently fades out in the middle of a sentence. This type of panic also becomes very obvious during dictation. Such students suddenly begin to leave large blanks and put down completely incoherent phrases in between. The harder they try, the more tense they become and the less they can hear. The only remedy for this situation is for both teacher and student to relax completely. The student may be asked, for instance, to stop taking dictation for several lines, and then begin again. Above all, the tense student must not be made to feel that a particular oral test or exercise is a vital factor in success or failure.

Age Differences

Teaching the pronunciation of strange sounds is easier with younger students. Children of elementary school age love making strange noises, mimicking other people, and using secret code languages among their friends. They delight in the unusual sound combinations and rhythms of nonsense and counting rhymes and invent strange inversions of people's names. Most elementary pupils, then, are uninhibited in imitating the sounds of a new language, although even at this stage they mimic with varying degrees of accuracy according to their natural talents.

Even at junior high school age, mimicking of sounds causes little embarrassment if teacher and students have a friendly and sympathetic relationship. If the teacher, however, seems odd and peculiar to children of this age, they will mimic ironically. They will be unwilling to identify themselves with this person to the degree of imitating the new way of speaking, which they find equally ridiculous.

In mid-adolescence, students are much more self-conscious. Boys are very conscious of voice changes and are sometimes loath to draw attention to their voices by active participation in oral work, particularly in coeducational classes. Both boys and girls of this age hate to make fools of themselves in front of their peers, and this is what they may feel they are doing when making sounds which are not customary in their native language. They also feel they are not being themselves. This natural reluctance and inhibition can be overcome by a friendly, sympathetic classroom atmosphere, where the teacher sees to it that no student, however poor in production, is ever embarrassed in front of other students.

At this self-conscious stage, choral repetition provides a screen against undue personal attention, and the language laboratory booth or cassette recorder at home provide isolation where students may feel free to come out clearly and distinctly with strange sounds until, by sheer familiarity, they begin to find them natural and acceptable. Comments on personal efforts at pronunciation are best given, at this age, in a private conference out of class, or worked into general explanation and practice for the whole class. Unless the class as a whole is made to feel at home in the acquiring of an authentic accent, it may become the accepted thing among the group to retain a native-language pronunciation as a sign of solidarity.

It is partly because of the peculiar psychological and emotional problems posed by adolescent development that many language teachers support the introduction of a foreign language at a preadolescent or early adolescent stage. Children then become accustomed to strange sounds and ways of expression before the period of greater self-consciousness. In the fun of hearing and using the language freely in group activities, the child has a happy experience of taking on foreign ways and foreign speech, which creates a positive attitude toward further language learning. At whatever level the language study is begun, a class which has been accustomed to hearing and using the language continually from the very first lesson, within the amount of material the student can handle with confidence, will pass through the adolescent stage without suffering to any serious extent from inhibitions and anxieties about oral work.

Attitudes
Another important factor in successful language learning is the attitude of the language learner toward the speakers of another language.[6] If students hold the speakers of the language they are learning in low esteem, they will not want to identify themselves with—or risk having others identify them with—this cultural group. They will therefore prefer to retain a "foreign accent" as a sign of their true identity when speaking the language.

Maintaining a High Level of Pronunciation
After studying a language for a certain period, students seem to reach a plateau in pronunciation. This baffles many teachers. The students have assumed the correct articulatory positions for some of the more difficult sounds but still retain a foreign accent. The plateau is a commonly observed feature in learning curves. Students should be discouraged from accepting this level of achievement as the limit of their learning capacity in pronunciation. Psychologists have shown that two things can set a learning curve on an upward trend again:

6. See Gardner and Lambert 1972. See also chapter 14 below.

a new method of attack or increased incentive.[7] With this in mind, an imaginative teacher should be able to introduce some new method of attack at this stage to promote greater effort in improving pronunciation. A competition to see which student can learn to recite a simple poem most acceptably, or which group of students can present a short dialogue to the rest of the class with articulation and intonation which most resemble those of the native speakers on the tape, or an opportunity not previously provided to record on tape a skit they have prepared—new approaches such as these can stimulate fresh interest and renewed effort.

An even more discouraging situation frequently presents itself at the intermediate level of foreign-language study. Students who have acquired an acceptable, even creditable, pronunciation often show a distinct deterioration at this stage. The students are surrounded by a native-language atmosphere, and the better students are continually hearing poor pronunciation from their classmates or even, in some cases, from the poorly prepared teacher. There are several explanations for such deterioration: first, there may be a lack of vigilance on the part of the teacher, who is preoccupied with the problems of new work to be covered; second, perhaps less time is being spent on aural-oral activities, with the result that the student no longer hears authentic native speech with the same frequency; and third, it is possible that no credit is now being given for oral production, since more and more of the quizzes and tests have become wholly written in form. Students will soon follow their teacher's lead in assessing the relative importance of the various sections of the work.

The remedy, then, lies in rectifying each of these deficiencies. Regular oral practice, in the classroom or with taped material out of class, is essential at all stages if the gains of the elementary level are to be consolidated and retained. The more frequently advanced students can listen to native speech the more attuned will their ears become to the precise qualities of authentic articulation and intonation. At advanced stages, students can still profit from regular reading practice from a well-known script where full attention is being paid to pronunciation. If the text chosen is too literary in style, the practice will not lead to transfer in a conversational context. A text containing conversation with some narrative, or a scene from a play, are better choices. To ensure the retention of an acceptable pronunciation, the teacher must continue to turn an attentive ear to the way students are speaking during class discussions and other oral activities. Eval-

7. See R. S. Woodworth and H. Schlosberg, *Experimental Psychology,* rev. ed. (New York, 1954), p. 538.

uation of their level of articulation and intonation at regular intervals, as part of their overall grade, should continue throughout the language course.

- **What has been your own approach to maintaining a high level of pronunciation and intonation in a non-native language?**

Areas of Controversy

Should students be given practice in all elements of the phonological system as an introduction to the course?

Some teachers and some textbooks allot several weeks to a complete study of the sound system of the language at the beginning of the course, on the assumption that the first words and phrases the students will learn will contain so many different sounds that students will inevitably practice errors if they have not been well prepared beforehand.

A phonological introduction of this type is too abstract for children of elementary school age, for whom the language lessons should be lively and exciting with much mimicry and active use of the language. Young children will learn sounds as they are mimicking phrases and singing songs. All that is needed is an incidental articulatory recommendation[8] and occasional drilling in areas of special difficulty. At junior high school age a long phonological introduction can also be frustrating. Students are eager to come to grips with the learning of the new language, which means to them being able to say something as the speaker of this other language would say it. This initial eagerness can easily be blunted if the experience of saying something meaningful in the new language is postponed for several weeks while the students practice sounds which, out of the context of communication, seem pointless and odd.

At senior high school level, a short phonological introduction may serve to make the students aware of the particular problems they will be encountering, and this applies to adult beginners also. Even at a more mature level, however, a thorough treatment of sounds isolated from acts of communication will suffer from apparent irrelevance. Much of what will be brought forward and practiced will not receive, at this initial stage, the attention it would receive later—after the student has become conscious of its importance in understanding and producing utterances. At this later stage, students who have become

8. The difference between articulatory descriptions and empirical recommendations is explained in the *PG*'s, chap. 5.

self-conscious about the deficiencies of their oral production will welcome a further opportunity to find out what they should be doing.

Should a phonetic or phonemic script be used in teaching pronunciation?

Some methodologists advocate the teaching of the phonology of the language with the aid of a phonetic script[9] (usually the symbols of the International Phonetic Alphabet or I.P.A.) or a phonemic script (several systems of phonemic symbols are in use).[10] Phonetic symbols are usually printed in square brackets, for example, [e]; and phonemic symbols are placed between slashes, for example, /e/.

Each phonetic symbol represents a precise sound, and advocates of the I.P.A. notation maintain that such symbols become a guide to exact pronunciation for the student. They have the added value that, once learned for one language, they serve as a guide to the pronunciation of other languages. This advantage is more illusory than real. Certain sounds in two languages may differ only to a slight degree (thus making the use of the different phonetic notation that a linguist would require pointless for language learners), yet they may differ sufficiently to make it imperative for students to learn this slight difference if they wish to acquire a near-native accent.

Phonemic symbols indicate, within a certain band of tolerance, the contrasting sounds which are essential to comprehension of meaning in a particular language. Since the phonemic system of one language does not coincide with that of another, the set of symbols used for one language will not act as a sure guide to the learner of another language. Some supporters of the phonemic system use I.P.A. symbols between slashes for the phonemes of a language where these are close to the type sounds of the I.P.A. system; others use symbols which are closer to the orthographic conventions of the language being studied. There is still no one accepted system for phonemic notation.

We shall not in this discussion consider the relative value of the use of phonetic as opposed to phonemic symbols. We concentrate instead on the question: Should a system of notation of sounds different from, but more consistent than, the conventional spelling system of a language be taught to language students as an aid to the

9. Sweet (1899) says, "The main axiom of living philology is that all study of language must be based on phonetics" (p. 4). This was the heyday of the phonetic movement. Palmer (1921) strongly supports the use of a phonetic script in the early stages and sets out nine arguments for and against it (pp. 100–101).

10. Rivers and Temperley 1978, Appendix B (pp. 352–54) gives eight American and four British phonetic or phonemic alphabets for transcribing English.

development of correct pronunciation? This problem will not be relevant to the teaching of languages where the orthographic system and the sound system are consistently related, with one symbol or group of symbols always representing one sound or phonemic distinction. (In this case, the orthographic symbols of the new language may be used as a guide to pronunciation from the start.) In some languages, however, this is an extremely important consideration, either because of the apparent illogicality of the spelling system (as in some aspects of English) or because one sound may be rendered by as many as nine different letters or combinations of letters (as in French).[11] Once again, it will be necessary to distinguish clearly the level of study at which students are beginning the language.

At the elementary school level, the learning of a phonetic or phonemic notation before learning the orthographic system of the language can be confusing. Students in the early elementary school years are still consolidating their reading, writing, and spelling skills in their native language. For this reason, among others, there is usually less reading and writing in the new language than for older students, except for a written form of what is being used in active oral work, and perhaps some variations of this. Even in the later elementary years, two orthographic systems pose sufficient problems without the introduction of a third form of notation.

At high school and college level, phonetic or phonemic symbols are sometimes taught in association with introductory lessons on the phonological system of the language. After students have been drilled very thoroughly in the production of certain sounds, phonetic symbols are used for clarification of differences and for explanation. It is undeniable that phonetic symbols, when made available to students in this way, can help them to pronounce words which are spelled in an unexpected fashion. Some teachers have found, however, that phonetic or phonemic spellings learned thoroughly in the introductory stages can remain with the students as a constant source of interference when they begin to use the traditional spelling system. These teachers doubt the value of setting up two distinctly different symbolic systems for the same words and phrases, particularly for the adolescent age group. For this reason, and because students easily forget the sound-symbol associations of the phonetic or phonemic system when they are not being actively drilled in them, some teachers feel that the time spent in learning the phonetic or phonemic system sufficiently well for it to be useful might be better spent in giving the students more practice in the correct pronunciation of the sounds,

11. For examples, see the *PG*'s, chap. 6, R27.

and in the association of each sound with the various spelling equivalents in the traditional writing system.

At junior and senior high school level, students with no previous experience of a foreign language may not see the relevance of a special system of notation for sounds at first. The phonetic or phonemic notation can usefully be introduced at a later stage, when a plateau is reached or a deterioration in pronunciation is threatening to develop. At this stage it may arouse a fresh interest in sounds and provide a new method of attack for an old problem, which will push the learning curve up for a further period. It can then be used at more advanced levels as a system of reference for remedial work in pronunciation and for help with exceptional spellings.

Adult students may find a phonetic or phonemic notation helpful after some initial experience with the language because it renders them independent of their teacher and enables them to push ahead in individual study, without learning all kinds of erroneous pronunciations which will have to be corrected at a later date.

The advantages and disadvantages of introducing a phonetic or phonemic script need to be weighed carefully in the light of the particular situation in which the teacher is working.

Is a near-native pronunciation desirable for, or attainable by, the majority of foreign-language students?
There was a period when an English gentleman learning French prided himself on not stooping to adopt the effeminate and obviously degenerate way of speaking of the French. Since he always insisted that any individual worthy of his attention should speak to him in English anyway, it was of no importance that he could not understand or make himself understood in French.

This attitude to the tongue of the foreigner is now a thing of the past in most countries. Except in certain special cases, where a reading knowledge of the language is required without there being any probability of the learner's ever meeting a person who speaks the language, languages are now taught for oral communication as well as for reading and writing.

Communication is a two-way process. Students who have acquired native-language approximations to foreign-language sounds will inevitably be disconcerted when they hear native speech. They may or may not be understood, depending on how much experience the native speaker has had with foreigners with this particular variety of accent. If the students ask questions, they will usually not understand the answers. If they are asked questions by native speakers, they will not be able to reply, because they will not understand what is required of them.

If communication skills are an objective of the language course, then true communication beyond the confines of the classroom must be the ultimate aim. This involves the acquisition of an accent in which the phonemic distinctions are respected and the stress and intonation patterns make the meaning clear. Furthermore, certain distortions of pronunciation are more irritating than others to native speakers. There are, for instance, pronunciation variants the native speaker associates with lack of education or finds slightly ridiculous. Faults like these should be particularly avoided by language learners.

Because of differences in ability to mimic, and lack of opportunity to hear native speech frequently, many students may be hindered in their efforts to develop a near-native accent. Most students can, however, develop an accent which is acceptable (not irritating) to a native speaker and learn to recognize important distinctions so that they can comprehend what a native speaker is saying. Whether they do in fact acquire these skills is dependent on the teacher's understanding of the bases of speech production, on careful and conscientious drilling of those areas where the sound systems of the native language and the foreign language most distinctly diverge, and on frequent use of tapes recorded by native speakers when the teacher does not have near-native facility with the language.

Annotated Reading List

Wilkins, D. A. *Linguistics in Language Teaching*. Cambridge, Mass.: MIT Press, 1972. Chapter 2, "Phonetics and Phonology," discusses intonation, phonetics, phonemics, and generative phonology, with particular attention to the problems teachers face. Examples are taken from English, French, and Spanish.

Brown, Gillian. "Practical Phonetics and Phonology." Chapter 2 of J. P. B. Allen and Corder 1974. Gives a rapid course in these areas for those with gaps in their preparation; deals with articulatory phonetics, segmental phonology, rhythm, and intonation.

———. "Phonological Theory and Language Teaching." Chapter 4 of J. P. B. Allen and Corder 1975. Applies both generative theory and phoneme theory.

FOR SPECIFIC LANGUAGES

Prator, Clifford H., Jr., and Robinett, Betty W. *Manual of American English Pronunciation*. 3d ed. New York: Holt, Rinehart and Winston, 1972.

Trim, John. *English Pronunciation Illustrated*. 2d ed. Cambridge, Eng.: Cambridge University Press. For General British pronunciation.

Politzer, Robert L. *Teaching French: An Introduction to Applied Linguistics*. 2d ed. New York: Blaisdell, 1965. Chapter 5 gives a clear outline of the material of articulatory phonetics, useful to teachers of any language. Chapter 6 has valuable material on teaching French pronunciation. Similar chapters are found in the following:

————. *Teaching German: A Linguistic Orientation*. Waltham, Mass.: Blaisdell, 1968.

Politzer, Robert L., and Politzer, Frieda N. *Teaching English as a Second Language*. Lexington, Mass.: Xerox, 1972.

Politzer, Robert L., and Staubach, Charles. *Teaching Spanish: A Linguistic Orientation*. Rev. ed. New York: Blaisdell, 1965.

Delattre, Pierre. *Principes de phonétique française à l'usage des étudiants anglo-américains*. Middlebury College, Vt., 1951.

Valdman, Albert. *Introduction to French Phonology and Morphology*. Rowley, Mass.: Newbury House, 1976.

Wangler, H.-H. *Instruction in German Pronunciation*. 3d ed. St. Paul, Minn.: EMC Corporation.

Navarro Tomás, T. *Studies in Spanish Phonology*. Coral Gables, Fla.: University of Miami Press, 1968.

Magner, T. *Applied Linguistics: Russian.—A Guide for Teachers*. Boston: D. C. Heath, 1961.

Contrastive Structure Series. Charles A. Ferguson, General Editor. Chicago: University of Chicago Press:

Moulton, William G. *The Sounds of English and German*. 1962.

Agard, Frederick B., and Di Pietro, Robert J. *The Sounds of English and Italian*. 1965.

Stockwell, Robert P., and Bowen, J. Donald. *The Sounds of English and Spanish*. 1965.

TEACHING TECHNIQUES AND EXERCISES

Rivers, Wilga M., et al. *Practical Guides*. Chapter 5: "Teaching the Sound System."

For Tone and Intonation

Brazil, David; Coulthard, Malcolm; and Johns, Catherine. *Discourse Intonation and Language Teaching*. London: Longman, 1980.

Research and Discussion

1. If you are not a native speaker of the language you are teaching, make a tape of your production. (Read a section of a play,

then recount an anecdote from your own experience without any prepared script.) Ask a native speaker or near-native speaker to list for you the particular weaknesses in pronunciation, stress, or intonation on which you should concentrate for improvement.

2. Take a contrasting pair of vowels in the language you will teach, e.g., /ü/y/ or /i/ɪ/, and work out a series of practice exercises for teaching this distinction along the lines sketched on pp. 133–34.

3. Take a consonant sound which your students find difficult to pronounce, e.g., /r/ or /l/. Study the way it is produced in the language you will teach and the way the similar sound in the students' native language is produced. Work out some practical hints you would give your students to help them produce the target language sound correctly.

4. Find some rhymes or poems that will be easily understood by elementary students, in which certain sounds are repeated in various contexts. Draw up some lesson plans to show interesting ways in which this material could be used in class.

5. Make a tape of the production of some of your students. Ask a native speaker of the language to identify those utterances where the meaning was not clear. Examine these segments and identify any weaknesses in pronunciation, stress, and intonation which may have caused these problems of comprehension. Study the sections on pronunciation in the textbook and laboratory tapes your students have been using to see whether these points are given sufficient practice.

6. Make a tape of the production of some of your students. Ask a native speaker of the language to identify those faults in pronunciation, stress, and intonation which are irritating. Look at your textbook to see whether these areas have been dealt with adequately. Design some exercises to improve the production of your students at these points.

7. If the language you will teach shares many cognates with the native language of your students, they can augment their vocabulary rapidly by correctly pronouncing these cognates. Work out some exercises to show students the sound-symbol correspondences they will need to observe to convert words from their native language into foreign-language words and to give them practice with cognates they have not met before.

8. Take a section of a tape in a language you have never heard before. Copy it with spaces at points where the speaker pauses. Play your spaced tape and record in the spaces your imitation of what you heard. Listen to the original with your imitation and rerecord several times, attempting to approximate the original more closely. Write a

short account of how you felt during the experience and what you learned about the process of imitation of sounds and rhythms.

9. Listen to a tape on which a student has recorded responses to a grammatical exercise in the language you will teach. Analyze the problems of pronunciation the student demonstrated while concentrating on the exercise. What weaknesses would you call to this student's attention? What advice would you give the student for detecting such weaknesses while listening back to a tape? What advice would you give the student for overcoming these weaknesses?

*10. If you have studied generative phonology, try to work out some exercises based on rules by which variants are derived from underlying forms to help your students to improve their pronunciation of problem areas of the language.

6· Listening Comprehension

Speaking does not of itself constitute communication unless what is being said is comprehended by another person. The greatest difficulty for travelers in strange countries is not primarily that they cannot make themselves understood; this they can frequently do by gesture, by writing, or by pointing to something written in a bilingual book of phrases. Their major difficulty, and one that leads to considerable emotional embarrassment, is that they cannot understand what is being said to them and around them. Even if the native speaker enunciates the words slowly and distinctly, elements of stress, intonation, and word grouping (often exaggerated in an earnest attempt at clarity) add to the confusion of the inexperienced foreigner. As a result, there is no communication, and the traveler's speaking skills cannot be exercised to great advantage. Enjoyment of and participation in community life and thought are further curtailed by inability to comprehend announcements, broadcasts, lectures, plays, and films.

Teaching the comprehension of spoken language is of primary importance if the communication aim is to be achieved. A frequently neglected area, listening comprehension has its peculiar problems which arise from the fleeting, immaterial nature of spoken utterances and the complicated ways we process what we hear.

THEORETICAL CONCEPTS BASIC TO LISTENING COMPREHENSION
In chapter 5, the special problems of discrimination of sounds, stress, and intonation are discussed, but these are only a few of the elements involved in understanding what is being said to us.

Information Theory
Useful ideas for teaching listening comprehension can be drawn from the research of communications engineers concerned with the maximum efficiency of telephonic and telegraphic equipment. Their work has dealt particularly with the nature of the message to be communicated, the qualities of the channel by which it passes from emitter to receiver, and the state in which it is received and interpreted by the listener.[1] We are not concerned here with detailed mathematical

1. See diagram in chapter 7 (p. 184).

explanations of information theory, which had a profound influence on psychological research in the sixties, but rather the lines of thought that can be extracted from it for the teacher. (Information theory should not be confused with information processing, which is the term used for the activity of the mind in extracting, processing, storing, and retrieving the meaning of verbal and nonverbal material. This concept, which is basic to much contemporary research in perception, artificial intelligence, and cognition, is discussed later in this chapter.)[2]

The speech emitted by the communicator, which contains the message, has phonic patterning distinctive for each language. This conventional patterning limits the acceptable sequences of sounds for that particular language and determines their frequency of occurrence. As children learning their native language, our students come to expect certain sound sequences and not others. They are therefore disconcerted by the sounds of a new language until they have had sufficient experience with them to build up a frame of expectations. The phonic patterning of a language has not only acceptable sound sequences but anticipated degrees of loudness, levels of pitch, and lengths of pause. With experience the child learns to recognize groupings of these features as clues to meaning. Unexpected variations are clues to emotional states and the attitudes of the speaker to the message or the receiver.

Some sequences recur with great frequency, and in certain contexts alternatives are inconceivable. Such items are considered to contain little "information" in the technical sense of that term. *Information* in this sense does not refer to meaning but to the *range of possible alternative items which could occur* in a certain position in speech. As Weaver has put it "the word information in communication theory relates not so much to what you *do* say, as to what you *could* say. That is, information is a measure of one's freedom of choice when one selects a message."[3] The concept of information in terms of probabilities is mathematical but the basic idea is useful for extrapolation to comprehension situations. If in a given situation any other word would be most unlikely to occur, the word used may be said to give little information; if the range of words which could possibly be used is great, then the particular word one hears conveys a great deal of information. If I hold a book in my hand and state, "This is a book,"

2. For a detailed discussion of information processing in computer-simulated artificial intelligence research, see B. S. Melvin and W. M. Rivers, "In One Ear and Out the Other: Implications of Memory Studies for Language Learning," in J. F. Fanselow and R. H. Crymes, eds., On *TESOL '76* (Washington, D.C.: TESOL, 1976), pp. 155–64.

3. C. Shannon and W. Weaver, *The Mathematical Theory of Commmunication* (Urbana: University of Illinois Press, 1949); p. 100.

the word "book" conveys little information. Possibilities have been reduced by visual and situational clues which help to delimit the alternatives. On the other hand, if I say of someone who is not present, "He is reading," the word "reading" conveys much information because of the great number of words which could easily have occurred in that situation.

In our own language, we have learned to recognize a number of factors which reduce the possibility of occurrence of certain linguistic items. Syntactic relationships limit the possible items in certain positions in the sentence to those belonging to particular categories (e.g., *the* is not normally followed by *are,* except in such sentences as "the *are* is illegible"). Similarly, we become accustomed to combinations of sounds of high frequency (e.g., we expect to hear "tomorrow morning," we do not expect to hear "tomorrow daytime"; "glug" sounds like an English word, "ygu" does not). Clichés, conversational tags, and greetings like "Good morning" and "How are you?" become so familiar that they hardly need processing.

The effect of these factors in reducing the amount of information conveyed in any one utterance is of great importance because the human organism has a limited capacity for receiving and processing information. When someone is conveying to us a message which is not entirely expected or obvious, we often say, "Wait a minute! Not so fast!" or "Say that again! Who did you say it was?" These expressions make it clear that we can absorb only a certain amount of information at a time.

Redundancy

In order to reduce to manageable proportions the amount of information in any one sound sequence, each language has developed a certain amount of redundancy. (Redundancy also allows the speaker to elaborate the message.) It has been estimated, for instance, that the English language is 50 percent redundant.[4] Were this redundancy eliminated, the human organism could not absorb information at the rate at which it would be emitted in normal speech. Redundancy in languages is to be found in elements of sound and in morphological and syntactic formations which reinforce each other in the conveying of meaning. A French sentence may begin with "Est-ce que," which signals a question for which the response will normally be "Oui" or "Non." At the same time the voice will continue to rise in pitch until the end of the sentence, this being also an indication that a question of this type is being asked. In English, the word *do* and yes/no question

4. Ibid., p. 104.

intonation perform similar functions. The listener who was not attending to the first words of the sentence will be guided by the rising intonation. Both of these features are conveying the same element of meaning, and there is therefore redundancy.

It is redundancy in language which helps us to piece together the information we hear. Even in communication in our native language we do not hear clearly everything that is said to us, nor do we pay full attention to every element of each utterance. In a second or third language, our perceptual difficulties are compounded by many items which we do not recognize or with which we are still unfamiliar. Artificially constructed messages, such as those frequently devised for use in language classes, often unwittingly reduce the amount of redundancy supplied by a speaker in a normal situation. In this way the perception of the foreign-language message is made more difficult, even for a person familiar with the language clues.

Body Language

Over and above the clues provided by sound sequences, we convey further elements of meaning by body movements, facial expressions, slight changes in breathing, length of pauses, and degrees of emphasis. These elements, usually classed as *kinesics* and *paralanguage,* vary from language community to language community, and even within language communities, at various levels of interaction and for subgroups within the culture. No full comprehension of oral communication is complete without taking these aspects into consideration as further delimitations of the message. In the classroom, or laboratory, these elements may be supplied by films or videotapes, so that the student can watch the expressions and gestures of the speakers as an aid to meaning. Such visuals are a help only if they are of a level of production acceptable to the student. Scripted and filmed in an amateurish way, they merely create the impression that the speakers of the language, whose ways are so different from those of the student, are quaint and rather ridiculous.[5]

Noise

The message itself may be studied in terms of the amount of information it conveys and the rate at which this information is encoded. Further problems arise, however, in the transmission of the message from communicator to receiver. If the message is transmitted with an accompaniment of irrelevant sound, or "noise," some of the message

5. Factors to be considered in the preparation and selection of visual materials are discussed in chapter 7.

154

may not be received by the listener. When recording and playback equipment is not properly serviced, with tapes and cassettes re-recorded at regular intervals, audial quality in the language laboratory deteriorates. As a result, students have problems discriminating sounds, and the message they receive is defective, with certain clues (particularly phonemic distinctions) reduced. A similar difficulty is sometimes experienced in some sections of a classroom which is acoustically faulty. This imperfect reception of auditory clues has the same effect as increase of information content. What was not heard clearly may mislead in the interpretation of what was heard earlier or is heard later, requiring extra processing before real comprehension is achieved; or, if something was not heard at all, expectations for what follows are reduced and interpretation becomes more complicated.

Even when the message is received clearly, unfamiliar elements of it may be perceived in much the same way as noise, so that some parts of the message will be lost in the process of transmission to the receiver. The language learner is then faced with several problems: the identification of patterns and their combinations in the somewhat mutilated message which has been received (this is made more difficult by the gaps); the reconstruction of the defective sections according to probabilities of occurrence; and the organization of these segments in a meaningful way. The organization which results will depend on the listener's previous experience with words, syntactic groupings, situational context, and the cultural elements reflected in the foreign-language usage. Degree of familiarity with these elements will determine what is selected from the stream of sound, which is providing information at a rate which makes it impossible for the listener to assimilate it totally.

Personal Factors in Listening

Probabilities of occurrence of certain sequences of sounds are built up through experience with a language. These probabilities determine what we hear; that is, we tend to hear what we expect to hear. A nonconventional, and therefore improbable, sequence of sounds will at first be interpreted as a familiar, or probable, sequence and in this way acquire intelligibility. Psychologists have found that if a nonconventional sequence of sounds is presented just below the threshold of audibility, the listener will organize it into a conventional sequence. In other words, a series of meaningless syllables with sentence intonation will be interpreted as an intelligible sentence, and a longer segment of meaningless discourse will often be given a sequential coherence. In other words, listening is a creative process, as we shall see later in this chapter. When a new language is being learned, many sequences of sounds have low probability of occurrence for the inexperienced listener and will therefore be misinterpreted, while others which have never before been encountered provide an accompaniment of "noise."

Ability to distinguish slightly familiar sequences from unfamiliar ones may also be affected by the emotional stress and anxiety which not infrequently accompany aural comprehension experiences in a foreign language. In a face-to-face communication situation, this anxiety is compounded by the fear of being embarrassed or appearing stupid. Furthermore, certain students become very tense in class when they are expected to depend on the ear alone. As a result of this emotional tension, the utterances they are hearing come to them as an auditory blur, and they become panicky. This panic decreases their ability to discriminate sounds and word groupings. Natural trepidation on the part of normal students who are not accustomed to paying close attention to aural messages can be overcome by the early introduction of much practice in listening to material which uses and reuses linguistic forms with which they are familiar.

Students trained to study the language through written texts are sharply challenged when suddenly confronted with listening comprehension material of a similar standard of difficulty to that which they are accustomed to study at their leisure in graphic form. The emotional tension associated with this experience is frequently compounded by the near approach of some examination for which this type of activity is preparing them. It must be clearly borne in mind by teacher and student alike that listening comprehension is not a skill which can suddenly be brought into the picture at an advanced level for students visually trained, nor can it be mastered once and for all and then ignored while other skills are developed. There must be regular practice with increasingly difficult material. This practice must, however, be regularly spaced over the language learning period and not massed urgently in great blocks at some moment preceding an examination. Facility in understanding what one hears increases with growing familiarity with the vocabulary and structures of the language. Systematically developed, listening comprehension can provide one of the most enjoyable activities associated with the language program and one which the students continue to enjoy after they have left the classroom.

- **After you have given a listening comprehension passage to a group of students, ask them to write down below their answers what they felt their main problems in comprehension were.**

LEARNING TO LISTEN TO ANOTHER LANGUAGE

Students learning a new language pass through several stages in the comprehension of speech. On first contact, the foreign-language utterances strike their ears as a stream of undifferentiated noises. As they listen, they gradually perceive some order in the noise: a regularity in the rise and fall of the voice and in the breath groups. As they learn some of the arbitrary associations of the particular language (i.e., vocabulary, structure of phrases, verb groups, simple expressions), they begin to distinguish the phonic and syntactic patterning— the recurring elements which give form to segments of speech. This is not yet comprehension, which requires selection from the stream of speech of what is crucial for the particular situation in which the utterance is heard.

Language learners next pass through a stage when they recognize familiar elements in the mass of speech but are unable to recognize the interrelationships within the whole stream of sound; this again is not full comprehension. The listener feels rather like a person walking in a fog which clears in patches and floats back to obscure other points. It is only with much practice that learners can pass beyond this stage.

As they hear much speech in the new language, language learners eventually acquire facility in recognizing the crucial elements which determine the message. They are aided in this by their growing knowledge of syntax, which enables them to "chunk" the language, that is, to group elements into coherent segments, thus reducing the processing load. At this more advanced stage, they may recognize the essentials of the message but not be able to remember what they have recognized. This is because they are unable to concentrate their attention on the crucial elements of the message long enough to rehearse them subvocally before moving on with the continuing voice. All their attention is taken up with recognition and selection. There is little capacity left for processing for retention.

Memory and Retention

After much experimentation, Broadbent developed an interesting theory of memory and retention.[6] The human organism, he maintains, has a limited capacity for absorbing information (in the information theory sense of this term). Since irrelevant items place an extra load on the system, information is at first filtered by the perceptual processes according to characteristics which events have in common.

6. D. E. Broadbent, *Perception and Communication* (London and New York: Pergamon Press, 1958).

Listening Comprehension

This filtered information is then absorbed into the immediate memory, which is a short-term storage mechanism. Information is easily lost from this short-term store if it is not recirculated through the perceptual processes at regular intervals. (Here we may think of the way we repeat a telephone number to ourselves on the way from the phone book to the dial.) Only *selected* items of information pass from this short-term store to long-term storage in the memory. The perceptual system has a limited capacity for absorbing information. Thus, when the perceptual processes are bombarded with items in quick succession, the immediate memory cannot recirculate what it is retaining, and these items are lost. As a result, the listener loses material which would have been useful in interpreting the overall message. We cannot say the listener did not comprehend this part of the message as it was uttered, but it has slipped from conscious memory and the material cannot be recalled. The listener may then ask: "Just a minute. There was something you said . . . just before that. . . . What was it?"

Comprehension of speech requires the retaining of information from a whole sequence of sounds, not just from the last sound heard. As a result, when material is unfamiliar, inexperienced students have a high-information content to absorb from each sound sequence. After a while, they are unable to retain through recirculation the relevant elements from preceding sequences while absorbing more information from the succeeding sequences. This stage, when students understand everything as they hear it but are unable to remember what they understood, must be recognized as a legitimate and normal phase of the learning process. If students understand that this is a common experience in language learning, they will not be alarmed at what they might otherwise consider a personal failure of memory.

- **Listen to a longer passage for testing listening comprehension. Would you yourself need to listen to it a second time before comprehending it or being able to recall the details? Could you answer the questions asked without listening a second time? Does the test provide for this?**

Information Processing

Since the time of Broadbent, psychologists have become very concerned with the way the human mind processes the information it receives from outside the organism. ("Information" is being used here in the usual sense of the word.) Cognitive psychologists study not only the way the mind processes the input, but how this material is then interrelated with existing knowledge, so that new knowledge evolves; how the information is stored; and how it is retrieved from storage at the appropriate time.

158

Neisser (1967, chap. 7) maintains that after we have imposed a structure on what we are hearing, we retain only what we have selected as relevant from the signal. The echoic signal fades, and we no longer have recourse to the raw data. We recirculate what we have selected to relate it to what we have heard and what we anticipate that we will hear. In this way we are constructing a message from the sound signal. We then recode the *gist* of this message for storage in long-term memory. It is the gist of our interpretation which is accessible to us for retrieval, not the original message. If in recoding we find ambiguities or inconsistencies, we may attempt to reconstruct the now faded signal by inferential processes and then recode our inferences. Reconstructing what we are retrieving into its full linguistic form also requires processing capacity and energy; while we are doing this, we often simplify and omit details which later questioning reveals we actually stored.

It is clear, then, that there are many points at which the original message may become distorted during processing. (Witnesses to the same scene, as we know, can tell very different stories and even differ in their own account on successive occasions.) If retaining and recalling a message heard in our native language requires so much effort and is such a chancy process, the difficulties must be far greater for a second or third language. Teachers must show much patience with students learning to perform these processes with unfamiliar material. Since telling the gist of what one has heard and then filling it out with detail as required is a normal process, this is the procedure which should be encouraged in questioning students on what they have heard. At first, teachers will be satisfied with the broad outlines which show that the students correctly interpreted what was said. Retention and recall of details may be expected later, as students extend their active knowledge of the language and storage of a greater quantity of material becomes much easier. Above all, verbatim recall should not be required, since of itself it does not necessarily indicate comprehension of what was heard.

- **For a third or fourth language that you do not know well, take a longer listening comprehension passage, with questions attached. Read the questions first. Then listen to the passage. Did knowledge of the questions help you with overall comprehension or did it encourage you to listen only for the details required by the questions? Listen again without thinking of the questions. Did this change your perception of the import of the passage?**

HEARING AND COMPREHENDING

"What was that? I didn't quite catch it?" This polite interruption demonstrates the difference between hearing and comprehending. In teaching students listening comprehension in a foreign language, we must realize that one is possible without the other. The listener in this case probably heard the actual sounds of the utterance quite clearly and even distinguished words. Linguistic information (identification of words and syntactic structures) was not necessarily the problem, but for some reason the listener was not able to construct a significance for them which seemed to fit the situational context. (The listener may also have preferred not to comprehend because the message extracted was displeasing. The remark with which this section begins is, in this case, part of a conversational gambit through which the listener allows the speaker the opportunity to reconstruct the original message in a way which is more acceptable.)

Listening is not a passive skill, nor even, as has traditionally been believed, a receptive skill. *Listening is a creative skill.* In order to comprehend the sounds falling on our ears, we take the raw material of words, arrangements of words, and the rise and fall of the voice, and from this material we create a significance. There is *meaning* in the linguistic arrangement the speaker has produced, the speaker's meaning, but *significance is in the mind of the listener.* That is why we can say of a person whose language we understand perfectly, "I find her quite incomprehensible." Even more difficulties of this kind arise with a language and culture with which we are only slowly becoming familiar.

Significance, which comes from the listener's side, is dependent on three factors.

1. There is the *linguistic information* which is extracted from the sound signal, that is, what listeners perceive aurally of sounds, words, and their arrangements in utterances. What the listener perceives is not necessarily what was emitted by the speaker, but once the listener has selected a sequence from the original signal, the rest of the sound signal slips from auditory memory and is no longer directly accessible for the reconstruction of an alternative message.

2. The *situational context* of the utterance affects what listeners perceive to be the relationship between what they have heard and what has been said and also their expectations of what will follow.

3. The comprehended message is dependent on what the listener perceives to be the *intentions of the speaker.*

If we look at this act of comprehension from the point of view of the listener in a real situation, we may invert the order of these factors. What we perceive to be the intentions of the speaker in a certain context determines what we select and retain from the sound signal as the significance of the message. This is why "You cunning fox!" can be perceived as a compliment in one situation and as a deadly insult in another. Unfortunately, in teaching situations it is often only the first factor, the linguistic content of the utterance (which in real life is really the last to be apprehended), that receives much attention. Consequently many students hear, but do not comprehend.

Significance begins, then, with interpretation of the speaker's intentions. This interpretation is dependent on what we know about the speaker or persons like the speaker (Parisian cab drivers, Texas oilmen), the expectations the situation (as a continuum) and previous utterances have aroused; and the nonverbal behavior of the speaker (deep breathing, flushed appearance, shrug of the shoulder, faraway look, and so on). Information about the speaker's intentions, beliefs, and attitude toward the listener is called *interactional content,* and experimentation has shown that we recall much more accurately the actual words spoken when interactional content is high. In other words, the interpretation we have stored parallels much more closely what was actually said in this case, because we have more insight into the meaning the speaker intended to encode.[7]

The more we already know, the less auditory information we need to create a significance from phonic material. Hence we can "understand" distorted, noisy signals, defective signals, or even an uncompleted signal if our expectations in the situation are sufficiently accurate. This shows we are creating a message, not receiving one, since we cannot "receive" what was never uttered. Furthermore, we do not register all we hear. If we did, our language processing system and our memory would quickly become overloaded and we would not be able to continue to function as comprehenders. In comprehending oral messages, then, we are not just extracting linguistic information but are selecting and matching what we have selected against probable messages that we are anticipating. similar to top down reading theory — "psycholing. guessing game".

Recognition Vocabulary

Schlesinger suggests that in listening we may not bother to process most of the syntax—that, for the most part, we move from apprehension of semantic elements directly, by matching, to the cognitive

---

7. J. M. Keenan, B. MacWhinney, and D. Mayhew, "Pragmatics in Memory: A Study of Natural Conversation," *Journal of Verbal Learning and Verbal Behavior* 16 (1977): 549–60.

(or comprehension) level. He considers that we resort to the analysis of the syntax of the sound signal only when there is ambiguity or when, for some reason, we have not extracted a clear meaning from the signal.[8] If this is so, foreign-language learners need a wide recognition vocabulary for rapid comprehension, rather than a sophisticated knowledge of syntax. Most of the latter, it seems, will not be needed for this task, because if we took the time to process each message in detail, we would never be able to keep up with the speaker.

To develop facility in comprehending spoken messages, students need much practice in aurally recognizing vocabulary they have been learning mostly in written form. Here games, competitions, and other activities which require quick word recognition, grouping, and matching are useful. Where this is appropriate for the language being learned, students should have much practice in recognizing cognates of words in their own language. This is not always as easy as we think, since most cognates have assumed very effective linguistic disguises. Students also need to acquire rapidity in "topping and tailing," that is, in extracting the meanings of apparently unknown words by word-breakdown methods. They need practice in rapid recognition of prefixes and suffixes and what these contribute to the meanings of words. They need practice in aurally associating word stems with related forms which may have different vowel or consonant sounds (e.g., poor, poorly, poverty, impoverished, poorer, poorness; do, undo, redo, undone, redid). They need to associate words in semantic fields, so that recognition of one taps the conceptual network[9] and makes associated words more readily available. This process is facilitated if vocabulary is acquired in a matrix of relevant material and there are frequent exercises in word associations.

- **Design a game or competition to develop (a) rapid recognition of numbers, dates, and prices in the currency of a country where the language is spoken; (b) compound words.**

The "Click of Comprehension" Presumes Knowledge of "the Script"

Comprehension also requires a deep knowledge of the theme of the speaker's discourse, because much of comprehension is drawing inferences. A great deal of what we "comprehend" is not in the linguistic information we are receiving at all. Researchers in artificial

8. I. M. Schlesinger, *Production and Comprehension of Utterances* (Hillsdale, N.J.: Lawrence Erlbaum Associates, 1977), pp. 155–59.
9. The operation of semantic or conceptual networks is discussed in W. M. Rivers and B. S. Melvin, "If Only I Could Remember it All! Facts and Fiction about Memory in Language Learning," in Burt, Dulay, and Finocchiaro 1977, pp. 166–67.

intelligence have become keenly aware of this as they try to program computers to comprehend human language.

We may hear: "He went into a restaurant. After the salad he felt better." Comprehension of this sequence requires us to know that one sits down at a table in a restaurant; a waiter brings a menu; one orders; the waiter goes away to order the main dish; in America, the waiter frequently brings a salad for the customer to eat while waiting for the main dish to be prepared. None of this information is in the linguistic signal. The information we possess as a background to what we comprehend has been called a *script*. Schank and Abelson, who coined the term, work even more detailed scripts than this into the information banks of their computer programs for experiments on comprehension.[10] Because we possess this type of information about real life, we are able to make inferences we would not otherwise be able to make. In an American setting, then, "after the salad" allows us to infer that the person to whom the speaker is referring has already ordered a meal. "The possession of a script allows a speaker to leave many things unsaid with the certainty that the listener will fill in such gaps by default."[11]

Clearly, this is one of the obstacles to comprehension when we listen to a message in a foreign language. If the ways of life, customs, and values of the speakers of the language are very different from our own (or if the area is very specialized, e.g., genetic engineering), we do not possess the same script as the speaker. As a result, we do not understand, because we do not possess sufficient information to make the necessary inferences.

Similar to the notion of a script is what other psychologists call our "currently activated knowledge of the world." Note that, even if we possess the knowledge of the world we require for comprehension of certain utterances, it is of no use to us unless it is activated as we listen—in other words, unless we have picked up cues which direct our attention in a certain direction. In the usual social interaction, this orientation is supplied by the situation in its broadest sense. Where such cues are lacking, existing knowledge can be activated through titles or statements of topic. Newscasters give headline statements before they give details of the news. In conversation, we do this with *topic focus*. We say, "About your cousin's trip, it's raining in Haiti."

10. R. C. Schank and R. P. Abelson, "Scripts, Plans, and Knowledge," in *Thinking: Readings in Cognitive Science,* ed. P. N. Johnson-Laird and P. C. Wason (Cambridge: Cambridge University Press, 1977), pp. 421–32.

11. "Introduction to Inference and Comprehension," in Johnson-Laird and Wason, *Thinking,* p. 353.

From the teaching point of view, we activate prior knowledge through *preparatory discussion* of related topics and by making sure that key words are known and have been recently brought to conscious awareness. To do this, we do not need to place before the student a list of such words, but the well-prepared teacher with an integrated plan of activities will see that such key words have been used in some recent discussion before they appear in listening material. An unfamiliar key word must not appear near the beginning of a listening passage, since this can cause early confusion for the listener. It must be set in a context where its meaning becomes clear.

In natural communication, part of the script is what we know about the speaker and the situation and what we are absorbing from nonverbal behavior. With a foreign-language listening experience on tape or cassette, we often know nothing of the speaker; the situation and its antecedents are not clearly specified; and we cannot see the nonverbal behavior of the speaker. The comprehension of the utterance is thus made much more difficult for the student. To supply students with background for listening material, we should give them, before they begin listening, explanations as to who is speaking to whom, the nature of their relationship, and their expectations in the situation. With the wider availability of videotapes and films, students will have the additional aid to comprehension that a natural situation provides: a chance to observe movements and expressions.

- **Examine some dialogues in the textbook being used in the class you are teaching or observing. What aspects of this material do you understand better because you are familiar with the culture of the speakers of the language? What kinds of explanations would need to be given to the students before studying these dialogues?**

Inferences

In extracting significance, we have to make many *bridging inferences* which help us to understand the logic of the sequence. For this we need to be able to recognize logical connectives and relational words *(because of, since, therefore, not necessarily)* and words which establish temporal order *(before, after, at the same time)*. Exercises should be developed to help students recognize these types of expressions rapidly in their aural form and draw the inferences from their use.

When we understand what elements make for easy or difficult comprehension, we will see that success is not entirely dependent on knowledge of actual details of the language. We must help the students to bring into play some of the factors that operate in native-language comprehension: toleration for vagueness and ambiguity as the message unfolds; deduction from context, situation, and speaker in the situation; drawing inferences and inferring meaning of unfamiliar words; bridging and drawing conclusions not actually in the linguistic input.

False Recognition Memory

We store in memory our *interpretation* of what we have heard; later, we usually cannot distinguish the interpretation from what we actually heard. This has implications for the testing of listening comprehension by multiple-choice items and true-false statements. In these types of tests, students who did not comprehend will select statements which were never uttered and yet be certain they heard them. Multiple-choice and true-false items, well designed, can be more than hit-or-miss elimination items; they can pinpoint genuine misinterpretations on the part of the students. They must, however, be carefully thought out to provide plausible alternatives to the correct interpretation of the speaker's intention.

- **Take a set of multiple-choice questions on a listening passage. Ask half the students in one class to read them and select answers without listening to the passage. Give the listening passage with the multiple-choice questions to the rest of the class. Compare the results for the two groups. What did you learn about the quality of the multiple-choice questions for this test? What advice would you give a teacher about constructing such items?**

Attention Focus

If we begin by misinterpreting the significance of what we hear, we will continue to draw inferences from the wrong cues and finally develop a quite erroneous interpretation of the whole. Since we will have selected what to retain and interrelate, we will no longer have access to the auditory image of the material we have rejected and thus be unable to reconstruct an alternative significance.

For this reason, several sections of discourse (with ample context) are better for testing aural comprehension than one long discourse. In this way, an initial error will not ruin the whole test for the student, as may happen with one lengthy passage. The student has a new opportunity with each section of the test. Several passages also constitute a better test because they tap several different semantic areas and thus make possible a much fairer assessment of the student's real knowledge of the language.

Levels of Difficulty

Carroll has pointed out that listening comprehension ability tests correlate highly with intelligence tests, because both test "processes of inference, deduction, and problem solving that often accompany the reception of language."[12] For this reason, it is difficult to decide on levels of difficulty of listening comprehension material, since it is not purely a matter of the difficulty level of the language material for the student (breadth of vocabulary, complications of syntax, length of segments, and so on). The result of a listening comprehension test is often all or nothing—the student perceived the significance or did not. This does not necessarily mean that the student did not understand the words or grammatical structures or would not have understood another passage of comparable length. Here we have another strong reason for testing students through a variety of passages in any one test, so that a passage which was found to contain unanticipated difficulties for a number of students may be dropped from the final score.

Testing the Results of Listening

In testing listening comprehension, we are not testing some vague entity called "the listening skill." We are testing comprehension of significance which has resulted from the listening experience (not "knowledge of the language" in itself). Students need knowledge of the language to comprehend, but comprehension goes far beyond this.

Rather than trying to give students practice in, and testing them on, something we call "listening comprehension," we should be testing "learning (comprehending) by listening,"[13] listening which requires the listener to act in some way,[14] and the results of listening.

The most effective practice in listening will therefore be in a purposeful context:

- students listen for instructions which must be carried out in some practical way;
- students listen to subject matter which must be learned and which itself will be tested (thus testing how well it was comprehended);
- students listen as part of a global act of communication, as part of a conversational interchange, which can only continue when there *is* comprehension;

12. J. B. Carroll, "Defining Language Comprehension: Some Speculations," in Carroll and Freedle 1972, p. 3.

13. T. G. Sticht, "Learning by Listening," in Carroll and Freedle 1972, p. 294.

14. G. A. Miller and P. N. Johnson-Laird, *Language and Perception* (Cambridge, Mass.: Harvard University Press, 1976), p. 703.

- students take part in a continuing activity (e.g., a series of episodes of a soap opera they are creating) where successive groups of students can perform their part of the activity only if they comprehended the preceding segment.
- **What other "purposeful contexts" can you add to this list?**

DEVELOPMENTAL STAGES
Students will need to develop their own listening strategies, but they can be assisted in the early stages to penetrate the dense fog of the new language through suitable activities appropriate to the four stages through which they will pass:

Stage 1: Identification
Stage 2: Identification and selection without retention (that is, listening for pleasure with no questions asked).
Stage 3: Identification and guided selection with short-term retention (where students are given some prior indication of what they are to listen for).
Stage 4: Identification and selection, with long-term retention.

In the usual language-learning situations, language skills should not be taught in isolation. Listening comprehension activities should spring naturally from, or provide material for, oral practice or reading; they can also provide a stimulus for writing activities. Listening comprehension should be tested at all stages along with the other areas of language study.

When various skills are integrated into free-flowing activities, in which one provides material for the other, students learn to operate confidently within the language, easily transferring knowledge acquired in one area for active use in another. It is most important that the teacher not compartmentalize the learning, even if, to some extent, this is inevitable in materials preparation and in talking about activities, as we are doing in this book. Integration of the various aspects of language use requires careful preparation on the part of the teacher, so that opportunities for natural movement from one language modality to another evolve continually during each lesson.

Similarly, the stages to be discussed in the following pages should not be regarded as rigidly sequential. While new material is forming the basis for identification practice, more familiar material is being used for identification and selection without retention, and material with familiar elements in recombinations and variations is being provided for identification and selection with retention. Suitable activities for all stages will therefore be presented at all levels.[15]

15. A detailed chart of activities for each of these stages at elementary, intermediate, and advanced stages for specific languages will be found in the *PG*'s, chap. 3.

Listening Comprehension

All material used for listening comprehension, even in the earliest lessons, should be authentic; that is, it should consist of utterances with a high probability of occurrence. Teaching students to comprehend artificial language combinations which would rarely be heard from a native speaker is a waste of time and energy, and can only confuse the student when later confronted with natural speech. Natural speech can be brought into the classroom in the form of recorded conversations of a spontaneous nature with native speakers, if native speakers themselves are not available to help.

Stage 1: Identification
Students learn to discriminate sounds and the elements of meaning conveyed by stress, pitch, and intonation (see chapter 5). They learn to identify words and phrases in their structural interrelationships, time sequences, logical and modifying terms, and phrases which are redundant interpolations that add nothing to the development of the line of thought and can be passed over quickly as the student selects what is relevant to the main message. (That we do ignore such redundant interpolations becomes clear to us when we try to transcribe a tape of authentic speech in our own or another language.[16] We must listen many times before we can transcribe every syllable and hesitation expression. Each time we listen, we hear new segments we had ignored when we were attending to the message.)

Dialogues are particularly appropriate for this stage. These should be short, written in authentic speech forms with a normal amount of redundancy, and heard and repeated at a normal conversational speed to provide practice in aural identification of common word groupings, phonological and structural patterns, and clichés of everyday speech. For practice in identification, students may listen to dialogues they have already learned, as they are given at a rapid conversational speed. These are often recorded with a variety of voices (male and female, high and low-pitched, young and old).

Where dialogue memorization is employed as an introductory technique, the students are continually hearing the material they are learning repeated by the model, by other students, and by themselves. In this way, they form an auditory image of these short utterances so that they are able to recognize them without analysis. The danger in this situation is that such recognition may remain at the echoic level, the students only dimly aware of the meaning of what they are saying. To ensure that the phrases they are learning will be useful also at the

16. Transcriptions of authentic speech taken from tapes are presented and analyzed in the *PG*'s, chap. 3, examples C35–37.

selective level, frequent opportunity must be provided for their application to communication situations within the class group, where actual degree of comprehension can be clearly demonstrated by an appropriate response, either physical or oral.

Responses to material heard, if oral, should as a general rule be in the foreign language. If students are habitually asked to demonstrate comprehension by translation into the native language, a further danger develops. They will acquire the habit of analyzing the elements of every utterance for comparison with what seem to be the most nearly appropriate categories of their native language, and they will not learn to perceive short utterances, and segments of longer utterances, as meaningful in themselves. They will also not develop facility in listening to and registering an ongoing stream of sound for retention. As they listen to an utterance, they will be busy decomposing the first segment they have heard in order to retain a native-language version of it, when their attention should have been fully engaged in forming an auditory image of the second segment and in selecting from it the elements relating it to the first.

In the early stages, the teacher should concentrate on teaching the immediate apprehension of a segment of sound, not on long-term retention of it: that is, on recognition, not on total or delayed recall. Students, for instance, may not be able to recall a sequence of utterances in a dialogue but may yet be able to respond promptly and appropriately to an item from the dialogue. They will not be capable of total recall until a strong frame of expectations has been built up in the language. It is debatable whether time should be wasted on memorizing a long series of dialogue sentences, as the value of the dialogue lies in the potentiality of the segments to generate new utterances, rather than in the devised sequence itself.

The uses of a dialogue for improving listening comprehension have not been fully exploited until the student is hearing recombinations of the material in the current and earlier dialogues, particularly in the context of actual situations, as in dramatizations acted out by groups of students or in actual conversational exchanges among students. A sense of reality can also be created by filmed situations where such recombinations are used.

In many classes, of course, dialogues are not used. No matter what the approach, however, the beginning lessons should provide frequent opportunities for hearing certain segments of language to develop familiarity with the phonological and syntactic patterning. Action sequences performed to oral cues, direct method discussions of what can be seen, handled, and demonstrated, these also provide considerable practice in hearing segments of language repeated until they are rapidly recognized.

Stage 2: Identification and Selection without Retention
This is the stage when students listen for pleasure, learning to select for comprehension, without being expected to answer questions on what they have comprehended. At this stage, students listen to a connected sequence with a development of thought which they try to follow. The students and the teacher are satisfied if they have followed the passage as delivered, without worrying about ability to recount or discuss what they have heard. The most suitable materials for this stage are simple plays or sketches depicting everyday situations in which the characters use the common, repetitious speech of conversation. The parts should be recorded with normal diction, not the artificial diction employed on the stage. Also suitable are dramatic readings, by several participants, of stories with a considerable amount of conversation. This kind of listening practice provides opportunities for introducing interesting material about the culture and the preoccupations and ways of the people. It should also be entertaining.

At a more advanced stage, students may listen to group conversations where two or three native speakers with easily identifiable differences of voice discuss a subject of interest to the student. In the excitement of the discussion the speech will be slightly slurred, but this will be compensated for by the hesitations, interruptions, and repetitions characteristic of natural speech. Conversations and discussions of this type may be taped and used over and over again. Simulated telephone conversations, with clear distinctions of voice, are also worthwhile, for they give practice in listening to slightly distorted speech with no visual clues to counteract the effect of the distortion.

At this stage, in laboratory work, the same tape should be repeated several times (in the same session or in successive sessions) to give the students further practice with the same material.

Where reading material is used from the first lessons, reading extracts should contain a considerable amount of conversation, and from these the students should be encouraged to prepare and act short sketches which are essentially recombinations of words and phrases from the reading extracts, which their fellow students recognize with ease.

Listeners cannot concentrate their attention with the same intensity on every constituent of an utterance. The familiar expressions in the recombinations form a matrix, from which students select certain

170

Developmental Stages

elements which are interrelated from segment to segment and which outline the developing pattern of the ideas they are pursuing. If students are confused by an effort to comprehend every element as they hear it, thus concentrating their attention fully on every constituent, they will not perceive these interrelationships, and what they have not perceived they will not retain. It is in listening comprehension particularly that the teacher can easily underestimate students' difficulties. To teachers of a language the comprehension of elementary material is immediate and effortless. They must try to see the processes involved from the students' point of view. They must provide plenty of opportunity for their students to hear well-rehearsed material, while requiring the abstraction from it of different lines of thought.

Recombinations of listening-comprehension material can, with a little ingenuity, be included in games requiring a physical or an oral response. Often these can take the form of guessing games. Games imaginatively devised give the students comprehension practice in a situation where interest is heightened by the competitive element and their attention is distracted from the skill being practiced. If comprehension is thus demonstrated in a real situation, where it is an instrument rather than an objective, the teacher will have tangible evidence that the students have passed beyond the recognition stage to that of selection. A few minutes of listening-comprehension games[17] at regular intervals will enable the teacher to reintroduce systematically material which is not currently being practiced. In this way, retention of material from earlier lessons will be constantly reinforced by active recapitulation without tedium.

Stage 3: Identification and Guided Selection with Short-Term Retention

Material similar to that for stage 2 may be used, with clearly distinctive voices and lively themes. At this stage the students are given some questions, not a great number, beforehand. They listen for the answers which they mark on a question sheet as they hear them or, at a more advanced stage, after they have listened to the whole passage. The passage should be repeated so that the students may have further practice in listening and selecting, and may have an opportunity to verify their answers.

17. A number of listening comprehension games are described in the *PG*'s, chap. 3. See also *PG*'s, Index, under Games.

171

Stage 4: Identification and Selection with Long-Term Retention
This is the final stage. Here students are encouraged to listen freely to all kinds of materials. They listen for pleasure or profit. They may wish to listen to plays, songs, sound-tracks of films, poems, news bulletins, discussions of subjects of topical interest, speeches by important political figures, or literary or cultural material related to other course work. At this stage they should have practice in listening to regional accents and all types of voices. After a period of listening, students are expected to be able to talk or write about what they have heard.

Practice at this stage may be in individual situations divorced from a conversational context (although active communication practice continues at the same time). Students may listen in the language laboratory, take home recorded cassettes, or listen in a local cinema or theater.

Groups of schools in the same supervision area should cooperate in the production of materials for listening comprehension, freely exchanging tapes which they have had the opportunity to make. One school may be able to tape an interview or conversation with a native speaker who has visited them. This material should be immediately circulated to other schools in the district. In areas where contact with native speakers is rare, no opportunity should be lost to build up, through cooperative action, a supply of semi-informal material in the foreign language. In this way students will have the opportunity to hear a variety of voices of differing quality, and accents representative of several regions and educational backgrounds.

Since telephone conversations are a normal activity in which speakers of a language engage at regular intervals, opportunities should be provided for all students to practice this activity. This may be at specified hours with the instructor, an assistant who speaks the language well, or cooperative native speakers in the community (retired, isolated, or merely friendly). Lonely foreign students may also enjoy an opportunity to chat with foreign-language students and perhaps make friends. Once the opportunities are arranged, it is up to the student to make the contact sufficiently interesting for the volunteer, so that the activity does not languish.

PRESENTATION OF LISTENING COMPREHENSION EXERCISES
Physical aspects of the classroom or laboratory presentation, such as speed of utterance, length of segments, length of pauses, acoustics of the room, and comfort of the students exert a decisive effect on the value of the exercise. The teacher should study these elements carefully.

Speed of Speech

All utterances for listening comprehension should be delivered at normal speed from the earliest lessons. Normal speed does not mean rapid native speech. After all, in any language there are people who speak fast and people who speak slowly; both groups are speaking normally. Pimsleur, Hancock, and Furey studied the speech rate of French radio announcers (the average being similar, they found, for American announcers). They found that speech rate varied a great deal among French announcers and also fluctuated among samples of the same speaker at different times.[18] From this research, they have drawn the following proposed set of standards for teaching purposes, all of which represent "normal speed of speech," depending on the speaker and the occasion.

Standard Speech Rates[19]

FAST = above 220 wpm
MODERATELY FAST = 190–220 wpm
AVERAGE = 160–190 wpm
MODERATELY SLOW = 130–160 wpm
SLOW = below 130 wpm

The desirable speed of delivery in the classroom from the early stages is one which would not appear to a native speaker to be unduly labored—a speed which retains normal word groupings, elisions, liaisons, consonant assimilations, phrase and sentence stress, and intonation—in other words, a natural rhythm. Utterances which are delivered at an unnaturally slow pace become distorted, and the auditory images stored by the students will not be immediately useful when they hear normal speech. It may be argued that in a foreign-language situation native speakers will, on request, speak very slowly; but, in so doing, they often exaggerate what to the listener are already confusing liaisons, elisions, and phonemic distinctions of the language. They may even try to incorporate, in an unsystematic fashion, what they believe to be the distinctive characteristics of the language of their foreign listener. This labored delivery, running contrary to the expectations of the foreigner, is often as difficult to interpret as undistorted speech at normal speed.

If the foreigner is clearly not understanding, the listener reduces the response to what has been called "foreigner talk"[20] and keeps to

18. P. Pimsleur, C. Hancock, and P. Furey, "Speech Rate and Listening Comprehension," in Burt, Dulay, and Finocchiaro 1977, p. 30.
19. Ibid., p. 31 (wpm = words per minute).
20. C. A. Ferguson, "Towards a Characterization of English Foreigner Talk," *Anthropological Linguistics* 17 (1975): 1–14.

bare essentials. Recent research in "foreigner talk" in various languages has revealed certain common characteristics. We simplify sentences to basic forms and keep these short; we reduce verbs to the most simple forms of the present tense or infinitive, omitting articles and avoiding any complications of word order or syntax. (The author recently heard an airport official say loudly and firmly to a bewildered foreigner: "You want airplane. You go that way.") The student of the language will wish to avoid getting into situations where native speakers take this extreme measure or even resort to their best efforts in the foreigner's native language in order to communicate. Once the native speaker has given up and resorted to the native language of the foreigner, it is often difficult for the inexperienced foreign-language user to get the exchange back on track. It is important, then, that students encountering normal speech should be able to take it in their stride, being accustomed to hearing it. They will thus receive valuable input for their future development.

Even in the very early stages, familiar material can be understood when spoken at normal speed. It is obvious that difficulties will arise when unfamiliar material is included, thus increasing rapidly the amount of information to be assimilated. As students advance and unfamiliar words and phrases begin to appear more and more frequently in comprehension material, they should be embedded in much easily recognizable material so that the student is able to concentrate on comparing the new elements with the surrounding context and deducing their meaning. These new elements are more easily assimilated at this stage because their characteristic phonological and structural patterning is recognized by the trained ear of the student.

Pauses

It seems that the *length of the segments* emitted in each breath group and the *length of the pauses* between the segments are of more importance for comprehension than the actual speed of delivery within the segments. (A fast speaker differs from a slow speaker more in the length and frequency of pauses than in actual speed of articulation.) The amount of information in a segment increases rapidly with the length of the segment, a greater number of words allowing for a greater number of alternatives: the longer the segment, the greater the strain on auditory memory. During the pause between segments, the organism can rehearse what it has heard, thus strengthening the memory trace. Research has shown that the auditory memory span for foreign-language material is considerably less than for native-language ma-

terial, probably on a ratio of nine words to fifteen.[21] With segments
of from eight to ten words (less in the early stages) the mind can
recirculate the material during the pause, relating it to what preceded
and anticipating to some extent what will follow. The ways the words
"chunk" or form natural semantic and syntactic groupings will, of
course, affect the absolute amount we can recall.[22]

Pauses are supplied in natural speech by hesitations, a certain
amount of hemming and hawing, some restating, and by certain conventional expressions that contribute nothing to the meaning of the
utterance but have a high frequency of occurrence because of this
function of extending the pauses in a normal utterance. (Here, we
may think of such expressions in English as *you know, like,* and *sort
of.*) Since artificially prepared material usually omits these common
features of natural utterances, it tends to deliver information at a
much higher rate than normal speech. A slight lengthening of the
pauses in prepared materials will supply the extra time that the organism requires to absorb the information presented to it, without
adding a time element not available in normal conversation.

- **Listen to the tapes supplied with the book in use in the class you
  are teaching or observing. Are the pauses in the model and cue
  items, or after these items, long enough for inexperienced students
  to process what they are hearing? Are the pauses prolonged to the
  degree that students have to keep on recirculating the material so
  long before they use it that they forget some of it?**

Repetition

For ease of comprehension, exercises should contain a certain amount
of repetitious material. This may take the form, for example, of explanations or descriptions in slightly different versions. Such repetition is another characteristic of normal speech. In conversation and
other forms of extempore speech there is redundancy of content as
well as linguistic redundancy. Because redundancy of content has
been eliminated, the listener to a close-knit discourse or the reading
of a well-written paper, even in the native language, must make a
concentrated effort. This fact is often overlooked, with the result that
listening-comprehension materials in the foreign language may con-

21. R. Lado, "Memory Span as a Factor in Second Language Learning," *IRAL*, 3,
no. 2 (1965): 127.
22. According to G. A. Miller, we can cope with about 7 items (plus or minus 2). If
these 7 are "chunked" according to some organizational principle, we can cope with
more material. See "The Magical Number 7 plus or minus 2: Some Limits on our
Capacity for Processing Information," *Psychological Review* 63 (1956): 81–96. Syntax
organizes many items into groups for us.

tain features which make them even more difficult to follow than similar material in the very familiar native language.

Areas of Controversy

Should the learning of a language begin with massed listening practice?

Infants listen and clearly comprehend a great deal before they begin to produce intelligible utterances. Children thrust into bilingual situations similarly pass through a listening phase before they attempt to construct utterances in the second language. Observations like these have led some researchers to advocate that the learning of a new language should begin with a prolonged period of listening before the student is required to speak the language, even in simple form. They advocate a "latent period" or "pre-vocal stage" of some duration.[23] Winitz and Reeds go so far as to say that "foreign languages instruction should discourage speaking until a high degree of comprehension is achieved, that is until the student can understand a nontechnical conversation and decode it with ease"—a recommendation that goes far beyond the native language acquisition analogy on which they base their arguments.[24]

The best-known programs experimenting with a pre-vocal stage have been those of Asher,[25] Winitz and Reeds, and Postovsky (all with adults), and Olmsted Gary (with elementary school children).[26]

In Asher's approach, the Total Physical Response, language learners listen to commands to which they respond with actions, moving from simple orders like "Go to the door" to very complex sequences

---

23. Valerian A. Postovsky, "Why Not Start Speaking Later?" in Burt, Dulay, and Finocchiaro 1977, pp. 17–26. Quotation is from p. 20. See also V. A. Postovsky, "Effects of Delay in Oral Practice at the Beginning of Second Language Learning," *MLJ* 58 (1974): 229–39.

24. Harris Winitz and James A. Reeds, "Rapid Acquisition of a Foreign Language (German) by the Avoidance of Speaking," *IRAL* 11 (1973): 295–317. Quotation is from p. 296.

25. Shirou Kunihira and James J. Asher, "The Strategy of the Total Physical Response: An Application to Learning Japanese," *IRAL* 3 (1965): 277–89. James J. Asher, "The Strategy of the Total Physical Response: An Application to Learning Russian," *IRAL* 3 (1965): 291–300. "The Total Physical Response Approach to Second Language Learning," *MLJ* 53 (1969): 3–7; and "Children's First Language as a Model for Second Language Learning," *MLJ* 56 (1972): 133–39.

26. Judith Olmsted Gary, "Delayed Oral Practice in Initial Stages of Second Language Learning," in Burt and Dulay 1975, pp. 89–95; and "Why Speak if You Don't Need to? The Case for a Listening Approach to Beginning Foreign Language Learning," in Ritchie 1978, pp. 185–99.

of actions. They are not expected to imitate what they hear or to produce utterances of their own. In experimental situations with Japanese and Russian, Asher found that students who learned in this way achieved a higher level of listening comprehension than those who were expected to speak early in the program. He also claimed that his subjects retained what they had learned over surprisingly long periods.

Winitz and Reeds combined aural input with pictures representing what was being said, and tested comprehension by requiring students to select from four illustrations the one demonstrating what they had heard. To this visual accompaniment Postovsky added writing (taking of dictation and writing out of pattern drills and dialogues). To encourage active listening, Gary used pictorial-audio matching, physical response–audio matching, and graphic-audio matching (in which students select from written multiple-choice items the graphic representation of the aural input which they have previously seen in association with a picture). Gary thus included reading but not writing, which she considered a productive mode, like speaking.[27]

Postovsky's experiments in Russian for adults were conducted in intensive, day-long programs at the Defense Language Institute at Monterey, and speaking was delayed for 240 hours of instruction (seven weeks of intensive study). In a daily program of twenty-five minutes of Spanish instruction for elementary school children, Gary maintained the pre-vocal approach for fourteen weeks, followed by seven weeks of partial delay in oral practice (that is, for the first half of each lesson). Ingram, Nord, and Dragt, in a college Russian course, experimented with 270 hours of delay before oral practice was introduced (that is, thirty weeks of nine class hours per week).[28]

Both Postovsky and Gary make clear that students were not prohibited from speaking spontaneously, if they wished, as individuals, during the prolonged periods when they listened and performed other activities (some certainly did begin to speak), but that they were *not required* to speak.[29] Postovsky also presumes that subvocalization occurred during writing practice, particularly dictation, and that this assisted in the assimilation of linguistic structure.[30] In other words,

27. Gary, "Delayed Oral Practice," p. 92.

28. F. Ingram, J. Nord, and D. Dragt (1974) at Michigan State University, described in Gary, "Why Speak?" pp. 193–94.

29. Postovsky, "Why Not Start Speaking Later?" p. 22; Gary, "Why Speak?" p. 185.

30. Postovsky, "Effects of Delay," p. 237. Postovsky claimed for his experimental groups better pronunciation than for groups which spoke from the beginning. This could have resulted from subvocalization in response to native models.

the term "pre-vocal" refers to the principle that students not be expected to imitate, repeat, and perform oral drills, as in an audio-lingual approach, or to create utterances along the lines of what they have been hearing, as in a direct method approach. The listening materials used in the pre-vocal stage are, however, based on morphological and syntactic features to which students are introduced in a carefully developed sequence that is further practiced in the associated activities—writing, physical response, or reading of multiple choice options. (Gary gives examples of information questions and declarative statements.[31] Winitz and Reeds moved from nouns like "pencil" and "cup," to the teaching of morphological and syntactic elements of German, as in "the man has the hat," "the big knife," and "the girl goes over the bridge."[32] Postovsky's students practiced structural variations of Russian in writing.)

Results showed, not surprisingly, that the experimental groups surpassed the control groups in the level of listening comprehension achieved, and also, for the experiments which included selections from written options, in reading. Since listening and reading involve similar processes,[33] one would expect the development of listening strategies through intensive practice to carry over to reading, especially when listening comprehension has been tested through choice from among written alternatives, thus providing practice in reading. Furthermore, if, as Carroll has suggested, there is a nucleus of knowledge of the structure and lexicon of the language, basic to and pervading the operation of all the language skills,[34] then it should not surprise us that practicing this basic corpus in one modality will make it more readily available for use in another.

The basic question which these experiments leave unanswered is whether intensive listening for a considerable period at the beginning of the course will result at a later stage in more rapid development of speaking ability—a hope implicit in all of these reports. (Postovsky, for instance, states that the goal of his courses is communicative competence and oral fluency.) No significant results for a higher level of speaking skill have been reported for the experimental groups.[35]

31. Gary, "Why Speak?" pp. 186–87.
32. Winitz and Reeds, "Rapid Acquisition," pp. 303–13.
33. Discussed by Wilga M. Rivers, "Linguistic and Psychological Factors in Speech Perception and their Implications for Teaching Materials," in *SMT*, pp. 131–44. Also in Pimsleur and Quinn 1971, pp. 123–34.
34. John B. Carroll, "Foreign Language Testing: Will the Persistent Problems Persist?" in O'Brien 1973, p. 12.
35. Gary, "Why Speak?" (p. 194), quotes Ingram, Nord, and Dragt as claiming that "a continuing focus on listening for comprehension of newly introduced materials is readily transferred to . . . speaking," but no data are given in support of this conclusion.

Consideration of certain facts about listening and speaking may throw light on this question and provide some direction for further experimentation or alternative interpretations of existing studies.

Recent psycholinguistic research makes clear that listening and speaking are not decoding-encoding processes which are mirror images of each other. It would seem, in fact, that listening and speaking operate quite differently and may even involve quite different grammars[36] (see p. 267 below). Consequently, the knowledge of the language we require for comprehension of oral output may be quite different from that required for expressing our meaning in speech and writing. Schlesinger even goes so far as to state that comprehension of language moves, for the most part, directly from perception of the intake to semantic interpretation, bypassing any syntactic analysis. The implication of this for the language learner is that knowledge of lexicon may have greater importance for the listener than detailed knowledge of syntax, which is, however, essential for precise expression of a speaker's intention. (Yet the listening material in the experiments discussed is syntactically oriented.)

In listening (and reading), expectations and inference help us create a meaning from semantic clues, so that it is often unnecessary to recognize or comprehend the significance of morphological or syntactic elements, many of which are redundant. On the other hand, our own utterances will usually not be comprehensible, and will frequently be unacceptable, if we do not use these elements correctly ourselves. With listening in a situational context (or accompanied by a visual representation of meaning), many clues other than linguistic ones help us interpret the intended meaning—kinesics, physical surroundings, relationships of persons, knowledge of real world probabilities (see p. 163 above). Many aspects of a sketch provide students with clues to meaning that the teacher did not anticipate, and some of these clues may be misleading. It is very difficult, therefore, to judge how much of the "meaning" has been extracted solely from the sound signal. When the teacher demonstrates a physical response while uttering a sound sequence, the same uncertainty applies.

Even in the face of little evidence, proponents of a pre-vocal stage continue to voice the hope that massive listening practice will lead to accelerated acquisition of speaking fluency, once oral practice is introduced. Yet research into the listening process indicates that we store the gist of what we hear, the core of meaning, and that surface structure features are not stored. When we ask listeners to restate a

---

36. T. G. Bever, "Psychologically Real Grammar Emerges because of its Role in Language Acquisition," in Dato 1975, p. 66.

179

message they have received, they give it back "in their own words," not verbatim. In fact, close attention to surface structure features in listening interferes with the process of developing meaning. It overloads the temporary memory store, thus hindering rehearsal of essential elements of meaning which are being retained in order to relate them to material still to come. Listening would not, then, appear to be the ideal way of learning those morphological and syntactic elements distinctive to the new language, which will be essential later for production of utterances. On the other hand, writing exercises which do not contain an excessive number of elements not represented in speech are more likely to impress on the learner morphological and syntactic features for productive use. This type of written practice is evident in the Postovsky model. Writing from spoken input requires processing, segmentation, and attention to detail, all performed at a slower pace than listening to speech.

We must not forget, however, that aural comprehension is an essential element of an act of communication which has frequently been neglected in language classrooms. That students should have confidence in their ability to comprehend all kinds of spoken messages should be a goal of instruction from the early stages. The experiments of Postovsky and Gary, among others, have laid a timely emphasis on the need for developing confidence in listening from the beginning, on the importance of bringing students into contact with authentic materials, and on the value of extensive early experience with the rhythm (stress, intonation) of the new language. The experimenters also emphasize the motivational value of the early feeling of achievement which comes with comprehension, and the relaxing of tensions which result from allowing students themselves to decide just when they will attempt to speak.

Certain disadvantages of the pre-vocal stage as proposed are: putting off the moment when students must try to express themselves (always traumatic for some); brushing aside the desire of many students to express themselves orally in the language (this is particularly important in second language situations); and the use in the experiments described of short uncontextualized segments which do not appear to have any immediate usefulness as communication (e.g., "the table," "the boy walks to the chair," or "Das Messer ist über dem Brot").[37]

Basically, the decision on how to approach the initial stages of language learning will be determined by the goals of the language

37. Examples from Winitz and Reeds, "Rapid Acquisition," and Gary, "Why Speak?"

instruction, the age and maturation of the students, and the intensity of the course. As Ervin-Tripp has said, we should not "blindly assume that there is one method for all ends, or even that the superficial features of skill practiced will inevitably match the knowledge acquired."[38]

Carroll's advice on this subject is set out in his theory-derived principle that "the more numerous kinds of associations that are made to an item, the better are learning and retention. . . . This principle," he continues, "seems to dictate against the use of *systems* of language teaching that employ mainly one sensory modality, namely, hearing."[39] This is the error that the researchers we have discussed have tried to avoid. Any teacher seeking to follow their lead should do likewise.

Annotated Reading List

Rivers, Wilga M., et al. *Practical Guides*. Chapter 3, "Listening," gives samples of authentic speech in the various languages and examples of exercises, games, and tests based on the theoretical concepts discussed in this chapter, with a detailed chart of listening comprehension activities for elementary, intermediate, and advanced levels.

————. "Linguistic and Psychological Factors in Speech Perception and their Implications for Teaching Materials." In *SMT,* pp. 131–44. Detailed account of information processing, with applications to the teaching/learning situation.

Rivers, Wilga M., and Melvin, Bernice S. "If Only I Could Remember it All! Facts and Fiction about Memory in Language Learning." In Burt, Dulay, and Finocchiaro 1977, pp. 162–71. Recent research in memory is applied to language learning and teaching.

Miller, G. A. "The Magical Number Seven, Plus or Minus Two: Some Limits on Our Capacity for Processing Information." *Psychological Review* 63 (1956): 171–72. Reprinted in Miller 1967, pp. 14–44. A very readable article based on information theory, in which the notion of "chunking" is introduced and discussed.

Oller, John W., Jr. "Expectancy for Successive Elements: Key Ingredient to Language Use." *FLA* 7 (1974): 443–52. Takes the view that the native speaker's knowledge of the first language is based on a grammar of expectancy that incorporates pragmatic knowl-

38. Susan Ervin-Tripp, "Structure and Process in Language Acquisition," in Alatis 1970b, p. 340.

39. John B. Carroll, "The Contributions of Psychological Theory and Educational Research to the Teaching of Foreign Languages," in Valdman 1966, p. 105. Italics in the original.

edge of the world, and that the learner of a new language should be able to take advantage of previously acquired expectations about situations and events in the world while learning a new grammar of expectancy for the coding of information.

*NONVERBAL COMMUNICATION

Knapp, Mark L. *Nonverbal Communication in Human Interaction*. 2d ed. New York: Holt, Rinehart and Winston, 1978. Discusses the effects on human communication of such factors as personal space, physical appearance and behavior, touching, facial expressions, eye contact, and vocal cues.

Research and Discussion

1. Make or obtain a tape of authentic speech in informal discussion (in any language you know well). Take one small segment (the equivalent of about eight sentences) and try to transcribe it word for word, syllable for syllable, repeated syllable for repeated syllable, with all the hesitation expressions, and er's and ah's. Mark each pause with a slash.

What did you learn about natural speech from this exercise?

2. Take a passage for listening comprehension for the level of a class you are teaching or observing. Design a multiple-choice test of comprehension and then a true-false test for the same passage. Administer the tests to parallel sections of the same class (not streamed sections). Compare the results on the two tests. Was there any great discrepancy in results? What did you learn about false recognition memory from this project? What did you learn about the items you constructed?

3. If you know a third or fourth language less well than your second language, go to the language laboratory and listen to some stimulus items for drills or grammatical exercises in this language. Is there enough context provided to enable the student to comprehend the model or stimulus sentences for the exercise? From what you have learned in this chapter, what other criticisms would you make of the exercises from the point of view of listening comprehension?

4. Devise a task which tests the results of listening or learning by listening.

5. Record a radio or television newscast in the language you are teaching (or obtain one from the cultural services of the embassy or consulate). How would you use it as a learning experience for your students? Design a lesson around this newscast and then try it with a class.

6. Listen to some conversational material in the language you are teaching, observing hesitation expressions and pause fillers. How do these differ from the ones you use in your native language? Design some lessons to teach students to fill pauses (thus giving themselves time to think out what they want to say by using acceptable hesitation expressions in their new language.

7. Listen to a newscast from a country where the language you are teaching is spoken. What information about the life and institutions of the people would the listener need to possess to draw the full significance from this newscast?

8. On the tapes that accompany the book used in the class you are teaching or observing, listen to the listening comprehension sections. How do you estimate the "level of difficulty" of these passages? Do you consider that they proceed from easier to more difficult? What criteria did you use for establishing "level of difficulty"?

9. Listen to a newscast in a language which is not your native language. Record it while you are listening. Replay the newscast several times and write down the names of places and personages in the news which you did not recognize when you heard it the first time. Did you know the foreign pronunciation of these names? Does the pronunciation follow the regular phonological rules of the language? Write down several other names of people and places frequently discussed. How would these be pronounced according to the phonological rules of the language? Work out an exercise or activity to train students to pronounce and recognize names as they would appear in this language.

*10. Watch a short scene from a film or videotape with the sound-track below the level of audibility. Study the nonverbal behavior of the participants, making notes on what you think they are expressing by their gestures, facial expressions, and slight body movements. Watch the film again with the sound track audible. Did you interpret the nonverbal behavior correctly? If possible, watch a third time, again without the sound track, and see whether you observe different things this time.

7· The Speaking Skill:
Learning the Fundamentals

COMMUNICATION MODEL

Let us first examine the following model of a communication system, which derives from the work of Shannon and Weaver.[1] Although originally used as a basis for the study of problems of telegraphic communication, it provides many interesting insights into interpersonal communication through speech.

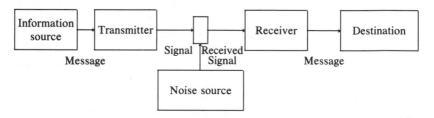

In this model, an information source emits a message, which is encoded for transmission as a signal. This signal passes through a channel to a receiver, which decodes the message for use at its destination. Paralleling this telegraphic model, Carroll supplies an organismic communication model:[2]

Intentive behavior of speaker ⟶ Encoding behavior of speaker ⟶ Message ⟶ Decoding behavior of hearer ⟶ Interpretive behavior of hearer

In chapter 6 we discussed the characteristics of a message, the passage of a message through a channel and the problem of "noise," the reception of the message, and its decoding by the receiver (that is, the right-hand side of each of these models). In discussing the development of the speaking skill, we are concerned with the selection of the message to be sent and the encoding of the message for transmission (that is, the intentive and encoding behavior of the speaker).

1. W. Weaver, "Recent Contributions to the Mathematical Theory of Communication," in Claude E. Shannon and Warren Weaver, *The Mathematical Theory of Communication* (Urbana, Ill.: University of Illinois Press, 1949), p. 34.

2. John B. Carroll, *The Study of Language* (Cambridge, Mass.: Harvard University Press, 1953), p. 88.

THREE ASPECTS OF LANGUAGE

Many of the controversies about language teaching stem from the fact that there are several different ways of looking at language and we may not be talking about language in the same way as others. As an analogy, we may consider three ways of looking at an instrument. First, there is the form of the instrument: its shape, the materials of which it is made, and how these are combined to cope with stresses or provide particular types of surfaces. Then we may consider the potentialities of the instrument: Is is suitable for digging? Can it cut? Can it be used for carrying other objects? The more ingenious its construction, the more we discover and experiment with possible uses. Finally, we may take the instrument and begin to dig to see how it performs: Does it really throw up the dirt in this dry garden bed? Does it reach right down to the roots of this rhododendron? Does it stop exactly when and where I want it to stop among the roots of these roses?

Three views of language down the centuries have distinguished language-as-product from language-as-tool and language-as-activity or process.[3]

We consider *language-as-product* when we make the language an object of study. We analyze specimens of the language, as linguists do, and examine the system of rules (phonological, syntactic, morphological, and semantic) by which it operates. Sometimes we stop to examine our native language which we may have been using without reflection for years. We identify parts of speech and observe the operation of syntactic rules; we parse and analyze; we study dialectical variations, neologisms, and what happens to the sound system in different contexts.

Language-as-product is sometimes referred to as *langue* (see p. 68), or as the language *code,* and such study can be intensely interesting. Naiman, Fröhlich, and Stern report the case of a man who learned thirty-two languages (from Spanish, Russian, and Chinese to Tagalog, Iroquian, Thai, Hittite, and Sanskrit). He did not learn to speak all these languages; for some he studied the language system for its intrinsic interest. "I've never lost my interest in languages," he said. "It's the fun I get out of it."[4]

The grammar-translation approach emphasizes language-as-product when students study grammar rules and paradigms. So does contrastive linguistics, which compares language systems.

---

3. For a detailed discussion of the development of these views and their significance for different linguists and psychologists, see Hörmann 1979, pp. 2–14.

4. The case of Mr. E is described in Naiman et al. 1978, pp. 87–96.

Language-as-tool, a concept which goes back to Aristotle, emphasizes the ways we can use a language to operate upon the environment (upon things, upon people, upon ourselves in the self-directive function of thought). Each language has great potentiality for conveying our intentions—our personal meaning. We may wish to ask, to order, to state, to hypothesize, to deny, to persuade. We will need to know how to do these things in a new language so that we can express nuances and subtleties of meaning. For instance, we may wish to ask in one of a number of different modes. We may wish to ask for a certain sum of money; we may wish to ask whether a certain sum of money might be made available; we may wish to demand a certain sum of money in a peremptory fashion; by the form of our question we may wish to persuade someone to give us the money; we may be trying to obtain money from someone by deceitful means; or we may express our desire indirectly, by merely wishing we had access to a certain sum of money. The language we are learning can provide us with the means to ask in these various ways. By the availability of certain forms it can induce us to use the approach which is most appropriate in the new culture. As we learn a new language, we have to internalize its potentialities as an instrument. How to forge such an instrument for our use is the special emphasis of this chapter.

With *language-as-activity* or *language-as-process* we go beyond linguistics into pragmatics and social psychology. Can we use a language to effect our purposes, whether in oral or written form? Do we perceive the messages the senders intend us to perceive? (Listening and reading are as much a part of language in use as are speaking, writing, or signing.) We may understand the system of a new language and know how to formulate or recognize the formulations of the various options available to us for expressing specific meanings, but we may still "not understand a word they're saying" or feel unable to say what we really want to say. Our timing may be the problem. Perhaps we have difficulty putting together the right formulations fast enough to keep an interlocutor's attention. Our pronunciation, stress, or intonation may be correct from one point of view, but misleading in the particular situation in which we are using it.

We need to learn how to conduct communicative episodes: how to initiate interaction with speakers of the language, how to respond to the initiative of others, how to avoid and how to terminate communication. We need to internalize the "good manners" of the language (how to ask the acceptable and expected questions, how to greet, console, keep interaction moving). We need to know what levels of language we should use in different circumstances, when to speak, when to remain silent, how to look for covert meanings behind words and gestures. This is speech as a social event, and, as such, it can be learned only through experience with language in use. (Chapter 8 will take up this area in practical detail.)

WRITTEN AND SPOKEN LANGUAGE

The teaching of languages has traditionally concentrated on language-as-product, by making students aware of certain aspects of the code (vocabulary of the new language, phonological and morphological features, syntactic rules), often without providing adequate practice in the selection of messages by students themselves and in the process of encoding these for transmission. As a result, after years of study, students have known a great deal about the language they were learning without being able to use it to express their intentions.

Until recently, the new code was usually studied in its written form. Before the era of the record player and the recorder, the printed script was the most convenient form in which it could be dissected, the parts examined in detail, and interrelationships explained and practiced. This emphasis on language-as-product has continued in many places because of teachers' unwillingness to change their pattern of book and chalkboard instruction. Because of its enduring nature, the written code has also acquired a certain prestige as the standard against which the spoken code should be measured and evaluated; it is still considered by many to represent the "correct" form of the language.

The written code, once learned, has not proved to be of great use for oral communication: it is too elaborate and cumbersome. It is also too intellectually demanding for informal communication, because it is less redundant than the spoken code as people normally use it. (Compare the reading aloud of an official report or announcement and the animated discussion of it later among the people it concerns.) In courses emphasizing written language, aspects of the spoken code which are not noted in the written code have frequently not been taught beyond a very superficial level. Such features as pitch, intonation, stress and duration, assimilation, juncture, elisions, liaisons at word boundaries, and expressive features like tone of voice and gesture are often all but ignored. Yet all of these features play an important part in conveying the full import of a spoken message.

As we shall see, an act of speech involves more than knowledge of the code. It involves the selection of integrated patterns of elements of the code for the expression of an intention, and the assembling of the necessary features without undue hesitation (this is the process of encoding). In many languages, expressing intentions in speech also involves the selection of different sentence types and syntactic patterns from those of written language and a different choice of lexical items. Teachers must know and understand these differences between spoken and written forms of the language they will teach,[5] or their students, if they talk at all, will "talk like a book."

The teaching of the speaking skill is more demanding on the teacher than the teaching of any other language skill. For this reason, many teachers give up the attempt to teach it and concentrate on what they call a more "intellectual" approach to language teaching: the deciphering of the written code and the analysis of its features, or the discussion of the content of written texts. (These are, of course, legitimate techniques, for which speaking is not the main objective. See chapter 9.) Students taught in this way acquire much passive knowledge of the language which can, and frequently does, become active when the students are plunged into a situation where only the new language is used. However, there are much more direct ways to foster the speaking skill.

WE LEARN TO SPEAK BY SPEAKING

Other teachers persuade themselves that if they speak the new language exclusively in the classroom, the students will, at some time, begin to speak it fluently too; this they justify by the argument that the students now have the opportunity to learn a second or third language as they learned their native language as a child. This reasoning ignores the fact that little children learn to speak their language by continual prattling for most of their waking hours, frequently using incorrect forms; that they are continually being spoken to, often in specially adapted language, and encouraged in their efforts to produce speech; and that their efforts at uttering comprehensible speech enable them to gain things for which they feel a great need (physical satisfactions or their parents' attention and praise). Students of a new language will not learn to speak fluently merely by hearing speech in class, although this is most important for familiarizing them with accepted forms and the flow of authentic speech, as well as for giving them practice in the receptive side of communication. Teachers will need to give their students many opportunities to practice speaking. They will need to use their imagination in devising situations which provoke the use of the language in the expression of the student's own meaning, even when the student has very limited resources on which to draw. From these early experiments with the language, students become aware of the extraordinary potentiality for the creation

5. Differences between written and spoken forms of French, German, Hebrew, Spanish, and English are discussed in detail in the *PG*'s, chap. 1.

of new meanings that recombinations and rearrangements of language elements provide. They realize language is a valuable tool which can be used in many ways.

The active practice of speech cannot be left to a "later stage," when students presumably "know the language" from the dissection and reassembling of the written language. By this time, many students will have developed certain inhibitions about making strange sounds in public, and will find it difficult to express themselves orally in the complex forms of the literary code they have been taught. Students should be given the opportunity, throughout their period of language study, to develop ever greater skill in encoding their thoughts in ever more complicated structural patterns of the new form of speech, and in consolidating the muscular control involved in the acceptable production of sound sequences. The prolonged practice they require in working with the code must not be delayed. For these reasons, speaking the language should be a natural activity from the first lesson.

Motivation

The early introduction of the speaking of the language is also important for reasons of motivation. Students come to the study of another language with the strong conviction that "language" means "something spoken." They are often discouraged and lose interest when they find that studying a language is just like other subjects: "learning a whole lot of stuff from a book," and that being able to speak the language is some far-distant goal, attainable only after years of uninteresting and uninspiring labor. Pimsleur, in his study of under-achievers in foreign-language study,[6] found them anxious to speak the language. They considered it "fun" and felt it to be "important." Students who come away from their first lesson able to say something useful in the new language, no matter how simple it may be, feel great satisfaction, and their attitude toward language learning becomes much more favorable. They are also encouraged by family and community approval of this evidence of their nascent skill.

ANALYSIS OF AN ACT OF SPEECH

To teach the speaking skill, it is necessary to understand the processes involved in speech. Through speech, one expresses emotions, communicates intentions, reacts to other persons and situations, influences other human beings. At a subvocal level, speech enables us to examine and rearrange impressions and associations so that we see

6. P. Pimsleur, D. M. Sundland, and R. D. McIntyre, *Under-Achievement in Foreign Language Learning,* Final Report (Columbus: Ohio State University Research Foundation, 1963), p. 24.

new relationships and evolve new purposes. Spoken language is, then, a tool in everyday life. In the teaching of the speaking skill, we are engaged in two processes: forging an instrument and giving the student practice in its use. Our students already know how to use a similar instrument—their native language. Finding at first that the new instrument is cumbersome and frustrating, they tend to slip back, whenever possible, to the use of the instrument to which they are accustomed.

The teaching of the speaking skill thus involves *two levels of activity*. The forging of the instrument requires much practice in the obligatory associations of the new language: lexical items, morphological and syntactical patterns, sentence types. At this level, students are asked merely to manipulate the elements of the new language code, so that they can express a number of possible meanings suggested to them by the exercise or the teacher. When they have acquired facility with these customary associations, they need practice in setting in motion a number of interacting systems of a hierarchical nature. Speaking to express a personal intention is not a sequential or linear process, one item generating the next throughout the utterance. It is a hierarchical process. The intention demands a certain overall construction or sentence type (an exclamation, a statement, a question) referring to the past, the present, or the future, to the existent or the nonexistent, in absolute or modified form. Speakers select the general construction of an utterance and, according to their purposes, combinations of segments within it. This they do speedily and with little apparent effort. They may even pause in the middle of an utterance and completely reframe it—as we do when we begin a statement and change it in mid-utterance into a question.

Students who are to speak a language so as to express their personal meaning need much practice in this process of generating new sentences to suit their purposes. In authentic communication the process is not always an initiatory one. The form of the utterance one person is generating has frequently been determined by some utterance of another person to which the speaker is reacting. Typically this occurs when one is answering a question.

As well as sentence type, the speaker must choose the *style of language* in which to express the message. This is sometimes called register or level of discourse. In the *Five Clocks,* Joos (1961) discusses at length what is involved in the choice from among five styles of English speech: intimate, casual, consultative, formal, and frozen.

Similar styles can be established for other languages.[7] Once a choice of style has been made, certain subordinate choices of lexical sets and structural patterns will follow.

A further complication arises when we consider *registers* of language. Certain types of language are acceptable, even expected, for certain situations and for specific purposes. A specialized vocabulary and style of speech is used, for instance, in sporting broadcasts which would not be appropriate for pleading in court or for telling a folk story to a young child. Even apart from the questions of style and register, the emotional or evaluative tone of the utterance will impose further limitations.

Finally, the speaker has to articulate the whole utterance by muscle movements which will enable the listener to get the full import of the message. These muscle movements determine not only the individual sounds in complicated relationships with other sounds in the flow of speech, but also duration, stress, and intonation and juncture phenomena, along with such expressive features as pauses, hesitations, voice quavers, loudness, and facial expression.

In a language with which we are familiar all these elements are so integrated that selection at one level sets the appropriate operation in action for selection at the next level. It is this smooth integration of processes which the student of a new language has to learn by assiduous practice in shaping the tool, and then in trying it out in all kinds of contexts.

FORGING THE INSTRUMENT

At the first level of activity, the forging of the instrument, the aim of the teacher is to present students with a functioning language system which becomes more and more sophisticated in its operation, and to give students well-designed practice in the various functions, individually and always ultimately in combination, so that when they wish to express something in the new language they can concentrate on what they want to say rather than on the details of how to say it acceptably.

Many of these details consist of arbitrary associations, juxtapositions, and oppositions of elements (often of morphology and word order) which must be learned to a degree of automaticity if the subtle distinctions of syntax are to convey their full meaning. This requires intensive practice, which may not be intrinsically very interesting but is nevertheless unavoidable if students are to progress beyond a nearly

7. Examples of these five levels for different languages are given in the *PG*'s, chap. 1.

incomprehensible pidgin. Where such practice can be built into a competitive activity or a game, students will repeat the activity a number of times much more willingly. Variety of presentation of practice, using a recorder, pictures, objects, actions, or songs will assist. But essentially, students need to be convinced by their teacher that what they are learning is indispensable for the undistorted communication of meaning. (Here the type A and B exercises of chapter 4 are important.)

Students are accustomed in some other areas of study to understand principles, memorize facts related to these principles, see these principles in operation in a few examples, and then move on to new topics. Often, missing one topic or not learning it thoroughly will not prevent the student from mastering the next. This is not true of language learning. It is the task of the language teacher to convince students that quite small distinctions affect comprehensibility, and what is learned on the first day will, in all probability, be required on the last in acts of communication. Everything, then, needs to be retained and to be readily available for recall. This often means repetitive practice until certain structural elements are thoroughly assimilated. Frequent reentry into class activity of what has been learned earlier is essential if students are to acquire the ability to use this seemingly endless mass of detail.

Although steady practice in forging the instrument is essential, it will not achieve its purpose unless students are made aware of the pertinence of what they are practicing to situations beyond the classroom. They must be given the opportunity to apply what they have learned in acts of communication among members of the class group. We cannot wait until our students have a sure grasp of all the structures of the language before giving them practice in communication. If they are to do more than glibly reel off mechanically acquired sequences, they must be trained continually in using these sequences to generate new utterances in *situational contexts*.

Functions of Language in Use

To use an instrument freely in the performance of tasks, we must understand the functions it can perform and what various mechanisms do, either directly or by meshing with other mechanisms, to cope with these functions.

Halliday has elaborated the basic functions language performs for children learning their first language (Halliday 1975, p. 37). This analysis can act as a useful guide for teachers of a second or third language who wish to provide their students with a well-honed instrument that they can use for all kinds of purposes. Although the adult uses these simple functions for the most part in combination in macro-functions[8] (as an instrument user also does), understanding and acquisition of the mechanisms of the simple functions is essential if use of the new language is not to remain confused and mysterious.

The basic functions Halliday proposes are as follows.

1. *Instrumental:* the "I want" function. Students need to be able to express their desires and needs. Going beyond babyhood, they must learn how to express these wants in the more subtle forms languages provide. Certainly, "I want," "I would like," "Would you be so kind as to give me," "Please let me have," "Could you possibly find me," and so on are among the most basic expressions a language speaker needs.

2. *Regulatory:* the "Do as I tell you" function. This is the language of rules, instructions, orders, and suggestions. These are learned early in most classes through simple orders and action games. Again the adult function requires more subtle forms of expression and is basic to using language to help others perform tasks, as well as for organizing joint activities.

3. *Interactional:* the "Me and you" function. For our second-language learner, this includes the learning of many culturally acceptable patterns of greeting, leave-taking, thanking, extending good wishes, excusing oneself, and generally making the persons with whom one is communicating feel at ease. Many of these expressions can be learned in simple dialogues and they should be used regularly in classroom contacts.

4. *Personal:* the "Here I come" function. This function has received new emphasis through humanistic techniques which encourage the students to talk about themselves, express their feelings, and share emotions and experiences (see Moskowitz 1978). In bookish language classes, this function is often very much neglected in favor of function 7 (the informative function), so that later, as language users, these students are stilted and seemingly distant with those with whom they are trying to communicate. Common exclamations which release tension and cover confusion can be practiced early in classroom interaction.

5. *Heuristic:* the "Tell me why" function. Again, frequently neglected in language classes are abundant opportunities to practice asking questions. Question forms are a constant problem to users of a new language, yet, in many classes, teachers ask all the questions and the students merely give information. This is easily

8. Halliday's macro-functions are the ideational, interpersonal, and textual (1975, p. 52).

rectified if students work in small groups, do interesting things in the foreign language together, and teach each other. Many games which require the participants to ask questions are very easily adapted as classroom activities and should be used again and again.

6. *Imaginative:* the "Let's pretend" function. This is the use of language for supposing, hypothesizing, and creating for the love of sound and image. "If I were this," "Suppose you were that," "It might be possible"—this type of language draws students out into the creative. The writing of short poems can be encouraged early.[9]

7. *Informative:* the "I've got something to tell you" function. This is the realm of the declarative affirmative and the declarative negative. Statements are not neglected in most language programs, but attention should be paid to the use of compound and complex sentences, not just simple sentences, and the ability to express vividly as well as precisely. The possibility of using present, past, and future in the easiest forms should be available early in the course.

- **Can you think of any other functions of language in use which adolescent and adult language-learners need?**

How Does the Student Acquire Structures for the Basic Functions?

Language teachers down the ages have faced a choice between an inductive or a deductive approach (see chapter 2, p. 25). All, or nearly all, have included in their teaching some form of practice of basic forms and structures. The various ways this has been approached may be summarized as follows.

Inductive Options

1. Students encounter a new structure in a meaningful context in a dialogue. The dialogue may be presented orally or accompanied by a filmstrip or pictures. The students practice use of the structure orally through substitution and conversion exercises. They then establish a generalization or rule as a summary of what they have been doing. They may continue practice in written exercises or further oral exercises, if student uncertainty shows the teacher that this is necessary. They then try out what they can do with the new structure in variations of the dialogue, directed dialogue, chain dialogue, im-

9. For proposals along these lines, see D. Birckbickler, "Communication and Beyond," in Phillips 1977, pp. 78–82.

provisations related to the dialogue, or games which force use of the structure.

2. Students encounter a new structure in a meaningful context in a reading passage. (In the early stages, these are usually conversational in tone.) Through questions on the content of the passage, the teacher forces use of the structure. If it is obvious that students have not worked out how the structure operates, their attention is drawn to a paradigm, a schematic explanation of the rule, or a statement of the rule with examples. The teacher improvises further examples of the structure in use in sentences related to the content of the reading. Students then do written exercises which contain vocabulary and situations drawn from the reading passage. Finally, they give oral reports or write original paragraphs on related subjects which draw on the structure just learned.

3. The teacher demonstrates the new structure through activity in the classroom, using objects, pictures, actions, sounds, or mime. Students imitate the teacher's production and then demonstrate their comprehension by variations on what they have heard, demonstrating their meaning through action or other visual means. If students have not fully grasped the workings of the structure, the teacher gives further oral examples which focus on the point at issue, or demonstrates its operation schematically on the chalkboard. Students continue to use the structure creatively in conversational exchanges or role-playing activities, built on situations which require use of the structure. (This is called *active grammar* practice.)

4. Students attempting to communicate spontaneously with each other need a structure they do not know. The teacher supplies it. Other students need the same structure. The teacher supplies the structure again. Students attempt to use it, with the teacher correcting discreetly when they misuse it. Students continue to have recourse to the teacher on those occasions when they are not sure that they are using the structure appropriately.[10] (Students may later refer to a textbook or programmed notes to review what they have been using in class. This is usually an out-of-class activity.)

5. Students study example sentences and discuss regularities of structure they can observe in these sentences. With the teacher's help they establish a schematization of the operation of the structure. They then do exercises, orally or in writing, in which they apply what they have just discovered.

6. Students listen to examples of the structure in use and then do guided written exercises which involve use of the structure. When

10. This is similar to the counseling-learning approach of Curran (1976).

they have grasped the operation of the structure, they try to use it in conversation with other students.[11]

Deductive Options

1. The students study a rule or paradigm. They look at examples of its use. The teacher explains the operation of the rule. Students ask questions and construct some new examples of the rule in operation under the direction of the teacher. They then work through exercises in the textbook orally or in writing (or first orally and then in writing). Next, they translate from the native language into the target language a set of sentences or a passage which has been carefully constructed to contain examples of the various aspects of the structure in operation. Alternatively, they read a passage into which examples of the structure in operation have been woven. Through question and answer on the passage, the teacher is able to test the students' understanding of the operation of the structure. If necessary, the teacher gives further explanations of the structure being learned, and the students do further practice exercises.

2. Students study in programmed materials before the class session a schematization of the structure, or a rule or paradigm, with examples. The materials may be accompanied by cassettes. They try to use this structure themselves in conversational practice during the class session. The teacher gives further explanations when necessary. Students then use the structure over and over again in some role playing or game selected to promote use of the structure. (They may write the roles as a group activity and then act out what they have written.) They may move on to demonstrate their comprehension of the structure in reading materials.

3. Students study rules, with examples, and practice exercises with the assistance of a computer. Class sessions are devoted entirely to conversation and discussion in which students try to use what they have been learning.

Whichever of these options is adopted, the following *principles* should be observed.

1. Structures must be experienced in *possible and probable linguistic contexts,* whether in oral or written discourse. Forms and structures viewed in isolation may be interesting oddities, but students cannot be expected to know what to do with them.

11. Postovsky (see above, chap. 2, n. 34) advocated listening with writing before speaking.

2. Practice of structures should be in *possible and probable situational contexts,* so that students can learn use along with form and relationships.

3. Practice should be *creative,* in that students should have the opportunity to create meanings of their own through use of the structure.

4. Students must *understand what they are doing* when they are practicing variations of the structure. They must understand what changes in meaning are created by small variations of the structure.

5. Students must see the *relationship* of the structure they are learning *to what they have learned* and practice it as a further extension of possible meaning within the corpus.

6. Students must see the *relationship* of this particular structure *to the overall grammar* of the language. (If it is a tense, how does it fit into the way this language expresses time relationships?)

7. It is helpful for students to understand how this structure is similar to or differs from a seemingly equivalent structural element in their native language. Since information is stored in memory in conceptual networks independent of the forms of any language, the student needs to find the *appropriate conceptual network* to which to attach the functioning of the new structure. Without guidance, the student may attach the new structure to the conceptual network of an inappropriate native-language structure and later find it hard to make a switch.

8. Thorough practice is necessary for forging the instrument, but overlearning through unimaginative, repetitious, and boring activity causes fatigue and distaste on the part of the student. *Variety of approach* is essential if students are to concentrate their energies on mastering the use of structures. Teachers must use imagination in designing a variety of activities for structural practice, even if the textbook is disappointingly monotonous.

9. All student practice must be carried out with *awareness of the meaning* of what is being said or written. Requiring creative additions to or conversions of the exercise which can follow only from understanding of the whole is the best way of ensuring that this is so.

10. A class consists of individuals who have gradually been welded into a group with some knowledge of each other's activities and some interest in each other's affairs. Communication among them is possible. No structural element may be considered to have been learned satisfactorily until the student shows confidence in using it in a natural way to *communicate with others* in the class.

- **Can you think of other inductive or deductive options for practicing basic structures? Discuss the advantages and disadvantages of the various approaches in light of the ten principles elaborated. Which option do you favor and why?**

Specific Areas Where Practice Is Needed

1. For fluent oral communication, practice is essential in the *prosodic features* of the new language: stress, intonation, juncture phenomena (such as liaisons, elisions, internal juncture, release of final consonants), and syllabification. Incorrect production of these features is a frequent source of miscomprehension even when students have mastered the structures required for the basic functions and can pronounce individual sounds acceptably. Unfortunately this is the area where interference from native-language habits, or from habits acquired more recently in learning another foreign language, is the strongest and the most persistent, possibly because students have rarely studied with conscious attention these aspects of their speech. Often teachers fail to give much explanation of these distinctive aspects of the language. Students are expected to acquire them by imitating the speech of the instructor in classroom activity or in dialogue learning. If imitated prosodic patterns are to be retained, they will need to be brought to conscious awareness and practiced frequently in the context of appropriate utterances. Students should be encouraged to listen carefully to these aspects of native speech, whether on recordings or in the speech of the teacher and any native contacts they may have. In a second-language situation, conscious imitation of the rhythm of the speech they hear in the street, from friends, or on broadcasts will help them develop and maintain acceptable and comprehensible patterns.

2. *Sentence types related to the basic functions.* Frequently neglected in the endeavor to build in facility in the handling of grammatical features is practice in selection of overall *sentence patterns*. Attention is often focused almost entirely on isolated forms or segments of sentences. In oral practice or a game format, students can create new utterances of a particular sentence form by supplying lexical items which suit their purposes and imaginings. Students may be encouraged to vie with each other in the production of affirmative and negative statements, questions, conditional utterances required by the game. In the excitement of the contest they forget that this is another practice in structure. Also valuable for the development of fluency in speaking is practice in *expanding sentence frames* with dependent phrases which elaborate the message: this also can be a competitive or chaining activity within the class group. Students will

accept much more intensive practice if it takes the form of an amusing, even exciting, occupation. Exercises of this type are normally practiced orally, without the support of a written script, so that students become confident in oral construction. The teacher who feels the need for some visual representation during the preliminary establishment of the sentence frames to be used may employ vanishing techniques on the chalkboard, gradually eliminating elements of the visual support until students can work without it.

DIALOGUES AND DRAMATIZATIONS

Many students who were well trained in using language structures have found themselves completely at a loss in conducting a conversation with a native speaker of the language because the books from which they (and their teacher before them) learned the language forms failed to emphasize the characteristic features of everyday spoken language and persistently used outdated or pedantic turns of phrase. Such students may be perfectly at home with the language of an ode or a classical play, yet find their ears assailed by unfamiliar phrases as soon as they hear two native speakers in discussion. They may be able to talk fluently about peasants and palaces, carriages and wooden ploughs, but be quite unable to ask for air to be put in the tires of their car or the price of a new film for their camera.

Vocabulary items are, of course, easily acquired when needed, but language learners are disconcerted when the structure of informal speech does not parallel the meticulous requirements of the literary style to which they are accustomed, as happens in so many languages. The familiar compliment "You speak the language better than we do" may be taken to mean: "You express yourself in a formal idiom which no native speaker would ever use." The student does not learn to speak a language fluently by continual practice in question and answer on a reading text—a very common procedure in language classes. This technique has its place in the discussion of ideas in a literary context, but does not provide adequate preparation for informal conversation. Even naming objects in the classroom has limited usefulness. In ordinary conversation we do not usually name objects about which we are talking because context makes our meaning clear. Expressions like "Put it down" are more frequent in informal situations than fully elaborated sentences like "Put the box on the ground."

Conversational speech is characterized by the frequent repetition of well-worn expressions (clichés); by tags and formulas now empty of precise denotation; by expletives and exclamations which give the speakers time to reorganize their thoughts and select the form in which they wish to express these thoughts; by pauses and changes in structure as an utterance proceeds. Were these omitted, speech would proceed much more rapidly, and it would be beyond the capacity of the listener-speaker to assimilate much quick-fire conversation. We have only to listen carefully to our friends gossiping over their morning tea or coffee to realize how frequently the same hackneyed phrases and exclamations recur. Recognition of these features of informal communication has been the basis for the advocacy of the dialogue as a device for elementary classes.

Why The Dialogue Is Useful

In dialogues students learn important features of conversation such as: greetings; expressions of impatience, dismay, or surprise; conventional expressions of agreement and polite disagreement; common forms of question and noncommittal answer; expletives and exclamations which give the speaker time to search for the correct form to express the meaning; appropriate levels of language for specific situations and relationships.

In a dialogue, expertly written, the informal language is learned in an *immediately useful form:* a form which the student can practice by turning to a neighbor, or apply in contacts outside the classroom. Everything in the dialogue is meaningful and relevant to the situations of everyday life. The clichés of the language are embedded in typical acts of communication instead of being learned artificially in lists as isolated phrases. Students learn to return conventional expression for conventional expression in a natural way. Most important of all, they learn to speak in the first and second persons, whereas in discussion of reading texts they nearly always use the third person. They learn to ask questions as well as answer them, to speak in short sentences, to reply in incomplete sentences which do not repeat all the elements of the question, to make short rejoinders.

In imitating the teacher or a native model as they learn a dialogue, students practice the rhythm, the intonation, the stress, the liaisons and elisions, the assimilations of the spoken language, and learn to understand and reproduce these at a normal speed of utterance. All the elements of the sound system recur in their natural context and are practiced without being artificially isolated and distorted. Grammatical structures introduced into dialogues are encountered in a natural matrix of meaning even before being explained or drilled. Later they can be studied in a more formal and systematic way.

Apart from the pragmatic value of teaching contemporary speech in an immediately usable form, the dialogue has other *psychological advantages*. When students act out roles, some of the embarrassment of making strange sounds is eliminated, as they take on the person-alities of people who speak the language in everyday situations. A set of sentences or a prose reading becomes very boring if students are asked to repeat or read it over and over again, whereas a role in a miniature drama can be acted out by the same or different students again and again with a conscious effort at improvement. Different groups of students will vie with each other to produce the best reen-actment of the scene, enabling the class to listen to the same phrases a number of times without tedium. Students will enjoy learning roles by heart. They will set about assiduously writing *variations of the basic situation,* using the now-familiar phrases. Some books provide a number of variations of scene based for the most part on the same restricted set of phrases, and these variants can be studied as fresh material until the basic sentence segments have been thoroughly as-similated. Students then find they have abundant material on hand for writing their own original skits and sketches.

In classes where dialogue learning is not part of the method used, an introductory textbook should be chosen in which the early lessons consist of much *conversational material* which can be *dramatized* in the classroom. The material should frequently reuse the most useful conversational phrases. This material can be acted out by the stu-dents, just as dialogues are. The very act of doing what the characters are depicted as doing, while saying what they are reported to have said, gives deeper meaning to the words and phrases of the new language, so that later they are more easily recalled in situations where they are appropriate. Starting from the textbook material, students can write short dramatizations, using what they have learned to create variations of the situations for their favorite characters.

Features of Well-Written Dialogues

The interest of students is more readily aroused if situations in dia-logues and material for dramatization involve persons of *a similar age* to that of the students. These young people should be engaged in activities appropriate to their age group in the natural setting of life in a country where the language is spoken. Behavior as well as language should be *authentic and contemporary,* so that students can identify with the characters and be willing to enter into the roles they are enacting.

Writers of dialogues or informal introductory material for language learning should ensure that students understand the *situational con-text* (the place, the time of day, the type of activity involved), the *relationships* among the characters (approximate age, sex, occupa-tions, authority patterns), and the *emotional overtones* of their conversation (friendly, formal, hostile, teasing, reprimanding). All of these factors have an important bearing on the level of language used and the choice of vocabulary. They must be clearly appreciated by the students if they are later to be used appropriately.

Care should also be taken to reintroduce familiar words and phrases frequently to help students with recall. Dialogue sentences are difficult to recall when pronunciation difficulties, unfamiliar words, and structural novelties are concentrated at about the same point. Any two of these coinciding will cause problems for the student. One of the marks of a well-written dialogue is the scattering of these three problem factors in different parts of any sentence that students are to learn thoroughly and be able to use.

Types of Dialogues

The dialogues in textbooks can mostly be classed as conversation-facilitation dialogues or grammar-demonstration dialogues. Some mix the two functions and this usually makes them less useful. Also valuable in the classroom are recreational dialogues, or skits, which the students themselves compose and perform. (Skits will be considered in chapter 8 as examples of spontaneous expression.)

The *conversation-facilitation dialogue* provides students with immediately useful segments of language, with which they can begin to communicate. These should be short and centered around one situational episode. Several short conversation-facilitation dialogues may be included in one unit. Often they are memorized because of the usefulness of the segments. The phrases learned are then used in a number of variations of the situation and with differing lexical content. Frequently, formal memorization as an individual task is unnecessary, because the continual use of the segments in various class activities results in their retention by the students. The segments are then used over and over again in the students' recreational dialogues, in association with new segments from later dialogues, and should eventually reappear spontaneously when the students are engaged in communicating their own messages.

Grammar-demonstration dialogues perform a similar function to that of the conversationally-oriented reading passages with which some textbooks begin. They are carefully seeded with different aspects of a grammatical structure to be studied (e.g., all the persons of the verb in a particular tense; adverbs in various positions in the sentence). They provide the examples in context from which the students will work out the generalizations or rules about structural operation and function. They are usually longer than conversation-facilitation dialogues and may have longer, more involved sentences.

202

Because of the necessity to introduce into the dialogue certain grammatical forms for study, they are often more stilted and artificial in their development.

Since grammar-demonstration dialogues are to be used ultimately for grammatical study, there is no great gain for students in memorizing these dialogues. Actually, because of their length and complications, such memorization becomes a tedious chore, and the memorized dialogue is easily forgotten when the student undertakes the memorization of the next one. Inductive option 1 (p. 194) explains the usual procedure for exploiting a grammar-demonstration dialogue.

If the grammatically seeded dialogue also contains useful conversational expressions, exclamations, and everyday greetings, the teacher would be well advised to extract these from the longer dialogue and write short conversation-facilitation dialogues using this material, which students will then learn thoroughly and use actively.

Learning the Conversation-Facilitation Dialogue
Since conversation-facilitation dialogues are written to provide useful material for student-to-student communication in the first few weeks, they are often memorized. Students then use the greetings, exclamations, simple conversational clichés, and situationally useful sentences to improvise other scenes similar to that in the dialogue they have learned.

Certain techniques have been evolved for the memorization of short dialogues in the classroom,[12] where the teacher serves as a model for pronunciation, intonation, and other prosodic features. (It is inadvisable in the early stages for students to memorize dialogues on their own, without a teacher or tape model.)

The dialogue is first acted out in the native language or through mime, with visual aids such as flash cards or stick figures drawn on the chalkboard; this sets the students thinking along the right lines. During the memorization which is to follow, a native-language version of the dialogue is sometimes available to the students, either in their textbooks or posted for them to see. This native-language version is in contemporary language the students would use, giving idiomatic equivalents for whole phrases rather than presenting a stilted attempt at equivalence for words in the foreign language. If the native language is being avoided in the teaching, the stick-figure version is kept in view to help the students with meaning.

12. The techniques described in this section are set out in considerable detail in Patricia O'Connor, *Modern Foreign Languages in High School: Pre-Reading Instruction* Washington, D.C., 1960).

The dialogue is next presented in the foreign language several times with the same visual aids, so that the situation becomes quite clear to the students. Now comes the task of memorization of the dialogue sentences. A dialogue for memorization should be short, consisting usually of three or four exchanges between the characters. Each of these utterances is memorized by the students, by mimicking the teacher, until a point of accurate reproduction is attained. Each utterance is presented orally by the teacher, who repeats it several times clearly and distinctly at a normal conversational speed, and with correct intonation, usually from different parts of the room. This is the recognition stage, when students concentrate on distinguishing the patterning in the stream of sound. After the students have had the opportunity of hearing the sentence several times, they are invited to imitate what they have heard. Each utterance in the dialogue should be short, since otherwise students have difficulty in remembering all the sounds in the correct order.

As students imitate the teacher's rendering of the utterance they try to memorize it. Some teachers employ at this stage a technique called the *backward buildup:* the sentence is divided into meaningful segments (two or three, depending on the structure of the utterance). The students repeat the last segment several times with correct end-of-phrase intonation, then they repeat the second-last segment with the last segment, and finally they repeat the whole sentence. This technique is justified by its advocates on several grounds: The student memorizing the utterance moves from the unfamiliar to the familiar and, for this reason, does not falter before reaching the end of the phrase; since each practice carries the student through to the end of the utterance, the appropriate intonation pattern is retained throughout. Some teachers object to the backward buildup, maintaining that students are not practicing language at each step in an immediately usable form. Later they will need to repeat it from beginning to end, and not with final segments isolated. Since the students have practiced the last segment most frequently, it is this segment that they will recall most vividly, yet this is not the segment they will need in order to produce the utterance promptly when required. The forward movement of an utterance also provides cues for succeeding features. These objections can be met if the utterance is broken into segments which would still be meaningful in another context, and if the complete utterance is well practiced in its normal sequence after the early processes of memorization.

The memorization of the dialogue can proceed from choral repetition (by the whole class) to group repetition (by halves of the class and then by rows). If the smaller groups falter, the teacher returns to large group and full choral repetition, testing progress in memorization by a return to small-group repetition. As the small groups become more accurate and ready in response, the teacher calls on individuals to recite. It is at this point that the teacher discovers the real stage of memorization which has been reached by the majority of the students, since chorus repetition disguises many weaknesses and inaccuracies in the undifferentiated torrent of sound. When several individuals falter, as they will at first, the teacher returns to group repetition, drilling the weaknesses which have been uncovered. The process continues in this way until the majority of the students in the class can demonstrate a near-perfect knowledge of the utterance. The teacher then takes up the next utterance, teaching it in a similar fashion and linking it frequently in repetition with the preceding utterance.

If this learning work is not to be mere parroting, the teacher must make sure at frequent intervals that the students are well aware of the meaning of what they are saying. This becomes easier when several utterances have been memorized, because the learning procedure can now include an interchange of question and answer or statement and rejoinder. This interchange takes place at first between teacher and class, then between large groups, between small groups, and finally between individuals. The teacher takes care to see that roles are frequently reversed, so that all sections of the class have the opportunity to ask the question as well as answer it, to make the statement as well as give the rejoinder.

As soon as a segment of dialogue is learned well enough, students are given the opportunity to use it in near-spontaneous situations, where they enter into a conversational interchange with a classmate. This interchange can take the form of *directed dialogue,* where the teacher suggests that a student should ask a classmate a particular question and that the classmate should respond in a particular fashion. Directions for this type of exchange are sometimes given in the native language to ensure that students are fully aware of the meaning of the conversation that is to take place. When the directions are given in the target language, students will need practice in the technique of directed dialogue before they are able to listen to a direction in one person of the verb and, turning to their classmate, use another person of the verb. They are being asked to perform a transformation which is particularly difficult in languages where the verbal inflection changes from person to person.

When students have acquired a considerable number of basic utterances, they may enjoy *chain dialogue.* In this procedure, one student asks a neighbor a question, the neighbor replies and then immediately asks a question of the next student in the row. This activity gives students an opportunity to practice sentences from a number of dialogues in a relaxing, yet slightly competitive, atmosphere similar to that of a game. When one chain peters out, another may be started in a different part of the class. If conducted at a smart pace, with frequent changes of direction, chain dialogue can provide valuable practice without boredom.

Caveats about Dialogues

Dialogue sentences will soon be forgotten, and their usefulness will prove to be very limited, unless frequent opportunities are taken to reintroduce and practice utterances from earlier lessons. Students will readily reproduce these utterances with ones they are currently learning if they are encouraged to do so from the beginning. They will take pleasure in showing how many expressions they can use when they are given opportunities to try to communicate spontaneously with each other. The sentences they have learned also provide material for exercises on various structural features and combinations of features and, at a later date, for oral reports in class and for practice in reading and writing. Techniques for developing these skills are outlined in chapters 9 and 10.

The teacher must look upon the utterances in dialogues as foundational sentence types and gradually train the students to use them, with variations, for more and more situations outside those of the dialogue sequence. Teachers who are satisfied with glib repetition of sentences, with fine accuracy and an apparent apprehension of appropriateness of context, may well experience considerable disappointment after some months. Students who, to their delight, have performed very well in class exercises may prove incapable of putting their knowledge to use in actual comprehension and communication, divorced from the sequence in which the utterances were learned. Mere learning of dialogue sentences can never be an aim in itself. As a technique, it is justified only when it provides students with a ready supply of language elements for use in communication.

- **Write a conversation-facilitation dialogue for the language you will teach; then write two or three variations of it, using approximately the same material.**

THE AUDIO-VISUAL APPROACH

Some teachers firmly advocate the use of some form of visual aid in teaching speaking, especially in the early stages. Where the visual element is accompanied by recorded voices, the term "audio-visual" has come to be used. "Audio-visual" is not synonymous with "audio-lingual." Some audio-visual materials are constructed according to the principles of the audio-lingual method, the dialogues being learned in association with pictures. Other materials are derived from the direct method. Still others bear no relationship to either method. Audio-visual materials are now being used with computer-assisted instruction also.

In its simplest form, the audio-visual approach has been employed for many years in classrooms where objects, pictures, actions, and gestures have been systematically used with aural-oral work to illustrate meaning, as in direct method teaching. With the easy availability of filmstrips, slides, films, and video and audio tapes, it is now possible to bring into the classroom a more vivid representation of the foreign culture than the teacher was able to do with pictures and objects.

Advocates of an audio-visual approach believe that the picture associated with the recorded voice eliminates the need to use the native language, because a direct bond is established for the student between meaning, as demonstrated in the image, and the foreign-language utterance. The intention is to train the students to think in the foreign language from the first lessons. The need for a script is eliminated, because the spoken words become associated with the picture stimulus, which can then be used to evoke the sequence of utterances. In this way the strain on the auditory memory is less than with a purely aural presentation with oral practice. With the elimination of the script, certain problems of native-language interference in pronunciation, arising from similarities in appearance of words, are avoided, at least in the early stages.

Student motivation is also considered to be a strong factor in favor of the audio-visual approach. Young people today are accustomed to looking and listening for long periods. With well constructed pictures or films, they find language classes more interesting and enjoyable. When they see the situations for which the phrases they are learning are appropriate, they feel they are learning something which is useful and practical. As they associate phrases with people and incidents in the pictures, rather than learning them as abstractions, they realize that these utterances serve real purposes.

The picture, with accompanying voice, has a greater sensory impact than lines on a printed page, or even than that of the voice alone. With films particularly, the student can also see the gestures and facial expressions which play an essential role in clarifying that part of the meaning which is conveyed by intonation and tone of voice. Through observation of the personal relationships portrayed, the student also acquires some understanding of the register or level of language for which particular utterances are appropriate. The attention of the students is kept focused on the picture, so that all the members of the class are concentrating on the same thing at the same time. This centering of attention is particularly helpful for weaker students, who, in a reading-writing or even in a purely aural-oral situation, frequently find their minds wandering to other things than the point on which the teacher is concentrating.

As well as the advantages outlined, the audio-visual approach maintains the specific advantages of aural-oral work. The students hear the language continually and speak it often. They hear the sounds of the language from the first lesson in meaningful sequences with the appropriate intonation patterns and, as they concentrate on situation and meaning, they begin to pronounce and speak without self-consciousness.

Audio-visual materials available commercially do not always meet this fine ideal. They are not necessarily the asset for teaching they should be. They should be examined carefully before being adopted for class use. If the extra expense and effort of using equipment is to be justified, picture and tape must be fully integrated with the learning material in the text, in such a way that the contribution of the one consolidates that of the other.

An Audio-Visual Lesson with Filmstrips

In this type of lesson, a series of pictures, with accompanying recorded voices, illustrates a short situational episode. This is shown several times to give students the opportunity to absorb image and sound and associate the two. As they watch and listen, the students attempt to deduce the meaning of what they are hearing.

Next, students repeat utterances after the recorded voice while watching the image. The teacher may point to sections of the picture in order to make the meaning of certain words and groups of words clear. After the utterances on several frames (forming a meaningful sequence) have been learned, the students are tested by being asked to respond to alternate frames in response to the voice, and finally to respond to the visual images only. At this stage, the roles in the dialogue may be taken by parts of the class. If the students falter in their reproduction of the dialogue, the teacher returns to the filmstrip and gives the students further practice. After the students have shown their command of the learning material in the unit, they are asked to demonstrate their understanding and control of it by using utterances in communication situations within the class group. They are rapidly drawn into using variations of these utterances to reflect their own experiences and relationships.

Since the situations depicted are intentionally of a type the students themselves might experience, the language learned in this way is immediately useful in these early attempts at personal communication. It is at this point that any misconceptions the students may have acquired about the actual meaning of what they have been learning become apparent. When students are working with pictures continually before them, it is sometimes difficult for the teacher to be sure that they are not merely producing responses they have associated with a certain visual stimulus without being aware of the exact meaning of what they are hearing or saying. Sometimes the situation in an image could be associated with several closely related responses, and the students are not sure which of these is intended. When students are endeavoring to communicate with others, or to make a meaningful response to what the others have said to them, they are forced to establish for themselves a clear interpretation of each group of language sounds, and the teacher has the opportunity to direct and guide them where their interpretation is faulty.

Immediate application is not the final learning stage with audio-visual materials. Even strongly associated aural and visual impressions weaken when the student leaves the classroom. This is especially true of the student with a poor auditory memory. In the method as described, students do not have access to a script to refresh their memory when they are trying to rehearse to themselves what they have been learning.[13] For these reasons, material must be reintroduced in class activity and repracticed regularly until it is obvious that the students have assimilated it completely.

Selection of Materials

There are other factors of importance in evaluating audio-visual materials, apart from the principles basic to their design. The *quality* of the visual image and of the reproduction of the recorded voices will affect the efficiency of the learning.

In evaluating the acceptability of the audio-visual aids offered with courses for school use, the teacher must consider the degree to which the images convey the actual message contained in the utterances. In many audio-visual materials, *sketches* are used rather than photographs. In drawing a sketch, the artist can pay particular attention to the production of a clear, unambiguous outline which does not contain details likely to distract the attention of the learner from the meaning of the utterances with which it will be associated.

13. The question of the value of withholding the script of what is being learned orally, especially in the early stages, is discussed at some length in Rivers (1964), chapter 10.

Sometimes the artist will attempt to indicate meaning by using certain symbols. An interrogation mark may be used to show that a question is being asked, or that the speaker is puzzled, or an exclamation mark may indicate astonishment. Facial expressions depicted help the student to interpret the symbols. The artist may place a balloon over the head of a person in the picture in order to show what he or she is dreaming or thinking. A symbolic representation may be devised to make apparent the sequence of events in time. Since the impact of the visual image is strong, it is essential that the meaning the student absorbs from the image be the one that was intended by the writer of the materials. Unfortunately this is not always the case, and the symbols may mislead the students. Teachers should remember, with audio-visual materials, that wrong impressions of this kind are all the more difficult to eradicate because of the greater sensory impact. They should at all times verify that the correct significance has been extracted by the students.

For a successful audio-visual presentation, the picture must be pleasant in line and coloring, with details which will not make it appear old-fashioned with the passage of time. Ultrafashionable hemlines, hairstyles, and vehicles are traps in this regard. Care must also be taken not to make the pictures too obviously humorous, since jokes wear very thin after their initial presentation. Unintentional humor in the drawings can also make the pictures seem ridiculous.

Materials designed to accompany the learning of common situational phrases often contain cultural elements which introduce the student to the ways of behavior and the social attitudes of the people who speak the language. In an attempt at simplicity, a picture may tend toward caricature, thus reinforcing stereotypes of the speakers of the language which the students may already hold or arousing new prejudices.

Audio-visual course materials have, in the past, concentrated on the establishing of basic structural and lexical knowledge. This is partly because of the limitations of the medium. It is difficult to convey by image and voice alone certain relations of opposition, concession, condition, and the like. Illustration cannot always make clear the use of certain function words. The range of language patterns which may be communicated directly by means of an image, without explanation, is to some extent restricted, although the degree of restriction may vary from language to language. For these reasons, images on filmstrips for teaching new language are most useful in the early stages.

Films

Sometimes the visual material used in class is a film of the situation in which a dialogue takes place. Here students can identify with the persons depicted, in a living experience in the other culture, and hear and observe the total response, with facial expressions, gestures, hesitations, and pauses. This type of presentation is useful for language teaching at the elementary stage so long as the film is not so cluttered with background material of cultural interest (places, ways of dressing and reacting, the objects associated with daily life) that the actual dialogue becomes of secondary interest to the students. Films for early language teaching should be specially made to concentrate attention on language of a level accessible to the elementary-level student.

At the intermediate and advanced levels, films become more important. They give a vivid representation of the life of the people and the places where they live, thus providing much useful information as a background to reading and as a basis for oral discussion. They are very useful for practice in listening comprehension. As they watch a film, all students can be fully immersed in the language for an hour or two.

Films can provoke thoughtful analysis of the culture of the speakers of the language, raising interesting questions about relations between people of different social classes, age groups, sexes, and races. Students see people from city and country at work and play and in their homes. As people interact, absorbed in what they are doing, body language and gestures which may seem artificial if discussed and taught in isolation are seen in their natural setting as communicators of meaning among native speakers. Eventually, films will be studied at the advanced level for their intrinsic interest as a form of artistic expression.

Tapes

Mention has been made of the importance of the *audial quality* of the accompanying tapes. A checklist of desirable features to look for when choosing tapes is included in chapter 13. In addition to these features, tapes to accompany filmstrips or slides should contain signals to indicate to teachers when they should turn to the next frame, so that there may be no confusion during a class lesson. Pauses should be carefully planned so that neither teacher nor class is misled into believing that the utterance associated with a particular frame has been completed, when only half of it has been given. The most useful materials are those in which the tape is synchronized with the projector, so that a new frame is introduced automatically at the right moment.

Problems with Audio-Visual Materials

Audio-visual materials, useful as they are, have potential disadvantages. Materials and equipment may prove to be costly. Teachers need training in the use of the necessary equipment and, if the equipment is not synchronized, in passing smoothly from the operation of one piece of equipment to another. Where the teacher is not proficient in such operations, disrupting breakdowns may occur. As a result, the operation of projector and recorder may demand of the teacher an undue expenditure of time and effort, which will reduce the value of the learning experience for the class.

Where a school is unable to spend money freely, available projectors and recorders must serve a number of purposes, often having to be booked well in advance and transported from classroom to classroom. This can become even more of a problem when parallel classes, and classes at more than one level, wish to use audio-visual materials as part of their normal program. If audio-visual materials are adopted as the basis of instruction, the language teachers must take steps to ensure that at least one set of equipment is available for their exclusive use, housed, if possible, in a room in which the language classes will be regularly scheduled. The audio-visual language room should not be a language laboratory with individual booths, however, or the teacher will find it very difficult to promote real interaction among the members of the class. A language classroom must provide possibilities for breaking the class up into small groups, for acting out scenes, for students to see and talk to each other.

The language laboratory serves a different purpose from the language classroom. It is most useful for intensive individual practice and listening comprehension. When audio-visual materials are used in the laboratory, it is important that the screen be so placed as to be clearly visible to all students. In many modern laboratories, the visual material is projected by closed circuit television or from videotape onto individual screens in the booths, and students listen individually with headphones. In the latter case, the students feel more immediately involved with the situation.

All audio-visual lessons must be carefully planned to ensure that the additional sensory elements are exploited to the full, with proper preparation and follow-up activities. Of themselves, however, equipment and well-designed materials will not ensure effective language lessons. Of much more importance is the imagination and energy of the teacher who is using the materials, so that there is variety and interesting classroom activity. The visual element should be considered an aid in the learning process and not an end in itself. The success of the audio-visual course will be demonstrated in the ability of students to use in free communication with each other what they have learned in close association with the visual image.

Areas of Controversy

Is dialogue learning too mechanical, leading only to parrot learning of phrases which the student cannot apply in other situations?
This common criticism of dialogue learning is certainly applicable when its techniques are employed without clear understanding of the reasons why dialogues are being used and what this type of learning is expected to achieve. Students will learn phrases by heart and recite them with acceptable articulation and intonation, without any clear idea of what they are saying, and as readily forget them while they embark on the learning of a new series. In these circumstances dialogue learning is a piecemeal, time-consuming, futile activity. If the method is to achieve its objective of enabling students to use freely the most common forms of expression of the language to convey their own meaning, the students must be continually kept aware of the import of what they are repeating. The most impressive dialogue-learning lessons, where memorization proceeds smartly under the direction of a competent drillmaster, may be the least effective. Students are allowed to sink into a repetition mood where prompt echoing is all that is required of them. This they can do without great effort, while their minds are elsewhere. A few keen students set the pace for the rest. It is often after a lesson of this type that the most disappointing results are seen at the stage of individual exchange.

An examination of the techniques of dialogue presentation employed in such cases usually reveals little attention to meaning during the learning phase. Since many of the students have been reciting only sequences of sound combinations, they cannot put these to use outside the dialogue framework. To avoid such a situation, the teacher must ensure that students have a clear idea of what the dialogue is about before they begin to work with it. This can be achieved, as has been suggested in this chapter, by a native-language presentation or miming of the dialogue, with situational props to make it more vivid. If the same situational props and visual aids are used then for presenting the dialogue in the new language, students will associate the various phrases with the meaning sequence they apprehended in the earlier presentation. In an audio-visual presentation, a group of frames or scenes forming a coherent segment should be projected several times at the beginning so that the students may become aware of the situation and the import of the individual utterances.

To ensure that students are continually aware of the meaning of successive utterances, the teacher may refer from time to time to a native-language version or to sketches with stick figures discreetly posted so that they can be seen by all members of the class. Occasionally the teacher may check whether the members of the class realize which part of the conversational interchange they are practicing and, when the utterances are clearly segmented, the meaning of particular segments within an utterance. Where some segments are familiar from earlier units, these should be used as a guide to the meaning of the whole utterance. This does not mean that teachers should give word-for-word translations of what is being learned, nor that they should require students continually to translate what they are learning. For an initial period, students may not be conscious of the specific meaning of every element in an utterance (this will come later with wider knowledge), but they will understand the overall meaning of the various segments of the utterance and their function in communication. Finally, as soon as a useful section of the dialogue is well known, students must be encouraged to use it in actual situations involving communication of meaning to another person.

Further flexibility in the use of learned phrases will be developed if students are encouraged to try them out in variations of the dialogue situation which force them to think about what they are saying. These variations may require, for instance, changes of persons of the verb, changes from singular to plural, changes in relationships, or a slightly different vocabulary to create a new situation. The action or discussion may move from the street to the supermarket or to the football field and still be substantially the same. Students then improvise their own situations, using what they have been learning.

Memory for the phrases learned in dialogues will be consolidated if these phrases are continually reintroduced in later lessons and not allowed to slip into disuse like so much useless impedimenta.

Is the dialogue method or the direct method preferable as an introduction to the study of a new language?
Some teachers find dialogue learning too mechanical and fail to see what advantage it has over a direct-method approach of oral learning of phrases, with variations, connected with the activities of the classroom. Direct-method learning is active and vocal. The students hear the new language all the time and endeavor to use it from the beginning in a context where it has meaning.

Several objections to the direct-method approach are raised by the supporters of the dialogue method. The first objection is that the classroom is too limited an arena for language practice. With dialogues, the students move in imagination and dramatized activity out of the confines of pen and paper and chalkboard into situations similar to those they will meet on leaving the classroom. The language becomes less of a "school" matter and is seen as appropriate to many aspects of social life. The second objection that has been raised is that in a natural development of discussion around activities and incidents in the classroom it is difficult to keep the language used by the teacher within the confines of a limited number of structures. The variety of the phrases which spring naturally to the lips of the fluent teacher (and the direct-method teacher needs to be fluent in the language) become confusing for the student. With a variety of phrases and alternatives at their disposal, it is maintained, the students do not practice any of them thoroughly.

With the dialogue method, the teacher and students keep within materials which have been carefully prepared to promote a steady growth in control of language structure and from which confusing alternatives have been eliminated. The less fluent teacher can work within such material and learn with the students. The students get thorough practice in everything they learn, hearing the correct version from the teacher or tape model and practicing afresh when they make mistakes. The transition to reading is effected more easily than with the direct method because the structuring of the materials makes it clear which structures should appear first in reading matter. The limitations on the amount of language material contained in the dialogues also makes transition to writing more feasible than in the more amorphous situation of the direct method. On the other hand, this tight structuring and control can lead to bewilderment when the audio-lingual student discovers that outside of the classroom, or at more advanced levels, people express these meanings in a variety of ways— a discovery that the direct-method student made at the beginning.

The attitude toward errors differs also in the two approaches. The advocate of the dialogue method, at least in its audio-lingual phase, tries to structure the situation so that students will not make mistakes. Even while practicing communication, students try to keep to expressions and structures they know well. When mistakes are made, students are given the correct version as soon as possible so that mistakes will not become ingrained. In the direct method, on the other hand, the teacher tries to encourage the efforts of the students to communicate by not correcting them every time they make a mistake. As a result, the students are uninhibited in their flow of language.

Clearly the advocates of the dialogue method value accuracy while the direct-methodists value fluency and confidence. The former prefer a structured progression while the latter seek whatever material will attract and keep the attention of the students. Since there is so much to be learned at the beginning, one can enter into the material at many different points and organize it in many different ways.

this all applies to L.C.

Wilkins labels these two approaches *synthetic* and *analytic* (Wilkins 1976, pp. 1–2). The synthetic approach breaks the global language down into an inventory of grammatical structures, presented progressively, and a limited number of lexical items. In the analytic approach "much greater variety of linguistic structure is permitted from the beginning and the learner's task is to approximate his own linguistic behaviour more and more closely to the global language" (ibid., p. 2).

Both approaches have a long and honorable history. With either, success will depend on the imagination and resourcefulness of the teacher in conveying a feeling of reality and in arousing and maintaining the enthusiasm of the students for the activities proposed.

Should dialogues be designed so as to provide the first introduction of structures to be drilled?

It has been customary in introductory textbooks for passages for reading to contain examples of the grammatical structures to be studied in that particular unit. In many textbooks which begin with dialogues, the same practice is followed, so that the students have a certain familiarity with a grammatical pattern before practicing its use and studying the circumstances of its occurrence.

Some writers of textbooks, however, have decided against this common practice. They feel that it requires the adoption of one of two positions, both of which are unsatisfactory. The writer may, on the one hand, distort the natural development of a dialogue in order to introduce all the structural examples the students need to see in preparation for their grammatical study. On the other hand, a dialogue situation may dictate the order in which grammatical structures are to be studied and produce a haphazard, piecemeal sequence of topics in which the students cannot recognize grammatical relationships.

Some textbook writers use dialogues purely for rapid teaching of conversational phrases. Marty maintains that the principal value of dialogues is motivational: they give students an early sense of achievement and great satisfaction in being able to express themselves fluently and acceptably in everyday situations. Side by side with a course in dialogue learning he advocates a systematic study of the structure of the language, organized in a logical progression.[14]

In this regard, we may look at the objectives of the course and the age of the students. Late-adolescent and adult students have been trained to seek order in their studies and may feel the need for materials which clearly serve specific purposes. On the other hand, younger students, with less clear goals, need integrated material which can act as a basis for a variety of activities interwoven into the one lesson. The material to be taught first, for these students, should be chosen for its adaptability to active classroom practice. Certain persons of the verb may be of more interest in such a situation than others; certain tenses or aspects may be indispensable for communication, even though they have traditionally been reserved for teaching later in the course. Similarly, older students in a communication-oriented course will profit from less emphasis on structure and more emphasis on practice in realistic linguistic exchanges, thus acquiring confidence and fluency in expression.

Distortion of dialogues may be avoided by teaching the most immediately useful aspects of a grammatical feature without trying to include every possible example of its use in the dialogue, or even in the unit. At a later stage, when students have acquired a considerable knowledge of the features of the language and are more mature, areas of grammatical interest may be studied in detail as part of a systematic presentation of the structure of the language.

Annotated Reading List

Carroll, John B. *Language and Thought.* Foundations of Modern Psychology series. Englewood Cliffs, N.J.: Prentice-Hall, 1964. Chapters 1, 2, and 4 give a concise picture of the nature and function of language and the production and understanding of speech.

Rivers, Wilga M., et al. *Practical Guides.* Chapter 1, "Structured Interaction," gives examples of the different types of dialogues and dialogue-related activities for specific languages and propose many ways of exploiting the dialogue in class.

Rivers, Wilga M. "From Linguistic Competence to Communicative Competence," in *SMT,* pp. 36–48. Discusses ways of bridging the gap from skill getting to skill using.

Paulston, Christina B., and Bruder, Mary N. *Teaching English as a Second Language: Techniques and Procedures.* Cambridge, Mass.:

14. F. Marty, *Linguistics Applied to the Beginning French Course* (Roanoke, Va.: Audio-Visual Publications, 1963), p. vi.

Winthrop, 1976. Section 1, "Grammar," deals with mechanical, meaningful, and communication drills, and how to use them in class.

Allen, Edward D., and Valette, Rebecca M. *Classroom Techniques: Foreign Languages and English as a Second Language.* New York: Harcourt Brace Jovanovich, 1977. Chapters 5, 6, and 9, "Teaching Grammar: General Procedures," "Teaching Grammar: Techniques Arranged by Grammatical Categories," and "Speaking," describe with examples many activities which are useful for forging the instrument.

Maley, Alan, and Duff, Alan. *Drama Techniques in Language Learning.* Cambridge: Cambridge University Press, 1978. Describes many dramatic activities which give students the opportunity to use their own personality in imaginative ways in association with others, thus creating the material on which part of the language class is to be based.

*Learners' Strategies

Naiman, N.; Fröhlich, M.; Stern, H. H.; and Todesco, A. *The Good Language Learner.* Research in Education Series, vol. 7. Toronto: Ontario Institute for Studies in Education, 1978. Provides case studies of successful language learners and an investigation into the critical variables which distinguish good language learners in a formal second-language learning situation.

Research and Discussion

1. Record a short informal chat with a friend in your native language. Transcribe it word for word, pause for pause, and extra syllable for extra syllable. (This is a demanding and time-consuming process, if you are to record it exactly as spoken.) Make a list of features of the spoken output that you have observed.

2. Record a short informal chat in the language you will teach with a native speaker of that language. Transcribe it word for word, pause for pause, and extra syllable for extra syllable. Make a list of features of the spoken output of the native speaker. Listen again to the recording. What are the most striking differences between your spoken output and that of the native speaker?

3. Study the Shannon and Weaver communication system model and the Carroll organismic communication model on p. 184. Think carefully about each segment and list under each segment all the disciplines from which one would need to draw to fully understand its role (e.g., physics, acoustics, depth psychology, sociology, pho-

netics). Discuss your conclusions with others in the class and add to your list.

4. Study Appendix B, the "Adult Learner's Daily Diary." Make a list of things important for language teaching which it drew to your attention. What aspects of your own language learning experience did this diary recall to you? Can you now add to your list of things to be aware of in teaching?

*5. What language learning strategies are discussed in the literature in the field? Can you add others you have observed or which you have employed? Observe a class for several days, talk with the students and the teacher, and look at some written work. (Monitor a language laboratory session if this is possible.) Do you now have any strategies to add to your list or any changes to make in what you had already noted?

6. Take a modern play in the language you will teach or a modern novel with a great deal of conversation. Study the levels of language used in relation to situations and participants.

7. Which aspects of the grammar of the language you will teach did you find most difficult to learn to use correctly and effortlessly? Which of the inductive or deductive options in this chapter would be, in your opinion, the most productive for teaching each of these aspects of the language? Why?

8. Take two widely used textbooks which employ the dialogue approach. For how many units do they use dialogues? How many weeks of study would this normally represent? (Consult the Preface or Instructor's Manual.) Examine the way the dialogues are written and the application activities proposed in relation to the criteria in this chapter. How do they measure up? What improvements would you propose? Which book would you now prefer to use?

9. Find a textbook in which the author has produced a dialogue which mixes grammar-demonstration and conversation-facilitation material. Write one or two conversation-facilitation dialogues with material extracted from it. Rearrange the remaining material as a dialogue demonstrating one aspect of grammatical structure.

*10. The French developed a *méthode audio-visuelle* at CREDIF (Centre de recherche et d'étude pour la diffusion internationale du français) in Paris. What materials came from this project? For what levels of instruction? What were the principles on which the *méthode audio-visuelle* was based? Try to find some schools or individual teachers who have used this method and report their impressions of the effectiveness of the materials.[15]

15. You will find reports by some teachers in professional journals. Detailed information about the method can be found in D. Girard, *Les Langues vivantes* (Paris: Larousse, 1974); also published in English as *Linguistics and Language Teaching* (London: Longman, 1972).

For the original statement of the principles and practice of the CREDIF *méthode audio-visuelle* and its relationship to research on *le français fondamental,* see CREDIF, *Voix et images de France. Livre du Maître* (Paris: Didier, 1962) and the Supplement to *Teaching with Voix et images de France,* part 1, prepared by the staff of the Center for Curriculum Development (Philadelphia: Chilton Books, 1963). The method was developed by P. Guberina and P. Rivenc.

8· The Speaking Skill: Expressing Personal Meaning

The forging of the instrument is not enough to prepare students for acts of communication in the foreign or second language; they also need much practice in its use. They may have some knowledge of the code, but they have to develop facility and fluency in encoding their own meaning. The ideal way for them to develop the speaking skill to the fullest is to live for a period among the people who speak the language. They are then forced to use what they know to supply their physical and emotional needs, that is, in genuine communication. For many students this is not possible. In a foreign-language situation, even casual contact with native speakers may be rare.

We can, however, impart to our students in the classroom basic attitudes and foundational skills upon which they can build rapidly when the opportunity for personal communication in real-life situations presents itself. They will be greatly hindered in their progress if the teaching they receive forces them into a translating frame of mind, where they seek one-to-one equivalences between the foreign language and their native language for everything they wish to say. Furthermore, overtraining in the use of language patterns, to a point of inflexibility, will leave them unprepared for the constant variation in selection of linguistic means which is essential for the expression of their own purposes. If the teacher is to facilitate rather than impede the student's progress in communication, the nature of the speaking skill must be taken into account, as well as the psychological factors involved in its use.

AN ACT OF COMMUNICATION

We have already discussed the hierarchical nature of speech and the fact that the form of an utterance is dependent on the communication situation (see pp. 190–91). In an act of communication we are influenced by environmental cues as well as by our own intentions. We have certain expectations as to the response of the person to whom we are addressing the message; some of these expectations are culturally based. We frame our message and select the linguistic elements to express it so as to arouse in the receiver the meaning we are trying to convey. Thus we express the same message with different elements if we are addressing it to a child, an intimate friend, a person in authority, or a stranger. We select different elements when the receiver is sympathetic from those we would select for a hostile listener or one who needed to be persuaded.

In speaking, we are not conveying to the receiver a meaning clothed in words, but by our words we are arousing within the receiver associations and expectations which will enable that person to form an interpretation of the intention of our message. If we do not choose our words carefully, and if our anticipation of the reaction of the receiver has been ill founded, the message decoded may be quite different from the message we intended to convey. This is a frequent occurrence in native-language communication. If there are two receivers of the message, they may decode two different messages from the same signal. Misinterpretation is even more likely to occur when the speaker is using a non-native language for communication with a native speaker of that language. The cultural associations of the linguistic items,[1] and of the accompanying prosodic, paralinguistic, and kinesic elements (intonation, stress, tone of voice, facial movements, gestures), may be quite different for listener and speaker.

By the combination of elements in the utterance we convey our attitude to the basic message (whether we are simply giving information, for instance, or being humorous, ironical, disapproving, cautious, and so on). Feedback from the listener (facial expressions, tension, interruptions) gives us indications of the meaning being extracted. As a result, we may adapt the message in mid-utterance (we may change the form of the basic framework; we may expand, we may omit sections we had intended to include, we may repeat, emphasize, or modify) in order to arouse the kind of reaction we are seeking. As the emitters of a message, we may be reacting to a previous message. In this case, the form and choice of items in our message may be to a large extent predetermined by what we have just heard. Nevertheless, we proceed to adjust and readjust according to the reaction of the listener.

Nida maintains that receivers of messages are often encoding parallel messages as they listen. They are choosing from alternatives the meaning they think the emitter is trying to convey. This, Nida says, is shown by the fact that when the speaker pauses, listeners often supply what they consider to be the appropriate words.[2] Sometimes their choice is accepted by the speaker. Sometimes it is rejected, thus demonstrating that the meanings being aroused in the receiver are not those that the emitter intended. The difficulties of conveying the mes-

1. The cultural context is discussed in chapter 11.
2. E. A. Nida, *Toward a Science of Translating* (Leiden: E. J. Brill, 1964), pp. 122–23.

sage are compounded when either emitter or receiver, or both, are using a language they do not know very well.

Not every act of communication involves a rapid-fire exchange. There are hesitations, cliché expressions which fill the pauses, much repetition, and frequent indefiniteness as the speaker seeks the most suitable combination of elements to express a particular meaning.[3] By contrast, students in formal learning situations are generally expected to respond promptly, accurately, and without hesitation in oral exercises in class or laboratory. Communication of personal meaning, they soon discover, is quite another process. They have to develop skill in recombining elements they are learning into novel utterances, each unique in its final form, and each purposeful and intentional in its construction. This process does not proceed automatically and effortlessly. It usually involves some searching and fumbling, and some pausing to select the desired construction and the most appropriate words to convey the meaning intended. Teachers need to be patient and encouraging while students go through this process, as polite listeners are in a normal act of communication. By expecting completely accurate grammatical forms and sentence structure and thoroughly appropriate choice of lexical items when students are learning to express their own meanings in the new language, teachers are often demanding a higher level of expression in the language class than that achieved in conversation in the native language.

Students will not need to construct in a novel way all the segments they use in their personal utterances. This would make personal expression in any language an arduous process. They recombine elements, with lexical variation appropriate to the circumstances of the utterance. Many commonly used expressions (*last night, in class, despite everything*); subject-verb combinations (*I'll go, he can't*); clichés of conversation (*wouldn't you know it! you're welcome*), and conventional sentence openers and closers (*I just wanted to know, by the way; isn't it? you know*) will come to mind from class practice, dialogue learning, or recent reading. Selected lexical elements will frequently fit into practiced frames (*he's going to Sydney; my aunt's going to Boston*). Features of this type may be considered the foundational supports, scaffolding frames, or cornerstones of personal utterances. Knowing them well allows the speaker time for selection of the really novel elements and for expressive rearrangements, without losing the attention of the listener. They provide a framework for the utterance and fill pauses unobtrusively while the speaker is as-

3. Examples of authentic speech illustrating these features are given for French, German, Spanish, and English in the *PG*'s, chap. 1.

sembling elements essential to the intended meaning. What has been practiced in class and laboratory can prove useful for facilitating spontaneous expression, but ultimately ability to converse in a new language is developed only by frequent practice in conversing in that language. Language use is a process or activity and must be practiced as such.

PSYCHOLOGICAL FACTORS IN COMMUNICATION

Desire to Communicate

Certain psychological factors which enter into interpersonal communication are highly relevant to the process of developing ability to communicate in the target language. Spontaneous verbal expression is not solely the product of knowledge of and skill in using a language code. It presupposes that *the student has something to communicate*. Silent students in the classroom often have "nothing to say" at that moment. The teacher may have introduced a topic which they find uninteresting or about which they know very little, and as a result they have nothing to express, whether in the native language or the language they are learning.

As well as having something to say, the student must have the *desire to communicate* this message to some person or group of persons. Students who find their teacher unsympathetic and their classmates uncongenial may well feel that what they would like to say can be of little interest. Others may be very conscious of their limitations in the new language and feel that, by expressing themselves in it, they are laying themselves open to censure or ridicule. For many reasons like these, students may prefer to remain silent.

Comprehension as Well as Expression

Since conversation is essentially interaction between persons, comprehension plays a role, as well as skill in expression. Students may have acquired skill in expressing themselves in the new language code, but have had little practice in understanding the language when it is spoken at a normal speed of delivery in a conversational situation. They therefore make a noncommittal acknowledgment of the fact that they have been addressed in order to extricate themselves from an awkward situation. Since they have not comprehended sufficient elements in the message to be able to make any further contribution to the discussion, or to be stimulated into meaningful responses, the conversational gambit lapses. In a classroom situation the teacher is then obliged to initiate another possible interactional episode along new lines. Students need much practice in listening to the language before attempting sustained conversation. They also need practice in seizing on the elements of a preceding utterance and incorporating these into their response. This will provide them with the breathing space necessary for the formulation of their own contribution to a continuing verbal exchange. (For instance: *"Where's your cousin?"* *"My cousin? Oh! He's in Germany."*)

Personality Factors

In a class group, the teacher must be alert to recognize personality factors which are affecting participation in discussion in the language. Some students are talkative, others are shy or taciturn. These characteristics affect student performance in the oral part of the lesson. Nida noted among missionaries that the talkative extrovert learned the language faster than the quiet, studious person (Nida 1957, p. 26). Some students are by nature cautious or meticulous; others are unduly sensitive and therefore easily embarrassed or upset if found to be in error or not understood. Students in these categories often prefer to say nothing rather than run the risk of expressing themselves incorrectly, whether in a first or a second language.

Limitations of Expression

In attempting to use the new language to express their own thoughts, students find themselves in an abnormally constricting situation, where their choice of expression is severely limited. At the age at which many of our students are studying a foreign language, they are accustomed to being able to demonstrate orally the maturity of their thought and the breadth of their knowledge. Finding themselves now limited to expressing themselves in childishly simple language, they feel frustrated and exasperated.

Teachers must be aware of this inhibiting factor and conscious of their own advantage of fluent expression in the new medium. They need to show great restraint in their own contributions to the conversation or discussion, patience with the students' attempts to use the new tool, and respect for the fact that, although their students may be limited in their powers of expression in the new language, they are not really the immature persons this limitation might make them appear to be. In the earlier stages the teacher should not expect students to express in the foreign language sophisticated ideas and concepts for which they cannot possibly know the accepted forms of expression and which they cannot be expected to discuss with any degree of refinement within the narrow confines of their foreign-language knowledge. At the early stage, students speak more in the narrative and descriptive vein than in the philosophical or polemical.

225

They ask questions and express their feelings, rather than hypothesize.

Correction of Errors

Psychological experiment has shown that people are more likely to continue a conversation when other people agree than when they disagree.[4] In many societies, cultural patterns have conditioned people to keep their ideas to themselves if expressing them could cause unpleasantness and embarrassment for themselves or for the people with whom they are conversing. The student who is continually corrected by the teacher for every little mistake will withdraw from the unequal contest. A little reflection will make the teacher conscious of the fact that many slips in conversation do not indicate lack of knowledge. Continual correction in areas where the student really knows what should be said can be very irritating, especially as teachers often jump in before students have had time to correct themselves. When the student hesitates long enough to show inability to continue, or has made a mistake in pronunciation or structure which hinders comprehension, or is clearly not conveying the meaning intended, the teacher may supply items or corrections in a low, supportive voice which does not interrupt the flow of thought. The student speaking usually picks up the helpful correction without pausing. These tactful offers of assistance sometimes lead to questions from students, either during or at the end of the session. Such questions should be answered at the time students show interest in them, unless this is clearly going to distract the students' attention from the train of thought or disrupt the activity.

For consistent errors within the group which impede communication (incorrect verb forms or tenses, misuse of the article, pronoun, or other important grammatical features; mispronunciation of phonemes which a native speaker would find unacceptable or misleading), the teacher should make unobtrusive notes. These faults may then be discussed with the whole class as part of a review session a little later on. In this way errors give direction to reteaching and practice. If the errors indicate that individual students clearly require some extra help (as with consistently incorrect production of an important sound or apparently basic misunderstanding of a grammatical concept), these students may be invited to a private session with the

4. W. S. Verplanck, *Journal of Abnormal Social Psychology* 51 (1955): 668–79, quoted in Carroll 1964, p. 46.

teacher.[5] Often a few minutes are reserved at the end of conversation sessions for individual or small group discussions of serious mistakes made consistently.

In view of the emotional and personality factors which are involved in a verbal exchange, expression of personal meaning in a new language can be developed only in a relaxed and friendly atmosphere, where students feel at ease with the teacher and with each other. Material for discussion must be such that the student has something to say, or can make some contribution which will stimulate others to add information or to disagree. Students themselves will raise issues which concern them. The teacher must adopt an encouraging rather than a correcting attitude: assisting the development of the verbal exchanges in such a way that all students are involved at some time, as far as their personalities permit. Above all, the teacher must resist the temptation to dominate the discussion and must tactfully discourage others from doing so. Helping a group to keep discussion open to all and free-flowing is an art the teacher must cultivate.

ACQUIRING BASIC LANGUAGE MATERIAL

Since students need some language material with which to create their own utterances, the early stages of language learning, in most methods, involve much presentation and practicing of new language forms and sequences. Through intensive practice exercises, students become sensitive to interverbal associations and learn to produce correct utterances without having to work out each time how to put the elements together. In these exercises, language elements are learned in their normal sequence in useful utterances, and practice is provided in the rapid construction of various sentence types.

As oral responses are elicited by a variety of cues, the teacher tries to maintain a brisk tempo, so that students will learn to produce language patterns as wholes and not as laborious constructions from basic elements. This type of brisk drill can become an end in itself, and both class and teacher will then be satisfied with the glib production of correct responses in practiced sequences. This type of result can be produced without a great deal of effort and concentration on the part of the students, who soon understand what is required of them. Consequently, some critics of oral drill have maintained that students trained in this fashion emerge unable to conduct even a simple conversation in the target language and are quite at a loss to

5. An interesting discussion of correction in relation to fossilization of errors is found in N. A. Vigil and J. W. Oller, "Rule Fossilization: A Tentative Model," *LL* 26 (1976): 281–95.

understand phrases that are not heard in the exact form in which they were practiced.

The teacher must be continually alert to the danger of developing mechanical responses without the students' being aware of the purpose and function of particular exercises. Theories of transfer of learning[6] suggest that mechanical practice makes a certain skill available only when an identical situation demands its exercise. Situations do arise where language responses are appropriate in the identical form in which they have been practiced in drills, but such occurrences are rare. If learning is to transfer to wider contexts in spontaneous utterances, the student must be conscious of the interrelationships within the structure being practiced, and of the parts of the pattern that have to be manipulated (transformed, substituted, expanded) to achieve specific purposes. They must participate with alert understanding, and with full awareness of the crucial element in the pattern which is undergoing modification as the drill proceeds. In this way they will be more likely to understand what kinds of meanings are created by variation of each element, and thus realize how these may be used for the expression of their own intentions. "It is what the mind is *doing* during language-learning activities that will determine what is stored, in what form, and whether it is retrievable and usable in new contexts."[7]

FROM STRUCTURED PRACTICE TO SPONTANEOUS EXPRESSION

Awareness of the intention of practice exercises is only one small step in the direction of facility in communicative expression. The next and most important step is the opportunity for students to demonstrate that they can use the structure they have been practicing in situations where they are engaged in communication with others.

In the early stages, members of the class may ask each other questions related to their personal lives. If these questions involve some humor and good-natured teasing, they become less artificial, so that students can concentrate on meaning rather than mere form of utterance. Students may recount events or incidents. They may give short personal commentaries on pictures or objects. They may describe persons and objects which involve the guessing of identity, or of some other element such as occupation or function. A game or competition may be introduced which induces students to produce the desired structure at frequent intervals. In a game, the element of competition

6. Theories of transfer are discussed at length in Rivers 1964, pp. 121–29.

7. W. M. Rivers and B. S. Melvin, "If Only I Could Remember It All! Facts and Fiction about Memory in Language Learning," in Burt, Dulay, and Finocchiaro 1977, p. 165.

and the excitement force out oral expression so that students forget their inhibitions about making mistakes and being embarrassed in front of their fellows. The trainee teacher should begin to make a collection of such games and competitions,[8] noting beside each one the structural pattern and vocabulary area which the students would be practicing during this activity.

Quite early, students can begin to give short oral reports to the class. These may at first be guided by a simple outline which will keep them from trying to make their way too soon in uncharted areas of the language. By the time they begin to develop their own subjects without an outline, their whole experience in the language class should have impressed upon them the importance of trying to incorporate expressions and structures they know well and can handle confidently. This is an orientation which the teacher must continually foster in the early weeks, so that every attempt students make at using the language for their own purposes will be a further occasion for consolidation of basic knowledge and for confident variation within recognized boundaries.

Students may tell in their own words the essence of what they have heard in a listening-comprehension exercise or what they have read. This will not be mere repetition if they are expected to reconstruct the material in some way, telling it from the point of view of a different person or varying the situation in which it was supposed to have occurred. They may attempt to tell a story to the class as they would tell it to a very young child. This is a very useful exercise because it compels students to keep to simple vocabulary and structure, instead of trying to put into the foreign language the complicated expression and structure they would be using in telling stories in their native language. In all such oral work, students should be taught that whenever they are at a loss to express themselves in the new language, they should consciously simplify what they want to say, reducing it to basic patterns with which they are familiar. This is what a foreigner does intuitively when in the language environment. It is also what native speakers do when communicating with inexperienced speakers of their language.

Ingenuity is required in the classroom to create situations of the type the students would encounter in real life outside the classroom: opportunities for them to discuss with each other subjects in which they can be presumed to share an interest; to recount to each other facts and incidents of home, school, and community life; or to com-

8. For ideas, see Crawshaw 1972; Hubp 1974; Schmidt 1974; and Lee 1974. These are adaptable to various languages.

ment on and tease their fellow students about current happenings. Experimentation has shown that listeners remember both surface form and content of utterances much more when they know something of the speaker's expectations, intentions, beliefs, and attitude toward the listener. This is called "interactional content."[9] When the interactional content of foreign-language utterances in the classroom is high, students will retain much more of what their teacher hopes they are learning in conversational practice.

Some have questioned whether situations structured in the classroom can be considered real and actual. To our students who spend a large part of their waking hours in school, classroom situations are as real as any others in their day's experience. Furthermore, they are communicating with individuals with whom they normally communicate in out-of-class activities. Where suitable material is available in the textbook, students will have vocabulary and expressions at their command for the discussion of simple relationships, personal interests and emotions, and everyday activities. Where this is not so, the teacher will have to provide supplementary material before the students will have the means for such interpersonal interaction.

ENCOURAGING EXPRESSION OF PERSONAL MEANING
In chapter 7, we discussed the functions language performs for the user and proposed these as essential in the forging of the instrument (p. 192). In a similar vein, if students are really to be able to communicate, their personal use of the language from the beginning must be purposive. They must be using the new language for the purposes for which they normally use their own language. (In simple terms, as soon as a student asks in the new language for classroom materials he or she needs, the process has begun.) This approach swings the focus in the class from the teacher to the learner. Language teachers must learn how to promote language-using activities in which there is as much student involvement and as little teacher direction as possible.[10]

What are the Normal Purposes of Language in Communication?
We use language for a number of communicative purposes. We greet each other, make polite enquiries, ask conventional questions, express

9. J. M. Keenan, B. MacWhinney, and D. Mayhew, "Pragmatics in Memory: A Study of Natural Conversation," *Journal of Verbal Learning and Verbal Behavior* 16 (1977): 549–60.

10. For a discussion of the progress of the language lesson from teacher-directed practice to student-directed practice, and then to autonomous activity and spontaneous interaction, see Wilga M. Rivers, "From Linguistic Competence to Communicative Competence," chapter 3 of *SMT*, or *TQ* 7 (1973): 25–34.

certain expected reactions (*Oh! I'm so sorry you're not well!*); we make arrangements and change them; we issue invitations; we congratulate; we persuade, promise, discourage, or refuse. We express our feelings;[11] we hide our intentions; we talk our way out of trouble; we talk people into doing things for us; we talk about ourselves and our affairs. We ask for and give information. We seek and give instructions. We talk for hours for the sake of talking, in personal contact or by phone. We discuss ideas and solve problems together. We work out plans and projects. We act out social roles; we entertain others; we show them what we can do. We share celebrations and festivities. We also share memories, experiences, and imaginings. We play with language in games and competitions; we sing and act. We create language.[12]

The criterion for an activity designed to promote spontaneous use of language to express personal meaning is the degree to which it approximates some normal use of language in everyday life. So many language-learning activities have no obvious connection with language use as the student has experienced it. A salutary exercise for a language teacher (or a textbook writer) is to examine learning materials and activities to see how they reflect or require normal uses of language within the classroom community. The result of such an examination is too often surprise and disappointment. The remedy is at the stage of textbook selection (or preparation). Few classroom teachers have the time or experience to rewrite materials. (For guidance in textbook selection, see chapter 14, pp. 475–83).

- **Add to the list in this section any other normal activities that involve the oral use of language.**

CONTEXT AND MEANING

Spontaneous expression does not mean just idle chatter. It means saying appropriately what you want to say in whatever circumstance, even if what you want to say is a conventional greeting, a cliché, or a frequently heard utterance like *Will you open the door, please.* Learners of a new language will need to know how to express their intentions appropriately (that is, comprehensibly) for many purposes. "For many purposes" implies "in many contexts."

There is no meaning without context. There is always a context for language. What we may consider "no context" for language material

11. Moskowitz (1978) provides words and expressions indicating feelings and emotions in English, German, Latin, Spanish, French, Italian, and Hebrew.

12. For a full discussion of these categories of language use, with many suggestions for activities which incorporate them, see chapter 2 of the *PG*'s, or the shorter version, in "Talking Off the Tops of Their Heads," in Rivers, *SMT,* or *TQ* (1972): 71–81.

is itself a context and will affect the interpretation of it. A sound cannot be uttered without an emitter who emits the sound for some reason. A sound cannot be heard without a receiver who will interpret the intentions of the emitter and the circumstances of the emission in some way or other.

The various levels of complexity of any utterance provide context and contribute to the meaning the receiver derives from it. At the phonological level, sounds, intonation, stress, duration will indicate to the listener the educational level of the speaker, geographical origin, emotional or physical state, and communicative intent (persuasion, rebuke, request for information, imposing of authority). At the syntactic level, the relationship of an utterance within a complete discourse or of an element within an utterance has an important bearing on meaning. Selecting a different order of words within an utterance, or of utterances within a discourse, will change this meaning. It is not just at the semantic level that meaning is conveyed, and even here meaning is not as simple as it appears. In the appropriate context, not only linguistic but social, and with the appropriate intonation and tone of voice, *"Don't tell her!"* can mean *"Please do,* but if there's trouble don't drag me into it," or *"Do tell her,* because I won't and someone has to."

THE FUNCTIONAL-NOTIONAL COMMUNICATIVE APPROACH

The central problem of teaching to promote spontaneous expression in a language is knowing in what contexts learners will want or need to express themselves. The next problem is to decide the linguistic resources they will need in order to make appropriate choices to achieve the purposes of their communications. These are problems which have been taken up by the Committee of Out-of-School Education and Cultural Development of the Council for Cultural Cooperation (CCC) of the Council of Europe, whose interest is specifically in adult language learning.[13] Wilkins has called their approach a *"communicative approach to language learning* since it assigns higher priority to the content of communication than to its form."[14] This approach "ensures that the learner is taught only what is relevant to his or her needs and that this knowledge is easily activated in actual

13. See *Systems Development in Adult Language Learning* (Strasbourg: Council for Cultural Cooperation of the Council of Europe, 1973). Contributing experts: J. L. M. Trim, R. Richterich, J. A. van Ek, and D. A. Wilkins.

14. D. A. Wilkins, "Learning a Language is Learning to Communicate," in *Education and Culture,* no. 28 (summer 1975), special issue, "Modern Language Learning by Adults" (Council for Cultural Cooperation of the Council of Europe), p. 18. Italics in the original.

language behaviour.''[15] It responds, therefore, to the requirements of individuals with specific needs, which are presumed in the CCC context of adult learners to be largely oral. Speaking and understanding thus receive the main emphasis.

The Council of Europe project has developed a *threshold level,*[16] which sets out in specific detail exactly what students with minimum requirements will know and be able to do in particular situations. The *situations* in which they will need the language have been analyzed into *social roles* (stranger/stranger; friend/friend); *psychological roles* (neutrality, equality, sympathy, antipathy), *settings,* and *topics.*[17] Reading and writing at the threshold level are limited to very functional tasks, such as reading road signs, public notices, and menus; or writing for accommodation and filling in forms.

The *communicative functions* the language learners will need to fulfill at the threshold level are likewise specified (imparting and seeking factual information; expressing and finding out intellectual, emotional, and moral attitudes; getting things done; and socializing). What is involved in each of these has been studied in detail and the semantic and syntactic features required for each are listed. (For instance, for identifying in English, the student will need demonstrative adjectives and pronouns; personal pronoun subjects + BE + NP; declarative sentence types; and short answer forms like *Yes, he is.*)[18]

Next, the concepts or *notions* people use in oral communication are identified (general notions for any situation, specific notions which are topic-related). These are used as a basis for deciding the linguistic items in a specific language which the student will need to learn. The notions listed include such areas as spatial and temporal properties and relations; action/event relations; qualities of size, shape, texture; possessive relations; and logical relations. (For instance, for the evaluative quality *rightness/wrongness,* the student will need for productive use in English the words *right* and *wrong;* the expressions: *This is the right thing to do; What's wrong?; It is wrong to be lazy; What's the matter?;* and the constructions: NP + should (not) + VP; while receptive (or comprehension) knowledge requires also the construction: NP + ought (not) to + VP.)[19]

Finally, a *lexicon* has been established for the threshold level, consisting of about a thousand words for production and reception and another five hundred words purely for recognition purposes.

15. Ibid.
16. See van Ek 1975 and 1977. For French, see Coste et al. 1976.
17. Van Ek, pp. 10–11.
18. Ibid., p. 35.
19. Ibid., p. 56.

To make the system operational, the CCC has examined forty-four categories of adults who need another language, setting out the degree to which they require, to varying degrees of proficiency, the skills of understanding, speaking, reading, and writing in specific types of situations. For instance, athletes, sportsmen, and related workers will need to understand and speak to a fair degree of competence a language of everyday communication and a very specialized language as well; they may also need to read and write some documents in the specialized language, but this part of their language activity is less important. Pilots, deck officers, and engineers (on ships and planes) will need to be able to speak, understand, and read to a high degree of competence a highly specialized language resembling a private code, and may have to enter data in logbooks in a highly specialized language with fairly simple syntax. Postmen and messengers who are responsible for sorting, registering, and distributing the mail will, on the other hand, need to be able to read written documents in connection with their activities to a high degree of competence and draft instructions in writing reasonably well, but will not need to understand or speak the language.[20]

Once the needs of language learners are identified in this precise fashion, units can be designed to meet these needs and credit assigned for complexes of units, so that a *unit/credit system* is established for adult language learning. If this unit/credit system is widely adopted, it will be transferable across boundaries so that it becomes clear what the learner may be presumed to know at a particular level. Units can be combined in complex ways to suit particular needs.[21] The unit/credit system is intended to provide the means whereby individuals can match their learning to the profile of their own needs.[22]

- **What levels of competence in understanding, speaking, reading, and writing a foreign language and what kind of language do you think policemen, firemen in the inner city, or miners would require?**

Notional Syllabuses

One of the features of the CCC system is the presentation of the structures of the language from a semantic point of view, not through a systematic study of articles, adjectives, tenses and so on, as in the traditional language syllabus. This approach is based on the work of Wilkins (1976) on notional syllabuses. Wilkins believes that the semantic approach is necessary if languages are to provide the learner

20. *Systems Development*, pp. 68–84.
21. J. L. M. Trim, "A European Unit Credit System," *Education and Culture* 28 (1975): 5.
22. Wilkins, "Learning a Language," p. 20.

with adequate communicative capacity. "The notional syllabus," he says, "is in contrast with the [grammatical and situational syllabuses] because it takes the desired communicative capacity as the starting-point. In drawing up a notional syllabus, instead of asking how speakers express themselves or when or where they use the language, we ask what it is they communicate through language. We are then able to organize language teaching in terms of the content rather than the form of the language. . . . A general language course will concern itself with those concepts and functions that are likely to be of widest value."[23]

Wilkins analyzes language needs within three categories: the *conceptual* or semantico-grammatical; the *modal,* by which the speaker's attitude is conveyed; and the *functional,* which derives from the speaker's purpose in communication. Material to be taught is thus established from a study of the needs of specific language users.

Since the forms required to express semantic needs are very varied, this means that structures will not necessarily be presented for learning purposes in a strict ordering from the simpler to the more complex, although order of difficulty will be taken into consideration where there is a choice of variations for which it is appropriate. Wilkins proposes a cyclic presentation of concepts and functions, so that students, as they advance, will be learning to express notions in more and more subtle ways to meet the needs of interpersonal relations and the particular medium of expression (Wilkins 1976, pp. 59–62).

Since a notional syllabus is clearly designed to help students communicate their personal meaning appropriately, it cannot be taught by the same old techniques, although some of these may be useful. Wilkins places the emphasis in a teaching situation on the use of *authentic language materials* to develop a varied and useful receptive repertoire, and on *role-playing* as a means of developing facility in communicative interaction (ibid., p. 78).

Notional syllabuses are still at the theoretical and experimental stage, and materials will gradually become more readily available to implement them. Notional materials will meet the criterion of ensuring that "the learner knows how different types of meaning are expressed, so that he can then adapt and combine the different components of this knowledge according to the requirements of a particular act of communication" (ibid., pp. 55–56). Emphasis thus falls on sociolinguistic and stylistic variation, which is determined by the conditions under which the act of communication is taking place (ibid., p. 57).

23. Wilkins 1976, pp. 18–19. Those interested in an in-depth study of this approach are referred to this book, and to C. J. Brumfit and K. Johnson (1979).

TWO TRADITIONS OF LANGUAGE STUDY

Halliday speaks of two traditions in the study of language down the centuries: language as thought and language as action. The former stresses rules and grammaticality, the latter "represents language as choices, or as a resource; it stresses the semantic interpretation of discourse, and uses . . . the criterion of acceptability or usage."[24] The former stresses uniformity (universals of language), the latter variety (differences between languages and language varieties). The latter includes variation theory, which looks upon variability in form of utterances as choices in relation to context. "The essence of variation theory," as Halliday sums it up, "is the notion that language is inherently a variable system, so that even within one individual speaker variation is the norm rather than the exception"[25]

The work of Wilkins clearly falls into the second tradition, as does the work of sociolinguists like Dell Hymes, who has studied what he has called "communicative competence" (Hymes 1974, p, 75). This is Wilkins's communicative capacity. The variation to which both Halliday and Wilkins refer is not of the slip of the tongue variety nor the "performance errors" of Chomsky (1965, pp. 3–4). They believe, as does Hymes, that there are rules of communication (just as there are rules of grammar) which members of a speech community have internalized. Like the grammar rules of one's native language, one cannot usually articulate these rules; one operates in conformity with them and knows when they are violated. Common expressions like: "She *knows* I didn't mean *that!*"; "I will not be spoken to like that!"; or "Who do you think you are speaking to?" indicate the acknowledgment of shared pragmatic rules, and a non-native speaker will sometimes be told: "You can't talk like that to your host (boss; a policeman; a lady; a workman)!" The variation to which Wilkins and Halliday refer is rule-governed or learned behavior which is appropriate in some circumstances but would not be in others.

- **In what circumstances (with what kinds of interlocutors, in what relationships) would you use each of the following?**
  Open the door. / Open the door, please. / Please open the door. / Would you please open the door. / Would you mind opening the door, please? / It's stuffy in here. / Would you mind very much if the door was open? / I wonder if we could open the door? / Would you have any objection to having the door open? / Do you think we could open the door? / Would it be possible to have the door open? / Would it be any inconvenience to you if we opened the

24. M. A. K. Halliday, "Ideas about Language," in *Aims and Perspectives in Linguistics* (Brisbane: Applied Linguistics Association of Australia, 1977), p. 37.
25. Ibid., p. 46.

door? / Goodness! the door's shut! / Please! You're nearest. / Go on!

Can you think of any other variations to add to this series to suit a different set of relationships, a different level of formality, or a different attitude on the part of the speaker?

Communicative Competence

Hymes speaks of two kinds of structure in the speech community. "The traditional structural linguistic view," he says, "sees structure in the speech community as . . . 'replication of uniformity'; sociolinguistics sees structure in the speech community as . . . 'organization of diversity.' The most novel and difficult contribution of sociolinguistic description must be to identify the rules, patterns, purposes, and consequences of language use, and to account for their interrelations."[26] These rules native speakers acquire as children during the early process of socialization within their speech community. The child acquires, along with a system of grammar, "a system of its use, regarding persons, places, purposes, other modes of communication, . . . patterns of the sequential use of language in conversation, address, standard routines." This is "the child's *socio*linguistic competence (or, more broadly, communicative competence)."[27]

These communicative rules can be learned by the non-native speaker through a period of immersion in the life of a group of speakers of the language, either in a country in which the language is spoken, or in an enclave of speakers of the language in another country, so long as this enclave remains in frequent contact with the contemporary culture of its broader linguistic community.

Where such immersion is not possible, the teacher must be aware of the need to develop this ability to communicate acceptably according to the sociolinguistic rules of the speech community, and must include this "organization of diversity" as an essential element of the program. This becomes difficult if the materials being used have not been prepared with this important aspect of communication in mind. Communicative competence is not just the ability to chatter fluently in the new language within the framework of sociolinguistic rules of the native language. Where they are available, native speakers or near-native speakers with considerable experience of life in the other community should be brought into the classroom. Students should

26. Hymes 1974, p. 75. "Replication of uniformity" and "organization of diversity" are terms which Hymes is quoting from A. F. C. Wallace, *Culture and Personality* (New York: Random House, 1961).
27. Ibid. Italics are in the original.

also be encouraged to seek out native speakers on their own initiative with whom they can interact on a personal basis.

SPEAKING SKILL AT THE ADVANCED LEVEL

As students move into the advanced stage, many teachers give up regular practice in speaking the language. The class often becomes absorbed in reading and writing, with oral work limited to discussion of subjects of which the students have little previous knowledge. Students, still uncertain and hesitant in expressing themselves, are often pushed prematurely into situations where they are expected to discuss in the target language literary or philosophical concepts and problems for which they do not know the accepted terminology and turns of expression. Very often they have had no adequate preparation for this type of discussion, even in their native language. As a result, a pall of silence falls over what has in previous years been an eager and vocal group, and the teacher, in desperation, falls back on lecturing in the target language. Maintaining and developing fluency in expressing personal meaning at an advanced level is certainly a demanding task, and many teachers give up the struggle, completely baffled as to how to proceed.

At the advanced level, conversation calls into play a multiplicity of structures and lexical items which have been learned over a period of years. The student must select from this stored knowledge the lexical items, accepted phrases, and structures most appropriate to the expression of the intended meaning. Skill in rapid selection can be developed only by much practice in retrieving learned items—in their complicated interrelationships—from the memory store and adapting them to new requirements as meanings are expressed with more and more finesse and nuance.

This practice in selection is facilitated if the conversation is about subjects on which ideas spring readily to mind, and students can more easily (and eagerly) maintain their viewpoint. If they are forced into a position where the development of ideas on subjects about which they know very little is the all-important factor, they will fall back on native-language means of expression which are less demanding for them. For practice in selecting rapidly from what they have available, students require opportunities to discuss subjects of their own choice, where the production of ideas is less arduous and most of their attention is on the process of selection. Students who study another subject in the target language have subject matter to discuss and should be encouraged to talk freely in class. If the subject matter is literary criticism or analysis, contemporary culture, or business practices, teachers need to ensure that students have the means (specialized vocabulary, specific structures) to make discussion feasible and not unduly laborious.

Practice in the selection of appropriate language elements will involve experimentation and trial-and-error learning. Students should be encouraged to try out new combinations to create novel utterances, as they would do if they found themselves in an environment where the language is spoken. In this situation they would make every effort to express their meaning by using all the linguistic means at their disposal. The more daring they are in such linguistic innovation, the more rapidly they progress. In the classroom, the students have the additional advantage of a mentor who guides them in distinguishing acceptable from unacceptable combinations.

Variable Achievement in Expressive Use of Language
If we wish our students to speak with ease in another language, we must see that they are given ample practice, at all levels, in expressing themselves in situations as close to spontaneous expression as possible. Preoccupation with other aspects of the work must not be allowed to whittle away the time spent in this activity. Nor must teachers allow themselves to become discouraged at the slow rate of development of real facility and fluency. They must recognize the fact that individual students will reach varying levels of self-expression in speaking the language. These students have achieved greater or lesser degrees of fluency in their native language. Some have wide-ranging vocabularies and a sure choice of felicitous expression; others express themselves badly with much repetition and many clichés; still others are at a loss for words when asked to explain or describe anything out of the usual run of their daily experience. In the native language, some speak rapidly, others slowly and deliberately.

Teachers are, by their choice of profession, an articulate group. Without realizing it, they often expect of students a greater degree of control of the language they are teaching than these same students show in their native language. They may even expect more consummate expression than some native speakers display in a natural situation. By their methods of testing, too, teachers often reward the imaginative and the extrovert, under the illusion that they are rewarding fluency of expression in the language. (Testing oral production is a difficult problem, which will be discussed in chapter 12.) Teachers of advanced students must keep these factors of individual differences in mind and encourage each student to participate as his or her personality allows. Then, and only then, will the class atmosphere lend itself to spontaneous expression and interest in communication.

CONVERSATION GROUPS, COURSES, AND CLUBS

The Structured Conversation Group

In situations where the only available practice in speaking is in school, conversation groups are a regular feature of the program. We may hope that students will seize opportunities out of class to practice unstructured communication together, and the most enthusiastic certainly will, but there is a valid place for conversation practice in a situation where the teacher can help and guide. In a high school there may be scheduling difficulties for small groups. In such cases, half the class may be sent to the language laboratory for individual practice in listening to tapes or records of plays, stories, and poems studied in class, for making notes of news broadcasts taped from radio programs, for listening to the sound track of a film which has been or is to be shown in class or club, or for remedial exercises in pronunciation. If no laboratory is available, much of this listening practice can be provided by a tape recorder in the classroom, around which half the class gathers. The other half of the class will then remain with the teacher, preferably in an informal arrangement, for practice in free oral expression. If neither of these arrangements is feasible, the class will be divided into small groups, and the teacher will spend some time with each.

Conversation groups of this kind require careful preparation and special techniques. They cannot be expected to produce good results if the teacher vaguely hopes that the mood of the group will carry all the participants forward in a steady flow of chatter. This may happen on the first occasion, but limitations of vocabulary and paucity of ideas soon make the sessions repetitive and tedious. It is useful for the teacher to plan a series of conversation topics and activities which require use of the language.

Where it is possible to link the conversation group with consideration of aspects of the target culture, the topics may follow a systematic progression based on readings, films, or visits from native speakers. A recent magazine or newspaper article distributed beforehand will provoke discussion. If short films on aspects of life in the foreign culture are at the teacher's disposal, these may serve to stimulate conversation. Students will be encouraged to bring in material they have discovered on aspects of life, thought, and beliefs of speakers of the language, or on recent events in countries where the language is spoken.

When the purpose of the class is general fluency and extension of the areas of vocabulary within which the student can operate, general topics of interest to the student will be chosen. (This may occur where there is a parallel course on the culture of the speakers of the language, or where it is considered inadvisable for political or other reasons to consider the foreign culture in depth.) For this general discussion group, the topics chosen may be considered conversation areas in a very broad and flexible sense, and they should be announced in advance. Some teachers like to issue, several days beforehand, sheets of relevant vocabulary for preparation. Lists of words in a short context in the target language, which relate to various aspects of the topic, with perhaps some exclamations or fill-in expressions, are sufficient. Students may look these up in a dictionary beforehand, if necessary. The topic chosen is then taken as a wide, elastic area within which all may range, and the students are expected to come prepared with ideas within that area which they will introduce into the conversation as either reminiscences, anecdotes, or provocative statements. General discussion groups of this type may be introduced quite early and topics used to develop useful vocabulary in semantic fields along with flexibility of expression. On one such occasion, for instance, the topic may be announced as the *sea*. For that day, any conversational gambit which relates to the sea is permissible: experiences at the seaside, fishing, sea travel, scuba diving, sailing, pollution of the oceans, saving the whale, sea tales, sea monsters, films or books about the sea, and so on. The topic itself is merely a focus to give the conversation direction and to provide some community of ideas. The course the conversation takes is spontaneous and not guided by the teacher, who does, however, inject it with new interest when it seems to be flagging. No two sessions centered on the same topic will ever evolve in the same way, since it is whatever the students feel like talking about or wish to share with each other that is the real topic of the day. Should they deviate from the topic in pursuit of a common interest, the topic will have served its purpose in stimulating a line of thought or discussion, and a natural conversation will have developed.

Topics of similarly wide scope which will serve as starters are: national holidays, love and marriage, sports, travel, leisure-time occupations and hobbies, how to improve the school program or solve national or local problems, favorite authors or films, the contemporary family, careers, extrasensory perception, and such personal topics as "What irritates me most" or "The funniest (happiest, weirdest) experience of my life." The imaginative teacher will soon have a list long enough to cover most of the sessions, and the students will certainly suggest more.

Once a conversational group becomes a place for giving oral reports, it ceases to achieve its purpose, since most of the students settle back happily to become listeners, which is not the purpose of the class. Just as the setting should be informal and the group small (eight students is a good number), so should the atmosphere be one of relaxed camaraderie, where students feel free to tease each other and the teacher and are thus eager to hear what is said, to interrupt, and to question. The students should be encouraged to come to the group with the firm intention of making and taking opportunities to make their voices heard.

The role of the teacher in such a group requires alertness and self-discipline. The teacher must not talk too much, resisting any temptation to use the session as a forum for giving a lecture in the foreign language. Nor should two or three people be permitted to do all the talking. If such a situation arises, the teacher must be ready to step in and tactfully swing the conversation to another student by asking a question or raising a problem related to what has just been said, watching for opportunities to launch the shy or taciturn. The well-prepared teacher has ready a few provocative questions to throw into the ring when conversation is beginning to lose pace, always remembering the stimulating effect of hearing the teacher produce the unexpected or the controversial.

To what degree should the teacher correct inaccurate speech during such sessions? It is obvious that continual interruption to correct every mistake will discourage, frustrate, and inhibit the students, so that they lose their train of thought and cease to speak freely; yet such a conversation session should be an occasion for improvement. (The recommendations on p. 226 should be kept in mind.)

The Conversation Course: Oral Survival

After students have acquired a basic competence, some may wish to concentrate their efforts on the development of facility and fluency in oral communication. For these, a course can be designed that meets four or five hours a week, in which listening and speaking predominate.

The *aims* of the course will be to increase the students' confidence in their ability to communicate in a target-language setting; to make active the knowledge of the language they already possess; and to help them to acquire further means (cultural, pragmatic, semantic, syntactic, kinesic) for conveying the full force of their personal messages.

Reading matter of a readily accessible level may be included in the course as a reference tool, to provide material for more informed discussion of aspects of the target culture, but it must not obtrude into the course to the detriment of the time devoted to oral communication. It is preferable to use for this purpose articles from magazines and newspapers that the students would currently be reading, were they indeed in the target-language environment. Any such reading is individual preparatory work, done out of the classroom.

Grammar will not be formally studied, but it will be actively practiced in communication activities when the students feel the need for clarification of specific structures or syntactic relationships. (An uncluttered grammar book, without exercises, is useful for private reference when the student feels the need to check on usage.) Students will endeavor to broaden their knowledge of *vocabulary* through their attempts to express their meaning in many different domains.

An important segment of the course will be practice in *listening* to native speech, produced by persons of different sexes, age groups, or regional origins. Material for this listening practice may take the form of serial episodes of a continuing story; recordings of authentic conversations with native speakers about their life, work, and views on subjects of interest to the students; broadcasts of news, commercials, interviews, and reportages; episodes from radio or television soap operas, plays, or situation comedies; films in the language; and contemporary songs. Whenever possible, the students will be brought in contact with native speakers of the language, through classroom visits for discussion, group meals, or involvement in some activity with a local community.

The course will run more smoothly if its activities are loosely based on a theme. "How to survive if parachuted into an area where the language is spoken" is one such open-ended theme. Students learn how to get a room, buy food, or deal with police, garage mechanics, or shop assistants. They learn how to accept invitations and how to behave when visiting or staying in a home; what is expected of them in casual social contact and later, when relations become more intimate. They learn to react emotionally in acceptable ways.

They acquire skill in these kinds of behavior through *role playing* in simulated situations. Different groups of students may act out their own versions of these situations. The simulation may also take the form of serial episodes in the life of a group of characters interacting in the target setting; different groups of students will take turns in applying their imagination to acting out the relationships of the characters in a developing drama.

The students learn to ask acceptable questions and *discuss many subjects* as they would be discussed with speakers of the language. They learn to answer questions about their own culture and to view it in relation to another.

The theme of "survival in the target country" provides scope for *personal research* on regions within the country: how to get there, what to expect when one arrives. This personal research will be presented to the whole group in oral form by the student, as a basis for active discussion.

Above all, the course must evolve in accordance with the *interests and initiative of the students*. This requires a flexible teacher who becomes in reality another member of the group—ready to help when needed, but willing to stand aside and let the ideas of the students blossom and mature.

How can such a course be evaluated? Clearly, the *evaluation* must be based on ability to communicate: to understand and to convey personal meaning effectively and confidently. This requires a lengthy oral interview for each student. The interview may be supplemented by a listening comprehension test based on authentic conversational material, a carefully selected scene from a contemporary play, or a broadcast interview. Any personal research projects undertaken by the students will be evaluated on the basis of an oral presentation followed by wide-ranging discussion with the other students, the quality of the students' response to discussion rating equally with the oral presentation.

The Language Club

Speaking ability can also be developed in the language club, where students practice communication in an informal atmosphere. As in the country where the language is spoken, a spirit of linguistic innovation and enterprise, within the acknowledged limitations of the level of language use individual students have reached, can provide students with much practice in selection and variation of structures and vocabulary learned in the classroom, while helping them develop confidence and self-assurance. In the atmosphere of the club this all seems fun. The program of the club should be designed with the intention of creating a setting where the students are engaged in activities they would normally enjoy in the native language or sharing the kinds of activities their counterparts enjoy in the foreign culture. Students prepare one-act plays and skits, organize competitions and games, see films, take part in mock television programs or panel discussions, sing songs, engage in informal conversation over coffee cups, meet native speakers of the language, or celebrate festival and national days of the country or countries whose language they are learning.

The club should be the spearhead for stimulating awareness of other languages. The club members can organize foreign-language days, with displays, dances, competitions, ethnic foods, sports, and games, concentrating on activities which involve all the participants in some elementary contact with the language. The club members can keep bulletin boards and display cases supplied with items in the language. They can design and sell bumper stickers, buttons, and T-shirts. They can organize outings and inexpensive weekend camps where the language is used. Above all, they should share with others their excitement and pleasure in language use.

Although the activities of the club have the basic aim of providing opportunities to use the language, they should be such that the students will enjoy themselves while absorbing some of the spirit and culture of the country where the language is spoken. Songs should be modern in harmony, rhythm, and theme, or folk songs which still appeal musically to the young people of today. Art songs of a more serious nature may be excellent for those who have a developed taste for music, but the language club should be a place of enjoyment for all, irrespective of tastes, so that the language will be readily practiced.

In club sessions, language teachers must put all their effort into making the practicing of the language attractive, and not dilute their efforts with other, sometimes conflicting, aims. Plays, for instance, should be presented for fun, with fluency of speech of paramount importance, rather than perfection of costuming and stage presentation. In this way, three or four one-act plays can be learned and rehearsed, and more people involved in the acting, in the same amount of time that would be required for the thorough staging of one such play. For a successful club from the point of view of language use, variety and informality should be the keynote in all activities.

THE NATURAL AND THE NORMAL

Is it possible to develop *natural use of language* in a conversation group or course? This question is often raised. Some maintain that any teacher-initiated conversational interaction is not natural, because the classroom is an artificial environment to begin with. This is a specious argument, since a classroom is an environment, and what normally takes place within it is a feature of that particular environment. Whether we can reproduce in this specialized environment the type of interaction which takes place between people in social, work, or home environments within a multidimensional community is another question.

We should distinguish between *normal uses of language* in interaction and natural or spontaneous language use. As we have seen (p. 230), there are normal communicative purposes for which we use language. These can be taught as can the language forms appropriate for expressing them. Natural use of language springs from the will and desires of the individual. This can be encouraged or stimulated, but not taught. Natural language use presumes natural, uninhibited relationships. We may wish to establish such relationships with all our students. We may succeed with some, even most, but before natural use of language in interpersonal interaction can burst forth in our classrooms there must also be natural relationships among the members of the class. The students themselves will decide when they feel sufficiently at ease to behave "naturally" with each other and the teacher.

When students do begin to use the language naturally in class, we may not like the experience. Authentic communicative use of language in class presumes equality of relationships and acceptance of difference. The teacher cannot suddenly take refuge in a reinvoked authority posture and expect "natural language use" to continue. This is one of the reasons why many teachers find the conversation group or course the hardest to teach. Without natural relationships on the part of all, including the teacher, the group can be very stiff, the session can drag, some students may do all the talking, or the teacher in desperation resorts to a question-answer or lecture format.

We aim at promoting natural language use by stimulating and encouraging student-directed and student-initiated activities. These may evolve from teacher suggestion and teacher preparation, but at some stage the students take over and natural use of language develops. This breakthrough cannot be organized or mandated. When it does occur, the teacher is elated, aware of success in the task, and the students themselves realize that they have really been communicating and interacting.

We can all promote normal uses of language in conversation groups and courses. We can strive to break down barriers and create a relaxed atmosphere where students feel free to express themselves. The flowering of natural language use will come in its own time; it cannot be forced. When students do begin to interact naturally, if only for a few minutes, we must be quick to recognize the change and let the natural interaction take over until its energy is spent. Being able to withdraw and leave students space and room to take over and learn through their own activity is the mark of the real teacher.

TAKING THE LANGUAGE OUT OF THE CLASSROOM
Practice in normal uses of language and natural interaction are fostered by encouraging students to seize opportunities to use the language away from the classroom.

In bilingual and second-language situations (see Preface), the student should be encouraged to become a participant in the life of the community where the language is spoken. In a *bilingual situation,* this means rendering needed services to the bilingual student's mother-tongue community by helping its members in their relations with the other-language group: acting as interpreter, helping with the filling in of forms and the writing of letters, sharing one's newly acquired knowledge with others by teaching older people to read or younger people to take their first steps in the language of the unfamiliar community.

In a *second-language situation,* students should be involved in projects which bring them into active contact with speakers of the language and require that they talk with them. They may be assigned the task of reporting on the history of the town, or its current problems. They may be sent to discuss town organization with local officials and be encouraged to attend town meetings, sessions of the local council or school board, and political rallies. They may visit local schools to observe classes and discuss educational policy with the teachers. They may report back to the class on comparison shopping which has involved discussion with shopkeepers. They may help in hospitals or day-care centers.

The students can work with children in after-school activities (children are great teachers, and foreign speakers are less embarrassed when corrected by small children with whom they are working). They can join clubs: photography, bird-watching, scouts, or whatever interests them. They can offer services: baby-sitting; working one evening a week at the local library; doing shopping or yard work for old people and keeping in touch with them by phone (another useful area of practice). They should listen purposefully to radio and television to gather information or to let the language envelop them until comprehension is no longer a problem and they begin to understand the culture. (Here, class discussion will help with their interpretation.) Involving students in projects like these should be an active concern of the teacher who knows the community as the students do not.

In the *foreign-language situation,* these kinds of activities are not usually possible. Where there are ethnic pockets of speakers of the language in the vicinity, their potential should be studied and exploited. The language can still be taken out of the classroom through weekend or week-long language camps run by the local teachers (with the involvement of any native speaker who may be passing through or visiting the community). Short trips to an area where the language is spoken are often feasible, or periods of study may be arranged on an exchange basis with a school in the other-language area. These visits should involve, where possible, family exchanges so that students from each area get to know each other well and can keep in touch later. The experience of family living not only makes the use of the language more real and purposeful but gives vivid insight into the culture of the native speakers.

Students should engage in tape correspondence with speakers of the language. They should see any films in the language which are shown at local theaters, and attend performances by visiting theatrical groups. Even where opportunities such as these are not available, language tables can be organized, where students talk with each other and their teacher, over a meal, in an informal atmosphere. And finally, there is short-wave radio. Teachers should know when programs in the language may be heard and keep their students informed, discussing afterwards the content of the program with those who have listened. As with all other aspects of language teaching, the possibilities for out-of-school language use are limited only by the imagination and initiative of the teacher and the courage and confidence of the students. One is fostered by the other.

Independent Improvement in Speaking When Opportunities for Communication Out of Class Are Rare

Not to be underestimated in the development of facility in expressing one's meaning in another language is the role of listening. In a foreign country, students would hear the language spoken continually. Expressions, rhythms, phonological patterns: all would strike the ear and impress themselves upon the memory. The learner-listeners can imitate and frame their utterances on the basis of what they have heard. Slowly and with increasing confidence they advance to the stage where their speech begins to approximate the speech of those around them. This constant hearing of the language throughout the day is missing in the school environment, and the students begin to flounder. As they try to express themselves in a more mature fashion, dearly won control of structure and idiomatic expression often proves too frail, and students yield to the temptation to disguise native-language forms of expression in foreign-language dress.

Advanced students must be given opportunities for careful and attentive listening to authentic language materials at frequent intervals, either in a laboratory, or with a tape recorder or record player. Suitable types of listening materials for advanced levels have been listed in chapter 6. Carroll points out that "normal speech involves a perceptual self-monitoring process.''[28] Students who have a distinct auditory image of what speech in the new language should sound like will be able to monitor their own speech more critically, with a greater possibility of adjusting it gradually to the model of native speech which they hear so frequently in recorded form. This monitoring gradually becomes a barely-noticed but habitual accompaniment of the expression of personal meaning.

Also useful in developing the mechanics of fluent speech is frequent repetition, after a model, of conversational utterances of some complexity. Students who do not have ready access to a laboratory or tape recorder can gain great benefit from frequent reading aloud of conversational material (e.g., dialogue of an informal character from modern novels or plays). Such utterances may be practiced after the teacher, then read aloud at home until the phrases trip off the tongue without effort. Repeating and reading aloud help develop those interverbal associations so necessary for rapid production of speech. It is lack of such well-established associations in a language one is learning which causes a certain hesitancy in articulating the next word in a group of words.

Repeating and reading aloud also give practice in the mechanics of pronunciation in larger contexts. Students can concentrate on smooth transition from sound to sound and from word to word, according to the conventions of rapid speech in the target language. They can also concentrate on reproducing appropriate intonation patterns. In reading conversational material, students can practice all of these phonological features without the added complication of selecting the most appropriate expressions to clothe their ideas. Later, when trying to express their own meanings, students will be able to reproduce these practiced sound sequences without undue effort, and thus give their full attention to the process of selection of syntax and lexicon.

As students become more and more independent of the teacher, they should be encouraged to practice talking to themselves and thinking in the language as often as possible. They can describe to themselves things they see on the way to school, recounting to themselves what they have done during the day or what they intend to do. They can express their exasperations as they dress or when they miss the bus or their feeling of exhilaration on a fine spring morning. In this way they will provide for themselves some of the practice they would have in the foreign country, because much of what passes for interaction in everyday life is little more then egocentric monologue.

28. Carroll 1964, pp. 45–46. Krashen has taken up this question of the monitor. See S. D. Krashen, "The Monitor Model for Adult Second Language Performance," in Burt, Dulay, and Finocchiaro 1977, pp. 152–61.

Facility in speaking will also draw much from increasing fluency in reading and the active application of language knowledge in writing. As students read widely, their vocabulary and their understanding of cultural concepts will be greatly broadened, so that the knowledge available to them for selection as a basis of spoken expression will also be expanded. Wide reading and practice in putting some of the material read into an uncomplicated written form will consolidate their familiarity with many language items and make these more readily available for selection in oral expression. To capitalize on the potential contribution of other skill areas, the teacher should promote active class discussion of what has been heard and read, and encourage the presentation of short oral reports on reading done out of class. These oral reports should be given without a script and followed by free-wheeling discussion with the other students on the substance of the report.

Many students of a language have become remarkably fluent, despite the lack of opportunities in their situation to interact with native speakers, because they have persisted in using the language in every possible context until it came trippingly off the tongue.

Areas of Controversy

Is speaking a foreign language a skill worth cultivating when students meet few native speakers and live far from lands where the language is spoken?

Teachers who make this objection usually round it off by adding: If we teach our students to read and write the language well and to understand the grammar, they will learn to speak it quickly enough when they are in a situation where the speaking of the language is important for them.

This type of reasoning ignores pedagogically sound reasons for teaching the speaking skill. One of these has already been discussed: students (and the parents) feel that learning a language is something to do with speaking. They expect to learn to speak it. Early introduction to the aural-oral skills increases their interest in and enthusiasm for language learning. Besides this, listening and speaking are basic to some of the most interesting and exciting activities in the language classroom. Dull indeed would many lessons be without them. Nor must we forget that we are teaching a generation which spends more of its leisure time watching television than reading books. To such students, oral expression seems a most natural activity.

These motivational factors apart, there are other valid reasons for an aural-oral approach to language learning. When we read and write, we draw upon what we know of the language orally. In reading, we recognize the oral equivalent behind the script, and as we read we supply many elements of intonation and vocal emphasis which are not in the printed text. We read more fluently because we are able to recognize whole phrases which we could say aloud. In writing, in its commonest forms, we put in graphic form what we would say; even at a refined level we often repeat phrases over to see which sounds best before making a choice. Students cannot do this if they have been taught only to write things down in the target language, not to say them. Their efforts at composition become exercises in concoction where they piece language elements together and rearrange them according to rules they have learned.

Oral exercises permit of much more student participation in sustained practice than written exercises do, in a situation where the teacher has immediate and direct access to the production of each student and is able to correct and guide it. The vividness of oral practice reinforces the visual impression of the textbook. The more senses we involve in learning, the greater the retention.

Finally, many people who have learned a language only through reading and writing are severely inhibited when the opportunity arises to practice speaking it. They are uncertain of pronunciation and intonation. At the first signs of incomprehension, they withdraw in embarrassment. They are unfamiliar with many of the commonest phrases they hear around them, and consequently they begin to feel insecure in the knowledge they do have. Once they have overcome their reticence and have found they can understand and be understood, they progress, but the initial stage is often too painful for them and they do not persist. If as young students they had been forced to use the language frequently in front of others in a friendly atmosphere, they would have lost many of these inhibitions early and would have been eager, rather than reluctant, to try out their skill in a real situation.

Students who have been taught all through their study of a language to understand and speak it will not only profit in this area but will usually develop into much more fluent readers and writers as well.

Can a teacher who is not fluent in the language teach the speaking skill?

Despite the fears of many teachers who learned the language by a grammar-translation method with little oral work, it is possible for a teacher who is not a fluent speaker of the language to teach the speaking skill by an audio-lingual approach. It is much more difficult for such a teacher to use a direct-method or natural approach, where the teacher must talk continually and use much ingenuity to ensure that students understand.

In an audio-lingual, or structural, approach, teachers are expected to keep strictly within the limits of the material the students are learning, drilling it thoroughly and allowing the students to hear and use it as often as time will allow. Teachers lacking in confidence can use a tape recorder in the classroom to give the students the opportunity to imitate an authentic accent. They can then learn with the students by continually hearing the correct sounds from the model. The audio-lingual method discourages teachers from doing all the talking in the foreign language themselves. They are expected, rather, to use class time for maximum opportunities for participation by all the members of the class. Their deficiencies will not show up as much in the classroom if they have prepared each section of work well, working with the tape recorder at home before presenting any material to the class.

Teachers who are in this position should heed the following advice.

• They will need to pay very careful attention as they compare their own articulation and intonation with that of the tape model. If they have been badly trained, they will have acquired certain inaccuracies and incorrect articulatory habits of which they will very probably not be conscious and which will be hard to eradicate. They may find it helpful to seek the criticism of other, better prepared teachers as they try to detect these weaknesses. Once these are identified, they must practice to improve, both at home and in class. If their weaknesses are very important phonemically, they will do well to warn the class that where there is a discrepancy between what they say and what the students hear on the tape, the tape should be accepted as the model. Above all, teachers should not be too proud to admit their faults. If they find students have imitated some of their weaknesses, they should be ready to correct the class and their own production and work with the class toward the elimination of the inaccuracy. With authentic models, students can acquire a better pronunciation than their teacher, so long as they are alerted to the situation.

• They should watch for personal inhibitions about speaking the language. Such an inhibition means taking refuge in the use of the native language when the students should be having steady practice in listening to and using the target language. As a result, the students will later be as unwilling as their teacher to speak the language.

• They should use techniques which encourage their students to use the new language as much as possible, so that the lesson does not

252

depend on the teacher's oral contribution. For variety, the better students can be used to lead drills and dialogue practice, especially if these students have acquired, from imitation of the tape, a better pronunciation than their teacher's.

- They will need to be patient and persevering in improving their own oral skills. They should practice talking to themselves; listen to foreign-language tapes, records, and films; and attend inservice training schools and workshops, or meetings of cultural societies.

With the right attitude toward this problem, the teacher should be able to correct the situation as time goes on without too much inconvenience to the first aural-oral classes. Later classes will profit as the language skills of the teacher develop and mature.

Is the acquisition of an extensive vocabulary the most important aspect of learning a language if one is to speak it fluently?

In a grammar-translation approach great store is set by the learning of many foreign-language words. Textbooks begin each lesson with lengthy bilingual vocabulary lists, and students learn these lists by heart night after night. In many cases, the vocabulary learned for one unit is not reentered in later units and students rapidly forget a great deal of it until they are threatened with a test. They then go over it as rapidly as they can in order to pass the test. In an audio-lingual approach, by contrast, vocabulary learning is given a minor role until the students have a sure control of the basic structural patterns and are able to express themselves freely within a limited area of language. The direct method falls somewhat between these two extremes. The students learn words for many objects about which they can talk and for many actions they can perform. These words are associated not with translation equivalents but with pictures, actual objects, or actions, the amount of vocabulary still being much less than in the traditional grammar-translation approach.

There are various reasons for this underplaying of vocabulary learning. The number of words one can learn in a foreign language is seemingly endless, and it is difficult to know exactly which word one will need next—it may well be a word of very low frequency, but of considerable importance to the learner. Without knowing the circumstances in which our students are likely to use the language, it seems more difficult to decide which vocabulary areas will ultimately be the most useful for them[29] than which basic structures are indispensable. Many common objects, whose foreign names the students soon learn,

29. Constructors of frequency counts soon discover the degree to which the use of concrete nouns in particular is a function of the situation in which an utterance takes place. As a result, what would normally be regarded as common concrete nouns may

are rarely talked about in normal conversation. Vocabulary for any specific area in which the student is involved is more readily acquired when circumstances require its use.

Excessive vocabulary learning early in the course gives students the impression that the most important thing about learning a language is accumulating new words as equivalents for concepts which they can already express in their native language. They often fail to realize that meaning is expressed in groups of words and in combinations of language segments, and that the meaning of an individual word is usually difficult to determine when it is separated from a context of other words and phrases. Traditional vocabulary lists rarely provide contexts of this type. Students are thus unprepared to use the words they have learned as isolated units in any approximation to authentic communication.

Once students have acquired some basic vocabulary, this can be used for giving practice in morphological variations and syntactic structure, which are fundamental to expression of meaning in speech or writing. When well-known lexical items are used in grammatical exercises, students are able to concentrate on elements of syntactic structure without distraction. After a structural pattern has been well practiced in the audio-lingual approach, further vocabulary is usually included in a clear context in a testing series in order to draw the student's attention away from the feature being practiced. Thus the instructor can tell whether the students are able to use in an accurate but effortless way the structure they have been practicing. In current audio-lingual practice, vocabulary building is mainly conducted in association with practice in communication.

Hesitancy in speaking a language, or in reading or writing it for that matter, is often a question of slow vocabulary recall. This is inevitable when the student has been asked to learn an indigestible number of items out of context. In an approach where everything is learned thoroughly by being used in aural-oral practice, then reentered in reading and written exercises, the vocabulary that has been learned is not allowed to fall into disuse and remains readily available for recall. New vocabulary can then be introduced in an attention-catching way in oral activities, where students are attempting to use what they know in real communication and, therefore, concentrating on choice of the appropriate word. Alternatively they encounter the new words in interesting reading material in which a context of familiar words makes the meaning of the new vocabulary clear. In both textual

be rated as of very low frequency or may not appear at all in the particular corpus of utterances under examination. See Halliday, McIntosh, and Strevens 1964, p. 194; and "Vocabulary Learning" in chapter 14 below.

materials and classroom activity, continual reentry of vocabulary throughout the course is essential to long-term retention.

In some recent approaches, listening plays a very important role in the initial presentation of the language, and students learn to recognize many words before they are expected to produce any of them orally. In this type of class, students acquire much recognition vocabulary, reproducing only as much of it as they feel they need or can control in classroom communication. Here more vocabulary is presented than in an audio-lingual approach, but in ways which allow it to sink in over time.

In the native language, children acquire vocabulary slowly at first, making maximum use of each item for their purposes. During this early period, their recognition vocabulary increases through much listening. Later, when they can use certain basic structural patterns (or their own version of them) and are determined to communicate about the many exciting new things they are encountering, their vocabulary increases by leaps and bounds. In many classrooms, students do not have sufficient opportunities to acquire a wide recognition vocabulary through constant listening (although more and more teachers are realizing its importance). For these students, the phase of rapid vocabulary expansion comes when they move into wider reading. The more they read, the more their recognition knowledge of vocabulary increases. A part of this becomes active as it is used in speech and writing. Just as in the native language, students must not be expected to be able to use actively, without hesitation, all the recognition vocabulary that has been acquired. The limitations of their current active vocabulary will not hinder them unduly in the expression of their meaning unless they continually attempt to express themselves beyond their level of control of the new language. They must realize that, mature as they are, they are still like children in their knowledge of this language. They must try to simplify what they wish to say, attempting to express their meaning with correct use of uncomplicated structural patterns and a general all-purpose vocabulary. In the early stages, this will mean learning to use circumlocutions and paraphrases when they do not know the precise term (as all nonnative speakers do constantly, even when they know a second language quite well). In this way as they learn more vocabulary, they will be fitting the new words into appropriate and correctly combined syntactic structures, instead of stringing them together in the hope that they will make comprehensible sentences.

There seems to be a parallelism between prevailing emphases in linguistics and the tenets of contemporaneous language-teaching approaches. When phonetics and phonology were the center of interest, teachers put pressure on students to attain near-native pronunciation. With a change of emphasis to syntax, grammar became central. As semantics became a major preoccupation, a new classroom emphasis on vocabulary emerged. (See also chapter 3.) Natural Language Learning emphasizes the learning of much vocabulary which is used in classroom communication, the study of grammar being largely a matter of individual pre-class preparation.[30] In Community Language Learning, Curran's Counseling-Learning model (Curran 1976), students select their own vocabulary, with the help of a counselor, since they decide what they wish to say or discuss. The vocabulary will then be as wide-ranging or as limited as their needs dictate. Suggestopedia (Lozanov 1978) gives considerable emphasis to vocabulary learning, claiming that 2000 words can be acquired in twenty-four days.[31] These words are presented in dialogue form and then practiced in classroom communication. It is not clear how so many words, continually increasing in number, can all be reentered satisfactorily in communication activities in the time normally available. (Suggestopedic courses are, of course, intensive, with four lessons per day, which is more time than most teachers have at their disposal.)

As with every aspect of language learning and teaching, we must seek balance. There are many competing facets of a language to be developed. The aims of specific courses, based on the interests of the students concerned, should guide the teacher in deciding how much emphasis to give to one aspect of language learning rather than another at a particular time. (See also chapter 14: "Vocabulary Learning.")

Annotated Reading List

Wardhaugh, Ronald. *The Contexts of Language*. Rowley, Mass.: Newbury House, 1976. Chapter 4, "The Functional Context," discusses what is involved in speech acts and verbal exchanges; and chapter 6, "The Social Context," discusses social variation in speech.

Rivers, Wilga M. "Talking Off the Tops of Their Heads." In *SMT*, pp. 21–35. Also in *TQ* 6 (1972): 71–81. Proposes a model of language teaching, distinguishing skill-getting from skill-using. Discusses the relationship of intensive practice to autonomous interaction and sets out normal uses of language in communication.

————. "The Natural and the Normal in Language Learning." In Brown 1976, pp. 1–8. A revised version appears in Schulz 1977.

30. Tracy D. Terrell, "A Natural Approach to Second Language Acquisition and Learning," *MLJ* 61 (1977): 325–37.
31. Lozanov 1978, pp. 321–22.

Outlines the normal functions of language and distinguishes normal use of language in communication from natural language use. Discusses the place of each in language learning.

Rivers, Wilga M., et al. *Practical Guides*. Chapter 2, "Autonomous Interaction," discusses fourteen categories of language use in communication, with proposed activities for each.

Birckbickler, D. W. "Communication and Beyond." In Phillips 1977, pp. 53–94. Deals with creative language use: the dimensions of creativity, the relationship between creative and communicative capacities, and techniques for encouraging and stimulating creative communication in the classroom. Extensive bibliography.

Stanislawczyk, Irene E., and Yavener, Symond. *Creativity in the Language Classroom*. Rowley, Mass.: Newbury House, 1976. Gives many creative activities for class use, with examples in English, French, and Spanish.

Burney, P., and Damoiseau, R. *La Classe de conversation*. Paris: Hachette, 1969. Describes many oral activities and games.

Dobson, Julia M. *Effective Techniques for English Conversation Groups*. Rowley, Mass.: Newbury House, 1974. Discusses the dynamics of conversation groups and suggests many activities to keep them moving.

*Wilkins, D. A. *Notional Syllabuses*. Oxford: Oxford University Press, 1976. Develops a rationale for an approach to language syllabus design which starts from content rather than form. Discusses in detail the conceptual, modal, and functional categories such a syllabus would entail and how it might be taught.

Research and Discussion

1. Keep a diary for one day. Note the purposes for which you and your friends have been using language during that day. Compare these with the purposes listed in this chapter and add to the list.

2. List typical activities in which you (or teachers you have observed) commonly engage in the classroom. Decide for each whether it is a useful activity. If it is useful, how could it be converted into a more normal type of activity (in the sense in which "normal" has been used in this chapter)?

3. Make a tape of a session of a conversation group in which you are involved, either as teacher or as student. From listening to the tape, what can you discern of the dynamics of the group? What percentage of the time did the teacher talk? Did all students participate? Did the teacher allow students time to formulate their utterances? Was there any need for correction? Was there any correction?

How was it done? Did the conversation lag? If so, why? What suggestions would you make for improving the sessions of this group?

4. You have been selected to teach a language to an adult class of migrant farm workers. Analyze their language needs in their working situation, along the lines of the CCC classifications, and decide the relative importance for them of the different language skills. What semantic categories would you select as a basis for your teaching and how would you teach these categories to this group? (See references in notes 13, 14, and 16 on pp. 232–33.)

5. You have been asked to take responsibility for the language club. How do you intend to involve the students in running their own club? Set out the types of activities you would propose to the students for one semester or term. Examine your list to see whether these activities will stimulate natural use of language. Are there ways in which you can relate language club activities more directly to the surrounding community?

6. Work out the detailed syllabus of an Oral Survival course for a semester or a term. (Consider first the students' objectives and how they may be achieved. Are your proposed activities open-ended, that is, do they provide opportunities for the students to develop them in their own way when their interest is aroused? Is your syllabus flexible enough to allow for student initiative and autonomous activity?)

7. In the situation in which you teach or will teach, how can the language be taken out of the classroom?

*8. Conduct an enquiry among students who have spent a year (or semester) of study in a country where the language they are learning is spoken. (Alternatively, enquire among students who took part in a short-term school trip of this type.) From your discussions, what are the problems of such study projects? Did the students meet local people who spoke the language? How can this best be accomplished? Were there lasting effects from the project? If so, what were they? Write a report advising an inexperienced teacher on how to organize such a project to ensure effective results.

9. You have decided to adopt a notional approach to the development of teaching materials. Select one communicative function your students need to develop, e.g., persuasion, or showing others how to perform a specific task. Work out what language forms and vocabulary the student will need to perform this function, keeping in mind the semantico-grammatical, modal, and communicative aspects of the function. Develop a unit to teach and practice this communicative function for the language you will teach. See Wilkins 1976 and references in note 16 on p. 233.

9· The Reading Skill

Up to this point we have been laying great stress on the listening and speaking skills. This insistence has been necessary to redress an imbalance which many teachers, because of their bookish interests and traditional training, have tended to perpetuate. Recent intensive discussion of ways of developing the listening and speaking skills from the beginning stages of foreign-language study has sometimes given the erroneous impression that advocates of active oral methods neglect the reading skill. As a result, foreign-language teachers are sometimes accused of wishing to produce "language illiterates," that is, fluent chatterboxes who can speak the new language but have nothing worthwhile to say because they have never been given the opportunity to share the thinking of the great minds of another culture and so to widen the horizons of their knowledge and understanding. This unfortunate impression stems from the fact that many new techniques are described and demonstrated as they would apply to elementary-level classes. This does not imply that later teaching must follow the same pattern. The emphasis on early teaching is, however, relevant to the work of more advanced students in that the ability of students ultimately to think in a foreign language and understand it without mental translation, in both oral and graphic form, is largely the result of the way in which they have been taught to approach their language study in the early stages.

Clearly, reading is a most important activity in any language class, not only as a source of information and a pleasurable activity, but also as a means of consolidating and extending one's knowledge of the language. The main difference in the attitude to reading in recent years has been the emphasis on providing guidance for students in developing their skill in reading, rather than merely expecting it to develop somehow of its own accord. Contemporary teachers of languages try to understand the processes involved in the reading of a written text, especially a text in a non-native language. They then plan learning experiences to help their students develop habits of reading which will lead them to direct comprehension of the text, without resort to translation into their native language. They realize that, if this aim is to be achieved, progress must be unhurried but steady and the teaching of the skill continuous.

Why Reading?

Justification for an emphasis on the development of the reading skill is not hard to find. In many countries foreign languages are learned by numbers of students who will never have the opportunity of conversing with native speakers, but who will have access to the literature and periodicals, or scientific and technical journals, written in the language they are learning. Many will need these publications to assist them with further studies or in their work; others will wish to enjoy reading in another language in their leisure time to keep them in touch with the wider world.

The reading skill, once developed, is the one which can be most easily maintained at a high level by the students themselves without further help from a teacher. Through it they can increase their knowledge and understanding of the culture of the speakers of the language, their ways of thinking, their contemporary activities, and their contributions to many fields of artistic and intellectual endeavor. To imagine that all students who have learned another language at school will do this, however, is a blissful illusion. Unless students have been taught to read the target language fluently, without deciphering it laboriously word by word, and to approach a book or magazine article independently with confidence, it is unlikely that they will want to continue to read in that language after they have completed their studies.

Ability to read another language with direct comprehension and with fluency should be cultivated in progressive stages, and practiced at first with carefully selected material which students can read with ease and enjoyment. Rushing students too soon into reading material beyond their present capacity for fluent comprehension with occasional contextual guessing, which is the ultimate goal, destroys confidence and forces students back to deciphering with a dictionary or word list. This deciphering allows students to piece together the denotational meaning of discrete elements, but they frequently remain insensitive to the overall meaning which evolves from the way these elements interact within the discourse. They tend to miss the mood, tone, or special intent of the passage while extracting detailed information from particular segments. Later, when they have gained confidence, they will be ready for a wide range of materials selected primarily for content and pertinence to their interests, without specific attention to level of reading difficulty.

What Is "Reading"?

Before considering efficient approaches to the development of skill in reading, it is essential to distinguish two activities which go by this name but must not be confused with each other. A student who stands up in class and enunciates in the conventional way the sounds symbolized by the printed or written marks on the script may be considered to be "reading." The "reading" may be comprehensible to a listener, without the reader drawing much in the way of meaning from what he or she is enunciating. Such an activity is one aspect of reading for which the student may usefully be trained, but it is a minor goal. The student must also be taught to derive meaning from the word combinations in the text and to do this in a consecutive fashion at a reasonable speed, without necessarily vocalizing what is being read. This is *reading for comprehension*. The reader may have learned to extract meaning from a text in the native language, but is now faced with a different language code and a fairly unfamiliar one at that. There may even be a quite different script or form of symbolization to cope with.

According to Fries, the student is "developing a *considerable range of habitual responses* to a specific set of patterns of graphic shapes" (Fries 1963, p. 121). When learning to read our mother tongue, we acquire essential space and direction habits: we learn to recognize the shapes of letters in the alphabet of our native language and become skilled at reading these in the direction our language prescribes. We also learn to recognize certain patterns of arrangement (such as paragraph divisions) and become familiar with the punctuation marks and their functions. When we come to read in another language, we already understand what the process of reading signifies. We are alert to the fact that reading involves recognition of certain patterns of symbols and that these represent particular sounds which form words we use or hear spoken. We have also come to recognize with ease particular words which clarify the function of other words close to them, and words which indicate logical relationships among segments of sentences or sections of discourse. We have also learned to identify rapidly word groups which have a meaning transcending the meaning of the individual units of which they are composed. This means that we have learned to extract from the printed patterns three levels of meaning: lexical meaning (the semantic content of the words and expressions), structural or grammatical meaning (derived from interrelationships among words, or parts of words, or from the order of words), and social-cultural meaning (the evaluation that people of our culture attach to the words and groups of words we are reading) (Fries 1963, pp. 104–12).

If the foreign language employs the same alphabet as the native language of the students and is a cognate language, (as is the case with English, French, Italian, Spanish, or German), well-practiced

261

reading habits may hinder the students at first as they try to extract from the foreign-language text these three levels of meaning. They will see familiar combinations of letters which signal distinctively different sounds. They will recognize some combinations of letters, identical or very similar to those of their native language, which signal different lexical or social-cultural meanings. They will sometimes encounter a word order which has a different structural or grammatical meaning from that which their native language has taught them to expect.

The language teacher often assumes that, because students have already acquired reading skill in their native language, reading in another language will not be difficult for them. In practice, the main elements transferred from the student's training in native-language reading are a certain comprehension of what reading is about, an appreciation of the organization of a written text, and a certain awareness of the importance of letter and word combinations. Unlike children learning to read their native language, foreign-language students are not recognizing symbols for words and expressions already very familiar to them in their spoken form. If they are forced to read complicated material in the language too early in the course, they find themselves adrift in a flood of words and expressions they may never before have encountered. Where there is a similar alphabet, they are impeded by interference from well-established native-language habits (this becomes very clear when they read aloud). Structural clues are all awry. Forced to decipher with the aid of a dictionary, they attach inaccurate lexical meanings to units, and units within segments, and are misled in interpretation by their previous cultural experience.

Some teachers argue that experience with a considerable quantity of reading material is essential from an early stage of language learning in order to expand the students' knowledge of the language. This will give them, it is felt, experience with a much wider range of expressions and structures than they could gain from listening and speaking, which are limited to time spent in laboratory or classroom. Let us examine, at this point, one of the practices commonly observed in elementary language classes where students spend much of their time reading. The student deciphers a part of the text with the help of a bilingual dictionary or word list, then hurriedly writes a native-language near-equivalent above each unfamiliar word in the text and rushes on to find out further trivial details of a banal story (as often as not artificially constructed to include certain grammatical forms). Students who do pause to reread skip through a hodgepodge of text, their eyes leaping from foreign words to interlinear native-language glosses. We may question whether real knowledge of the language, beyond casual acquaintance with some isolated elements of it, is attained by a deciphering process like this.

Reading is certainly an important activity for "expanding knowledge of a language," but only under certain conditions. We may ask ourselves several questions. First, have the differences between spoken and written language been taken into account in relation to the course objectives? Have the students been made aware of these differences, so that they are expanding their knowledge of both spoken and written language and not of some unrecognized conglomeration of the two? Furthermore, have students learned to read with confidence and comprehension through a carefully organized series of reading experiences, so that they can draw the maximum of new linguistic knowledge from coherent discourse and not just add a few more isolated items to an already undifferentiated stock?

WHEN SHOULD READING BEGIN?

This again will depend on course objectives. Later in this chapter we will consider courses where reading is a major objective. Here we are concerned with the development of reading skill in communication-oriented general purpose (sometimes called "four-skills") courses.

In our treatment of the speaking skill (chapters 7 and 8), we have emphasized the importance of aural-oral learning in the beginning stages of the course, whether by variation and adaptation of dialogues or by direct or situational methods of oral activity of a less formal nature. Some methodologists, in their anxiety to establish good habits of pronunciation and intonation untainted by native-language habits, have advocated a purely oral period of learning of considerable length (some weeks or even months) before students are allowed to see a printed or written representation of what they are learning. This they feel will lead to a near-native command of articulation and intonation.[1] Experienced teachers, however, have found that, even after a long period of aural-oral training, deterioration in the newly established habits of sound production is often observed as soon as students are presented with a script with symbols similar to those of their native language.[2]

Early advocates of the direct method, under the influence of phoneticians like Passy and Sweet, tried to concentrate attention on proper acquisition of the sounds of the language with a prolonged oral introduction, using a phonetic script as a visual support. This enabled

1. D. Muller, "The Effect upon Pronunciation and Intonation of Early Exposure to the Written Word," *MLJ* 49 (1965): 411.
2. F. Marty, *Language Laboratory Learning* (Wellesley, Mass.: Audio-Visual Publications, 1960), pp. 75–76.

them to include aural discrimination and recognition of sounds, same-different exercises, and phonetic dictation techniques in the early lessons. Nonetheless, the same problems of regression in pronunciation and intonation seemed to arise when the students were finally introduced to the normal printed text, with the added problem of interference of the phonetic script with the new spelling system.

A prolonged time lag between an oral introduction to a language and the graphic presentation of the material learned can cause other problems. Students deprived of any visual support tend to make surreptitious notes of what they think they are hearing, in a form which frequently represents the sounds inaccurately. It is difficult for them later to correct the mistakes which they have been learning according to this system of their own. To relieve students' anxieties about the accuracy of what they remember of work learned orally in class, parents and friends sometimes write down for them what they seem to be repeating, or provide them with old-fashioned elementary textbooks in which they seek out the spelling of what they remember of the class work. Some students with poor auditory memory become overanxious when they are expected to retain everything they hear without the established associations and structural clues on which they are accustomed to rely in the native language. As a result, they develop a psychological block against learning the language. Even students who enjoy the purely oral period find it hard to practice out of class unless take-home cassettes are provided, or laboratory facilities are readily available, and hours of valuable practice may be lost. Finally, where no script of any type is provided for the students, neither reading nor writing exercises can be introduced to provide variety of activity during class and give the overburdened teacher some relief from the strain of continually eliciting oral language use.

A compromise can be reached which allows for reading early in the language course, without sacrificing the undoubted benefits of initial oral training (notably the development of good habits of sound production and the training the student receives in depending on the ear rather than the eye). The introduction to the foreign language may, for most courses, be in oral form, for one week, two weeks, even four weeks, depending on the age and maturity of the students and the experience and confidence of the teacher. Then the script is introduced systematically in relation to the oral forms of the language. For some time all new work is still presented in its oral form first, with the graphic form as a support after the preliminary oral practice.[3] In this

3. Gladys C. Lipton, "To Read or Not to Read: An Experiment on the FLES Level," *FLA* 3 (1969): 241–46, demonstrated that, at least for gifted students of French in grade 4 of the New York City Schools, the introduction of reading after a preliminary oral

way the script helps to consolidate class learning during later individual study. It also serves to clarify certain problems and provides variety of practice.

Where communication is the main objective, it is essential that the bulk of class time be devoted to aural-oral practice, to provide plenty of listening opportunities and to eliminate the students' early inhibitions against expressing themselves in the language. From the first introduction of the written form of the language, students should be encouraged to read directly in the language without translation. This approach is facilitated when the printed script represents at first only variations of material which has been learned orally, and when graphic symbols are continually associated with the oral version, thus providing extra material which students may use orally in a spontaneous, creative way. Students listen or repeat after a model as they read in the early stages, so that from the beginning they associate correct pronunciation with the sound-symbol combinations in print, and learn to segment correctly, superimposing elements of stress, pitch, and intonation that the printed script does not indicate. The script will then become a help to learning, not a hindrance.

Teachers must beware of presuming that students know a section of foreign-language work thoroughly because they are able to read and discuss it with the book in front of them. As a result, the teacher may reduce prematurely the amount of practice provided in the active use of language forms. The script is a prop which students must learn to do without. They must be continually provided with opportunities to use material they have read in the book in an active interchange of communication while their books remain closed. Only in this way can they prove to themselves and their teacher that they have mastered a particular section of the work and need no further practice.

Where the new and the old languages use the same script, both teachers and students need to be constantly alert to possible interference from reading habits associated with familiar combinations of symbols. Deterioration of pronunciation in the direction of native-language phonology and the development of pronunciations based on the spellings of words can become a problem when students are reading with their attention on meaning rather than form, which is, of course, the ultimate aim. Students should be aware of these problems and have opportunities also to practice reading aloud from the script from time to time as a counteractive measure.

presentation (in this case from the second day of instruction) led to superior performance in auditory comprehension, the effect being even more marked for boys than for girls. This result confirmed the theory "that better achievement results are obtained when more of the senses are brought into play during the learning process" (p. 244).

The introduction of reading permits the introduction also of some writing exercises. Reading and writing thus reinforce each other and consolidate the aural-oral learning. The teaching of the four skills concurrently, with emphasis in the early stages on listening and speaking, provides for greater variety of classroom activity for both teacher and student than a purely aural-oral program. Where reading is the major objective of the course, there will naturally be much more reading from the beginning, but even then a certain amount of aural-oral activity in association with the reading (reading aloud after the teacher, listening to the teacher reading the passage) helps the student to segment the new text into meaningful groupings, thus facilitating the development of direct reading skills.[4] Reading aloud in association with reading by the teacher (or a recorded model) also makes the passage to oral proficiency more feasible, since students develop a feeling for the sounds of the language, for intonation, and for the flow of fluent phrases.

- **Discuss the specific problems of a completely different script or a syllabary. Share any experiences you have had in making students familiar with such a script.**

THE PROCESS OF READING

Reading is sometimes referred to as a passive or receptive skill, but if we examine the abilities that come into play in fluent direct reading with comprehension of meaning it is clear that readers are far from passive during this activity. If they have had a purely aural-oral introduction to the language, they must now learn to recognize the sound patterns represented by the graphic symbols and identify their combinations as language units already encountered. They must be able to recognize structural clues: the indicators of word classes (or parts of speech) and of persons and tenses of the verb; the words that introduce phrases and clauses and the particular modifications of meaning these indicate; the adverbs and adverbial expressions which limit the action in time, place, and manner; and the indicators of interrogation and negation. They must be able quickly to distinguish word groupings and their relations with other word groupings. As they take in these various clues at a glance, they must be able to anticipate what will probably follow while holding in their immediate memory inconclusive elements from what preceded. Goodman calls fluent reading a "psycholinguistic guessing game" which requires "skill in selecting the fewest, most productive cues necessary to pro-

4. For a discussion of the practice of listening and reading in association, see W. M. Rivers, "Linguistic and Psychological Factors in Speech Perception and their Implications for Teaching Materials," in *SMT* pp. 131–44.

duce guesses which are right the first time."[5] This is far from easy for a person reading in a foreign language.

These abilities must be developed to such a degree that they operate almost automatically. The mind is then free to assimilate the message being communicated by the interrelationships in the coding, and to deduce from the context the meaning of unfamiliar elements through their relationship to the whole message. This process is made even more difficult for the reader of a new language when the reading material contains many items not yet encountered in their oral form. Familiarity with language items in their oral form facilitates early foreign-language reading, which then becomes a rapid recognition process that leaves more mental energy available for the complex and demanding task of comprehension of sequential meaning.

According to recent research in cognition, speech perception and speech production are different processes, independently represented in behavior. Perception of spoken or written messages is primarily dependent on apprehension of semantic meaning, moving from what one perceives in the sound sequence or in the written script to the idea, with recourse to knowledge of syntax only when the meaning is not clear or an ambiguity or misdirected interpretation is detected.[6] In a second- or foreign-language situation, where the reader does not have full control of the syntactic system of the language, even this recourse to syntactic analysis may be bypassed by resorting to inference from what one has understood. In production, on the other hand, the speaker or writer expresses the intention (or idea) through the operation of the syntactic system, fine details of which may be necessary to give structure to the full semantic intention of the speaker.

It is useful, then, in teaching reading to make a distinction between *recognition* and *production grammar*. The syntactic details the reader needs in order to extract the important elements of the message are fewer and may be different from those which are important when producing one's own messages in speech or writing. In a course primarily concerned with reading, only the details important for extraction of meaning need be emphasized. In a general or four-skills course,

5. Kenneth S. Goodman, "Reading: A Psycholinguistic Guessing Game," *Journal of the Reading Specialist* 6 (1967): 126–35. Reprinted in *Language and Reading: An Interdisciplinary Approach*, ed. D. V. Gunderson (Washington, D.C.: Center for Applied Linguistics, 1970), pp. 107–19.

6. For a fuller discussion of this viewpoint, see T. G. Bever, "Psychologically Real Grammar Emerges because of its Role in Language Acquisition," in Dato 1975, pp. 63–75; and I. M. Schlesinger, *Production and Comprehension of Utterances* (Hillsdale, N.J.: Lawrence Erlbaum, 1977).

on the other hand, students will learn to be alert to certain grammatical details in their reading that are different from those they need for the production of comprehensible messages.

- **Which grammatical features in the language you teach are particularly important for rapid recognition in reading? Which are important in speech production but cause no great difficulty in reading?**

DEVELOPMENTAL STAGES

In many schools the reading of printed texts, in and out of class, has been the main feature of language courses for years; yet, for most students, direct and fluent independent reading does not seem to have been the end product. What is needed is a carefully designed program of developmental stages:[7] at each, students practice certain aspects of reading so that they gradually acquire sufficient confidence to be able to continue on their own, without returning to laborious deciphering. Material for each stage must be selected with the aims of that particular stage in mind. Most students, but not all, will need to pass through each stage. For these students, jumping a stage will lead to regression in reading technique rather than to accelerated progress. Reading can, however, be individualized, and those students who are obviously reading confidently and fluently while their classmates are still unsure should be given material of interest to them to read on their own.

Six stages of reading development will be described in detail. In an aural-oral or direct method program, students usually begin with stage 1 (reading of material already heard or practiced orally) and stage 2 (reading of recombinations and variations of material heard or learned orally), before they move to stage 3 (where they begin to encounter new language material in their reading). Courses which emphasize the reading objective, or where the teacher prefers to move from reading and writing to oral skills, will normally begin with the techniques of stage 2 or 3, depending on the maturity of the students. As has been emphasized throughout this book, course objectives determine approach and techniques, and course objectives are determined by the type of student, the needs of these students, and the situation in which the teaching and learning is taking place.[8]

7. See G. A. Scherer, "Programming Second Language Reading," in *Advances in the Teaching of Modern Languages,* ed. G. Mathieu, vol. 2 (London: Pergamon, 1966; originally published 1964).

8. For a detailed discussion of the relationship of objectives and situation, see W. M. Rivers, "Educational Goals: The Foreign Language Teacher's Response," in NEC 1979, pp. 19–51.

Stage 1: Introduction to Reading

There are several ways of approaching reading. The audio-lingual and direct method approaches will be considered first. In an audio-lingual approach, dialogue sentences are learned through oral imitation, then these same sentences are read in graphic form. This reading is at first choral, the class reading after the teacher or a taped model. Next comes unison reading in smaller groups (the group memory helping the individual student to avoid the pitfalls of unfamiliar sound-spelling combinations). After a successful period of unison reading, individuals are called upon to read. As with small children learning to read their native language, when memorized or partially memorized material is being read it is essential to ensure that the student is actually reading from the text, and not merely repeating sentences by heart upon recognition of initial words or phrases. The teacher may ascertain whether students are reading, rather than reciting, by pointing to particular words or phrases on a chart of sentences and calling upon individuals to read them.

In a direct method approach, early reading is usually based on the type of material students have been learning through classroom experience: that is, they are reading what has already become familiar through oral activity. These early reading passages may be experience-oriented, with the teacher writing down what the students wish to say and then using this as reading material. Some approaches begin with conversational reading material, developing oral work through dramatization of an informally written reading text. This approach skips stage 1.

The student must become familiar at this first stage with the conventional way in which the phonemes of the new language are represented in graphic form. Where a completely unfamiliar script is involved, some teachers prefer to use a romanized script at first so that students will not be deprived of a visual prop during the period of establishing a basic foreign-language repertoire. The unfamiliar script is introduced later when students are able to recognize with reasonable ease the phrases it represents. Where the script differs only in the use of a limited number of symbols, or where there is a one-to-one equivalence between phoneme and symbol in the new alphabet, there is no need to delay its introduction any longer than for a familiar script.

Sound-symbol relationships may be taught directly, rather than being left for some haphazard assimilation to take place. Explanations of these relationships are followed by reading and writing exercises on specific sound-spelling combinations. Spot dictation is also useful; in this procedure the teacher reads a short sentence to the class, asking the students to write down a particular word in the sentence which exemplifies the rule under study. Alternatively, the teacher may read a sentence and pause for the students to pronounce a particular word. (This is an introductory procedure only, to focus attention on sound-symbol correspondences, and must not be continued beyond the initial stages, since students must learn very early to make the assimilations and juncture adaptations of an ongoing discourse.)

For a systematic study of sound-symbol relationships it is sometimes necessary to introduce into spelling exercises words which have not yet been encountered in oral work. Where the relationship constitutes a simple one-to-one equivalence of phonemes and written symbols, the occasional introduction of a new word is not unduly demanding for the student, for most of the material is very familiar. In fact, it may be a challenging diversion to attempt to construct the spelling from known rules. Rare words which the student will never again encounter should be avoided since they overload the memory with useless material.

For languages where the sound-spelling relationship is a complicated one (with perhaps as many as four or five possible spellings for one phoneme) a thoroughly systematic study can be time-consuming and confusing at this stage. The learning of all the possible relationships becomes for the students an abstract task at a time when their energies should be devoted to learning living language which they can use immediately. With mature, linguistically sophisticated students who realize there are difficulties in this area, such a study may be accepted as an orderly approach to an inescapable problem, but beginners as a rule should not be bothered with the less frequent and less useful correspondences.

If the problem of sound-symbol correspondences is to be approached inductively rather than deductively, students will be oriented from their first contact with the text to observe sound-spelling relationships, watching particularly for variations from the anticipated pattern, and listening for mistakes in application on the part of their fellows. As these variations and slips are noted, the basic relationships between sound and symbol can be briefly analyzed and identified. When a number of words with similar sounds have been learned, these words may be studied in close association by writing on the board some of the sentences in which they have occurred. The students themselves will supply the sentences, continuing until they feel the list is representative of the various spellings they have encountered for a particular sound. After the different spellings have been highlighted in this way, the students may practice reading the sentences with careful attention to the correct pronunciation of the sound under study. Students may then copy the sentences into their books, adding to their list as more examples accumulate. At intervals, students may be asked to reread their lists with the new examples which have been added to them. As time goes on, it will be found that all the important sound-symbol combinations have gradually been noted, but in order of frequency of occurrence rather than in some artificial, presumably more systematic fashion. As students read their lists aloud, each sound-symbol learning session becomes also a review of pronunciation.

- **In your experience, which sound-spelling relationships cause the most problems for students of the language you teach? Have you any suggestions as to how they may be taught more effectively?**

Stage 2: Familiarization

At the second stage, students read material they have been using orally, but this time with recombinations and variations. The students may read recombination narratives and conversations developed from dialogues, or short anecdotes and episodes which use the type of material students have been actively producing in oral activities in the classroom. When the course begins with a considerable amount of listening, rather than active speaking, the early reading material will consist of variations on the material to which the students have been listening. In this case, early reading may be performed while the students are listening to the content being read expressively (and dramatically, where conversational material occurs).

At this stage a limited number of new lexical items and some slight adaptations of structure may be introduced to give the students practice in deduction of meaning from context. Students may be encouraged to write their own recombinations within the limits of what they have been learning. After correction, these scripts may be distributed to provide practice in reading for other members of the class.

Since recombination passages are being used at this stage to establish efficient reading habits, unfamiliar words or spelling combinations which will cause difficulty will be carefully prepared beforehand by the teacher, either directly preceding the reading practice or by discreetly including them in the work of a preceding lesson. (In a systematically prepared textbook such problems should not occur.) The passages will then be read or dramatized for the class by the teacher, or by a tape model, and the students will read them after the teacher or model several times to ensure that their later individual reading will be comprehensible and unhesitating. The recombination passages will then be discussed orally, the teacher asking questions which the students do not see, or which they can later read in their books. After this oral discussion of subject matter, the students will reread the passage as correctly and expressively as they can. Since the aim at this stage is to ensure correct production of sounds to correspond with the written script, such passages will not be assigned for home- or private-study reading, or for individual reading or dramatization in the classroom, until they have been carefully prepared under the teacher's guidance.

At stage 2 the student is taught to read in word groups. Fundamentally this means thinking in word groups. The student must learn to look ahead and recognize sections of the thought as it develops (what Nida has called "meaningful mouthfuls").[9] In a dialogue approach, this orientation will be developed with the learning of word groups or phrases as wholes in the oral study phase. In a text where dialogues are not used, teachers will give students opportunities to repeat the text after them in coherent word groups. During intensive oral practice in the classroom, whether for pronunciation or structural manipulation, the teacher must see that the students are on all occasions repeating meaningful segments. Where a backward-buildup technique is employed (as described in chapter 7), this principle should also be observed. When later, in recombination passages, the students encounter these same constructions in a new guise (with variation in lexical content or in a different position in the sentence), they must be encouraged to read them as groups of words which have an essential relationship and whose combination represents a single thought.

In native-language reading, fluent readers look ahead to the next word group, or even further, and relate it to what preceded before reading it aloud. This determines the stress and intonation patterns they will use. (In fact for perfection of oral reading, they need to study the whole passage before attempting oral interpretation.) It is more difficult to do this with a foreign-language text unless the material of which it is composed is very familiar. Students therefore need much practice in reading in "meaningful mouthfuls," never producing orally a new segment until they have identified the word grouping to which it belongs in relation to the ongoing discourse. With recombination conversations or dialogues, a moment to set the scene—to outline briefly the general development of thought or action—and a few moments to glance over the whole passage will help the student, when reading in detail, to anticipate what follows and so to identify more confidently the next word group. In this way techniques that facilitate fluent reading will be acquired.

9. E. A. Nida, *Toward a Science of Translating* (Leiden: E. J. Brill, 1964), p. 128.

It cannot be overemphasized that familiarity with the context and the semantic area which is basic to the reading material is essential in early practice, if students are to develop habits of fluent direct reading. As Frank Smith puts it, "There is a trade-off between visual and non-visual information in reading—the more that is already known 'behind the eyeball,' the less visual information is required to identify a letter, a word, or a meaning from the text" (F. Smith 1973, p. 7). Knowledge of what the writer is talking about helps the student in contextual guessing of the meaning of unfamiliar words.

Above all, word-for-word translation must be avoided. Otherwise, students will think this is what reading is about, and they will then continue to translate word-for-word (mentally if the teacher later tries to discourage overt translation), thus greatly hampering the transition to direct extraction of meaning. Where there is a genuine problem which context does not clarify, the teacher may supply or ask for a translation of the particular phrase or word which is creating the block; this is merely a quick lift over the obstacle which avoids confusion and saves time but does not interfere with the generally direct approach to the text.

Teachers using a text not based on dialogue learning or oral practice in the classroom of the direct method type (in other words, a text which plunges directly into reading material of an informal nature) will prepare the students carefully before expecting them to read the passages in the book. They will first give adequate oral practice in the use of vocabulary items and structures before students meet these in the text. They will then ensure that students have a great deal of practice in reading after them, or after a model, before attempting to read on their own. They will see that the students have some idea of what they are going to read about, so that they may be helped in anticipation of meaning. And from the beginning they will train students to read only in word groups and to identify a whole group before they begin to articulate it.

At the second stage, as in the first stage, we are giving training in techniques of reading which are going to determine the approach of our students for many years to come. Sometimes we underestimate the amount of help our students need in developing reading techniques. We do not read fluently what we cannot say aloud with ease. Even though in rapid direct reading we have passed beyond the stage of sounding out all the words subvocally, when we encounter material which baffles us we often fall back on the strategy of reading it aloud to ourselves to help us determine the meaning. Students should be given opportunities to read very familiar material aloud: earlier dialogues, conversations, and reading passages. This provides practice in segmenting, that is, in reading in word groups which form meaningful units—a subskill which is essential to later rapid reading. If students are encouraged to compete in groups in acting out conversations and dramatizing reading passages, they will happily read and reread the same material for their classmates, without experiencing any boredom or tedium. Simple poetry is also useful in this regard.

Reading aloud of unfamiliar material is, however, another question. In many classes it is common practice to demand this of the students, the reading then being followed by questions on what has been read aloud. This practice does not help the student to develop confidence in drawing coherent meaning from a text, that is, in reading for comprehension, which is the ultimate aim of learning to read in any language. The student's attention is on many things, and concentration on an acceptable oral rendition distracts attention from the content.

Reading for comprehension in its truest sense is not decoding to speech, but precedes decoding to speech (F. Smith 1973, p. 7). For this reason, reading aloud an unfamiliar passage can demonstrate the student's ability to relate rules of sound-symbol correspondence to graphic material, accompanied by the activation of appropriate articulators, without indicating a high degree of comprehension. This lack of real comprehension will be evident in occasional misapplication of stress, juncture, and intonation rules in particular, since these indicate the appropriate allocation of words to meaningful segments in the comprehension phase which preceded the oral production. If individual reading aloud has to be practiced in preparation for some examination (in which case, it is usually used as a means of assessing pronunciation of certain features), comprehension must come first through a preliminary silent reading before the reader can render the text orally with full expression of meaning. It is the silent activity which may rightfully be termed "reading"; the second activity is a different process, which we may call "reading aloud." Individual oral reading, continued beyond the early practice in sound-symbol correspondences and correct segmentation, can have the effect of encouraging students to look closely at individual words, or even syllables, rather than at words in context where true meaning lies. In this way, it can inculcate reading habits that are ultimately detrimental to efficient extraction of meaning directly from graphic material.

Experimentation has shown that concentrating on sound-symbol correspondences and hearing oneself read aloud actually hinder students in extracting a message from a text by preventing them from rehearsing adequately the elements of the evolving meaning as they proceed and from retaining what they have extracted long enough to relate it to later parts of the text. We must remember that the "mean-

274

ing" at one point in a discourse may be radically modified by later information, even by something we read much later, so that holding elements in immediate memory until the full meaning has been extracted is an important step in reading comprehension. For these reasons, asking questions on what has been read aloud, without allowing the student a few minutes to reread the passage silently, is making unrealistic demands on a language learner.

The problem of choosing a suitable textbook is discussed in chapter 14. If the text in use for the early stages does not provide recombinations of familiar material or matter for reading practice with considerable redundancy, it should be discarded, unless the teacher is prepared to write such recombinations for distribution to the class. Without adequate training at stage 2, students will be rushed into reading material in which they cannot recognize even a basic framework of meaning, and they will be well on the way to becoming decipherers, not readers.

In their anxiety to hasten the day when their students can read on their own, well-meaning teachers often destroy the developing direct-reading habits of their better students by putting into their hands supplementary readers, simple enough in content but containing vocabulary, structures, and even tense forms different from those the students have learned and practiced in class. There is time for these at a later stage. Students should not be presented with reading material which is other than a carefully varied recombination of known elements, with a few easily identifiable novelties, until the teacher is reasonably confident that their knowledge of the language is sufficient for them to read most of it without recourse to a dictionary.

Stage 3: Acquiring Reading Techniques

At the third stage, students may be introduced to more sustained reading under the guidance of the teacher. They are now being trained by the teacher to do without the teacher. While class instruction in grammar, vocabulary, and common expressions continues, the students will be introduced to the pleasure of reading simple narrative and conversational materials which develop an uncomplicated but entertaining theme. These will be accompanied by illustrations which assist the student to guess the meaning of any unfamiliar items.

Materials of this type, preferably written by native speakers,[10] should be within the limits of vocabulary and structure being learned by the students, except for the gradual introduction of a few unfamiliar

10. When simple texts are written by non-native authors, the material should always be checked by a native speaker for authentic expression. Many published texts show all too clearly that this simple precaution has not been taken. As a result, expressions

lexical items, the meanings of which may reasonably be inferred from the illustrations, cognates, or the context. Where the new language is a branch of the same language family as the native language of the students, the texts may be liberally seeded with cognates which are easily identifiable in their written form, or with words from the growing international vocabulary for aspects of modern life which is becoming a feature of most languages. Opportunity is thus provided for incidental learning of the regular ways in which such words are adapted to fit into the phonological, morphological, and orthographic systems of the new language. Novel items should be repeated often enough throughout the text for them to be assimilated by the reader.[11] Since the memory span for foreign-language material is shorter than for native-language material, the segments which students will be expected to hold in their immediate memory in order to follow the text easily should be somewhat shorter than in the native language. Because these reading materials will be used for practice in effortless direct reading, the degree of difficulty of the foreign-language expression should be less than that of other sections of the text in which new grammatical structures are being introduced. If fluency in reading is to be the aim, the action described in the reading passages should be easy to follow without requiring students to retain a great deal of detail as they proceed.

There is some controversy among textbook writers whether simple reading matter of the kind appropriate to this stage should be written around familiar situations in the learner's culture or placed in the background of the second culture. If situations common to young people in both cultures are chosen, with a background of foreign ways and places, the material will be of greater interest to the student despite the simple style in which it must of necessity be presented. This will also provide an early introduction to the new culture, enabling the student to identify with people of similar age and interest in a country where the language is spoken.

At this third stage, students need practice in quick recognition of structural clues. As they try to read in word groups without translation, they must develop the art of distinguishing indicators of tense, affirmation, negation, question, and exclamation; words which modify the meanings of other words; relationships of time and cause and effect; and conditional statements. During reading practice, the teacher will find many opportunities to give incidental training in

no longer current in the country where the language is spoken continue to be learned by successive generations of language learners.

11. The subject of density of new words in graded or programmed reading material is discussed in NEC 1963, pp. 30–32.

recognition grammar as problems arise in the text, but the reading lesson must always remain first and foremost the student's time for reading, with the teacher in the background to help, not direct. Recognition grammar is less complicated than production grammar. Many things become clear in context because of redundancy and other clues to meaning—temporal, spatial, or rational. The teacher need only emphasize those aspects of the grammar which can lead to misinterpretation or ambiguity for the reader.

Students should not yet be left to read entirely on their own, as a homework assignment, as is so often the case. Since their habits of direct reading are still fragile, they will inevitably revert to deciphering and translation with the help of a dictionary as soon as they find the material difficult. They should therefore continue reading under the guidance of the teacher. Materials for this stage, having been designed specifically for the development of efficient reading habits, should not be used for grammatical instruction, writing practice, or for any form of intensive language study which will destroy their interest for the students. They should be kept for amusement and enjoyment.

Sometimes the teacher will begin with a short preparation of the general vocabulary or background area, or with an introduction to the story in simple language to excite the interest of the students in what follows. This preparation can often be achieved by discussing a picture on a related theme. When the actual reading begins, part of the story will sometimes be read to the students by the teacher; at other times, sections will be read silently while students look for answers to questions provided beforehand. After a preliminary reading roles may be read by students, with a narrator reading the descriptive or explanatory passages. Parts of the story may also be dramatized by students for the rest of the class. After class treatment of the material, students will be in a position to reread it as a whole with confidence. For this final exercise, three techniques are suggested: the class may reread the complete story silently as the teacher reads it aloud; the class may listen, with books closed, to a rereading of the story by the teacher; or the students may be encouraged to reread the story silently within a certain space of time to encourage them to concentrate on the flow of the narrative.

Many modern textbooks supply extra reading material of the type proposed in this section, either within the lesson units or in supplementary readers for use with the textbook. Where this is not the case, the teacher will need to search for easy readers within a similar frequency word count[12] or general area to that used by the textbook writer. The development of good reading habits is dependent on the teacher's prescribing, at this stage, readers simple enough in expression for the students to follow without too much thought and effort. Unless such material can be found, it is preferable to keep the students at stage 2 for a longer period, for consolidation of reading habits, rather than to force them prematurely into reading material which is beyond their level of development.

- **Draw up a checklist of desirable features you would look for in a textbook for developing reading skill for stages 2 and 3.**

Stage 4: Practice

At the fourth stage the student's reading activities may be classed as intensive and extensive. Intensive reading is related to further progress in language learning under the teacher's guidance. Extensive reading develops at the student's own pace according to individual ability.[13]

Intensive reading will provide a basis for explaining difficulties of structure and for extending knowledge of vocabulary and idioms. It will also provide material for developing greater control of the language in speech and writing. Students will study short stories and extracts from novels, chosen for the standard of difficulty of the language and for the interest they hold for this particular group of students. Poems, if their meaning is not obscured by unusual word order or arcane expressions, are also valuable. Since this reading matter will be studied in considerable detail, it will not serve as the ideal vehicle for further practice in direct reading. This purpose will be served by the material chosen for extensive reading.

Material for *extensive reading* will be selected at a lower level of difficulty than that for intensive reading. Where frequency word counts are available for the language being learned, extensive reading will conform to a lower level of the word count than reading for intensive study. Otherwise, authors will be selected whose choice of structure is habitually less complex and whose vocabulary range is less extensive. The purpose of the extensive reading program will be to train the student to read directly and fluently in the target language for enjoyment, without the aid of the teacher.

Where graded texts are available, structures in texts for extensive reading will already be familiar at this stage, and new items of vo-

12. For frequency word counts and their application to reading texts, see the *PG*'s, chap. 6.

13. Harold Palmer proposed the distinction between intensive and extensive reading in 1917 (Palmer 1917, p. 137).

cabulary will be introduced slowly, in such a way that their meaning can be deduced from the context or quickly ascertained. The student will be encouraged to make intelligent guesses at the meaning of unfamiliar items. For this reason, extensive readers need not contain end vocabularies with glosses in the native language. Some less common words may be explained in the target language in footnotes at the bottom of the page or in the margin. A monolingual foreign-language dictionary will be available on the teacher's table for consultation. This will discourage students from seeking native-language equivalents for every unfamiliar element they encounter. The material for extensive reading will consist of authentic short stories and plays, or informative or controversial articles from newspapers or magazines. With some texts, a few adaptations of vocabulary and structure may be made to bring them within the level of difficulty required, as long as this does not rob them of their authentic flavor. Occasionally material may be specially written for this level.

West makes a useful distinction between *observational reading* and *searching reading*. In observational reading, "the reader goes through the matter observing every word (or almost every word) and waiting to see what ideas arise." In searching reading, "the reader skims over the surface of the printed matter definitely searching for certain required items" (West 1941, pp. 8–9). The first approach is that of the person learning to read and may be expected at various stages of foreign or second language reading, depending on the difficulty of the material. The second approach is that of the practiced reader and is the goal toward which our students should be aiming. As West puts it: "The efficient reader does not drift through the page, like a boat carried by the stream: he drives through it looking for something. The speed of his reading depends on how much he is wanting to get out of the matter. If he wants only one or two points out of a mass of verbiage or irrelevant matter, he reads fast or he skims. If he wants nearly everything that is there, and almost every word is important, he reads slowly" (ibid., p. 79). Our learner-readers need experience in both types of reading, and this experience is provided by the introduction of both intensive and extensive reading materials. Both are valuable, so long as their distinct purposes are kept in mind.

For the development of fluent reading, students must be encouraged to read a great deal. This will only be possible if the subject matter provided is of real interest to them and suitable for their age level. It must approximate as closely as possible the type of material the students would be interested in reading in their mother tongue. If they are at the age when adventure and excitement are important to them in their native-language reading, then they must find these elements in their second-language reading. The background should provide an authentic picture of the culture of a country where the language is spoken, with emphasis on present-day life and preoccupations. If the exotic and outlandish are stressed, the students will be unduly puzzled by the behavior of the characters about whom they are reading, and their ability to deduce meaning from context will be impeded. The student's mind must be kept leaping ahead and anticipating (as in native-language reading). In this way the reader is distracted from the fact that the material is in a foreign language. Students are surprised and delighted when they realize for the first time that they have been reading directly in the language without being conscious of it.

The style of writing in extensive readers should entail a certain amount of repetition without monotony. Novelties of vocabulary, where these do occur, should not coincide with difficulties of structure. The readers must be attractive in appearance with clear print, and the stories and articles should divide naturally into sections which are not too long, so that students have a sense of achievement as they reach the end of a new section. These factors of physical arrangement of material may seem trivial, but their importance in increasing the students' enjoyment in reading must not be underestimated.

The student is now learning to read without the teacher's continual support. The teacher's role at this point is to interest the student in the reading matter and to be available for help and consultation. Sometimes a story or article may be introduced in class before students are left to read on their own. The teacher prepares students for some difficulties, arousing interest in the subject matter, reads the first section with the students, and then leaves them to continue individually at their own pace. Students may be encouraged to read together in pairs, approximately matched for reading ability. They should certainly be allowed to murmur to themselves as they read, since this helps some students to recognize what they are reading. Sometimes questions will be set beforehand for which students have to find answers in the text. At other times, students will come to the teacher as they finish a section to do a quick true-false or multiple-choice test to show that they have understood the script before them.[14] These tests should be based on the important lines of development in the reading material, not on finicking details which test accuracy of memory rather than comprehension.

At this stage, various techniques may be employed to move students from observational to searching reading. They may be given problems

14. For a discussion of testing reading comprehension, see chapter 12 below. Examples of multiple-choice and true-false tests for reading comprehension, with full discussion of the pitfalls are given in the *PG*'s, chap. 7.

for which they must find answers in several pages of text within a limited period of time. Individuals may be given different sections of a text to read, from which they must draw certain information to be shared with others to piece together the evolution of a situation or the resolution of a problem.[15] Anything which excites and interests the students to seek out information from a text will encourage rapid reading, particularly if a competitive or cooperative atmosphere can be created.

As students show by their comprehension that they have successfully read particular texts, they may be encouraged to do supplementary reading in magazines and newspapers available in the classroom. Magazines specially written for learners of particular languages are often available. Teachers should know of these resources and see that their students have ready access to them. These specially written magazines are often produced at several levels of difficulty. Above all, students should be encouraged to read at the level at which they feel most at ease and at which they can enjoy the reading for its content. If the students or the teacher are overambitious in this regard, steady development of reading skill will be greatly hindered, and the inexperienced reader will become satisfied with picking out details here and there through a return to a deciphering or literal translation process.

Some teachers become concerned because their students, when reading extensively, are not conscious at all times of the exact meaning of every item in each sentence. They forget that such close attention to detail is not necessarily a feature of native-language reading when a person is reading for pleasure and not seeking for accurate and detailed information. Children, especially, gain much practice in reading in the native language with books containing many words and expressions which they do not stop to identify precisely. By encountering these words in varying contexts on a number of occasions, however, they do come to class them sufficiently to feel at home with them when they meet them again, and eventually they are able to use them actively with a precise denotation. If students are being encouraged to develop habits of fluent reading in the target language, a certain vagueness of this sort with some words must be accepted as part of the procedure.

Acceptance of the flexible, changing nature of meaning in context is essential to the development of efficient reading techniques. Willingness to withhold judgment, to resist a tendency to closure, to fill

15. B. F. Freed describes in detail this technique in "Communication Techniques and Teaching Reading," *FLA* 9 (1976): 552–57.

in the gaps by inference: these require a certain courage on the part of the anxious reader. It is important, then, to have much reading for pleasure, reading for reading's sake, which is not tested at all, that is, reading to develop confidence in reading.

Students should not be expected or encouraged to stop whenever they meet a new or rather unfamiliar word to insert a native-language gloss between the lines. This habit must be consistently discouraged if they are to learn to think in a second language. If they feel they must write in a gloss, this should always be relegated to the margin. On the other hand, students may be encouraged to increase their vocabulary by keeping individual notebooks in which they copy words they wish to remember. These words should be copied down in complete phrases or sentences, so that the students are continually reminded of the context in which they would be appropriately used. This practice will be more frequently associated with the language-learning activities of intensive reading, but students may be encouraged, after completing an extensive reading assignment, to note down certain new words and expressions which they have marked in their books as recurring rather frequently or of particular interest.

- **Examine a textbook which is intended for stage 4 of reading development: Does it provide material for observational or for searching reading or for both? How does it tally with the standards proposed for reading material in the Textbook Evaluation Checklist in chapter 14?**

Stage 5: Expansion

At stage 4 we have begun to wean the students from dependence on the teacher in the area of reading. At stage 5 we expect this independence to be established, but we are more conscious than the students themselves that they have been nurtured on artificial food and that they are not yet strong enough to eat of any meat that comes their way. For intensive and extensive reading, they will now be introduced to material which has not been adapted in any way to make it more accessible to them. At most, it will have undergone some judicious cutting, to eliminate sections containing excessively difficult vocabulary or complicated structure. As at stage 4, the principle will be respected that material selected for intensive reading (that is, as a basis for extension of active knowledge of the language) will be of a greater degree of difficulty than that recommended to the students for fluent reading at an individual pace for their own pleasure.

Intensive reading material will be the basis for classroom activity. It will not only be read but will be discussed in detail in the target language, sometimes analyzed, and used as a basis for writing exercises. At this stage, some teachers fall into the monotonous pattern of setting a section of reading material for homework preparation every night; they then begin the lesson each day by asking students to translate what they have prepared, sentence by sentence, around the class. This becomes a tedious chore, completed in a purposeless way, and soon destroys any pleasure in the reading assignment. Teachers must work continually for variety of presentation in the classroom.

Sometimes sections of intensive reading material may be set for preparation beforehand, the students being supplied with questions to think about before they come to class. Sometimes students may read the passage together in class while the subject is still fresh and interesting. In either case, students must be encouraged to read whole sections for meaning before attempting to extract the details. In any well-knit writing, details cannot be extracted in linear fashion. (As common experience demonstrates, persons who are very fluent in a non-native language are often at a loss to find native-language equivalents for particular phrases until they have assimilated the meaning of a whole portion of the text.) When students need help in ascertaining meaning, they should be trained to consult a monolingual foreign-language dictionary, so that they may find what the word really means to a native speaker, instead of being satisfied with the loose fit of a native-language gloss.

The ability of the students to talk and write in the foreign language about the material chosen for intensive reading will be very dependent on the teacher's choice of texts. If the material for study is distinctly harder than that at the fourth stage, if the vocabulary is complicated and esoteric with too many new items per page, if the subject matter is too abstract or highly descriptive, students will feel swamped. They will lose confidence in their ability to read a text directly without the support of the teacher or a dictionary, and will often fall back on translation instead.

This is not yet the stage for selecting texts because of their historical significance in the development of the foreign literature. The main purpose of the reading assignments is still the consolidation of language skills. At a later stage, when their specific areas of interest have crystallized, some students will wish to make a specialized study of the foreign literature. Even at the advanced stage, however, the language class should still attract those whose interests are primarily scientific, sociological, political, or linguistic as well as those who are interested in literature for its own sake.

The literature chosen for intensive study should be predominantly contemporary or at least twentieth-century in flavor. (This permits the use of some writers of the nineteenth century whose attitudes and language do not set a barrier between them and the modern reader.) The material selected should parallel the type of material the advanced student would enjoy in the native language: short stories, short novels (mystery stories, detective novels or whatever interests the students), plays, poems where the theme is not too much obscured by experiments with language, articles on scientific discoveries, artistic achievements, political developments, and aspects of contemporary community life in a country where the language is spoken. Film scenarios for which the films are available for viewing are also useful.

Apart from their intrinsic interest for twentieth-century minds, texts of this nature will keep students in touch with contemporary turns of speech and consolidate the work of earlier years in preparing them to understand and be understood in a conversation with a native speaker. It will be soon enough for them, when they specialize at a higher level, to read the great works of the seventeenth and eighteenth centuries. Indeed, if they have already had a superficial introduction to these works at too early a stage, their interest in them may well be dulled when they encounter them again in literature courses. If we provide texts with outmoded vocabulary and syntax as the basic element of the students' diet, we cannot blame them if they assimilate these elements and speak to us, or write for us, in the outworn phrases of a former day.

One of the aims of the earlier stages of language study has been to give the students insight, through their language experiences, into the cultural attitudes and behavior patterns of another people.[16] Many students begin their study of a language with deep-rooted prejudices against the foreign people, based on derogatory stereotypes current in the community. If we choose, at this consolidating stage, material for study which is not contemporary or at least reasonably close in ways of thinking to our own century, or material which is distinctively provincial, atypical, or subtly satirical, without making clear that such texts are of special historical, anthropological, or sociological significance, we may confirm the students in their prejudices. Instead of developing a growing sympathy with their contemporaries and peers in another culture, the students will feel condescension and even contempt for people who seem to them so peculiar, even ridiculous, and obviously ill adapted to the pressures and demands of our age (see Gardner and Lambert 1972).

Information about the foreign culture and its historical background can be imparted by the social studies or history teacher. But only in the language class can students have an experience of another culture

16. For a full discussion of this subject, see chapter 11 below.

by actually participating in it, as they do when they read directly in the language as a native speaker would do. They can read with greater comprehension if they are brought into contact with that part of the culture which represents the spirit of their own century. Modern authors reflecting the strains and conflicts of our complex age will stimulate the thinking of the students and make them eager to continue their reading beyond the minimum demands of the school program.

This emphasis on contemporary material of varied origins applies even more particularly to the student's *extensive reading*. The library should be well stocked with reading material, selected with attention to level of difficulty but varied in subject matter. The teacher should now be able to recommend to individual students reading material which corresponds to their tastes and interests. Some students may pick up a novel or play of which they have heard, or which has recently been made into a film. Others may be encouraged to undertake a course of reading in the language related to some research topic of personal interest to them or required for another course. A standard encyclopedia in the target language, and some serious magazines kept on file from year to year, will provide much reference material of this type. Thus, habits of using the language for one's own purposes will be fostered, and continue as a source of pleasure and profit after the students have left the classroom. Students who leave school without having had the experience of reading on their own and enjoying target-language material of their own choice are ill prepared to do so on their own initiative in later life.

Extensive reading, at this stage, can be made the basis for oral reports to the rest of the class, or full class discussion. It may be the source for written compositions in which students deal with specific issues arising from the material in the book. The class may, on occasions, be divided into groups to read interrelated material. Each group may prepare some part of a project on some aspect of the culture, or on some topic they have been researching, and present a group report to the rest of the class. In this way all members of the class share in what each group has learned from its reading. This type of class project gives point and purpose to extensive reading by building reading practice into a matrix of purposeful activity. The attention of the reader is thus directed toward the extraction of information from the text, rather than toward the reading process itself.

No matter how the teacher organizes the extensive reading program, some record of it should be kept for grading purposes, so that the students will know they are getting credit for the effort they are making. Students will soon set a low priority for any activity which they believe rates low in importance in the mind of the teacher. Comprehension of what has been read can also be tested through purposeful activity: the performance of some task using information derived from reading or the completion of some project. If cooperative tasks are regularly performed by groups of students, the teacher will soon learn to allot grades equitably for successful participation in such group activities.

For *supplementary reading* the library should keep a plentiful supply of foreign-language magazines of a popular and readable type; these should be on display and readily available to students with a few minutes to spare. In such magazines, they will read about similar matters to those they are encountering in their favorite native-language magazines. Pictures and well-designed advertisements will lead them on to read for pleasure more material than they realize or had intended. This, once again, is building for future autonomous reading.

- **Begin for your future use a list of suitable reading material for both intensive and extensive reading at stage 5. With each title make a note of its particular advantages or disadvantages.**

Stage 6: Autonomy
Students with a good background in reading in their course work should be able to move into stage 6 of reading development: the stage of independent reading. They should feel confident enough to pick up a book, magazine, or newspaper and read it for their amusement and enlightenment, with only occasional resort to a dictionary. They will not feel moved to do so, however, if they have not been encouraged during their language course to read on their own with ever-increasing confidence.

Areas of Controversy

Is reading literature in the original language in which it was written more profitable than reading it in translation?
Many teachers, when asked why they believe students should study a foreign language, will reply that they wish their students to have the experience of reading the literature of another people in the original—not only the belles-lettres, but newspapers, magazines, and books of general interest. They believe that reading literature in the original language will give their students the opportunity to penetrate, to some extent, the thought processes of another people and, through experience of their ways of expressing themselves, to share some part of the heritage of their culture.

This is a very worthy aim. We may, however, ask ourselves whether this is in fact the experience that most foreign-language students have in the area of reading. In classes where the reading skill is not taught carefully through various stages of development, students are often thrust too soon into attempting to read advanced foreign-language texts. Even though these books may contain material which should be of interest to the students, it is very frequently expressed in language which they cannot possibly understand without help. They are thus forced into an activity which can only be tedious: the laborious deciphering, with the help of a dictionary, of many pages of text full of unknown words and expressions. All their attention is devoted to this time-consuming activity, so that the most they gain from the experience is a certain amount of information of which they retain only what is necessary for the comprehension of the central theme. It is very probable that students who read in this way would acquire much more appreciation of the literary qualities of a particular work, and much more favorable attitudes to the foreign culture and the ways of thinking of the foreign people, from the reading of a well-written translation, with the teacher available to add thoughtful words of explanation and elucidation.

This is not to say that the reading of a translation has as much to give the reader as the reading of a work in its original language. The original will not, however, give readers more than they will get from a good translation unless they have learned to read fluently and to assimilate meaning directly from the text, without reverting at every step to their native language. A program such as the one outlined in this chapter will make the foreign literature accessible eventually to students who continue with the study of the language to stage 6. As they pass through the earlier stages, they will find the reading of foreign-language texts, carefully selected for their readability at the stage they have reached, a pleasant and rewarding activity. This in itself is important if they are to persist with the language long enough to read literature in its original form with ease, understanding, and enjoyment.

Annotated Reading List

Rivers, Wilga M., et al. *Practical Guides*. Chapter 6 (Reading I: Purposes and Procedures) and chapter 7 (Reading II: From Dependence to Independence) discuss different kinds of reading courses, word counts and frequency lists, techniques, and materials for the six stages of reading development, the assessing of reading comprehension, and vocabulary building.

Thonis, Eleanor W. *Teaching Reading to Non-English Speakers*. New York: Collier-Macmillan, 1970. Discusses approaches to reading, techniques for developing reading skill and teaching content in a non-native language, materials selection, and evaluation of reading growth.

West, Michael. *Learning to Read a Foreign Language and Other Essays on Language-Teaching.* London: Longman, 1941. West believes that foreign-language study should begin with reading as the most realistic objective. He discusses materials preparation and classroom techniques to develop fluent direct reading. Although parts of the book deal with West's experiences in Bengal prior to 1926, it is a delightful classic which provides much valuable guidance for all engaged in the teaching of languages.

Scherer, George A. C. "Programming Second Language Reading." Chapter 5 of *Advances in the Teaching of Modern Languages,* vol. 2, ed. G. Mathieu, pp. 108–29. London: Pergamon Press, 1966. Useful discussion of the mechanics of programming materials for foreign-language reading and criteria for choosing reading texts for various levels. Discusses briefly the six stages in the development of the reading skill. Another version may be found in NEC 1963 Report of the Working Committee II: "Reading for Meaning."

Paulston, Christina B., and Bruder, Mary N. *Teaching English as a Second Language: Techniques and Procedures.* Cambridge, Mass.: Winthrop, 1976. Chapter 5, "Reading," gives many useful suggestions for the conduct of reading lessons which are appropriate for the teaching of any language.

Gunderson, Doris V., ed. *Language and Reading. An Interdisciplinary Approach.* Washington, D.C.: Center for Applied Linguistics, 1970. Contains articles on the reading process by such well-known experts as J. B. Carroll, K. S. Goodman, H. Levin, and R. Shuy. Although the articles deal with native-language reading, they contain useful information for anyone concerned with teaching reading.

Mackay, Ronald; Barkman, Bruce; and Jordan, R. R., eds. *Reading in a Second Language: Hypotheses, Organization, and Practice.* Rowley, Mass.: Newbury House, 1979. A comprehensive collection of articles by experienced teachers on the reading process, and ways of teaching and testing intensive and extensive reading from the elementary to the advanced level.

TEACHING OF LITERATURE

"The Times and Places for Literature," report of Working Committee II, in NEC 1967, pp. 52–102. Discusses the study of literature and how it should be taught, particularly in relation to the level of control of the foreign language by the student.

Moody, H. L. B. *The Teaching of Literature with Special Reference to Developing Countries*. London: Longman, 1971. Examines the place of literature in the language course in a foreign-language situation and the selection of texts. Discusses in detail ways of approaching the study of poetry, prose, and drama, and the link with composition. Examples from English and American literature.

Research and Discussion

1. Examine an elementary-level textbook. How soon is reading introduced? How is it introduced? Do you recognize any developmental stages in the way reading is treated in this book? What suggestions would you make for improving the book?

2. Take a reading passage from an elementary textbook. What structural clues in this text would students need to be able to recognize to draw meaning from the text? How would you plan a lesson to teach students to draw information from these structural clues without turning the reading lesson into a grammar lesson?

3. Examine the oral material (dialogue or active classroom discussion) in the first five lessons of an elementary textbook. Try to write an interesting recombination narrative, using only the vocabulary and structures introduced up to that point in the text.

4. Take a passage intended for intensive reading. At what level would you use this passage? Develop a lesson plan for exploiting this material with an eye to increasing the students' knowledge while providing interesting and varied activities.

5. Take a book of short stories designed to be read at the intermediate level. Examine the themes and situations in the stories. Are they of universal appeal or culture-specific? With what aspects of the culture would readers need to be acquainted? For what age level would you consider this anthology appropriate and why?

6. Examine an intermediate-level textbook. What tasks could you devise for your students for which they would need to draw on reading material supplied in the book? What material could you yourself provide which would better meet the needs of a task-oriented approach?

7. Examine several magazines in the language you will be teaching. Which one (or ones) would you consider most appropriate as supplementary reading (a) at the intermediate level, (b) at the advanced level, from the point of view of content interest, structural difficulty, and vocabulary scope?

8. Take reading passages from books in several different disciplines (one scientific, one humanistic, one philosophical). Study the

linguistic characteristics of these texts. What differences do you detect, if any, in the use of grammatical structures, tenses, or sentence types? Approximately what proportion of the vocabulary items would you consider specialized and what proportion general? Could a common basic course be devised to meet the needs of students who wished to read in these different disciplines?

*9. How should literature be used in a language class? (For references, see Annotated Reading List.)

*10. Take several literary texts frequently read at the advanced level in the language you will be teaching. Apply the procedures of one of the available readability formulas to these texts. List the texts in order of readability. Do any of them appear to be altogether too difficult for students at this level? Compare the most readable of these texts with a story frequently used at the intermediate level. How do these two rank by the criterion of readability?[17]

17. For a suitable readability formula, see E. Fry's "Graph for Estimating Readability—Extended," in Madsen and Bowen 1978, pp. 238–39.

10· The Writing Skill

To be literate in the native language implies the ability to read and write. It is these skills that students, for centuries, have practiced in class. This approach to native-language learning has transferred to the foreign-language classroom, without much consideration of its appropriateness or inappropriateness for students who do not already have the spoken form of the language at their command. Writing exercises keep students busy and out of mischief. Conventional written exercises are easy to construct. The inexperienced or poorly qualified teacher may take them directly from the textbook, with which an answer booklet is usually provided. They may often be corrected as a group procedure in the classroom, and they yield a wide spread of evaluative grades for the teacher's records.

With so much writing in foreign language classes over so many years, one would expect to find highly effective methods for teaching this skill and marked success in learning it. Unfortunately, examination papers in composition the world over are, with few exceptions, disappointing. Many college and university students with four, five, even six or more years of study of another language behind them are still unable to express themselves in a clear, correct, and comprehensible manner in writing. We would do well to examine critically the role of writing in foreign- and second-language learning, to analyze what is involved in the process of writing another language, and to trace out the steps by which this skill can be progressively mastered.

At this stage it may be well to recall two facts often ignored by language teachers, who traditionally have expected students to write something as a demonstration of learning: first, that many highly articulate persons express themselves very inadequately in writing in their native language, and, second, that only a minority of the speakers of any language acquire the skill of writing it with any degree of finesse, and then only after years of training in school and practice out of school.

We must realize that writing a language comprehensibly is much more difficult than speaking it. When we write, we are, as it were, "communicating into space." When we communicate a message orally, we know who is receiving the message. We know the situation, including the mood and tone it requires of us, even if it is as impersonal as "someone in the office" taking a phone message. We receive feedback from the interlocutor or audience (oral, emotional, or kines-thetic) which makes clear how the message is being received and if it is being comprehended. With spoken messages, many things are visible, or are part of shared knowledge, which cannot be taken for granted in writing. The novice writer has to learn how to make such things explicit and unambiguous, once and for all, through syntactic arrangement and lexical choice, whereas in speech the omissions, ambiguities, and misconceptions can be clarified by action, restate-ment, or expansion on the part of the speaker or even of the inter-locutor. It must not surprise us, then, that many students are hesitant to begin to write on some ill-defined subject which seems to have little purpose but its own existence, with no clearly indicated recipient for the message. For expressive writing they need preparation and specialized instruction.

After they have left school, the vast majority of students will never be required to write in a non-native language for anything but the most straightforward of purposes: an occasional letter or short note at most. Those few who will later write the language for career pur-poses will be expected to write correctly in a specific form, as, for instance, in the writing of business letters dealing with precise op-erations (much of which is now done by computers), or in the pre-paring of reports on clearly defined proposals or projects. For this they need specialized training.[1] Only at undergraduate or graduate level will students attempt to write essays in the new language, and then only some students for whom it is clearly important. Even for these, their instructors will bless them if they can write accurately and idiomatically, without attempting flights of fancy or a literary style which is beyond their capacity. It is in listening comprehension and reading that students need to be able to handle the language at the most sophisticated level, because in these areas they will have no control over the complexity of the material they encounter. These are the skills also through which they can improve their knowledge of the language independently at a later stage. In speaking and writing, the non-native speaker rarely achieves the same degree of mastery as the native speaker, even after living in a country where the language is spoken. What students most need in these production areas is to be able to use what they know flexibly, making the most of the resources at their command to meet the occasion.

This does not mean that writing has little to contribute to language learning. Apart from its intrinsic interest or value, it is an essential

1. Specialized courses for persons studying in non-native languages are discussed in Mackay and Mountford 1978.

classroom activity. As we shall see, it is of considerable importance for consolidating learning in the other skill areas; it provides a welcome change of activity; and it will always remain useful as part of a program of testing. Except for students who intend to continue their studies in their second language, writing should be considered the handmaid of the other skills, not the major skill to be developed.

Traditionally, writing activities in language classes have taken the form of the writing out of paradigms and grammatical exercises, dictation, translation from native language to target language and from target language to native language, and imitative and free composition. These activities have at times been the major forms of testing, acquiring, as a result, an undue importance in the eyes of both students and teachers. This has had the unfortunate consequence of reducing the amount of time spent on activities more generally useful to the majority of students, such as listening, speaking, and reading.

It will be readily admitted that the taking of dictation and the writing of grammatical exercises and paradigms, useful as they may be, are means rather than ends, and that skill in these intermediate activities does not necessarily ensure ability to comprehend and communicate in natural settings. Nor can the ubiquitous translation exercises be considered ends in themselves. Few of our students become professional translators, and for those who wish to do so we should provide, at the advanced level, specialized courses in the art of translation. For the rest of our students, continual emphasis on translation from the earliest stages inculcates the naïve belief that languages have a basic one-to-one equivalence which must be identified, with the dictionary as an indispensable tool. This attitude hinders the forging of direct links between meaning and foreign-language expression, a process which is essential for rapid comprehension of oral and written communication, for fluent speaking, and for idiomatic writing. Some translation exercises do have a place in foreign-language teaching, but the value of each type of translation exercise and the degree of emphasis it will receive must be considered carefully in relation to the whole program for developing ability to use language for real-life purposes.

WRITING ACTIVITIES IN THE CLASSROOM[2]

Up to this point in our discussion the term "writing" has been used, without definition, to refer to several activities which are obviously quite distinct in the demands they make upon the student. These may

2. Examples of activities and exercises for each of the categories of writing described in this section will be found, with detailed commentary for specific languages, in the *PG*'s, chaps. 8 and 9: "Writing and Written Exercises," I and II.

be classified as writing down or notation, writing in the language, production, expressive writing or composition, and translation.

In its simplest form, writing may be just *notation:* copying in its conventional graphic form something already written, or reproducing in written form something which has been read or heard. This act may involve nothing more than the ability to use the writing system of the language (already an important skill where a different script must be learned). It may require ability to associate with well-known graphic symbols unexpected sound sequences which for the student have no clear meaning and no significant interrelationships. An activity like this is sometimes used to sensitize students to a new phonological system and to important sound discriminations they must be able to make. Where the spelling system of the new language does not correspond in a one-to-one relationship with the sound output, reproduction in writing from spoken output can be a necessary long-term activity. For effective spelling practice of this type, students must, of course, be presented at all times with meaningful units in context.

Writing in the language becomes more complicated when it involves writing meaningful segments of language which might be used in specific circumstances by native speakers. This is the type of writing which is involved in grammatical exercises, the construction of simple dialogues, uncomplicated translation exercises, dictation, and the cloze procedure. This activity we may call *writing practice.* Writing practice moves from the more guided types of exercises, where elements of structure and vocabulary are manipulated, expanded, transformed, and restated in various ways, to more flexible production in writing, where students begin from the material provided and develop it out in an individual way. These flexible production activities may be related to what has been read or heard. They may also be preparatory to oral production in the form of short talks, oral reports, or dramatizations using material being currently studied.

In its most highly developed form, writing refers to the conveying of information or the expression of original ideas in a consecutive way in the new language. This we will call *expressive writing* or *composition.* Composition may be for practical purposes (the writing of instructions, reports, résumés, concrete descriptions, or essential correspondence connected with everyday affairs), or it may be more creative. The ultimate goal in creative expression will be to express oneself in a polished form which requires a nuanced vocabulary and certain refinements of structure. Finally, as a different form of written expression, we have fine *translation,* which is to some extent a meticulously controlled activity and to some extent creative, depending on the type of translation and its purpose.[3]

In our language classes, all of these stages of writing have some place, although many students will only approach expressive writing at a relatively unsophisticated and unpretentious level, preferring to remain with the practical. With the time at our disposal at the elementary level, we will concentrate on giving our students training and practice in writing down what they would say in various circumstances, with some attention to the differences between the conventions for spoken and written style. At the more advanced level, we will encourage them to express themselves with some finesse in oral discussion of more significant subjects, and then to write their ideas, with careful attention to lexical and structural choice.

Skill in writing in an elegant fashion in a foreign language, according to the canons of an educated elite, is an aim impossible of realization at the high school stage and demands a mastery of the foreign language which many high school teachers themselves do not possess. For undergraduate or graduate students it will be necessary to decide, after due consideration of their objectives in learning the language, to what level of felicitous expression the students need to be trained. For most students, ability to express their meaning clearly and accurately will be sufficient; specialized composition classes will meet the needs of the few who require more than this.

These distinctions among types of writing activities reflect the major areas of learning involved in the writing process. Students must learn the graphic system and be able to spell according to the conventions of the language, if what they write is to be comprehensible and acceptable to a native speaker. They must learn to control the structure according to the canons of good writing. They must learn to select from among possible combinations of words and phrases those which will convey the meanings they have in mind, and, ultimately, they must be able to do this so that nuances in the appropriate linguistic register are expressed through their writing. To reach this stage, students must have such a control of the mechanics of good writing that they are able to concentrate all their efforts on the process of selection among possible combinations.

At each stage, emphasis will be placed on writing something that will be read by someone, preferably not just by the teacher. Material may be copied or reproduced for display on a bulletin board (if individuals are copying different passages, this becomes more inter-

---

3. Translation is discussed in relation to testing in chapter 12, pp. 375, 381. For a detailed discussion of translation as a teaching device and the teaching of translation, see *PG*'s, chap. 9.

esting). Dialogues written as recombinations will be acted by other students. Students will write instructions for activities or information as part of a game, competition, or out-of-class activity, in each case supplying something which other students will need to read in order to proceed. Even at an elementary level, they will write items of news which may be posted on a bulletin board, passed around in multiple copies, or gathered together for a weekly class news sheet. To give students a sense of purpose in their writing, the teacher must think out ways of making the exercises themselves purposeful.

- **For what useful purposes can students write in the language in your situation?**

INTEGRATION OF THE SKILLS

Writing is not, then, a skill which can be learned in isolation. In the apprentice stage of writing, what the student must learn, apart from the peculiar difficulties of spelling or script, is a counterpart of what has to be learned for the mastery of listening comprehension, speaking, and reading—a nucleus of linguistic knowledge. The activity of writing helps to consolidate the learning to render it available for use in these other areas. Writing gives the student practice in manipulating structural variants and in selecting and combining lexical elements, adding the reinforcement of the kinesthetic image to the auditory and visual. Where a new script is involved, writing helps the student distinguish one form from another.[4] It is impossible to reproduce forms correctly if one cannot visually detect the differences among them. As one becomes familiar with forms and shapes, rapid recognition for reading purposes is facilitated. Written questions based on a reading passage encourage the student to read the text more attentively and discover areas which were misinterpreted on the first reading.

In its more advanced form of composition, writing is dependent on progress in the other skills. Accurate, idiomatic writing is quite different from the mere piecing together of language elements in some artificial patchwork which would never be encountered outside the classroom. Only by hearing and reading a great deal of the language as it is spoken and written by native speakers can language learners acquire that feeling for the appropriate use of language forms and combinations which is basic to expressive writing. What they are unable to say over to themselves, they will be unlikely to write with ease, and until they have read a great deal they will not be familiar with the way native speakers express themselves, for various purposes, in writing.

4. Hints on teaching students to write a new script are given in the section "Writing a Different Script," in chap. 8 of Rivers and Temperley 1978, pp. 266–67.

It is obvious, then, that the most effective writing practice, and the most generally useful, will have a close connection with what is being practiced in relation to other skills. Writing practice will at first be a service activity, consolidating work in the other areas. While the students are using it to reinforce other learning, they will be mastering the technical details of the art of writing. The higher levels of composition will be possible only when the student has attained some degree of mastery of the other skills. It will be well for the teacher to keep in mind that some will never reach a high standard in composition in another language. These students should not be driven into a state of frustration by examinations heavily weighted in favor of the writing skill, when it is evident that they have achieved a satisfactory mastery of the skills of listening comprehension, speaking, and reading.

Many writing weaknesses in advanced classes can be traced back to lack of systematic practice during the earlier stages of the language course. Often students in elementary classes are encouraged to try their hand at creative writing in the foreign language for fun, while the teacher turns a blind eye to the monstrosities they create. Students are soon in over their heads, and develop the habit of attempting to express themselves in strange words, often sought out in an inept way in a dictionary, before they have any adequate control of language structure. Believing that they are writing acceptably, they contrive expressions on the pattern of native-language forms, happily constructing hybrid phrases without realizing that these are quite incomprehensible in the context of the new language. To be sure, attempts at writing creatively can and should be encouraged from an early stage, so long as students have a clear realization of the limitations of knowledge within which they are composing. They then try to use in original combinations structures and expressions they have already learned in oral practice and reading, often creating interesting and amusing pieces of expressive writing. In so doing, they use and reuse in novel combinations much language material which otherwise would gradually be slipping from their active memory. Meanwhile, they continue systematic study through the various types of activities we have outlined, which will now be discussed in detail.

WRITING DOWN: NOTATION

Copying
Copying (sometimes called transcription) is often despised by teachers as an unworthy and unchallenging occupation for language learners. This attitude is unfortunate, since it ignores the fact that there are

many aspects of another language which are very strange to learners, and with which they need to familiarize themselves thoroughly if they are to write the language confidently. Where there is a new script to be learned, a disdainful attitude is less likely to arise, because accurate copying is obviously needed for purposes of recognition and reproduction. Where the script is the same as in the native language, and where there are many similarities between the two languages, careful copying focuses the student's attention on the differences between the native and target languages. The work to be copied should consist of sections of work already learned orally and read with the teacher. As students are copying, they should repeat to themselves what they are writing. In this way they deepen the impression they have acquired of the sounds the symbols represent, and they have further practice in producing fluent sentences. Particular attention should be paid to diacritical and punctuation marks which are distinctive elements of the written language.

In languages where sound-symbol correspondences are particularly complicated, copying activities may be continued side by side with more advanced writing practice. Students who have made lists of short sentences containing words with different spellings for the same sounds may copy these lists several times, concentrating on the variations in spelling. If they are assigned lists of words to be learned because of their peculiarities of orthography, they may be asked to copy the words several times as they are learning them, thus imprinting the graphic outlines more firmly in their minds. In the early stages, credit should be given for accuracy in copying, in order to encourage students in careful observation of details.

Reproduction

At the reproduction stage, students will attempt to write, without originality, what they have learned orally and read in their textbooks. This they will be able to do all the more successfully if they have been trained in habits of accuracy during the copying stage. If sound writing habits are to be firmly established, the learning situation should be structured so that the students will write correctly, not incorrectly, particularly since it becomes impossible for the teacher to check every item that is written down. Students will initially be asked to reproduce from memory only sentences and phrases which they have learned to copy. As a first step they will be asked to rewrite immediately each sentence they have copied without reference to their copy or to the original. They will then compare this version with the original for correction. Next they will be asked to write down sentences they have both learned and copied, as they are dictated to them.

Writing Practice

When dictation procedures are employed for reproduction, it is well for the teacher to realize that two skills are being exercised at once: listening and writing. Since all the skills are finally integrated in language knowledge, this is not necessarily a disadvantage, but the teacher must be aware of the fact that what is being required of the student is more than a simple exercise in writing. Where particular difficulties of spelling are being emphasized, the spot-dictation procedure may be adopted: a complete sentence will be read, but only the word or words which are repeated will be written. To avoid confusion in this exercise, some teachers supply an outline with blanks to fill in.

At a further stage, the teacher will call for the writing of a learned phrase as a response to a question, or as a description of a picture. Here students will be demonstrating understanding of meaning and memory for learned response, as well as ability to distinguish aurally and write accurately. Where the direct method is being used, the students will be asked to reproduce in writing, at a cue from the teacher, sentences which have been practiced orally in classroom activity and read in the textbook. At the reproduction stage, the students' writing activity does not require variation of learned phrases, since the emphasis is entirely on accuracy of reproduction.

WRITING PRACTICE

Recombination

At the recombination stage, students are required to reproduce practiced sentences with adaptations. This parallels in conception the recombination stage in oral work and reading. The work for recombination in writing, however, will always be a little behind what is being spoken and read. The writing of recombinations of practiced sentences requires not only the ability to manipulate grammatical structures to express meaning (which is also basic to the speaking skill), but also a sound knowledge of the intricacies of representing graphically what the student is required only to recognize in reading. More effective results will be achieved in writing exercises if there is a continual integration of practice in all the skills. At first, the students will have already heard, produced orally, and read in their textbook recombinations of the type they will write. When the students have demonstrated that they can say over to themselves correctly what they are to write, they will be asked to construct recombinations themselves. In this way, the beginning student is much more likely to write correctly.

The Writing Skill

At this stage, writing practice may take a number of forms. Students will write out grammatical exercises of different kinds: making substitutions of words and phrases, transforming sentences, combining them in various ways, expanding them to include further information within the limits of what they have learned, contracting them by substituting pronouns for nouns or single words for groups of words. (Many of the exercises discussed in chapter 4 can be used in this way.)[5] The writing of grammatical exercises not only gives valuable practice in accurate and correct construction of sentences but consolidates what has been learned orally. It is a useful home study exercise, ensuring that the student gives careful thought to work studied and practiced in class during the day.

Although fill-in-the-blank and multiple-choice exercises have their uses as a rapid check of how accurately certain grammatical features have been learned, they provide little or no practice in writing the language. To learn to write, one must write—and write full sentences, not isolated words. For the teacher, this naturally means more work to correct. If students are trained from the beginning, however, in disciplined rereading and checking of what they have written, this burden can be reduced. They may occasionally check each other's work, but only for class exercises, to ensure immediate confirmation of the correctness of the response and to save some teacher time. Where a grade is involved, the teacher must also check the work to make sure that the grading is equitable.

When students have acquired some confidence in writing simple substitutions and transformations, they may be asked to make novel recombinations around a theme presented to the class in a picture or a series of pictures. These pictures will represent situations in connection with which the students have learned phrases orally or in their reading. The recombinations may take the form of variations of dialogues, which, after correction, may be acted out in the classroom. At first these recombinations will not involve much new vocabulary. Later they may provide the occasion for some expansion of vocabulary into new areas. This vocabulary will be introduced orally and then learned in some group exercise or game before being used in writing. The teacher will see that students are not required to make a recombination which involves a structural change and new vocabulary at the same point in the sentence. The simple rule of one problem at a time will decrease the possibility of error and make for more effective learning. Correctness in writing may be further ensured if recombinations are first constructed orally in class. Students will not

5. See also *PG*'s, chap. 4: "Oral Practice for the Learning of Grammar."

be asked to write such recombinations unsupervised until they have had sufficient practice to ensure success.

Recombination Dictation

Recombination dictation—a mixture of recombination and reproduction—consists of rearrangements of dialogue sentences, or narratives constructed from the conversational material or from pattern sentences used in classroom oral practice. Since dictation involves ability to recognize these recombinations aurally and retain them, as well as reproduce them graphically, such dictations must be constructed carefully so that problems of aural recognition do not coincide with problems of graphic representation. At this stage, work to be written from dictation should not contain distinctly new elements. Elements recombined should be ones which have already been practiced and learned thoroughly, studied in graphic form, and used in some kind of writing practice, with, at most, the addition of some simple analogic variants of these. The dictation will then serve as a form of review, the possibility of error will be reduced, and the students will be encouraged by their progress.

The teacher should dictate at a normal speed of utterance, not distorting the phrases and the flow of speech in any way. Segments dictated should consist of meaningful word groups. Each phrase should be repeated clearly only once before students are expected to write it. Since some students become flustered when expected to retain what they have comprehended aurally long enough to write it accurately, students should be encouraged to repeat aloud to themselves what they have heard before attempting to write it from dictation, and then to repeat it again as they write it. This oral repetition helps them to retain what they have heard long enough for them to write the complete phrase. After they have had time to write the whole phrase, the same segment should be repeated to allow students an opportunity to check what they have written and correct any inaccuracies. At the end of the dictation of the whole passage, time should be allowed for rechecking of accuracy of writing before the passage is reread a final time, with normal intonation and fluency. This period for checking forces students to do some thinking for themselves before the final reading, and makes them more alert to the sections of the final reading which they most need to hear again.

If the procedure outlined is adopted from the early stages of learning the language, students will be trained to retain whole phrases in their immediate memory. The dictation practice will then be reinforcing practice in listening comprehension as well as providing practice in accurate writing. As students advance in language learning, phrases dictated will gradually be lengthened, until the students are eventually able to retain complete sentences in their immediate memory and write them down correctly.

PRODUCTION: GUIDED WRITING

At the guided writing stage, students will be given more freedom in the selection of lexical items and structural patterns for their written exercises. This will, however, be within a framework which restrains them from attempting to compose at a level beyond their state of knowledge. They will begin with outlines which allow for some individuality, but which also help them to keep to what they have learned. They will gradually move on to composition which is so closely associated with what they have read or heard that, without feeling unduly restricted, they will still be using and reusing what they know. As their control of writing techniques increases, they will be ready to move into the composition stage, where they will be attempting to express their personal meaning in the new language.

Early in the production stage the student may attempt completion exercises, where parts of sentences are given and the structural pattern for the completion is thus established. Each student will, nevertheless, be expected to construct an individual answer in the choice of a completion. Some types of drills provide useful guides for writing. Replacement exercises may be devised in which a section of the sentence can be replaced by a number of different phrases, giving the student the opportunity to express new meanings. Expansion of a simple sentence by the addition of modifying words and phrases, or the inclusion of further information, can give practice in developing meanings within a framework. Along the lines of a substitution drill, the student may take a given sentence and see how many different meanings can be expressed by lexical changes, within the limits of the structure provided.[6] Another form of outline supplies lexical items in their unmarked form in a fixed order which forces the student to use certain grammatical structures.[7] This restricts the semantic area within which the students may express themselves but leaves them free to vary such elements as person, tense, and number.

As students advance in skill, they may be allowed more freedom in their choice of expression. The framework will now come from

6. Examples of strictly controlled and more creative uses of substitution tables for developing writing skill may be found in C. B. Paulston, "Teaching Writing in the ESOL Classroom: Techniques of Controlled Composition," *TQ* 6 (1972): 40–45.

7. "Unmarked form" is a linguistic term. It refers to the base form to which morphological variations are made (*bat:* bats). "Dehydrated sentences" of this type (e.g., Cat/love/mouse) are illustrated in the *PG*'s, chap. 9, W45–49.

stories and articles they have been reading. At this stage they will be learning something about the differences between the conventions for spoken and written style. They may answer questions on a text read or heard, the questions requiring more and more individuality of response as their skill in writing increases. They may write summaries of stories they have studied in class, heard in the laboratory, or enjoyed for extensive reading. They may rewrite a story, or a part of a story, from a different angle. (This exercise may be designed so as to require a different tense; the story may be rewritten in the first person as told by one of the characters; or one of the characters may give explanations or explain the reactions of others, thus forcing the student into using indirect discourse.) A story may be rewritten in dialogue form or a dialogue rewritten as a narrative. The setting or main personalities of a story or dialogue may be changed in such a way as to require certain changes in the description, in the action, or in the tone of the conversational exchange. The skeleton of a story or dialogue may be supplied for development by the student, or an outline given for a description or narration based on a picture or a succession of pictures. As a variation of this procedure, a series of questions may be so constructed that in answering them the students write a continuous narrative. If pictures are used, the writing activity may be associated with intensive work in vocabulary building. With some imagination, the teacher will not be at a loss for finding ways of guiding students in elementary composition.

Writing at this stage is still under supervision. The teacher should see that the students do not lapse into the habit of writing native-language versions which they then translate inexpertly into the target language. As at all stages in developing the writing skill, problems which may arise in the exercise are anticipated in oral group work so that students know what is expected of them. Most of their difficulties are thus overcome before they are left to their own resources. Students work without bilingual dictionaries, endeavoring to use what they know or what they can learn from the model on which their guided writing is based. In this way, they are likely to adapt and paraphrase in order to reuse language material from previous lessons, rather than rush to a dictionary every time they need an expression which does not come readily to mind.

Until students have acquired the technique of relying on variations of what they have learned for the expression of their own ideas, and have begun to appreciate the role of the outline or basic text in stimulating ideas (while serving as their guide to authentic expression), they should continue to do their initial writing with the teacher available for assistance. In an unsupervised situation they will be required at first only to rewrite or improve work which has been prepared in class. These restrictions are essential if students are to be trained in good writing habits. Left to their own devices too soon, they will hasten to the dictionary and attempt a standard of expression beyond their state of knowledge. As a result, their developing skill in this area will soon deteriorate.

- **Can you think of other forms of framework from real-life materials which would provide useful guides for composition at this stage?**

EXPRESSIVE WRITING: COMPOSITION

The final stage of composition involves individual selection of vocabulary and structure for the expression of personal meaning. In a second or foreign language, students are still not able to use as wide a range of expression as a native speaker. Their knowledge of the second language is still very inferior to their knowledge and control of the native language. If asked to write on subjects which are too general, too philosophical, or too literary, they will be frustrated by their desire to write at the standard they have reached in native-language composition, at a stage when their resources of expression in the new language are still comparatively limited. If they have been carefully prepared, however, through the preceding stages, they will have developed an attitude of mind which will prevent them from committing the worst excesses of clothing native-language expressions and structures in foreign words.

The key word for students in this dilemma is "simplify." They must clothe their thoughts in simple, lucid language which is well within their command. Encouraged to use a monolingual rather than a bilingual dictionary and to think before they write, they will be more likely to use what they know, checking on its accuracy and examining the possibilities of suggested alternatives, rather than seeking inexact and misleading equivalents for notions they have not yet encountered in their experience with this new language.

At this stage they will be increasing their understanding of the differences between speaking and writing in the language. Apart from observing the conventional differences between spoken and written language, they will be trying to express themselves more concisely, more descriptively, less casually. This will severely test their control of structure and their precise understanding of lexical meaning. The composition stage provides teacher and student with the opportunity to identify persisting areas of misunderstanding on an individual basis, so that remedial practice may be undertaken where necessary.

When students have reached what is considered to be an advanced language class, the teacher will need to exercise great care to see that they are not plunged abruptly from guided writing into the limitless sea of free expression. The transition has to be gradual. Exercises in composition will at first be closely linked with material being read and discussed. Students will be asked merely to describe, narrate, explain, or summarize. As they become more accustomed to expressing themselves within voluntarily accepted restrictions, they will be asked to comment on or develop ideas beyond those in the material read. Only when their skill in writing lucidly, comprehensibly, and accurately is established may they be expected to imitate the style of great writers, write literary criticism, or discuss ideas at a philosophical or sociological level. For these types of exercises, they need a specialized vocabulary and training in concepts which go beyond what the language teacher is aiming to supply. Time taken out for these things reduces the time available for developing overall proficiency in handling the new language.

It is as well to remember that not all students have a ready flow of ideas when asked to write, even in their native language. Composition exercises which are not closely related to intensive reading assignments should be so designed that they do not become tests of originality and invention (although imaginative students with a good grasp of the language should never be discouraged from going beyond what is required from the less inspired). Precise descriptions of persons, places, and things provide excellent training in exact expression, as do instructions and arrangements. The writing of an original dialogue, using the vocabulary area of some recent reading, keeps the student practiced in the style of spoken language. Further practice in a more casual style of writing may be provided by the keeping of a personal diary or by international correspondence on an individual basis. (In the latter case, students are appropriately instructed in the accepted formulas for letter writing.) Students may have read to them, or be asked to read, parts of stories, which they are then required to complete for themselves; in this way, they have already been initiated into the appropriate vocabulary area and level of language before they attempt to write on their own.

Composition exercises may profitably be linked with assignments for extensive reading. As each book, story, or play is completed, the student is asked to submit, for correction and evaluation, a short composition based on it. This composition may consist of a summary of the contents with a personal commentary, or the narration of some aspect of the story assigned previously by the teacher. Students with imagination and a flair for invention will be encouraged to use their originality in selecting their own approach, and in this way they will be able to demonstrate the level of expression of which they are capable.

Extensive reading assignments may direct students to articles of current interest in foreign-language magazines or newspapers. To ensure that students do not become bogged down in reading which is too complicated or esoteric, the teacher will be well advised to discuss the selection of articles to be read, with due regard to the special interests of the readers. Otherwise, discouraged students will take little pleasure in what had promised to be an interesting activity. Where newspapers in the language being learned are freely available, students may be asked to submit at regular intervals short written accounts of items of news they have read. These reports may also be given orally, without consulting the written text, thus providing subject matter for class discussion and further exercise in the speaking skill.

In classes where students have been encouraged to undertake group or individual projects to deepen their understanding of the culture of the people who speak the language (as described in chapter 11), they will have valuable practice in composition as they draw up reports of their research in such areas as geography, history, sociology, art, music, education, political institutions, conditions of work, lives of famous men and women, and so on. For such projects the students should be required to draw their information from sources in the target language so that they may use authentic forms of expression in their written and oral reports. They should be asked to submit short reports on sections of their research for correction at regular intervals, rather than one long report at the end. The teacher can then guide them in the progressive improvement of their writing efforts. These reports, like those on extensive reading, should also be given orally to the class at some stage and used as a basis for further discussion.

CORRECTION OF WRITTEN EXERCISES

Many experienced teachers will say: "This is fine. This is what we aim to do, but is it possible?" The practical problem is that, to be effective, systematic training in writing requires systematic correction of individual scripts. With the usual class size, this can impose an intolerable burden on the most willing teacher. Approaches to the correction load must be developed which will give the most help to the student while making reasonable demands on the teacher.

Ideally, individual efforts at writing should be read by the teacher as soon as possible after completion, then corrected and sometimes rewritten by the students without delay. A great deal of uncorrected writing is merely a waste of time and energy. Inaccuracies and misconceptions become firmly fixed in the student's mind and are difficult to eradicate at a later date. Short writing assignments, given at frequent intervals and then carefully corrected and discussed, provide the most effective form of practice.

The following suggestions may be useful for the stage when students are launching out into the area of free expression in the non-native language. First, the students should be asked to write only one or two well-planned, carefully written paragraphs until they have acquired some skill in writing without a framework. The approximate number of words may even be stated, so that the more enthusiastic will not stretch their concept of a paragraph beyond reasonable limits. The teacher can cope with the correction of one or two paragraphs where complete compositions would take up far too much time. Second, from the very early stages of their writing experience students should be rigorously trained to study their own scripts systematically in order to eliminate as many errors as possible before submitting them for the teacher's perusal. Carelessly presented scripts should be refused and given back for rewriting. In this way the teacher will make a considerable saving in correction time, and students will be given valuable training in habits of accuracy which will serve them well in later work or study situations. Third, the teacher should anticipate certain common types of errors by giving regular practice in class groups in the use of tenses, ways of combining clauses with sentences, and conventional phrases used for making smooth transitions in thought. Fourth, teacher and class should agree on some system of symbols to be used in correcting compositions.

Teachers waste much time writing in comments and suggested improvements on composition scripts. The student who looks these over in a cursory fashion gains little from the teacher's laborious effort. Correction time is reduced by underlining errors and using a letter symbol to indicate the type of mistake made, whether lexical, syntactical, morphological, or orthographical, with special attention to errors which would make the composition incomprehensible to a native reader. The symbols should correspond to precise categories of errors, so that the students realize quite clearly the types of corrections they should make. When this system is used, the teacher returns the scripts to the students in class, allowing sufficient time for individual correction of mistakes under supervision, and for discussion of the implications of the commonest faults. If class size permits it, students may resubmit corrected versions for further checking. By making the students think through the errors they have made, the teacher will be using the compositions for teaching, and not merely for unsystematic practice or for constant testing.

The Writing Skill

Students will learn more quickly if at the end of each composition the teacher notes one or two particular areas on which the student should concentrate next time in order to improve. Perhaps a particular student needs to pay attention to the use of articles or to the selection of tense forms. The teacher will note down the kinds of problems recommended for special effort and check next time the progress this student has made in these areas. Thus students will understand what they must do and be working at the progressive elimination of weaknesses, rather than give up in discouragement before the seeming immensity of the task.

An organized correction system also helps the teacher to evaluate the work more quickly and systematically. An overall intuitive grade for written composition can be seriously influenced by neatness and clear writing. The grade should be a composite one, allowing a certain percentage for syntactic choice and accuracy; for lexical choice; for expression of time sequences; for general idiomaticity or feeling for authentic expression; and for arrangement of ideas. Where a symbol system is used, the teacher can more quickly assess the relative degree of error in the different areas. The emphasis given to each area will vary as students acquire more skill, so that at an advanced level considerable weight will be given to ability to communicate ideas, and to structural and lexical choices which make the composition read like a piece of authentic writing in the language.[8]

- **Devise a symbol system that you will use for composition correction.**

How Much Writing?
The listing of so many possible forms of written exercises may confuse inexperienced teachers, who, having glimpsed the core of the problem (that thorough, graded practice is required if students are to be able to write well in the foreign language), may believe that writing practice should occupy a large part of the teaching time at their disposal. This would bring us back to the traditional situation of the silent classroom, disturbed only by the busy scribbling of pens on paper. The amount of time that should be allotted to practice in writing will depend largely on the objectives of the course. Writing may be very important for one group of students but much less important for others. The decision on how much writing to include will, then, be made independently according to the needs of each group of students.

What is clear is that writing is a skill which must be taught and practiced. It cannot develop haphazardly to any degree of usefulness.

8. For a proposed weighted assessment scheme for expressive writing, see the *PG's*, chap. 9, W61.

It is most efficiently acquired when practice in writing parallels practice in the other skills. Writing provides an excellent consolidating activity. Through it the teacher can bring welcome variety into classroom work. It is also useful for setting homework exercises and for some class tests. It must not, however, be allowed to absorb so much time that aural-oral training and further development of the reading skill are neglected. If, as has been suggested, it is considered a service activity for most students rather than an end in itself, the teacher will find that the problem "how much writing?" soon solves itself. The type of writing in which the students are engaged will become more sophisticated as they acquire greater facility in the exercise of the other skills.

Areas of Controversy

Should an absolute standard of accuracy be required in writing exercises?

Accuracy in written exercises becomes an obsession with some teachers, to such an extent that it distorts their assessment of the relative merits of the written assignments of students. Often teachers demand of their students a standard of accuracy in writing which many educated native speakers of the language do not display. Many students who are the pride of their teachers in creative writing classes in their native language are notoriously careless about details of their writing. (It is significant that some of the scripts submitted to publishers by university professors and professional writers need considerable editorial revision.) It is obvious, then, that skill in writing consists of something more than mere accuracy.

If the teacher takes accuracy as the main criterion, the following anomalous situation may well arise. Student A writes an excellent composition in the foreign language, one which a native speaker would comprehend and enjoy. It has an idiomatic flavor, the structural patterns are varied, lexical items have been selected with a feeling for nuance of meaning. The student is, however, careless. Some words are misspelled. A number of accent marks and inflectional elements, not pronounced in speech but essential in a written script, have been omitted. In a few cases where there are several possible sound-symbol combinations, the wrong one has been chosen, although it is obvious that the student knows how the words are pronounced. In accordance with the teacher's "one mark off for each mistake" system, student A receives a very low grade for the composition.

Student B, on the other hand, is meticulous. This composition contains only a few common structural patterns used over and over again. The lexical range is very small. There are, however, no mistakes in spelling, in inflections, in diacritical marks, or in punctuation. The teacher gives a high grade for student B's assignment.

We may now ask: Which of these two compositions shows the greater development of skill in writing? Without doubt, the work of student A, yet this does not show in the evaluation.

The problem is a real one. If the teacher does not insist on accuracy in writing, many students will hand in careless work. Doing work of this type will confirm them in bad habits of writing which will be very difficult to change. Teachers who insist on accuracy will get at least an approximation to accuracy from most of their students. They will be training them to be observant of small details of the written system of the language, and they will also be training them to check through their work very carefully to detect their own inaccuracies. At the written practice stage, especially, unless teachers insist on accuracy they will be unable to judge whether the students have really assimilated the structural features they have been taught. For these reasons, insistence on accuracy is important.

On the other hand, sheer accuracy must not be rewarded at the expense of real knowledge of the foreign language and ability to use it resourcefully and flexibly. The answer to this problem lies in the awarding of a composite grade for compositions. Part of this grade will be given for accuracy of writing (correct grammatical forms, spelling, diacritics, and so on); another part will be allotted for variety of structure; another for lexical choice; another for idiomatic quality (authentic turn of phrase). In this way the inaccurate student will be penalized for inaccuracy but given credit for ability to communicate ideas in language which a native speaker would use. The accurate student will be rewarded for accuracy, but will not necessarily be graded at a high level if his or her composition reveals a lack of knowledge of the potentialities of structure and lexicon and little finesse of expression.

Annotated Reading List

Rivers, Wilga M., et al. *Practical Guides,* chapters 8 and 9, "Writing and Written Exercises." Gives examples in French, German, Spanish, and English of exercises and activities for copying and reproduction, writing in the language, production or guided writing, and expressive writing or composition, with particular attention to developing flexibility in using written language. Shows how writing can be integrated with listening, speaking, and reading. Discusses translation as a teaching/learning device and as a specialized study.

Allen, J. P. B., and Corder S. Pit, eds. *Techniques in Applied Linguistics*. The Edinburgh Course in Applied Linguistics, vol. 3. London: Oxford University Press, 1974. Chapter 6, "Reading and Writing" (pp. 155–201), integrates reading comprehension and writing in a principled way, with reading comprehension as a preparation for writing, and writing as the learning of the rhetorical conventions appropriate to different kinds of discourse.

Paulston, Christina B., and Bruder, Mary N. *Teaching English as a Second Language: Techniques and Procedures*. Cambridge, Mass.: Winthrop, 1976. Chapter 6, "Writing" (pp. 203–49), discusses techniques and procedures for controlled composition and free composition. Examples are in English, but the discussion is applicable to any language. Similar material may be found in Christina B. Paulston, "Teaching Writing in the ESOL Classroom: Techniques of Controlled Composition," *TQ* 6 (1972): 33–59.

Allen, Edward D., and Valette, Rebecca M. *Classroom Techniques: Foreign Languages and English as a Second Language*. New York: Harcourt Brace Jovanovich, 1977. Chapter 11, "Writing," gives examples in English, French, German, and Spanish of appropriate exercises and activities for controlled and free composition.

Widdowson, H. G. *Teaching Language as Communication*. Oxford: Oxford University Press, 1978. Chapter 4, "Composing and Writing" (pp. 111–43), discusses preparation and exploitation exercises and the extension of composition into writing by a process of gradual approximation. Advocates an integrated approach which represents skills and abilities as aspects of a single underlying activity. Examples in English.

*TRANSLATION

Nida, Eugene A. *Toward a Science of Translating*. Leiden: E. J. Brill, 1964. Discusses the theoretical and practical aspects of translation, with many examples drawn from experiences in translating the Bible. (Revised edition: Nida, Eugene A., and Taber, Charles R., *The Theory and Practice of Translating*. Leiden: E. J. Brill, 1969.)

Newmark, Peter. "The Theory and Craft of Translation." In Kinsella 1978, pp. 79–100. State of the art, with extensive bibliography.

Research and Discussion

1. (*a*) Take a piece of informal writing in the language you will be teaching (a conversational section from a detective novel or a newspaper interview). Rewrite this passage in formal style.

(*b*) Take a piece of formal writing in this language and rewrite it in informal style or as a conversational dialogue.

Which did you find easier to do, *a* or *b? Why?* What problems did you encounter in this exercise?

2. If the language you teach involves the learning of a new script, devise a self-teaching unit which could be used to help students write comprehensibly in this script.

3. Obtain from an intermediate-level class you are observing, or teaching for the first time, a set of original compositions. Study these compositions carefully. From this perusal, would you say that these students have been given systematic developmental practice in writing? What advice from this chapter would you give them in order to improve their writing? What advice can you add from your own experience?

4. Take an elementary-level or intermediate-level reading passage.

(*a*) Devise a series of questions which could be used to help the student write a coherent paragraph on the material in the passage.

(*b*) Devise a framework of questions or a guided outline which would help the student to use the material in the passage to create an original continuation of the narrative.

(*c*) Devise an exercise which would enable the student to use the material in the passage in the creation of his or her own story.

5. Take several dictation passages which were used during the past year to test parallel sections of a course (or as alternative passages for an examination; or as final test passages for a particular course in several successive years). Do you consider these passages comparable in difficulty for the level for which they were selected? Try to work out a practical system for deciding on comparable levels of difficulty. Apply various criteria and compare the ways in which the passages rank according to these criteria. What have you learned from this experience which could be useful to a classroom teacher or course head?

6. (*a*) Take several compositions written in the target language by students. Assess them on an alphabetical scale (A to F with pluses and minuses) according to a subjective evaluation of their **overall quality.**

(*b*) Devise your own weighted evaluation scheme based on categories like those on p. 308 (or the scheme described in the *Practical Guides,* W61).

(*c*) After a few days, reassess the same compositions that you used for *a,* according to the scheme in *b.* Does the second system alter their comparative ranking?

(*d*) Write down what you have learned from this experience.

7. Devise three classroom activities for the elementary (or intermediate) level for which students, individually or in groups, would need to write at least a few sentences in the language in order to participate.

8. Take several compositions in which students have gone far beyond their linguistic means in expression, so that they have had to fall back on native-language structure in target language lexical disguise. Apply the dictum "Simplify" to these compositions. Could students with this approach have expressed the same (or similar) ideas within the limits of language they had learned at the particular level they had reached?

*9. Design the first month of a high school or college course (five class meetings per week) which would begin with listening, reading, and writing (without speaking). If you have the possibility of doing so, try your course plan out on a beginning class and write a case report on your experiences, the students' reactions to the course, and the results your students have achieved in listening, reading, writing, pronunciation, and speaking. The report should compare your results with those of a same-level course using an audio-lingual or a direct-method approach, and another using a four-skills approach.[9]

*10. Select passages suitable for translation exercises for elementary, intermediate, and advanced levels. What criteria did you use to decide on the appropriate level for each passage? Can you propose other criteria which might be used?

9. See also V. A. Postovsky, "Effects of Delay in Oral Practice at the Beginning of Second Language Learning," *MLJ* 58 (1974): 5–6; and Postovsky, "Why Not Start Speaking Later?" in Burt, Dulay, and Finocchiaro 1977, pp. 17–26.

11· Cultural Understanding

Prominent among formulations of objectives in language teaching we usually find some such statement as the following: "to increase international understanding by enabling the student to enter into the life, thought, and literature of people who speak another language." The priority given to this objective may vary from one period to another, but it has long been present in the thinking of language teachers.

In 1904, in his book *How to Teach a Foreign Language,* Jespersen stated that "the highest purpose in the teaching of languages may perhaps be said to be the access to the best thoughts and institutions of a foreign nation, its literature, culture—in short, the spirit of the nation in the widest sense of the word."[1] In 1933, the Secondary Education Board of Milton, Massachusetts, declared that the primary practical value of language study was "the breaking down of the barriers of provincialism and the building up of the spirit of international understanding and friendliness, leading toward world peace."[2] In 1956, the Modern Language Association issued a policy statement, "F.L.'s and International Understanding,"[3] which lists three contributions which the learning of another language can make to the achievement of international understanding and cooperation: "direct intercultural communication . . . , experience of a foreign culture . . . , information about a foreign culture," and adds: "The third contribution of language learning to international understanding would be inefficient, . . . were it not for the two other contributions which it *uniquely* makes." Furthermore, the President's Commission on Foreign Language and International Studies (1979) declared in its report that "an international perspective is indispensable" and that "foreign languages, as a key to unlock the mysteries of other customs and cultures, can no longer be viewed as an educational or civic luxury."[4]

1. Quoted from 12th impression (1961), p. 9.
2. Extract reprinted in M. Newmark, *Twentieth Century Modern Language Teaching* (New York: Philosophical Library, 1948), p. 104.
3. *PMLA* 71, no. 4, pt. 2 (September 1956): xvi–xvii.
4. *Strength Through Wisdom: A Critique of U.S. Capability,* Report to the President from the President's Commission on Foreign Language and International Studies (Washington, D.C., 1979), pp. 5, 6.

It may be well to ask ourselves whether such idealistic aims have been realized in practice, whether international understanding can be said to have been promoted by the considerable amount of language teaching in schools around the world. Diligent learning of foreign words and phrases, laborious copying and recitation of irregular verb paradigms, the earnest deciphering of texts in a second or third language (many of them inauthentic and banal), even lively chatter in the language about trivial details of one's daily life—these can hardly be considered powerful devices for the development of international understanding and goodwill. It may be that many hours of tedium and limited comprehension in classrooms around the globe have produced a great deal of international misunderstanding, especially since many language teachers, willing as they may be to promote the understanding of other cultures, have received little serious preparation for this aspect of their work.

Whether they realize it or not, language teachers cannot avoid conveying impressions of another culture. Language cannot be separated completely from the culture in which it is deeply embedded. Any listening to the utterances of native speakers, any attempt at authentic use of the language to convey messages, any reading of original texts (as opposed to those fabricated for classroom use), any examination of pictures of native speakers engaged in natural activities will introduce cultural elements into the classroom. By failing to draw students' attention to these cultural elements and to discuss their implications, the teacher allows misconceptions to develop in the students' minds. When they misunderstand the culturally determined bases for the reactions and behavior of other peoples, students can develop contempt for and hostility toward the speakers of the language they are learning. Mere fluency in the production of utterances in a new language without any awareness of their cultural implications or of their appropriate situational use, or the reading of texts without a realization of the values and assumptions underlying them—these so-called skills are of little use even on a practical level, and certainly leave open to question the claims of language study to a legitimate place in a program of liberal education.

WHAT IS CULTURE?

We have stated that language is deeply embedded in culture. To some this may be an unusual concept. They would say that a language is the key to the cultural heritage of another people or that knowledge of another language enables individuals to increase their personal culture through contact with great minds and works of literature. They would prefer to define culture as "that training which tends to develop

315

the higher faculties, the imagination, the sense of beauty and the intellectual comprehension."[5] For a long time this was the accepted definition of the world "culture," and it was generally agreed that the study of another language had a contribution to make to this aspect of personal development. With the rapid increase in anthropological studies, however, the word "culture" has taken on a much broader significance.

The culture of a people, as the word is used in this chapter, refers to all aspects of shared life in a community. Children growing up in a social group learn ways of doing things, ways of expressing themselves, ways of looking at things, what things they should value and what things they should despise or avoid, what is expected of them and what they may expect of others. These attitudes, reactions, and unspoken assumptions become part of their way of life without their being conscious of them. Yet culturally determined features may be recognized in their actions, social relationships, moral convictions, attractions, and revulsions; through the institutions their social group establishes and conserves; and in the art and literature which the members of the group produce and appreciate. A language is learned and used within such a context, drawing from the culture distinctive meanings and functions which must be assimilated by language learners if they are to control the language as native speakers control it. There are variations within the group which express individual preferences or the orientation of some subgroup, and the literature of the group may reflect some of these alternatives or some evolving area of the culture. Despite such variations, certain patterns of behavior and value systems may be discerned which are integral parts of the cultural whole.

For depth of cultural understanding it is necessary to see how such patterns function in relation to each other and to appreciate their place within the cultural system. This should not, however, become just another theoretical or abstract area of study. If language learners are to communicate at a personal level with individuals from other cultural backgrounds, they will need not only to understand the cultural influences at work in the behavior of others, but also to recognize the profound influence patterns of their own culture exert over their thoughts, their activities, and their forms of linguistic expression.

In a country where there is one predominant culture, students will have learned, as they grew up, to react in certain ways and to value certain things. Their first encounter with a different set of behavior

5. From the report of the committee on "Position of Modern Languages in the Education System in Great Britain" (1928), as quoted in Massachusetts report, 1933, reprinted in Newmark (1948), p. 104.

patterns and a different set of values may come as a shock, causing them to consider the speakers of the language they are learning as strange, bad-mannered, rather stupid, or even morally lax. In a society where different forms of address are used according to the social status of the person being addressed, an important preliminary question in a social situation may be "How much do you earn?" In another society such a question may be considered the height of effrontery. Visitors to English-speaking countries have been known to judge acquaintances as indifferent to their welfare and brusque in personal relations because they have mistaken the customary greeting of "How are you?" for a genuine enquiry about the visitor's state of health; they have been disconcerted when their English-speaking acquaintances have not waited for a serious reply to the query. In a society where individuals must never admit that what they are wearing is valuable or in good taste, the reply of "thank you" to a compliment on their personal appearance may be considered an indication of a certain conceit or lack of breeding, whereas it is the normal response of an American. In each of these situations, the simple remark or question is only comprehensible within the structure of relationships and social education in the society.

In every language, even at the elementary stage of learning, features such as these emerge to puzzle and perturb the monolingual student. Feigenbaum tells of African students learning English who were shocked when, in a dialogue they were reading, a person refused a drink when it was offered a second time. In many societies this would indicate that the visitor had not enjoyed the drink the first time,[6] whereas in others such a refusal is considered polite behavior in a formal situation or a natural response in an informal situation.

Why Teach Culture?
The MLA Seminar Report (1953), "Developing Cultural Understanding through Foreign Language Study," suggests that "the understanding of the culture of a specific country is not, in and by itself, all that the cultural aspect of language study should contribute to a general and liberal education."[7] The authors suggest three ends which should be kept in view: students should gain an understanding of the nature of culture; their culture bondage should be reduced; and they should achieve a fuller understanding of their own cultural background.

Many of our students live in a monolingual and monocultural environment. This can be the case even where the larger society is

6. I. Feigenbaum, "The Cultural Setting of Language Teaching," *ETF* 3, no. 4 (Winter, 1965): p. 11.

7. *PMLA* 68, no. 5 (1953): 1203.

pluralistic. As a result, it is not surprising that they are "culture-bound." The MLA report defines the culture-bound person as one "whose entire view of the world is determined by the value-perspectives he has gained through a single cultural environment—who thus cannot understand or accept the point of view of another individual whose values have been determined by a different culture. . . . He makes premature and inappropriate value judgments. He is limited in his understanding of the world.[8] The study of a language should bring home to students the realization that there are many ways of looking at things, many ways of doing and expressing things, and that differences do not necessarily represent moral issues of right and wrong.

Familiarizing students with another culture is not, however, proselytizing. Students are not expected to surrender or lose confidence in their own culturally related ways of thinking and valuing. Instead, they begin to bring these to a level of conscious awareness and examine them as they may never have done before in relation to those of others. The study of another culture thus becomes a liberating experience in that students are encouraged to develop tolerance of other viewpoints and other forms of behavior while understanding better those of their own society or cultural group.

Culture and Language

The native language is learned along with the ways and attitudes of the social group, and these ways and attitudes find expression through the language. In this way the language is an integral part of the functioning social system. The psychologist Osgood has set out a theory of language "meaning" which maintains that the full meaning of words for individuals is the result of the sum total of experiences they have had with those words in the environment in which they learned them.[9] Since members of a cultural group have had similar experiences, the meaning of a word is shared by them all, but it may differ in certain respects from the meaning this word has for other groups. It is because of this interrelationship of language and culture that one-to-one equivalences can rarely be established between words and expressions in two languages, once one has passed beyond the stage of physical identification of objects. Even here there will be divergences, as the speakers of one language will have identified certain criterial attributes and categories, according to their environmental needs, which may not correspond with the attributes and categories of another language.

8. Ibid.
9. Osgood's theory is described and discussed in detail in Rivers 1964, chap. 12.

318

As Hjemslev has said: "Each language lays down its own boundaries within the amorphous 'thought-mass' and stresses different factors in it in different arrangements, puts the centers of gravity in different places and gives them different emphases."[10]

Where words seem to correspond in meaning in their *denotation,* or referential capacity, they may well diverge considerably in their *connotation,* or the emotional associations which they arouse. Even such a universal concept as "mother" may have in one culture strong emotional overtones which are incomprehensible in a culture where children are regarded as belonging to the tribe or clan rather than to their individual parents. Cultural patterning may also lead to expectations of different emotional reactions from various sections of the social group, as in societies where men and women are expected to react differently to the cry, "Spider!" The institutional system may add strong connotational elements to certain words. The word for "communism" should be easily identifiable in a number of languages, yet the full meaning, denotational and connotational, which a speaker or writer wishes to convey may be very poorly represented in translation by the mere insertion of the "equivalent" word. The misunderstanding is compounded when the word is considered in context and the interplay of nuances within the phrase and in the earlier and later parts of the discourse is taken into consideration.

Osgood found that the affective meaning of seemingly equivalent words across cultures could be compared by considering their relative strength on three two-dimensional scales: evaluation (good-bad), potency (strong-weak), and activity (active-passive).[11] This hypothesis has enabled him to compare the affective meaning of words across twenty-five world communities varying in language and culture.[12] Through this study Osgood found that a large part of the "meaning" of words is along the evaluative dimension (good-bad, right-wrong, acceptable-unacceptable) and that human languages have many more terms for evaluating things than for making other semantic differentiations.[13]

Since value judgments are acquired in the culture in which the individual has grown up, and are accepted without much question by

10. Louis Hjelmslev, *Prolegomena to a Theory of Language,* trans. Francis J. Whitefield (Madison: University of Wisconsin Press, 1961), p. 52.

11. Osgood developed a psychological instrument, the Semantic Differential, with which he measures differences among concepts as between individuals and social groups. See Osgood, Suci, and Tannenbaum 1957. The Semantic Differential is discussed in Rivers 1964, pp. 134–35.

12. C. E. Osgood, W. H. May, and M. S. Miron, *The Cross-Cultural Generality of Affective Meaning Systems* (Urbana: University of Illinois Press, 1973).

13. C. E. Osgood and M. M. Richards, "From Yang and Yin to *and* or *but,*" *Language* 49 (1973): 400.

most members of a major social group or within a subgroup, students need to be conscious of the values and attitudes held by the speakers or writers with whom they are interacting. This is not by any means a simple problem in the modern world, where the same language may be claimed as a mother tongue by peoples of divergent or diverging cultures, each expressing a social reality only dimly perceived, if not ignored, by most other speakers of the language. This is the case with the English of England, Wales, the United States, Canada, Jamaica, Australia, or Singapore, for instance; the French of *la francophonie* (France, Quebec, Senegal, Louisiana, Tahiti, etc.); or the Spanish of Spain, Cuba, Bolivia, Mexico, and many other nations.

THE COMPONENTS OF MEANING

In a useful analysis, Bever speaks of "the different kinds of knowledge that are components of every concept indicated by language."[14] These he distinguishes as semantic meaning, cultural ideas (of which linguistic ideas are a subset), and personal ideas.

Semantic meaning represents the denotational or referential aspect of meaning, which is shared across cultures because human beings have had similar experiences in a common physical reality. The terms used to describe this experienced reality may indicate different categorizations which have been adopted by different cultures (e.g., when does "green" become "blue"?). Nevertheless, each aspect of meaning at this level can be expressed in all languages, even though the ways in which it is expressed may vary (e.g., the French *gant de toilette* may have to be expressed in English through an explanatory phrase such as "a washcloth in the form of a pouch into which the hand is inserted").

Cultural ideas are much more of a stumbling block in the conveying of meaning across languages. Cultural ideas are not critical to the semantic meaning but represent the nonsemantic aspects of a concept which derive from shared life in the culture. "She is in mourning" conveys the notion of the wearing of black to an Italian, but the wearing of white to a Korean. The semantic meaning conveyed to both is the visible expression of grief at the death of some person. The cultural idea of black or white as appropriate for mourning does not affect the essential semantic meaning of the term "mourning," although lack of knowledge of the cultural idea implied by the statement may result in inappropriate behavior and miscomprehension ("She's not in mourning! She's wearing white!").

14. T. G. Bever, "Perceptions, Thought, and Language," in Carroll and Freedle 1972, p. 101. The discussion in the remainder of this section is derived from Bever's categorization of meaning, as discussed in this article.

Linguistic ideas refer to the way the structural forms of a language shape the message conveyed and perceived. "Will we go now?" may be expressed in French by "On y va?" The reactions of the parties involved may be the same, but the form of the message in French throws the stress on the going and the immediacy of it, as conveyed by the present tense of the verb. The English expression makes clear who is involved in the going and the joint nature of the decision.

Personal ideas further cloud the issue, and these must be taken into consideration, both in interpersonal relations and in interpreting artistic expression (in songs, paintings, poems or other forms of literary expression). With one family "I can't go out! My aunt's coming!" may be clearly understood because visits by aunts are always preceded by thorough housecleaning. In another family, one would expect: "I can see you tonight as long as I'm home by ten. My aunt's coming." In this case no special preparation is required for visits by aunts or even presence during their entire visit, because they are considered members of the immediate family group who integrate effortlessly into the situation as they find it. The ideas implicit in the statement at this level are idiosyncratic and culture-independent to a large degree (although not entirely since there may exist cultures where aunts do not visit families, either because they already live with them in an extended family arrangement or because girls are married off into distant tribes).

From this point of view, students acquiring another language must learn how to express the semantic meaning (through acquisition of vocabulary, idioms, verb forms, articles, and so on); they must learn the connotative meaning of these expressions as used in the new culture (the evaluative and reactive aspects of meaning), along with the special linguistic devices employed within a culture for the expression of these meanings. They must then be able to distinguish these culturewide meanings from the personal ideas of the members of the new culture with whom they have individual contact.

When students have learned to make these distinctions of meaning, they will begin to observe many things for themselves which will help them to understand and absorb the new culture. Such understanding is an important prerequisite to relaxed and appropriate reaction to speakers of other languages. Once students have realized that a new language is much more than a code to be cracked in order to transform ideas back into the familiar ones of the native language, they have gained an important insight into the meaning of culture. As they strive to understand another culture, they will learn much by comparison and contrast about their own culture and its relationship to their use of their native language.

To sum up, learning to understand a foreign culture should help students of another language to use words and expressions more skillfully and authentically; to understand levels of language and situationally appropriate language; to act naturally with persons of the other culture, while recognizing and accepting their different reactions; and to help speakers of other tongues feel at home in the students' own culture.

- **From the language and culture you intend to teach, find examples which illustrate each of Bever's aspects of meaning.**

CULTURE OR CIVILIZATION?

Traditionally, many language departments have offered courses in the "civilization" of the country (or countries) where the language is spoken. "Culture" and "civilization" should not be considered synonymous terms. "Civilization," as traditionally taught, has included such areas as geography, history, artistic and literary achievements, political, educational and religious institutions, accomplishments in the sciences, and major philosophical concepts basic to the operation of the society. These represent the institutionalized, and frequently the metropolitan, aspects of the culture. Emphasis usually falls on what educated persons of a certain level of society regard as the best their culture has to offer—what they see as the flowering of the culture through many generations.

"Culture" in the contemporary teaching of languages includes these aspects, but much more attention is paid to the everyday lifestyle of ordinary citizens and the values, beliefs, and prejudices they share with their fellows within their linguistic and social groups, with due attention to intragroup differences (of social class, for instance). This requires the consideration of the assimilated aspects of a culture which individuals are usually unable to describe in words, although they recognize them as typical and react affectively to their presence or absence.

These everyday patterns of living, the "deep culture" as Brooks has called it,[15] pervade the teaching at the earlier levels when emphasis is on situations of everyday life. Students are encouraged to perceive the way members of another culture experience it every day. They are discouraged from making value judgments about isolated details, which ultimately can be understood only within the cultural system. When students have a certain grasp of the language, and a basic

15. Nelson Brooks, "Teaching Culture in the Foreign Language Classroom," *FLA* 1 (1968): 204–17. "Deep" and "formal" culture are defined on pp. 211–12. Another useful article by Brooks is "Analysis of Language and Familiar Cultures," in Lafayette 1975.

understanding of the cultural attitudes of the people, they are able to understand more fully the evolving relationship between the "formal culture" (or civilization)[16] and aspects of contemporary society, and the relationship and interaction between this formal culture and the deep culture of everyday living.

PROBLEMS OF TEACHING CULTURE

There are certain problems in attempting to teach a culture, whether one's own or that of another language group.

1. Students who have experienced a uniform culture often suffer from *culture shock* when confronted with different ways of thinking, acting, and reacting. It is important to convey cultural concepts dispassionately and objectively, so that students do not feel that the teacher considers everything in the new culture to be "better" or "worse" than in the students' native culture. Students try to understand why things are as they are in the new culture, and, in so doing, they learn to understand why they are as they are in their own culture.

2. In attempting to fit complicated cultural systems into a simplified framework which is comprehensible to an early level student, we run the danger of imparting or reinforcing *stereotypes* of attitudes and behavior. Too much emphasis on the exotic or the "different" in superficial details (e.g., isolated surprises on encountering certain aspects of behavior) makes another culture seem weird and irrational.

- **Discuss the stereotypes commonly accepted by your linguistic group about the people whose culture you intend to teach. What aspects of their culture are reflected in these stereotypes? How would you explain within the wider framework of the systems and subsystems of their culture the customary behavior which has led to these stereotypes?**

GOALS FOR THE TEACHING OF CULTURE

Seelye proposes seven goals of cultural instruction toward which classroom activities and materials should be directed.[17] Students should be able to demonstrate that they have acquired certain understandings, abilities, and attitudes:

1. That they understand that people act the way they do because they are using options the society allows for satisfying basic physical and psychological needs;

16. Brooks does not equate "formal culture" and "civilization" in quite this way.

17. Seelye 1974, chap. 3, "The Seven Goals of Cultural Instruction." Seelye's discussion of each of these goals should be read in full. Seelye acknowledges his debt to F. and H. L. Nostrand, whose nine kinds of "understanding of a culture" are given in Nostrand, "Empathy for a Second Culture," in Jarvis 1974a, p. 307.

2. That they understand that such social variables as age, sex, social class, and place of residence affect the way people speak and behave;
3. That they can demonstrate how people conventionally act in the most common mundane and crisis situations in the target culture;
4. That they are aware that culturally conditioned images are associated with even the most common target words and phrases;
5. That they are able to evaluate the relative strength of a generality concerning the target culture in terms of the amount of evidence substantiating the statement;
6. That they have developed the skills needed to locate and organize material about the target culture from the library, mass media, and personal observation;
7. That they possess intellectual curiosity about the target culture and empathy toward its people.

- **(*a*) Are you satisfied with Seelye's list? Would you add, delete, or reword anything?**
  (*b*) What kinds of tests would enable you to judge whether your students had achieved each of Seelye's seven goals? (In your discussion of this question, use examples from the culture associated with the language you expect to teach.)

CULTURE IN THE CLASSROOM
We must focus on both appropriate content and activities that enable students to assimilate that content. Activities should encourage them to go beyond facts, so that they begin to perceive and experience vicariously the deeper levels of the culture of the speakers of the language.

Describing and Explaining the Culture
In the past, the commonest method of presenting cultural material has been by *exposition and explanation.* Teachers have talked at great length about the geographical environment, the history of the people, their literary, artistic, and scientific achievements, the institutions of their society, and even about small details of their everyday life. These cultural talks, sometimes supported by the showing of films or slides, can occur as isolated, slightly irrelevant interpolations in the general language program, or they may be part of a carefully planned and developing series.

A *cultural series* usually begins at the elementary stage with discussions of the daily life of the peer group in the other language community—their families, their living conditions, their school, their relations with their friends, their leisure-time activities, the festivals they celebrate, the ceremonies they go through, dating and marriage customs. At intermediate and advanced levels, attention may be drawn to geographical factors and their influence on daily living, major historical periods, how the society is organized, production (primary and secondary), transport, buying and selling, workers' conditions, major institutions (education, the law, government, religion), aspects of city and country life, the history of art, music, dance, and film, great men and women of whom the people are proud, achievements in science and exploration, and the roots of the prevailing philosophy. These aspects of the culture are sometimes presented through short talks by the teacher, but more frequently through reports on research projects[18] presented by groups of students or by individual students. In the beginning, when cultural readings are supplementing basic language practice, these talks may be prepared by the students in their native language. As soon as they have sufficient command of the language, however, they try to present them in the target language and engage in discussion of the material they have presented with other students. These presentations should be accompanied by visual illustration in the form of charts, diagrams, maps, and pictures, with films and slides where these are available.

Several objections have been made to this method of introducing the culture of the foreign people: first, that it is an activity more appropriate to other subject areas (social studies, history, art appreciation, for instance); second, that it consists of the absorption of a number of uninterpreted and often unrelated facts, interesting in themselves, but throwing very little light on basic beliefs, values, and attitudes; and third, that it takes students away from the fundamental task of language learning and communication. At its worst, this method becomes a cut-and-paste activity, keeping students busy for the class hour; at its best, it provides much valuable background information for the real task of penetrating the foreign culture. At the early stages some work of this kind has motivational value, since language learning must of necessity proceed slowly; reading in the native language about another country and another people provides an interesting out-of-class activity at a stage when most of the classwork consists of learning to express oneself orally in simple, basic language. At a more advanced stage, when students are able to present material of this type to their fellows in the language they are learning, it can become an exciting exchange of ideas, both in class and at

18. A useful discussion of research projects in the area of culture is found in F. L. Jenks, "Conducting Socio-Cultural Research in the Foreign Language Class," in Altman and Hanzeli 1974, pp. 95–123.

meetings of an out-of-class language club. If native speakers can be invited to attend, the discussion becomes all the more illuminating.

Experiencing the Culture through Language Use

The question arises: Can we take time in our language classes for the teaching of cultural background in this way? There is another approach which does not take time from the essential work of language learning: the insight into culture proceeds at the same time as the language learning—in other words, teaching for cultural understanding is fully integrated with the process of assimilation of syntax and vocabulary. Since language is so closely interwoven with every aspect of culture, this approach is possible, but only when teachers are well informed and alert to cultural differences. Well-prepared teachers bring an awareness of cultural meaning into every aspect of their teaching, and their students absorb it in many small ways. This awareness becomes a part of every language act in the classroom, as students ask themselves: How do we say it as a native speaker says it? How do we do it as they do it in the country where the language is spoken? What is the underlying significance?

Through language use, students become conscious of correct levels of discourse and behavior; formulas of politeness and their relation to the temperament and social attitudes of the people; appropriateness of response in specific situations (within certain social groups, among people of certain age groups). Gradually they begin to perceive the expectations within the society and to glimpse the values which are basic to the various forms of behavior. From the beginning, the teacher should orient the thinking of the students so that they will feel curious about such differences and become observant as they listen and read, applying what they have perceived in their active oral work.

Dialogues, Skits, and Minidramas

One of the commonest devices used in the early stages of language learning is the *dialogue*. Carefully constructed, it lends itself to acting out culturally based situations. Each dialogue should be constructed around an experience compatible with the age and interests of the students, one which will clearly demonstrate behavior culturally appropriate for speakers of that particular language. As students become familiar with the dialogue and act it out, they learn through *role playing* how to interact with all kinds of people, as they did in their own culture in childhood games. For a short spell, they have the experience of feeling Japanese or Russian or French, of reacting as a person of that culture would react. Such experiences are more valuable than many lines of comment and explanation. Even in books which do not begin with dialogues, the early lessons are frequently written in a dramatic style which lends itself easily to transformation into acted dialogue. In others, situations are proposed which students then act out in a culturally authentic fashion. Students who, in a conventional teacher-student situation, would feel foolish if asked to respond in a foreign way with an accurate imitation of the sounds of the language and with appropriate gestures, lose such inhibitions when acting a role. Here they are identifying with persons of the other culture, seeing things as they would see them, and naming things as they would name them.

Masks and Puppets

Even more complete identification with the outward behavior, social attitudes, and implicit values of another culture can often be achieved by the use of masks in the role playing or by presenting the situation through puppets. These devices protect the participants from violating their own codes of behavior or appearing foolish to their peers, because it is clear that it is not they but the modeled characters who are responsible for what is expressed or performed. Students readily identify with puppets and become very imaginative and daring as they develop character traits and exploits for them.

Authenticity of Situational Material

These experiences are valuable for cultural understanding only insofar as the dialogue or dramatic reading faithfully reflects behavior in the target culture. Some textbooks deliberately begin with dialogues which reflect common, everyday experiences of the students in their native culture, on the principle that they will not find this disconcerting since they recognize a familiar situation behind the strange forms. Such texts fail to capitalize on the natural curiosity of the beginning language learner about all things foreign, and deprive the class of the excitement that comes with novelty. Acting out dialogues of this type confirms the impression of many students that the new language is the native language in another dress: an unnecessarily confusing way of saying what the student can already express satisfactorily in any case.

In other textbooks one finds dialogues which are deliberately kept "culturally neutral." Whether this is possible is another question. Just as psychologists use ambiguous drawings to discover the attitudes and prejudices of the subject, so "culturally neutral" situations will inevitably be interpreted by the students as familiar patterns of their own culture. They will then presume that, in such situations in the new culture, people behave and think and react as they do in their own culture. The teacher will have to add what is missing through gesture, action, pictures, and situational variation. At least with "culturally neutral" dialogues, the well-informed teacher has a better opportunity to enrich the textbook material than with the culturally familiar.

Even dialogue material which seems to depict authentic situations and relationships in the new culture must be examined with the greatest of care. The dialogues may represent an interesting situation or relationship in the target culture, but be expressed in a type of language which would never be used in such circumstances or among people of the type depicted.[19] Even if the language is appropriate, the whole situation may develop in such a stilted way that students feel foolish acting it out. Finally, in an attempt to include cultural material, the writer may have so overloaded the dialogue that it becomes an artificial showcase and quite unusable as a natural interchange. Dialogues should cover the major situations of interest to the students without becoming pedantic or unreal.

Role Playing

After students have learned and acted out dialogues or dramatized situations from their early reading, they are encouraged to try to use what they have learned freely and spontaneously in communication situations in and out of the classroom. They may also use the material in developing their own skits. Some fear that in this way students will be associating first-language behavior with second-language forms. This will be true to a greater or lesser extent depending on the orientation the students are receiving throughout their language instruction. If they are encouraged to look upon much of their language learning as role playing, they are more likely to carry this over into classroom conversations and skits, endeavoring by content, intonation, gesture, and reaction to simulate a situation in the second culture. They will be able to do this more successfully as their knowledge of the cultural behavior and attitudes of the people increases.

19. Feigenbaum, "Cultural Setting," gives a very striking example of this type of dialogue (p. 12). It is intended as part of a lesson in American English for Frenchmen.
Pierre: Good Sunday, Henry. How are you?
Henry: I am well, thank you. And you?
Pierre: Very well. One told me that your brother passed the examinations for the second part of the baccalaureate degree.
Henry: Yes, it is true. He decided to continue to study for the philosophy degree. We are very happy that he may complete his studies in high school.
Pierre: Will you be with your family at our house for dinner on Tuesday? My mother will prepare snails, brains, and a special stew of hare. . . .

Three role-playing devices which will hasten this process are culture clusters, cultural assimilators, and simulation games.

Culture Clusters[20]

The distinctive behavior of a speaker of the language in a specific situation is analyzed into component parts about which the students are informed in several culture capsules. These capsules are classroom demonstrations of the components of the behavior through the showing of pictures or through action with any necessary cultural objects. Later, the students act out a scene into which is integrated what they have learned in the capsules. For instance, students may learn about different types of shops, about bargaining, and about ways in which one completes a purchase or declines to buy. These isolated pieces of knowledge are then integrated into the acting out of a shopping incident.

Students become more conscious of the subtleties of behavior in differing cultures when two classes studying different languages combine to act out the same situation as it would evolve in a second and in a third culture.

The Culture Assimilator[21] and Minidrama

A confusing or frustrating situation in the second culture or one that contrasts the second culture with the students' own culture, is described in narrative form, the narrative coming to an end before the problem is resolved. Students then act out the situation, resolving it as they think it would be resolved in the second culture. Various groups may present dramatizations of different solutions, and these versions will then be discussed in the light of what is known about the culture. This encourages students to think about the implications of cultural attitudes and values. (A complete culture assimilator consists of a large number of such items; through them, students build up an understanding of behavior within the culture.)

Simulation Games

These can be used at a more advanced level when students have considerable knowledge of culturally appropriate behavior. Students

20. Culture clusters were proposed by B. Meade and G. Morain, "The Culture Cluster," *FLA* 6 (1973): 331–38. Culture capsules of which the clusters were formed were first proposed by H. D. Taylor and J. L. Sorensen in "Culture Capsules," *MLJ* 45 (1961): 350–54.

21. See F. E. Fiedler, T. Mitchell, and H. C. Triandis, "The Culture Assimilator: An Approach to Cross-Cultural Training," *Journal of Applied Psychology* 55 (1971): 95–102.

are supplied with a packet in which they find the description of a group of people whose personalities, relationships, and social roles are clearly defined. A situation is outlined in which an important decision has to be made by the members of the group. All documentation that will be needed for the role-playing activity is supplied (copies of letters, school reports, proclamations, arrest warrants, or whatever). The students take the roles of particular participants, acting as such persons would do in the second culture. Maintaining these roles, they participate in a group decision-making process and carry through a joint plan. (Possible situations for simulation games would be the following. A person in the village is receiving threatening anonymous letters, and the villagers gather to decide on joint action, knowing that one of their number may be the writer of the letters. A big industrial company has decided to close down its operation in an inner-city area where the large majority of the inhabitants are dependent on work with the company for their livelihood; people in the neighborhood undertake joint action to safeguard their future. The members of a small community who have become aware of plans to overthrow their present government by force decide what they should do.)[22]

Students may invent their own situations and the various persons involved. They then prepare a packet for the class. As with culture assimilators, groups of students within the class may work together on their own development of the situation, act out their versions, and discuss which presentation most authentically represents cultural viewpoints, relationships, and general behavior.

Popular Activities within the Culture

A sense of reality is brought into the classroom when students have the opportunity to enjoy the types of activities native speakers of the language enjoy. Some schools have introduced their students to national sports, which they teach in the language (e.g., soccer or curbside bowls). Members of many language classes celebrate festivals with national or regional foods, cooked from recipes in the language they are learning. Even where such activities may seem too ambitious, it is always possible to introduce students to the songs and dances of the people.

22. For further ideas for simulation games, see L. Q. Troyka and J. Nudelman, *Taking Action: Writing, Reading, Speaking, and Listening through Simulation-Games* (Englewood Cliffs, N.J.: Prentice-Hall, 1975).

Songs and Dances

The types of songs people sing in moments of happiness, in moments of fervor, or in moments of depression reflect the things they prize, the things that amuse them, the things they fear. As with all cultural material, songs must not be treated merely as a kind of end-of-the-hour relaxation, although they certainly are appropriate for this. Students must understand on what occasions these songs are sung, whether they are learned at school or at home, or acquired in social festivities as part of the group's heritage. They must learn to sing them as they are sung in the land of their origin, with appropriate action and, where possible, with the musical instruments that would normally accompany them. Where songs are associated with particular areas or great historical events, when they reflect social problems and tensions, opportunity should be taken to learn them within a context of explanation, illustration, and discussion which will breathe cultural life into them.[23]

From the wealth of material available we select songs with the preferences of our students in mind. Musically, they should appeal to the young people of today. Some songs of earlier periods fit into this category. Nevertheless, much of what our students would prefer to sing will be contemporary, revealing to them the aspirations and preoccupations of their peers in the other culture. The lyrics should not be expressed in language too difficult for the students at the stage they have reached, or in language specifically dialectal. Scripts of the words should be made available. If the teacher or student cannot lead the singing with voice or instrument, records or cassettes will prove useful for giving a lead. Opportunity should be provided for those who wish to do so to perfect their knowledge of the song in the language laboratory or from a take-home cassette.

Every language class should have a repertoire of songs which the students come to love and sing spontaneously. A splendid opportunity to give students this feeling of participation in another culture is lost when teachers waste precious time teaching songs from their own culture which have been translated into the foreign language. A few stilted words and phrases may remain with the student, but nothing else that is of value. Every culture has a rich repertoire of songs that are authentic, attractive, and a pleasure to sing. Teachers should begin collecting the most suitable of these from their first initiation to teaching, so that they may have ready in their files appropriate songs for all occasions and for all levels of instruction. Singing games, and

23. An interesting use of songs for developing cross-cultural understanding is described in G. L. Robinson, "The Magic-Carpet-Ride-to-Another-Culture Syndrome: An International Perspective," *FLA* 2 (1978): 135–46.

dances which are accompanied by singing, are also suitable activities for younger students.

Pictures

From the first days of teaching, the teacher should also collect pictorial material which will bring many of the lessons to life. Suitable pictures with an authentic cultural setting are available from some publishers and appear in some textbooks, but teachers do not need to look far for ones of their own. Many may be found in the pages of illustrated magazines. Often advertisements in magazines portray natural situations and the activities of people of different ages, social groups, and occupations. Travel posters are attractive as classroom decoration, but only a few go beyond the scenic, the exotic, or the nostalgic. Since travel posters are designed to have an uncomplicated, unambiguous visual impact, their usefulness is usually limited as a source for discussion of another culture.

In choosing pictures for teaching purposes, the teacher must avoid those that are cluttered with too much detail. The pictures should be illustrative of one main aspect of cultural behavior which is clearly depicted, without caricaturing the life of the people. It is important that pictures used in the early stages should show life as it is lived at the present time, unless it is made clear to the students that for some specific reason they are being shown pictures of the life of bygone days. Sometimes it is hard for teachers to resist the picturesque element in pictures of people in national costumes which are no longer worn, engaging in activities of a premechanical age. Such pictures can, however, be the source of considerable cultural misunderstanding.

The same comments apply to the use of *films* and *filmstrips*. Film is a vivid medium of presentation; for this reason, it is imperative that it should not give a distorted picture of the life of the people. Again, it is easy to yield to the temptation to portray the unusual rather than the typical. Many films, filmstrips, and transparencies have been made for use in schools. Only a few of these are suitable for a program where cultural understanding is integrated completely with language learning. With the ease of travel at the present time, many teachers prefer to make their own slides for use with their classes. Those who do should be careful to select the kinds of subjects that will lead to fruitful discussion of cultural differences and similarities.

Textbooks should be selected that integrate pictorial material with the text and the proposed activities. One sunset over the sea may resemble another, but an argument over cards in a café or people scrambling into a bus at rush hour may show features that are more typical of one culture than another. The best culturally oriented pictures in textbooks portray some situation which students can discuss and perhaps recreate, with appropriate language and gesture.

Textbook pictures should avoid showing the life of only one segment of society—for instance, the urban upper-middle class—or they will give a very misleading impression of how the speakers of the language live. Pictures should give a rounded view of society, not forgetting nondominant subcultures where these represent a significant segment of the population. (Pictures are discussed at greater length in chapter 7 above.)

Advertisements can also provide a cultural study of their own. Designers of advertisements are astute students of their own culture and know how to tap hidden springs of emotion through images and allusions. Advertisements should not be taken as picturing reality within a culture, although some do. They provide material for a very interesting study of the myths of the culture (such beliefs as: "We don't allow anyone to kick us around"). They play up the things people cherish, despise, or find amusing or poignant. They focus on unacknowledged snobbery, secret admirations, current fads, group fears, and cultural nostalgia. A contrastive study of the way advertisers have appealed to people of different cultures to sell the same product can be particularly illuminating. Through such a study students may discover many things about their own culture of which they had not been conscious.

Using the Bulletin Board

Another means of making life in the country where the language is spoken seem real and contemporary is the keeping of an up-to-date bulletin board in the language classroom. On this board will be affixed news of current events, new ventures, and achievements in countries where the language is spoken. Occasionally the teacher will pin up a reproduction of some outstanding work of art. The students will be given an introduction to the humor of the people by the displaying of cartoons and comic strips, carefully chosen to exclude jokes which depend on subtle puns or turns of speech which are not yet familiar to them. Cartoons without words are often culturally rich. Proverbs, too, can be posted. Proverbs contain the folk wisdom of a race and are often a significant index of its value system, with its ambivalences reflected in seemingly contradictory sayings. Advertisements from current magazines can teach a great deal of useful modern vocabulary, some of which has not yet appeared in published dictionaries, and always attract students' attention if the objects advertised are ones they value. A well-kept bulletin board will provide for much incidental learning while students wait for lessons to begin, or fill in a few moments during a wet lunch hour. It can also provide material for conversation during the lesson: the teacher adding judicious cultural comments on what has been affixed, as the students ask questions.

Keeping Up with the News

The daily news is a rich source of cultural information. Why does one nation react to particular events in one way, and another nation quite differently? How could a particular event have occurred at all? Why didn't people prevent it from taking place? Questions like these arise spontaneously from a discussion of the news, and the teacher has the opportunity to explain much of cultural importance to an interested audience.

News may be recorded from short-wave broadcasts and made available in the language laboratory or played on a recorder in the classroom. Should this not be possible, it may be extracted regularly from newspapers or news magazines airmailed from the countries concerned. Groups of students may be assigned the task of preparing brief synopses of the news from these sources for the bulletin board or for class discussion. If none of the above resources is available, students may bring in reports from their native-language press which deal with events in, or events which concern, the countries where the language is spoken. There are many more items of this type available in local newspapers and magazines than is generally realized.

Native Speakers in the Classroom

From time to time native speakers should be invited into the classroom. At quite early stages students can ask questions and understand what a native speaker has to tell them. They should be encouraged to prepare questions in order to establish a picture of who their visitor is, what he or she does, and other interesting facts about the visitor's life and work.

When students are able to understand stretches of more complicated discourse, a discussion between the classroom teacher and the native speaker can illuminate many differences in points of view. Students should be encouraged to ask questions about things which have puzzled them. If the native speaker is of the same age as the students, they can ask him or her about the activities and interests of their counterparts in the environment of the other culture. All students may have personal contact with native speakers by means of international correspondence. As soon as the students are able to put together a simple written or taped account of their doings, they should be encouraged to enter into correspondence by letter or tape with students of their own age who speak the language they are learning. More can be learned about the life of the speakers of another language in this way than from many hours of formal instruction.

If suitable classroom visitors are rare in a particular district, much can be learned from *taped discussions* with native speakers. More and more teachers while abroad are recording conversations with native speakers of different occupations and interests; they then use this living, and often lively, material to supplement what they themselves can supply in class. A high-quality portable recorder should be packed away every time the teacher has the opportunity to travel. Even if opportunities to record personal discussions do not arise, much can be recorded from radio or television. And when the rare native speaker does visit the classroom a recorded conversation should be kept for repeated use in later years.

Where the school is close to a community which speaks the language being learned, the students should be encouraged to interact with these local native speakers in a natural setting. This is best done by involving the students in some form of service to the second-language community, such as working in an after-school young people's club, helping older monolinguals with problems such as filling in applications, tax forms, or the like, or advising them on problems they may be having in the wider community. In this type of interaction, the students of the language learn much about the way speakers of the language think and react. The student visitors can then join in festivals in this local community, eat in local restaurants, see films in local theaters, and take an interest in ethnic radio and television broadcasts. As time and opportunity permit, students may begin to collect from members of the local community interviews about life experiences for discussion and preservation in the school.

Reading about the Culture

As the student's control of the language increases, much of the cultural content of the course will come from reading, some from films, and some from classroom discussion of what has been read and viewed. Serious thought must therefore be given to the type of reading material which is to be presented. With the cultural objective in mind, the choice seems to lie between factual and expository materials which throw light on the system of culture in its various forms of expression, and literary materials which have been selected, not only for their aesthetic worth, but also because of their potential for stimulating discussion.

Both types of material are valuable. Students need an understanding of the basic features of the culture in order to understand the literature they read; they need to penetrate beyond surface detail to its inner significance, to the appeal or message it has for those for whom it has been written. A penetration to the level of values must arouse controversy and lead students to examine more objectively their own value system. Such a process can be of considerable interest at the adolescent stage, when students are asking themselves many questions of a philosophical and ethical nature. If materials about the basic culture and literary materials are to be used side by side, then one must illuminate the other.

The suitable textbook, at the *intermediate* level, will contain cultural information which will lay the foundation for later reading of works of literature, while also providing interesting reading for students of more eclectic interests. Suitable cultural material may be found in articles from recent magazines and books of a general nature. These reading materials should be supplemented by short stories, poems, and scenes from plays. The literary items will be selected because they are representative of contemporary attitudes and situations, are expressed in twentieth-century language, and develop themes of interest to young adolescents. The writer of the textbook will show by the development of material that some rational sequence of cultural insights and interrelationships has been established, and that the reading material has been selected with a view to clarifying these insights. Materials selected haphazardly and arranged with no consistent development will not serve the purposes of informed teachers but will merely exasperate them. Poorly selected and badly arranged materials merely confirm prejudices and reinforce those stereotypes, or facile generalizations, about the speakers of the language which students have already acquired from less informed members of their own community.[24]

At the advanced level, the language class frequently becomes a class in literary history and criticism conducted in another language. This discourages students whose bent does not lie in literature from pursuing their study of the language. Study of literary movements and literature of earlier centuries is best kept for students who wish to specialize in foreign literature at undergraduate or graduate level. If cultural understanding is to be realized, students must continue to read the thought and invention of their contemporaries, or such classical literature as is timeless in content and easily accessible in language. Even at the advanced level of study, students need to be aware that what they read in fiction does not necessarily depict in faithful detail the reality of life for every individual in the foreign country.

24. Rivers 1964, pp. 140–41, discusses the question of stereotypes.

The ordinary life of an average citizen rarely provides the specific elements sought by the writer of a novel, play, or short story. There will be individual variations and, in some cases, deviations from the social pattern, but the general atmosphere and the attitude of the writer to his or her subject will reveal much of interest to the advanced student who has already received a grounding in cultural interpretation.

TYPES OF COURSES FOR TEACHING CULTURE

More and more, at the advanced level, students are being offered courses directly concerned with the culture of the country, or countries, where the language is spoken. These may be of several kinds.

1. A sequenced presentation of all aspects of the culture, with reading, exposition, discussion, illustration by films, slides, maps, and other visual means, and personal research projects. A course of this type is usually conducted in the target language.
2. A contrastive study of the target culture and the culture of the language learners. Similar means are used to those for course 1. Readings and other informational material may be in either language. Students study articles on the same subject by representatives of the two cultures, what each says about the other, how newspapers and magazines from the two cultures vary in their interpretation of events and in the kinds of materials they present, how writers and poets deal with similar themes in the two cultures, and so on. The course is often conducted in the native language of the students, with much of the reading and some of the explanations in the foreign language.
3. Interdisciplinary courses in which students study the history, sociology, fine arts, or philosophy of the country or countries where the language is spoken. Students read and study original documents in the language. The course may be given in the target or the native language.
4. A conversationally oriented course in which students learn much about the country and the culture so that they may interact orally in a more effective and sympathetic way with speakers of the language. All activities (role playing, discussions, oral reports) are conducted in the target language and are closely linked with situations in the target culture. In this case, both students and teacher use the target language.
5. Contemporary culture studied through literary texts. These are chosen to illustrate themes or values of the culture, as well as for their specific literary quality. Literature is taken in its broadest sense, and the course may include popular fiction, folklore, bal-

lads, children's rhymes, or anything else that can illuminate the thought and life experience in the culture. The course may be conducted in the target language or in the language of the students, although the former is more common.

6. A course similar to number 5 will use film as the medium for study of the culture. Again, films will be selected which are representative of aspects of life in the culture, not those which reflect deviant or completely untypical behavior and situations. The films should be in the target language, preferably without subtitles. Target or native language will be used for discussion, depending on the types of students attracted by the course.

WHO SHOULD TEACH CULTURE?

Teachers of the culture of a linguistic community need (1) informed insight into the culture to be taught, (2) informed insight into the culture of the language learners.

This is a tall order. Native speakers of the language are often considered essential for this task because of their presumed intimate knowledge of their own culture. Unfortunately, many native speakers who teach their mother tongue do not possess this *informed* insight into their own culture. As a result they may present the myths of their culture—the stereotypes to which many members of their culture unthinkingly subscribe (e.g., many a conformist society views itself as exceedingly individualistic, and the interplay between conformism and individualism within such a society is very complex). They may recount facts and anecdotes which they have never recognized as manifestations of a patterned system of relationships or beliefs within their society. They may present an idealized view of their society which their students consider chauvinistic. They may be insensitive to or intolerant of cultural variations within their society, thus presenting the viewpoint of one class, sex, race, or religious or political group. They may be equally intolerant of the variant culture (and language) of descendants of immigrants of their linguistic group who may be in their classes or of a local community of speakers of the language. Alternatively, as immigrants into a new culture, they may denigrate their own because they are dazzled converts to the new. Finally, they may offend their students through misinformed comments on the culture around them. Because of their superficial acquaintance with the culture of their students, they may fail to recognize where explanations are imperative, particularly at those danger points for misunderstanding where the two cultures seem to come very close, but where the similarity in outward practice disguises an important divergence in inner significance.

On the other hand, teachers presenting another culture to students of the same cultural background as themselves also have their problems. To avoid confusion I shall refer to this group as foreign-language teachers.

Foreign-language teachers, who have the advantage of sharing the culture of their students, will usually understand and anticipate the reactions and prejudices of their students. They will be sensitive to the degree to which members of their own culture are willing to accept criticism or the implied criticism many perceive in the pointing out of cross-cultural contrasts. Like the native speaker, however, they may not be sensitive to the feelings of some of their students who have been brought up in other social groups within their society. Or they may be quite ignorant of variants of the foreign culture and language in which certain members of their class have been raised. They may know many facts about the foreign culture without having sufficient insight into the deeper significance of these facts within the cultural system. As a result, they may be inclined to teach "civilization" rather than culture, finding this more accessible to a foreigner; or they may avoid all but the most superficial cultural references because of their feeling of insecurity in this area. Like the native speaker, they may be dazzled by the culture they are teaching and offend their students by presenting it as "better" or grander than their own, or denigrate it in comparison with their own and that of their students. Those who have spent a short period visiting a country where the language is spoken may have been struck by a number of picturesque, exotic, or humorous customs which they may not have recognized as outward manifestations of functions and interrelationships within the cultural system. Their teaching of culture is then reduced to anecdotes which amuse but do not illuminate.

Whether native speaker or foreign-language teacher, those wishing to present another culture in a way which may foster intercultural understanding and appreciation will need to study. They will need to acquire specialized knowledge of how cultures are organized—their value systems, their institutions, their interpersonal relationships, their adaptation to their environment. Where possible, such teachers should have lived for some time in both the culture to be taught and that of their students. If this is not possible, they must compensate for the lack by disciplined reading. They must examine what responsible students of the culture have said, weighing differences of interpretation in the light of the status and recognized scholarship of the writers, while taking into consideration possible biases deriving from the writers' social class, political and religious views, and, in some cases, propaganda intentions. They must read what the people living

339

in the culture read (books, newspapers, magazines), listen to radio and television broadcasts where accessible, and watch films made for local consumption. Whenever possible they should make contact with native speakers, discussing all kinds of subjects with them and, if at all possible, visiting in their homes and meeting their families. In this way they will educate themselves in cultural interpretation.

Finally, the teachers of another culture must develop sensitivity to the attitudes of the students toward their own and other cultures, moving delicately toward attitude change where this is warranted. Above all, native speakers and foreign-language teachers alike must overcome any temptation to demonstrate the superiority of one culture over another. They are not in the classroom to confirm the prejudices of their students nor to attack their deeply held convictions. For these reasons, any presentation of cultural material must be objective, analytic, and informative.

THE CONTEMPORARY OUTLOOK

A program which seeks to develop systematic progress in cultural understanding side by side with growing mastery of the language will ensure that language learners are able to communicate with the speakers of the language in the fullest sense of the word. Students will learn to recognize what people of different cultures have in common beneath surface variations, while appreciating that their deeply rooted differences of outlook are related to a life pattern which is an essential development from their experiences as a group in a particular environment. The student who has achieved this type of understanding will form a contrast to many in the past who, after years of language study, have been able to do no more than clothe their "cultural offensiveness in the best local diction" (NEC 1960, p. 35).

Areas of Controversy

Does each language have a world view?

Since linguists have discovered great variations in the ways in which languages codify experience (different ways of looking at time and space, different categories for many types of physical objects and experiences, different ways of grouping people), and anthropologists have described widely different behavior patterns and attitudes in many cultures, some scholars have hypothesized that the categories of the native language determine the way individuals look at reality, and that this in turn affects some aspects of their behavior.

This thesis, traceable to von Humboldt, was firmly held by Sapir, who said, in discussing translation: "The environing world which is referred to is the same for either language; the world of points is the same in either frame of reference. But the formal method of approach to the expressed item of experience, as to the given point of space, is so different that the resulting feeling of orientation can be the same neither in the two languages nor in the two frames of reference'' (Sapir 1949, pp. 153–54). In other words, we see the physical world, finally, as our language trains us to see it, and we can only describe it as our language permits us to describe it.

In his collected writings, *Language, Thought, and Reality* (1956), Whorf gives a number of examples which he considers support this hypothesis. Whorf draws his illustrations from the language and culture of the Hopi Indians of the Southwest of the United States, which he had studied intensively for some time. He observes, for instance, that the Hopi language does not have forms or expressions for dividing up the stream of time as do European languages. On the other hand, the verb form indicates the validity the speaker intends the statement to have, and aspects and modes of the verb show whether the occurrence is momentary, continued, or repeated. Whorf infers from these facts that Hopis view the passage of time differently from people who speak languages which have very complicated tense systems. He says: ''The background linguistic system (in other words, the grammar) of each language is not merely a reproducing instrument for voicing ideas but rather is itself the shaper of ideas, the program and guide for the individual's mental activity, for his analysis of impressions, for his synthesis of his mental stock in trade'' (Whorf 1956, p. 212). The Hopis, according to Whorf, have a view of the world which is determined by the language they learn as children.

Sapir and Whorf's viewpoint has been disputed by other scholars. Some criticize Whorf's exposition as being unsystematic and consider his observations on the Hopi language not sufficiently inclusive to establish the existence of a world view. Carroll quotes research demonstrating that distinctive features of the Hopi way of looking at things which appear to spring from the categorization in their language have also been observed in non-Hopi speakers (Carroll 1964, p. 109). When it comes to determining the metaphysical implications of grammatical features, there can be considerable diversity of interpretation, most of which may be considered merely personal, that is, hypotheses drawn from the data which are then established by examination of the same data.

One thing would appear to be undeniable: that different languages establish different categories for various aspects of reality. These categories develop because they are particularly appropriate to the environment, needs, and development of the people. As an example, we may quote the many words for different kinds of snow in the Eskimo language. For Eskimo activities it is of great importance to identify the type of snow. Learning the categories established in the language helps individual members of the culture to make identifications which they might not have made otherwise. The division of garden plants into "weeds" and "flowers" in English causes us, as novice gardeners, to observe differences which might otherwise have escaped our observation because they held no particular significance for us. As a result, we "see" things differently.

Students learning a foreign language have to assimilate many new categorizations and codifications if they are to understand and speak the language as its native speakers do. This does not mean that the native language of the students could not have established such distinctions for them. All languages which have been closely studied seem to possess the potentiality for expressing all kinds of ideas and making all kinds of distinctions. For a particular way of looking at things, one language may have a grammatical form which does not exist in another language. The other language may have to use a circumlocution to express the same aspect of reality because, for some reason, the speakers of the language do not feel the need to express this nuance as frequently as the speakers of the first language. The second language does, however, possess sufficient flexibility to meet the situation when it occurs. Should the particular concept acquire greater relevance to the life pattern of the speakers of the second language, new words or, less frequently, new members of grammatical categories will be created or borrowed from some other language.

Carroll has set up a modified hypothesis of linguistic relativity which seems to fit the facts more closely than that of Whorf: "Insofar as languages differ in the ways they encode objective experience, language users tend to sort out and distinguish experiences differently according to the categories provided by their respective languages. These cognitions will tend to have certain effects on behavior."[25] This seems to be as far as we can go in the present stage of knowledge; it does not go far enough to justify the assertion that each language imposes on its speakers a distinctive world view.

Annotated Reading List

Seelye, H. Ned. *Teaching Culture: Strategies for Foreign Language Educators*. Skokie, Ill.: National Textbook Co., 1974. Discusses

25. J. B. Carroll, "Linguistic Relativity, Contrastive Linguistics, and Language Learning," *IRAL* 1, no. 1 (1963): 12.

nature of culture, goals of cultural instruction, teacher and student activities, and constructing appropriate tests. Extensive bibliography.

Dodge, James W., ed. *Other Words, Other Worlds: Language-in-Culture* (NEC 1972). As well as discussing theoretical aspects of teaching culture, the report discusses Greek and Roman culture, French-Canadian, German, Italian, Japanese, Russian, and Spanish-American cultures.

Smith, Elise C., and Luce, Louise Fiber, eds. *Toward Internationalism: Readings in Cross-Cultural Communication*. Rowley, Mass.: Newbury House, 1979. A series of studies of cultural differences and cross-cultural empathy; stereotypes; differing role expectations; and styles of communication (both verbal and nonverbal).

Lafayette, Robert C., ed. *The Cultural Revolution in Foreign Language Teaching: A Guide for Building the Modern Curriculum* (CSC 1975). Discusses ways of analyzing cultures (with examples from French and Hispanic culture); ethnicity (particularly the German and Black heritage); ways of teaching culture; how to evaluate cultural learning; sexism in textbooks; and teacher preparation.

Seelye, H. Ned. "Analysis and Teaching of the Cross-Cultural Context." In Birkmaier 1968, pp. 38–81. Discusses the scope of culture; culture and literature; cross-cultural communication; interdisciplinary approaches to culture; Nostrand's Emergent Model; techniques; and testing. Extensive bibliography.

Morain, G. G. "Cultural Pluralism." In Lange 1971, pp. 59–95. Discusses plural goals in teaching cultures; student motivation; subcultures; cross-cultural understanding; textbooks; the place of culture in the curriculum; and how to measure cross-cultural understanding. Extensive bibliography.

Nostrand, H. L. "Empathy for a Second Culture: Motivations and Techniques." In Jarvis, 1974a, pp. 263–327. Discusses how we may select what to teach, techniques for teaching culture (elaborating eleven experiential and nine cognitive techniques); sources and resources for obtaining materials; and the preparation of the teacher. Extensive bibliography.

Rivers, Wilga M. *The Psychologist and the Foreign-Language Teacher*. Chicago: University of Chicago Press, 1964. Chapter 12 deals with meaning and its relationship to the culture of the society, the problem of stereotypes, and practical applications to classroom teaching.

343

THE ETHNIC EXPERIENCE

Born, Warren C., ed. *Language and Culture: Heritage and Horizons* (NEC 1976). Detailed accounts of the experiences and contributions of French, German, and Spanish speakers in the United States.

Research and Discussion

1. Examine dialogues in some recent textbooks for the language you will be teaching. Is the target culture represented to any degree in these dialogues? How much of the information they contain is culturally significant? How much is trivial? How much is misleading? Is the target culture presented in any other way in these textbooks? Is this presentation adequate?

2. Take a commonly used elementary- or intermediate-level textbook. How is the target culture presented in this book? Is the cultural material implicit or explicit? Is the emphasis on factual information or abstract qualities of the culture? Is the point of view from which the material is presented sociological? literary and artistic? historical and geographical? contemporary? or some other? Are there elements of chauvinism? How are the following represented: social classes? religions? subcultures? sexes? age groups? educational institutions? occupations? regions? family relations? values? attitudes toward institutions of the state? ecological concerns? leisure-time pursuits? the rhythm of life (special occasions, stages of life)? societal change? Are the cultural characteristics depicted stereotypical or oversimplified? What improvements would you propose for a new edition of the book?

3. For a week, study television commercials and soap operas in your own language. List the social, racial, ethnic, and sex stereotypes of your own culture that you have detected. List the stereotypes of social behavior and personality types of persons of other cultures which were depicted. Examine the two lists and write paragraphs describing the way your own culture is being presented and the way each of the other cultures in your list is made to appear. What have you learned about your own culture from this study? (If you have the opportunity to watch television commercials and soap operas in the language you will teach, you may apply this question to the depiction of the target culture by native speakers and the way they view persons of other cultures, including your own.)

4. Find a folktale or song (in the language you will be teaching) which would be useful in presenting to students some aspect of the

culture. Analyze the cultural elements it contains and draw up a lesson plan showing how you would use this material.

5. Using Wylie and Stafford's *Beaux Gestes* (1977) as a basis, make an inventory of the gestures you yourself use to express similar reactions. If the language you intend to teach is not French (and not your native language), make a similar inventory for speakers of that language. If possible, discuss this inventory with a native speaker. (For Spanish, you may consult Green 1968.)

6. Take a varied group of common products which are advertised in your own country and also in the country of the target culture. From magazines and newspapers, make a comparative and contrastive study of the way these products are presented to the potential customer. What can you learn from this study about the way advertisers view the consumers from each culture (e.g., their values, their attitudes, their reflectiveness, their vulnerability)?

7. Develop, for a group of your students who will be spending a short period in contact with the target culture, a questionnaire which will help them to penetrate the deeper cultural significance of what they will encounter and experience.

8. Gather a group of poems in the target language which seem to you to convey cultural values and attitudes. Look for poems in your own language which convey similar or contrasting values and attitudes. Develop a teaching unit, showing how you would use this material with your students.

9. Look for ten paintings which seem to you to demonstrate aspects of the target culture. Develop a teaching unit which shows how you would use these paintings in your class.

*10. Investigate whether there is, in your area, a community of speakers of the language you intend to teach. Form a group to undertake the collection of materials written in the language by members of this community (biographical and historical accounts of the community's life and development; poems, stories, and songs; extracts of interest from a community newspaper in the target language; notices of events of importance to the community; etc.), and prepare an anthology for the public library and local school libraries. During your investigation, find out what services your students can render to this community and ways members of the community can interact with your students.

12· Testing:
Principles and Techniques

Many conventional scholastic tests, according to one critic, are inappropriate, mysterious, unreal, subjective, and unstructured (Strevens 1965, pp. 89–90). Most of us have taken tests that fit this description. Many teachers continue to set tests of a kind familiar to them without asking themselves the basic questions: What is my purpose in testing these students? How is the test related to the objectives of this course? What do I expect this test to show? What precisely is being tested by this method of testing? Am I really testing what my students have been learning? By using these tests am I actually finding out what my students know? Answering these apparently simple questions involves a fundamental understanding of the principles of testing. We shall therefore examine the implications of each of these questions in turn.

KNOW WHY YOU ARE TESTING

Many aspects of language study may be tested—at a number of levels and in a variety of ways. The selection of material for a test and the way this material is to be tested will depend on the purposes of the test, as determined by course objectives. The teacher will need to reflect on questions like the following. What are the objectives of this course? What kinds of competencies do I want these students to be able to demonstrate? (Ability to communicate? If so, at what level? Ability to read? If so, what kinds of materials? To what level of comprehension? With knowledge of a specialized vocabulary? For use in what mode—aural recognition? graphic recognition? oral or graphic production?) Is the test intended to indicate how well certain material has been learned by the students, or is it an elimination test to select a few outstanding candidates from a large group of students from different institutions? Is the test to be the determining factor in placing a new student in a class at the appropriate level? Is the test being given with a special intent, such as selecting those who will be most efficient as oral interpreters or those who are likely to be successful as translators of articles for scientific journals, or is it to determine which students are capable of visiting another country and surviving orally?

If tests are to be effective in grouping or ranking candidates as required, decisions like these must be made before the test is designed.

We may need to administer prognostic or aptitude tests, proficiency tests, achievement tests, or diagnostic tests. For each there will be a different approach to the construction of test items. We shall consider these kinds of tests in turn and discuss appropriate principles of construction for each.

Aptitude Tests

Aptitude tests have been developed in an attempt to identify students who will have difficulties in learning another language. The authors of these tests insist that they should not be considered instruments of exclusion from foreign-language study, since all students can profit from some experience in this area. Although some progress has been made, these tests have not as yet been perfected as prognostic tests. Rather, they provide a chart of predicted strengths and weaknesses which may serve as a guide in placing students in faster-moving or slower-moving groups. The analysis they provide can be useful to the teacher who is trying to help particular students with problems in some areas of language learning. Some students may be weak in auditory memory or have difficulty with abstract discussions of grammatical structure. Others may not read well in their native language and so have difficulties with reading in another language. Some may find memorizing new vocabulary a problem. Some students may be aurally oriented, others graphically oriented. They may feel hostile toward language learning or toward speakers of a particular language. Data from aptitude tests can also aid the teacher in identifying underachievers in the foreign-language class.

Some researchers, recognizing that language teaching, widespread as it is, has clearly been unsuccessful with many students exposed to it, have sought to develop batteries of tests which might be used to predict probable success or failure in this undertaking. Traditionally, measures of general intelligence and of achievement in studying the native language were considered the best predictors of success with a foreign language. Pimsleur found these to be inferior to other measures,[1] which he worked into his Language Aptitude Battery (discussed below).

Before any decision can be made about the best predictors, we must consider the method by which the foreign language will be taught to the particular students whose success or failure we wish to predict, and the type of course to be followed. If the foreign-language course is to be a silent one consisting mainly of reading, translation, and the learning of rules and paradigms, different abilities will be called into

1. "Testing in Foreign Language Teaching" in Valdman 1966, pp. 176–77.

347

play than in a course where the foreign language is taught primarily for oral communication. Most of the research in aptitude has been conducted with a view to establishing ability factors involved in learning a foreign language for active oral use. As this type of prediction is of considerable concern to the organizers of intensive foreign-language courses for persons to be sent overseas on business, diplomatic, military, or foreign-aid assignments, some of the experimental testing has been conducted in conjunction with such training. Other testing has been carried out in universities and high schools. Since the academic and nonacademic situations are not comparable, we shall concentrate in this discussion on appropriate tests for the normal school situation.

After extensive testing, Carroll and Sapon designed a Modern Language Aptitude Test (MLAT)[2] based on the factors they considered most important in learning a language: *phonetic coding* (ability to "code" auditory phonetic material in such a way that this material can be recognized, identified, and remembered over a period longer than a few seconds); *ability to handle "grammar"* (being sensitive to the functions of words in a variety of contexts); *rote memorization ability;* and *ability to infer linguistic forms, rules, and patterns* from new linguistic content with a minimum of supervision or guidance.[3] To test these abilities, they constructed the following subtests.

1. Number Learning: the candidate aurally learns an artificial number system constructed of nonsense syllables, and is then asked to write the appropriate numerals for numbers dictated fairly rapidly.
2. Phonetic Script: the candidate learns from a printed script symbols for certain English sounds given aurally and is tested on this learning.
3. Spelling Clues: a type of vocabulary test with English words spelled in an approximation to their sound (e.g., *mblm* for *emblem, knfrns* for *conference*), with multiple-choice items from which the student is to select the English word corresponding most nearly in meaning with the disguised word (e.g., *mblm: symbol; knfrns: discussion meeting*).
4. Words in Sentences: the candidate is expected to detect the functions of words and phrases in sentences and identify in other sentences words which perform the same function.

2. J. B. Carroll and S. M. Sapon, *Modern Language Aptitude Test, Form A,* and *MLAT—Elementary* (New York: The Psychological Corporation, 1959 and 1967).

3. J. B. Carroll, "The Prediction of Success in Intensive Foreign Language Training," mimeographed (Cambridge, Mass., 1960), quoted in W. Lambert, "Psychological Approaches to the Study of Language," *MLJ* 47 (1963): 60.

5. Paired Associates: the learning of a twenty-four-item foreign (Kurdish) vocabulary list with English equivalents; after a two-minute learning period, students select from multiple-choice items the English equivalents of the Kurdish words.

Pimsleur developed a Language Aptitude Battery (LAB)[4] with six subtests weighted as indicated (total 117 points).

1. Grade-Point Average in academic areas other than foreign languages—16 points.
2. Interest in learning a foreign language, registered on a five-point scale—8 points.
3. Vocabulary: a test of knowledge of native-language vocabulary, in this case English—24 points.
4. Language Analysis: a test of ability to discern the function of language elements in a number of forms in an unknown language (Kabardian) for which English equivalents are given, (a discovery procedure type of test)—15 points.
5. Sound Discrimination: the candidate learns aurally three Ewe words which are similar, though not identical, in sound and is expected to recognize these words when given orally in sentences—30 points.
6. Sound-Symbol: recognition of the graphic form of English non-sense words the candidate has heard spoken (e.g., students choose among *tiksgel, tigskel, tiskgel,* or *tigksel*)—24 points.

Pimsleur's research in schools led him to believe that ability to handle verbal materials, important as it is, is not sufficient in itself to ensure success in learning another language. He laid great stress on motivation to learn the language and auditory ability.[5] The latter ability is obviously of great importance when the course is conducted on an aural-oral basis.

It is important to remember that foreign-language aptitude tests are useful for both predictive and diagnostic purposes. They do not tell us who will succeed or fail in learning a foreign language. They attempt to predict the rate at which certain students will be able to acquire a language, other factors being favorable. If the test predicts that particular students will need much more time than others to reach an acceptable level of language mastery, the question must be faced: Is ability to use the language worth expenditure of so much time for these students? The answer will depend on the students' objectives. if personal motivation is very high, or career objectives require knowl-

4. Paul Pimsleur, *Language Aptitude Battery* (New York: Harcourt, Brace & World, 1966). See also Pimsleur in Valdman 1966, pp. 179–80.

5. P. Pimsleur, D. Sundland, and R. McIntyre, "Under-Achievement in Foreign Language Learning," *IRAL* 2, no. 2 (1964): 135–36.

edge of this language, students will be compensated for the amount of effort they exert and will thus persist.

From the diagnostic point of view, the aptitude test gives some indication of the student's strengths in three areas which Carroll considers to be the most clearly identifiable abilities in language-learning aptitude: phonetic coding, grammatical sensitivity, and inductive ability.[6] Students weak in one of these areas may then be helped by variation in the instruction and instructional materials or by special guidance in their approach to learning.[7]

In the present state of research it would be unwise to use the available aptitude tests as definitive instruments for deciding which students will, or will not, be allowed to undertake the study of a foreign language, except in specialized institutions where for financial and professional reasons only those with the greatest possibilities of success can be accepted. At school or college level, all students can profit from some experience of foreign-language learning as part of their general educational program. Some will learn more slowly than others; some will continue the study longer than others. Aptitude tests can help the teacher to understand the particular problems which certain students are facing, and to identify students who could be learning more quickly if they were willing to apply themselves more diligently, that is, the underachievers.[8]

Proficiency and Achievement Tests

Tests may also be devised to establish the level of *proficiency* which a student has reached. Such tests may be required to determine the level of language skill of majors or concentrators completing their courses, and of student teachers or practicing teachers who have studied at different institutions. They may be used for placement into an appropriate high school class of students who have studied a foreign

6. See J. B. Carroll, "Implications of Aptitude Test Research and Psycholinguistic Theory for Foreign-Language Teaching," *International Journal of Psycholinguistics* 2 (1973): 5–14. Carroll reports obtaining multiple correlations as high as .84 between measures of aptitude and achievement in foreign-language learning.

7. The discussion in this paragraph draws from Carroll's "model of school learning," which he summarizes as follows: "Success in learning is a function of whether the student takes the amount of time he needs to spend on learning a task. The amount of time he *needs* to spend is determined by his aptitude and the quality of instruction he is offered. Poor-quality instruction requires him to spend more time, particularly if he has difficulty in understanding instruction. But the amount of time he *actually* spends on learning is a function of the amount of time he is allowed (his 'opportunity to learn') and his willingness to spend that time (his 'perseverance')." "Learning Theory for the Classroom Teacher," in Jarvis 1974b, p. 116.

8. For a discussion of underachievers, see Pimsleur et al., "Under-Achievement."

language in elementary school, or for placement at the appropriate undergraduate level of high school graduates. In their design, proficiency tests are related not to the actual studies undertaken by the particular persons to whom they are administered, but rather to the level of skill in the language which is considered desirable in a successful candidate.

Some states require that teachers and prospective teachers demonstrate a certain level of proficiency in the four skills before being permitted to teach in their schools. They may also be required to demonstrate knowledge of the culture of the people who speak the language, of applied linguistics, and of teaching methodology, as in the 1961 Modern Language Association Foreign Language Proficiency Tests for Teachers and Advanced Students[9] of French, German, Italian, Russian, and Spanish. (These tests have long formed part of the certification procedures of New York State.) The National Teacher Examination, administered by the Educational Testing Service (ETS) in French, German, and Spanish, is another proficiency test of this type (without the professional training sections). The ETS also administers a standardized Language Proficiency Interview to establish the candidate's level of oral communicative ability in terms of the ratings used by the U.S. government agencies (see Appendix A). Apart from certification requirements, it is useful for teachers and advanced students to know how the level of proficiency they have attained rates in comparison with their peers and with recognized teaching demands. When this level proves to be rather low, teachers and trainees should take immediate steps to improve their ability to use the language. Teachers cannot expect their students to achieve anything approaching authentic use of the language they are learning, if they lack such ability themselves.

Proficiency tests differ from tests of *achievement* administered to groups of students from different institutions who are presenting themselves as candidates for a common terminal examination at the end of a certain period of study, or to students from multisectioned courses who are taking a common mid-semester or semester test or final examination. These achievement tests are usually based on an avail-

---

9. Although the material in the professional training sections of the MLA Proficiency Tests for Teachers and Advanced Students is now reflective of another era, both James and Jorstad in 1973 found that the MLA total scores and "speaking about pictures" section of the speaking test correlated at a highly significant level with communication of meaning (as rated by native speakers) in random samples of videotapes made by senior-year student teachers in microteaching sessions and tape-recorded interviews. (The correlation was higher for the French test than for the German.) See report of results from their 1973 unpublished Ph.D. dissertations at the University of Minnesota in H. L. Jorstad, "Testing as Communication," in Jarvis 1974b, p. 235.

able course of study, however sketchy, and students expect to be tested on what they are supposed to have been learning. Such tests have a considerable influence on methods of teaching, since teachers try to ensure that their students are adequately trained in the particular areas which will be tested. Achievement tests often test what the students are presumed to have been learning, rather than what they have actually been learning. For this reason they may be faulty testing instruments for many, since results may not reflect the level of achievement each student has demonstrated through classroom work and progressive tests on course content.

For some languages *standardized achievement tests* are available. These tests, constructed by organizations outside the schools, are designed for different levels of achievement. They are usually prepared by experts, pretested, and revised where defects have been revealed by item analysis of the results of the pretests. They are then administered each year to large groups of students from different types of schools in different areas. From the scores that are obtained, *norms* are established so that valid cross-comparisons may be made of the achievements of groups of students in the same year and in different years. Parallel series are sometimes available so that comparisons may also be made of level of achievement at different stages of a teaching sequence. Such tests enable teachers to see how the standards they have set for their own classes compare with those of other teachers. (Some widely used proficiency tests are also standardized.)[10]

Diagnostic Tests

Tests set by teachers for their own classes, particularly informal tests and quizzes during the course of the year's work, have a different purpose. They are designed to indicate to teacher and students areas of strength and areas of weakness. The results of these tests will show what sections of the work should be retaught or restudied and where further practice is essential, thus indicating clearly to the teacher whether the students are ready to move on to new work. Such tests may be called diagnostic tests. Diagnostic tests are most useful if corrected thoroughly, returned promptly to students, discussed in class, and rewritten where necessary by the students.

When the time for a periodic class test arrives, teachers may well ask themselves why they are giving this test. The answer for many teachers is obvious: such tests have always been given; they are

10. For a lucid discussion of the statistical principles behind norming, percentiles, standard deviations, and how to interpret standardized scores, see Valette 1977, pp. 43–64.

necessary in order to assign the students a grade for the work they have been doing; the administration demands it. With this administrative requirement before them, teachers with very little training in test construction regularly prepare well-intentioned but poorly designed tests which for the most part reveal what the students do not know and what they may not have been taught in their particular class. To many students these tests seem to have been prepared with the intention of tricking them in subtle ways and exposing their insufficiencies to public view. As a consequence, they become tense and overanxious as each test approaches.

The test should be regarded as a natural step in the learning process. It should serve a twofold instructional purpose: as a guide to the students and a guide to the teacher. The test should help the students by confirming what they do know, while revealing areas of weakness which need special effort and possibly relearning. The students should be encouraged to look on the test as a help, not a hurdle. When opportunities are provided for students to retake parts of the test to show they have really mastered the material, each test can become an incentive for self-improvement.

Well-designed tests are also a guide to the teacher, revealing areas in which the teaching has not been effective: sometimes because of the intrinsic difficulty of the material for these particular students; sometimes because the teacher has not provided sufficient time for the practice the students require. A test should not be an end in itself. It is another step forward, to be followed by reteaching and relearning, with variation from the original presentation to emphasize more adequately the areas of difficulty or misunderstanding which have been revealed.

Diagnostic tests are an essential part of *individualized instruction* programs. In this case, the students take the tests for each unit when they feel ready for them. The tests help them to see whether or not they are ready to move on to the next unit, assignment, or packet, and enable the teacher to develop a cumulative grade for credit. If the test reveals that certain students are not ready for new work, analysis of the individual test results indicates which areas need additional study. Sometimes diagnostic unit tests are provided in self-correcting format, so that students may see how they are progressing whenever they wish to check. Provision of two (or more) forms of the same level of test allows students to go back over work they have not mastered and retake the unit test to improve their grade. This approach has also proved useful in nonindividualized classroom settings.[11] Since foreign-language learning is cumulative, everything is to be gained from encouraging students to learn thoroughly at each stage. The opportunity to retake tests to improve their grade increases students' motivation to persevere in learning more difficult (though not necessarily more interesting) aspects of the language. This is an essential part of the concept of *mastery learning:* providing all students with the opportunity and sufficient time to learn the work to a high level of mastery.

Norm-Referenced and Criterion-Referenced Tests

Norm-referenced tests rank the achievement of students in relation to that of other students, the norm being the mean score achieved by the group. In standardized tests, the norm represents the mean level of achievement attained by many students in many administrations of the test, since with large numbers this tends to approximate a normal distribution, represented by a bell-shaped curve. The results usually state the percentile level each student has reached; for instance, students may score at the ninetieth percentile if they attain a level achieved by only 10 percent of the students who have taken the test.

In a classroom testing situation, the teacher does not have the numbers to expect a normal distribution among the students. Self-selection, tracking, or elimination of weaker students at previous levels will have skewed the distribution of probable attainment in the class, usually toward the upper levels. The practice which is sometimes called ''grading on the curve'' is therefore not justified for small numbers of students. It is preferable for the teacher to rank the scores achieved by the students and then to study the spread of scores to see how they group, before deciding how these raw scores are to be converted into grades. The final decision on grades will depend on the degree of difficulty of the test and the purposes for which the results of the test will be used. (Are the results to be used to place students in a higher level course or in an honors section? To determine a terminal pass on the course? To indicate mastery of the material? To indicate to the teacher that reteaching is needed?)[12]

Criterion-referenced tests are based on a completely different rationale and serve a different purpose. Criteria, or sets of objectives which the students must each attain, are established and each student is expected to master all of the objectives usually through the per-

11. Samia Spencer and Paulette Pelc, ''Testing: A Hurdle or a Means of Learning,'' in Rivers, Allen, et al. 1972, pp. 281–84.

12. For a readable and informative discussion of the interpretation of scores, see Harris 1969, pp. 121–34. Material applies to any language.

formance of specified tasks, although some students will need more time than others to do so. For convenience of administration, or other reasons related to the needs of a particular group of students, a criterion mastery level is usually set (a certain percentage of items correct, for instance) and the students are expected to demonstrate knowledge to this level of mastery. Criterion-referenced tests are used for courses where students must all demonstrate a certain level of mastery of a specified body of material. For example, a high level of listening comprehension in a non-native language is required by many air-control personnel in noisy situations when they are performing other tasks, and anything less than this high level is unacceptable; cabin attendants on international flights, on the other hand, may need to be able to make certain announcements in a non-native language, comprehend and respond to certain types of questions, and give certain instructions, each one being expected to perform these tasks to a high degree of language control.[13] The score on this type of test is interpreted in terms of the kind of performance that the individual student has demonstrated as it relates to the preestablished criteria, with no attempt at comparison with the achievement of others.

In school situations, criterion-referenced tests have been used for mastery learning in individualized instruction programs. (An achievement level of 90 percent is often used.) In these programs the requirements of the final test are often worked out, in consultation with the students, as contracts. Reaching clearly defined criteria may also be required of all students in regular classroom instruction for certain aspects of the work for which a high degree of mastery is indispensable. Clearly, students of Russian, for instance, need to master the Cyrillic alphabet, just as students of Arabic need to master a new writing system.

In criterion-referenced testing, students know in advance exactly what knowledge they will be required to demonstrate on a particular test and they may not continue beyond this test until they have demonstrated that knowledge. An unsuccessful attempt at the test acts as a guide to areas of weakness which must be given attention. Students' scores are not ranked nor are they compared with those of other students. The students' efforts are directed entirely toward personal mastery of the material of the course.

13. The rationale for criterion-referenced tests and the ways they differ from norm-referenced tests are clearly explained in F. A. Cartier, "Criterion-Referenced Testing of Language Skills," *TQ* 2, no. 1 (1968), reprinted in Palmer and Spolsky 1975, pp. 19–24. Readers will recall the discussion of the needs of particular categories of adults for specific language skills at specific levels and with specific content in the Unit-Credit Approach of the Council of Europe (in chapter 8 above, pp. 233, 234).

Further discussion of the pros and cons of criterion-referenced testing will be found in the articles and books in the Annotated Reading List. Tests of this type must be used with care in language teaching. Frequently criteria are set out in the form of behavioral or *performance objectives*. These can overemphasize easily described and conveniently testable atomic elements of language structure or factual details of passages for reading or listening comprehension, for which there is one undisputed answer. Such criteria neglect the real essence of language knowledge demonstrated through use—a much more elusive thing to test. Because of the continual feedback to both student and teacher on progress and current problems, criterion-referenced testing has considerable merit for classroom use, so long as teachers foresee and compensate for its potential weaknesses.[14]

KNOW WHAT YOU ARE TESTING

One important concept in testing is that of *validity*. A valid test is one that actually tests what the designer of the test intended it to test. Validity in foreign-language tests is not attainable without a great deal of thought and analysis before the test is constructed. *Knowledge of a language* implies possessing the means to set in motion a complex of skills of different kinds. Each skill has a number of different aspects, and exercising it is dependent on facility in manipulating a multiplicity of small elements which are closely interrelated in actual language use. On the other hand, *control of a language* means being able to use it in an integrated, global fashion for understanding and communicating (in either the aural-oral or the graphic mode) as nearly as possible as a native speaker would use it, respecting the same social conventions and cultural values. This kind of control implies possession of the types of skills acquired in learning to know a language.

R. L. Jones expresses the complexities of language learning very succinctly: "It is a skill, yet it also requires conceptual ability. It depends a great deal on memory, but it also depends on psychomotor coordination and social and cultural sensitivity. Success in language learning correlates highly with general academic achievement, as well as with personality type. The acquisition of a second language is a highly complex process which no one fully understands."[15] In other words, language learning involves both *skill getting* and *skill using*.[16]

14. A full discussion of the insufficiencies of some performance objectives for foreign-language learning will be found in W. M. Rivers, "Individualized Instruction and Co-operative Learning: Some Theoretical Considerations," in *SMT* (1976), pp. 245–48.

15. R. L. Jones, "Testing: A Vital Connection," in Phillips 1977, p. 237.

16. Skill-getting and skill-using are explained by the schema C_1 in the *PG's*, chap. 1.

Know What You Are Testing

Students need knowledge of many small details and facility in acti-
vating this knowledge within interacting systems, yet they need to be
able to do this in original ways which are neither irritating nor offen-
sive to their listeners (or readers). They also need to be able to perform
in the language with a certain fluency and coherence, if they are to
keep their interlocutor's attention. Paradoxes abound when we try to
analyze exactly what we and our students are attempting to do in this
joint language teaching/learning enterprise. Yet such an analysis is
precisely what we need when we are planning a testing program.

Discrete-Point and Integrative Testing

Testing knowledge of the details of a language (grammatical structures, word order, acceptable production of certain sounds, items of
vocabulary, or spelling) has been called *discrete-point testing*. The
form of the test focuses the attention of the student on specific points.
Properly constructed, a discrete-point test should require that the
student relate the point at issue to a context of language (even if only
within one sentence) in order to respond to the item correctly. Testing
degree of control of the language in actual use is called *global* or
integrative testing. An integrative test requires that the examinee pay
less attention to "specific structure points or lexicon than to the total
communicative effect [of the utterance or material]. It entails a
broader and more diffuse sampling over the total field of linguistic
items and thus depends less upon the specifics of a particular course
of training. [The test tries] to ascertain how well the examinee is
functioning in the target language."[17] An integrative test need not be
a full test of communication, like an oral interview, but it must involve
functioning language, that is, meaningful discourse with an evolving
message. The response usually requires the exercise of several skills
in interaction. For this reason integrative tests are sometimes referred
to as tests of *overall language proficiency*.

A fill-in-the-blank structure test, properly constructed, may be a
valid test of knowledge of irregular plurals or tense forms, but would
not be a valid test of ability to communicate in writing. Writing in
possible responses in a partial dialogue validly tests ability to under-

17. The terms "discrete-structure-point" and "integrative" applied to testing were
proposed by J. B. Carroll in "Fundamental Considerations in Testing English Language
Proficiency of Foreign Students," in *Testing the English Proficiency of Foreign Students*
(Washington, D.C.: Center for Applied Linguistics, 1961), pp. 30–40. Reprinted in Allen
and Campbell 1972, pp. 313–21. Quotations in this paragraph are from Allen and Campbell pp. 318–19. For a discussion of the discrete-point/integrative controversy, see J.
W. Oller, Jr., "Language Testing," in Wardhaugh and Brown 1976, pp. 275–300, and
chap. 3 of J. W. Oller, Jr., *Language Tests at School* (London: Longman, 1979).

stand certain sentences of the language, to anticipate the direction of a discourse, and to construct appropriate sentences for particular meanings, but it is not a valid test of the student's ability to convey personal meaning in a spontaneous conversational exchange. Discrete-point tests test skill getting, while integrative tests test skill using. Both kinds of tests have their place and serve specific purposes at various levels. Teachers must know the differences between them, and the purposes each serves, in order to be able to construct tests which validly test the learning objectives of their students.

At the elementary level, discrete-point exercises and tests act as a learning guide to both student and teacher as to the rate of acquisition of essential grammatical structures and vocabulary. Even at this level, however, they should be accompanied by integrative tests of listening, speaking, reading, and writing, that is, listening to complete episodes, even though short; expressing oneself in one's own words in brief conversational exchanges, while remaining within areas of language and content with which one is familiar; reading consecutive passages of discourse which have a rounded content (anecdotes, descriptions, explanations, incidents); and writing something of interest in one's own words. (These activities are discussed more fully in chapters 6–10 above.)

- **Can you propose an integrative test for assessing ability to use the tense system of the language appropriately?**

Objectives of the Course

Before deciding what to test and how to test it, teachers must first consider the objectives of the course. Is the purpose of this course essentially to develop reading comprehension? listening comprehension? oral communication? To provide remedial practice in grammar? To introduce students to the culture of the speakers of the language? Or to do all of these things but to a lesser degree of control? Such an analysis is the first step in ensuring the validity of the test for the students in a particular class.

Having identified the objectives of these particular students, the teacher then sets about identifying the skills needed to perform the kinds of language tasks these objectives imply and the way the attainment of control in these areas can be demonstrated. Then, and only then, does the teacher begin to select the types of tests, appropriate for the level and kinds of students in the class, which validly test their ability to perform in the specific area.

358

Dictation

Very probably the students will need to be able to understand the spoken language. Teachers have often presumed that this ability can be sampled through administering a dictation test; consequently, dictation has been one of the commonest types of tests in language classrooms. If we examine the dictation test, we see that it undoubtedly tests recognition of elements of the language when spoken. Dictation as a test, however, warrants much more penetrating analysis than this.

Dictation can test recognition of grammatical segmentation of discourse and of elements of the vocabulary of the language as they cluster according to the sense of the discourse. It can test ability to keep up with evolving meaning (that is, to project probable meanings derived from what has been said and then to match these against what is actually uttered); this process draws on auditory memory and ability to store language material and recirculate it while attending to the further development of the meaning. Dictation also involves the ability to write the language accurately, correctly associating symbols with sounds, and making any adjustments required by the syntax of the written language, even though these may not be present in the sound signal. It requires ability to adjust to different kinds of voices, levels of language, speed of speech, dialectal variations in sound production, and individual idiosyncrasies of articulation. Finally, it requires intelligent guessing from context to complete the discourse where the sound signal was not clear or some element was not recognized by the person taking the dictation. All of these operations must be performed during the test at a pace established by the examiner, not the examinee (except in cases where the dictation is on tape and the student is allowed to stop the tape or replay segments at will).

Clearly, then, dictation can be a very demanding test. It is an integrative test which requires that the student demonstrate precise knowledge of structure and lexicon without taking the escape route of paraphrase or ellipsis. Some teachers consider it the best all-round test for rapid placement of a diverse group of students with very varied preparation. It is, however, not necessarily the fairest test for this purpose, since students given intensive training in dictation can improve their score over those not so trained. It favors the meticulous student who can write and spell very accurately at the expense of the student who may be very fluent in oral expression but has had less training in accurate writing.

It is maintained by some that dictation is an excellent test of comprehension of meaning—that one cannot write a passage from dictation without fully understanding what one is writing. This is not necessarily so. With some languages for which there is a regular and predictable relationship between the sound and the spelling systems, it is quite possible to write down accurately a dictated passage without paying too much attention to some of the elements dictated and without worrying unduly about the overall meaning of the passage. Even where there is not such a close relationship, students taking dictation are notoriously inattentive to the meaning of what they are writing and have to be positively coerced into keeping in mind the relevance of the segment they are writing at a particular moment to the import of the whole passage. Their attention becomes concentrated on segments, despite constant reminders. This is not pure obduracy on their part, but is due to the considerable strain on the cognitive system of performing so many operations at once in a language which one is still learning. (It is true that some of the problems this creates can be solved later in the editing process, when the student is rereading what has been written.) Further, students who understand perfectly what they have heard at the moment they hear it may be unable to retain the meaning long enough to write the segment down in full, either because of the fallibility of their auditory memory or because of pure cognitive overload.[18]

Dictation can, unfortunately, be a test of temperament. Nervous or anxious students, or students who know they have problems retaining auditory material, often suffer emotional blocks and lapses of memory which do not affect the more stolid and self-assured or the aurally oriented. Sometimes even a kind of panic develops, and the dictation finishes as a series of long blanks or a garbled rendition which makes no sense at all. Knowing the students, the classroom teacher can take steps to avoid some of these problems, but they can result in very low scores for some students in placement or proficiency situations.

Material for dictation must be selected with great care. Success in the dictation can be far too dependent on lexical factors, if comprehension of the passage is too closely tied to recognition of certain key items of vocabulary. Since we hear what we expect to hear, failure to recognize such items can lead to a consistent misinterpretation of the rest of the passage. This problem is compounded when the dictation is in a language with a great number of homophones and homonyms and many peculiarities of spelling which disguise the pronunciation for those graphically trained. It is also hard to assess the level of difficulty of a passage of discourse for a group of students

18. For a discussion of processes of listening in cognitive terms, see Wilga M. Rivers, "Linguistic and Psychological Factors in Speech Perception," in *SMT* pp. 131–44.

with very varied preparation. Where large numbers of students are taking a placement or proficiency examination, dictation should not be given by an examiner in person to groups of more than thirty, and preferably to less. Even where taped dictations are administered, unless an extremely large language laboratory is available, or many rooms are wired for reception, the dictation will inevitably be given at successive sessions at different hours. This entails the selection of a number of passages of comparable difficulty. So far, no objective system has been developed for estimating levels of difficulty of different passages in relation to levels of study, not to say levels of achievement of students. Subjective judgment can be very misleading in this regard, particularly where native speakers are assessing levels of difficulty of dictated material for non-native speakers from different language backgrounds. If the test is to be equitable, selection of alternative passages must be given serious attention before the administration of the test.

The dictation test as a placement device is a rough sieve which has its uses because of the ease of administration and mechanical nature of its correction. The "one wrong word = one mistake" method is sufficient for most purposes. If all errors are counted, even when there are several in one word, the student who omits a word has an advantage over a student who makes an attempt but misses a morphological adjustment while making a spelling mistake at the same time.

As a diagnostic test, dictation is useful as part of the ongoing program, especially where passages are constructed to test work being studied. These incidental tests sometimes take the form of spot dictation where the student fills in blanks in a script (of one word or groups of words) from oral input. Spot dictation resembles the cloze test, which is discussed later in this chapter, but it is less demanding since the student hears what is missing from the script. In-class dictation can pinpoint for the student and the teacher areas of weakness in grammar and spelling. For proficiency or achievement testing, dictation should be used only as part of a group of tests aimed at determining all-round skill in handling the language, with due attention to the way the dictation is administered.[19]

- **What have been your own reactions to dictation? In your native language? In a second or third language? How helpful did you find it to be?**

---

19. For eight different ways of using the dictation device in teaching, see the *PG*'s, chap. 8.

Reading Comprehension

Reading comprehension is often tested by asking the student to *translate* a passage from the foreign language into the native language. It is clear that it is necessary to understand the original passage in order to be able to render it accurately in the native language. It is not so clear that ability to give an idiomatic version of the passage in one's native language is an essential element in reading comprehension. It is possible for students to understand the passage very well and yet do very badly on a test of this type because they are not very skilled at expressing nuances of meaning in their first language. It is a valid type of test if we wish to test comprehension of the foreign language, knowledge of stylistic differences and of cultural contrasts between the foreign and native languages, and also felicity of expression in the mother tongue. In this case, it is an interesting and challenging integrative test. The grading of such a test is to some extent subjective, since the "perfect translation" exists in the mind of the translator, as in the mind of the examiner, without there being any perfect match between the two. It is a suitable test for advanced classes, where translation as a craft is studied and practiced[20] and students learn to understand better the potential of their native language as well as that of their new language. If we wish to test reading comprehension alone, however, we must devise a different type of test.

A common test of reading comprehension requires the *answering in the foreign language of foreign-language questions* on a section of discourse. On the surface, this appears to be a more valid test of reading comprehension than the preceding one. Actually it is even less satisfactory. Unless the test is very carefully designed, it is often possible to answer the questions on the text from the text itself without knowing the meaning of a number of lexical items. X is mentioned in the question: we identify the sentences about X in the passage and are able to answer the question about X (where it is, what happened to it) without knowing what X really is. Since the answers must be in the foreign language, they can often be supplied very accurately by piecing together sections of sentences from the text—an exercise in quick wit and transcription as much as reading comprehension. The less quick-witted may merely write their answers badly, in which case the teacher does not know whether to give credit for the comprehension which is apparent despite the incorrect writing, or deduct marks for inaccurate writing, in which case something other than reading comprehension is being evaluated. At their worst, questions in this type of test may refer to isolated sections of the text which

20. Translation as a specialized study is discussed at length in the *PG*'s, chap. 9.

can be pinpointed from certain words in the question and do not test comprehension of the passage as a whole. (This is particularly the case where proper names, dates, and numerical allusions are involved.)

In an endeavor to overcome the defects of this type of reading-comprehension test, some examiners set *foreign-language questions on the reading passage to be answered in the native language.* This reduces the bias in favor of students who have great facility in expressing themselves in their native language, as in the translation test described, and enables students who are weak at composing sentences in the foreign language to gain full credit for understanding what they have read. The validity of a reading-comprehension test of this type depends very largely on the construction of the questions. If the questions require answers which may be located in strict sequence through the text, students are unduly assisted in answering them by being able to identify the next sentence as the one in which the next answer will probably be found. They may be able to answer many questions in isolation in this way, even though they have not understood the development of thought or the real implications of the passage. Sometimes the way the questions in the foreign language are framed enables quick-witted students to detect a sequence of events or ideas they had not really comprehended when reading the passage by themselves. Furthermore, despite the good intentions of the teacher, the questions may seem ambiguous to the student, who may lose marks for not supplying the answer the teacher expected or for not including all the details the teacher wanted to see in the answer. The students may be asked, for instance, "Did John know the thief was in the house?" A student who answers quite correctly, "No" may, under this system, be given one mark out of the four allotted, because the teacher expected him to write, "No, / he was watching television / and the noise of the shooting in the Western / covered the sound of the breaking glass / ." The answer "No" may have indicated that the student understood all of these details in the text, but the teacher may be unwilling to give full credit for comprehension because of insufficient evidence for it in the answer. A test of this kind tests reading comprehension. It also tests the ability to interpret the teacher's requirements. To some extent it tests volubility, since many people (often highly intelligent people) do not go into details when answering questions, considering the details to be self-evident. It usually allows little room for diversity of interpretation. Finally, it tests docility, full credit going to the student who not only understands the passage but also recognizes what the teacher requires and supplies it in dutiful fashion.

Reading comprehension alone is more validly tested by selection of the correct answer from multiple-choice items in the foreign language which have been based on the reading passage. In this case the student shows ability to comprehend not only the reading passage but also the fine distinctions between the choices offered. No other skill has to be demonstrated at the same time. This type of test, however, must be prepared with great care. The choices must be constructed in such a way that they contain elements from the reading passage arranged so that each provides a plausible response for students who have misinterpreted the text in different ways; in other words, each must provide a real choice and a cause for hesitation for the student who is not quite sure of the real import of the text. The choices anticipate errors in comprehension that students may make. On the other hand, there must be no ambiguity from the point of view of the student; the correct answer must be such that it will be chosen without hesitation by a student who has really understood the text. If there are several possible interpretations, credit must be given for alternate points of view.

Effective choices of this type are demanding and time-consuming for the classroom teacher to construct. Often two or three valid choices can be constructed, but the fourth is so obviously unrelated that it is rejected by most students and ceases to act as a choice. Asking a native speaker to construct the choices is not the answer, unless the native speaker is an experienced teacher of the language to non-native speakers. It is often difficult for a native speaker to perceive the kinds of problems the students are having with the text. Until teachers have accumulated, over a number of years, a series of well-constructed sets of multiple-choice questions, or have discovered some commercially produced series of a suitable standard, they would be well advised to intersperse multiple-choice tests with the more easily constructed type, foreign-language questions with native-language answers, always provided that these have been constructed with attention to the pitfalls already discussed. Teachers working with classes at the same level should exchange personally constructed material to reduce the burden of preparation and to ensure a greater supply of suitable tests. A well-constructed set of questions may be kept and reused on a number of occasions, so long as students have not been allowed to take copies from the classroom. Experience with student responses on previous occasions will enable the teacher to drop ineffective choices and eliminate ambiguity.

Listening Comprehension

Objections similar to those set out above may be raised when *listening comprehension* is tested by means of printed questions in the foreign language to be answered in writing in the foreign language. Once again, students may understand perfectly what they hear but receive no credit for it because they have misinterpreted the printed question before them, or because they have not written the answer correctly or accurately. Some teachers who realize that in this type of test they are testing three things at once (comprehension of spoken language, comprehension of the printed word, and ability to express oneself in the foreign language in writing) try to compensate for this plurality of effort by awarding some marks for evidence of listening comprehension, irrespective of the correctness of the written response, assessing the written expression separately. In this case, students receive no credit if they understood the spoken word and would have been able to express the answer in writing but misinterpreted the printed question. They also receive no credit for listening comprehension if they express themselves so awkwardly in writing that their answers are misinterpreted by the examiner. If students are to be tested for listening comprehension alone, this skill must be separated out and credit given for evidence that students did in fact comprehend what they heard.

In the earlier stages, listening comprehension may be tested with the use of pictures and objects. Three comments may be made by the teacher about the picture, two of which are not appropriate. Students will then mark A, B, or C on a sheet to show which one they consider to be the appropriate comment. (Note that four comments begin to make demands on auditory memory which penalizes some students.) Alternatively, they may hear a remark in the foreign language and be asked to choose from three oral rejoinders the one which would be an appropriate response. With both pictures and oral rejoinders it is important to avoid all ambiguity. The comments or rejoinders must be short and should be repeated, again because of the element of auditory memory involved in holding a quantity of material in the mind for a comparatively long period.

At more advanced stages, when students who have acquired some facility in reading the foreign language are asked to listen to more sustained discussions or longer narratives or descriptions, multiple-choice items written in uncomplicated language will serve the purpose better than purely oral choices, because the length of the listening passage makes individual variations in auditory memory an important factor.

In chapter 6, we spoke of testing the results of listening (see p. 166). Students may be required to carry out instructions by drawing, completing drawings, or filling in information on maps, charts, or diagrams. They may sketch the environment in which actions or dialogue took place (e.g., positions of objects and persons in relation to each other, or possible stage settings), or such details may be added to an outline sketch. Students may identify relationships between persons heard speaking or the reasons for the discussion between them (the source of disagreement, the problem to be solved, or the solution proposed). Sometimes the material heard must be comprehended in order to write a continuation, conclusion, or explanation, thus linking listening with writing. With a little imagination, teachers can invent other tasks which depend on what was heard. The results of listening are also tested in the oral interview, which is discussed later in this chapter.

To sum up, if a test is to be valid in the sense that it is testing what the test constructor wishes it to test, teachers must proceed through certain stages. They must first decide exactly what they wish to test. They must then work out how they propose to test it. Next, they must analyze the type of test they have selected to see whether it really tests what they intended it to test, but they must also decide what other skills are required of the student while taking the test. After this careful analysis they will be in a position to modify or redesign the test, to ensure that evidence of the degree of control of the specific skill or knowledge they wish to test can be clearly discerned in the mode of response and that credit can be given for this skill or knowledge without confusion with other abilities. The teacher may, of course, wish to test control of several aspects of language use at the one time, or some form of overall language proficiency. The design of the test must then allow for this interaction so that the grade that emerges really reflects this composite or global operation.

UNDERSTAND HOW YOU ARE TESTING
Many teachers are proud of the fact that they are conducting communication-oriented classes; yet they evaluate their students' learning solely through "pen-and-paper" tests. This unfortunately common practice betrays a lack of reflection on *how* they are testing.

The Oral Interview
The most valid test of ability to speak in another language would seem to be obvious: students are placed in communication situations and assessed on how they cope. This is the concept behind the oral interview. However, neither the decision as to what is a "communi-

cation situation'' nor the assessment of the student's performance is a simple matter.

In the oral interview, we are testing the speaking skill. We are also testing listening comprehension, to some extent self-assurance and composure, and even, if the activities during the interview are not very carefully thought out, quick-wittedness and ability to talk about almost any subject without preparation. Were we to have discussed another subject, the responses of the student may well have been of a quite different standard, and the noncommittal or apparently taciturn student who had nothing to say might have been quite voluble. When we finally allot a global mark for this interview, we have presumably taken into account ability to comprehend the spoken language, ability to frame a ready response, and ability to express this idea intelligibly in the foreign language (with comprehensible pronunciation, stress, intonation and juncture, acceptable grammatical features and structural segmentation, appropriate lexical items in suitable collocations, and some approximation to the conventional courtesies of the culture).

As very little time has been available for deciding on the global assessment, we have arrived at some subjective counterbalance of these various elements, and we would usually be unable to say whether all elements were given—or ought to have been given—equal credit. If a second examiner protests that the student's pronunciation was rather defective in certain areas, we will probably agree without much hesitation to lower the assessment one or two notches; if someone else observes that, despite poor production, the candidate seemed to understand everything that was said, we may raise the grade again. Two examiners talking with the same candidate usually produce slightly different, sometimes substantially different, evaluations depending on which aspects of the speaking skill they consider important; the decision then drifts toward the assessment of the examiner with the most decided views. The same examiner confronted with the same candidate on some future occasion may estimate the degree of skill in quite a different fashion. (This indicates the unreliability of the test.) Some of these problems can be overcome with proper training of the examiners, but the effects of time of day, fatigue, and a cumulative impression left by previous interviews remain.

Despite these shortcomings, the fact remains that we must test communicative ability in an act of communication. One of our major problems is to decide what level of communicative ability we expect from the student at a particular point in the learning process. If the student says: ''I don't know,'' and ''Really?'' from time to time, this can pass for communication in many situations. Do we expect more than this? Some voluble examiners do not even realize they are doing all the talking. We need activities during the oral interview which reflect what the world regards as communicative activity. We need to decide on communicative levels at which the student can interact, and to devise an assessment scheme which clearly reflects what the student can do.

The best-known levels system of this type is the Foreign Service Institute Rating Scales of Absolute Language Proficiency, where expected achievements of a functional nature are described in detail for five levels of speaking (and reading). These ratings, numbered from 1 to 5 (with allowance for further discrimination at each level by the use of a plus), move from elementary proficiency, through limited working proficiency, minimum professional proficiency and full professional proficiency, to native or bilingual proficiency. They are based on the needs of career officers in the foreign service and armed forces, and personnel in other government agencies like the Peace Corps. The candidates know what communicative competencies they will be expected to demonstrate for each level. The interview is then geared to providing opportunities for the candidate to demonstrate these competencies. Two examiners are always present, one interviewing and the other making notes, which serve as a concrete basis for the discussion which precedes the final assessment.

Expectations for candidates begin with such elementary acts of communication as: "Can ask and answer questions on topics very familiar to him; within the scope of his very limited language experience can understand simple questions and statements if they are repeated at a slower rate than normal speech. . . . Should be able to order a simple meal, ask for a room in a hotel, ask and give street directions." At the next level, limited working proficiency, the candidate "can understand most conversations on nontechnical subjects and has a speaking vocabulary sufficient to express himself simply with some circumlocution." At the level of minimum professional proficiency, the candidate "can participate effectively in all general conversation; can discuss particular interests with reasonable ease; comprehension is quite complete for a normal rate of speech." For full professional proficiency, the candidate "can understand and participate in any conversation within the range of his experience with a high degree of fluency and precision of vocabulary, but would rarely be taken for a native speaker"; he can even interpret for others in an informal way, from and into the language. During the interview, the candidate is drawn out by the examiner from level to level until it is clear that a plateau has been reached. Full details of these ratings scales are given in Appendix A. Also in Appendix A is the breakdown used for rating different aspects of overall proficiency in speaking. Even with such a breakdown, the evaluation is still essentially a subjective one, although evaluators can be trained to reach basically comparable assessments.

A similar approach, with precise specifications, has been worked into the *unit/credit system* devised by experts of the Council for Cultural Cooperation of the Council of Europe for the teaching of languages to adults, to which reference has been made in earlier chapters. According to Porcher, "evaluation has meaning only in relation to the teaching objectives to which it is applied. . . . The first step must be an operational description of objectives, and not a general discourse on vague aims. . . . This involves deciding what a learner *must be capable of* by the end of his learning experience. Expressed in these terms, an objective includes, in its definition, the very means for evaluating it."[21] At the threshold level, which sets out "the minimum that is required in order to function adequately in those communication situations in which . . . 'general beginners' are most likely to need the ability to use a foreign language," learners will be expected "to be able to cope, linguistically speaking, in temporary contacts with foreign language speakers in everyday situations . . . and to establish and maintain social contacts" (Van Ek and Alexander 1977, p. 1). What these situations are and precisely what type of coping the students should be able to demonstrate are set out in full detail in the manual *The Threshold Level* (Van Ek 1975) and its French companion volume *Un Niveau-Seuil* (Coste et al. 1976) (where the approach is through speech acts). Halfway to the threshold level is *Waystage* (Van Ek and Alexander 1977), at which the learner will be able to impart and seek factual information (through identifying, reporting, correcting, and asking); to express and find out intellectual attitudes (agreement, disagreement, denial, knowledge and ignorance, etc.), emotional attitudes (like, dislike, intention, want, etc.), and moral attitudes (forgiveness, approval, regret, etc.); to get things done, and to socialize (ibid. pp. 13–14). In the Council of Europe approach, stress is laid on the sociolinguistic aspects of communicative competence discussed in chapter 3 above. (For further information on the unit/credit system,

---

21. *A European Unit/Credit System for Modern Language Learning by Adults.* Report of Symposium organized by the Government of the Federal Republic of Germany, 1977 (Strasbourg: Council of Cultural Cooperation of the Council of Europe, 1979), pp. 76–77.

the reader should consult the Council of Europe publications listed in the footnotes and bibliography.)[22]

Detailed systems like the FSI ratings and the Council of Europe unit/credit approach cannot be transferred in their original form directly to a school or college situation, since they are based on the specific needs of the learners for whom they were devised. However, they provide a useful model for the development and testing of communicative proficiency. Although the details may not be transferable, teachers should draft similar functional expectations for students in their local educational situation. In this way, oral testing will have a firm basis in language use in specific contexts.

Types of Activities in an Oral Interview

1. The first task during the interview should be one which sets the candidate at ease. Ways which have been tried are the following.

(a) *The student sets the pace.* Sometimes students are issued with a list of questions or topics of a general nature (about themselves, their interests, their environment) which they may prepare. The examiner then selects one of these questions to begin the interview or asks the candidate to choose the topic. The examiner then leads the candidate out into wider, unprepared but related topics. With this approach, students are less nervous at the beginning of the interview and feel greater confidence because of the opportunity provided to show what they can do.

(b) The interview begins with *a simple, practical task tied to something concrete.* Candidates may be asked to describe objects and their uses, or to show how to perform some simple task, during which they describe their actions and the reasons for them. They may discuss a picture. If the picture is ambiguous in its intent, this provides more scope for the imaginative student.

(c) The interview may begin with the *reading of a simple passage* in the language (after a moment or two to look it over). This calms the nerves through the opportunity it provides to perform an accustomed task (without having to look the examiner, or examiners, in the eye) while becoming accustomed to the situation and the surroundings. The passage should be of a level of difficulty which makes it quite comprehensible for the student. While the student is reading, the examiner has the opportunity to note unobtrusively the level of acceptability of the student's pronunciation, stress, and intonation.

22. With the exception of Coste et al. 1976, these reports have now been published for and on behalf of the Council of Europe by Pergamon Press (Oxford, New York, Toronto, Sydney, Paris, Frankfurt).

A five-column checklist of points to observe makes rapid decision easier for the examiner. The examiner's pencil hovers over the center column which represents average achievement. While the examiner is listening, the pencil slides to the right toward "good" or "very good," to the left toward "poor" or "very bad." Later, after the student's departure, the chart provides a profile from which to draw conclusions about pronunciation as a counter to the subjective impression the examiner has gained while conversing. (Evaluation of pronunciation is discussed in more detail in chapter 5, pp. 137–38.)

2. Once the student is relaxed, more demanding tasks may be introduced.

(*a*) The student may be asked to *role-play* with the examiner some situation for which the participants and setting are clearly described. The situations proposed may be designed to determine whether the student knows the accepted ways of behaving in certain social relationships within the culture, or, on a more practical level, how to supply needs, obtain services, or find solutions to pressing problems.

(*b*) Students may be asked to explain their views on some topic of current interest, or on some subject, book, or film discussed in class, and be provoked into a defense of those views by the examiner's expression of a contrary position.

(*c*) The student may be invited to question the examiner in a *reversal of roles*. This enables the examiner to see how the student handles question forms, as well as statements, and to what degree the student understands connected discourse at varying levels of complexity and at various speeds of utterance.

(*d*) Some part of the interview may be based on realia, such as restaurant menus, phone books, mail-order catalogues, maps, or airline schedules. The candidate is asked to find information and explain it to the examiner, who appears to find it difficult to understand or believe.

(*e*) Candidates may be given a few minutes to study some *situational problem,* presumably encountered in the foreign environment, and then be *expected to talk their way out of it* over the objections and protestations of the examiner. (This may be a job interview for which the candidate has minimal qualifications; a police station situation in which the candidate must explain some extraordinary behavior which led to the interrogation; or a family situation in which the candidate must explain an absence of several days, which worried the members of the family.)

(*f*) Where there are two examiners, the student may be led into using more complicated forms of utterance by being asked to *interpret informally* to one examiner through the medium of the target language what the other examiner has said in the native language. (This technique is sometimes used in FSI interviews.)

3. A *group oral test* may be devised. Several students who are being examined together are given topics to discuss among themselves. They may even be given viewpoints to maintain in the discussion or roles to play while maintaining those viewpoints (such as an immovable supporter of the status quo or a wild-eyed radical). The examiners listen to the discussion and assess the level of communicative ability to each candidate.

4. Some part of the examination may be conducted over the telephone. The student is deputed to find out certain information during the phone call and report it to the examiner.

5. The real skill in conducting an oral interview is to interest the candidates so that they forget they are in a testing situation. The examiners then draw them on in a natural way into more and more expressive use of the language in order to assess the real level of mastery that has been achieved. This requires sympathy and imagination on the part of the examiners and some sophistication in developing dialogue which elicits more complex structures and more precise choice of words.

- **What other activities would you add to this list of possibilities for an oral interview? Which types of activities would you ban, as a result of your own experiences as a candidate?**

Assessing the Oral Interview

We have already discussed the subjective element in assessing communicative proficiency. Experienced oral examiners (like examiners of written compositions) develop a sense of level of achievement expressed as a global score, which takes into consideration listening comprehension and the acceptability and comprehensibility of sound production (both of which are essential elements in ability to communicate); correctness and flexibility in the use of more and more complex grammatical structure; breadth and appropriateness of vocabulary; and fluency (not speed, but ability to produce what one wishes to say smoothly and without undue hesitation and searching). These together form an amalgam which may be called "feeling for the language." (Does it sound as English, German, Swahili, or Arabic sound when spoken by native speakers? Is it pleasant and expressive even if clearly non-native? Is it appropriate for the type of social relationship and situation?)

Experienced examiners realize that, although they can arrive at this undifferentiated amalgam with confidence, to continue to rate it consistently at specified levels in a way which is fair to all candidates is

Understand How You Are Testing

most difficult. Even with the best of intentions, the examiner's overall judgment tends to slide up or down the scale as a result of a number of seemingly unrelated factors (the twentieth candidate! distraction, personal cares intruding, the unattractive personality or appearance of a candidate, coffee break, an unfortunate remark that set the interview off on the wrong track, late afternoon heat). As a result, even experienced examiners, and certainly inexperienced examiners, need some kind of breakdown of factors to be considered. Where there are several examiners working independently with candidates from the same group, it is useful to have taped interviews from previous years which can be used for group practice sessions with the breakdown chart before the examining session begins. The examiners arrive at independent judgments about the tapes and then discuss the reasons for their decisions. These sessions continue until there appears to be a reasonable consensus of judgment.

An oral interview breakdown chart must be simple to be useful. Its purpose is merely to readjust the judgment of the examiner, who may be so wrapped up in the task of promoting a relaxed exchange that he or she may not notice and recall certain aspects of the exchange. (For this reason, it is important, where feasible, to have two examiners at each interview. One becomes fully involved in promoting the communicative exchange; the other observes and evaluates.) A simple breakdown makes possible unobtrusive note-making; this is important because nervous candidates always interpret any note-making as having negative implications.

The author has used for some years the simple chart reproduced here. Equivalents for the value terms across the top of the chart can

	Awful	Poor	Average	Very Good	Excellent
Listening comprehension					
Conveying of meaning					
Pronunciation, intonation, stress					
Grammar (accuracy and complexity)					
Variety of expression and fluency[23]					

OVERALL ASSESSMENT =

23. The author finds "variety of expression" to be an important element in the breakdown, because in the intense concentration of eliciting oral production from the student and getting meaning from what is said, it is easy for the teacher to be operating

be found in any system: letter grades, numerical grades, value grades (distinction, satisfactory, etc.). Depending on the level of the student, the form the interview takes, and the degree of difference between cultures, one might wish to add a section, "Cultural appropriateness." A weighting of factors can be agreed upon among the examiners, depending on the level of the students and the emphases of the course.

From this rapidly checked chart emerges a profile which the examiner can then compare with those for other candidates, in order to check on consistency in the final grades and to keep on track during long sessions of interviewing. The chart may also be used for diagnostic purposes by the classroom teacher, who can explain to the students the reasons for the differences in grades and give advice on areas for improvement. This additional benefit is most important psychologically in achievement testing and classroom situations. It allows for concrete explanations, which reduce student suspicions that the teacher is merely playing favorites in some ingenious way.

The breakdown chart and weighted assessment scheme in Appendix A, used by the Educational Testing Services and various government agencies, is slightly different from the one given here, and the instructions supplied to examiners are very detailed. An explicit system of this type is essential for proficiency examinations for large groups of candidates who will be interviewed by any of a number of different examiners, some more experienced than others.[24]

Testing Details of Language Knowledge

All the elements we have just seen to be implicit in a global assessment of communicative ability can be examined and evaluated apart from an act of communication through discrete-point tests of a more objective type. Students who can perform acceptably in these areas in separate tests should get credit for this knowledge. Whether they can continue to use these elements effectively when they are thinking about what they want to say will be shown by the communication assessment. The counterbalance of an objective score for detailed knowledge will make for more reliable evaluation in the final assessment of what the student has learned. It is also an encouragement to the student to perfect such knowledge. As Carroll from his long experience with language testing has observed, "As far as the foreign language teacher is concerned, the teacher is responsible only for

at an interlanguage semantic level and not notice that the way the student expressed meanings was simplistic and repetitive in the actual linguistic means employed.

24. For a detailed account of the administration of the oral ratings system by the Foreign Service Institute of the Department of State, see Claudia P. Wilds, "The Oral Interview Test," in Jones and Spolsky 1975, pp. 29–38.

developing in the student those basic competencies on which successful use of language depends. The FL teacher cannot be held responsible if a student possessed of all the basic language competencies fails to use them in practical situations."[25] Especially, we may add, if the teacher has continually encouraged and provided opportunities for such practical use. The experience of many has shown that the student with a solid knowledge of grammar and lexicon blossoms as a language user quite rapidly when in an environment where use of the language becomes necessary or desirable for personal reasons.

Further checks can be made on the students' conception of the *pronunciation* of words, if the teacher so desires, by objective tests in which students group words according to sound features or distinguish words which differ in pronunciation from others in a group. Taped *aural-discrimination* tests (where students select among several alternatives on an answer sheet the equivalent, in graphic form, for the sound or word they heard on a tape) reveal which sounds the students are confounding and, therefore, which sounds they are probably not distinguishing in their own production. Items for tests of these types are described in some of the books in the Annotated Reading List at the end of this chapter and in the text of chapter 5 above.

Features of *sound production* can also be evaluated by the teacher at intervals during the year, in the course of class work. Students will be imitating sounds, participating in oral exercises, acting out dialogues and skits, conducting conversational exchanges of various types, reading aloud from their books. The alert teacher will keep a cumulative record of the production of each student. This will provide a fairer picture of the student's capabilities than an assessment made in an artificial test situation, when the student may be tense and anxious.[26]

Even when teachers believe they are concentrating the student's attention on a single aspect of the language, they may be demanding too many decisions at one point. A common type of question in foreign-language tests consists of a series of *sentences to translate* from the native language to the foreign language. This apparently innocent device has become the bugbear of many students. The author of the sentences frequently becomes preoccupied with the structures and vocabulary most likely to cause problems for the students and

25. John B. Carroll, "Foreign Language Testing: Will the Persistent Problems Persist?" in O'Brien 1973, p. 11.
26. A Pronunciation Checklist, which is useful for this purpose, is provided in the *PG*'s, chap. 5.

tries to weave four or five of these into one sentence. The result is usually a very stilted and artificial sentence, which can be regarded only as a linguistic curiosity. A quick glance at an old textbook for the teaching of German to speakers of English reveals the following sentences for translation: "Steer courageously the ship through the rolling sea," "My brother has something beautiful and I have nothing ugly," "We do not go to the Dutch captain's, we go to the Russian major's," and "It would be necessary for you to dwell on the seashore."[27] It is difficult to conceive of situations where these sentences could prove to be useful utterances, yet in classrooms all over the world teachers continue to concoct monstrosities almost as ludicrous as these, because they consider them an effective way to test their students' understanding of grammatical relationships and lexical range. For grading sentences of this type, the teacher usually makes a superficial count of the difficulties which have been deliberately included, perhaps four or five to each sentence. Marks are then allotted accordingly. Closer examination reveals that each sentence requires as many as ten or twelve decisions on the part of the student. Students may choose the appropriate lexical equivalents but neglect to make the necessary morphological adjustments to these words; they may choose the right tense for a verb but forget to make some other adjustment which use of this tense entails, or forget that this particular verb has some irregularity of form in this particular tense. Having solved several of these problems, they may have paid little attention to some special problem of word order, forgotten to use some idiomatic turn of expression, or mispelled a word. It is not surprising that the student who gives up the unequal struggle and leaves blanks at various points in the sentence is often credited with a higher score than the student who has tried to solve most of the problems. A test that includes questions of this kind is usually attempting to test too many things at the same time in an artificial way; it therefore fails to provide students with a fair opportunity to show what they really know.

The first step in alleviating the pressure on the student in tests of detail is to test range of vocabulary separately from knowledge of grammatical structure. Only the most common lexical items which have been used frequently by the student should be employed in tests designed primarily to ascertain knowledge of morphology and syntax. Similarly, tests designed specifically to determine variety and range of vocabulary should not involve at the same time decisions on tenses,

27. In case the reader finds it hard to believe that such extraordinary sentences for translation are still being used, the author attests to having seen such distortions of English for translation into French, Russian, and German as recently as 1979.

grammatical agreement with other words in the sentence (particularly where this involves the use of rare forms), or unusual word order. Where two difficulties which are different in kind coincide, only the most alert student may be expected to deal with both effectively in the anxiety-creating atmosphere of the test. The very fact that students are anxious to do well in a test often hinders them from seeing more than one point at a time—they are so pleased with their one discovery. Concurrence of difficulties can mean that the student who has learned what has been taught is ranked on the same level with the student who knows only some sections of the work, whereas one of the main aims of testing should be to distinguish clearly between the two.

The Cloze Test

An easily constructed, easily corrected integrative test which can be used to assess both feeling for the language and knowledge of detail is the cloze test. Based on the gestalt concept of closure (that human minds tend to complete the incomplete according to expectations of the complete form that they have developed through experience), the cloze test is constructed by omitting every *n*th word in a continuous passage of discourse. This may be every fifth, sixth, or seventh word. The first sentence of the passage is usually given in its entirety to provide some background for what follows (and sometimes the last sentence is left complete as well). The students are expected to read the test carefully, filling in all the omitted words according to their projections of the evolving meaning. This tests their knowledge of many aspects of the language in a context of meaningful discourse. Students are guided by syntactic, morphological, and semantic clues, of which there are many because of the redundancy of natural sequential language.

It is advocated that the omission of words follow some arbitrary scheme, like every *n*th word, to avoid subjective overemphasis by the teacher on certain aspects of the language (favorite structural problems, a concentration on vocabulary, or whatever). Adjustments may be made if the arbitrarily selected blank deletes a key word which is vital to the meaning but cannot be deduced from the context. (Problems of this type can sometimes be avoided by careful selection of a title for the passage.)

The cloze test is a challenging exercise which students find more interesting than dealing with isolated items. It has been shown to correlate highly with tests of reading comprehension, listening comprehension, and dictation (which also involve projecting expectations), and with the TOEFL test (Test of English as a Foreign

Language, administered to many students of English wishing to study in the USA).[28] This supports Carroll's observation: "In recent work on the comprehensive measurement of language skills, we have the paradox that the more we attempt to measure *different* language skills, and the better our measurements of those skills, the higher the correlations among the skills, and thus the more they appear to converge toward the measurement of a *single* all-embracing skill . . . especially if we adjust for unreliability through statistical techniques. . . . It is tempting to conclude that there is indeed only one basic foreign language skill—that we can epitomize as simply 'knowledge of the structure and lexicon of the language.' But perhaps it is incorrect to draw this conclusion."[29] Be that as it may, the cloze test appears to be a useful placement device for large groups of students, as well as a convenient measure of overall proficiency or achievement.

There are several methods for presenting and correcting cloze tests.[30]

1. The student may select completions from multiple-choice options. This limits the cloze test to language processing through reading and does not involve other language activities such as writing or cognitive scanning of stored vocabulary.
2. The student may fill in the blank with any appropriate word, but only the expected word will be counted as correct. This makes for easy correction of a placement test and has not been shown to be significantly different from method 3 (see next item) in ranking non-native speakers. (It is not advisable for a class test where the correction of the test will later be discussed with the students, since students will resent the fact that credit has not been given for a plausible alternative.)
3. The student may write in any appropriate word and will receive credit for any word which makes sense in the context. (This is psychologically more satisfactory for class use.)
4. Multiple-word deletions are made in the text, and the student inserts appropriate word groups.
5. The deletions are made deliberately to test knowledge of certain grammatical features, such as tenses or prepositions. This makes

28. For a summary of research on the cloze test, see J. W. Oller, Jr., and C. A. Conrad, "The Cloze Technique and ESL Proficiency," *LL* 21 (1971): 183–96.

29. Carroll, "Foreign Language Testing," pp. 11–12.

30. For research on scoring methods for the cloze test, see J. W. Oller, Jr., "Scoring Methods and Difficulty Levels for Cloze Tests of Proficiency in English as a Second Language," *MLJ* 56 (1972): 151–58.

the cloze test more like a fill-in-the-blank overall structure test,[31] except that the items occur in continuous discourse longer than the sentence. This type of cloze test, not surprisingly, correlates highly with other tests of grammar. It provides useful diagnostic information, not easily discernible in the regular cloze test, on difficulties students are experiencing in specific areas of morphology or syntax.

6. A contextual test has been proposed, along the lines of the cloze test.[32] In this test, "high redundancy points in the string (affixes, function words, etc.) are suppressed and must be supplied in order to reconstruct an integral text."[33] Authentic texts are used, "because such material is much more likely to provide the frequencies, patterning, and constituent order typical of a given language style-level and register."[34]

7. The initial letter may be given for the word required for each blank. This solves in most cases the problem raised in methods 2–3. The approach is appropriate for elementary-level students or as a familiarization device.

- **Can you think of any other possible variations of the cloze test which would be worth trying?**

TEST WHAT THE STUDENTS HAVE BEEN LEARNING

With a changing emphasis in teaching objectives and methods, there is always the danger that a time lag will develop between ways of teaching and ways of testing. Certain forms of testing have become so established with the passing of time that teachers who were tested by these methods themselves tend to accept them without questioning their value. Many teachers do not even pause to analyze what is really being tested by the types of questions they are asking and the types of exercises they are setting. They are merely dismayed at the results achieved by their students and complain about deteriorating standards and the laziness of students.

At a time when foreign-language teaching was consciously patterned on the teaching of Latin and Greek, emphasis was laid on a thorough analysis of the grammar of the language according to the traditional system, on the learning of rules, and on the developing of

---

31. Hints on constructing fill-in-the-blank "overall structure tests," which require the student to understand the surrounding context in order to be able to complete the item correctly, are given, with examples, in the *PG*'s, chap. 8.

32. See J. Bondaruk, J. Child, and E. Tetrault, "Contextual Testing," in Jones and Spolsky 1975, pp. 89–101.

33. Ibid., p. 92.

34. Ibid., pp. 91–92.

skill in applying these rules deductively. The memory was trained, or so it was believed, by the learning of long lists of foreign words with their native-language equivalents and by the reciting of innumerable conjugational and declensional paradigms. Teachers of the classics considered that to be able to translate a passage from the native language into a reasonable approximation of Latin or Greek was a suitable demonstration of the kind of mastery that was sought: the understanding and memorization of rules and their deductive application. The same test of skill was soon applied in modern language classes.

At the present time, what is being demanded of foreign-language students by the community which supports their education has changed in most areas. They are now expected to demonstrate that they can understand, speak, or at least read the language they are learning. (Ability to write the language beyond a basic level is not usually required of non-native speakers except when they are studying alongside native speakers in a country where the language is spoken.) After a period of study, students are expected to be able to understand general conversation, radio or television programs, instructions, or directions; to be able to say something comprehensibly in the language; and to be able to read a foreign-language newspaper, book, or article in their field without constant use of a dictionary.[35]

Despite this change in approach, many tests, particularly those which have become community institutions and serve many schools, have not changed to a marked degree. They remain, with notable exceptions, as they were years ago.[36] In the schools, teachers tend to construct their class tests on the same lines as these communitywide tests so that their students may be better prepared to face, at a later date, what are considered to be the most important tests of all. As a result, numbers of students are being taught one way and tested in another. These students are no longer being tested on what they have been learning.

---

35. A survey of objectives in language classes, conducted in fifty countries and fifty American states in 1978, showed that active communication rated high in the USA, Canada, Western Europe, Japan, Australia, and New Zealand, whereas developing countries like Thailand and Brazil were more interested in reading for updating their knowledge of modern scientific and technological developments. The complete report may be found in Wilga M. Rivers, "Educational Goals: The Foreign Language Teacher's Response," in NEC 1979, pp. 35–49.

36. Many state- and nationwide examinations have adapted to changing times, as, for instance, the New York State Regents Examination, which is regularly reviewed to bring it into line with current objectives.

Translation of Passages of Prose or Poetry

One of the traditional ways of testing knowledge of the foreign language has been through the translation of a passage of prose or poetry from the native language into the foreign language. This type of test accorded well with the way in which the classical languages were taught. It is, however, inappropriate for students who have been taught active oral use of the language to express personal meaning. They are now asked to examine a passage of prose in their native language in the utmost detail, to break it down into its smallest elements of meaning, to find foreign-language equivalents for these meanings, and then to construct an acceptable segment of discourse which retains the spirit and style of the original. This is a valuable and interesting task, for which students may be prepared through specialized training, but it is completely different from the tasks encountered in most modern-language classes today.

Any prose passage presents many problems for the translator, some obvious, some not so obvious. Some of these the teacher has consciously included in the test, others may have been overlooked in choosing the passage. If the student has not been trained in translation method and in comparative stylistics, what is finally produced can rarely be called a translation; it is frequently no more than a reexpression of the forms of the student's native language with a lexical overlay from the target language. If students are to be asked to translate, they should be taught to translate in an efficient manner—a procedure possible only when the student has a considerable grasp of the structure, lexical possibilities, and cultural context of both languages.[37] Translation cannot be considered a comprehensive test in all teaching situations. It is not a fair test for students who have been trained from the beginning to seek a direct grasp of structure and meaning in the foreign language, because it forces them into ways of thinking that can only retard their progress toward free and fluent expression of their own meaning in communication. It is a specialized art, which deserves the full attention of those who require it or are interested in it, and wish to become proficient at it. For these, translation of passages of discourse of this type constitute a valid test.

Translation of Stimulus Sentences

Where students have been trained in the early stages to produce acceptable target-language utterances as equivalents to stimulus ut-

---

37. The specific problems of translation are discussed in greater detail in Wilga M. Rivers, "Contrastive Linguistics in Textbook and Classroom," in Alatis 1968, reprinted in *SMT*. Translation as a teaching/learning device and as a specialized study is discussed at considerable length in the *PG*'s, chap. 9.

terances in the native language, they may be tested in this form in writing. In appearance such a test resembles the sentence translation exercise described earlier, but in principle it is very different. The sentences for which the student is asked to give target-language equivalents in this case are uncomplicated. Each contains one language problem only—a problem which is of common occurrence and easily recognizable by the student. The vocabulary in which the utterance is phrased is of high frequency in classroom use or in the textbook, and the utterance is of a type the student would be likely to hear or use. The student is being asked to express as a whole in the target language the meaning of the native-language stimulus utterance, not to construct element by element a supposed equivalent. The student produces the utterance rapidly and moves on. Such sentences as "He's here," "Isn't he here?" "Aren't they here?" serve as stimuli of this type. A series of items like these is a legitimate applicational test of work which has been learned through dialogue memorization, intensive practice exercises, or controlled oral practice of grammatical structure in the classroom. It is not appropriate for a class that is proceeding on direct-method lines, without use of the native language at any time. This type of test can be continued to an advanced level as a test of the mastery of structural patterns. The student is expected to give equivalents for a large number of utterances in a short time, as a quick recall. If students are allowed to pore over such sentences for a long period, they will be tempted to break them up into translation segments in their search for tricks and hidden difficulties, and the objective of direct expression of meaning in the target language will not be realized.

Grammar Tests

One kind of grammatical test which has been common is the *fill-in-the-blank* type. Sometimes this kind of exercise appears in textbooks and in tests as a conglomeration of foreign-language expressions with native-language inserts. This is to be avoided, since students need to get the feeling for complete sentences in the language and they learn from everything they do. Fill-in-the-blank items often involve little more than the quick recognition of some structural clue in part of the sentence (in most cases in the segments preceding or following the blank). As a result, many items can be completed quite successfully by a quick-witted student who has a minimal knowledge of the structural pattern required and a very vague idea of the meaning of the sentence. This is particularly the case when multiple-choice answers are offered for selection. This type of exercise is little improved when foreign-language clues are given instead of native-language clues.

Many students learn to make the required adjustments to foreign-language words without bothering to find out their meaning or to examine their relationship to the whole sentence. Sentence-completion items can be of value only if the completion requires a thorough understanding of the whole sentence. Clue words, which have a vital bearing on the correct decision, should be embedded in the item, usually some distance from the blank. With this careful kind of construction, the whole item can be kept in the foreign language, and the student is forced to study the complete sentence rather than concentrate only on the manipulation of segments.[38]

Certain types of *structure drills* can be converted into test items. Students may be asked to make transformations of sentences, as they do in conversion exercises. They may be asked to expand, contract, and combine sentences in various ways. They may be required to choose from a list of alternatives a correct form as a response to a particular situation (this type of item being acceptable only if no incorrect forms, only inappropriate ones, are supplied). They may be given an outline to expand which has been structured in such a way that they are forced to use certain structures and grammatical forms which they have been learning.

Composition

When the students have attained some control of a body of material, even at an elementary level, they may be asked to express themselves in a written *composition,* in which they can combine elements they have been learning in novel combinations to express their own meaning. An outline helps the less imaginative, although the more confident should always be given the choice of developing their own sequence of ideas. Once students have realized that what they must do is recombine elements they know, not seek out new material in their dictionaries, they often surprise and delight the teacher with their ability to express their ideas in original and amusing ways. The grading of such compositions (discussed in chapter 10 above) is more subjective than for the usual types of tests, even when a weighted assessment scheme is used.[39] In this way, the composition is somewhat like the oral interview, discussed earlier. The written composition acts as a counterbalance and corrective to a diet of objective and multiple-choice tests, providing the opportunity to evaluate the students' feel-

38. Techniques for drafting valid fill-in-the-blank items for English SL/FL, French, German, Hebrew, and Spanish are discussed with examples demonstrating the pitfalls, in chapters 4 and 8 of the *PG*'s (examples G5–7, W9–14, and W19–27).

39. A weighted assessment scheme for grading free compositions is proposed in chapter 9 of the *PG*'s (W61).

ing for authentic expression in the language (as opposed to sterile accuracy) and their control of the interplay of a variety of disparate elements. It is also an important form of communication which many students enjoy.

• **Devise a breakdown scheme for assessment of written compositions.**

A new emphasis requires a new approach to testing and a search for types of items which test what we are teaching and what we hope our students are learning. A great deal of research is at present being put into the designing of new types of tests, particularly integrative tests of communicative ability and tests of overall language proficiency. Teachers should keep in touch with these developments through their professional literature. With the principles enunciated in this chapter in mind, they should themselves experiment with new ways of testing, endeavoring to cover all the areas which they are emphasizing in their teaching in a way which is consistent with the approach taken in the classroom.

Weighting the Sections of the Test
In establishing a final grade, the teacher should ensure that it reflects what the students have been learning. Care in constructing tests is not sufficient guarantee that this will be so. Some areas of language study require tests which contain many more items than others. Having assessed a series of tests, teachers must then see that the system of "adding up marks" has not given a distorted picture of the individual student's achievement. If a vocabulary test contained fifty items, a listening-comprehension test twenty items, and a structure test twenty items, while an oral interview was assessed out of ten possible points, "adding up the marks" will imply that knowing fifty words is five times as important as being able to communicate effectively, and more than twice as important as understanding the spoken language and knowing how to use structural patterns. Knowledge of vocabulary will already have been assessed as an integral part of each of the other tests, which again increases its share of the total. At this point, the teacher must decide what weight to give to each kind of work tested. This decision will depend on the objectives of the course, the percentage of time that has been devoted to each area, and the stage of learning that has been reached.

Weighting, a simple arithmetic procedure, corrects the imbalance caused by the number of small items in sections of the test. Inexperienced teachers sometimes need to learn that the total of marks in a test is not some rigid reflection of reality; it is often a particularly deceptive objectivization of the defects of the test itself. Where the test does not reflect what the teacher knows of the proficiency of the class (that is, if the test items have proved too difficult and confusing for the candidates, or if the test has obviously been too simple), the teacher should make suitable statistical adjustments in the records. These adjustments will not alter the ranking of the candidates but will standardize the whole range of marks, making comparisons with other test entries more realistic. Guidance for this type of statistical treatment of a range of marks is provided in several of the books in the Annotated Reading List for this chapter.

TEST TO FIND OUT WHAT THE STUDENT KNOWS

At first reading, the heading of this section may appear so self-evident that it does not warrant discussion. This is far from being the case. It expresses an attitude which, unfortunately, is reflected in too few of the tests and quizzes which are administered, whether for languages or for other subjects of the curriculum. Questions are often framed in such a way that the successful student is the one who is best able to interpret the teacher's intentions. Questions may be so interrelated throughout one section of the test that a mistake early in the series inevitably causes a succession of mistakes, and the student loses credit much in excess of what was warranted by the original error. This is particularly true of badly constructed listening and reading comprehension tests (whether of the multiple-choice, question-answer, or true-false types), cloze tests which depend on key words early in the passage, dictations, and translation tests of consecutive discourse. Tests may be so limited in scope that they provide for certain skill areas and leave others unconsidered. Such imbalance occurs when all testing is of the reading-writing variety while a great deal of the class work has consisted of listening and speaking. Items may also be directed to finicky points of grammar and largely ignore those areas the student knows well.

The method used for determining the total test score may prevent the teacher from differentiating clearly between those who have learned an acceptable amount and those who have not. A distinct difference in grading is observable between an assessment based on deduction of points for student errors and one based on addition of points for what the student knows. "One mark off for each mistake" deducted from a predetermined total can mean that a student who has tried hard but made a number of mistakes of varying degrees of importance receives less credit than a student who omitted portions of the work here and there and was therefore not in a position to make so many mistakes. If tests are of the objective type, where students check off letters for multiple-choice options, this kind of discrepancy between points deducted and points allotted is not important. It is also less observable in a test where items are not interdependent than in a test which proceeds in a sequential development.

A special problem arises where several classes at the same level are streamed, according either to predicted ability or to achievement in earlier years. The purpose of the streaming is to enable students to study with other students who work at approximately the same pace. As a result, one or two of the streamed groups will inevitably advance more rapidly than the others. The intended effects of such streaming (permitting students to learn at a pace which they find comfortable) are obviated when the department or the administration insists on the construction of one test, graded identically, for the assessment of all groups. The test may be geared to the achievement of the fast-moving group, in which case it is inevitable that the students in the slower-moving groups will perform very badly, their enthusiasm will be dampened, and discouragement will set in. If, on the other hand, the test is geared to the average student, it will provide no challenge for the students who have been moving more quickly. In either case, the test will not help the teacher to find out what a number of the students know of the language they have been learning. There are several possible solutions to this problem. The teacher may set a *progressive test* with sections which move from the more elementary to the more advanced areas of the work. In this case, the fast-moving group may be required to complete the whole test, while the slower-moving groups complete only certain earlier sections. Alternatively, the teacher may set separate tests geared to the level of achievement of the different groups, adding some symbol to the report card to show the standard represented by the test assessment.

There is no reason why students should not proceed in this way over a period of years, with differentiated classes taking different lengths of time to reach various specified levels of language control. This approach is facilitated if the content of the different levels is clearly spelled out in terms of grammar to be covered and approximate size of vocabulary to be acquired, with the level of difficulty of reading and listening material and the degree of communicative facility set out in functional terms (e.g., Should be able to read the news items on the front page of a newspaper, *or* Should be able to listen to a news broadcast and recount the contents, *or* Should be able to participate without hesitation in a conversational exchange on the activities in which he or she participates at school or during the weekends). Students are then given credit for the level of mastery they have achieved, rather than the number of years they have studied the language.[40]

CONSTRUCTION AND USE OF OBJECTIVE TESTS

Earlier in this chapter it was pointed out that certain aspects of language learning can be tested by carefully constructed objective tests. These are especially useful when it is considered desirable to test such things as aural discrimination of sounds, comprehension of spoken language and of written texts, range of vocabulary, or understanding of the function of elements of grammatical structure. Objective tests are generally considered more reliable, in the statistical sense of the word, than traditional tests, for they are scored in an identical fashion even if corrected by several different persons. Reliability, however, is never a virtue by itself. The reliable test must also be a valid measure of what the examiner intends to measure and, from the teaching point of view, a valuable learning experience also for the students.

Objective tests have several practical advantages over tests of a more traditional character. Although they take much longer to prepare, they are more easily and rapidly corrected, and when both preparation and correction time have been taken into account, they represent a great saving where large groups of students are involved. They may be machine-corrected if numbers warrant it, as in a placement test for entry into a large program. If numbers are small, they are quickly corrected by visual scrutiny or with the aid of a cardboard key with holes punched for the appropriate answers. Teachers are thus able to test more frequently without fearing the burden of many hours of laborious correction. With objective tests, more questions can be answered by students in a test period because time is not taken up with a lot of redundant writing, much of which is mere copying from the test paper. Consequently, questions can range over a much broader area of the work studied, giving students more opportunity to show what they have learned than in the more limited procedure of a few questions sampling all the work studied.

40. This approach to providing opportunities for students to learn at a slower or faster pace as they are able is basic to individualized instruction (see Altman 1972 and Logan 1973). The problem of evaluating variable progress through levels is discussed in Grittner and LaLeike 1973, chap. 4: "Evaluating Student Performance and Progress."

There are several types of objective tests which may be used in language classes: true-false, multiple-choice, fill-in-the-blank or completion, and matching tests.[41]

True-false tests involve the acceptance or rejection of a statement or utterance heard or read. They are useful as tests of listening or reading comprehension, or of knowledge of historical, literary, and cultural facts related to the context in which the language is used. Since the choice is a two-way one, the probability of a chance success is much higher than in a multiple-choice test with four options. Even when a third choice, "Don't know," is added, there is little guarantee that students will not prefer to guess the answer. A heavier penalty for a wrong answer than for "Don't know" may discourage this to some extent, although it makes correction a little more complicated. For these reasons, true-false tests are probably best used for rapidly checking whether students have prepared certain work, or as a guide to students as to their understanding of texts they have been reading on their own. Where a more penetrating discrimination of student achievement is sought, a more elaborate type of test is advisable.

Multiple-choice tests provide answers to questions on, for example, listening or reading comprehension material, lexical meanings of words, appropriateness of rejoinder in spoken language, or items of cultural interest. Of the choices offered (usually four), only one is appropriate; the others are based on probable errors which the student is likely to make by not discriminating between words of similar sound in listening comprehension, by confusion of vocabulary or misinterpretation of structural relationships in reading comprehension, by not distinguishing between words which are similar in spelling and form in vocabulary tests, or by mishearing or misreading the question under consideration. Contrary to the belief of some persons untrained in probability theory, a well-constructed multiple-choice test with a large number of items, each with three or four choices, does not make it easy for students to guess their way through to success. Apart from the restricted statistical probabilities of successful guessing, over a large number of items, well-designed choices of answer in a multiple-choice test seem plausible to the student who does not know the work thoroughly and will therefore not be chosen on a purely chance basis. The arrangement of the appropriate choices on the answer sheet (the choices are usually labeled A, B, C, D) should be randomized, so that students cannot hit upon a pattern of response, however unintentional on the part of the constructor, which will help in guessing (for instance,

41. Examples of these types of tests for English SL/FL, French, German, Hebrew, and Spanish are given, with hints on effective construction, in the *PG*'s, chap. 3 (C59–66), chap. 5 (S15–21), chap. 7 (R58–66, 72–77), and chap. 8 (W9–28).

an equal number of A's, B's, C's, and D's as correct choices). The use of a table of random numbers is useful in establishing the order of placement of the correct choices.

The *fill-in-the-blank* type of test may be multiple-choice or it may require the student to write in an appropriate word. These tests are useful for assessing knowledge of grammatical structure, use of tenses, levels of language, and vocabulary. The teacher must ensure that the sentences are quite unambiguous and can be completed appropriately by only one word, or the advantages of quick correction are lost. Where choices are given, they must represent real possibilities for the student who has not taken into account all the clues in the item, and there must be no possibility of the student's arriving at the correct decision by a process of elimination. Write-in completion tests are less objective than multiple-choice completion tests, because students may make errors other than those which the teacher has foreseen, and the possibility of ambiguity must be even more rigorously controlled.

Matching tests are commonly used as vocabulary tests. Students are asked to match synonyms, antonyms, names of objects with names of groups or classes of objects, names of objects with occupations, and so on. Tests of this type can also be used for testing knowledge of facts about the foreign culture or for sound-symbol correspondences. It is in matching tests that there is the greatest possibility of reaching correct decisions by a process of elimination. This danger can be avoided by providing unequal lists for the matching process, or by providing several items which may be matched with more than one item, and others which do not match at all.

Objective tests require skill and ingenuity in their construction. With a little imagination and humor, items can be made interesting as well as useful. If students are not allowed to retain their question papers, tests may be reused in successive years, with items improved where experience and item analysis have shown them to be ineffective or defective. In revising a test, the teacher should eliminate any item which essentially tests the same thing tested by another item and therefore distorts the score. These doublings are not always obvious to teachers at the stage when they are constructing the test and earnestly seeking valid items. Once an effective test has been produced in certain areas, notably in testing grammatical structure, parallel forms of the test can be created without a great deal of difficulty by converting items from the lexical point of view without altering other relationships

In the Annotated Reading List below, the reader may glean many practical hints of this type for the effective construction and revision of objective tests; other ideas will come with experience. If the position of objective tests is to be justified in a language-learning program, however, it must be remembered that they test only certain aspects of language study (passive knowledge rather than active use) and that they must be combined with other, more subjectively evaluated, integrative tests of language use to give an all-round picture of the student's achievement. Teachers must avoid taking the easy way out if their students are to use the language with facility.

DESIGNING CLASS TESTS

All teachers have to undertake the preparation of their own tests at regular intervals. As they prepare a test, they should keep in their minds the image of the particular class for which they are constructing the test. This will act as a corrective to a natural tendency to compose the test around what they themselves know of the subject. They should design the test with careful attention to what this particular class has been learning: what has been taught to the class and not what the teacher intended to teach or feels should have been taught. No test will be efficiently constructed if the teacher designing it does not have a clear picture of what the students may realistically be expected to know.

The test constructor should decide, after careful consideration, which skills and competencies are to be tested, and settle on the best ways to test these particular abilities and not something else. Some short tests are designed to establish the students' grasp of a particular area of the work (these are sometimes called quizzes); some are intended as all-round tests at the end of a unit of study. If the test is a comprehensive one, the teacher should examine it carefully to see that it reflects adequately the objectives of the course and the amount of time spent on practice of the various skills, and that the test items for each skill reflect the way in which this skill was presented and practiced in class. There should always be some integrative activity, to enable the student to demonstrate overall control of the language. Finally, the material and items in a language test should be authentic specimens of language which would be used in normal communication, oral or written.

From the practical point of view, teachers should ask themselves the following questions:

Are the instructions in the test so clear that the students cannot possibly misunderstand what they are expected to do?
A foreign-language test is designed to find out what students know of the language, not whether they are alert, intelligent, or able to read

the teacher's mind. Unless the students have been thoroughly drilled in certain instructions in the target language, or have every opportunity to ask questions in cases of uncertainty, instructions should be given in the native language. A weak or nervous student may mis-interpret instructions in the foreign language and be prevented by this error from demonstrating to the teacher what he or she knows. As student confidence grows, instructions will be converted into foreign-language equivalents. If the question requires a particular format for the answer, misunderstanding may be avoided by the inclusion of a sample question and answer, so long as the sample demonstrates only the way the question should be answered, without supplying information which will give clues to the correct answers to later questions.

Is there any ambiguity in the test items?
The test must be scrutinized to ensure that each question will prompt the response the teacher is looking for and not leave the way open for other responses which will not be acceptable as a demonstration of learning in this particular area. No item should be included which allows of several possible answers unless it is clear to the student that all of these will be acceptable. It is very difficult for the teachers writing the tests to detect certain types of ambiguity, because they are conscious of their own intentions in the creation of the items. For this reason, it is advisable to submit any test to one or two colleagues for criticism before it is produced in its final form.

Is the test so constructed that the student begins with easier items and proceeds to the more difficult?
This is an important psychological principle in testing. If the test is carefully graded in its development, weaker students who do not complete the test will omit only the items on which, in all probability, they would not have been successful. Weaker students often become anxious when they feel unable to answer some of the questions satisfactorily. As a result, they become tense and find it difficult to answer even the easier questions. In a graded sequence, they do not reach this stage until the later part of the test, when they have already moved confidently through the items which the teacher expected them to be able to complete correctly. A graded sequence also enables the teacher to test at several levels when the class consists of students of a wide range of abilities, or when the same test is to be used for several classes which have been streamed according to speed of learning.

Do the items test ability to use the language rather than mere knowledge about the language?

The learning of rules or generalizations about language structure and usage does not ensure ability to use the language effectively in speech or writing. Since teachers tend to teach and students tend to study in the way in which a test is framed, items which require students to write about the language rather than to show how it works have a very damaging effect on language study. If the language is being taught through use, students must not be expected to be able to make formal statements about its structure. Formal descriptions of the way a language functions should be expected only of students who are studying the language at an advanced level, with an objective which is primarily linguistic; this is usually a university-level study.

Are the items in the test linguistically useful?

Test items should concentrate on what is normal usage, not on unusual forms about which even a native speaker may show hesitation. They should consist of complete utterances, unless there are valid reasons for using segments of utterances. An "utterance" in this sense does not mean a complete sentence, in the traditional sense of the term, but a linguistic sample which is meaningful when used on its own. Words in isolation can be ambiguous and obscure in meaning, and many students have learned to make adjustments to such isolated elements without having any clear idea how they function in context. When elements being tested are placed in a linguistically useful utterance, the student demonstrates more knowledge than when dealing with the same element in isolation, and feeling for appropriate context is strengthened by this further experience. Items which present students with a mixture of target-language and native-language forms force them into concentrating on disconnected elements of an utterance and hinder them in their efforts to think in the language. Incorrect forms for identification or correction should be avoided. While students are pondering the answer, these incorrect versions are being impressed on their senses and may be learned incidentally, quite contrary to the teacher's intentions.

Does the test concentrate exclusively on bits of information, or is some opportunity provided for the student to put it all together or to see authentic language material as a meaningful whole?

It is easy to prepare and correct test items on particular, circumscribed points of structure, vocabulary, or the sound system. This breaking up of the language into discrete elements can be useful for checking the student's accurate knowledge of details, many of which are essential for comprehension and comprehensibility. Knowledge of a language, however, goes beyond a succession of discrete items, and these details in combination form new meanings. Every test should provide the opportunity for students to see and use language as a whole, a vehicle of meaning which functions only when its parts are interacting harmoniously. If the teacher constantly tests isolated elements, students will learn the language in a fragmentary way. An oral interview (even brief); a composition, or original skit; a listening or reading experience of sufficient length and coherence to hold intrinsic interest for the student; a problem to solve, an enigma to resolve, or a task to perform; the opportunity to contribute some original ideas about material read in class—any of these will draw together language in a normal language activity.

PERSISTENT PROBLEMS OF TESTING

In conclusion, it is well to reflect on what Carroll has identified as the persistent problems in foreign-language testing:

> (1) The problem of *validity*—that is, making sure that the measurements and assessments we obtain reflect what we want them to reflect.
> (2) The problem of *scope*—that is, making sure that we measure or assess all the varied components of foreign language competence and skill.
> (3) The problem of *efficiency*—that is, obtaining the best assessments we can obtain within the limits of time and resources available for the construction and administration of the assessments.
> (4) The problem of how tests relate to the wider context of instruction—for example, the degree to which testing either enhances instruction or, contrariwise, distorts it through undesirable feedback effects from the tests.[42]

- **Which of the problems above seem to be the most persistent in your situation?**

Annotated Reading List

Valette, Rebecca M. *Modern Language Testing.* 2d ed. New York: Harcourt Brace Jovanovich, 1977. A complete study of testing, indispensable for all teachers. Instructions on test construction and evaluation for the various types of tests for the four skills, for culture, and for literature, with a section on testing in bilingual and

42. Carroll, "Foreign Language Testing," p. 8.

ESL programs. Examples in English, French, German, Italian, and Spanish.

Harris, David P. *Testing English as a Second Language.* New York: McGraw-Hill, 1969. Very thorough guidance for the teacher in constructing, administering, and interpreting tests for all four skills and vocabulary learning, with practical advice on the pitfalls. A final section on computing basic test statistics. Useful for teachers of any language.

Rivers, Wilga M. "Testing and Student Learning." In *SMT,* pp. 49–63. Discusses testing as an important step in student learning which must be related to the student's expectations and objectives in learning the language. Distinguishes between tests for micro-language learning and tests for macro-language use. Urges a testing program which helps the students develop their confidence in personal use of the language, rather than one which merely screens or ranks them.

Jorstad, Helen L. "Testing as Communication." In Jarvis 1974b, pp. 223–73 (with bibliographic references). Discusses norm-referenced and criterion-referenced tests and the specific problems of individualized programs; discrete-point and global testing, with special attention to oral communication, reading, and culture. There is an extensive discussion of grades and reporting systems and input from students and parents in program evaluation.

Jones, Randall L. "Testing: A Vital Connection." In Phillips 1977, pp. 237–65 (with bibliographic references). Discusses language testing objectives; performance tests for speaking, listening, reading, and writing and for overall language proficiency, with some consideration of cultural and sociolinguistic factors. Gives many suggestions for appropriate types of tests.

Valette, Rebecca M., and Linder, Cathy. "Measuring the Variables and Testing the Outcomes." In Phillips 1979, pp. 199–232 (with bibliographic references). A useful guide to practicing teachers on available tests of aptitude, learning styles, attitudes, and motivation; on methods of placement, how to determine bases for assigning grades, and suitable forms of tests for all aspects of language learning. Concludes with advice on administering and interpreting tests.

Clark, John L. D. "Measurement Implications of Recent Trends in Foreign Language Teaching." In Lange and James 1972, pp. 219–57. Deals with the problems of evaluation raised by such trends as individualized instruction, consideration of learner variables, behavioral objectives, programmed and computer-assisted instruction, the teaching of culture, and interdisciplinary programs.

Palmer, Leslie, and Spolsky, Bernard. *Papers on Language Testing 1967–1974*. Washington, D.C.: TESOL, 1975. A varied collection of articles on test development for various skill areas and for overall proficiency (with discussion of some specific tests for ESL). Theory and interpretation of language tests and the specific problems of dialectal and bilingual students are considered. Although the examples are in English, the information in the book is of importance for teachers of any language.

Brière, Eugène, J., and Honifolis, F. B., eds. *Concepts in Language Testing: Some Recent Studies*. Washington, D.C.: TESOL, 1979. A research-oriented discussion of cloze tests, direct and semidirect tests of speaking ability, performance tests, and the concept of validity.

Oller, John W., Jr. *Language Tests at School*. London: Longman, 1979. Emphasizes the differences between pragmatically oriented language tests and discrete-point tests. Practical suggestions are given for preparing, administering, scoring, and interpreting dictation tests, cloze and essay tests, as well as tests of productive oral production. Along with analysis and critique of discrete-point tests, proposals are made for improving their construction. An excellent reference for any aspect of testing.

*Allen, J. P. B., and Davis, Alan, ed., *Testing and Experimental Methods*. Vol. 4 of the Edinburgh Course in Applied Linguistics. London: Oxford University Press, 1977. A thorough and detailed study of basic concepts in testing, the construction and analysis of language tests, and the design and interpretation of experiments. Essential reading as a foundation for a specialized study of testing.

Research and Discussion

1. You have been asked to prepare a final oral examination for elementary-level students. You decide to make it an activity- and task-oriented examination. Describe the activities and tasks you propose to use to assess both listening comprehension and oral proficiency.

2. You have been put in charge of a course of Language for Special Purposes. Your students need the language to read advanced experimental material in nuclear physics and for no other purpose. Design a battery of tests which will enable you to assess their competence to operate as abstracters for a research institute. (See p. 470.)

3. Look at the kinds of tests given in (a) social studies and (b) mathematics or general science in the school where you are teach-

ing or observing. What can the language teachers learn from these tests (positive or negative)?

4. Using Appendix A as a guide, draft ratings scales of absolute language proficiency for two of the following: (a) a course in the native language of a local ethnic community for policemen and firemen who will be in contact with this community; (b) certification for teachers of foreign languages and second languages at high school level; (c) acceptance of students into a year abroad program which involves study in a foreign university; (d) a screening procedure for bilingual secretaries for companies involved in international import and export.

5. Tape an oral interview with several of the students in a class you are observing or teaching and assess their communicative abilities, using the breakdown chart on p. 373. Exchange tapes with another member of the class and then meet to discuss your evaluations of each other's students. Was the breakdown chart usable in its present form? Was it sufficient for the type of assessment you wished to make? Devise an oral assessment breakdown chart you will use yourself in the future.

6. On pp. 390–93 is given a series of questions that teachers should ask themselves about tests they have designed. Draw up a similar series of questions teachers should ask themselves about the way they are testing their courses at present.

7. Of the various types of tests discussed in this chapter, which ones do you consider appropriate for individualized instruction? Which do you consider inappropriate? Which could be used for computer-assisted instruction? In what way?

8. Carroll speaks of the problem of the degree to which language tests can distort instruction through undesirable feedback effects (see p. 393). What form does the final examination take for the students in the course you are teaching or observing? What feedback effects from the form of the examination can you detect in the instruction? In the students' learning patterns? Which of these effects are desirable and which are undesirable?

9. Study the factors predictive of language-learning aptitude posited by Carroll-Sapon and Pimsleur. Do you think these are necessary and sufficient categories for predicting success in today's communication-oriented courses? Which subtests would you drop and why? What subtests would you propose which seem more applicable? How could the factors you propose be tested?

   *10. Study one of the following Council of Europe publications: *Waystage, The Threshold Level,* or *Un niveau-seuil* (for details, see Van Ek and Alexander 1977, Van Ek 1975, and Coste et al. 1976). Describe a series of tests which would assess functional proficiency at the level you have selected for an adult immigrant who is working (a) in a restaurant, (b) as a taxi driver.

13· Technology and Language Learning Centers

Language teachers have been quick to seize upon the possibilities opened up by the easy availability of recording equipment, both audio and visual. Where once it was difficult to provide opportunities for students to hear much authentic speech in the language they were learning, now through tapes, cassettes, and broadcasts (shortwave where necessary) such material is obtainable even in isolated areas. For those with the funds and facilities, videotapes and computer-assisted instruction further extend students' potential for learning a language at their own pace and in their own way. With the refinement of technology, many teachers have been able to move beyond the assistance of a tape recorder in the classroom to elaborate media or language resource centers where students can practice the language in groups or individually, on the spot or in other locations of their choice; or can be provided with take-away material on prerecorded cassettes.

The most common type of center is still what has come to be known as the language laboratory, although its design, its technological resources, its mode of use, and its name may vary from institution to institution. More recently, the term *language learning laboratory* has been preferred; for in many places the laboratory is one section of a media center or an instructional technology center and serves the needs of students in all language-related courses (communications, drama, literature, among others). Even where this is not so, the language learning laboratory of today is more than a room with a fixed set of booths equipped with headsets. It houses and often provides separate facilities for film and slide projectors, videotaping equipment, videoplayers, shortwave receivers, rear-view and opaque projectors, computer terminals, and record players. It may even provide for the student's use an oscillographic pronunciation monitor (to provide students with a visual demonstration of the distance between their pronunciation and that of a native speaker) or a speech compressor-expander (to enable them to hear the language spoken at a rate they can comprehend or prefer for comfort).

THE LANGUAGE LEARNING LABORATORY IS NOT A METHOD

There is no such thing as a "language laboratory method" as some people have falsely assumed. A tape recorder, a film projector, or a videoplayer are tools, like the textbook or the chalkboard. They can be used by a teacher accustomed to any method, but to varying degrees of effectiveness. Unless the teacher has considered carefully the role of technological aids in the teaching/learning process, and given some thought and care to appropriate materials, their use will be so much time wasted.

Although we tend to think of the language learning laboratory primarily as useful for listening and speaking skills, it can also be helpful for reading, writing, and translating, and for the appreciation of literature, particularly poetry and drama. It clearly contributes to the understanding of another culture by providing vicarious contact with speakers of the language, through both audio and visual means.

The use of tapes or other audio-visual aids does not of itself guarantee the effective development of any language skill. With materials originally prepared with other aims in mind than those of a specific class in a particular situation, work in the laboratory can be ineffectual, confusing and frustrating for the students. Before launching into laboratory use with any course, teachers need to study carefully and critically the proposed materials, even those which come with a very attractive textbook. They should listen to them and try to work with them themselves to see whether they are pedagogically useful as well as interesting and varied. They must then plan their use of the laboratory materials as they do the material in the textbook, not "going through them" as prepared, but selecting and rearranging according to a teaching/learning sequence which provides maximum participation in useful activity for each student in accordance with the goals of the course.

THE LANGUAGE LEARNING LABORATORY IS A PATIENT HELPER

Just as the language laboratory is not in itself a method, neither is it a teacher. It will not do the teacher's work or even reduce the amount of work the teacher is called upon to do. It will help the students learn by providing them with as much practice as they find they need—practice which one teacher cannot offer a number of students individually to the same degree. It will help teachers who are not native speakers by providing material they cannot provide themselves. It will supplement for students the general diet of the textbook, in as palatable a way as the teacher's enthusiasm and vigilance ensure.

In learning another language, mental comprehension is not enough. Students must practice the interaction of complex elements of the language until they can put them together freely and effortlessly. Sometimes teachers look only for signs of mental comprehension of each element before moving on to teach the next. As a result, grammatical structures and idiomatic expressions have to be taught and retaught several years in succession as students continue to make the same mistakes. In a large class group it is impossible to give each student all the individual practice that is necessary. With the use of taped material, much of this practice takes place in a situation where an accurate model and immediate comparison of the student's production with a correct response can be made available. The student can be provided with carefully sequenced learning practice and a way of verifying progress. The laboratory also provides for prolonged listening practice, in a situation where the student can listen over and over again to the speaker, without having to apologize for lack of comprehension. It must be remembered, however, that the work of students in the laboratory will be only as good as the program, or courseware, with which they are asked to work. Hardware can do nothing for the student without well-prepared learning materials.

LABORATORY WORK MUST BE DESIGNED AS A SIGNIFICANT PART OF THE LANGUAGE PROGRAM

If students are to be expected to take the practice in the language laboratory seriously and to devote to it the amount of time and concentration required to draw the maximum profit from it, they must perceive it as a significant part of the language program. In some second-language situations for students from other countries or immigrants who have already studied the language for a number of years, the instructor may consider that students will learn authentic use of language more effectively by spending time with native speakers in the community rather than in a language laboratory. This is rarely the case in a foreign-language situation, where the laboratory usually supplies the major contact with native speech. Laboratory work should be checked in some way that gives it the importance of regular class work in the eyes of the students. A short quiz at the end of the practice session, with a cumulative laboratory score included in the semester grade, will keep the students more aware of the necessity for regular attendance than the signing of an attendance sheet. Evidence of attendance in no way indicates that serious practice took place.

There are *several approaches* to the interrelating of laboratory work with the classroom and textbook program. To some extent these reflect the level of the students. although some are alternative possibilities for the same level. The needs of beginning students differ from those of advanced students. Having considered these possibilities, teachers will select their textbook and tapes and plan the laboratory program with due regard to the needs of the students in a particular type of course in a local setting.

1. The laboratory does not teach. New learning takes place in the classroom in a personal interaction between students and teacher. This approach is frequently adopted at the elementary level. Sessions in the laboratory are practice sessions, interspersed with meetings of the language class and supplementary to these. In a laboratory session, students practice work which has been taught in a previous class lesson or for which they have been prepared by the teacher. The teacher will then draw on what has been practiced in the laboratory for further linguistic development. If the class has not reached the stage where the work programmed for a particular laboratory session is significant for the students, this tape will be postponed or adjusted to the existing situation. Otherwise, students forced to practice actively what they have not understood will find the session frustrating.

This approach does not imply that practice material in the laboratory will be the same as in the textbook, with the students going over exactly the same exercises they have already practiced in class or for home study. It means that the work in the laboratory will require application in creative and demanding exercises of what has already been learned, thus helping students to consolidate this learning. These practice exercises will be accompanied by new material of interest to the individual student (for listening, pronunciation, and speaking, for instance) of a type the teacher cannot supply in the group situation. In this approach, tapes programmed in individual lessons by commercial publishers are difficult to use, since such tapes are prepared on the assumption that, in widely diverse schools, teachers will be teaching and students will be learning at an ideal pace. Teachers should look for tapes which contain a variety of materials and then select and dub this material onto lesson tapes to suit their purposes and the rate of progress of their students.

2. The laboratory program is distinct from the textbook material and the class work. In this approach, the laboratory program provides an ongoing, self-instructional program in language structure, pronunciation, listening, and reading comprehension, and vocabulary, thus liberating the classroom for active communication activities which build on what has been learned out of class and practiced in the laboratory. The student's individual work is facilitated when computer-assisted instruction is available along with the audio facilities of the laboratory, but this is not essential. This approach may be applied equally well with a carefully programmed textbook, which students study individually in association with taped language ma-

terial. Further explanations and additional help are often recorded on the tapes. Students consult the teacher as the need arises (see "Programmed Instruction," p. 111 above).

3. In a combination of the approaches outlined in paragraphs 1 and 2, the language material is first studied by the student in programmed form, then discussed and practiced in class before the student goes to the laboratory for consolidating practice in variation and further creative application. In the next class session, the students have ample opportunity to use the material in communicative interaction.

4. The laboratory is used solely for activities other than grammatical practice—activities for which students need much individual work at their own pace, such as extensive listening to authentic materials, oral composition on the subject of the listening practice, writing of summaries of or commentaries on material heard, dictations, extracting from recorded material information on cultural subjects for projects, preparing regular news bulletins from radio broadcasts. This is normally the approach at the advanced level.

5. The laboratory is regarded as a resource center like the library. Students borrow practice materials from the laboratory as they feel the need, or on advice from their teacher, and work with them for as long or as short a time as they require to master the content. When they feel they are ready, they take a quiz to check their progress, going back to the material if further practice is needed. This approach is adopted in some individualized programs and in most advanced-level programs.

ADVANTAGES OF A LANGUAGE LEARNING LABORATORY

Since a language learning laboratory is such an expensive tool, it is as well to consider what advantages students may derive from it to justify the expense.

1. Each student has the opportunity to hear native speech clearly and distinctly.
2. Students may hear this authentic native speech as often as they need or desire.
3. The taped lesson provides a constant and unwearying model of native speech for the student to endeavor to comprehend and to imitate.
4. In the laboratory the student may listen to a great variety of voices, both male and female, old and young.
5. In the laboratory booth, or alone with a cassette-player at home or in the dormitory, students achieve psychological isolation which releases them from some of the inhibitions they feel about

    making strange foreign-language sounds in front of other students. They can practice alone until they feel ready to produce utterances publicly.

6. Students may hear and use the foreign language throughout the playing of the tape, instead of wasting time waiting for their turn in a large group, as in the usual classroom.

7. The student can take the chance of making mistakes without fear of the judgment of teacher or peers.

8. The tape can provide a realistic situational setting (with noises, interruptions, music, the voices of well-known personalities) in a way the teacher cannot hope to reproduce in the classroom. With a visual component in the carrel, this culturally appropriate situational effect is even stronger.

9. Students may hear different varieties of the language (e.g., British or American English; Parisian or Canadian French; continental or Brazilian Portuguese).

With recording-playback facilities:

10. Students are able to compare a specimen of their own production with that of a native model.

11. Students may practice each language element as many times as they wish before moving on to the next. (This is facilitated by a playback loop system.)

12. Tapes provide means for testing oral production in the foreign language in a more detached, objective fashion. Tapes of test utterances may be compared with each other and reconsidered carefully in a way which is impossible in a series of personal interviews.

13. The laboratory provides teachers with a ready means of improving their own pronunciation and intonation where this is desirable, or of keeping their skill in these areas at a high level when they are not able to meet and talk with native speakers.

14. Students can study at their own pace, concentrating on the parts of the work for which they need most practice, rather than being forced to keep pace with their fellows.

15. Students may study on their own, with any available local assistance, self-instructional courses in the less commonly taught languages which would otherwise not be available to them.[1]

16. If a speech compressor-expander is available, students may adjust listening to the speed at which they can most comfortably com-

---

1. For a discussion of self-instructional language programs of this type, see *System* 7, no. 1 (1979): 3–44.

prehend it, varying the speed as they acquire more skill, without reference to the needs and capabilities of other students.

TYPES OF LANGUAGE LEARNING LABORATORIES

Level 1: Listen-Respond Laboratory

The simplest form of listen-respond laboratory is a classroom with a tape recorder in operation. Some form of amplification will probably be needed if the tape recording is to be heard clearly in all areas of the classroom. Certain advantages are gained when the school establishes a special room, acoustically treated, in which groups may be brought closer to the tape recorder and to which individual students may go to listen to recordings. Such a room will be situated away from distracting noises—from busy roads, playing fields, workshops, or frequently used corridors. (An extra facility is provided when students are able to borrow recorders and taped material to take away to practice in a quiet place of their own choosing.)

A further refinement is the addition for each student of headphones plugged into the tape recorder, or recorders, or into a single or multiple jack box attached to these. This addition enables each student to hear more clearly without being distracted by other students. Listening units of this type may be installed on some kind of moveable tray or table and taken from room to room, or, for more distraction-free listening, installed permanently in an acoustically treated room.

This simple form of laboratory is not expensive to install and maintain. It enables students to hear at frequent intervals authentic native speech, with a variety of voices and accents. Teachers who are not native speakers cannot provide such excellent models themselves; and if their own language training has been deficient, they find this aid invaluable.

With this type of installation the students can practice correct articulation, intonation, and phrasing in imitation of a native model. For practice in aural comprehension they can listen to dialogues, news bulletins, simulated telephone conversations, lectures, short stories, or interviews with native speakers. Their appreciation of literature can be deepened by listening to poems and literary extracts read by fine readers, and scenes from plays performed by professional actors. Songs may be learned from recordings by famous singers. More prosaic, but nonetheless essential, will be work with grammatical drills and exercises for which they will hear the correct responses immediately following their own production.

There is, however, room for improvement to the simple listen-respond system. Because of the earphones they are wearing, the students are not able to hear their own voices clearly. They will be tempted, almost without realizing it, to mumble, thus developing bad speech habits in the new language. Their pronunciation cannot be corrected immediately because they cannot hear the teacher speaking to them. In this type of installation there is no possibility for students to work at their own pace, because there is one non-stop lesson tape.

Level 2: Listen-Respond Laboratory with Activated Headphones
The value of the laboratory is greatly heightened by the addition of a microphone and activated headphones for each student. As students speak into the microphone, they hear their own voice amplified through the earphones much as another person would hear it, and with a similar volume to that of the program to which they are listening. This gives them a surer basis for comparison of their utterances with those of the native model. With this addition, the laboratory is called "audio-active." When these facilities are installed in separate, acoustically treated booths, the students profit in several ways. They hear the program more clearly because they are freer from extraneous noise and the voices of their fellow students repeating aloud. It is easier for them to concentrate. Certain types of students, too, gain confidence from the impression of isolation, and this helps them to overcome their diffidence about pronouncing foreign sounds. When they feel that they have achieved a fair approximation of the sounds, they are less nervous about taking part in oral work in class.

This type of language laboratory is completed by the addition of a console with one or more tape decks for the emission of the program. The console is wired to permit two-way communication between students and teacher. The teacher not only listens to the student's utterances but is able to make helpful comments, which are heard only by the student addressed. A further facility enables the teacher to address the whole group over the broadcast system in order to give instructions or guidance. Some consoles are wired so that groups of students may be put in touch with each other for group discussions or for purposes of mutual evaluation. The usefulness of the laboratory is increased if the initial wiring of the console permits the broadcasting through several channels of different programs to specific booths. In this way, various languages or several levels of the same language can be provided for at the same time.

If there are several tape decks at the console, the teacher is usually able to record the utterances of individual students from their booths. This can be very useful for testing oral production or for enabling students to listen more objectively to their utterances where no other playback facilities are available.

Students should also be given some opportunities to listen to authentic speech in less favorable conditions than through the headphones. The laboratory should therefore be wired to permit the broadcasting of parts of the program from room amplifiers, when only one class group is using the laboratory. This feature is particularly useful where songs are used as a diversion from the concentration of the main program. Students will join in the singing of songs if they are broadcast to the whole room but will feel embarrassed by the sound of their own voices if the music is coming only through the headphones.

Level 3: Listen-Respond-Compare Laboratory

The addition of individual recording facilities at each student place increases the scope of the laboratory. The students are now able to record their utterances and compare them with those of the native model. With the installation of dual-track tape recorders, students can record the master program sent out to them from the console on one track, and their own imitation or responses on a second track as the tape proceeds. Later, they are able to replay their recordings for comparison. Frequently the master track is already recorded for them before the session begins. This makes for greater flexibility since students can work independently. Each time they feel they could improve their work, they can rewind part of the tape and rerecord a section of the work, erasing their first effort as they do so. This process does not affect the master model on the first track in any way. They are then able to compare their own efforts with the tape model as often as they like. They can listen and rerecord, listen and rerecord, working at their own pace, without interrupting the work of their fellow students or being forced to wait for them to catch up. (This extra advantage is not available when students take away a single-track cassette for use with an ordinary cassette recorder.)

Where financial considerations prohibit the installation of recording-playback facilities of this type in every booth, serious consideration should be given to the installation of such facilities in at least a few of the booths. The students in each class can then, by a system of rotation, have the opportunity to playback and rerecord at certain intervals (perhaps every third or fourth session), thus studying their oral production more objectively. In this case they will need to be supplied with prerecorded tapes which are much shorter than those for the normal broadcast program for the listen-respond booths, so that they will have time to work through the tape several times with a view to self-improvement.

Listen-respond-compare facilities can be used for all the purposes listed for the listen-respond system, but their additional advantage is obviously in the area of improvement of pronunciation, stress, and intonation, and oral reading of prose and poetry. Because students can stop and start the tape when they please, this system is also useful for such exercises as advanced listening comprehension, simulated conversation with a tape model, practice in taking notes of foreign-language lectures, and learning roles in foreign-language plays.

Where recorders are available in student booths, it is usual to have wiring which permits the starting and stopping of all recorders from the console. This permits the making of multiple copies of tapes for individual work in the booths, which is an important time-saving consideration when a high-speed machine for making multiple copies is not available. Such a facility is also useful for giving timed tests, for which students record answers with their individual recorders.

Level 4: Listen-Respond-Compare Laboratory with Remote Control
A further development in language laboratory design removes the recording facilities from the student booth to a central location or core. The program source may also be in the same location, remote-controlled from the console. Often such a facility is computerized. This system simplifies the purely manipulative operation of both booth and console. It also facilitates maintenance, since the equipment for a number of laboratories may be in one place. Students are still able to hear the master program, record the master and their own responses, and play back both the master and their own version. Since they have less equipment to handle in the booth, the risk of mechanical difficulties hampering their work is reduced.

With remote control, the student has only to move switches or push buttons in the booth for all the necessary operations of listening, recording, playback, or rerecording. In some individualized systems there is a telephone type of dial in the booth; by composing the correct number the student can be connected with a particular tape in the central location. Under this system, student booths for practice can be established in different parts of a building, or in different buildings. Sometimes the students can obtain access from home or dormitory by dialing an allocated telephone number through the regular telephone service.

In some institutions, amplification is also installed in a certain number of classrooms from which the teacher may dial for a particular program in the central stack. In this way each teacher may interpolate illustrative or practice material into particular lessons as needed, or teachers in different classrooms may simultaneously give one test (usually aural) to several classes at the same level of instruction. This amplification is also useful when used in conjunction with a specially constructed wall in the classroom from behind which illustrative material is projected to accompany the audio material.

LABORATORY DESIGN

The popular conception of a language laboratory as a rectangular space filled with even rows of partitioned booths facing a console in the front of the room derives from the traditional classroom arrangement. With modern equipment, language learning laboratories can be of any shape, divided into sections as one wishes, with equipment in any position in the room or in another location.

The console is sometimes at the back of the room, so that the teacher can see what is going on without distracting the students' attention. Some laboratories are circular with the console in the center and the booths in concentric circles, with appropriately placed aisles for easy access. Booths may be placed around the walls with students facing the wall for more privacy, the central space then being available for regular classroom sessions or for small-group activity. Equipment may be installed so that it ascends to the ceiling or folds back into the classroom desks after its use during the lesson. This is the concept of the electronic classroom, where the teacher can incorporate work with tapes into any lesson at the most appropriate moment. The console itself may be in a central core section, with radiating classroom laboratories which can be surveyed from the console through one-way viewing partitions; in this arrangement what is going on at a multipurpose console does not disturb the students. The laboratory may have the appearance of a pleasant living room, with colored walls and comfortable armchairs, since equipment can be wired unobtrusively and conveniently into all kinds of furnishings. Laboratories may be scattered in various buildings in the school or university, with some booths in the library, every activity being initiated by remote control from a console or tape core in a central location.[2]

The design of the laboratory should evolve from an analysis of pedagogical needs and students' study patterns; the technological components are then selected to provide for the varied objectives of the program. Whatever form the design may take, provision must be made for a maintenance and planning space; a tape, cassette, or disc library; a recording studio with high-quality equipment and enough space for videotaping; a projection room for preparation of materials

2. The transformation of a conventional language laboratory into a center serving many purposes is described in detail in J. A. Rallo, "Foreign Language Resource Center: A Step Forward," *NALLD Journal* 4, no. 3 (1970): 14–22.

for laboratory and classroom use; and office space for the laboratory director and technical personnel.

INSTALLING A LANGUAGE LEARNING LABORATORY

Teachers who are called upon to advise on the installation or renewal of a language laboratory in their school should read some of the excellent books available on types of installations and their purpose, and the particular features to look for in the choice of equipment. They should then visit installations of various kinds and see them in operation in a school situation before making any decision. The comments of teachers who are using these installations will soon draw attention to the advantages and disadvantages of various features. It is only by such visits that a judgment can be made as to whether the type of installation the school has in mind will perform the kinds of functions desired. It is also the best way of studying ease of operation and the kinds of problems a particular type of installation leaves unsolved.

If *audio-visual courses* are to be used in the school, other considerations will arise. Audio-visual courses (discussed fully in chapter 7) require the constant use of films, filmstrips, slides, or videotapes in association with classroom teaching and with the practice sessions with taped materials. For maximum efficiency, audio-visual equipment needs to be installed in the classrooms; and, for individual practice, it is desirable to have in the booths viewing equipment which can be controlled by each student. If individual viewing facilities cannot be provided, the laboratory must be so constructed that the necessary slides or films associated with oral practice can be projected, without undue effort on the part of the teacher, on screens which are clearly visible to all students from their booths. Proper provision for the requirements of audio-visual courses will need to be discussed very thoroughly in the laboratory planning stages.

Having carefully established the purposes for which the laboratory is to be used, the teacher responsible for the laboratory should plan the future installation with these purposes in mind. In this planning the help of a qualified independent consultant, familiar with foreign-language teaching aims and methods as well as with the technical aspects of the installation, can be most useful. Language teachers often do not have the expertise to assess comparatively the technical quality and the flexibility in use of the many commercial systems currently available.

Throughout the planning stages the teacher should pay particular attention to the audio quality of the equipment to be installed. Discrimination of foreign-language sounds is much more difficult for the student than comprehension of the native language and requires the highest quality of reproduction available for the price. Chrome and fine woodwork and an impressive array of gadgets will soon use up money which should be spent on high-quality microphones, headphones, and recording equipment.

Particular attention should also be paid to the durability of the essential parts of the equipment. The teacher should seek out companies which are making equipment specially designed for the almost continuous use it will receive in the language laboratory. Standard equipment built for other purposes may appear cheaper at first, but will prove costly in maintenance and replacements.

Factors to Be Considered When Installing a Laboratory

No school should embark on the installation of a language learning laboratory without having weighed the following factors.

1. *The initial expense of installation is only part of the financial commitment involved.* Laboratories need continual maintenance and regular overhaul, with eventual replacements of expensive parts, if a high level of efficiency and audio quality is to be maintained.

2. There should be available a *person qualified to keep a continual check on equipment,* to make minor running repairs, and to perform necessary routine maintenance. The company installing the laboratory should be requested to supply a schedule of necessary maintenance operations. Without them equipment cannot be kept in fine condition, and with the passage of time frequent breakdowns and expensive repairs will be inevitable. Certain small operations, like the cleaning of the recorder heads, must be carried out very regularly if the sound quality is to be satisfactory. Some person within the school can be trained to do these things, since they do not require the competence of a technician. Emergency breakdowns are another matter. If the school does not employ a technical assistant, it is as well to have a contract with a local repairman who will undertake to come on call. Otherwise, booths will be out of order for lengthy periods—with resultant disorder for the language teacher. At intervals of six months a thorough overhaul of all equipment will be necessary. Since most companies contract to provide such a service only during the first year after installation, the cost of the regular overhaul must be included in estimates of the maintenance budget in succeeding years.

3. *The laboratory will be an unjustifiable expense if it is not used effectively.* Before a laboratory is installed, extended, or replaced, the department head should ascertain the attitude of the staff to its use. It may be necessary to conduct an evaluation study of the effectiveness of methods and materials already in use, and of changes

which must be made in the program if language laboratory or audio-visual work is to be fully integrated with it.

If it is a question of replacing an existing, outworn laboratory, the amount of use the laboratory has received during the preceding year should be ascertained, with an assessment of the types of facilities which have been the most valuable from the point of view of both students and teachers. Perhaps the replacement laboratory should be of a different type from the existing laboratory, not only as shown by recent use but also because of new developments in technology which have opened up possibilities for a different type of use. This period of discussion is ideal for examining the school's library of materials for various languages to determine whether these too need replacing. There may be a need for materials more in line with the objectives and methods of the present faculty or in order to exploit more effectively the new type of equipment to be installed.

This is also the time to conduct inservice workshop sessions for teachers who have not been accustomed to incorporating work with recorded materials into their programs. For the inexperienced, such training should include actual manipulation of the equipment to dispel the irrational reluctance of some teachers when confronted with knobs, switches, and revolving tapes or discs. These sessions should be conducted in association with discussions by the more experienced teachers on the most effective and innovative use of the equipment which has been selected. Particular emphasis should be given to criteria for selection of recorded materials (see p. 413) and techniques for adapting them to the age level and specific objectives of existing and proposed courses in the various languages.

With forethought and planning, much antagonism, frustration, and ineffectiveness on the part of the staff can be avoided, and the laboratory will be accepted and used instead of being the costly disappointment it has sometimes proved to be.

THE DIRECTOR OF THE LABORATORY

As soon as the installation of the laboratory becomes a real possibility, one teacher should be put in charge of it as director. The director's duties are administrative and organizational: advising on equipment and installation; ordering tapes and encouraging their use; scheduling classes; setting up and cataloguing the library of materials; supervising maintenance, replacement of equipment, materials preparation and adaptation, recording and filming, and the implementation of the system of study devised by various instructors; training students and teachers in the use of laboratory equipment in relation to course development; and studying the latest innovations in laboratory facilities with an eye to future improvements.

The director will find that equipment is kept in better condition if certain rules for behavior in the laboratory and some clear instructions for the orderly handling of tapes and equipment by both students and teachers are established and enforced. The provision of an orientation tape for new teachers and students which gives some guided practice in the use of the equipment will eliminate many problems which might otherwise arise in the first few weeks of the school year. Similarly, a library of standard reference works on laboratory use and some subscriptions to journals in this area will stimulate interest in exploring the potential of the equipment.

CHOOSING TAPED MATERIALS FOR THE LABORATORY LIBRARY

It is important not to rush ahead and buy a great quantity of taped material in order to fill the shelves of the laboratory library. The same care in choice is required with sets of audio- and videotapes or films and slides as in the setting up of a library of books. Taped and filmed materials are expensive. Money must be invested wisely in those which will best serve the purposes of the courses to be offered.

Textbooks for adoption should be studied thoughtfully in association with the taped materials offered by their publishers or the possibilities within the school of making tapes to accompany them. Most publishers will send demonstration tapes for examination. A textbook which has proved very suitable in other circumstances may be found to be quite unsuitable for use in association with a laboratory. If listening and speaking skills are not primary aims of the course set out in the textbook, then a choice must be made between the textbook and the use of the laboratory. Many teachers are misled in this matter because publishers now issue tapes of lessons for nearly all available textbooks. If the texts were not originally designed with the specific conditions of laboratory study in mind, the tapes made to go with them can prove exasperating to the student. An exercise designed to be studied by the eye at leisure often consists of segments too long and too varied in vocabulary and structural content to be absorbed aurally and held in the student's mind long enough for reproduction. A succession of segments often requires several changes at once, which demand an impossible performance of mental and verbal gymnastics. The only way for the teacher to appreciate the effect of such exercises on the student, and to assess their effectiveness, is to play one of the lesson tapes in the laboratory and try to produce the responses required in a limited interval of time without looking at the

412

textbook. The difficulty the teacher experiences will be much greater for the student, to whom the work is unfamiliar.

Checklist for Materials Selection
In considering tapes to be bought for the laboratory library, or to be used in conjunction with a textbook, the following qualities should be considered.

Production

Clarity of recording
Fidelity
Accent in the foreign language (standard native, near-native, un-
acceptable to native speaker)
Speed of speech (fast native, normal native, slow but acceptable
native, unnaturally slow, distorted)
Quality of speech (distinct, slurred, high-pitched)
Intonation (normal, unnatural, exaggerated)
Tone of voice (pleasant, uninteresting, bored, condescending, un-
intentionally humorous)
Extraneous noise in the recording

Material Recorded

(a) *Consecutive discourse and dialogues for imitation*
Clarity
Naturalness of subject matter and speech
Interest of material for level required
Standard of difficulty for level required
Authenticity of cultural setting
Usefulness of vocabulary and structures used
Length of segments for repetition
Value of segments as conversational building blocks
Background (music, "noises off")
(b) *Practice Exercises*
Designed for laboratory use or traditional exercises originally de-
signed to be read or written
Instructions unambiguous with sufficient examples as a guide to
students
Sufficient context to make the model and cue sentences compre-
hensible
Length of segments for repetition or manipulation (five to eight
syllables is quite sufficient at an elementary level; at a more

413

advanced level, eight to twelve syllables may be acceptable if the material has sufficient inbuilt redundancy)

Structural content of each segment (one structure, two, three?)

Number of examples of a similar pattern for practice before making a change

Number of changes from one segment to the next (minimal structural change, several changes at once?) Does the formula adopted best achieve the purpose of the exercise?

Vocabulary range (if this is too extensive, it can prove distracting and confusing)

Stimulus items that can elicit only one correct response (this is important if the practice is to be self-correcting)

Correct response given immediately after interval for student response

Length of interval for student response (this is not a vital consideration in evaluating a commercial tape, as the interval can be shortened or lengthened when copying from master to program tape; some commercial tapes do not include an interval, but leave it to the teacher to insert one; some types of equipment have a pause button with which students can put in their own length of pause)

Test Items

Items that are valid for the purposes of the test

Instructions that are clear and explicit

Adequate context to make the required operation clear

Sufficient context to make the meaning of key words clear

If several changes are required, an operation that is feasible in view of the limitations of auditory memory

Sufficient time allowed for the student to reflect

Enunciation clear and distinct

Acceptable audial quality throughout the test

Subject area of items familiar to the students

Length of items (and of whole test) such that fatigue will not set in and vitiate the results

Several passages for listening comprehension, rather than one long discourse

Practical Considerations

Does the material merely record what is already in the textbook and has been practiced in class or does it provide for creative use of what has been learned?

Are there review units which would be useful for students requiring extra practice?

Do the tapes and visuals contain new material of a type the teacher would have difficulty providing?

Is there sufficient supplementary material to warrant the extra expenditure for the tapes and visuals?

Is the recorded material of a type which could still serve as useful supplementary material (for individual study in the laboratory or for program tapes) if the textbook should be changed?

Acquiring Supplementary Materials

Careful consideration should be given to the acquisition of a well-designed set of materials on basic structures of the language, prepared for use with any textbook. These can supplement textbook tapes or provide remedial exercises. They are particularly useful in situations where teachers cannot prescribe their own textbooks but are obliged to use texts for which the accompanying tapes do not provide enough well-designed grammatical practice.

Some money should be set aside, too, for the acquisition of tapes and records of songs, poems, scenes from plays, and conversations and interviews with native speakers. These will be useful for certain sections of the program tape, the designing of which will be discussed later in this chapter. They will also provide useful listening practice.

It must be remembered that a substantial sum will have to be allocated for blank tapes or cassettes of good quality. Cheap tape will not stand up to the wear and tear of constant use. There will be a need for program tapes to be broadcast from the console and for tapes for student record-playback positions. Other tapes will be needed for some experimental programs designed by the teachers, for recording visiting native speakers or radio news bulletins, and for testing purposes.

Where tapes and cassettes are copied for loan to students, these must also be included in the estimate. Two lending systems are common. A complete set of tapes may be issued to the student for the semester on payment of a deposit which covers the cost of the tapes and is refunded when the tapes are returned at the end of the semester. Alternatively, students are issued, on payment of a deposit, with one tape, with the week's work recorded on it. This tape is returned and exchanged for a tape on which is recorded the next week's work. The returned tapes are then erased as the third week's work is copied onto them for the next exchange. (With some equipment, students may copy material onto their own cassettes in the booths.)

Since a wide variety of carefully constructed materials is now available commercially, inexperienced teachers are ill advised to make their own master series. The designing of effective lessons for the laboratory requires much time-consuming and meticulous work. The pitfalls are manifold. If the teacher has no training in materials preparation, most of this work may be useless when the practice material is tried out on students. Even a person experienced in designing written exercises will find a completely new technique is required if the student is to be dependent on the ear and if oral, not written, responses are to be elicited. If the material is repetitive and boring, the students will simply tune out.

Teachers who have had the necessary training and have been using the laboratory for some time may wish to prepare materials for purposes for which commercial materials are unobtainable. In this case, "Preparation of laboratory materials" should appear on the teacher's timetable along with class teaching assignments, preferably in blocks of several hours. Proper time and thought can then be given to lesson tapes which will be useful to other teachers as well, and to a succession of students for several years. To complete this work, the teacher will need to have access to a properly equipped recording studio where the material prepared may be put on audio- or videotape without extraneous noise and distraction.

Where inexperienced teachers are asked to prepare tapes to accompany a prescribed textbook, they should first put considerable study into the matter of the construction of effective oral exercises and dialogues and, if possible, attend seminars or workshops before attempting to work on their own. In this way many snags will be avoided and time will not be wasted on materials which are frustrating to the student and disappointing to the teacher who prepared them.

USING THE LANGUAGE LEARNING LABORATORY
Once the laboratory is installed and the teachers have had some training in its operation, a great deal of thought and effort will still be necessary before it will produce results. Added to the vagaries of the equipment, there will now be the human element, in some thirty or more individual segments. If this element is ignored, the whole enterprise will be sabotaged.

It is important to prepare students from the beginning for the kind of work they will be doing in the laboratory. This orientation may be given in class or by means of an *introductory tape*. Students should realize that they will learn to understand a foreign language only by hearing it spoken frequently, and that they will not learn to speak it with any variety of expression unless they have frequent and systematic practice with regularly recurring combinations of language elements, which they must learn to use to create new utterances. They must not be led to believe that the laboratory is a short and effortless road to language mastery, but must see it as one part of an integrated learning process, demanding work and concentration on their part. Many students in a foreign-language situation are confused when they first hear authentic native speech spoken at normal speed. They must understand that this confusion will pass as their ears become more accustomed to the language and as their knowledge increases.

Having been prepared for the laboratory work, the students must then be given explicit *instructions for the operation of the equipment* from their booth positions, and practice in performing different kinds of exercises. The more familiar they are with procedures before actual lesson tapes are played, the less likely they are to feel nervous or frustrated during the first few sessions.

The Time Factor

An important question to consider is the length of time students can be expected to concentrate on practice in a laboratory situation. Such purely physical factors as discomfort from headphone pressure have to be taken into account, as well as span of attention at different ages and for different individuals. In the laboratory, much more than in the usual classroom lesson, each student is expected to give full attention to active participation. This can be very fatiguing, particularly when the student cannot control the speed of the tape presentation. Twenty minutes of such concentrated attention without a break is ample at high school or college level, with ten or fifteen minutes for younger children. In some schools where the laboratory is close to the language classrooms, classes are scheduled in the laboratory for twenty-minute periods as part of the lesson several times a week. This ensures regular practice. It can, however, be very disrupting, since students spend a considerable amount of time moving from place to place and settling down in the changed environment.

Students who are able to control the equipment and those who are working on their own with cassettes will find out for themselves how much active oral practice they can tolerate and still concentrate. They will also discover how many times they need to go over the same tape in order to master the material. The teacher should discuss with them early in the course the advantages of shorter periods of spaced practice rather than one lengthy period just before the next class lesson.[3]

3. The New York City experiment, conducted by Sarah Lorge for the New York State Education Department from 1959 to 1963, demonstrated that shorter, more fre-

Program or Lesson Tapes

Commercial companies often provide programmed tapes for use in laboratory sessions. Many of these are well designed. Others, unfortunately, are not. For the full value of any set of tapes to be realized, the teacher must be very familiar with the contents of each program in order to ensure that the class is ready for the next programmed tape in the form in which it has been recorded, or in order to delete or vary some of the content of less well-designed tapes. This requires careful lesson preparation. Sometimes material must be selected by the teacher from various sources and a special lesson tape prepared to meet the particular needs of the students at that time.

In designing lesson or program tapes, the teacher should strive for a balance of activities, with variety to avoid monotony. The tape may be unwearying in dispensing material, but students are all too human in their reaction to sameness and lack of imagination. A well-designed lesson tape will contain interesting material for listening comprehension and for practicing fluent production of phrases with correct intonation; there may also be a few exercises in problems of pronunciation. Some grammatical practice will follow, moving from imitation of new syntactic structures to practice with variation, and then to activities requiring creative participation. Finally, there will be some activity of a recreational nature, such as singing, a problem-solving game, or a competition. The order of these components should not be fixed for every tape, but varied to provide an element of surprise.

For each activity, instructions to the student should be explicit and unambiguous, with sufficient examples to dispel any perplexity about how to proceed. Many experienced teachers believe that instructions on tapes should be in the native language so that students will be in no doubt about what they are expected to do. This will depend to some extent on the students' level of experience. A more useful approach is to give instructions in the native language and then in the target language for the first and perhaps second tape, with subsequent tapes moving over to instructions entirely in the target language. In this way, the student will not be confused during the early laboratory sessions, while later tapes will provide consistent practice in listening to the target language. Continuing with instructions, often the same ones, in the native language after an initial familiarization period is unnecessary, except perhaps for some tests where the evaluation of

quent periods of laboratory practice were more useful than one long session once a week. With the introduction of flexible scheduling, the allocation of short laboratory sessions at regular intervals becomes more feasible for many schools. See Sarah W. Lorge, "Language Laboratory Research Studies in New York City High Schools: A Discussion of the Program and its Findings," *MLJ* 48 (1964): 409–19.

learning should not be dependent on the student's understanding or misunderstanding of instructions.

Where dispersion of practice over several days is difficult to arrange, the program tape should be planned to allow for a distinct break after some fifteen or twenty minutes of work. The break provides a good opportunity to introduce attractive music and songs of the foreign culture as a relaxing change of pace. If the laboratory sessions are of twenty minutes or less, it may not be possible to include on each tape practice in all of the areas suggested, but even a shorter tape should be varied in content. Shorter tapes scattered through the week should still provide at some time practice for each of the types of exercises listed. If recording-playback facilities are available, the amount of material in the lesson tape will be reduced, and time allowed during the session for playing back and rerecording at least some sections of the work.

As the course advances and wider discrepancies become apparent in individual achievement, the teacher with a console wired for more than one program channel should try to provide a second tape, with more difficult work for the more rapid learners or, alternatively, simpler exercises or variations of more difficult exercises for those who are lagging.

Master Tapes
The master tapes of commercial materials, as well as the originals of tapes produced in the school or college, should not be used regularly on the tape decks in the laboratory. The master tapes provide source material from which the sections required for a particular week are copied onto a programmed lesson tape which has been carefully planned to fit into the lesson sequence. It is copies of these lesson tapes which are subjected to the hard wear and tear of regular laboratory use. If these copies break or are damaged in any way, the damage is not irreparable because the original masters are still available for recopying. The masters, carefully catalogued, are kept in the tape library, where they will not be in danger of accidental erasure, either by overproximity to a bulk eraser or by human error.

Pauses
As the work in the laboratory gets under way, the teacher should observe the reaction time of students in response to grammatical exercises. Some commercial materials are based on the theory that the response should be made very smartly, and the pause allowed for response is consequently very short. In the first weeks, when students are becoming familiar with laboratory techniques, this short pause

can be disconcerting or exasperating and may need to be lengthened slightly. With other prepared materials the pauses are at times very irregular and even far too long. This again is frustrating and time-wasting for the student who is waiting to respond to the next cue on the tape.

These situations can be rectified by the teacher when the material is being copied on to the lesson tape. Adjusting the pauses is a simple matter of the operation of the stop lever on one or the other of the recorders during the copying process. Some commercial materials do not provide any pauses on the master but leave it to the teacher to insert pauses of an appropriate length during the copying process. Where students have full control of the equipment but are not recording on a lower track, they may themselves introduce the pause they require by operation of a pause mechanism. As students become more experienced and fluent, they should not require long pauses. If the tape is well constructed, they will be carried forward by the steady progress of the tape to respond promptly, without requiring a long time for reflection on the construction of the responses.

The Laboratory and Creative Production
It is difficult for the work in the laboratory to give practice in spontaneous expression in a foreign language, since stimulus questions are usually designed to extract a similar answer from all students. The rationale behind this is that the tape can then provide students with the opportunity to compare their responses with a model answer for immediate correction. Some conversation-type exercises have been designed with a low voice on the tape indicating to the student the basic information required in the response to be framed. This technique does permit of a model response on the tape with which students can compare their own. This type of structure for conversation, however, merely duplicates the directed dialogue or "indirect speech to direct speech" conversion exercise (e.g., Prompt: "Say you will be late," Response: "I'll be late"; Prompt: "John asks her to wait for him," Response: "Wait for me, Mary"). It does not, however, provide opportunities for originality or creative response.

Some experimentation has been put into developing conversational tapes, with spaces for responses, which are so designed that original utterances will not make the continuing line of the conversation irrelevant. For instance, the taped voice may say: "What time will you be home this evening? . . . I'll call you tomorrow morning. Would you like to play tennis? . . . We can decide what we'll do tomorrow."[4]

4. A detailed example of a situation tape of this type is given in the *PG*'s, chap. 1, C33.

With a tape of this kind, students practice participating actively in the conversation (situations common to daily life are selected) without interpolation of "correct" responses. Students may work over the tape several times, improving the quality of the exchange or the originality of the responses. If a series of such tapes reintroduces personalities with names and distinctive voices, students begin to feel as though they know the people with whom they are conversing and become quite absorbed in the task. The tapes may later be discussed with an instructor or submitted for advice on improvement. Situation tapes of this type allow some choice of response, although students are still working within a controlled framework.

Where laboratory sessions are scheduled as part of the language course, teachers may compensate for the limitation on spontaneous production by sending one section of the class to work with tapes, while the remaining students gather together to practice the real give-and-take of conversation. Techniques for conversation groups are discussed in chapter 8 above.

Maintaining Student Interest and Attention

Some teachers complain of absenteeism or discipline problems in the laboratory. One of the commonest reasons for such trouble is student boredom. It is inevitable that students will be bored if lesson tapes have not been carefully planned to retain their interest, just as they become bored with an unplanned, repetitive lesson. With headphones on and the continuous demands of the tape, they cannot even take refuge in daydreams as they do in class. Uncooperative behavior soon results. Exercises may be too easy so that the students are soon weary of repetitive activity which might have been useful at an introductory stage. Equally disastrous is the provision of material which is too difficult or fast-moving for the students concerned. This results in vague mumbling, repeating of fragments of what has been asked for, or an impotent silence. In such situations some of the students withdraw from the unequal contest with the tape and begin to play with wires, experiment in communication with other booths, or damage parts of the equipment in their exasperation. Others just do not put in an appearance next time or bring their science homework with them.

Antagonism and resistance also develop when students are kept for long periods at a type of activity which does not demand some thoughtful contribution on their part. They feel brainwashed. If this type of reaction is observed, teachers should consider how the exercises on the tapes can be redesigned to require an original and creative response which warrants the students' attention and effort.

421

Sometimes reduced participation is due to sheer physical fatigue because no breaks have been introduced at reasonable intervals, or there is no variety of activity. An exercise involving writing can provide the necessary change of position and physical activity. This written exercise may be in the form of a multiple-choice questionnaire on a listening comprehension passage, a short dictation, notes taken on an aspect of the culture which is discussed or dramatized, or answers to a quiz or a problem-solving exercise given on tape. Students may be asked to perform some task in response to oral instructions: they may draw a diagram; locate on a map particular places or indicate the direction taken on a trip or on a walk in town; construct a plan of a place being described; or complete a sketch of a person, place, or incident, according to information obtained from listening.

Above all, the teacher must study the length of time which is being devoted to activities which require basically the same kind of response, making sure that provision has been made for the students to participate actively in a number of different ways.

The Language Learning Laboratory is Inanimate

Having learned to use the laboratory with reasonable efficiency, the teacher must keep in mind that it is an inanimate aid and can be overused as much as any other aid. The laboratory is important for providing regular and individual practice in comprehension, pronunciation, and the manipulation of language forms; but free and fluent use of the language must still be practiced frequently in face-to-face communication situations in and out of the classroom. Students do not feel a spontaneous desire to communicate their thoughts to a machine, except perhaps to curse it in their native tongue. The opportunity the laboratory provides for all students to practice elements of spoken language, as their individual need dictates, with immediate correction available, frees both students and teacher to use the classroom lesson to the full for the more difficult task of active communication. It is for the teacher to realize and exploit this opportunity.

THE LANGUAGE LEARNING LABORATORY AT ALL LEVELS OF LANGUAGE STUDY

To date, the laboratory has been most frequently used for elementary language classes. For one thing, space has often been limited. The benefits for beginners in practicing correct pronunciation and grammatical structures in imitation of a native model have been obvious, so these classes have been given priority in scheduling or allotting space. Often this leaves little time for the more advanced classes. Fortunately, take-away cassettes have changed this picture.

Most commercial publishers now provide tapes for beginning courses and for many aspects of the intermediate-level course. A few offer materials for more advanced levels. Remedial pronunciation materials for use at intermediate or advanced levels are available for most languages, and listening comprehension materials for these levels are appearing on the market with greater frequency. At the advanced level, however, teachers must often prepare their own materials to suit their special needs.

At the Advanced Level

Many teachers have found that recorded material, often available on disks, can be used effectively to improve reading and literary appreciation, particularly of poetry and drama. Where there is a visual capability, films and videotapes can bring plays alive through performances by famous actors and actresses. Films may also be studied as a separate artistic and literary genre, or in association with the literary texts on which they were based, to bring out differences of interpretation and impact.

Similarly, the types of materials a laboratory can make available are invaluable for introducing students to aspects of the modern culture and the preoccupations of the society in areas where the language is spoken. Culturally significant materials may be on tape, records, film, or videotape or may be recorded regularly from radio or television broadcasts. Media centers also house overhead projectors, slide projectors, and epidiascopes to make diagrammatic, photographic, and print materials available for class or individual study.

Students at the advanced level need constant practice in listening and speaking in order to keep up their fluency; yet many advanced courses are devoted almost entirely to reading and writing, or to a discussion of literary texts conducted at such a sophisticated level of expression that it becomes a lecture by the instructor with one-sided pseudo-discussion, because the students cannot express their opinions or sustain their viewpoint adequately in the second language. Both lecture and discussion may even be in the native language of the students rather than the language of the texts, because it seems clear that this is the only way out of the dilemma. Courses demanding creative effort from the students are essential if advanced students are to attain a level of mastery which will enable them to express themselves fluently and comfortably in any situation. For this, listening is as important as speaking, reading, and writing.

Listening comprehension of completely uncontrolled and unedited materials is not easy and needs continual practice for maintenance, particularly in foreign-language learning situations. This is what the laboratory or cassette-on-loan can supply most usefully at the advanced level. Normal native speech (not adapted or modified in any way for the learner) in authentic conversations and discussions, with a variety of regional accents and types of voices; news broadcasts and news commentaries; interviews with well-known personalities, specialists in specific fields, or men and women in the street; plays recorded by professional actors; sound tracks of films and documentaries; informational radio and television programs, broadcast advertisements, and segments of situation comedies and soap operas; recorded telephone conversations—materials like these should be acquired over a period of time for the use of advanced students. Some can be acquired commercially or through trade or diplomatic representatives; others can be recorded informally with visiting native speakers and by exchange of materials with teachers in other countries. When native speakers are invited, the talks they give should certainly be taped for further listening practice and, if suitable, used again in later years. Much of the listening at this level will be for the pleasure of the content. Occasionally it will be tested, but continual testing will turn a natural activity into just another routine chore.

The laboratory can also be used for the development of writing skills by providing opportunities, again on a library basis, for practice in advanced dictation. Notetaking and the writing of reports can be further developments from exercises in listening comprehension. Background material on authors and works being studied, particularly in the form of discussions with the authors themselves, with actors, or with critics, are often available in recorded form. Students may listen to these and make notes as a basis for written composition. Where lectures are given in class on literary or cultural subjects, a résumé tape may be recorded to be used by the weaker students who have not been able to follow the lecture and take notes at the same time. Memorizing poems with the help of a native model is not to be despised as a way of spurring interest in the perfecting of pronunciation and intonation. Listening to and repeating poems and prose helps students to develop an appreciation of the melody and rhythm of sound patterns and the importance of variations of word order.

Career-oriented students should be given opportunities to practice both simultaneous and consecutive translation or interpretation in the laboratory, comparing their recorded efforts later with a written script. Students intending to study in the language at university level should be given frequent practice in listening to lectures in their discipline and taking notes on the content. (Where the media center also records lectures in various disciplines for individual study by students, such material is readily available. Otherwise, steps should be taken to record lectures in those departments which frequently enroll foreign students.) This lecture practice should be self-paced, so that the students can listen to segments several times until they understand them. If the students are also learning to read in their discipline, the recordings should be related to the areas from which the readings have been selected. Finally, opportunities should be provided for students interested in the same area to discuss in small groups the material they have read and heard, thus preparing them to participate in tutorial or discussion sections.

The variety of programs available in the laboratory at the advanced level will reflect the imagination, resourcefulness, and initiative of the teachers using it.

HAS THE LANGUAGE LEARNING LABORATORY FAILED?

When language laboratories were first developed, there was much talk about machines replacing teachers and students learning languages with an ease and rapidity which had never been observed in conventional classroom situations. Developments in hardware continued apace, adding to the early tape-recording equipment the conveniences of remote control and selective access; fast multicopying machines for tapes and, later, cassettes; closed circuit television, videotapes, and videodiscs; shortwave receivers for recording material from distant countries; computerization of the organizational aspects of the laboratory; computer-assisted instruction with an audio component and a screen sensitive to touch, so that students need only point to a word to get a correction and explanation on the computer screen; computerized scoring so that lights at the console reveal to the teacher how many students have pressed the right button for multiple-choice selections; push-buttons enabling the teacher to dim the room or activate or stop films, filmstrips, slides, or music without leaving the console. None of these things can assist learning without effective courseware, that is, a learning sequence which is carefully designed and executed, yet interesting enough to retain the student's attention and encourage perseverance.

The evolution of courseware has not kept pace with the evolution of equipment. Much language programming is still steeped in the theories of the fifties. Furthermore, teachers trained in language, literature, or linguistics departments usually know very little about the kinds of operations that can be programmed for the newer kinds of hardware and have thought even less about their potential for facilitating language learning. As a result, they tend to transfer to the cassette, the videotape, or the computer a pale version of a classroom or textbook lesson. Not surprisingly, without the human ability to adapt to changing moods and needs, the machine so programmed performs less effectively than the experienced teacher. The machine does not "fail" unless the equipment breaks down. The failure has been in effective use of the available technology.

What can we learn from past experience?

1. The conventional language-learning laboratory has been hamstrung by a lack of *well-designed recorded materials at accessible prices*. Teachers need more than a set of tapes of indifferent quality to accompany a particular text. They need a great variety of materials from which to draw to serve many purposes. This problem becomes even more acute for computer-assisted instruction for which there are as yet only a few complete programs for specific languages, each of which has absorbed an enormous amount of professional time in the making. Despite this tremendous effort on the part of the authors, the resulting programs may not be congenial in methodology and objectives for all those who might wish to use this type of instructional aid.

2. At no level of instruction have school administrators been willing to pay for the *great amount of faculty time required* merely to prepare and dub lesson tapes appropriate to the interests and purposes of specific sets of students at particular times, let alone the vastly greater amounts of time needed for planning their own audio- or videotapes (and finding and supervising suitable persons for recording them); for recording radio broadcasts and converting these into useful teaching material; or for preparing film sound tracks for preparatory study where films were used. In far too many instances, there has not even been enough money to pay for adequate laboratory supervision, so that this too was added to the teacher's load.

3. The materials available for the laboratory have been tied too closely, in most instances, to *a particular approach to language teaching and to a particular theory of language learning*. Consequently, teachers wishing to use the laboratory in another way have had to prepare materials of their own from the base up (a process for which they were allotted neither the time nor the money), ignore the laboratory, or, to please the administration, implement a laboratory program which, as their students soon realized, had little or nothing to do with "the real work."

4. *Convenience* has been another inhibiting factor. In most schools, teachers must schedule the use of equipment well ahead of time, then use it at that particular class hour, whether it is appropriate or not. The film may or may not have arrived; it may be the wrong film; the film breaks or is wound backward; some of the laboratory booths are out of order; slides are incorrectly oriented for showing; the tape

begins at the wrong speed—many are the possible aggravations and delays in using equipment. In other words, teachers have not been supplied with *simple-to-operate equipment, readily available at the times it is needed,* or with aides to prepare it and properly trained maintenance staff.

5. Very few language teachers have been given more than a perfunctory introductory *training* in the use of hardware and often no training in the preparation of courseware or the selection and adaptation of existing courseware to the needs of their students and their programs. It is no wonder that, to many teachers, any form of audiovisual aid seems to be an extra, a luxury which can be omitted when time and money run short. Since they are not using very effectively what is already available, further developments in this area will leave them untouched (hiding behind the classroom door), unless they are made aware of the many possibilities for enrichment of learning which these developments provide. Furthermore, they need practical training (preservice and inservice) in writing at least segments of programs, recording or dubbing tapes, making visuals, coordinating these with appropriate sound tracks, and designing lessons which incorporate these materials usefully and conveniently.

6. *We tend to teach as we were taught.* If our future teachers are to be conscious of the potential for improved learning provided by carefully programmed machines, they must have had a convincing experience themselves in using such aids at college level. At this level, however, where financial provision has frequently been the most generous, we find the greatest unrealized potential. Instructors of undergraduates, with notable exceptions, are among the least convinced that the time and effort involved in programming technological aids are worth the investment. As a result, it is at this level that student attitudes toward the language learning laboratory have most rapidly deteriorated. There is therefore a need in colleges and junior colleges for convincing demonstrations of the potential of media and for considerable encouragement for instructors to experiment in innovative ways, if language teaching is to keep up with other subject areas in this regard.

7. If the language learning laboratory, foreign languages resource center, electronic classroom, closed-circuit television outlet, computer terminal, or simple cassette recorder in the classroom or dormitory are to assist the language learning of individual students, there must be much *research into new approaches to programming* consistent with a diversity of approaches to course content and language teaching. There is a need for the production of many *experimental segments, modules,* or *units,* demonstrating these new approaches,

which will be readily available to teachers who are willing to incorporate them in their courses and make suggestions for further development. With this help, inappropriate techniques and content could be detected and changed before becoming frozen into expensive programs which may take years to complete.

8. Going beyond the conventional textbook reviews in professional journals, we need *user's reports* in which teachers share, not only comments on the quality of audio-visual materials and their appropriateness for particular courses and levels, but also accounts of how they were used, the ways in which students reacted to them, and proposals for more effective use. The same kinds of users' reports on equipment and its use, published in widely circulated teachers' journals, would be helpful to less experienced laboratory users.

9. *Language teachers should meet with media technicians* in detailed discussions of ways in which the needs of language learners can be served more effectively by using the full potential of the equipment. Both groups would benefit from this exchange in developing their work.

10. Before requesting or rejecting expensive equipment, teachers should analyze *what the expensive equipment does* which makes it effective as an aid to language learning and then study less costly ways of doing the same thing. Teachers must not be pressured into adopting and using elaborate equipment which cannot achieve more than simpler and cheaper devices or the teacher in the classroom. Where equipment is to be replaced, all those concerned should discuss the aspects of the equipment which have proved most useful for language learning and the ways in which it could be used more effectively for the purposes of their courses. Only then can rational and defensible decisions be made as to the kind of equipment which should take its place. Money economized on unused, or rarely used, functions of the equipment should then be diverted to the building up of the collection of courseware and the provision of assistance, without which chrome, polished wood, and extra circuits are of little value.

11. Above all, we must be able to demonstrate in a convincing way, through *improved student learning,* that the cost of the equipment (hardware, courseware, and maintenance) is justified. To convince others, we need concrete results in terms of specific, realizable objectives, among which we may include, as an important element, student attitude toward language learning.

Areas of Controversy

Is a library system preferable to a group system for language learning in a laboratory?

Ideally students in the laboratory should be able to practice at their own pace. Under a library system this is possible. Students take out the tapes or cassettes which follow on from what they completed in the preceding session, continuing with as much of the next section as they can assimilate. They work over the material several times if they are slow learners, or move on to new material after the first hearing if they are confident they can use it effectively. If students prefer not to stay in the laboratory, they check out the recorded material and take it elsewhere to work on for as long or as short a time as they feel they need. In some schools and colleges this system operates with the help of student assistants, who check out tapes and cassettes; supervise sessions, see that material is returned; and take responsibility for handouts, attendance sheets, or progress tests, if these are in use.

The library type of operation is particularly suited to more mature students and is the most frequent at college and university level. Some experienced teachers maintain that the average high school student needs considerable guidance under this system to ensure that the material is being used in the most effective way. Some students are disorganized in their study habits; others are overcautious and spend far too much time on each section; while still others are overconfident and feel that they know the work thoroughly when they have just begun to learn it. Guidance in approaching individual study sessions should be given in the preceding class lessons, so that students know exactly what they should be getting from any particular tape. Tests which the students may take as they complete a section will provide some check on the way each student is working. Results will indicate to the teacher which students need more individual supervision, and which students need to work again with a tape they have not thoroughly assimilated.

In many high schools, the library system is not practicable because of the numbers of students involved or the complicated scheduling it implies. It certainly creates difficulties in the integration of work into the classroom program if some students cannot practice assigned exercises on the same day as others. Where this is the case, the pattern of regular laboratory sessions for class groups is usually adopted, with the teacher supervising and helping students individually from the console.

429

With listen-record-compare facilities available to students, individuals may still work at their own pace in a group system, recording and rerecording as they wish, with the teacher available for consultation when problems arise. With listen-respond equipment only, the group system has been called lockstep, because all students must keep pace with the lesson being broadcast from the console. Even within such groups, however, certain adaptations can be made to provide for differences in rate of learning. With a little thought and effort, the teacher may prepare two or even three program tapes constructed around the week's work, channeling them to different groups of booths. Most consoles allow for such a procedure. One of these tapes will provide the regular diet of practice material for the average learner; a second tape will concentrate, with more repetition and review material, on the needs of the slow learner; a third tape will provide extra material of a more challenging nature for the fast learner. On each tape the basic material will be the same: namely, the section necessary to practice what has been learned in class, and preparatory to the application work in the next class lesson.

For a library-type operation, students must have individual access to the program source they need, either through program selectors connected to several tape-decks at the console, by remote control to a central core, or through the option of borrowing cassettes as they do library books. Even in schools where the main laboratory facilities are of the listen-respond type, there should be several positions with recording-playback facilities where students may work to improve their pronunciation or record oral production. In this way, all students will have an opportunity from time to time to concentrate on their own problems for as long as they need.

Should group sessions in the laboratory be monitored?

In many schools a feature of laboratory work is the monitoring of student responses by the teacher at the console. Most consoles are wired so that the teacher not only can listen to individual students but also can speak to them directly to give advice or help. With full recording facilities, where students are working with individual copies of the master program, students are asked to stop their tape recorders while the teacher is speaking to them, so that their work is not disturbed.

In a group situation the teacher's communication from the console usually cuts out the reception of the master program, interfering with the continuity of the student's work. Even when the program continues at a lower level of sound, the student cannot follow it and still pay attention to the teacher's comments. If the interruption comes at a moment when there is some change in what the program requires of them, students may have difficulty in taking up their work again in an orderly way. The teacher's comment must usually be very brief because of the ongoing broadcast, and students who are reintegrating themselves into the program sequence have little time to think about the suggestions made, or to practice the correct pronunciation or grammatical form called to their attention. For these reasons, many experienced teachers question the value of monitoring.

On the other hand, some students feel that they are speaking in a void in the laboratory and are glad to hear the teacher's voice from time to time encouraging or helping them. This gives them the impression that someone is listening and is interested in what they are saying. Other less industrious students need to feel that the teacher is aware of their participation or nonparticipation. Since most students prefer to know when the teacher is listening to them, some word, even a short expression of commendation, should be spoken to each person monitored, so that the students will not have the impression that the teacher is either spying on them or ignoring them.

Students unmonitored in the laboratory may well be reinforcing their faults. It is hard for students to detect the defects of their articulation and intonation without guidance. They can continue to accent wrong syllables and slur others, while convinced that they are repeating what was said on the tape. Even when they realize where they are wrong, they often do not know what to do about it. Other students can continue to make grammatical errors in their responses without observing how their utterances differ from the model.

In view of the inevitable interruption with monitoring, the teacher should listen carefully, and analyze the fault to be corrected before speaking to the student, so that the interruption may be as short and as useful as possible. The monitor must avoid interrupting the student to correct some trivial slip of the tongue, or some minor fault which is not relevant to the main purpose of the particular exercise. If a long explanation is required, the teacher should make a note of this and discuss it with the student at the end of the session. The note may then be given to the student as a reminder for the next session. If many of the students are making the same mistake, the teacher can stop the master tape at the console, discuss the fault with the whole group, and then wind the tape back to a position preceding the fault, so that all may profit from another repetition. (This is not possible with student-controlled recorders.)

Monitoring enables the teacher to keep a record of the achievements and particular difficulties of individual students. Teachers monitoring their own classes should keep the class list at the console and evaluate the students' work at regular intervals in order to arrive at a more objective grade for their oral production. With a large group, it may be best to monitor carefully one-half of the students each session, merely tuning in to the others briefly to see that they are not in any particular difficulty.

Clearly, students' individual work with take-away cassettes cannot be monitored. It is imperative in this case that some activity during the class session should elicit responses from the students which will reveal what they have been learning individually. Action may then be taken to counteract as soon as possible any effects of incorrect learning.[5] With individualized instruction, students will report individually to the teacher, who will test in some appropriate form what they have learned from the week's cassette.

Beyond any theoretical or idealistic justification, the decision to monitor or not to monitor comes down to financial and logistic considerations. The advantages of a minute or two of immediate instructor help for each student during a session must be weighed against the costs of using teacher or monitor time for this task and the extra costs of equipment which permits monitoring. Then the objectives of the laboratory program in relation to the general instructional program must be considered. In individualized programs, much teacher or monitor time is required for personal attention to the students' needs in other ways (checking on progress, explaining, interacting in small groups, or giving guidance on whether the student should proceed with the next unit). It may be considered that monitoring in the laboratory is less valuable than other activities, and the choice will be made accordingly. Most monitoring means a lock-step practice session for students (who may profit more from practicing and repracticing sections as they feel the need). If students are practicing at their own pace, the monitor spends much of the brief time available for individual student help trying to identify just which part of the tape a particular student is practicing. The monitor's time may be more usefully spent working for a longer time on pronunciation problems with individual students, while the others continue to practice on their own or check their responses from self-correction sheets or laboratory manuals.

Since there are cogent arguments both for and against monitoring, the decision in a particular case must be made in the light of local circumstances.

5. J. J. Higgins reports an investigation of students' failure to correct responses which clearly did not tally with the correct response given on the tape. He discusses the factors hindering the student in self-correction. See "Problems of Self-Correction in the Language Laboratory," *System* 3, no. 3 (1975): 145–56.

Do students learn more effectively in the laboratory if they record their responses?

Opinions are divided on the value of dual-channel recording-playback facilities for each student. These, of course, are not available on a single-track cassette recorder, which is a very common practice instrument.

Where recording-playback facilities are provided, students are supplied with tapes on which the lesson is recorded on the upper track. They play these tapes on their individual machines, recording their responses on a lower track at intervals corresponding to the pauses on the upper track. If a number of students are using the same tape program at the same time, they may record the lesson broadcast from the console on the upper track of a blank tape, recording their responses simultaneously on the lower track. (This is a lockstep operation in that each student must continue to record the tape without stopping for any reason.) In either case, when the program concludes, the students proceed to play back their tapes to compare their version with that of the native model. They are then free to record a second version of the responses, if they so desire, since this automatically erases the first version but not the model. During this second attempt, students concentrate on improving those sections where they have detected weaknesses. Sometimes more than half the session is taken up with this process of comparing and rerecording several versions.

At first glance this recording-playback procedure appears to be an ideal arrangement. Students are able to compare their efforts objectively with the recorded native model. They then have the opportunity, by rerecording, to apply what they have observed to the improvement of their weaknesses. By playing this second recording back, they can observe with a minimum of delay whether they have improved. They can continue to work at their own pace, playing back and rerecording a short section as often as they wish if they feel they can still make improvements in their production.

Experience has shown, however, that it is very difficult for students to diagnose their own errors, particularly in pronunciation. After reaching a rough approximation, they are often quite pleased with their efforts, even when these would be quite unacceptable or even incomprehensible to a native speaker. On the other hand, a student may be well aware of deficiencies in pronunciation but at a loss how to overcome them. The result is discouragement and less concentrated effort. In either case, students go on repeating their errors and establishing them just as firmly in their repertoire as they would in a laboratory without playback facilities. As for structure exercises, if the students have answered correctly they are wasting their time listening to the whole tape over again; if they have made mistakes, these have already been drawn to their attention by the immediate correction of the model voice, and students would be better employed repeating the exercise than listening to their mistakes as they play back the tape. An immediate playback loop, which enables students to hear the correct version and then reverse the tape just enough to correct each response immediately, is the most useful of the recording-playback devices.

Students enjoy hearing their own voices, and this is often cited as an additional motivational incentive provided by recording-playback facilities.[6] A lively interest of this type is short-lived, however. After some time, the process of playing back becomes routine and tedious. It may hold only a small part of the student's attention, particularly when the section to be played back is lengthy, with correct and incorrect responses interspersed. Continual playing back and rerecording is very time-consuming, and such time would be better employed in further active practice in the language.

Some teachers feel that recording-playback-rerecording activities are valuable only in small, well-regulated doses. According to this view, ten minutes may be set aside for such activities at the end of a long period in the laboratory, in which case only a specific section, usually a pronunciation or reading section, would be recorded and rerecorded by the student with a view to improvement. With shorter sessions, opportunities for comparison and rerecording would be provided during one session out of three or four. With either of these systems, students would be recording and comparing their best efforts after a period of practice, and would be more anxious to see what improvement they had made than in routine rerecording.

If comparison and rerecording is to be effective in improving pronunciation, students should be trained to detect particular differences in the foreign sound system, and to identify their own weaknesses in some systematic way. They need explicit instructions on how to rectify these weaknesses once they have detected them. During the playback session, the teacher should be readily available for consultation on problems of improvement. Recognizing faults in pronunciation is not sufficient; one must know what to do about them.

The area in which recording-playback facilities have an undoubted superiority over audio-active listening facilities is in testing aural-oral skills. A test tape can be made by each student during one laboratory

6. See, however, the discussion of the second Lorge experiment (1959–63), pp. 437–38 below. A factor in the reported results could have been the novelty of such equipment at the time. Fascination with hearing one's voice recorded can lead to more concentrated attention to the task.

session. With the use of a pause button, students are not all forced to reply with identical promptness, and so are relieved of anxieties. They can also erase and rerecord an incorrect response, as they would do in a written test. Later, the teacher playing back the tapes is able to assess more precisely the student's comprehension of and reaction to the aural stimulus because both the original recording and the responses are still available.

The question of whether to record or not to record is resolved for many teachers by financial considerations. Where complete recording-playback facilities cannot be provided in every booth in the laboratory, students can still have much valuable practice in listening and in active grammar assimilation. They are, however, more dependent on the teacher's vigilance in pointing out to them their areas of weakness in the production of sounds. It is important for teachers to analyze the kinds of activities in which they wish their students to participate in the laboratory, and then to use the type of equipment which enables the students to practice these activities most efficiently. Where several types of equipment are available, each will then be used fully for the activity for which it is most appropriate.

Is the language learning laboratory effective?

The first research study on language laboratories to attract widespread attention was the Keating *Study of the Effectiveness of Language Laboratories,* published in 1963. Keating's interest was administrative rather than methodological. His aim was to find out whether the money invested in laboratories by United States high schools, in response to an offer of matching grants from the federal government, was money well spent in view of the fact that it was presumably being drained away from other worthwhile areas of the curriculum.

Five thousand students in New York schools associated with the Metropolitan School Study Council (MSSC) were involved in the investigation during the period 1961–62. These schools were described as "relatively well favored, especially as regards expenditure," and they were therefore able to employ "superior teachers" (Keating 1963, p. vii) who might be presumed to know how to employ the language laboratory to its full potential. No attempt was made to find out whether the teachers had had any training in the use of a language laboratory (at that time, many teachers had not), and no record was kept of how they used it. No information is available on the kinds of materials the teachers used, except that some were commercially prepared and some were teacher-prepared. (Whether the teachers had training in the preparation of materials for laboratory use is not specified.) As an administration study, these elements were not important;

the interest was in "results . . . with the laboratory as it was actually being used" (Keating 1963, p. 37).

In testing the students, this study concentrated on reading comprehension, listening comprehension, and speech production. Results showed the no-laboratory groups, at four levels of instruction, to be superior at the end of the first year to the laboratory groups on all of these measures except speech production.

It does not surprise language teachers to find that students who spent 25 percent more time with their books proved to be superior in reading comprehension. It is even less surprising when we note that the reading comprehension test used was constructed in 1940, that is, before the advent of the laboratory and of the aural-oral emphasis in language teaching. It therefore contained material much more similar in content to that in traditional textbooks than to the materials used at the time in a laboratory.

The results in listening comprehension were more surprising, since this is a skill which teachers aim to develop through practice in the laboratory. Here again, the test used was constructed before laboratories were installed in the schools and was originally designed to test students accustomed to classroom discussion of reading-oriented texts.

The results in speech production also favored the no-laboratory group at the three upper levels, but not in the first year. This test was specially constructed for the experiment and was used in identical form at all levels. On close examination it hardly justifies its name as a test of "speech production;" it may be considered, rather, as a very limited test of pronunciation (of ten words in isolation), followed by a test of the ability to read ten short sentences with acceptable articulation and intonation, a skill which is cultivated by superior teachers in classrooms where reading is the primary objective. The speech production test was the only one of the three that attempted to test the oral facility which users of the laboratory aimed to develop. Interestingly enough, despite its shortcomings, this test revealed that the laboratory did develop good pronunciation and fluency in short phrases at the level at which specially prepared materials for the laboratory were available in 1961.

The investigator concludes: "While this study does not purport to demonstrate that the language laboratory cannot be used effectively, it does show that in schools of the Metropolitan School Study Council, a group of schools characterized by competent and well-prepared teachers, better results in certain important skill areas are being achieved in instructional situations which do not use the language laboratory" (Keating 1963, p. 39). Since he had stated earlier that lack of accurate information on how the laboratory was used at any one time was "the inevitable outcome of improvisation with the laboratory by relatively inexperienced teachers" (ibid., p. 38), a justifiable interpretation of the results of the investigation would appear to be as follows: the students of experienced and competent teachers teaching material to which they are accustomed achieve better results in tests constructed with this material in mind than do the students of inexperienced teachers experimenting with a new medium and new materials for which the tests are inappropriate.

Interesting light is thrown on the results of the Keating investigation by the report of the New York City experiment (1959–63), under the direction of Sarah Lorge,[7] the results of which were published soon after the Keating report. The New York City experiment consisted of two studies. The first study was designed "to test the extent to which the regular use of the language laboratory would lead to measurable improvement in competence in speaking French and in comprehension of spoken French" (skills for which the laboratory was being used at the time) "without significant loss in reading comprehension and in written aspects of language study."[8] Teachers in the classes involved in the investigation were instructed in laboratory techniques recommended by experienced teachers, materials designed for the laboratory were used in teaching, and special tests were devised to evaluate the listening and speaking skills.

The tests of speaking ability required answers to questions on a sight-reading passage. Scores were given for fluency, pronunciation, and intonation in sight-reading, and for appropriateness, grammatical correctness, and fluency in response to questions. Although it retained elements of traditional testing, this was a more valid test of "speech production" than the Keating test. The tests for listening comprehension were also specially designed. The no-laboratory groups were not at a disadvantage on these tests, since they were taught by an audio-lingual method with similar materials to those used by the laboratory groups.

The laboratory groups showed significant gains at the first- and second-year levels in fluency of speech and in intonation, and at the

---

7. *Foreign Language Laboratories in Secondary Schools,* a special report summarizing four years of research by the Bureau of Audio-Visual Instruction, Board of Education of the City of New York, for the New York State Education Department 1959–63. The report is discussed at length in Lorge, "Language Laboratory Research Studies."

8. *Foreign Language Laboratories,* p. 5. The first study was entitled "A Comparison of Results in the Teaching of French in High School Achieved with and without the Use of the Language Laboratory."

third-year level in listening comprehension. The laboratory groups also showed a significant increase in motivation to continue with the study of the language. The traditional skills of reading and writing did not appear to suffer because of the time taken for laboratory practice. (It must be remembered that the control group was also taught by the audio-lingual method which, at that time, underplayed reading in the early stages.)

Also of interest in interpreting the Keating report is the second study of the New York City schools.[9] The report showed that regular daily practice for twenty minutes produced significant improvement in speaking and listening skills, whereas a laboratory session once a week did not. The schools in the Keating investigation followed, with two exceptions, the once-a-week pattern. The New York City study also showed recording-playback equipment to be more effective than audio-active listening facilities for improving quality of speech. In very few of the MSSC schools in the Keating study were full recording facilities available to all students.

The New York City report concluded that "the mere installation of a language laboratory is no guarantee that improvement in linguistic skills will occur automatically. Good results demand: equipment of good quality with potential for a variety of learning experiences; teachers skilled in handling equipment; materials prepared specifically with regard to the goals of the course and techniques of laboratory learning; and careful allotment of laboratory time."[10]

Whether the Hawthorne effect[11] was operative in the use of recording-playback equipment in 1959–63 in New York City cannot be ascertained at this distance. Flint Smith also found a small advantage for the audio-active-record mode in 1969.[12] In contradistinction to these findings, Perelle reported for a 1975 study of college and evening school students that, in an unmonitored situation, "a greater gain in oral/aural comprehension was made by those students using listen-respond method than by those using listen-respond-compare method, indicating that student recording in a language is not effective in increasing conversational ability in first-year language students, and may in fact, be a hindrance." Perelle hypothesized that this effect was

9. The second study was entitled "The Relative Effectiveness of Four Types of Language Laboratory Experience."

10. *Foreign Language Laboratories*, p. 8.

11. The Hawthorne effect is a term used by psychologists. Very successful results in educational experiments are sometimes found to have been influenced by the enthusiasm of the participants and the experimenter for a novel approach.

12. W. Flint Smith, "The Language Laboratory and the Electronic Classroom: A Comparison of Their Relative Contribution to Achievement in Three Languages in the Comprehensive High School," *Dissertation Abstracts* 30 (1969): 1474A (Purdue).

due to the inability of the students to discriminate and categorize their errors, so that "the time spent reviewing . . . prior responses is apparently not only wasted but actually interferes with . . . attempts to obtain conversational proficiency."[13]

Teachers become bewildered when research projects like these yield contradictory results. These particular projects have been cited to show how difficult it is to compare results of research conducted in different institutions at different periods, using different materials in ways which are not clearly specified and possibly quite diverse. Since we are not told in any detail the kind of preparation students were given for work with tapes, what kinds of practice exercises students performed, and what kinds of follow-up activities were conducted by the teacher, we are in no position to determine to what degree the results of the tests in each case can be attributed to the use of a specific type of equipment. Teacher behavior and student activity with the materials are very influential in the learning process, yet these are variables which are very difficult to control or to compare across projects.

Before deciding that the Perelle study cancels out the results of the New York City study, we need to take into account some important differences. First, there is a difference of at least fifteen years between the studies. In 1959, as the New York City report states twice, the interest in hearing one's own voice was high and considered motivating. In 1975, many students had had this experience frequently in home and leisure activities; for most, it was no longer a novelty which would rivet their attention. Second, in the New York City study the recording practice was compulsory, teacher-supervised work within a high school context; in the Perelle study it was considered independent work for college and evening school students; although attendance, which was compulsory, was checked. There were doubtless many other differences. (In 1975, for instance, college instructors were better prepared linguistically to provide their students with active aural-oral practice themselves, without laboratory assistance, than were high school teachers in a large, citywide system in 1959.)

Such important contrasts between the situations in which the studies were conducted permit us to doubt that the results of one cancel out the results of the other. What they possibly do show is that use of various types of equipment may lead to very different results in different learning situations. This accentuates the responsibility of individual teachers to think out what is best for their own students

13. I. B. Perelle, "Level II vs. Level III Language Laboratories: An Investigation of Their Relative Efficiencies," *System* 3, no. 3 (1975): 157–63; the quotations are from p. 162.

in relation to course objectives, and the ability of the school and instructors to meet these needs.

The sixties drew to a close with rising controversy about language laboratories as a result of the Pennsylvania Foreign Language Project (1965–69), a full account of which was published by its director in 1970.[14] The project was concerned with "two related questions: (1) Given several alternative teaching approaches to foreign-language instruction, which of these is better? and (2) Which of the commonly used language-laboratory systems is most effective as an adjunct to foreign-language instruction?"[15]

The teaching approaches chosen were the "traditional" (modified up-to-date grammar-translation approach), the "functional skills" (or audio-lingual), and a modified audio-lingual approach with exposure to formal grammar, termed "functional skills plus grammar." The second and third approaches used the language laboratory systematically; the first did not (although a tape recorder was available in the classroom). The language laboratory systems studied were the tape recorder in the classroom, the audio-active (level 2) language laboratory or the electronic classroom, and the audio-record (level 3) language laboratory. Important for our purposes, in this complex study (more than one hundred classes were involved in the first year), are the findings on the effectiveness of the language laboratory, as used in a large number of typical high schools. The study found no significant differences between groups which could be attributed to different language laboratory systems. The tape recorder in the classroom seemed as effective as the "lockstep" language laboratory (where material was broadcast to all the class at once) at a fraction of the cost. The results showed no discernible effect of the language laboratory on listening, speaking, or writing, although students who did not use recorded material in any systematic way (the grammar-translation group) had a slight advantage in reading over the "functional skills" group but not over the "functional skills with grammar" group.[16] The project director considered the differences between these results and those from more closely controlled research, like the New York Study, to be due to the broader representation of "typical schools" in the Pennsylvania project. (Many fewer schools had language laboratories in 1959 in New York City, which acted as a selective factor.)

14. Philip D. Smith, Jr. *A Comparison of the Cognitive and Audiolingual Approaches to Foreign Language Instruction: The Pennsylvania Foreign Language Project* (Philadelphia, Center for Curriculum Development, 1970).

15. Ibid., p. 3.

16. Ibid., pp. 236–37.

The project report recommended that "the tape recorder be considered essential equipment in every foreign-language classroom," that the language laboratory be used for "individualized practice in addition to regular classroom instruction rather than as a type of classroom activity," and that recording equipment be used "for testing purposes rather than for use in drill activities."[17]

The Pennsylvania project was extensively evaluated and its conclusions were much debated.[18] Not unexpectedly, the problems of educational research already discussed in this section were raised (namely, the uncontrollability of *teacher behavior* in actual situations in the classroom and the consequent variability of student *experience*). The *text* variable was also widely discussed. Valette pointed out that the vocabulary and structures in the tests for the first year of French had been more extensively covered in the text generally used in the "traditional" classes than in either of the "functional skills" texts.[19] Carroll concurred in this observation, commenting that there is a great deal of linguistic content that must be learned by the student of another language. "Writers of audiolingual texts and materials," he said, "seem to have neglected, to some extent, the voluminous linguistic content that has to be transmitted to the learner. 'Functional skills' methods place too little emphasis on content, and too much emphasis on habit formation. Perhaps the commonly available language laboratory materials are cast in such a form that they slow down learning, particularly when they are used only to drill and review materials already presented in class." He commented further that "the comparisons among strategies rested partly on differences in the texts used as well as on differences in the conduct of classroom instruction."[20]

Materials and the way they are used—these remain the crucial elements in the success or failure of laboratory or classroom. The laboratory can add little to the impact of the classroom if all it does

17. Ibid., p. 240. L. M. Aleamoni and R. E. Spencer, in "An Evaluation of the Pennsylvania Foreign Language Project," *MLJ* 53, no. 6 (October 1969): 428, do not consider that these recommendations can be derived from the project data.

18. See specifically the series of critiques in *MLJ* 53, no. 6 (October 1969): 386–428, by John L. D. Clark, Rebecca M. Valette, Elton Hocking, Frank Otto, Lawrence M. Aleamoni, and Richard E. Spencer; and J. B. Carroll, "What Does the Pennsylvania Foreign Language Research Project Tell Us?" in *FLA* 3, no. 2 (December 1969): 214–36.

For a summary, with bibliography, of the most important arguments, see W. Flint Smith, "Language Learning Laboratory," in Lange 1970, pp. 194–208.

19. Rebecca M. Valette, "The Pennsylvania Project, Its Conclusions and its Implications," *MLJ* 53 (1969): 396–404, and "Some Conclusions to be Drawn from the Pennsylvania Study," *NALLD Newsletter* 3, no. 3 (March 1969): 17–19.

20. Carroll, "What Does the Pennsylvania . . . Project Tell Us?" pp. 235, 224–25.

is to repeat endlessly what has already been drilled in class. Variety of materials and variety of activity are the key to continued student intake and perseverance in the language laboratory.

(The reports of the Pennsylvania project and the extensive evaluation and commentary they have provoked are far too complex to be considered here in further detail. Some experts, like Carroll and Valette, have reanalyzed portions of the data and reported slightly different conclusions. For further information, those interested will consult the references in notes 17–19 above.)

Annotated Reading List

Stack, Edward M. *The Language Laboratory and Modern Language Teaching.* 3d ed. New York: Oxford University Press, 1971. An important book of reference on types of installation, essential equipment, and the administration and use of the laboratory. There are excellent chapters on the construction of suitable drills and tests.

Higgins, J. J. *A Guide to Language Laboratory Material Writing.* Oslo: Universitetsforlaget, 1969. Discusses with numerous examples for English the making of a syllabus, the writing of contextualized exercises for grammar, conversation, and pronunciation, and ways of checking and evaluating student production. Sections on "Brightening up the Tape" and "How to be a Producer."

Dakin, Julian. *The Language Laboratory and Language Learning.* London: Longman, 1973. A very practical book for the teacher or materials writer, with many ideas for language laboratory activities to develop listening comprehension and speech production. The numerous examples are in English.

Edgerton, Mills F., Jr., ed. *Sight and Sound: The Sensible and Sensitive Use of Audio-Visual Aids* (NEC 1969). Gives much useful advice on the use of sound recordings and all kinds of projected and nonprojected visuals, with ways of integrating them into one's teaching.

Howatt, A., and Dakin, J. "Language Laboratory Materials." Chap. 4 of Allen and Corder 1974, pp. 93–121. Materials for listening and speaking. Examples in English.

Dodge, James W. "Educational Technology." In NEC 1980. Discusses technological developments and their implications for language teaching, with detailed consideration of televised instruction, videotapes, and videodiscs; the potential of microelectronics, and the use of general purpose and personal computers. Bibliography.

Useful articles may be found in *System,* ed. Norman F. Davies (Oxford: Pergamon Press), and in *NALLD Journal,* ed. Dale V. Lally, Jr. (Newsletter of the National Association of Learning Laboratory Directors).

Research and Discussion

1. Examine the tapes in the library of the laboratory in the school in which you are teaching or observing. Is the collection sufficient for the needs of students at all levels? For all aspects of language learning? For supplementary study for individual students? Write a report for the language learning laboratory director suggesting the types of materials that should be acquired to improve the collection.

2. Prepare a program tape for a class in the school in which you are observing or teaching and use it in the laboratory. Administer a questionnaire to the students at the end of the session to find out their reactions to the content and format of the tape. What improvements would you make to the program after reading the students' comments?

3. Take a tape for grammatical practice in a language you do not know well. Work through it in the audio-active mode. Then work through a similar tape using audio-active-record facilities. Analyze your experiences. Did one system seem more useful to you than the other? Why?

4. If you were planning a set of remedial tapes for grammatical practice in the language you teach, what structures would you select for inclusion? Why do you consider laboratory practice would be particularly beneficial in these areas? What types of activities would you propose for the various structures?

5. Examine the tapes which accompany the textbook you are or will be using and write an evaluation of them along the lines of the checklist in this chapter, keeping in mind the level of instruction and the age of the students.

6. Arrange to monitor a session in a language laboratory. After the session, analyze your experience. How many students were you able to monitor? Did it take you long to identify student problems? Did you feel you were able to help many students? In what ways? Draw up a list of instructions and recommendations for monitors.

7. Prepare an orientation tape to familiarize students with the equipment in a laboratory to which you have access. Try the tape out on some inexperienced persons and observe their reactions. Ask them for suggestions for improvement. Redesign the tape in accordance with these observations and suggestions.

8. Examine some listening comprehension tapes for the advanced level. Evaluate them according to the criteria set out in this chapter.

9. Work out an outline for innovative use of the language laboratory facilities for a course you yourself have designed. (Be sure to state the purpose of the course and the type of student whose needs it will serve.)

10. Study the equipment in a language learning laboratory to which you have access. List the functions for which it provides. Observe in the laboratory for several hours. How many of the potential functions were used? Which were used most? Were these functions of a kind which could not have been provided in a classroom or library without special equipment? If you were to be consulted on replacement of the equipment, what would you advise on the basis of your observations?

4· And What Else?

LEARNING LANGUAGES EARLY OR LATE?

The "Optimal Age" for Learning a Second Language: Theoretical Considerations
There has been, and continues to be, much controversy about the optimal age for learning another language in school. For many years the views of Penfield and Roberts (1959) were very influential in this area. Penfield and Roberts considered that acquisition of a second language in a natural, apparently effortless way was possible only until puberty, when the brain lost its plasticity. The best years were between four and ten. Language learning after the early teens, they said, was "difficult, though not impossible, . . . because it is un-physiological" (Penfield and Roberts 1959, p. 255). Lenneberg developed this view further. He maintained that, as the individual matures, the left hemisphere of the brain gradually takes over most, but not all, language functions. After the brain has reached its mature state, at puberty, and cerebral lateralization is irreversibly established (Lenneberg 1967, p. 168), "automatic acquisition from mere exposure to a given language seems to disappear . . . and foreign languages have to be taught and learned through a conscious and labored effort.
. . . However," he continues, "a person *can* learn to communicate in a foreign language at the age of forty," because the cerebral organization for language learning ("the way the many parts of the brain interact") is in place and functioning (ibid., pp. 176, 170).

Krashen reexamined the clinical data used by Lenneberg and concluded that lateralization of the brain function for language may be completed by five[1]—the age at which the first language is considered by most child-language researchers to have been acquired. Krashen,[2] Rosansky,[3] and Rivers[4] have proposed that certain differences between adolescent and child second-language learning may be attrib-

1. S. D. Krashen, "The Critical Period for Language Acquisition and its Possible Bases," in Aaronson and Rieber 1975, p. 219.
2. Ibid., p. 220.
3. E. J. Rosansky, "The Critical Period for the Acquisition of Language: Some Cognitive Developmental Considerations," in *Working Papers in Bilingualism,* no. 6, ed. M. Swain, pp. 93–100 (Toronto: Ontario Institute for Studies in Education, 1975).
4. W. M. Rivers, "Language Learning and Language Teaching—Any Relationship?" in Ritchie 1978, p. 202.

utable to the onset of "formal operations," which, in Piaget's paradigm, occurs at about puberty. This would explain why adolescents and adults seem to need to understand the rules of a language in a conscious process of learning, whereas many young children seem to "pick up" a language without feeling the need for explanations or verbalization of the functioning of the language.

Even in the acquisition of a second language by young children there is much variability. Hatch, after a careful survey of experimental studies, observed that "the task of learning a second language is not as easy and effortless either psychologically or linguistically for some children as folklore would have us believe" (Hatch 1978, p. 14). Indeed, the notion that most young children pick up either their first or their second language through the pores as it were, without reflection, is highly debatable. To quote Hatch again, "Recent work in first-language acquisition . . . shows that the process is a very long, very demanding, and frequently frustrating one for the child. . . . The same can be said about second language acquisition" (ibid., p. 12). Contrary to the general belief, many small children show "an amazing meta-awareness of language"; they seem quite conscious of differences between the languages, in some cases correcting pronunciation errors and even explaining how sounds in the second language are produced and when morphological endings are used (ibid., p. 14).

The matter of a clearly identifiable "critical period" for acquiring a new language has not yet been firmly established by scientific investigation. Lenneberg speaks of the "diverse circumstantial evidence that puberty marks a milestone both for the facility in language acquisition and a number of directly and indirectly related processes in the brain" (Lenneberg 1967, pp. 168–69), while Penfield and Roberts's remarks are in an anecdotal epilogue, based, as Burstall points out, on logical inference rather than on direct observation or experimentation.[5]

Nor is the common belief that young children learn new languages faster than adolescents and adults without its critics. Burstall, after studying the research in this area, comes to the conclusion that "the research studies which have striven for a high degree of precision and control have failed to produce evidence favouring the younger learner"[6] of a foreign language. When "time on task," in Carroll's

5. Clare Burstall, "Factors Affecting Foreign-Language Learning: A Consideration of Some Recent Research Findings," in Kinsella 1978, p. 15.
6. Ibid.

446

sense,[7] is equivalent, that is, when the adolescent or adult spends the same amount of time on language learning and practice as children do, the more efficient language-learning strategies of the older learner seem to lead to more efficient language acquisition, particularly in the areas of morphology and syntax. The older learner's more highly developed concepts of knowledge of the world also facilitate the acquisition of a more extensive vocabulary.

In the studies of Snow and Hoefnagel-Höhle[8] on the learning of Dutch by English-speaking children (3–5, 6–7, and 8–10 years), adolescents (12–15 years), and adults, in a naturalistic situation (that is, without specific teaching of the language), it was the 12–15-year-old adolescent group that consistently demonstrated faster and more efficient learning than the younger groups, paralleled by the adults for the first few months of acquisition. The adult learners slowed down after a period and were overtaken by the 8–10-year-olds. The teenagers (12–15 years) achieved "almost native performance extremely quickly," while "the 3–5-year-olds scored consistently worse than the older group on all tests." "These findings," Snow and Hoefnagel-Höhle conclude, "are basis for rejecting the hypothesis that the period 2–12 years constitutes an optimal time for language acquisition."[9]

Early Language Learning in a Formal Situation

Burstall and her colleagues conducted a ten-year study of the teaching of French in primary schools for the National Foundation for Educational Research (NFER) in England and Wales (1964–74). The three experimental cohorts involved about 1,800 pupils whose learning of French was investigated from age 8 (the second cohort being studied through a full eight years of language study). Many variables were considered in this investigation: long-term development of attitudes toward learning another language; levels of achievement in relationship to attitudes; the effect of pupil variables on level of achievement and attitude (such individual variables as age, socioeconomic status, perception of parental encouragement, employment expectations, previous learning history, contact with France); the effect of teachers' attitudes and expectations; and the effect of the early introduction of

7. John B. Carroll, "A Model of School Learning," *Teachers College Record* 64 (1963): 723–33. Also discussed in Carroll, "Learning Theory for the Classroom Teacher," in *ACTFL Review,* vol. 6 (1974), ed. G. A. Jarvis, pp. 116–24.

8. Catherine E. Snow and Marian Hoefnagel-Höhle, "The Critical Period for Language Acquisition: Evidence from Second Language Learning," *Child Development* 49 (1978): 1114–28.

9. Ibid., p. 1122.

French on achievement in other areas of the primary school curriculum.[10]

When the eight-year-old beginners were compared at age thirteen with eleven-year-old beginners (eleven being a very common age worldwide for beginning foreign-language study), the eight-year-old beginners were found to be superior in listening and reading, but not in speaking or writing. At age sixteen, the early beginners were still superior in listening, equivalent in speaking, but not equal to the eleven-year-old beginners in reading and writing. Burstall concludes: "The most conservative interpretation which the available evidence would appear to permit is that the achievement of skill in a foreign language is primarily a function of the amount of time spent learning that language, but is also affected by the age of the learner, older learners tending to be more efficient than younger ones."[11]

Some of the effects noted by Burstall could have been the result of methods used for teaching the French classes, particularly at the secondary level. Burstall gives very lengthy quotations from students who say the French "went too fast"; that they did not understand what they were saying or what the teacher was saying; that the teacher did not give explanations, or explained in French or by actions which the weaker students did not comprehend; that the tape recorder used in the classroom was difficult to follow (too fast, muffled, practically inaudible); that they would have liked some printed script of what they were learning; and so on (Burstall et al. 1974, pp. 135–42).

We may note in the Burstall study that, although the students who had begun learning the language at age eight did not demonstrate after the eleventh grade a higher level of achievement in speaking French than those who began at age eleven, they did attest to more favorable attitudes toward speaking the language (ibid., p. 169) and they retained an advantage in listening comprehension. Some secondary school teachers commented on their "keenness to speak the language" and

10. Burstall et al. 1974, pp. 12–13. For a dissenting view of the results of the NFER study, see Michael Buckby, "Is Primary French Really in the Balance?" *MLJ* 60 (1976): 340–46.

11. Burstall et al. 1974, p. 123. For a small-scale study in the United States, with similar conclusions, see John W. Oller, Jr., and Naoko Nagato, "The Long-Term Effect of FLES: An Experiment," *MLJ* 58 (1974): 15–19. Mirjana Vilke, "Why Start Early?" in Freudenstein (1979), makes a pertinent comment on this point of view: "A negative attitude is expressed by those who believe that more mature children (at the age of 11 or 12), or even adults, are faster learners of foreign languages. This turns out to be true if language learning is reduced to the counting of structures and words memorised per hour. But the same could be said about many other school subjects . . . , and it could be a strong argument in favour of postponing the entire education until children become more mature" (p. 14).

their "confidence and fluency," which distinguished them from later beginners (ibid., p. 175). If spontaneous communication is the aim, then these long-lasting benefits from an early start are surely of considerable value, since they correspond to areas which are often the despair of high school and college instructors.

Nisbet and Welsh, in 1972, evaluated the effects of introducing French into primary schools in Aberdeen and concluded that: "the effect of primary school French appears to have been an attitude rather than an attainment. . . . The conclusion would appear to be that one should not expect primary school French to confer a lasting advantage, but that the justification for the inclusion of French should be within the context of the primary school curriculum—in terms of its contribution to the enlargement of interests and understanding and the development of a general language skill, rather than its effectiveness as a preparation for secondary school work."[12] Burstall observes that the Aberdeen results were probably affected by complete lack of articulation on transition to secondary level.[13] It is not surprising that students who begin a language at primary level do not show spectacular gains at a later stage when they are forced to begin all over again at seventh grade level. This matter of articulation between the primary and secondary schools has been a perennial problem whenever attempts have been made to teach foreign language in the early grades.

Traditionally, it has been considered axiomatic that young children acquire an authentic-sounding pronunciation in a new language much more readily than older language learners. This has also been a common observation with the children of immigrants. Research evidence in this area is conflicting and inconclusive. The results of Fathman's investigation of the learning of English by non-native children of 6–10 years and adolescents of 11–15 years in a formal learning situation showed that the adolescents acquired the morphology and syntax more rapidly than the children, who acquired the phonology more rapidly than the adolescents.[14] That young children become indistinguishable from native speakers in accent far more frequently than adolescents or adults was also the finding of Seliger, Krashen, and

12. Quoted in Burstall et al. 1974, p. 169. See also J. D. Nisbet and J. Welsh, "A Local Evaluation of Primary School French," *Journal of Curriculum Studies* 4 (1972): 169–75.
13. Burstall et al. 1974, p. 169.
14. Ann Fathman, "The Relationship between Age and Second Language Production Ability," *LL* 25 (1975): 245–53.

Ladefoged.[15] Both of these studies were in a second-language environment. In a formal teaching situation, Olson and Samuels found that adults learned to pronounce German more accurately than children.[16] Stern (1963) reported that eleven-year-olds in Swedish elementary schools acquired a more accurate pronunciation faster than seven-year olds.

Despite these isolated cases from formal teaching situations, the weight of evidence seems to favor younger children in the area of acquisition of authentic pronunciation. Fathman suggests that "the ability to learn certain aspects of a second language may be age related, [resulting from] maturational, physiological, or environmental factors. There may actually be different critical periods," she hypothesizes, "which are optimal times for learning different aspects of a second language. The preteen years may encompass a period during which ability to discriminate, to interpret or to imitate sounds is manifested most fully; whereas, after puberty the ability to learn rules, to make generalizations or to memorize patterns may be more fully developed."[17]

The multiple critical periods hypothesis is of some interest since language learners and their teachers become very concerned about pronunciation and intonation, despite the fact that their importance varies according to circumstances. In a second-language situation, "sounding different" and "having an accent" can make the difference between complete acceptance and a feeling of belonging, and a permanent experience of exclusion, even if only in insidious ways. In a foreign language situation, on the other hand, some degree of foreign accent can serve as a protection against criticism or irritation when the stranger does not behave as natives of the culture expect.

We cannot underestimate the strong connection between how we sound to ourselves and others and our feeling of identity. When we hear ourselves on tape, we often say: "That doesn't sound at all like me!" Experienced teachers in foreign-language classes have all observed the reversion by teenagers to an accent closer to their native-language phonology, when they reach the stage of strong peer-group identification and assertion of personal identity. For many adults,

15. Herbert W. Seliger, Stephen D. Krashen, and Peter Ladefoged, "Maturational Constraints in the Acquisition of Second Language Accent," *Language Sciences* 36 (1975): 20–22.

16. L. L. Olson and S. J. Samuels, "The Relationship between Age and Accuracy of Foreign-Language Pronunciation," *Journal of Educational Research* 66 (1973): 263–68.

17. Fathman, "The Relationship between Age and . . . Ability," p. 251. See also Herbert W. Seliger, "Implications of a Multiple Critical Periods Hypothesis for Second Language Learning," in Ritchie 1978, pp. 11–19.

sounding like someone else leads to a feeling of malaise and anomie. Guiora sums up this aspect of pronunciation very well as follows: "Superimposed upon the speech sounds of the words one chooses to utter are sounds which give the listener information about the speaker's identity. The listener can decide whether what one is saying is sincere or insincere. Ridicule the way I sound, my dialect, or my attempts at pronouncing French and you will have ridiculed me. Ask me to change the way I sound and you ask me to change myself. To speak a second language authentically is to take on a new identity. As with empathy, it is to step into a new and perhaps unfamiliar pair of shoes."[18] Small children readily take on other personalities in games of make-believe; they amuse themselves (and annoy their parents) by mimicking strange accents and talking in different voices. It is not, therefore, surprising that they feel much less inhibited than adults toward adopting a different-sounding form of speech.

Social and Psychological Distance
Arguments based on age-related biological data which support the early learning of languages in formal situations seem now to be inconclusive. Schumann[19] and Guiora[20] have posited social and psychological factors as the elements determining the successful acquisition of another language.

Schumann hypothesizes that the arrested acquisition of a second language at a pidginization stage, which is frequently observed among adults (that is, the continued use of simplified, reduced forms which suffice to convey denotative, referential information in communication) can be accounted for by social and psychological distance between the learner and speakers of the target language. Social distance is, for the most part, dependent on political, economic, and societal factors which determine the relations between the native- and target-language communities (factors such as dominance, assimilation, enclosure, or cohesiveness).[21] Psychological distance is determined by

18. A. Z. Guiora, M. Paluszny, B. Beit-Hallahmi, J. C. Catford, R. E. Cooley, and C. Y. Dull, "Language and Person: Studies in Language Behavior," *LL* 25 (1975): 48.

19. Schumann 1978, chap. 7: "Social and Psychological Distance as Factors in Second Language Acquisition," pp. 69–100. See also John H. Schumann, "Affective Factors and the Problem of Age in Second Language Acquisition," *LL* 25 (1975): 209–35; and Schumann, "Social Distance as a Factor in Second Language Acquisition," *LL* 26 (1976): 135–43.

20. Alexander Z. Guiora, Robert C. Brannon, and Cecilia Y. Dull, "Empathy and Second Language Learning," *LL* 22 (1972): 111–30.

21. These societal relationships are very complex. For a detailed discussion, see Christina B. Paulston, "Ethnic Relations and Bilingual Education: Accounting for Contradictory Data," in Troike and Modiano 1975, pp. 368–401 (also in Alatis and Twaddell 1976, pp. 235–62; and Schumann 1978, pp. 77–86).

affective factors, such as the resolution or nonresolution of language shock and culture shock, motivation, and the degree of permeability of language ego boundaries.[22] "To have permeable ego boundaries," according to Guiora and Acton, "entails having a well-defined, secure, integrated self or sense of self." Those with permeable ego boundaries can "move back and forth between languages and the 'personalities' that seem to come with them,"[23] without experiencing any sense of threat to their identity.

This theoretical position is complicated and deserves careful study in the original sources. It does, however, shed light on some differences between early and late language learners (and on the variability of achievement of language learners at any age). Small children are seldom bound by what their parents perceive as relations between communities speaking different languages; they play freely with children from other communities and make friends with them. They are also less acculturated to the ways of thinking and acting of their own community and, therefore, less disconcerted when children from other communities think or act differently. They are much more flexible and curious, less inhibited, and less threatened in their sense of identity. They are more open to new experiences and new learning than their parents, or even their older brothers and sisters, and all of these factors are conducive to good language learning. Naturally, these observations do not apply to all children or to all adolescents and adults. Hence the great variability in language learning that we observe at all ages.

- **Do you have a student in one of your classes who seems to have particular difficulties in learning a language? Do any of the psychological factors we have discussed seem to apply to this particular person?**

22. See Schumann 1978, pp. 86–99; Guiora, Brannon, and Dull, "Empathy"; and A. Z. Guiora and William R. Acton, "Personality and Language Behavior: A Restatement," *LL* 29 (1979): 193–204.

23. Guiora and Acton, "Personality," p. 199.

24. See also the following survey articles: V. J. Cook, "Second-Language Learning: A Psycholinguistic Perspective," *LTLA* 11, no. 2 (1978): 81; Clare Burstall, "Factors Affecting Foreign-Language Learning: A Consideration of Some Recent Research Findings," *LTLA* 8, no. 1 (1975): 5–25; and H. H. Stern and Alice Weinrib, "Foreign Languages for Younger Children: Trends and Assessment," *LTLA* 10, no. 1 (1977): 5–25. The articles by Burstall and by Stern and Weinrib are reprinted in Kinsella 1978. For a comparison of achievement in language learning in various countries, see Carroll 1975; Lewis and Massad 1975.

The "Optimal Age" for Learning a Second Language: The Realities

From the practical point of view it is not at all obvious that the concept of "optimal" age for learning a language is a reasonable one, even if one were to discover incontrovertible psychological or biological evidence for such a concept in the abstract. Scientific studies of language acquisition apart, it is becoming more and more apparent that the decision on when a child should begin to learn a second language can be made only after careful consideration of individual, social, and political factors.

If the child has come to live in an environment, where the second language is an essential medium for communication, and possibly education, then the optimal age is clearly that of entry into the environment.[25] Where the family or community fears that, if plunged too soon into using the second language, their young children will lose command of their first language and, with it, cultural identity or identification, the decision will be made on other grounds. In such cases, the parents may prefer to defer the learning of the second language until full use of the first has stabilized and the child has begun to value it. In this case the child will be taught in the first language, with the second language being introduced gradually after concept formation and literacy are well established in the first.

Where efforts are being made to encourage bilingualism in an area where two communities interact at the institutional rather than the personal level, a "home-school language switch" has been tried. In this case the child learns at school for the first few years in the second language, which is not the language commonly spoken in the home or in the immediate community. This is the St. Lambert *immersion* model, developed in Quebec province for English-speaking children in Montreal.[26] At second or third grade level the child begins to study in the home language for an hour a day, in addition to the second language. Year by year the amount of subject matter taught in the home language is increased, until a bilingual balance is reached, with

25. The author recognizes that the question of bilingual education, which is important and complex, is dealt with very cursorily in this chapter. This is because it warrants a complete book (more complete treatments are recommended in the Reading List), yet it is important that all foreign-language teachers should have given it some thought. They should know some of the problems and the various models that have been proposed in differing situations. They should also know where to look for further information. Bilingual education is now being called Mother Tongue Teaching in the United Kingdom and Western Europe.

26. See Lambert and Tucker 1972. For a U.S. experience, see William Derrick and Khorsted Randeria, "Early Immersion in French," *Today's Education* (February–March 1979): 38–40.

half the curriculum being taught in one language and half in the other. In an alternative model, the child may move over into full education in the home language at some later stage, while maintaining study of the second language as an important part of the scholastic program. This "home-school language switch" has been more effective in promoting bilingualism in situations where the child's first language is being thoroughly maintained through family and community use, with no doubts cast on its ultimate value as a primary tool for communication.[27]

In cases where the community, and sometimes even the family, undervalue the first language, a home-school language switch for young children has usually resulted in a *submersion* experience, with the children being educated entirely in the second language throughout their school career, without any instruction in the mother tongue. This situation can result in the children's gradually switching to almost exclusive use of the valued language, their second language, while retaining only sufficient aural-oral ability in their first to maintain essential contact with monolinguals in their family or community circle. The latter has been the experience of many children of immigrant groups.[28]

In some cases, submerged children may become discouraged and drop out of school early, because they do not have any expectation of success in the majority culture. The problems of these children can be alleviated by special classes where they are taught fluent use of the majority language in both oral and written form, before they are dispersed among native speakers of that language.

To make the transition to the language of the majority for school learning less painful and less damaging educationally than the common submersion experience, *transitional* bilingual programs have been introduced. The children are educated in their home language while learning enough of the majority language to be able to move into full education exclusively in that language with children who are native speakers. The transition usually takes place at fourth grade, but this may vary according to the age at which the children began their

27. For a comparison of the results of the experiments in home-school language switching conducted at the St. Lambert school (English-speaking children learning in French in an area where English is valued) and in the Culver City schools (English-speaking children learning Spanish in an area where Spanish is not highly valued), see Paulston, in Troike and Modiano 1975. Paulston also discusses the results of teaching Indian children at Chiapas, Mexico, to read first in their native Indian language and then in Spanish.

28. For a concise account of the differences between immersion and submersion programs, see Merrill Swain, "Home-School Language Switching," in J. C. Richards 1978, pp. 238–50.

bilingual education. The transition is often delayed until the children and their teachers feel they are ready educationally and emotionally for this demanding experience. In an area where immigrant families are continually arriving, transitional bilingual programs may be necessary at all levels of the elementary school and into the secondary school.

Many bilingual programs are transitional by legislative mandate. In these cases, most tax-payers are willing to support only bilingual programs in which children of minority language groups are being prepared to enter a monolingual educational program with a view to a future career in the majority language. The community as a whole has little concern for, or may even oppose the notion of, preparing bilingual or multilingual citizens. In such situations, a special effort is needed if early bilinguals are not to lose linguistic skills which could be very useful to them in their careers in later life, as well as providing a valuable resource for the community. After bilinguals have been integrated into classes with speakers of the majority language, their pride in their language and their ethnic cultural heritage may be stimulated by the provision of special *maintenance* classes in the first language in areas like music and dance, art, and literature.

A genuinely bilingual program will educate together in both languages native speakers of the two languages concerned, so that children of both groups learn each other's language and something of each other's ethnic heritage. Thus future citizens will be learning to appreciate linguistic and cultural diversity through constant contacts and friendships with those from their community who have been brought up with different values and customs as well as a different language. This *two-way bilingual education* has been implemented in some places by alternating the days on which the languages are used for instruction or by teaching different school subjects consistently in one of the languages.

In a *foreign-language situation,* the decision on the age at which a new language will be taught will again be a sociopolitical one, based largely on the needs felt or perceived by the local community. The community may wish to develop a number of fluent bilinguals to represent it in contacts with other peoples, or there may be an indisputable need to prepare the entire population to communicate, at least minimally, in another language. The language to be learned may be that of a near neighbor, an important partner in trade, a nation exerting a strong cultural or political influence on the home community, or a country to which many students must turn for educational materials or advanced training. In many cases, the choice may fall on a major language of international communication, through which the citizens of this particular country may communicate with people of many tongues. (This is usually because few people in other parts of the world are learning their language.)

The age at which language study will begin in this foreign-language situation will depend largely on the level of achievement in the foreign language that the community desires for its future citizens and the amount of time for this purpose it is willing to see drawn away from other areas of study. Where the need is perceived to be most urgent, the study of the foreign language will be begun earlier, or time will be taken for intensive study when the students are older.[29]

Where there is no pressing need for members of the community to use another language within the national society or in contact with other peoples, the learning of a foreign language may be regarded primarily as an educational experience which opens the minds of students to other ways of thinking, expressing meaning, and valuing. Yet this experience is too often perceived by administrators and community authorities as an element of educational enrichment for some rather than as a necessity. Consequently, despite the earnest endeavors of researchers in seeking to ascertain the "optimal" age for beginning the study of a new language, decisions will generally be made on financial grounds, the most money going to those programs which are viewed as urgent priorities at a particular time.

The answer to the question, When should a child begin to learn a second language? is, then, not a simple one. There are multiple answers, even within one community, as circumstances change and evolve.

FLES (FOREIGN LANGUAGE IN THE ELEMENTARY SCHOOL)

FLES flourished in the United States during the fifties and sixties, but waned with the growth of bilingual programs. At present, it survives in some districts where pride in an excellent program has maintained its funding. Most language teaching in elementary schools is now in the teaching of English as a Second Language (ESL) to help non-English speakers cope with their elementary school education, or in the languages of ethnic communities to develop literacy and balanced bilingualism for young speakers of those languages. This is not to say that the study of another language is irrelevant to elementary education, but rather that, as new pressures were exerted on the schools, other areas were perceived to have priority by school authorities at the local level. In many cases, this was due to the per-

29. For a number of different models of school language study, see *CMLR* 33, no. 2 (November 1976).

sistence of problems foreseen by leaders of the FLES movement but never resolved.

Already in 1962, the following warning was voiced in a Modern Language Association statement of policy on FLES:

> *Cautions.* A FLES program should be instituted only if: (1) it is an integral and serious part of the school day; (2) it is an integral and serious part of the total foreign-language program in the school system; (3) there is close articulation with later foreign-language learning; (4) there are available FL specialists or elementary-school teachers with an adequate command of the foreign language; (5) there is a planned syllabus and a sequence of appropriate teaching materials; (6) the program has the support of the administration; (7) the high-school teachers of the foreign language in the local school system recognize the same long-range objectives and practice some of the same teaching techniques as the FLES teachers.[30]

To this last point we may add "and are willing to take into account the early language-learning experiences of their students in designing their courses, so that the former FLES students may continue to progress, instead of being held back until high school beginners have caught up with their level of knowledge." Unfortunately, these conditions were fully met in too few cases.

The 1979 Report of the President's Commission on Foreign Language and International Studies, having examined the state of foreign-language study in the United States and analyzed national needs, urges "school systems to encourage all students to master at least one foreign language and, ideally, to acquire a second." It further advocates "that language study begin in the early grades."[31] This recommendation makes it imperative for teachers to reflect on the FLES experience. School districts considering the introduction or reinstitution of full FLES programs, either in response to the recommendations of the President's Commission on Foreign Language and International Studies or because of pressing local circumstances, need not repeat the mistakes of the past.

30. *Second Statement of Policy on Foreign Languages in the Elementary School* (New York: Modern Language Association, 1962).

31. *Strength through Wisdom: A Critique of U.S. Capability.* A Report to the President from the President's Commission on Foreign Language and International Studies (Washington, D.C.: U.S. Government Printing Office, 1979), p. 29.

And What Else?

Why a FLES Program?

Elementary school foreign-language programs are often begun with no clear aims. "Learning a language is very good for children" is not convincing as a rationale and sets no goals for the program. If the endeavor is to succeed, teachers, administrators and parents must be convinced of the genuine educational worth of some experience with other ways of thinking and expressing oneself. They must be made aware that an understanding of the nature of language and the ways various languages operate to convey meaning can have a beneficial effect on the development and use of the students' native language. The FLES program should be so designed and implemented that the children do in fact achieve this new knowledge. This will depend on the way the language is taught, the types of materials used and the way in which the new knowledge is taken up and integrated with other learning activities of the elementary school day.

Where a fully developed program for the learning of one language is not feasible or desired, two other possibilities should be given careful consideration: an exploratory language course at an appropriate level, or the integration of some language study with a multicultural or a global education course.

Exploratory language courses, which may be for six weeks, or one or two semesters, provide an introduction to one language or to several languages through materials appropriate for the grade level (first grade, fourth grade, sixth grade, or whichever). Students learn how to pronounce the language; how to understand and produce greetings, commands, requests, and simple declarative statements; how to sing songs and play games in the language; how the language is written (if this is appropriate for the level); and how to perform simple everyday tasks commonly performed by people of that culture. The emphasis is not on the amount of language learned, which is admittedly limited, but rather on developing favorable attitudes toward language learning (whether of the native language or another language), consciousness of aspects of language use, and appreciation of cultural differences—all of which are important elementary learnings.

Multicultural and global education are growing areas in the elementary school program. Children need to learn to live with others who speak and act differently. They also need to have their minds opened to the concept of one world, in which all must cooperate to solve planetary problems and improve the quality of life for themselves and for many, very different others. Programs of this type can be enriched and given a concrete reality when they include a language component through which children can act out what it feels like to be one of these others.[32]

Which languages should be selected?
In areas of strong ethnic identification, or where two communities of different languages are living in close contact, the languages which children hear around them and which are spoken by some of their classmates, or by their parents and grandparents, will be the obvious choices. Where no such local imperatives exist, one of the major languages of international communication will be a good choice. These are most probably the languages the children will have a chance to study later, at high school or college level. They will also find them useful as an adjunct skill for future careers.

A strong case can also be made at this exploratory stage for a language very different from the child's native language. Distinctive differences help develop the child's ability to listen and observe (especially where very different sounds and a new script are involved). Through a language from a very dissimilar culture, children also become more aware of the many possibilities of expression that languages offer and the diverse ways people who speak different languages view the common reality of our world.

To whom should the foreign language be taught?
Since the aims of a foreign language program at this level are limited, and since elementary education should provide opportunities for children to explore all kinds of areas and modes of learning, all children should have the opportunity to experience what it is like to use another form of linguistic expression. Mimicry, acting out, practicing ways of expressing needs and ideas, singing songs with repetitive refrains, playing games, dancing, and imitating different ways of behaving in real-life situations are activities that can be enjoyed by all kinds of children, and none should feel left out. The language-learning experience, with its opportunities for developing an attitude of openness toward difference, should be a part of every child's education.

By whom should the foreign language be taught?
The most important qualifications for the FLES teacher are a love for young children and an understanding of the most appropriate ways to arouse their interest and assist their learning. Such a person, with a certain competence in the language to be taught, some training in

32. See Lorraine A. Strasheim, "An Issue on the Horizon: The Role of Foreign Languages in Global Education," *FLA* 12 (1979): 29–34; and Wilga M. Rivers, in NEC 1979, pp. 29–31.

language-teaching methods appropriate for children of this age, and the support of well-designed aural and visual materials, can create the type of learning situation which will make children want to learn more of the language, even after an interval of several years. A foreign-language specialist with no understanding of or interest in elementary school children can soon kill any incipient enthusiasm by boring or intimidating them. A native speaker from the community with elementary school training, and a willingness to learn how to teach the language to speakers of another language, is sometimes available. Other native speakers who love children may be willing to be trained as paraprofessionals to help the FLES teacher.

High school student volunteers who love the language and have achieved a high level of mastery of the elementary material will sometimes give their time to teach younger children, usually under the direction of an experienced elementary school teacher, a sympathetic and involved high school teacher, or a district supervisor or coordinator. (Many such volunteers discover that they love to teach and go on to train as teachers at college.)[33]

How should a FLES program be started?

Like any educational innovation, a FLES program should be preceded by a public awareness campaign in the local district. Through the media, meetings, and preliminary language experiences among the children, interested teachers will work to win the interest and support of parents, community, administrators, and teachers of other subjects. Where parents are opposed, the children will become discouraged; where the administration is unsympathetic, many details of scheduling and provision of materials and equipment will be difficult; the hostility or even the indifference of other teachers will dampen the children's enthusiasm; community apathy or opposition will cause funding problems.

Before the program is established, there should be much discussion of plans, visits to neighboring systems where successful programs are in operation, careful development of proposals appropriate to the local situation, training of all who will be associated with the project, and discriminating selection or development of materials to achieve the aims of the program. In all such planning, a district supervisor or coordinator can be invaluable. All the resources of the community should be tapped, so that the community will feel responsible for the success of the venture.

33. See Mary L. Williford, "The Answer: High School Foreign Languages Tutoring Program," *FLA* 12 (1979): 213–14 and 248 (FL Notes: "High School Students Teach FLES").

And afterwards?

Any educational innovation should be carefully evaluated to see whether the aims of the program are being achieved, and are being achieved in the most efficient way. Student learning (whether linguistic, cultural, or attitudinal) will be assessed in some form appropriate to the age and the type of educational experience being provided. If the goals of the program are limited, then the evaluation will be appropriate to the voluntarily accepted limitations of the program.

The *evaluation* may take the form of a round table discussion of the evaluative material among teachers, parents, administrators, local coordinators, and school board members so that all points of view are represented. The evaluation should lead to action. Changes in objectives, ways of improving the program, the level at which the program is to be introduced, types of materials and activities to be included, appropriate in-service training for language teachers and other teachers with whose work the language program interrelates— all of these should be regularly and openly considered if the program is to continue to be productive.

If the program is regarded as a continuing language-learning one, as part of a long sequence of study rather than an exploratory experience, attention must be paid to *articulation* between levels. The elementary school teachers must maintain regular contact with the junior and senior high school teachers to ensure that there will be a continuing program for those coming up from the FLES classes: a program for which materials will be selected so that they build on what has been learned at lower levels. Where the secondary program is too small to allow for special classes for the FLES students, the high school teacher must be prepared to divide classes into groups to ensure this kind of continuity. Nothing is more frustrating to enthusiastic young language learners than to find the hard-won knowledge of which they are so proud completely ignored or even denigrated.

Where elementary language-learners select another language on making the transition to junior or senior high school level, the teacher in whose class they find themselves should be aware of the fact that they have had previous experience with another language and be ready to capitalize on this fact in approach and speed of presentation. High school teachers should be aware of the methods and materials which have been used in the elementary schools in their district and not expect their students to switch without preparation to a completely different type of learning. Sympathetic and appreciative interest in each other's work on the part of both elementary and secondary level teachers will make for happier and more effective language learning by students on both sides of the gap.

ELL (Early Language Learning)

Perhaps a new term is needed to combat the image of obsolescence some associate with the FLES movement of the sixties. The term *Early Language Learning* (ELL) is being used more and more frequently to cover all forms of language learning by pre-teens: bilingual education, second-language instruction, foreign-language learning, exploratory language courses, and interdisciplinary language-learning activities. As a term, it also leaves the door open for a useful collaboration with teachers of the native language. Language arts teachers have much to contribute to ELL teachers, and their cooperation is essential if the learning of a new language is to be integrated with other language and culture related activities in the elementary school program.[34] Nor should the value of Latin in developing language consciousness be overlooked. A new and broader designation also frees this generation of ELL teachers from too close an identification with doctrines and methods of the earlier FLES movement that may not be as appropriate in the teaching atmosphere of the next decade.

Ethnic awareness and an increasing realization on the part of parents that their children's early learning years should provide them with opportunities to explore even those areas of learning which have sometimes been considered "difficult" are raising questions about the basic content of the elementary school curriculum. Future teachers should be prepared to meet any local demand with a reasoned and cooperative view of the value to all students of any form of language learning which develops understanding of communication by any symbol system, verbal or nonverbal, and opens minds to the diversity of human expression.

Vocabulary Learning

It would be impossible to learn a language without vocabulary—without words. One could learn about a language through some symbol system which would demonstrate relations and how they are realized, but this would be like examining the skeletal remains of a dinosaur and believing that one had actually encountered the creature. Language is not dry bones. It is a living, growing entity, clothed in the flesh of words.

Vocabulary has been considered at various points throughout this book. It has not been discussed fully, as a separate topic, within any

34. See Virginia Garibaldi Allen, "Foreign Languages in the Elementary School: A New Look; A New Focus," *Language Arts* 55 (1978): 146–49.

of the preceding chapters, because it pervades them all. Yet it does deserve detailed consideration as that aspect of language learning and use which continues to develop and evolve for as long as one has contact with a language—whether it be one's first, second, or third language.

Vocabulary cannot be taught. It can be presented, explained, included in all kinds of activities, but it must be learned by the individual. The vocabulary we understand and the vocabulary we can use varies in nature and in quantity from one person to another even in our native language. As language teachers, we must arouse interest in words and a certain excitement in personal development in this area (that is, motivation to learn ways of expressing meanings that are important to the individual student, even if not to others in the group). We can help our students by giving them ideas on how to learn vocabulary and some guidance on what to learn.

Part of the value of learning another language lies in learning about language: how language works and its function in relations between individuals and within the life of a community. Students need to learn that words do not label things but classify concepts. They enable a linguistic group to organize the ways they perceive concrete objects or distinguish abstract values, how they express the emotions they feel, or their ideas about the seen, the unseen, that which exists, that which no longer exists, the possible, or what may be imagined.

When we are learning our first language, we are developing concepts while we are learning the ways our language community expresses these concepts. We may later use the language in innovative ways to bring new concepts to our fellows. When we approach another language, we begin to understand and appreciate this role of language. We already possess many concepts and we seek ways of expressing them in the new language. Since language is embedded in a way of life and thought, a culture, we frequently find it is not easy to express these concepts in the new language; yet the language seems to lend itself with ease to the expression of concepts which are new to us, or are expansions or reductions of concepts with which we are familiar. To learn another language effectively, the learner must come to the realization that, except in a restricted number of cases, a word in a second language is rarely precisely equivalent in meaning to a word in the first language. Precise equivalences are quite limited. Even with a simple concrete word like a *stone,* each language may have different boundaries to the meaning the word expresses (when does a *stone* become a *pebble,* for instance, and when is it a *boulder?* When does a *cup* become a *mug?* Must a *cup* have a handle and only one handle? Is it always used for drinking? Is it a prized object?)

Not only may boundaries of meaning for apparently comparable words differ in ways which are difficult to define, but an apparently equivalent word may cover a much larger or a much smaller area of meaning in one language than in the other. This is the case, for instance, with French *prendre* and English *take*. *Take* can refer to the action of picking something up, but it can also signify transportation through space (among other things), whereas this meaning requires the use of a word other than *prendre* in French. Similarly, *prendre* has other meanings which cannot be rendered by *take* in English.

To add to the confusion, apparently equivalent words in two languages may "mean the same thing" but not be used in the same circumstances: in one language the word may be used only in very formal situations, in the other the parallel word may be acceptable only in the most informal situations or in moments of exasperation. In other words, there may be sociolinguistic rules governing word choice. Customary metaphoric extensions of the meaning of words also vary considerably across languages, as well as the emotional associations that the words bring with them (that is, connotation as opposed to denotation). Experiencing these differences will make students much more conscious of precise meanings in their own language. They should be encouraged to expand and refine their native language vocabulary as they explore that of another language.

- **Discuss examples from the language you will teach of distributions of meaning which differ from apparently comparable meanings in English.**

Learning How to Learn Vocabulary

1. Students need to learn *how to commit vocabulary to long-term memory.* This does not necessarily mean "memorizing," although some students may find this activity suits their learning style. First, we must arouse a desire to store and remember by constantly reentering vocabulary in class work and by providing activities (discussions, competitions, or games) through which students can demonstrate what they know and learn from each other. They must have many opportunities to associate within semantic fields what they have just encountered and what they already know, so that they can build up facilitative semantic networks within their cognitive system.[35]

Storage is one process, retrieval is another. Constant use of what has been stored makes it much more available for retrieval when appropriate situations arise for its use. Research has shown that the

35. For a discussion of semantic or conceptual networks, see Wilga M. Rivers and Bernice Melvin, "If Only I Could Remember it All! Facts and Fiction about Memory in Language Learning," in Burt, Dulay, and Finocchiaro 1977, pp. 162–71.

more modalities are involved in associations, the more readily items will become available in varying situations. Items should therefore be presented in association with visual representations (pictures, objects), aurally, and in association with activity of all kinds.

2. Students must learn to *discriminate variations in distribution and new boundaries* of meaning. Assimilation of these new facets of meaning is facilitated by awareness of the problem. The teacher may give explanations of contrast with native-language distribution, demonstrate schematically the distribution of meaning of apparently comparable words, or promote activity which requires for success that these boundaries be respected. (A student may learn the differences between *prendre* and *take,* for instance, by picking up an object and carrying it away, describing the action at the same time as it is being performed.) Much knowledge of this type will be acquired if questions asked require precise interpretation of what has been heard or read. (Such precision should not always be required in listening and reading, as chapters 6 and 9 have shown. The differences between extensive and intensive reading should be respected, and the same distinction applies to listening.)

3. Students do not always realize that words are constructed of *morphemes which share the burden of the meaning* among them. Many have not realized that this is so in their own language. Very early, students should learn to detect morphemes which recur in a number of words and which can help them to identify at least part of the meaning, thus assisting them in guessing from context the meaning of apparently new items (e.g., *in*/imit/*able; in*/apt; predict/*able; apt*itude). Exercises in "topping and tailing" (that is, dividing off prefixes and suffixes) as an aid to discovering the meanings of apparently unknown words can be interesting and profitable.

Once they have become adept at distinguishing elements of meaning within a word, students should be encouraged to watch for patterns in word formation (e.g., in compound words like *bottle opener, can opener, meat cutter, house painter, baby sitter*). As they become aware of the fact that the language is still developing and that these mechanisms for combining meanings are still at work in the creation of new words, they may be given exercises in *creating new words* themselves (e.g., *glass shatterer*). These may not always be terms in actual use, but they will be comprehensible to a native speaker because they are possible words of the language constructed according to the lexical rules by which it operates. This will also help the language learner to comprehend when a native speaker engages in word creation (e.g., "Where is that nail remover?" or "The sand was all gluggy").

Sensitivity to word formation will assist language learners in extracting meaning by making them conscious of the parts of speech to which words belong (e.g., commun*ism*, social*ism*, and capital*ism* are nouns; while social*ize*, civil*ize*, and merchand*ize* are verbs).

4. Students should learn *to penetrate disguises*. With languages of the same family or from areas where there has been considerable interaction, there are many borrowed words and cognates. Ability to penetrate the disguises these words have adopted in becoming assimilated within another language can often double or triple the vocabulary available to the student. Even in unrelated languages there is now an assimilated international vocabulary of considerable size and importance, particularly in contemporary areas of development and activity. (*Pollution, nuclear, hydrogen, jazz, jeans,* and *football,* for instance, can now be found, often thinly disguised, in most languages.) Not only should students learn to detect words like these that they already know, but also how to pronounce them according to the phonological rules of the new language. If they know these rules of assimilation, they can often meet their needs in communication by transforming words for currently important concepts into forms which a speaker of the other language will recognize in spoken or written form. They will also find that they themselves can now recognize many apparently new words in newspapers, in broadcasts, or in general conversation.

5. Students must learn *how to discover new words* for themselves. Practice in the use of dictionaries (unilingual and bilingual), thesauruses, and encyclopaedias should be a regular part of the language course. Search exercises can be developed which are amusing and informative. Since vocabulary expansion will be a continuing, individual activity for as long as the students remain interested in or need the language, we must see that they know how to use all the tools available to them.

This does not mean that students will be encouraged to open a dictionary as soon as they encounter a word of which the meaning is not clear. Part of their training from the very early stages will be in deducing the meaning of unfamiliar words from the context in which they are embedded. This is a normal process in augmenting native-language vocabulary. They will, however, need to know how to use dictionaries to find precise terms to express their own meaning and to check on that elusive word that even context cannot elucidate. For recognition purposes, context remains the best guide. For production, assistance may need to be sought elsewhere.

6. If students are not to become discouraged, they need to learn that *vocabulary is elastic* and that they can make much of the

little they know by paraphrase, circumlocution, and definition, as they gradually build up a more precise and varied lexicon. They should not, however, be permitted to settle down with a "getting by" attitude, but should be stimulated by all kinds of activities to develop greater expressiveness through the use of more and more carefully selected words and phrases.

7. Students must learn how to *augment their own vocabulary* steadily and systematically. They should begin early to keep individual lists of new words they encounter, words that interest them, and problem words which are continually tripping them up. These words should be written down in a short context as an aid to memory and also as a guide to use. If words are written down each time they are met but not recognized, the list will provide a kind of frequency indicator as well. Constant rereading of the list, with immediate efforts to use the words in some appropriate way, either in communication with others or in internal dialogue, will help to impress these words upon the mind and facilitate storage.

Students should seek opportunities to hear and use the language *outside of the class context.* Much hearing, reading, and using of the language in informal settings, where the student's concern is not with grading but with the giving and receiving of messages, will increase familiarity with many commonly used words and phrases, increasing the probability of long-term retention and of rapid retrieval when the need arises.

What Vocabulary Should the Student Learn?

What vocabulary to learn is a very difficult question. The obvious answer is: the words most frequently used in the language. Many efforts have been made to establish frequency counts of the words of various languages. Deciding which "words" to count is, of itself, a thorny problem. Are homonyms counted separately for each distinct meaning? Are words in idiomatic groups like "in order to" counted independently, or does the idiom count as one "word"? Are *be, is, are, was* considered separate words, or is one form of the verb selected for listing? In what types of discourse should the words be counted—spoken, written, formal, informal, technical, general interest, poetry, prose? Or should there perhaps be separate counts for each of these?

Many words for common objects and actions are not frequently heard or read but are readily available[36] to the native speaker when

36. Gougenheim uses the term *disponible* for "available" vocabulary in G. Gougenheim, P. Rivenc, et al., *L'Elaboration du français fondamental. Ier degré* (Paris:

needed; these words may not have a very high ranking in a frequency word-list. Sometimes a frequency count will not yield all the items in an indispensable series (e.g., days of the week, months, numbers, colors); nevertheless, these must all be acquired by a person learning the language. The corpus from which the frequencies are calculated sometimes distorts the ranking. *Microphone,* for instance, may appear frequently in a recorded corpus. In a written corpus one segment, selected as typical of scientific discourse, may center on the role of *corpuscles* in the *blood;* had another extract been selected, *planet* or *satellite* might have achieved unexpectedly high ratings instead. Words like these will reappear in a limited number of scientific works, whereas *experiment* and *theory* are more likely to be encountered in a wide variety of scientific books and articles. This question of range of occurrence must also be kept in mind. Many considerations like these make frequency counts a difficult and often unsatisfactory undertaking.

When these basic questions have been considered and the count has been completed, the first hundred most frequent words are, for the most part, found to be function words (like *to, at, for, from, when, why*), which certainly must be learned, and learned early, by the student of a new language. However, no useful information can be conveyed without content words (like *table, tomorrow, indispensable,* or *rapidly*). Which content words the student will need (after learning such frequent general-purpose words as *come, take, slow, before,* or *food*) depends on the type of situation in which the student will need to use the language. Will it be for reading technical material in a specific field, for listening to weather reports, or for chatting with a neighbor on inconsequential incidents of everyday living? Specific future needs cannot be predicted for most learners of a language, especially while they are still in school. (Where specific needs are known, there is less of a problem, although the problem still exists— there may be a basic Spanish vocabulary which is useful for American firemen, but all the situations which will arise cannot be predicted.)

Teachers and textbook writers usually try to provide in the early stages a general vocabulary of words in common use for everyday interaction. This vocabulary then acts as a vehicle for the practice of structural patterns and for conveying realistic messages in the situation in which the students find themselves. At later stages, the emphasis will be on learning to learn vocabulary, so that the students may retain from listening and reading material and classroom com-

Didier, 1964), p. 146. This book describes the method used for establishing the frequency lists of *Le Français fondamental.*

munication what seems most relevant and interesting to them as individual learners. Much of this vocabulary will be for recognition, in aural or graphic form. Practice in using the language actively in real situations will make clear how much of it is needed for the production of one's own messages.

Vocabulary Learning Must Be Active

The learning of vocabulary should rarely be a separate activity, except perhaps at the advanced level when it is being acquired for a specialized use. Even then, vocabulary will be more readily available for retrieval if it has been used in some meaningful activity: writing business letters, reading and making notes on scientific reports, drafting job descriptions, or whatever is appropriate for the course.

Vocabulary learning should always be *in a purposeful context.* Students should be involved in an activity which requires them to retrieve from their long-term memory store vocabulary which is appropriate in the circumstances. This requirement is basic to the popular "warmup" at the beginning of a lesson, when students discuss what they have been doing, current affairs, contemporary problems, or a picture (depending on the level). This introductory activity is free-wheeling and wide-ranging, providing the opportunity for students to draw on anything and everything they have at their disposal. As they become more experienced with the language, more sophisticated expressions will be employed, along with those common basic words which continually recur in speech or written texts.

Vocabulary-centered activities

There are many ways of playing with words which make new vocabulary salient and keep the students' attention concentrated on both meaning and appropriate use. Some approaches are suggested below; many others can be invented, or borrowed from leisure-time magazines or radio and television programs. Some of these are suitable for the elementary level; others for more advanced levels.

1. *Similarity and contrast.* Appropriate here are games and competitions involving synonyms and antonyms, contradictory and implausible statements, or subtle impossibilities (Have you ever seen a walking statue? an invisible cloud?) These can become chaining activities and serve as retrieval mechanisms in a relaxing moment.

2. *Whole to the part, part to the whole.* This may require a rapid-fire response to a cue—house: window; office: typewriter; watch: hand. It may be an alternating chain—arm—hand—clock—chime—

carillon—bells—school, and so on. Written lists may be supplied to be completed by the students.

3. *Object—function* or *Agent—function.* As each object is proposed, a function is suggested. These are useful at various levels, e.g., cake: for eating; brick: for building; lawsuit: for prosecution; carpenter: mends chairs; broker: sells shares.

4. *Person and an associated stereotypic object.* Churchill: cigar; king: crown; teacher: chalk.

5. *Descriptions.* Guessing games can be developed to evoke more precise vocabulary: What sings, has wings, is green?

6. *Collectibles.* Weekly tasks may be set, such as collecting words beginning with a certain prefix, having a certain root, or derived from colors or numbers; or collecting names of places with a clearly identifiable meaning (e.g., One Tree Hill, Black Snake Creek).

7. *Stories based on a sequence of randomly selected words* (e.g., feather, open, factory, laughter, pursue, obnoxious, silently . . .). Students may be required to develop the story using the words in the order given or alternatively in any order. This activity may be oral or written, group or individual. Trying to include a word in the sequence of the story makes students concentrate on its meaning and appropriate use.

8. *Cloze passages with multiple-choice proposals* for the blanks provide opportunities for careful consideration of the most appropriate word in a context. Reasons for the choices should then be discussed as a group activity.

9. *Malapropisms.* Students are given sentences with malapropisms (e.g., *extraneous* for *extenuating*); they rewrite these, inserting the correct word.

10. *Word puzzles.* Crosswords, acrostics, and scrabble are useful for concentrating attention on retrieval of previously encountered words.

- **Add to these types of activities others which would provide students with opportunities to play with words and retrieve less frequently used items. At what level would the activity you propose be used?**

LANGUAGES FOR SPECIAL (SPECIFIC) PURPOSES (LSP)

The purposes for which students are learning a particular language are paramount, and determine the approach to teaching and materials. This was stressed in chapter 1 (pp. 11–12). It is in the area of Languages for Special Purposes[37] that this process is most consciously

37. Strevens uses also the acronym *SP-LT* (Special-Purpose Language Teaching).

applied. Throughout the world, LSP is growing in importance. Studies are made of the contexts in which a specific language is used by scientists, technologists, social workers, agricultural advisers in developing countries, policemen, foremen, immigration officers, students studying abroad, migrant workers venturing beyond the boundaries of their own country, and so on. Strevens (in Kinsella 1978, p. 192) attributes the recent expansion of LSP courses to the "global trend towards 'learner-centered education,' " with its emphasis on learners' needs and interests. It may also be seen as a product of the rapid technological and societal changes and the increased mobility of populations which are features of our age. A further influence is the developing tendency for taxpayers in many countries to demand a reconsideration of programs of education at all levels in the light of current national needs and career possibilities.

In the teaching of foreign languages, LSP courses have been in operation for many years. They have been closely linked with the reading of material in specialized fields, as in German and Russian courses for science students and required language courses for doctoral candidates in the United States (usually in French and German). Courses in ESP (English for Specific Purposes) are in great demand in countries anxious to familiarize numbers of their students with the latest developments in their fields of study in the English-speaking world, and in other language areas whose research reports are rapidly translated into English. Teachers of English as a second or foreign language should be familiar with the many acronyms in use in ESP, and teachers of other languages will learn much from the analysis of needs that these imply.

EST (English for Science and Technology) has come to the fore because English is considered the major international language in these areas. Mackay and Mountford (1978, p. 6) quote from a 1957 UNESCO report that nearly two-thirds of engineering literature appeared in English at that date. Scientists and technologists from many countries, whose languages are not learned and used on an international level, routinely report their work in English. The findings of others become available in English, soon after their publication, through translating and abstracting services. Consequently, EST textbooks are pouring from the presses to supply English-language needs of economists, soil scientists, zoologists, mathematicians, computer experts, sociologists, and others.[38] These incorporate the results of research into the characteristics of style and the development of ideas

---

38. Books with readings in many areas are also available for French and German.

and arguments in scientific discourse.[39] In addition, more and more bilingual and multilingual dictionaries are appearing each year to meet the need for precise terminological equivalents in specialized fields. EST, the oldest subsection of ESP, has come of age.

EEP (English for Educational Purposes), for which Robinson (1980, p. 7) proposes EAP (English for Academic Purposes), prepares students to study other subjects in English as an Auxiliary Language (EAL),[40] or to undertake specialized courses in English-speaking universities. EAP goes beyond language study to training in study skills: listening to lectures and taking notes on these and on reading in the field; writing reports and papers (and learning the bibliographic conventions these require); answering questions on specialized material orally; taking part in group discussions; maintaining a point of view; interpreting graphs, diagrams, and tables, and so on.

EOP (English for Occupational Purposes) applies less to the requirements of highly educated professionals and more to the everyday needs of working people. This area, as LOP (Languages for Occupational Purposes), is important for languages other than English (e.g., German, French, Swedish, Dutch, or Arabic), since our epoch is witnessing a substantial migration of workers from less industrialized countries to areas of high production.[41] These workers need to be able to understand spoken and written instructions and to communicate in work situations with foremen and fellow workers. Telephonists must be able to understand various languages and give specific information in these tongues; nurses and operators of medical equipment also need to communicate in restricted but specialized ways with patients who speak other languages. The list of occupations in which some knowledge of another language for specialized pur-

39. See, for instance, Larry Selinker, Louis Trimble, and Robert Vroman, *Working Papers in English for Science and Technology* (University of Washington: Department of Humanistic-Social Studies, College of Engineering, 1972); John E. Lackstrom, "The Reading Comprehension of Elliptical Arguments in EST (English for Science and Technology) Textbooks," in Nickel 1976, vol. 1, pp. 225–35; Strevens 1977, p. 93; and Strevens, in Kinsella 1978, p. 194; John E. Lackstrom, Larry Selinker, and Louis P. Trimble, "Grammar and Technical English," in Lugton (1970), pp. 101–33; J. R. Ewer and G. Latorre, *A Course in Basic Scientific English* (London: Longman, 1969); and Trimble et al. 1978.

40. Certain countries where a number of major languages are spoken and where, for political reasons, none of these may be declared the national language still have English-medium schools where students of the various languages study, on a basis of equality, in English. English is then an auxiliary language (EAL). EIL (English as an International Language) recognizes the existence of varieties of English (Indian English, Jamaican English, Singapore English) which may be taught in such situations.

41. See *ELA*, no. 30 (1978): *Des Migrants confrontés au français;* and Coste et al. 1976.

poses is useful, even essential, is seemingly endless. We have already discussed the Council of Europe approach to occupational needs (see p. 234). Like many others, the Council of Europe experts believe that a basic course in the language (a threshold level) is essential before language learners concentrate on more specialized expressions related to their tasks. This permits of more flexibility in an actual communication situation. The curriculum guide of the New York State Education Department, *Modern Languages for Everyone* (Albany, N.Y., 1978), also proposes a basic course before making available a series of special interest courses, such as French for Travelers, German for Auto Mechanics, Spanish for Community Service, and so on. Most occupationally oriented courses lay primary stress on oral communication, which requires ability to produce utterances as well as to understand them. In this way, EOP/LOP courses differ from those for EST/LST (Languages for Science and Technology).

With the development of LOP, teachers have gone beyond the traditional reading approach of LST.[42] Students and teachers alike are realizing the need for LSP courses directed to the development of a high level of listening comprehension and comprehensible oral production; not only for work situations in factories and on farms, but also for the conduct of international business or communication with international agencies; for journalism; for the travel industry; for collaboration in research with colleagues in the same field, and for many other activities. The oral survival courses discussed in chapter 8 (p. 242) are, in this sense, LSP courses. For certain tasks, writing too may be of prime importance, especially in countries where a second language is a lingua franca, or a parallel national language in which forms, reports, newspapers, and textbooks must be written.

LSP courses are not developed by merely adding some specialized vocabulary to a general-purpose course—for instance, by having students learn a dialogue about repairing a carburetor, instead of preparing for a trip to Chicago. The precise requirements of the situation in which the students will find themselves need to be analyzed. Will they need to understand spoken or written language, or both? Will the language they must understand be very restricted in range (as with factory workers on an assembly line)? Will the communication channel be noisy (as for air controllers)? Will they need to understand but not speak or write the language (as with persons monitoring broadcasts or extracting items from newspapers on a specific topic)? Will they need to understand specialized material in a foreign language in

---

42. Techniques for LST reading courses are discussed in detail in "Reading for Information," in chap. 8 of the *PG*'s.

order to explain it to others in their native language (in which case translation becomes important)? Will they need to read in the language at all? Once questions of this type have been answered, the approach to the course can be selected. A further analysis of the language items and structures which will most frequently be encountered in the specific work context, or in specialized reading, will precede the writing, or selection, of learning materials. (Much research, for instance, is now being conducted into the nature of discourse in well-defined situations, e.g., between doctor and patient, between foreman and assembly-line worker, or between shopper and supermarket cashier.) What is required for LSP is not the learning of a special language, but the learning of "a restricted repertoire of words and expressions selected from the whole language because that restricted repertoire covers every requirement within a well-defined context, task or vocation. . . . What we have is the same language employed for similar and different uses employing similar and different usages" (Mackay and Mountford 1978, pp. 4–5). Hartley summarizes the requirements for LSP materials as "the linguistic core, the special register, and a list of priorities for the introduction of the most frequently used grammatical structures" (Hartley, in Perren 1969, pp. 26–27).

The need for LSP in second language and bilingual situations, even at the ELL stage, needs to be stressed. Children must be prepared, not only for everyday communication in the language, but also for integration into an ongoing school program in that language. This means acquaintance with the concepts and terminology their future classmates will have acquired in their earlier classes, as well as facility in performing arithmetic operations in the second language, and familiarity with mathematical formulas, grammatical categories (where these are prominent in the program), classroom and textbook instructions, testing procedures, and content area skills (like the ability to express ideas in writing and observe the accepted conventions; to interpret diagrams, and to seek information in encyclopedias and dictionaries).

Robinson points out that the true LSP course "will have only one student in it, since each individual student has different needs and purposes which an [LSP] course should aim to satisfy" (Robinson 1980, p. 12). This diversity of interests has been one of the major problems in LSP classes. Small group work within a larger class (mathematicians with mathematicians, and social scientists with social scientists) can alleviate the situation; but even broad groupings, like scientists, engineers, or humanists, are unsatisfactory, since chemists have little in common with botanists, and nuclear engineers are not interested in dams and bridges. The teacher will attempt to gather together a class of students of reasonably similar interests (a group with reading as a priority should be separate from one with aural-oral priorities, for instance) and then break down the large group into smaller special-interest groups. Where this is still unsatisfactory, the teacher must resort to individual assignments, giving students individual guidance and evaluation.[43]

Finally, the burning question remains: Who should teach the LSP course? The conventionally prepared language teacher is usually inappropriate for the task, without reorientation and supplementary training. LSP requires not only skill in language teaching, and especially in preparing language-learning materials, but also some knowledge of the demands of the specialized field or occupation. For this, close cooperation with a specialist or practitioner in the area is most desirable. Fortunately, with adult learners, the students themselves know the area better than the language teacher, and this real-world knowledge helps them to interpret what they are reading or hearing (see p. 163). They themselves will bring to the attention of the teacher what they need to express. The intelligent teacher draws freely on this knowledge to clarify difficulties and direct productive language use into relevant channels. Where it is desirable to make LSP a significant segment of the language-teaching operation, a retraining program in association with an expert in the field is indispensable.

- **Which type of LSP program is most appropriate for your teaching situation? How would you go about researching this question?**

THE TEXTBOOK

The importance of the textbook cannot be overestimated. It will inevitably determine the major part of the classroom teaching and the students' out-of-class learning. In its preparation, decisions have already been made about what the students will learn, how they will learn it, and what sections of the work will receive most emphasis. Naturally, concerned teachers will adapt the material in the textbook, supplement it in many ways, and add emphases of their own. They will not work their way through the textbook from beginning to end, making students study every section consecutively and do every exercise. Nevertheless, their work will be greatly facilitated if they are using a textbook which reflects their objectives and their preferred approach for achieving these objectives.

Inexperienced teachers need to be particularly careful in selecting

43. For individualized instruction, see Annotated Reading List to chapter 4 above.

a textbook. From a well-constructed textbook, they will learn much about presentation of material and areas where students will have problems. They will find the work of conducting an interesting and effective class considerably hampered if they select a poorly constructed book, no matter how well it may be printed and illustrated. It is essential for teachers to know for what qualities they should look before a textbook is adopted for class use.

When a textbook is being selected, the following major areas should be evaluated in relation to the local situation.

A. *Appropriateness for local situation*
   Purposes of the course in relation to content of textbook; age and abilities of students; length and intensity of course.
B. *Appropriateness for teacher and students*
   Method and techniques; supplementary aids; teacher's manual and students' workbook; convenience.
C. *Language and Ideational Content*
D. *Linguistic coverage and organization*
   Selection of linguistic material. Unit design, treatment of specific topics (grammatical, phonological, lexical)
E. *Types of activities*
F. *Practical Considerations*
   Physical features; price; availability
G. *Enjoyment index* (for students and teachers)
Note: *Major advantages*
      Major disadvantages

In the checklist which follows, significant questions are raised within each of these areas. After consideration of these specific aspects of the book and its contents, a broad-based evaluation may be made on a five-point scale as outlined below. Textbooks may then be compared, category by category, and an overall rating established for each. Teachers will weight those areas which are particularly important to them in their situation. For instance, in some situations, areas A and F may be of major importance; in others, where the course is of a general nature, teachers may feel that areas B and E will make a great difference to the success of the class. Some will feel that D is a very important consideration. Where a committee is deciding on the adoption of a textbook, the broad-based evaluation chart will make comparison of individual recommendations much more feasible. (If weighted points are added together for an overall rating when using this chart, the lowest will indicate the most desirable book.)

Chart for Broad-based Evaluation

Categories	1) Excellent for my purposes	2) Suitable	3) Will do	4) Not very suitable	5) Useless for my purposes
A) Local situation					
B) Teacher/student needs					
C) Language and Ideational Content					
D) Linguistic Coverage and Organization					
E) Activities					
F) Practical Considerations					
G) Enjoyment Index					

Note: Major advantages—

Major disadvantages—

Detailed Checklist for Textbook Evaluation

A. *Appropriateness for local situation*
1. What *objectives* did the writer have in mind? (See preface or foreword of book.) Are these the objectives of your course? (e.g., four skills? listening and speaking as primary goals? general reading? specialized reading?)
2. For what *level of study* was the book designed? (Look very carefully at a book which claims to be usable at several levels, e.g., junior high school and senior high school; senior high school and undergraduate level.)

3. For what *kind of course* is the book intended? (a. three hours per week, five hours per week, intensive? b. teacher taught? individualized? student study followed by class activity?)

4. *Pace of material.* Having studied the material in the book carefully, do you think it moves too fast or too slowly or just right for the class you have in mind? Would it require a great deal of supplementing? Would you have to leave out a lot of material to complete the course in the time you have available? Could the extra material be used for enrichment for the faster learners, or is it too repetitive? Would it provide extra practice for the slower learners? Is there so much material that the teacher would feel smothered or pressured?

5. Is material supplied for students of differing abilities?

6. Is the material of a kind that would *interest* students at the level and of the age you have in mind? (Is it too juvenile? Is it too dull? Does it make too obvious an effort to amuse? Is the material dated?)

B. *Appropriateness for teacher and student*

7. On what *method* is the book based? Is the method appropriate for your purposes? Is the method carried through well in the unit design? If you intend to present *new* work in oral form first, does the book make provision for this?

8. How much is the *native language* used in the exercises (or in other sections of the book)? Could the target language have been used instead?

9. Are *tapes or cassettes, films, slides, filmstrips, transparencies, large pictures, or flashcards* available with the book? If so, are they well constructed for teaching purposes or individual student learning? Is the technical quality acceptable? (See checklist for tapes in chapter 13 and guidelines for evaluation of pictorial aids in chapter 7.) Are they well integrated with lesson material in the book? Are the pictures useful for discussion? Do you pay extra for these? If so, are they reasonably priced? If not, can the book be used successfully without them?

10. Are *supplementary readers* available with this book? Are these satisfactory for the level of your class? Are they of a level of difficulty which can be easily read by students at this level? Do they repeat what is in the textbook or provide interesting variants of the material?

11. Is there a *student's workbook* for laboratory or home use? Is the work different from that in the textbook, requiring a cre-

ative response from the student? Is the sequence of material well planned, so that work which has not yet been encountered in the textbook does not suddenly appear in an exercise?

12. Does the book leave scope for *student-initiated participation,* or is it so tightly structured that it could only be used in a lockstep, teacher-directed fashion?

13. Is this the type of book that students could use for *independent study* or to catch up on work on their own?

14. Is there a *table of contents* setting out clearly which structures are introduced and in what order? (Check the way a particular structure which causes students problems is presented and practiced.) Is there an *index* to help students (and teachers) find grammatical explanations, special lists, or paradigms?

15. Does the publisher provide a *teacher's manual* with indications on how to use the book and suggestions for extra activities? Does this manual encourage teacher initiative or dominate the teacher?

16. Has the book been *pretested* in schools for a similar level to that of your students and revised before being printed in its final form?

C. *Language and ideational content*

17. Is the *language* in the lessons authentic (not stilted or artificial; not old-fashioned; free of unnatural language not used by native speakers; correct for the persons and relationships in the situation in which it is used; free of dated slang or obscure dialectal idioms?)

18. Is there an interesting *theme* through the book, or related themes for sections of the book?

19. Are the *situations* in dialogues or practice activities realistic and thought-provoking, or are they merely banal vehicles for linguistic material?

20. Is the content of the *reading material* interesting and worthwhile?

21. Does the material give an unprejudiced and balanced *picture of contemporary life* in countries where the language is spoken? Does it bring out contrasts between the foreign culture and the culture of your students? Similarities? Are cultural stereotypes avoided? Is any of the cultural material out-of-date? If customs of an earlier period are included, is this made clear?

22. Are there *chauvinistic, racist,* or *sexist* elements, implicit or explicit, in the text material, illustrations, or supplementary aids?

D. *Linguistic coverage and organization of material*

23. How is *pronunciation* dealt with? Is the treatment satisfactory? Is attention paid to distinctions between similar sounds in the native and foreign languages, and within the foreign language? Is the sound system taught as an interdependent whole? Are stress, intonation, and juncture considered?

24. Is the *grammar* presented through structures? Some other way? Does the type of presentation suit your purposes? Are the most frequently used *structures* introduced early, irrespective of any difficulty ordering, so that students can express themselves adequately? Are these common structures continually reentered? Are there *summaries* of grammar?

25. Are the *exercises* well-designed? Do they give adequate practice in what has been learned, or would they have to be supplemented? Do they introduce any material which has not been studied up to that point? Do the exercises move from simple to more complex? Are all exercise sentences ones that would be used? Do the exercises provide ample practice before a testing exercise is presented. Are there too many exercises in each unit for practical use?

26. Is *reading* introduced early or late? Is the timing of its introduction appropriate for your course? Does the reading material provide for progressive teaching of the reading skill? Is it interesting in content and written in language which is appropriate for your students? Is the content of the later reading material worthwhile?

27. Is the *vocabulary* well-presented? How much new vocabulary per lesson? Is the vocabulary reentered sufficiently within the unit and in successive units? Is it summarized in some way? At the end of the book? in a dictionary format in the target language or in a bilingual list? How is the *vocabulary* to be taught? Is incidental vocabulary glossed within the text? (At foot of page, in margin, between lines, at end of passage?) Is attention paid to word formation (prefixes, suffixes, common roots)? To cognates, synonyms, antonyms? To thematic groupings? To the semantic coverage of related words? Are prepositions, conjunctions, and common adverbs given sufficient attention? Is choice of vocabulary based on a frequency count? If so, is the level of the count for this book sufficient,

or too advanced, for your purposes? If not, does the vocabulary appear to be generally useful, or is it esoteric?

28. Is *writing* introduced early or late? How does the timing suit your purposes? Do the writing exercises provide for progressive development of this skill? Do you consider there is enough (too much) writing? Is there provision for original writing? If there is a new *writing system* to be learned, is this presented clearly and practiced adequately?

29. Does the *unit design* allow for *progressive development* of and practice in listening comprehension? speaking? reading? writing? What is the *proportion of working time* allotted to each skill in the unit design? Is this proportion appropriate for the objectives of your course?

30. Is adequate opportunity provided for *review* at regular intervals? Does this review give reference to elements learned earlier as well as to current work?

31. If *tests* are provided with the textbook, do they test what the students have been learning (that is, all items are drawn from material studied and practiced to that point)? Are they of an appropriate level for your students? Does the book teach one way and test another (for instance, provide for oral teaching of items which are then tested in writing)? Do the tests contain review items as well as current items? Is there a good balance in the aspects of the work they test? Are they of a suitable length for your purpose? Is provision made for integrative as well as discrete-point testing? Are alternative items proposed for retesting or for makeup tests?

E. *Types of activities*

32. If there are *dialogues,* do they represent realistic situations within the foreign culture? Is the language authentic for use in such situations and relationships? Are the sentences short enough for students to be able to use them actively? Are there segments within the sentences which can be useful in creating variants for communicative interaction? Are the dialogues cluttered with new structures which could more effectively be presented in some other way? Are the dialogues too lengthy to be useful in the classroom? Can other material than dialogues be dramatized?

33. Are there indications of ways in which students can be encouraged to use what they have learned in *actual communication* (in speech and writing)?

34. Is there *variety* in the types of exercises? Are the exercises interesting? Do they encourage students to create utterances of their own?
35. Are indications given of *extra activities* (games, songs, poems, crossword puzzles, things to look for) which would add variety to the lessons?
36. Is provision made for *student-conducted activity?* for group work without the teacher's direction?
37. Is some material introduced just for *fun* and relaxation while using the language: humor, problems to solve, anecdotes, rhymes, cartoons, curious customs?

F. *Practical considerations*

38. Is the book *part of a series* which would be adequate for the sequence of courses in your school? Are the other books in the series satisfactory for the purposes of your classes? Is the transition from level to level well worked out? Can this book be used satisfactorily even if the other books in the series are not used?
39. Are the *illustrations* in a style which is likely to make the book seem to your students old-fashioned, ridiculous, or just dull? Are they of a type which can act as a stimulus to class discussion?
40. Are there appropriate *maps* somewhere in the book? Are they too detailed or too sketchy?
41. Is the book *printed* in an interesting style? Is the type clear? Is the page layout attractive? Is the work set out so that it is easy to find what you want? Are the binding, cover, quality of paper, and clarity of illustrations satisfactory? Is the cover attractive? Would the book stand up to normal wear and tear? Is it too heavy to carry around with other course books?
42. Is the book free of *printing errors?* in the dialogues and reading passages? in the exercises? in the glossary?
43. Is the *price* reasonable for your school situation?
44. Is the book *readily available* in the area in which you are teaching?

G. *Enjoyment index*

45. *Would you enjoy working with this book* at this level? Is it hard on the teacher in any way? Could the teachers in your department (particularly the inexperienced ones) work with it? Does it provide scope for individual teaching styles?

Note: Major advantages—

Major disadvantages—

(This section provides the evaluator with an opportunity to articulate strongly felt impressions of an overriding nature, after so much consideration of detail.)

- **What additional aspects of a textbook would you wish to evaluate? Which of the above seem most important to you, and which least important to you? Why?**

PLANNING THE LANGUAGE LESSON

Most student teachers approach their first lesson with some trepidation. "Yes, I know a lot of things," they say, "but what do I do when I am actually there, in front of my first class?" The answer lies in the carefully planned lesson. In an effective lesson given by an experienced teacher it is always possible to detect a clear progression of activities. For expert teachers the underlying plan may have taken only a few minutes to elaborate as they walked down the corridor to meet their class, but the outline of it is clear to the student teacher taking notes in the back of the room. It will be some years before the inexperienced teacher can hope to do likewise. Some may never reach this stage.

In the meantime, the lesson plan should be thoughtfully established according to certain principles, so that each lesson will contain the necessary ingredients for developing the language skills of the students. The teacher should outline the plan in brief form on a small card which can be kept in the textbook for quick reference. Later, what has been achieved during the lesson can be marked on the card for use as a guide when elaborating the plan for the next lesson. A file of these cards should be kept and examined from time to time so that the young teacher can see how to improve planning for subsequent lessons. From a series of such cards it will become clear to the novice whether too much has been expected from the students too soon, or whether the pace has been too slow for the class. It will also be clear where reteaching has been necessary because too little time was spent on demonstration or practice in the first place. For their own edification, new teachers should also note on their cards whether the students found the lessons interesting or dull, whether they offered original contributions, or whether they accepted it all as part of the routine. Analysis of one's own performance in class helps the teacher to identify combinations of ingredients which have been effective in improving past lessons. (An inexpensive but effective way of analyzing one's own performance post facto is to make an audiotape of a complete lesson and then to listen to it critically.)

General Principles

1. The teacher is *not the slave of the textbook.* Teachers are trained professionals who know the capabilities of various classes and the objectives of their courses. The textbook provides the teacher with material which can be used in innumerable ways. It is essential to know what is in the textbook and to be able to select, omit, recombine, and supplement this material as the class situation indicates. The teacher should know the textbook well enough to be able to prepare students for what is coming, to refer quickly to other parts of the book when this is desirable, and to make up for any deficiencies. Experienced teachers tend to believe that the perfect textbook is the one they themselves have yet to write. While awaiting this great event they should take great care in selecting the one that most nearly meets the needs of the particular class, with due regard to the objectives of the course and the age and maturity of the students.

2. Each lesson must be based on *clearly established aims.* A lesson is not a haphazard collection of more or less interesting items, but a progression of interrelated activities which reinforce each other in establishing and consolidating the learning toward which both teacher and students are directing their efforts. As the lesson proceeds, some of these activities test, in an unobtrusive way, what other activities have been teaching; others reteach what has not been assimilated by the students; while still others refresh the students' memory and enable them to reuse essential material.

3. Each lesson should *move smartly,* the teacher leading the class from one activity to another with assurance, never allowing time to be wasted because of hesitancy or indecision, while always remaining alert to student needs. This brisk tempo will be possible only when the teacher has a sure grasp of the plan.

4. The class should *not* be kept for *too long at one type of activity,* even when the students appear to be enjoying it. The teacher should not wait until the students have ceased to enjoy what they are doing before calling a new tune. Too much drilling, especially of difficult if essential structures, can lead to emotional fatigue, absentmindedness, and boredom. It can also cause the students to become so fixed in the use of certain patterns that they are incapable of using

them flexibly in communication. Too much reading and writing means the neglecting of classroom opportunities for practicing communication skills. Too much unsystematic oral work can deprive students of opportunities for studying new material about which they may talk. A well-designed lesson will contain a number of different activities, with a return to certain types of exercises at intervals for further consolidation of learning. Frequent, spaced practice is more effective than great blocks of one activity for undue lengths of time.

     5. The teacher should plan to *do in class what cannot be done out of class*. This requires careful thought. It means that the student must have plenty of classroom time for practice in communication with the teacher's encouragement and help. This does not mean that *all* reading and writing will be done out of class—an unwise procedure when these skills are being acquired, as we have seen in chapters 9 and 10. The students will do out of class what the teacher knows they can do on their own with reasonable probability of success. Out-of-class work will consolidate learning done in class through some type of creative activity. It will also include preparation for work to be done in subsequent lessons.

     6. The lesson should be planned so that the class is on its toes, *never sure of what is coming next*. Nothing is more tedious for the student than lessons which always follow the same pattern. Many class sessions will inevitably contain very similar activities, but the ordering of the elements should be varied: some may be included today, some left out, a few reintroduced from time to time. Imagination must direct the final form of the plan.

     7. The teacher should be ready to *toss aside the plan* or change it as the lesson evolves. The mood of the class, the unexpected difficulty or simplicity of some section of the work, an interesting possibility which did not occur to the teacher when drawing up the plan, student initiative—all of these things, and many others, may lead to a change in the progression. Although ready to change the plan, the teacher should not do it as the result of a whim. The teacher will be conscious of any changes being made and the direction in which they are leading.

Ingredients

     1. After the introductory stages, usually aural-oral, when the course is getting under way, each lesson should provide *some practice in each of the four skills,* not necessarily in the same proportion. Not only does one activity consolidate the other, but a change of activity maintains the interest and energy level of the class. This does not mean that there will be practice in listening to, speaking, reading, and

writing the same material during the one lesson. What has already been heard or read in a previous lesson may be being used as practice material by the class or as the basis for communicative interaction. What has been discussed or practiced orally may be reappearing in a more developed form in material for reading or writing. There will be a continual interplay among new elements and familiar elements, so that what has already been learned is not allowed to fade from the memory.

2. Each lesson must have *variety and some spice*. Since there are many ways of presenting and practicing material in all the skill areas, the teacher has no excuse for keeping to a few well-worn techniques. The spice is provided by surprise items (a language game, an anecdote, some cultural information with a visual accompaniment, a culture quiz, a competitive test of what has been learned, or some pertinent contribution by a student which will interest or amuse the others).

3. The teacher should think up *games and competitions* which provide the same types of activities as exercises. The old game of Twenty Questions gives ample practice in interrogative forms. A chaining game, where each student in turn must change a certain element in the sentence, is very similar to a substitution drill. A game or competition which provides the same kind of practice is more amusing and spontaneous than an exercise, and students who are enjoying the activity will continue doing the same thing for a longer period without boredom.

4. A *repertoire of songs* well learned can always be called upon to bring variety to the lesson. A simple song, with uncomplicated words and some repetition, relaxes and refreshes the class. The period of singing need not be prolonged. Though often more appropriate at the end of the lesson, singing may provide a very welcome interlude in the middle of a period of hard work.

And So, the Plan

The danger in trying to set down a plan for a language lesson is that some inexperienced persons may take it to be *the* plan, and continue to follow it unswervingly from lesson to lesson. This would violate principle 6 (see p. 485).

The lesson usually begins with a *warm-up*, where students are encouraged to talk about subjects of interest to them (e.g., what happened during the weekend or a recent startling event in the news). Sometimes this warm-up is built around a picture or an object, selected for its potential for expanding the students' *vocabulary*. In their discussions, students use much material they have already learned and acquire new vocabulary in a meaningful context. With proper planning, the warm-up also provides an opportunity for students to use some of the structures they practiced the previous day, as well as experimenting with material they prepared out of class. Its most useful function is to encourage students to retrieve and reuse much material from previous units in a real exchange of ideas and comments.

• *New work* is now introduced in an interesting way. In a continuing sequence this will be building on previous work, so that students do not learn aspects of the language in unconnected segments, in a series of jolts and starts. New situations may be acted out with new structures and vocabulary or a dialogue segment learned (depending on the method the teacher is following). It may be the day for some training in direct reading, in which case a passage constructed of known elements with a few novel items—the meaning of which can be ascertained from the context—will be read or played on tape. After discussion of the content, students will read rapidly in silence and be ready to discuss the content, referring to the text when in doubt.

• Out of the new work will emerge some structures or syntactic arrangements which must be practiced in *oral exercises* of some form. As these are being practiced, some brief, concise explanations may be necessary. After the main point of the practice exercise appears to be assimilated, some individual response or a competition will show whether the students have thoroughly mastered what they have been learning. If they have not, the teacher will return briefly to practice, or reserve the point at issue for a second practice a little later in the lesson. Some teachers have found that if practice on material which has not been well assimilated is deferred till the next day, student performance shows considerable improvement over the work of the previous day. Once again, teachers will vary their approach on different occasions.

• There follows a period for the *practical application* of the material of the day. The teacher may engage the students in an interchange of communication using what they have been learning. Later, this work may be combined with elements from earlier lessons to make sure the students recognize the relations between what they have been learning and what they have already learned. The application may involve reading and discussing a passage for which the previous work has prepared the class. It may necessitate some form of written demonstration of understanding and assimilation. It may take the form of a dramatization or some type of role playing in front of the class. The teacher may initiate a game which enables the students to use what they have learned, while concentrating on the progress of the game or on the success of their team. If they are able to use material successfully during such an activity, the teacher has some evidence that they have assimilated it.

• There will now be some *preparation of the work for home study.* This will not necessarily be overt preparation. The teacher, knowing what the students will be asked to do as preparation for the next class, will see that those aspects of the preparatory work which could cause problems for the students have already been encountered before the end of the lesson. This may involve introducing into some activity new vocabulary which occurs in the study assignment, discussing a cultural aspect of a topic which the students may find puzzling, making sure that any grammatical terminology is well understood, or discussing orally a subject about which students will be asked to write a short composition or read some longer account. The teacher will make very sure that the homework is assigned well before the final bell, so that all students fully understand what is being required of them.

• The lesson will *end with a relaxing and enjoyable activity* in the target language: some acting out of situations, a rousing discussion of a controversial subject, a song, a short illustrated talk on some aspect of the culture, or an oral report from one of the students. No matter what form this activity may take, the teacher should plan the lesson so that the students will have time to relax and enjoy the use of the language before the lesson ends. The students should always leave the classroom in a cheerful mood, feeling that language lessons are among the best in the day.

CLASSROOM MANAGEMENT

During training, and in the early weeks of the first teaching appointment, the inexperienced teacher is bombarded with advice from colleagues on how to establish a satisfactory relationship with the students. The following suggestions provide nothing new, but give a short, nonexhaustive summary of what every good teacher discovers through experience. Attention to these hints may save the new teacher from some uncomfortable experiences.

To establish a good working atmosphere in the classroom, it is essential to *know the students' names* as soon as possible. Nothing arrests an incipient disruption so quickly as calling an individual by name. Many a young teacher has lost control of a class during an overlong initial period of anonymity. Furthermore, time should be devoted during the first week or two to getting to know the students as individuals—finding out something of their backgrounds, any languages they already know, any problems they feel they will encounter, and their expectations for the course. (If a dearth of expectations, or even some resistance, is uncovered, the teacher is already alerted that a special effort to motivate and interest will be required.) With this accomplished, the teacher can rapidly personalize questioning, individual involvement, and unobtrusive assistance.

A class which is *kept actively involved* has little time or energy for disruptive behavior or for that common sport of all students: diverting the teacher from the main business of the day into fascinating by-paths. Choral response; rapid change of roles from teacher to group and group to group; constant shifting of response from individual to group and from group to individual; group practice of poorly assim-ilated items; brisk alternation of oral and written work; questions asked of everyone, even the weakest, in no recognizable order so that students do not know at any moment when they will be called upon to participate; group practice in reading—all these techniques keep students' attention on the progress of the lesson. The teacher who constantly relies on individual responses, asking questions in order around the class, must expect a high proportion of students to be inattentive at some period during the lesson.

The teacher who feels the time has come for a *sequence of individual responses* and wants to ensure that all are finally interrogated should crisscross around the class in a pattern which cannot be identified by the students. This has the same effect as a random choice, while enabling the teacher to verify the progress of each student in turn. The teacher should always ask the question first, then name the student for the individual response; this induces all the students to think about the answer while waiting to see if they will be asked the question. Name first, question afterwards, is an invitation to the rest of the students to think of other things.

A student who answers a question sincerely should never be made to feel stupid or ignorant. The teacher should take all the useful elements from the answer, using them for further teaching, or as the basis of a question to another student. When an answer is unsatis-factory, the teacher should consider carefully whether the wrong an-swer was an indication of inattention or laziness on the part of the student or whether it was the result of some deficiency in the pre-sentation of the work or insufficient practice of the point at issue. When a student has given a wrong answer, the teacher should put the same question to another student and, on receipt of the correct an-swer, put the question again to the student who made the mistake. An alternative to this procedure is to ask the class to repeat the correct answer in chorus, since the point where one student has made a mistake is frequently the place where other students are weak.

Students should be encouraged to ask about things that puzzle them, even apparently simple things. Since what puzzles one usually puzzles others in the group, such questions often show the teacher where explanations or the presentation of material were insufficient. To avoid slowing the tempo of the class, the teacher should answer briefly, demonstrating in the subsequent practice what was puzzling the student. Where questions indicate the need for more than a brief reorientation, students should be encouraged to keep them to the end of the class session or for personal discussion with the teacher at a later stage. Frequently, a question is answered in later practice or demonstration and the necessity for further explanation fades away.

As the year progresses, *the problems of the bright, fast-working student and the dull, slow, frustrated student* will emerge. Bright students may be asked more difficult questions, invited to help others in group work, or encouraged to do extra, more demanding work on an individual basis. Slow students must not be humiliated or embarrassed if they are working to the best of their ability. Their deficiencies will not be very obvious to the other students in group work in the early stages or in the laboratory. Later, they must be encouraged to work thoroughly on some portions of each unit, even if they cannot keep up with the class at every point. They should be asked questions the teacher knows they can answer without difficulty to give them a feeling of success and of participation in the work of the group.

These two extremes are not representative of the majority of the students in the class. The teacher must become very well acquainted with the ability level of all the students, so as to encourage them to keep working to full capacity. Above all, the new teacher must avoid being monopolized by the talkative, fast-thinking, fast-learning student, who will learn with or without the teacher. Those who really need help with learning and the support and encouragement of the teacher to persevere must be recognized early, so that valuable time can be devoted to their needs.

Early in the course, the teacher must be able to *detect the potential nuisances* so as to keep them busy and involved in activities. A question aimed at the inattentive before disruption has started, or a call to participate in some activity, is a good preventive move. Sarcasm should never be used; it gives the teacher an unfair advantage over a student who, if nettled into replying, will be considered insolent. In dealing with problem students, teachers must never threaten what they cannot or do not intend to put into action. An extreme threat often obliges the teacher, in a calmer moment, to retreat from its implementation, and the unruly student has won the day. The student will remember this on a later occasion. Restlessness and inattention on a general scale are often an indication to the teacher that explanations are being unnecessarily prolonged, or that the class has been kept for too long at the same type of activity. A sudden switch from oral work to a written exercise, or from individual work to choral response or some other group activity, will usually recall the attention of the students.

The teacher must *always keep faith* with the students. If they have been asked to prepare some work for the day's class, the teacher must remember to check on it. If they have been told to expect a test, the test must be given. The conscientious and hardworking have reason to feel resentful if the teacher is continually forgetful in these matters, while the wily will soon learn how much work they can avoid without detection.

KEEPING ABREAST PROFESSIONALLY

When we speak of "a born teacher," we are referring to certain qualities of character and personality that enable some to gain the confidence and respect of students more quickly than others, to recognize the students' real problems, and to approach these with clarity and patience. Most teachers acquire these abilities through practical experience. There are, however, many other requirements for the language teacher in this modern age. Many need to improve their own skills in the language, others need opportunities to keep their communicative ability at a high level. As priorities of objectives change, so do techniques. New technological discoveries bring into the classroom new aids which the teacher must learn to use effectively. There may be new discoveries in linguistics or psychology which are relevant to language teaching. The teacher must keep abreast of developments and achievements in countries where the language is spoken. In some cases, important changes are taking place in the language itself (a new spelling or writing system, an expanding lexis, evaluation of structural variants, newly recognized simplification or complication of the phonemic system). The teacher should also be alert to reevaluate techniques, even seemingly indispensable ones, and be ready to change and adapt them from year to year to increase their effectiveness.

In all these things teachers are unwise to rely on their own resources. They should join professional associations, read and contribute to language-teaching journals, and participate in professional discussion at meetings and congresses. They should take advantage of the services put at their disposal for professional improvement: seminars, workshops, institutes, information centers. Teachers who remain alert professionally, evaluating carefully in the light of practical experience what they have heard and read, and contributing their own insights to the fund of professional knowledge, remain vital and interesting in the classroom, even after years of teaching the same subject. Each class is different. Each year the teacher's approach will be a little different, adapted to new classes and incorporating a little more of what has been learned from colleagues and from the experience of the previous year. Beginning teachers should set before them this dual aim: to keep abreast of developments in their profession and to keep growing professionally through continuous and systematic evaluation of their own experience.

Annotated Reading List

EARLY AND LATE LANGUAGE LEARNING

Krashen, Stephen D. "The Critical Period for LanguageAcquisition and its Possible Bases," in Aaronson and Rieber 1975, pp. 211–24. Discusses in detail the research on a critical period for second-language acquisition, with extensive bibliography.

Stern, H. H., and Weinrib, Alice. "Foreign Languages for Younger Children: Trends and Assessment," *LTLA* 10, no. 1 (1977): 5–25. Reprinted in Kinsella 1978, pp. 152–72. Survey article with extensive bibliography.

Schumann, John H. "Affective Factors and the Problem of Age in Second Language Acquisition," *LL* 25 (1975): 209–35. "Second Language Acquisition: The Pidginization Hypothesis," *LL* 26 (1976): 391–408. *The Pidginization Process. A Model for Second Language Acquisition* (includes both articles from *LL*). Rowley, Mass.: Newbury House, 1978. All three works discuss such concepts as social distance, psychological distance, and age in relation to second language learning.

Van Ek, J. A. *The Threshold Level for Modern Language Learning in Schools*. London: Longman (for the Council of Europe), 1977.

BILINGUAL EDUCATION

Alatis, James E., and Twaddell, Kristie, eds. *English as a Second Language in Bilingual Education: Selected TESOL Papers*. Washington, D.C.: TESOL, 1976. Discusses models of bilingual education, testing, training of bilingual education teachers, and insights from the social sciences and linguistics.

Paulston, Christina Bratt. *Bilingual Education: Theories and Issues*. Rowley, Mass.: Newbury House, 1980. The equilibrium and conflict paradigms are discussed. Different types of bilingual education programs in various countries of North America and Europe are analyzed in relation to these paradigms. Bibliography.

Tosi, Arturo. "Mother-Tongue Teaching for the Children of Migrants," *LTLA* 12, no. 4 (1979): 213–31. A survey article, with extensive bibliography. Special reference to the situation in the United Kingdom and Western Europe. See also Tosi, A., *Immigration and Bilingual Education*. Oxford: Pergamon, 1981.

Woodford, Protase E. "Bilingual/Bicultural Education: A Need for Understanding," in Jarvis 1974b, pp. 397–433. Discusses kinds of bilingualism, types of bilingual programs, how to implement a program, and teacher training. Extensive bibliography.

FOREIGN LANGUAGE IN THE ELEMENTARY SCHOOL

Andersson, Theodore. *Foreign Languages in the Elementary School: A Struggle Against Mediocrity*. Austin: University of Texas Press, 1969. Sets out a rationale for early language learning, with a history of FLES teaching in the United States from 1840 to 1967. Discusses the course of study and teacher training.

Freudenstein, Reinhold, ed. *Teaching Foreign Languages to the Very Young: Papers from Seven Countries on Work with 4- to 8-Year Olds*. Oxford: Pergamon, 1979. Discusses reasons for an early start, the types of activities that maintain the interest of young children, and the selection and training of suitable teachers. Recommended course materials for English, French, and German are described.

Donoghue, Mildred R., and Kunkle, John F. *Second Languages in Primary Education*. Rowley, Mass.: Newbury House, 1979. Discusses why second languages should be taught to young children; the characteristics of these children; and appropriate techniques and activities for teaching all the language skills in primary schools and bilingual education programs.

VOCABULARY LEARNING

Rivers, Wilga M., et al. *Practical Guides*. Chapter 7, "Building and Maintaining an Adequate Vocabulary," gives detailed activities for vocabulary learning, under the headings: Focusing on Form, Focusing on Meaning, and Expanding by Association. Topping and tailing, compounds, and disguised cognates are discussed in chapter 6, as are frequency word lists for the various languages. Developing aural recognition vocabulary is discussed in chapter 3. Chapter 9 gives examples of search exercises in the section "Exploring the Dictionary." Examples are in English, French, German, and Spanish.

Cornu, Anne-Marie. "The First Step in Vocabulary Teaching," *MLJ* 63 (1979): 262–72. Gives proposals for presentation of vocabulary, based on what research has shown about vocabulary storage. Useful for the intermediate or advanced level. Examples in French and English.

LANGUAGE FOR SPECIAL PURPOSES (LSP)

Robinson, Pauline. *ESP (English for Specific Purposes): The Present Position*. Oxford: Pergamon, 1980. Discusses the variety of contexts for which LSP courses are appropriate; register and discourse analysis; student needs; syllabus design; materials production; testing; and self-directed learning. ESP testbooks currently available are described and evaluated.

Strevens, Peter. "Special-Purpose Language Learning: A Perspective," *LTLA* 10, no. 3 (1977): 145–63. Reprinted in Kinsella 1978, pp. 185–203. Survey article with extensive bibliography. Sets out a taxonomy of special-purpose language teaching (SP-LT) courses and an analysis of communicative purposes. Another version, "The Teaching of English for Special Purposes," chapter 8 of Strevens 1977, gives spoken and written English examples of the communicative categories.

Mackay, Ronald, and Mountford, Alan, eds. *English for Specific Purposes: A Case Study Approach*. London: Longman, 1978. Discusses the theory and practice of ESP, with special attention to syllabi and materials. Several well-known writers explain their approach to textbook design. Case studies supply details of exercises and activities for different types of courses.

TEXTBOOK

Madsen, H. S., and Bowen, J. D. *Adaptation in Language Teaching*. Rowley, Mass.: Newbury House, 1978. For teachers who are required to teach from a textbook they do not find congenial or congruent with the objectives of their students, this book proposes techniques for supplementing, editing, or localizing content; expanding, pruning, or modernizing linguistic material; modifying the cultural and situational content; and adapting activities to the age and interests of the students. Practical guidelines for initial selection of a textbook are provided. Examples are in English, but principles apply to all languages.

Morrow, Judith C., and Strasheim, Lorraine A. "Supplementing the Textbook Attractively, Effectively, and Responsibly." In Schulz 1977.

Research and Discussion

*1. It has been demonstrated that successful acquisition of a second language in bilingual programs in different parts of the world is to some degree dependent on the prestige of the language being learned and the self-image of the learners. (See C. B. Paulston, "Ethnic Relations and Bilingual Education: Accounting for Contradictory Data" in Troike and Modiano 1975, pp. 366–401, and attached references.)

Visit a bilingual school or class near you. What kind of bilingual program does it represent? What kind of community does it serve? What are the relations of this community with the community of the dominant language? Write down your observations on how the students were learning and the level of language control they seemed to have reached. Have you any proposals for improving this program?

2. Draw up a detailed project for a six-week "exploratory language" course at fourth grade level. (Consider carefully what aspects of language you wish the children to explore and the kinds of activities you consider appropriate.)

3. Draw up for a first-year class in its sixth week of study a lesson plan which contains all the ingredients proposed in this chapter. Try it out on a class. Reflect on the students' reactions and then work out an improved plan which responds to any deficiencies in presentation that you observed.

4. Look for a textbook you think you would enjoy using. Prepare an evaluation along the lines proposed in this chapter. In what ways has your first impression of the book been modified by this close study?

5. Study professional journals from 1960 to 1965 and from 1970 to 1975, and write an account of the promise and the later evaluation of the achievement of FLES programs. What advice would you give to a person wishing to establish a FLES program?

6. Reread the ten educational pressures outlined in chapter 1, p. 13. Choose the one which, in your opinion, is most evident in your area at the present time. Draw up a detailed project for a language course which would respond to this pressure. (If you believe the major pressure is a different one from any of those listed, describe it and use it as the basis for your project.)

7. Draw up a list for future reference of sources of information which would be useful to teachers of the language you will be teaching. Include:

(*a*) titles of useful professional journals, with name of professional organization and address for subscriptions;

(*b*) addresses of consulates, cultural services, trade missions, or companies from which you can obtain booklets or other printed information, borrow or rent films or taped material, or buy posters or other illustrative material;

(c) addresses of nonprofit organizations from which films, video-tapes, or taped materials may be obtained;

(d) names and addresses of principal publishers producing text-books for your language;

(e) educational institutions with innovative programs in your language which would be worth visiting.

*8. In 1973 Rivers set out a series of *changing relations* and *changing directions* in the language teaching field. See "Students, Teachers, and the Future," *FLA* 8 (1975): 22–32; also in *SMT* (1976), pp. 256–59. Do you think these are valid today? Which would you retain and which others would you add?

9. Work out for each level (elementary, intermediate, and advanced) an appropriate activity for vocabulary learning which is different from those given in this chapter.

10. Study the following two statements of objectives in language teaching in relation to the local situation. Set out in detail the kind of course you would design for students in each situation. Then write out a concise statement of student objectives for the situation in which you will be teaching.

(a) *Finland.* "The country . . . is particularly isolated, geographically, historically, culturally, and linguistically. . . . Learning another European language is often principally a means toward securing a better job. From the teacher's point of view, it should, I think, be largely an attempt to extend the horizons of the students, giving them a deeper appreciation of their own culture. At the same time, the students very much need to acquire confidence when encountering people from other countries. . . . By learning English, they will be able to communicate with all speakers of that language, whether or not it is those speakers' mother tongue."

(b) *Mexico.* "To read—particularly scientific and technical English—so as to be able to extract information relevant to the practice of the student's profession and important to the development of the country as a whole. Also, to be able to understand and analyze the socio-political, economic and philosophical context in which the information or viewpoints are presented so as to better determine their applicability to the student's own environment."[44]

44. Personal communications. Twenty-five more statements of objectives in language teaching from different countries will be found in Wilga M. Rivers, in NEC 1979, pp. 47–49. These will be useful for class discussion.

Appendix A
Absolute Language Proficiency Ratings
Foreign Service Institute, United States Department of State, May 1963

The rating scales described below have been developed by the Foreign Service Institute to provide a meaningful method of characterizing the language skills of foreign service personnel of the Department of State and of other Government agencies. Unlike academic grades, which measure achievement in mastering the content of a prescribed course, the S-rating for speaking proficiency and the R-rating for reading proficiency are based on the absolute criterion of the command of an educated native speaker of the language.

The definition of each proficiency level has been worded so as to be applicable to every language; obviously the amount of time and training required to reach a certain level will vary widely from language to language, as will the specific linguistic features. Nevertheless, a person with S-3's in both French and Chinese, for example, should have approximately equal linguistic competence in the two languages.

The scales are intended to apply principally to government personnel engaged in international affairs, especially of a diplomatic, political, economic and cultural nature. For this reason heavy stress is laid at the upper levels on accuracy of structure and precision of vocabulary sufficient to be both acceptable and effective in dealings with the educated citizen of the foreign country.

As currently used, all the ratings except the S-5 and R-5 may be modified by a plus (+), indicating that proficiency substantially exceeds the minimum requirements for the level involved but falls short of those for the next higher level.

DEFINITIONS OF ABSOLUTE RATINGS

Elementary Proficiency

S-1   Short definition: Able to satisfy routine travel needs and minimum courtesy requirements.

Amplification: Can ask and answer questions on topics very familiar to him; within the scope of his very limited language experience can understand simple questions and statements if they are repeated at a slower rate than normal speech; speaking vocabulary inadequate to express anything but the most elementary needs; errors in pronunciation and grammar are frequent, but can be understood by a native speaker used to dealing with foreigners attempting to speak his language; while topics which are "very familiar" and elementary needs vary considerably from individual to individual, any person at the S-1 level should be able to order a simple meal, ask for a room in a hotel, ask and give street directions, tell time, handle travel requirements and basic courtesy requirements.

R-1   Short definition: Able to read elementary lesson material or common public signs.

Amplification: Can read material at the level of a second-semester college language course or a second-year secondary school course; alternately, able to recognize street signs, office and shop designations, numbers, etc.

Limited Working Proficiency

S-2   Short definition: Able to satisfy routine social demands and limited office requirements.

Amplification: Can handle with confidence but not with facility most social situations including introductions and casual conversations about current events, one's work, family, and autobiographical information; can handle with confidence but not with facility limited business requirements (e.g., a vice-consul can give a visa interview, a business man can give directions to a secretary, a housewife can instruct a servant, but each may need help in handling any complications or difficulties in these situations); can understand most conversations on non-technical subjects and has a speaking vocabulary sufficient to express himself simply with some circumlocutions (non-technical subjects being understood as topics which require no specialized knowledge); accent, though often quite American, is intelligible; can usually handle elementary constructions quite accurately but does not have thorough or confident control of the grammar.

R-2   Short definition: Able to read intermediate lesson material or simple colloquial texts.

Amplification: Can read material at the level of a third-semester college language course or a third-year secondary school course; can read simple news items with extensive use of a dictionary.

Minimum Professional Proficiency

S-3   Short definition: Able to speak the language with sufficient structural accuracy and vocabulary to satisfy representation requirements and handle professional discussions within a special field.

Amplification: Can participate effectively in all general conversation; can discuss particular interests with reasonable ease; comprehension is quite complete for a normal rate of speech; vocabulary is broad enough that he rarely has to grope for a word; accent may be obviously foreign; control of grammar good; errors never interfere with understanding and rarely disturb the native speaker.

R-3   Short definition: Able to read non-technical news items or technical writing in a special field.

Amplification: Can read technical writing in a special field or modern press directed to the general reader, i.e., news items or feature articles reporting on political, economic, military and international events, or standard text material in the general field of the social sciences.

Full Professional Proficiency

S-4   Short definition: Able to use the language fluently and accurately on all levels normally pertinent to professional needs.

Amplification: Can understand and participate in any conversation within the range of his experience with a high degree of fluency and precision of vocabulary, but would rarely be taken for a native speaker; errors of pronunciation and grammar quite rare; can handle informal interpreting from and into the language, but does not necessarily have the training or experience to handle formal interpreting.

R-4   Short definition: Able to read all styles and forms of the language pertinent to professional needs.

Amplification: Can read moderately difficult prose readily in any area of the social sciences directed to the general reader with a good education (through at least the secondary school level), and difficult material in a special field including official and professional documents and correspondence; can read reasonably legible handwriting without difficulty.

Native or Bilingual Proficiency

S-5   Short definition: Speaking proficiency equivalent to that of an educated native speaker.

Amplification: Has complete fluency in the language practically equivalent to that of an educated native speaker. To attain this rating usually requires extensive residence in an area where the language is spoken, including having received part of his secondary or higher education in the language.

R-5   Short definition: Reading proficiency equivalent to that of an educated native speaker.

Amplification: Can read extremely difficult and abstract prose, as well as highly colloquial writings and the classic literary forms of the language; can draft good prose and make informal translations from English into the language.

Appendix B

Learning a Sixth Language:
An Adult Learner's Daily Diary

I recently had the opportunity to begin learning another language, the fifth non-native language I had studied. For five weeks I kept a day-by-day diary of my language learning and using experiences. I present it here, just as I wrote it, as case-study material on non-native language learning processes, strategies, and affective reactions. My observations are admittedly those of a sophisticated language learner. The experience, however, made me much more sensitive to the problems a person encounters in learning another language. I hope that reading this diary will have a similar effect upon my readers.

The following background information is essential for the interpretation of the diary entries.

In January 1978, I spent five weeks in Spanish-speaking areas of South America. My aim was to begin the study of Spanish. I had already learned five languages. I had learned English as a native language and French which I now speak with bilingual confidence and fluency. I studied Latin for three years in high school and for one more year at the advanced level as an undergraduate. I studied Italian during my senior year in high school and have largely forgotten it; I do, however, listen to it quite often on ethnic radio programs in Boston and hear it spoken around me in the Department of Romance Languages and Literatures at Harvard; German—which I studied on three occasions, separeted by four- and ten-year intervals (the last about eighteen years ago)—I consider a language I can read, but I speak it only in simple, informal sentences when situations abroad demand it.

I took with me to South America an elementary textbook for Spanish, with a few accompanying tapes, and a Berlitz phrasebook. I was given six two-hour lessons by a university faculty member and his assistant, who taught me as a team. I worked on assignments they gave me, which I supplemented with information from my private textbook. I listened to radio and television programs and the conversations on social visits. I read the newspaper. (My hostess, "E," an American, was a close friend and spoke English with me.) I then went on an eight-day tour to a beautiful, but distant, area of the country with twelve Spanish-speaking tourists (all inhabitants of a neighboring city and all previously unknown to me), a guide, and later four university students (*las lolas*). After my return from the tour I had opportunities to use the language on social visits. I continued to study by myself with my private textbook and occasional work with tapes. I listened to television. I then spent five days on my own in another Spanish-speaking country and talked with

This diary by Wilga M. Rivers was published in a slightly different form in the *Canadian Modern Language Review*, 36, no. 1 (1979): 67–82. © 1979 *The Canadian Modern Language Review / La Revue Canadienne des Langues Vivantes*.

people I met on buses and planes, in airports, on trains, in the hotel, and in streets and shops. I listened to my transistor radio and continued to read newspapers and guidebooks in Spanish.

10 January

[On the plane to South America, I began to study the Berlitz phrasebook.]
1. I find myself making as many associations as possible with what I know: *sed*—sedative; *treinta*—trente; and also negative associations (*tardes, not* tardy).
2. I repeat things over and try using them in some sentence context, putting them together in little phrases.
3. I was not embarrassed to try out little phrases as soon as I knew them— e.g., with the (Portuguese-speaking) Brazilians in the plane who, themselves non-native Spanish speakers, were sympathetic and posed no threat. I tended to try them out as soon as I saw an appropriate opportunity—either aloud or mentally.
4. I found looking over a short pronunciation guide or a rapid overview of grammar helpful, before actually learning piecemeal.

11 January
In VM

1. I am feeling the need for function words (adverbs, prepositions) and for exclamations, fill-in expressions, polite responses, and words like *ayer-hoy-mañana*.
2. I look up conjugations—how to express past and future.
3. I look for short cuts based on previous knowledge of languages: *once* = Fr. onze; *lluvia* = pluie, therefore *llena* = pleine.
4. I feel the need for common words—bread, fruit, etc.
5. I notice a tendency to use German with the Spanish-speaking maid—*sehr gut,* etc.
6. I need to understand how things work, e.g., *ser/estar*.

12 January

1. I am listening hard to try to segment and recognize some of the segments or words within segments; I try to identify English, French, or Latin cognates.
2. I am still forming conscious associations for memory: *estoy* (était) *ser* (sera).
3. In my first class: I find it very tiring and demanding to make continual and prompt responses to questions and still remember the material. I find it easy to respond to a question, but harder to remember the question form and ask the question.

It is worthwhile and more interesting to make up one's own additions (to sentences proposed) with extra information or real information—one begins to think in the language in this way.
4. I am seeking for rejoinders and adverbial expansions—*Lo lamento, Desculpeme* (?) (I should have copied it down!) *Perdóneme.*

5. I spent half an hour in the language lab and found it demanding and tiring, requiring much concentration. I don't think it's true you can just parrot utterances.

6. Assignments are becoming more difficult and certainly unreal. You *cease to think in the language* when the exercises make you say things which are contradictory and do not apply to you, e.g., *yo soy norteamericana, yo soy chileno; soy estudiante, soy profesor.*

7. I feel a need to find out as many things as possible as soon as possible, so I am constantly looking up the textbook I brought with me for extra information beyond the loose-leaf assignments I am given.

8. I realize the value of practicing saying things over to develop fluency and to keep thinking in the language.

9. I feel an early need for some sound-symbol correspondences if I am to practice from written examples.

10. In the Vocabulary section of my private textbook, it would be useful to have the page numbers where the item may be seen in context.

11. I found I misinterpreted *tengo que aprender* as "I want to" from French *je tiens à* and I keep thinking this meaning, instead of *have to.* This shows the pitfalls of a purely direct method.

13 January

1. I am finding model examples useful to memorize as guides to rules—yo *estoy* enferma / yo *soy* simpática.

2. I check on special deviations from or correspondences with French rules, e.g., position of adjectives.

3. I feel the need for models for strange sounds. Descriptions are definitely not enough.

4. I feel a continual need to understand the larger picture into which the bits fit, so I realize the usefulness (indispensability to me) of the index to grammatical and other details in my textbook. Life without it would be most frustrating.

5. I use mnemonic associations: *sesenta,* soixante; *sententa,* septante; *noventa,* novena.

6. I continually need reference tables for pronunciation of sound/symbol correspondences or paradigms of verbs, lists of numerals, etc.

14 January

1. I ask directions to church. I come out with my little Spanish phrases quite confidently but cannot understand the replies. I finally got to the reception office at the Hotel Europa and they found an English speaker to help me.

2. In the hymns and prayers, I experience interference from practice in reading other languages as I try to read the Spanish script rapidly.

3. I try out my "Lesson 1" sentences on sympathetic people at E's party, as a party joke, with no embarrassment.

4. When I begin to say a Spanish sentence I tend to think in German (*ich . . . , aber*), that is, in my fourth, less fluent foreign language. Amusingly enough, I am told that I speak my little sentences with a German accent!

(perhaps I am unvoicing the voiced consonants?) This is interesting because I am deliberately avoiding what I recognize as interference from French: /y/ for /u/, etc.; and also what I see to be interference from English /I/ for /i/; /ɛ/ for /e/, palatal /t/ and /d/, diphthongs. Perhaps I am subconsciously slipping into German features, or perhaps it is the absence of the English and French ones which leaves the accent unidentifiable as these?

5. In listening, I am beginning to segment what I hear and recognize cognates with French and English. I feel the need for the adverbs and other function words and also fill-in words. I recognize the cognate ones and a few I have learned.

6. I am observing and recognizing pronunciation features: Mouth position as distinct from French and English; pronunciation of *j* and /b/, and becoming accustomed to the intonation of fluent speech.

15 January

I think the alleged German accent is because I am distinguishing two phonemes /b/ and /v/ instead of using /b/ or /b/ for both *Viña del Mar, beber,* etc. [I have been told since that it was probably because of my vowels, after all. By avoiding French and English vowels, I must have fallen back on other "foreign" vowels I had learned.]

16 January

1. I still think German! *Danke schön, ja, und so weiter.* Ridiculous since I am so unfluent in German and rarely, rarely use it.

2. I still can't understand, although I can put together new sentences (elementary) and write what I can say. I wrote two pages of biographical notes in class today. (My teacher used these as the basis for a notice in the newspaper about the lecture I was to give.)

3. Pronunciation drilling today revealed continued influence of French of which I had no idea—use of /y/ for /u/ and French stress on last syllable (*háblo* as *habló*) and occasional uvular *r*. All these are things I had had to work hard to acquire in French as differences from English.

4. Also occasional influence of Italian, which I thought was 90 percent forgotten, in the pronunciation of *ciento* as "chiento," for instance.

5. I find *intense* concentration is required (as well as careful attention to fine phonetic distinctions) in order to imitate correctly the models given, particularly as no articulatory help is supplied. It becomes a process of successive approximations. One does not hear one's own mistakes or misimitations unless they are the ones on which one is expressly concentrating one's intellectual attention. Personal and immediate correction and remodeling are essential before one has lost the auditory image of the sound one has made and, quite clearly, one cannot imitate correctly what one has not discriminated correctly at first. Therefore there is need for a clear model and a patient one who is willing to repeat and listen over and over again. I have two—a man and woman who take turns at modeling and remodeling until I reach a satisfactory approximation. The encouragement of their pleasure when I come near the target is also a help and their devoted interest in helping me reach

503

it. Many mistakes in pronunciation come from misconceptions on which I had worked hard and which came from rough approximations (expressed in English spelling) in the Berlitz book.

6. I found applying learned numbers to random figures, dates, and times of day required much more concentration than I had realized, and I fell into traps (confusing *sesenta* and *sententa,* for instance).

7. I find I *need* to ask questions, to ask for clarifications and to get them at the moment I need them if I am to progress. I do not feel at ease if they are left hanging.

8. I do make mental translations and these give me a feeling of security, yet I do find myself thinking directly in the language when I read, or go over an assignment, or create utterances in class.

9. I find practice exercises where one applies and reapplies new rules in variant situations to be useful and important to my learning. I do not find that they involve "parroting." Instead, they require active mental participation because even if only one element has to be substituted one has to recreate the complete sentence. This is where I find myself definitely re-creating, because if the element to be varied is near the beginning, I sometimes complete the sentence meaningfully, although not with the vocabulary supplied by the model, but a related word instead, e.g., "history" for "chemistry."

10. I like to try to say my own little things and usually begin by telling my teachers something about what I have been doing. These creative efforts come out rather slowly and gropingly, but seem to be understood and appreciated. I also add my own flourishes to exercise sentences, thus creating my own meaning, and even adding my own humor at times.

11. In listening, I do not hear it all yet, but grasp what my teacher is saying from a word here and there and the context (what element are we working with at the moment? so what is he probably saying?). I feel myself taking the plunge on surmise and hoping that I am plunging into the right spot in the right way. Mostly my surmise is correct, so perhaps I am putting together more elements than I realize *or* we do not need too many elements when context makes clear what is probably being said.

12. I feel I am "hearing" a few more segments on TV. Certainly my major problem in listening is a meager vocabulary.

19 January

1. I begin to construct short sentences in *English* like my Spanish sentences and to speak with my "foreign voice" with people who know only a little English or even some English.

2. I learn a great deal from advertisements and street signs. I am constantly reading them and pronouncing them over to myself and then continuing to repeat over nice sentences from them which contain useful turns of expression. I learn fruits, vegetables, meats, kinds of drinks, sweets, ices, recognize useful expressions in insurance, cigarette, or housing ads, shop signs for sales, etc.

20 January

On the way to S, I talk with a young man on the bus, a former Naval College cadet now working in the railways. His English is about equal to my Spanish and we communicate quite well about ourselves and the problems of the blacks in the USA.

21 January

1. Listening to TV. The frustration of feeling on the brink of comprehension in the sense of being able to segment and recognize phrasings and hear words here and there but just not having the vocabulary to know exactly what it is all about. I can guess from a word here and there, from expressions and from actions. Presumably when I know *words* I'll be able to understand. I can recognize numbers now. The same problems arise as I listen to conversations around me. But here I can get a better idea of or guess better what is being said because of the context in which I am myself involved and the situation (e.g., at table eating crabs: the *jaivas* at A).

2. I feel a desperate need for common verbs—going, coming back, putting, looking for, trying—many of which are irregular. I will have to settle down and learn them. I also need past tenses, and the verb "to go" for immediate future. I must learn *on, under,* etc.

3. I also feel the need for *Oh, Ah, Really, Of course* kinds of sounds—it's hard to know where to turn to find them.

4. I am very frustrated by the lack of an English-Spanish glossary in my private textbook and other books. I will have to buy a small pocket English-Spanish, Spanish-English dictionary.

5. I notice the local dropping of "s" at the end of words which is mentioned in the *Practical Guide to the Teaching of Spanish,* chap. 4, and which my teacher tells me is "very bad." However, even my well-educated friends do it in conversation. I am glad I knew about it.

6. I amuse people by wrong pronunciations which produce incongruous words—I try to say "beans" and end up with "sissy." My teacher roars with laughter when I say I saw a Japanese prostitute down by the wharf, instead of a Japanese boat.

7. I find I can read the newspaper and other informational reading material quite fluently already and feel I am reading directly in the language.

23 January

1. Verbs are a terrible trial. All those endings for all those tenses and persons! I make associations with French: je parl*ai:* / *yo hablé* to try to remember, also j'ai / *yo he,* il a / *el ha.* I have to pause to make this connection in order to produce the correct form in speech, yet it seems more reliable and more reassuring than having to remember in the void.

2. The problem of the illogicality or unassociatability of irregular forms which are so common. Why should *es* belong to *ser,* not *estar?* It will not stay in place. *Ser* seems to be an amalgam of three verbs—the *soy, era* and *fui* stems, then *fui* also belongs to *ir* which has the *ir* (*ido, iba*), *va* and *fui* stems. A terrible pest for everyone. Oh for Esperanto and its regularities!

3. I can read fluently now, except for the odd word here and there and can *recognize* the tenses (of course, they are in context).

4. My teacher laughs because I sometimes jump the gun pedagogically, as I did this morning. He asked me the day I was born. I replied and immediately asked him the day he was born: a question which he was just about to ask me to ask! I still add extra information to practice sentences, which my teachers find amusing. Teachers should encourage this. The numbers are beginning to come without reflection.

5. I still have problems *hearing* what is said, with a normal intonation at a normal pace, even when my teacher is only asking questions using things we have learned. I often guess (correctly) from the element or elements I do hear. Clearly students need a great deal of practice *hearing* the language. It isn't at all easy.

6. It is annoying that the textbook has only the irregular parts of the irregular verbs and not the regular parts. I suppose it makes you think, but I find it irritating and you miss out on the many opportunities of *seeing* the regular parts along with the irregular.

7. I find writing out lots of mixed verbs as they come to mind helps.

24 January
At the hotel in S
I felt I could understand the advertisements on the radio tonight.

25 January
[The beginning of the tour to the south with a Spanish-speaking group]

1. I find I am understood. This gives me confidence. I talk to taxi drivers and find I can amuse them. All that I learned in my six lessons was useful. It shows the value of learning a number of tenses at the beginning, as well as useful patterns into which one can build sentences.

2. I can understand members of the group when they speak to me and they understand me (what I can say at present). I am learning words hard. I check everything I want in the Spanish/English, English/Spanish dictionary which T lent me and in my textbook and the Berlitz book (which I find is very well constructed and most useful).

3. I find myself saying *Buon giorno* to people instead of *Buenos días*. Why the Italian now?

4. Half-understanding means one needs luck. The guide asks how many cases we have. I think he's asking how many we are for room allocation. I say *Una,* which fortunately is right for both!

5. I became very upset this afternoon, after a day with the group, because the guide had stopped telling me in his weak English what happened next and I felt stupid asking every time to make sure. (Finally I understood quite well that we were to eat at 8:30 p.m. but not that we were going out, instead of staying in the hotel, so I didn't bring my coat down.) I understand some of his explanations, but listening to guides standing in the middle of moving buses is always difficult, even in English. A very nice Swiss and his wife (he is a budding linguist) came to my rescue and asked me to have a drink with

them. He is quadrilingual (Irish mother, German father, grew up in Alexandria, married a French-speaking Swiss and has now been three years in South America). I settled down after the drink with my Swiss friends had relaxed me and I had regained my courage. During the dinner with the group I recounted funny stories in French and was able to make some conversation in Spanish with the help of a *vaino* with cinnamon and some white wine. I found I sometimes thought the Swiss was talking French when he was speaking Spanish, and I followed his Spanish quite well. Does this mean he has a French accent (or intonation) in his Spanish? At least he translated mutually for me and the Spanish speakers at crucial moments.

26 January

1. I understood at least *what was being talked about* on the radio this morning and can definitely segment, but there is still the problem of the vocabulary I don't know.

2. I feel sure now that in an immersion situation, at least for adults on their own, it is important to have someone to whom one may have recourse in one's own language (that is, in a nonteaching situation and in isolation) because one feels such an idiot when one cannot express one's own personality at least from time to time. It can be quite traumatic.

27 January

1. It was very reassuring that today I was able to listen in to a long conversation between the Swiss, the architect, and the social worker on the boat and could follow quite well what it was all about. I did not get the nuances of meaning because of all the words missed, but I definitely felt I was getting the segmentation of the language. (The Swiss explained the really interesting parts later. It was about what the local people thought of the present political situation.)

2. Now that the group knows me they are very helpful and I am gradually expressing myself more and being more like me. Being able to slip into fluent English or French with my Swiss friends occasionally is a help. (We talk about linguistics and many other interesting subjects.)

28 January

1. I worked on my Spanish in the bus while traveling through parts we had been through twice before. My procedure: (a) reading attentively and learning expressions from the reading, (b) checking in the dictionary on words and expressions I needed immediately, and (c) making up sentences based on (a) and (b), repeating these in my head and where possible trying them out on others in the bus. (I think this is the key: continually trying to construct new sentences with anything one is trying to learn); (d) checking in the grammar sections of the textbook I brought for all sorts of things I needed immediately, from demonstratives to reflexives, and particularly *irregular verbs,* and continually referring back to the verb forms of the different tenses. (Quite clearly this is basic, and I am particularly pleased that my teacher in our six rapid

lessons did give me past, present, and future and *I have to* and *I must* forms.) I still feel not having an English-Spanish section in my textbook is a distinct disadvantage and hobbles me in trying to create new sentences.

2. My tour companions are very helpful and look pleased when I produce a bright new sentence out of the blue. Their understanding of my effort and their pleasure at my having made the effort are certainly rewarding (reinforcing?).

3. I was in despair this afternoon because in the bus there were several rapid conversations in my vicinity (one a discussion on religion between the guide and *las lolas* from the Catholic University in S). I could tell what the subject was, but not what the arguments were at all. On the other hand I was encouraged when we returned to the hotel and sat around having an apéritif, because I was able to understand individuals, some of whom I had had difficulty understanding before, and was able to contribute to the conversation and make some of them laugh.

4. It was Ricardo's thirteenth birthday and we had all sorts of fun and games, champagne and birthday cake, singing, etc. I got the general drift of most of it because of actions and an obvious context, but again found around-the-table discussion hard. I do feel it is coming, however, and must keep plunging in.

Having A-M to translate table jokes at times is a help and makes me feel more "in."

5. Our Swiss friends have left us, which is probably a good thing for me, since I'll not have that "out" for the last four days of the tour.

6. German still pops into my mind, and in the morning I have to concentrate on what language I'm to use. I think I can say that the interference comes from the most recent of my two weakest languages. This is hard to judge. Is it because German is the non-Romance language and the Romance languages help as a source of possible positive transfer (admitting that I am well aware that there may not be direct transfer), so I can take a chance adapting the transfer according to rules I already know? Or does using my weakest language make me feel I am "talking foreign" and therefore seem appropriate? Of course, let's admit it, I've forgotten my Italian!

7. The emotional problems in all this are clearly important, as witness my breakdown on the first day. I, of course, benefit from my social and intellectual maturity, determination, and overwhelming desire to get as much out of this month as possible, and my knowledge of how to go about learning a language. How are these transferable to the average L_2 learner?

8. I'm fortunate in knowing (or being forewarned) of such features of local conversational Spanish as the tendency to drop final *s*. I have to compensate for this.

9. I am still misled by the *ll* and *j/g* plus *e* or *i* pronunciations. This shows that I am mentally visualizing unrecognized words in order to make any unnecessary adjustments to make them guessable from French or Latin, and also so that I can scan the lexicon I have stored. Unfortunately this process takes too long and the conversation moves on while I'm stuck on an earlier

word—which shows the value of practice in rapid recognition of words in oral form.

10. I find I'm thinking in Spanish when I speak my little sentences, although I consciously construct them in my head, with due attention to any rules I know first.

11. I'm also thinking in Spanish when I read, and it's true that reading "in Spanish" what one can read—that is, reading ahead for the complete contexts—helps enormously in deciphering the words; then, when I come to a block, I begin to go over the surrounding context in English translation to see if I can make it out before referring to the dictionary (which is only a last resort because I'm too lazy anyway). I don't worry too much about the tense forms I haven't learned because they become clear (or else don't matter), but it's those wretched little irregulars again which mess things up.

12. I am still filling in gaps in my knowledge of the *often, everywhere, nearly, perhaps, in front of, behind, inside* types of words. I've picked up rejoinders like *Claro!* and *Exacto!* from listening to others, but need more of the soothing noises for social occasions.

29 January

1. I have given the impression that only German and Italian seem to interfere. This is from the lexical point of view mainly. When I'm seeking a common word, *sehr* pops up instead of *muy* but in the correct word class, so it is really lexical interference. French acts as a guide lexically as does Latin—a guide to word formation; but French structure interferes much more than English structure—in fact I am tempted to use the seeming equivalent of the French *passé composé* for conversational past when the actual form required is much closer to ordinary English past tense. That this is an effect of the close correspondences between French and Spanish that occur elsewhere is very possible. Similarly I had problems at the beginning (and probably still do without knowing it) with transference of French stress (not English, which is more similar) and of French sounds in parallel words *una* as /yna/ for instance, and a French /lj/ for *millón*. I also tend to make participles in compound tenses agree with subjects or objects, which comes from French and is not Spanish.

2. Certainly ways of looking at *being* (*estar/ser*) and ways of expressing time are interesting problems.

3. The gender agreement part is no problem (once you know the gender) because of previous experience with French, Italian, German, and Latin. It's almost expected and it might be more of a problem if it didn't exist, since for me "speaking foreign" implies watching out for genders.

31 January

1. It is very frustrating that one does not use what one knows in the heat of producing an utterance in a situation which requires it immediately. So I go into a shop and make up some muddled sentence for "Where can I buy films?" and make various peculiar mistakes so no one understands until I wave the package of my former film under their noses and wave my arms

around saying *Dónde*. Then afterwards I remember I know perfectly well *se vende. Dónde se venden películas?* We should remember this. An oral interview does not always reveal what students know unless the students are feeling relaxed and at ease, and even then they may well be furious with themselves for making silly mistakes and forgetting useful expressions. The SI line, I guess [see *Practical Guides*, chap. 2].

2. When dealing with adult students, and probably bright high school students, we should familiarize them with the book, encourage them to look ahead and find out how certain things are expressed if they find they need them, teaching them how to use the grammatical index and dictionary correctly. I'm continually looking ahead beyond what I am learning to see how it fits into the total picture. Am I exceptional? At least for third-language learners this should be useful.

3. I still have problems with those wretched verbs and vocabulary—common things like *since, again, forget, remember, right away.* Is there a Spanish equivalent for *quand même?*

4. *Listening.* I am still struggling with understanding rapid speech between other speakers. In a one-to-one situation one can control the exchange either by one's own selection of topic, or by lack of comprehension, which results in slower, more careful speech from the other person. For normal rapid speech not addressed to me I am now trying to let it soak in without trying to understand and retain words as they come—like reading for comprehension. I remember what I have written about stages of comprehension and try to apply it. I am understanding better little by little. I understood the guide better yesterday when he was talking about a fort which I had read up beforehand.

5. It is very important to try out in new sentences what you have just learned, if not to others, at least in private talk to yourself.

6. I just came out with *"mais aber sed"* for *pero!*

7. When you don't know a language very well, people you talk to seem to fall into four groups: (a) those who treat you as some kind of idiot and wave their hands at you showing four fingers for 4; (b) those who come close and mouth everything at you in an exaggerated way, distorting syllables and raising their voices; (c) those who avoid you completely so as not to be embarrassed; (d) the helpful ones, who continue to speak normally, if simply, and show encouraging understanding, supply a word or two, or quietly correct.

8. Being with the same group of intelligent people for a while is rather inhibiting of attempts at expression, because you feel something of an idiot if you keep on saying simplistic things; and also because, since you do not completely understand, you realize your simplistic sentences may not hit the right spot, in which case they will be greeted with polite tolerance or explanations of what was really being discussed.

9. Quiet conversations with one person or a couple are best for expression. I've done a lot of concentrated listening in distorted conditions: at long dinner tables in crowded restaurants, shouted conversations in jolting buses (some-

times with the radio blaring), listening to the guide shout in the bus. All of this has been good because I'm beginning now to hear the words in quiet conversation and on the radio, and people are really not using complicated expressions.

10. Now that I can "hear" what they are saying, I can see that in the local Spanish they not only drop final *s* as in Punta Arena(s), but also in the middle of words and phrases: "E'paña" and "e'tá." It helps to know these things.

1 February

[First day of fourth week]

1. When I go into a post office or shop with a neat little sentence and there are complications, my mind goes a complete blank and I lose all the Spanish I thought I had and become a dumb tourist, not understanding a word and not being able to frame a sentence. (Even now my French deteriorates in similar circumstances.) This is maddening and must be what nervous students undergo when oral exams do not approximate their expectations. This should be kept in mind. Clearly what I am learning must become much more automatic to be useful in such situations. Just now I couldn't frame "I gave it to you" when the mail clerk couldn't find the letter I had just put stamps on and handed her. Well, quite obviously three weeks isn't much, even in a country where the language is spoken.

2. In plane to S: I find I can talk with much less inhibition to strangers in the plane, probably because I can say all the simplistic little things one says on first meeting—information about oneself, comments on the situation. These have already been said when one is with the same people for a while. I also find I can understand now what is being said to me, not necessarily all the words but enough cue words to know what it is all about.

2 February

Back in VM. I listened to a lot of television today. It is frustrating to feel myself on the brink of understanding, yet not understanding more than the general drift. I am now recognizing many words that I've learned. I tried listening and trying to project meaning and this helped with the general drift. Of course, the visual elements (facial expressions, dress and bearing of the various characters, and gestures and actions) help, especially in soap operas or "novelas." Then I tried a different training procedure: ignoring the continuing meaning and trying to train myself to recognize the words rapidly without trying to keep the developing meaning in mind. I am certainly understanding much more than before I went on the tour, but I'm not there yet.

3 February

When I'm in France I think in French all the time. Here I think in English and so have to switch consciously to Spanish when I need to speak it. This makes for a slow reaction, then a slow construction of the message, and occasional false starts like coming out with greetings in Italian or German or English. When quick reactions are required, "Yes" or a rejoinder like "Fine"

511

or "OK," I tend to insert English in the Spanish utterance (or French—I tend to say *Oui* rather than *Sí,* which is after all similar in sound as well as meaning and seems to fit without clashing).

4 February

1. I was listening to the Minister of Housing giving an economic report to the nation last night. I felt I was following and understanding in Spanish so long as I didn't take up valuable processing time to mentally translate and digest figures (percentages, GNP, balance of payments, etc.), except simple ones like 6%. If I did, I missed the continuing message. The best thing seems to be to listen and try to follow the words at this stage without worrying too much about processing and retaining the meaning over long segments (like stringing on beads without stopping to straighten up the string). Clearly one needs to do a great deal of listening without being required to recapitulate the meaning. There should be much more intensive listening practice provided, if fluent comprehension is to be developed. Without the latter, ability to produce sentences is rather useless.

I feel I am on the brink of a breakthrough in comprehension, but how much more intensive listening is required is not clear. Sometimes closing my eyes helps, because processing all the visual elements on the television screen takes up mental space. So close listening to the sound without the image *is* valuable, and this distracting aspect of the visual element should be kept in mind. The visual helps with clues but also hinders because it must be processed.

2. I have been learning about stem-changing verbs and writing them down with correct changes but wrong endings (for *ir, er, ar* etc.). Yet I know these! But I am clearly distracted by the stem changes. I make mistakes which do not reflect lack of knowledge. A note in the book—"Be careful: Note that these verbs are from different conjugations"—would have helped avoid this. Fortunately I picked up on it myself while checking verb paradigms, but will all students?

3. With material on tapes or cassettes, it is a real problem if you don't catch the model sentence properly to begin with. Model sentences should be repeated or, better still, students should have their own tapes or cassettes so they can run the tape back to the sentence they didn't comprehend and hear it over as often as they need to get it.

4. In early learning I like to repeat the correct version of an exercise item after the tape model to get correct intonation and pronunciation (4-phase), so time should be allowed for this. (This goes against something I said in the *Practical Guides.*)

5. More about practice exercises. Students need time to formulate the responses, particularly when the drill requires verb adjustments, stem-changing, and switching in different slots. They also should have the opportunity to go over any particular exercise until they feel comfortable with it (hence the value of individual control of tapes or cassettes). I certainly need this anyway.

6. I had lunch today with Gina Lollabrigida—and about 250 other people. The secret of social (cocktail) communication is to look pleasant, keep a

"listening" appearance, and follow facial and kinesic cues, saying *Exacto* and *Claro* at suitable moments. This is especially so when the noise level reaches that of the Concorde. Intonation indicates when you should be responding. These are the dangerous moments when you should keep your ears tuned for a cue word and take off from there, turning it into a question as soon as possible.

5 February

1. I went to a family service in Spanish at the church. I understood some of the sermon from expectations aroused by associations with some key words. Conducting the service and preaching was a young man about twenty years old who spoke Spanish rapidly and naturally.
2. I went to cocktails with E's neighbors in the building. There were five of us: the ophthalmologist and his wife, another neighbor, E and myself. I managed to conduct a conversation with them and to get the gist of most of what was being said, so the three and a half weeks have led somewhere. Verb endings of tenses in various conjugations are still a problem, naturally, despite my efforts to memorize a great deal in a short time. They don't come out automatically in the flush of trying to construct interesting sentences. I find I can make people laugh, even in simple sentences. Spanish seems easier to string together than French or German, or perhaps I just don't know any better yet!
3. Clearly for aural comprehension on tapes, single sentences require very careful listening and relistening to hear them accurately. Those preparing tapes should use longer contexts from the beginning. I am looking for an opportunity to listen to stretches of the language, but the tapes don't provide these, even though this is what they could most usefully supply to supplement a class lesson.

6 February

Ability to comprehend aurally seems to come and go at this stage, being dependent not only on degree of concentration. When I first begin listening to TV it seems something of a blur and I feel as though I've learned nothing. After a while (ten minutes or a quarter of an hour?) it begins to sort itself out a bit. I have to concentrate hard and consciously, otherwise my mind takes the easy road of receding from the effort and reverting to the blur. In other words, listening with comprehension is hard work and conscious work.

7 February

Four weeks today since my arrival in this country and three and a half weeks since I began learning Spanish. I find I can chat away in Spanish quite freely in unsophisticated conversation but am inhibited by my usually intelligent standard of comments when in sophisticated company. For instance, when we visited the director of the Museum of Fine Arts I couldn't think of how to say a single intelligent thing, although I understood the discussion. The one bright comment I did try to make came out half in French, and the director and E stared, clearly puzzled. On the other hand I chatted quite extensively with the girl from the Institute who accompanied me to a bookshop and the bank, and to her children.

9 February

I got in a hassle at the airport for my departure from the country because some official had never stamped my arrival! Habits are strong, so since the girl at the counter understood some English I continued to talk fast in English (always a mistake with non-native speakers as I should know from my own experiences). When she took me to see the police officer, who didn't understand a word of English, I suddenly burst into fluent (and flawless?) Spanish, which brought kindly amused smiles to both their faces and everything was smoothed out in the usual way in this culture—"No problems." It is interesting that in a sticky situation it never occurred to me to make use of my newly acquired Spanish (the obvious way to behave), presumably because of deep-rooted emotional convictions that link my native language with "talking my way out of trouble." How insecure one feels in relying on newly acquired skills when "important" outcomes are at stake.

10 February

Visiting a French-speaking family in L, I found my newly acquired Spanish interfering with my French for the first time, particularly function words like *pero,* as though my mind is now geared to searching my Spanish lexicon for function words instead of my French lexicon.

11 February

In C, I watched the mime in a "street theater" (children's theater) in the central square. I found I could understand what he was saying when he was explaining his purposes because he was speaking loudly and distinctly, since it was in the open air in a large area and presumably also because there were so many small children there.

12 February

1. I went to a service in the cathedral on Sunday morning and by concentrating was able to comprehend the subject matter and general development of the sermon, although not the details, because the semantic area (beginning of Lent and Lenten duties of Christians) was familiar to me and I could anticipate and guess meaning to fill in for lack of knowledge.
2. I went around the Temple of the Sun with a Quechua/Spanish-speaking guide and found I could comprehend on a one-to-one basis. In this situation, the speaker adapts to hesitancies, questioning looks and incorrect rejoinders by repeating, re-explaining, or elaborating, and there are visual objects being described and explained. I had also read information about Inca customs and practices, so again the area of discussion was not completely unknown, which clearly helps in leaping gaps of incomprehension and putting together a message.

3. I am improving gradually in following what is being said on the radio. I am still identifying the general subject matter without being sure of the details, but have more moments when I comprehend the details too.

13 February
1. On the way to MP in the train (a trip of three and a half hours each way) I was with a Peruvian girl, a Venezuelan, and an Argentinian. I was able to tell them about myself and conduct general (minor) conversation, with resort to English and French here and there. I was well accepted and included in the group.
2. I could understand the explanations of the Spanish-speaking guides, again aided by the visual element and previous knowledge of the subject.

14 February
My glasses were stolen in the park. I spent about two hours with various policemen in two commissariats, with one officer in particular (a handsome young man!) who took over the case, and I was apparently able to make myself perfectly clear, because I found out later that at least one of the officers actually spoke English very well but he didn't attempt to use it. This was a very good test of my ability to "survive" in the language when I had to and was not able to take the easy way out of asserting my superiority by loudly holding forth in English (thus treating the native as the "foolish foreigner," as I did on my return from MP to C when I found out from the hotel personnel that the airline had no record of me on the list for a twice-reconfirmed flight).

15 February
At the Airport at L
1. I had quite a lengthy conversation with a family group of Spanish speakers who will be emigrating to Australia in March. The importance of the conversation to the Spanish speakers (meeting a real Australian and finding out more about conditions in Melbourne) created a desire to comprehend. I was able to bring out my most practiced sentences (who I was, what I did, where I came from) and construct informative sentences from which the listeners were anxious to extract information (there was plenty of motivation to communicate on both sides). I was able to comprehend their questions and personal explanations, which were on a one-to-one or very small group basis (two or three persons) centered on me. Those who had already spoken with me would urge the others to give me time to put my sentences together.
2. At least from my five weeks' experience with Spanish I have acquired the ability to "survive" orally and in graphic form (since I can now also read the newspapers, information booklets, police reports, and notices without difficulty). The necessity of everyday contact has played a considerable role in forcing me to make an effort which it would have been more comfortable to avoid, and as a result my confidence has been boosted.

Abbreviations

ACTFL	American Council on the Teaching of Foreign Languages (2 Park Avenue, New York, N.Y. 10016)
ACTFL Review	*ACTFL Reviews of Foreign Language Education* (Skokie, Ill.: National Textbook Company)
ADFL	*Bulletin of the Association of Departments of Foreign Languages* (Modern Language Association of America, 62 Fifth Avenue, New York, N.Y. 10011)
AL	*Applied Linguistics* (Oxford: Oxford University Press)
CMLR	*Canadian Modern Language Review* (Ontario Modern Language Teachers Association)
CSC	Central States Conference on the Teaching of Foreign Languages. Annual Report (Skokie, Ill.: National Textbook Company)
EAL	English as an Auxiliary Language
EAP	English for Academic Purposes
EEP	English for Educational Purposes
EIL	English as an International Language
ELA	*Etudes de Linguistique Appliquée* (Paris: Didier Erudition)
ELL	Early Language Learning
ETF	*English Teaching Forum* (Washington, D.C.: United States International Communication Agency)
ETS	Education Testing Services (Princeton, N.J.)
FLA	*Foreign Language Annals* (American Council on Teaching of Foreign Languages, 2 Park Avenue, New York, N.Y. 10016)
FLES	Foreign Language in the Elementary School
GA	General American
GB	General British
IRAL	*International Review on Applied Linguistics in Language Teaching* (Heidelberg: Julius Gross Verlag)
LST	Language for Science and Technology

Abbreviations

LL	*Language Learning* (University of Michigan, Ann Arbor, Mich. 48109)
LOP	Language for Occupational Purposes (for English, EOP)
LSP	Language for Special (Specific) Purposes (for English, ESP)
LTDA	*Language Teaching and Linguistics Abstracts* (Cambridge, U.K.: Cambridge University Press)
MLA	Modern Language Association (62 Fifth Avenue, New York, N.Y. 10011)
MLJ	*Modern Language Journal* (National Federation of Modern Language Teachers Associations, U.S.A.)
NALLD	National Association of Learning Laboratory Directors
NEC	Northeast Conference on the Teaching of Foreign Languages. Annual Report (Box 623, Middlebury, Vt. 05753)
NFER	National Foundation for Educational Research (Slough, Berkshire, U.K.)
PG's	*Practical Guides to the Teaching of English/French/German/Hebrew/Spanish,* by Wilga M. Rivers and others (see Bibliography)
RELC	*Regional Language Center Journal* (Singapore)
SMT	*Speaking in Many Tongues,* expanded 2d ed., by Wilga M. Rivers (Rowley, Mass.: Newbury House, 1976)
TQ	*TESOL Quarterly* (Teachers of English to Speakers of Other Languages; Washington, D.C.: School of Languages and Linguistics, Georgetown University)

Selected Bibliography

Aaronson, Doris, and Rieber, R. W., eds. 1975. *Developmental Psycholinguistics and Communication Disorders*. New York: New York Academy of Sciences.

Agard, Frederick B., and Di Pietro, Robert J. 1965. *The Grammatical Structures of English and Italian*. Contrastive Structure Series, ed. Charles A. Ferguson. Chicago: University of Chicago Press.

————. 1965. *The Sounds of English and Italian*. Contrastive Structure Series, ed. Charles A. Ferguson. Chicago: University of Chicago Press.

Alatis, James E., ed. 1968. *Contrastive Linguistics and Its Pedagogical Implications*. Georgetown University Round Table on Languages and Linguistics. Washington, D.C.: Georgetown University Press.

————, ed. 1970a. *Linguistics and the Teaching of Standard English to Speakers of Other Languages or Dialects*. Georgetown University Round Table on Languages and Linguistics. Washington, D.C.: Georgetown University Press.

————, ed. 1970b. *Bilingualism and Language Contact: Anthropological, Linguistic, Psychological, and Sociological Aspects*. Georgetown University Round Table on Languages and Linguistics. Washington, D.C.: Georgetown University Press.

Alatis, James E.; Altman, Howard B.; and Alatis, Penelope M., eds. 1981. *The Second Language Classroom: Directions for the 1980's*. New York: Oxford University Press.

Alatis, James E., and Twaddell, Kristie, eds. 1976. *English as a Second Language in Bilingual Education: Selected TESOL Papers*. Washington, D.C.: Teachers of English to Speakers of Other Languages.

Ali Bouacha, Abdelmadjid, ed. 1978. *La pédagogie du français langue étrangère*. Paris: Hachette.

Allen, Edward D., and Valette, Rebecca M. 1977. *Classroom Techniques: Foreign Languages and English as a Second Language*. New York: Harcourt Brace Jovanovich.

Allen, Harold B., ed. 1964. *Readings in Applied English Linguistics*. New York: Appleton-Century-Crofts.

Allen, Harold B., and Campbell, Russell N., eds. 1972. *Teaching English as a Second Language: A Book of Readings*. 2d ed. New York: McGraw-Hill.

Allen, J. P. B., and Corder, S. Pit., eds. 1973. *Readings for Applied Linguistics*. The Edinburgh Course in Applied Linguistics, vol. 1. London: Oxford University Press.

————. 1974. *Techniques in Applied Linguistics*. The Edinburgh Course in Applied Linguistics, vol. 3. London: Oxford University Press.

————. 1975. *Papers in Applied Linguistics*. The Edinburgh Course in Applied Linguistics, vol. 2. London: Oxford University Press.

Allen, J. P. B., and Davies, Alan, eds. 1977. *Testing and Experimental Methods*. The Edinburgh Course in Applied Linguistics, vol. 4. London: Oxford University Press.

Alter, Maria P. *A Modern Case for German*. 1970. Philadelphia: American Association of Teachers of German.

Altman, Howard B., ed. 1972. *Individualizing the Foreign Language Classroom*. Rowley, Mass.: Newbury House.

Altman, Howard B., and Hanzeli, Victor E., eds. 1974. *Essays on the Teaching of Culture*. A Festschrift to Honor Howard Lee Nostrand. Detroit, Mich.: Advancement Press.

Andersson, Theodore. 1969. *Foreign Languages in the Elementary School: A Struggle against Mediocrity*. Austin: University of Texas Press.

Andersson, Theodore, and Boyer, Mildred. 1978. *Bilingual Schooling in the United States*. 2d ed. Austin, Texas: National Educational Laboratory Publishers.

Benamou, Michel. 1971. *Pour une nouvelle pédagogie du texte littéraire*. Paris: Hachette/Larousse.

Benseler, David P.; Schulz, Renate A.; and Smith, W. Flint, eds. 1979. *Teaching the Basics in the Foreign Language Classroom: Options and Strategies*. CSC 1979. Skokie, Ill.: National Textbook Company.

Birkmaier, Emma M., ed. 1968. *Foreign Language Education: An Overview*. Britannica Review of Foreign Language Education, vol. 1. Chicago: Encyclopaedia Britannica.

Bloomfield, Leonard. 1942. *Outline Guide for the Study of Foreign Languages*. Baltimore, Md.: Linguistic Society of America.

Bolinger, Dwight. 1975. *Aspects of Language*. 2d ed. New York: Harcourt Brace Jovanovich.

Bowen, J. Donald. 1975. *Patterns of English Pronunciation*. Rowley, Mass.: Newbury House. (For GA.)

Bowen, J. Donald, and Ornstein, Jacob, eds. 1976. *Studies in Southwest Spanish*. Rowley, Mass.: Newbury House.

Brooks, Nelson. 1964. *Language and Language Learning: Theory and Practice*. 2d ed. New York: Harcourt, Brace & World. (1st ed., 1960.)

Brown, George Isaac. 1971. *Human Teaching for Human Learning: An Introduction to Confluent Education*. New York: Viking Press.

Brown, H. Douglas, ed. 1976. *Papers in Second Language Acquisition*. LL Special Issue 4. Ann Arbor, Mich.: Research Club in Language Learning.

————. 1980. *Principles of Language Learning and Teaching*. Englewood Cliffs, N.J.: Prentice-Hall.

Brown, Roger. 1973. *A First Language: The Early Stages*. Cambridge, Mass.: Harvard University Press.

Brumfit, C. J., and Johnson, K., eds. 1979. *The Communicative Approach to Language Teaching*. Oxford: Oxford University Press.

Burney, Pierre, and Damoiseau, Robert. 1969. *La Classe de conversation*. Paris: Hachette.

Burstall, Clare; Jamieson, Monika; Cohen, Susan; and Hargreaves, Margaret. 1974. *Primary French in the Balance*. Windsor, U.K.: NFER Publishing Company.

Burt, Marina K., and Dulay, Heidi C., eds. 1975. *On TESOL: New Directions in Second Language Learning, Teaching and Bilingual Education*. Washington, D.C.: Teachers of English to Speakers of Other Languages.

Burt, Marina K.; Dulay, Heidi C.; and Finocchiaro, Mary, eds. 1977. *Viewpoints on English as a Second Language*. In Honor of James E. Alatis. New York: Regents Publishing Co.

Burt, Marina K., and Kiparsky, Carol. 1972. *The Gooficon: A Repair Manual for English*. Rowley, Mass.: Newbury House.

Byrne, Donn. 1979. *Teaching Writing Skills*. London: Longman.

Carroll, John B., ed. 1956. *Language, Thought, and Reality: Selected Writings of Benjamin Lee Whorf*. Cambridge, Mass.: MIT Press.

———. 1964. *Language and Thought*. Foundations of Modern Psychology Series. Englewood Cliffs, N.J.: Prentice-Hall.

———. 1975. *The Teaching of French as a Foreign Language in Eight Countries*. New York: Halsted Press/John Wiley.

Carroll, John B., and Freedle, Roy O., eds. 1972. *Language Comprehension and the Acquisition of Knowledge*. Washington, D.C.: V. H. Winston & Sons.

Catford, J. C. 1965. *A Linguistic Theory of Translation*. London: Oxford University Press.

Celce-Murcia, Marianne, and McIntosh, Lois, eds. 1979. *Teaching English as a Second or Foreign Language*. Rowley, Mass.: Newbury House.

Chastain, Kenneth. 1976. *Developing Second-Language Skills: Theory to Practice*. 2d ed. Chicago: Rand McNally. (A revision of *The Development of Modern Language Skills: Theory to Practice*. Philadelphia: The Center for Curriculum Development, 1971.)

Cherry, Colin. 1957. *On Human Communication*. New York: John Wiley & Sons.

Chomsky, Noam. 1957. *Syntactic Structures*. The Hague: Mouton.

———. 1965. *Aspects of the Theory of Syntax*. Cambridge, Mass.: MIT Press.

———. 1972a. *Language and Mind*. Enlarged ed. New York: Harcourt Brace Jovanovich. (Original ed. 1968.)

———. 1972b. *Studies on Semantics in Generative Grammar*. The Hague: Mouton.

Cohen, Andrew D. 1975. *A Sociolinguistic Approach to Bilingual Education*. Rowley, Mass.: Newbury House.

———. 1980. *Testing Language Ability in the Classroom*. Rowley, Mass.: Newbury House.

Coleman, Algernon. 1929. *The Teaching of Modern Foreign Languages in the United States*. Publications of the American and Canadian Committees on Modern Languages, vol. 12. New York: Macmillan.

Selected Bibliography

Corder, S. Pit. 1973. *Introducing Applied Linguistics*. Harmondsworth, U.K.: Penguin Education.

Coste, Daniel; Courtillon, Janine; Ferenczi, Victor; Martins-Baltar, Michel; and Papo, Eliane. 1976. *Un niveau-seuil*. Strasbourg: Council of Europe.

Council for Cultural Cooperation. 1973. *Systems Development in Adult Language Learning*, by J. L. M. Trim, R. Richterich, J. A. van Ek, and D. A. Wilkins. Strasbourg: Council of Europe. (Republished 1980 by Pergamon Press.)

————. 1977. *A European Unit/Credit System for Modern Language Learning by Adults*, by J. L. M. Trim. Strasbourg: Council of Europe. (Republished 1980 by Pergamon Press as *Developing a Unit/Credit Scheme for Adult Language Learning*.)

Crawshaw, Bernard. 1972. *Let's Play Games in French*. Skokie, Ill.: National Textbook Co.

Croft, Kenneth., ed. 1980. *Readings on English as a Second Language: For Teachers and Teacher Trainees*. 2d ed. Cambridge, Mass.: Winthrop.

Curran, Charles A. C. 1976. *Counseling-Learning in Second Languages*. Apple River, Ill.: Apple River Press.

Dakin, Julian. 1973. *The Language Laboratory and Language Learning*. London: Longman.

Dalbor, J. B. 1969. *Spanish Pronunciation: Theory and Practice*. New York: Holt, Rinehart & Winston.

Dato, Daniel P., ed. 1975. *Developmental Psycholinguistics: Theory and Application*. Georgetown University Round Table on Languages and Linguistics. Washington, D.C.: Georgetown University Press.

Davies, Alan, ed. 1968. *Language Testing Symposium*. London: Oxford University Press.

Delattre, Pierre. 1951. *Principes de phonétique française à l'usage des étudiants anglo-américains*. Middlebury, Vt.: Middlebury College.

————. 1965. *Comparing the Phonetic Features of English, French, German and Spanish*. London: Harrap.

Dil, Anwar S., ed. 1972. *Language in Sociocultural Change. Essays by Joshua A. Fishman*. Stanford: Stanford University Press.

Diller, Karl C. 1978. *The Language Teaching Controversy*. Rowley, Mass.: Newbury House.

Di Pietro, Robert J. 1971. *Language Structures in Contrast*. Rowley, Mass.: Newbury House.

Dobson, Julia M. 1974. *Effective Techniques for English Conversation Groups*. Rowley, Mass.: Newbury House.

Dodge, James W., ed. 1971. *The Case for Foreign Language Study*. New York: Northeast Conference and MLA/ACTFL.

Donoghue, Mildred R. and Kunkle, John F. 1979. *Second Languages in Primary Education*. Rowley, Mass.: Newbury House.

Eastman, Carol M. 1978. *Linguistic Theory and Language Description*. New York: J. P. Lippincott.

Fanselow, John F., and Crymes, Ruth H., eds. 1976. *On TESOL '76*. Washington, D.C.: Teachers of English to Speakers of Other Languages.

Farb, Peter. 1975. *Word Play: What Happens When People Talk*. New York: Bantam Books. (Original publication: Alfred A. Knopf, 1974.)

Ferguson, Charles A. and Slobin, Dan I., eds. 1973. *Studies of Child Language Development*. New York: Holt, Rinehart & Winston.

Finocchiaro, Mary. 1974. *English as a Second Language: From Theory to Practice*. New York: Regents Publishing Co.

Finocchiaro, Mary, and Bonomo, Michael. 1973. *The Foreign Language Learner: A Guide for Teachers*. New York: Regents Publishing Co.

Fishman, Joshua A., ed. 1968. *Readings in the Sociology of Language*. The Hague: Mouton.

—————. 1971. *Sociolinguistics: A Brief Introduction*. Rowley, Mass.: Newbury House.

—————. 1976. *Bilingual Education: An International Sociological Perspective*. Rowley, Mass.: Newbury House.

Freudenstein, Reinhold, ed. 1979. *Teaching Foreign Languages to the Very Young: Papers from Seven Countries on Work with 4- to 8-Year Olds*. Oxford: Pergamon Press.

Fries, Charles C. 1945. *Teaching and Learning English as a Foreign Language*. Ann Arbor: University of Michigan Press.

—————. 1963. *Linguistics and Reading*. New York: Holt, Rinehart & Winston.

Fromkin, Victoria, and Rodman, Robert. 1974. *An Introduction to Language*. New York: Holt, Rinehart & Winston.

Fry, Edward B. 1963. *Teaching Machines and Programmed Instruction: An Introduction*. New York: McGraw Hill.

Gaarder, A. Bruce. 1977. *Bilingual Schooling and the Survival of Spanish in the United States*. Rowley, Mass.: Newbury House.

Gardner, R. C., and Lambert, W. E. 1972. *Attitudes and Motivation in Second-Language Learning*. Rowley, Mass.: Newbury House.

Gattegno, Caleb. 1972. *Teaching Foreign Languages in Schools: The Silent Way*. 2d ed. New York: Educational Solutions.

George, H. V. 1972. *Common Errors in Language Learning: Insights from English*. Rowley, Mass.: Newbury House.

Gerli, E. Michael; Alatis, James E.; and Brod, Richard I., eds. 1978. *Language in American Life*. Washington, D.C.: Georgetown University Press.

Giglioli, Pier P., ed. 1972. *Language and Social Context*. Harmondsworth, U.K.: Penguin Books.

Gimson, A. C. 1970. *An Introduction to the Pronunciation of English*. 2d ed. London: Edward Arnold. (For GB.)

Girard, Denis. 1972. *Linguistics and Language Teaching*. London: Longman.

—————. 1974. *Les Langues vivantes*. Paris: Larousse.

Gleason, H. A., Jr. 1961. *An Introduction to Descriptive Linguistics*. Rev. ed. New York: Holt, Rinehart & Winston.

Selected Bibliography

Gouin, François. 1892. *The Art of Teaching and Studying Languages*. Trans. H. Swan and V. Bétis. London: George Philip & Son; New York: Charles Scribner's Sons.

Grazia, Alfred de, and Sohn, David A., eds. 1964. *Programs, Teachers and Machines*. New York: Bantam Books.

Green, Jerald R. 1968. *A Gesture Inventory for the Teaching of Spanish*. Philadelphia: Chilton.

Grittner, Frank M., ed. 1974. *Student Motivation and the Foreign Language Teacher: A Guide for Building the Modern Curriculum*. CSC 1973. Skokie, Ill.: National Textbook Company.

———. 1977. *Teaching Foreign Languages*. 2d ed. New York: Harper & Row.

———, ed. 1980. *Learning a Second Language*. Seventy-ninth Yearbook of the National Society for the Study of Education, pt. 2. Chicago: University of Chicago Press.

Grittner, Frank M., and LaLeike, Fred H. 1973. *Individualized Foreign Language Instruction*. Skokie, Ill.: National Textbook Company.

Gumperz, John J., and Hymes, Dell, eds. 1972. *Directions in Sociolinguistics: The Ethnography of Communication*. New York: Holt, Rinehart & Winston.

Gunderson, Doris V., ed. 1970. *Language and Reading: An Interdisciplinary Approach*. Washington, D.C.: Center for Applied Linguistics.

Hagboldt, Peter. 1940. *The Teaching of German*. Boston: D. C. Heath.

Hall, Edward T. 1959. *The Silent Language*. New York: Doubleday.

———. 1976. *Beyond Culture*. New York: Anchor Press/Doubleday.

Hall, Robert A. 1966. *New Ways to Learn a Foreign Language*. New York: Bantam Books.

Halliday, Michael A. K. 1973. *Explorations in the Functions of Language*. London: Edward Arnold.

———. 1975. *Learning How to Mean: Explorations in the Development of Language*. London: Edward Arnold. (New York: Elsevier, 1977.)

———. 1978. *Language as Social Semiotic: The Social Interpretation of Language and Meaning*. Baltimore: University Park Press.

Halliday, Michael A. K.; McIntosh, Angus; and Strevens, Peter. 1964. *The Linguistic Sciences and Language Teaching*. London: Longman.

Harris, David P. 1969. Testing English as a Second Language. New York: McGraw-Hill.

Hatch, Evelyn. 1978. *Second Language Acquisition: A Book of Readings*. Rowley, Mass.: Newbury House.

Hesse, M. G., ed. 1975. *Approaches to Teaching Foreign Languages*. Amsterdam: North-Holland Publishing Co.

Hester, Ralph, ed. 1970. *Teaching a Living Language*. New York: Harper & Row.

Higgins, J. J. 1969. *A Guide to Language Laboratory Material Writing*. Oslo: Universitetsforlaget.

Selected Bibliography

Hilton, J. B. 1973. *Language Teaching: A Systems Approach.* London: Methuen.

Hockett, Charles F. 1958. *A Course in Modern Linguistics.* New York: Macmillan.

Hörman, Hans. 1979. *Psycholinguistics: An Introduction to Research and Theory.* 2d ed., rev. Trans. H. H. Stern and Peter Lappman. New York: Springer Verlag.

Hornsey, Alan W., ed. 1975. *Handbook for Modern Language Teachers.* London: Methuen.

Hubp, Loretta B. 1974. *Let's Play Games in Spanish.* 2 vols. Skokie, Ill.: National Textbook Company.

Huey, Edmund B. 1968. *The Psychology and Pedagogy of Reading.* Cambridge, Mass.: MIT Press. (Original publication: Macmillan, 1908.)

Hymes, Dell. 1974. *Foundations in Sociolinguistics: An Ethnographic Approach.* Philadelphia: University of Pennsylvania Press.

Inhelder, Barbel, and Piaget, Jean. 1958. *The Growth of Logical Thinking from Childhood to Adolescence.* New York: Basic Books.

Jakobovits, Leon A. 1970. *Foreign Language Learning: A Psycholinguistic Analysis of the Issues.* Rowley, Mass.: Newbury House.

Jakobovits, Leon A., and Gordon, Barbara. 1974. *The Context of Foreign Language Teaching.* Rowley, Mass.: Newbury House.

Jankowsky, Kurt, ed. 1973. *Language and International Studies.* Georgetown University Round Table on Languages and Linguistics. Washington, D.C.: Georgetown University Press.

Jarvis, Gilbert A., ed. 1974a. *Responding to New Realities.* ACTFL Review of Foreign Language Education, vol. 5. Skokie, Ill.: National Textbook Company.

———, ed. 1974b. *The Challenge of Communication.* ACTFL Review of Foreign Language Education, vol. 6. Skokie, Ill.: National Textbook Company.

———, ed. 1975. *Perspective: A New Freedom.* ACTFL Review of Foreign Language Education, vol. 7. Skokie, Ill.: National Textbook Company.

———, ed. 1976. *An Integrative Approach to Foreign Language Teaching: Choosing among the Options.* The ACTFL Foreign Language Education Series, vol. 8. Skokie, Ill.: National Textbook Company.

Jespersen, Otto. 1904. *How to Teach a Foreign Language.* London: George Allen & Unwin. (Reissued 1961.)

Jones, Randall L., and Spolsky, Bernard, eds. 1975. *Testing Language Proficiency.* Arlington, Va.: Center for Applied Linguistics.

Joos, Martin. 1961. *The Five Clocks.* New York: Harcourt, Brace & World.

Keating, Raymond F. 1963. *A Study of the Effectiveness of Language Laboratories.* New York: Institute of Administrative Research, Teachers College, Columbia University.

Kellermann, M. 1981. *The Forgotten Third Skill: Reading a Foreign Language.* Oxford: Pergamon Press.

Kelly, Louis G. 1969. *25 Centuries of Language Teaching*. Rowley, Mass.: Newbury House.

Kloss, Heinz. 1977. *The American Bilingual Tradition*. Rowley, Mass.: Newbury House.

Kinsella, Valerie, ed. 1978. *Language Teaching and Linguistics: Surveys*. Cambridge, U.K.: Cambridge University Press.

Knapp, Mark L. 1978. *Nonverbal Communication in Human Interaction*. 2d ed. New York: Holt, Rinehart & Winston.

Koike, Ikuo; Matsuyama, Masao; Igarashi, Yasuo; and Suzuki, Koji, eds. 1978. *The Teaching of English in Japan*. To Professor Yoshio Ogawa. Tokyo: Eichosha Publishing Company.

Kufner, Herbert L. 1962. *The Grammatical Structures of English and German*. Contrastive Structure Series, ed. Charles A. Ferguson. Chicago: University of Chicago Press.

Lado, Robert. 1957. *Linguistics Across Cultures: Applied Linguistics for Language Teachers*. Ann Arbor: University of Michigan Press.

————. 1961. *Language Testing*. London: Longman.

————. 1964. *Language Teaching: A Scientific Approach*. New York: McGraw-Hill.

Lafayette, Robert C. 1975. *The Cultural Revolution in Foreign Language Teaching: A Guide for Building the Modern Curriculum*. CSC 1975. Skokie, Ill.: National Textbook Company.

Lakoff, Robin. 1975. *Language and Woman's Place*. New York: Harper & Row.

Lambert, Wallace E., and Klineberg, Otto. 1967. *Children's Views of Foreign Peoples*. New York: Appleton-Century-Crofts.

————, and Tucker, G. R. 1972. *Bilingual Education of Children: The St. Lambert Experiment*. Rowley, Mass.: Newbury House.

Lange, Dale L., ed. 1970. *Individualization of Instruction*. Britannica Review of Foreign Language Education, vol. 2. Chicago: Encyclopaedia Britannica.

————, ed. 1971. *Pluralism in Foreign Language Education*. Britannica Review of Foreign Language Education, vol. 3. Chicago: Encyclopaedia Britannica.

Lange, Dale L., and James, Charles J., eds. 1972. *Foreign Language Education: A Reappraisal*. ACTFL Review of Foreign Language Education, vol. 4. Skokie, Ill.: National Textbook Company.

Lee, William R. 1974. *Language Teaching Games and Contests*. London: Oxford University Press.

Lenneberg, Eric H. 1967. *Biological Foundations of Language*. New York: John Wiley & Sons.

Lenneberg, Eric H., and Lenneberg, Elizabeth. 1975. *Foundations of Language Development: A Multidisciplinary Approach*. Vols. 1 and 2. New York: Academic Press; Paris: UNESCO Press.

Léon, Pierre. 1962. *Laboratoire de langues et correction phonétique*. Paris: Didier.

Logan, Gerald E. 1973. *Individualized Foreign Language Learning: An Organic Process.* Rowley, Mass.: Newbury House.

Lourie, Margaret A., and Conklin, Nancy Faires, eds. 1978. *A Pluralistic Nation: The Language Issue in the United States.* Rowley, Mass.: Newbury House.

Lozanov, Georgi. 1978. *Suggestology and Outlines of Suggestopedy.* New York: Gordon & Breach.

Lugton, Robert C., ed. 1970. *English as a Second Language: Current Issues.* Philadelphia: Center for Curriculum Development.

Lumsdaine, A. A., and Glaser, Robert, eds. 1960. *Teaching Machines and Programmed Learning.* Washington, D.C.: Department of Audio-Visual Instruction of the National Education Association.

Lyons, John. 1968. *Introduction to Theoretical Linguistics.* Cambridge, U.K.: Cambridge University Press.

————. 1977. *Semantics.* Vols. 1 and 2. Cambridge, U.K.: Cambridge University Press.

Macaulay, Ronald K. S. 1980. *Generally Speaking: How Children Learn Languages.* Rowley, Mass.: Newbury House.

MacCarthy, P. 1950. *English Pronunciation.* 4th ed. Cambridge, U.K.: Heffer and Sons. (For GB.)

Mackay, Ronald; Barkman, Bruce; and Jordan, R. R., eds. 1979. *Reading in a Second Language: Hypotheses, Organization and Practice.* Rowley, Mass.: Newbury House.

Mackay, Ronald, and Mountford, Alan J., eds. 1978. *English for Specific Purposes: A Case Study Approach.* London: Longman.

Mackey, William F. 1965. *Language Teaching Analysis.* London: Longman.

Mackey, William F., and Andersson, Theodore, eds. 1977. *Bilingualism in Early Childhood.* Rowley, Mass.: Newbury House.

Madsen, H. S., and Bowen, J. D. 1978. *Adaptation in Language Teaching.* Rowley, Mass.: Newbury House.

Magner, T. 1961. *Applied Linguistics: Russian—A Guide for Teachers.* Boston: D. C. Heath & Company.

Marckwardt, Albert M. 1958. *American English.* New York: Oxford University Press.

Maslow, Abraham H. 1970. *Motivation and Personality.* 2d ed. New York: Harper & Row.

McLaughlin, Barry. 1978. *Second-Language Acquisition in Childhood.* New York: Lawrence Erlbaum Associates.

Miller, George A. 1967. *The Psychology of Communication: Seven Essays.* New York: Basic Books. (Republished as *Psychology and Communication.* London: Pelican, 1969.)

————, ed. 1973. *Communication, Language, and Meaning. Psychological Perspectives.* New York: Basic Books.

Mohrmann, C.; Sommerfelt, A.; and Whatmough, J., eds. 1961. *Trends in European and American Linguistics, 1930–1960.* Utrecht: Spectrum Publishers.

Mollica, Anthony, ed. 1976. *A Handbook for Teachers of Italian.* American Association of Teachers of Italian.

Moody, H. L. B. 1971. *The Teaching of Literature with Special Reference to Developing Countries.* London: Longman.

Moskowitz, Gertrude. 1970. *The Foreign Language Teacher Interacts.* Rev. ed. Minneapolis: Association for Productive Teaching.

———. 1978. *Caring and Sharing in the Foreign Language Class: A Sourcebook on Humanistic Techniques.* Rowley, Mass.: Newbury House.

Moss, N. 1973. *What's the Difference: A British/American Dictionary.* New York: Harper & Row.

Moulton, William G. 1962. *The Sounds of English and German.* Contrastive Structure Series, ed. Charles A. Ferguson. Chicago: University of Chicago Press.

Munby, John. 1978. *Communicative Syllabus Design: A Sociolinguistic Model for Defining the Content of Purpose-Specific Language Programmes.* Cambridge, U.K.: Cambridge University Press.

Naiman, N.; Frölich, M.; Stern, H. H.; and Todesco A. 1978. *The Good Language Learner.* Research in Education series, vol. 7. Toronto: Ontario Institute for Studies in Education.

Navarro, Tomás T. 1968. *Studies in Spanish Phonology.* Coral Gables, Fla.: University of Miami Press.

NEC. *See* Northeast Conference on the Teaching of Foreign Languages.

Neisser, Ulrich. 1967. *Cognitive Psychology.* New York: Appleton-Century-Crofts.

Newmark, Maxim, ed. 1948. *Twentieth Century Modern Language Teaching: Sources and Readings.* New York: Philosophical Library.

Newmark, P. P. 1981. *Aspects of Translation.* Oxford: Pergamon Press.

Nickel, Gerhard, ed. 1976. *Proceedings of the Fourth International Congress of Applied Linguistics.* Vols. 1–3. Stuttgart: Hochschulverlag.

Nida, Eugene A. 1957. *Learning a Foreign Language.* Rev. ed. Ann Arbor, Mich.: Friendship Press.

Nida, Eugene A., and Taber, Charles R. 1969. *The Theory and Practice of Translating.* Leiden: E. J. Brill.

Nilsen, Don L. F. and Alleen P. 1975. *Semantic Theory: A Linguistic Perspective.* Rowley, Mass.: Newbury House.

———. 1978. *Language Play: An Introduction to Linguistics.* Rowley, Mass.: Newbury House.

Northeast Conference on the Teaching of Foreign Languages (NEC). 1959. *The Language Learner,* ed. Frederick D. Eddy. (This and all other NEC volumes are obtainable from The Northeast Conference on the Teaching of Foreign Languages, Box 623, Middlebury, Vt. 05753; or from ACTFL Materials Center, 2 Park Avenue, New York, N.Y. 10016. See also Pell 1975.)

———. 1960. *Culture in Language Learning,* ed. G. Reginald Bishop, Jr.

———. 1961. *Modern Language Teaching in School and College,* ed. Seymour L. Flaxman.

———. 1962. *Current Issues in Language Teaching,* ed. William F. Bottiglia.

———. 1963. *Language Learning: The Intermediate Phase,* ed. William F. Bottiglia.

———. 1964. *Foreign Language Teaching: Ideals and Practices,* ed. George F. Jones.

———. 1965. *Foreign Language Teaching: Challenges to the Profession,* ed. G. Reginald Bishop, Jr.

———. 1966. *Language Teaching: Broader Contexts,* ed. Robert G. Mead, Jr.

———. 1967. *Foreign Languages: Reading, Literature, and Requirements,* ed. Thomas E. Bird.

———. 1968. *Foreign Language Learning: Research and Development,* ed. Thomas E. Bird.

———. 1969. *Sight and Sound: The Sensible and Sensitive Use of Audio-Visual Aids,* ed. Mills F. Edgerton, Jr.

———. 1970. *Foreign Languages and the "New" Student,* ed. Joseph A. Tursi.

———. 1971. *Leadership for Continuing Development,* ed. James W. Dodge.

———. 1972. *Other Words, Other Worlds: Language-in-Culture,* ed. James W. Dodge.

———. 1973. *Sensitivity in the Foreign-Language Classroom,* ed. James W. Dodge.

———. 1974. *Toward Student-Centered Foreign-Language Programs,* ed. Warren C. Born.

———. 1975. *Goals Clarification: Curriculum, Teaching, Evaluation,* ed. Warren C. Born.

———. 1976. *Language and Culture: Heritage and Horizons,* ed. Warren C. Born.

———. 1977. *Language: Acquisition, Application, Appreciation,* ed. Warren C. Born.

———. 1978. *New Contents, New Teachers, New Publics,* ed. Warren C. Born.

———. 1979. *The Foreign Language Learner in Today's Classroom Environment,* ed. Warren C. Born.

———. 1980. *Our Profession: Present Status and Future Directions,* ed. Thomas H. Geno.

O'Brien, Maureen C., ed. 1973. *Testing in Second Language Teaching: New Dimensions.* Dublin: Association of Teachers of English as a Second or Other Language, and Dublin University Press.

Oller, John W., Jr. 1979. *Language Tests at School: A Pragmatic Approach.* London: Longman.

Oller, John W., Jr., and Perkins, Kyle, eds. 1980. *Research in Language Testing.* Rowley, Mass.: Newbury House.

Oller, John W., Jr., and Richards, Jack. 1973. *Focus on the Learner.* Rowley, Mass.: Newbury House.

Osgood, Charles; Suci, G.; and Tannenbaum, P. 1957. *The Measurement of Meaning*. Urbana: University of Illinois Press.

Oskarsson, Mats. 1978. *Approaches to Self-Assessment in Foreign Language Learning*. Strasbourg: Council of Europe. (Republished 1980 by Pergamon Press.)

Palmer, Harold E. 1917. *The Scientific Study and Teaching of Languages*. London: Harrap. (Reprinted 1968 by Oxford University Press.)

———. 1921. *The Principles of Language-Study*. London: Harrap. (Reprinted 1964 by Oxford University Press. All page references are to the 1964 edition.)

Palmer, Harold, and Redman, H. V. 1932. *This Language-Learning Business*. London: Harrap. (Reprinted 1969 by Oxford University Press.)

Palmer, Leslie, and Spolsky, Bernard, eds. 1975. *Papers on Language Testing 1967–1974*. Washington, D.C.: Teachers of English to Speakers of Other Languages.

Papalia, Anthony. 1976. *Learner-Centered Language Teaching: Methods and Materials*. Rowley, Mass.: Newbury House.

Parker, William R. 1962. *The National Interest and Foreign Languages*. 3d ed. Washington, D.C.: National Commission for UNESCO, Department of State. (Preliminary ed., 1954.)

Parry, Albert. 1967. *America Learns Russian*. Syracuse, N.Y.: Syracuse University Press.

Paulston, Christina Bratt. 1980. *Bilingual Education: Theories and Issues*. Rowley, Mass.: Newbury House.

Paulston, Christina B., and Bruder, Mary N. 1976. *Teaching English as a Second Language: Techniques and Procedures*. Cambridge, Mass.: Winthrop.

Pearson, Bruce L. 1977. *Introduction to Linguistic Concepts*. New York: Alfred A. Knopf.

Pell, Mary and William. 1975. *Cumulative Index to the Northeast Conference Reports, 1954–1975*. Middlebury, Vt.: Northeast Conference on the Teaching of Foreign Languages (see annotation to Northeast Conference 1959).

Penfield, Wilder, and Roberts, Lamar. 1959. *Speech and Brain-Mechanisms*. Princeton, N.J.: Princeton University Press.

Perren, G. E., ed. 1969. *Languages for Special Purposes*. London: Centre for Information in Language Teaching.

PG's. See Rivers 1975; Rivers, Azevedo et al. 1976; Rivers, Dell'Orto, and Dell'Orto 1975; Rivers and Nahir (in prep.); Rivers and Temperley 1978.

Phillips, June K., ed. 1977. *The Language Connection*. ACTFL Foreign Language Education Series, vol. 9. Skokie, Ill.: National Textbook Company.

———, ed. 1979. *Building on Experience—Building for Success*. ACTFL Foreign Language Education Series, vol. 10. Skokie, Ill.: National Textbook Company.

————, ed. 1980. *The New Imperative: Expanding the Horizons of Foreign Language Education.* ACTFL Foreign Language Education Series. Skokie, Ill.: National Textbook Company.

Pillet, Roger A. 1974. *Foreign-Language Study: Perspective and Prospect.* Chicago: University of Chicago Press.

Pimsleur, Paul, and Quinn, Terence, eds. 1971. *The Psychology of Second Language Learning.* Cambridge, U.K.: Cambridge University Press.

Platt, John T. and Heidi K. 1975. *The Social Significance of Speech.* Amsterdam: North-Holland; New York: American Elsevier.

Politzer, Robert L. 1965a. *Foreign Language Learning: A Linguistic Introduction.* Englewood Cliffs, N.J.: Prentice-Hall.

————. 1965b. *Teaching French: An Introduction to Applied Linguistics.* 2d ed. New York: Blaisdell.

————. 1968. *Teaching German: A Linguistic Orientation.* Waltham, Mass.: Blaisdell.

————. 1972. *Linguistics and Applied Linguistics: Aims and Methods.* Philadelphia: Center for Curriculum Development.

Politzer, Robert L., and Politzer, Frieda N. 1972. *Teaching English as a Second Language.* Lexington, Mass.: Xerox.

Politzer, Robert L., and Staubach, C. 1961. *Teaching Spanish: A Linguistic Orientation.* Boston: Ginn & Company.

Prator, Clifford H., Jr., and Robinett, Betty W. 1972. *Manual of American English Pronunciation.* 3d ed. New York: Holt, Rinehart & Winston.

Pugh, A. K. 1978. *Silent Reading: An Introduction to its Study and Teaching.* London: Heinemann.

Reboullet, André, ed. 1973. *L'Enseignement de la civilisation française.* Paris: Hachette.

————, ed. 1978. *Pédagogie concrète du français langue étrangère.* Paris: Hachette.

Reichmann, Eberhard, ed. 1970. *The Teaching of German: Problems and Methods.* Philadelphia: National Carl Schurz Association.

Richards, Ira A., and Gibson, Christine. 1974. *Techniques in Language Control.* Rowley, Mass.: Newbury House.

Richards, Jack C., ed. 1974. *Error Analysis: Perspectives and Second Language Acquisition.* London: Longman.

————, ed. 1978. *Understanding Second and Foreign Language Learning: Issues and Approaches.* Rowley, Mass.: Newbury House.

Richterich, René, and Chancerel, Jean-Louis. 1978. *Identifying the needs of Adults Learning a Foreign Language.* Strasbourg: Council of Europe. (Republished 1980 by Pergamon Press.)

Ritchie, William C., ed. 1978. *Second Language Acquisition Research: Issues and Implications.* New York: Academic Press.

Rivers, Wilga M. 1964. *The Psychologist and the Foreign-Language Teacher.* Chicago: University of Chicago Press.

————. 1975. *A Practical Guide to the Teaching of French.* New York: Oxford University Press.

————. 1976. *Speaking in Many Tongues*. Expanded 2d ed. Rowley, Mass.: Newbury House.

Rivers, Wilga M.; Allen, Louise H.; et al., eds. 1972. *Changing Patterns in Foreign Language Programs*. Rowley, Mass.: Newbury House.

Rivers, Wilga M.; Azevedo, Milton M.; Heflin, William H., Jr.; and Hyman-Opler, Ruth. 1976. *A Practical Guide to the Teaching of Spanish*. New York: Oxford University Press.

Rivers, Wilga M.; Dell'Orto, Kathleen M., and Dell'Orto, Vincent J. 1975. *A Practical Guide to the Teaching of German*. New York: Oxford University Press.

Rivers, Wilga M., and Nahir, Moshe. *A Practical Guide to the Teaching of Hebrew*. (In preparation.)

Rivers, Wilga M., and Temperley, Mary S. 1978. *A Practical Guide to the Teaching of English as a Second or Foreign Language*. New York: Oxford University Press.

Robinett, Betty Wallace. 1978. *Teaching English to Speakers of Other Languages: Substance and Technique*. Minneapolis: University of Minnesota Press.

Robinson, Gail L. 1978. *Language and Multicultural Education: An Australian Perspective*. Sydney: Australia and New Zealand Book Company.

Robinson, Pauline C. 1980. *ESP (English for Specific Purposes): The Present Position*. Oxford: Pergamon Press.

Rogers, Carl R. 1969. *Freedom to Learn*. Columbus, Ohio: Merrill.

Roulet, Eddy. 1975. *Linguistic Theory, Linguistic Description, and Language Teaching*. Trans. C. N. Candlin. London: Longman.

Sapir, Edward. 1949. *Selected Writings in Language, Culture, and Personality,* ed. D. G. Mandelbaum. Berkeley: University of California Press.

Saussure, Ferdinand de. 1959. *Course in General Linguistics,* ed. C. Bally and A. Sechehaye; trans. Wade Baskin. New York: Philosophical Library.

Saville-Troike, Muriel. 1976. *Foundations for Teaching English as a Second Language: Theory and Method for Multicultural Education*. Englewood Cliffs, N.J.: Prentice-Hall.

Scherer, George A. C. 1955. "Programming Second Language Reading." In *Advances in the Teaching of Modern Languages,* ed. G. Mathieu, vol. 2. London: Pergamon Press.

Scherer, George, A. C., and Wertheimer, Michael. 1964. *A Psycholinguistic Experiment in Foreign-language Teaching*. New York: McGraw-Hill.

Schmidt, Elizabeth. 1974. *Let's Play Games in German*. Skokie, Ill.: National Textbook Company.

Schulz, Renate A., ed. 1977. *Personalizing Foreign Language Instruction: Learning Styles and Teaching Options*. CSC 1977. Skokie, Ill.: National Textbook Company.

Schumann, John H. 1978. *The Pidginization Process: A Model for Second Language Acquisition*. Rowley, Mass.: Newbury House.

Schumann, John H., and Stenson, Nancy, eds. 1974. *New Frontiers in Second Language Learning*. Rowley, Mass.: Newbury House.

Seelye, H. Ned. 1974. *Teaching Culture: Strategies for Foreign Language Educators.* Skokie, Ill.: National Textbook Company.

Sharwood Smith, J. E. 1977. *On Teaching Classics.* London: Routledge & Kegan Paul.

Sinclair, J. McH., and Coulthard, R. M. 1975. *Towards an Analysis of Discourse: The English used by Teachers and Pupils.* London: Oxford University Press.

Skinner, Burrhus F. 1968. *The Technology of Teaching.* New York: Appleton-Century-Crofts.

———. 1972. *Cumulative Record: A Selection of Papers.* 3d ed. Appleton-Century-Crofts.

Slobin, Dan I. 1974. *Psycholinguistics.* Glenview, Ill.: Scott, Foresman.

Smith, Elise C., and Luce, Louise Fiber, eds. 1979. *Toward Internationalism: Readings in Cross-Cultural Communication.* Rowley, Mass.: Newbury House.

Smith, Frank. 1971. *Understanding Reading.* New York: Holt, Rinehart & Winston.

———, ed. 1973. *Psycholinguistics and Reading.* New York: Holt, Rinehart & Winston.

Smith, Philip D., Jr. 1970. *A Comparison of the Cognitive and Audiolingual Approaches to Foreign Language Instruction: The Pennsylvania Foreign Language Project.* Philadelphia: Center for Curriculum Development.

SMT. See Rivers 1976.

Spolsky, Bernard, ed. 1972. *The Language Education of Minority Children.* Rowley, Mass.: Newbury House.

Spolsky, Bernard, and Cooper, Robert L., eds. 1977. *Frontiers of Bilingual Education.* Rowley, Mass.: Newbury House.

———, eds. 1978. *Case Studies in Bilingual Education.* Rowley, Mass.: Newbury House.

Stack, Edward M. 1971. *The Language Laboratory and Modern Language Teaching.* 3d ed. New York: Oxford University Press.

Stanislawczyk, Irene E., and Yavener, Symond. 1976. *Creativity in the Language Classroom.* Rowley, Mass.: Newbury House.

Steinberg, Danny D., and Jakobovits, Leon A., eds. 1971. *Semantics: An Interdisciplinary Reader in Philosophy, Linguistics and Psychology.* Cambridge: Cambridge University Press.

Stern, H. H. 1963. *Foreign Languages in Primary Education.* Hamburg: UNESCO Institute for Education.

———, ed. 1969. *Languages and the Young School Child.* London: Oxford University Press.

Stevick, Earl W. 1971. *Adapting and Writing Language Lessons.* Washington, D.C.: Department of State.

———. 1980. *Teaching Languages: A Way and Ways.* Rowley, Mass.: Newbury House.

———. 1976. *Memory, Meaning and Method: Some Psychological Perspectives on Language Learning.* Rowley, Mass.: Newbury House.

Selected Bibliography

Stockwell, Robert P., and Bowen, J. Donald. 1965. *The Sounds of English and Spanish*. Contrastive Structure Series, ed. Charles A. Ferguson. Chicago: University of Chicago Press.

Stockwell, Robert P.; Bowen, J. Donald; and Martin, John W. 1965. *The Grammatical Structures of English and Spanish*. Contrastive Structure Series, ed. Charles A. Ferguson. Chicago: University of Chicago Press.

Strevens, Peter. 1965. *Papers in Language and Language Teaching*. London: Oxford University Press.

———. 1972. *British and American English*. London: Collier-Macmillan.

———. 1977. *New Orientations in the Teaching of English*. Oxford: Oxford University Press.

Sweet, Henry. 1899. *The Practical Study of Languages*. London: Dent. Reprinted, London: Oxford University Press, 1964. (All page references are to the 1964 edition.)

Thonis, Eleanor W. 1970. *Teaching Reading to Non-English Speakers*. New York: Collier-Macmillan.

Thorne, Barrie, and Henley, Nancy, eds. 1975. *Language and Sex: Difference and Dominance*. Rowley, Mass.: Newbury House.

Titone, Renzo. 1968. *Teaching Foreign Languages: An Historical Sketch*. Washington, D.C.: Georgetown University Press.

Tosi, Arturo. 1981. *Immigration and Bilingual Education*. Oxford: Pergamon Press.

Trim, John. 1975. *English Pronunciation Illustrated*. 2d ed. Cambridge, U.K.: Cambridge University Press. (For GB.)

Trimble, Mary Todd and Louis, and Drobnic, Karl, eds. 1978. *English for Specific Purposes: Science and Technology*. Corvallis, Ore.: English Language Institute, Oregon State University.

Troike, Rudolph C., and Modiano, Nancy, eds. 1975. *The Proceedings of the First Inter-American Conference on Bilingual Education*. Arlington, Va.: Center for Applied Linguistics.

Trueba, Henry T., and Barnett-Mizrahi, Carol, eds. 1979. *Bilingual Multicultural Education and the Professional: From Theory to Practice*. Rowley, Mass.: Newbury House.

Turner, Paul R., ed. 1973. *Bilingualism in the Southwest*. Tucson: University of Arizona Press.

Vachek, Josef. 1966. *The Linguistic School of Prague*. Bloomington: Indiana University Press.

Valdman, Albert, ed. 1966. *Trends in Language Teaching*. New York: McGraw-Hill.

———. 1976. *Introduction to French Phonology and Morphology*. Rowley, Mass.: Newbury House.

Valette, Rebecca M. 1977. *Modern Language Testing*. 2d ed. New York: Harcourt Brace Jovanovich.

Valette, Rebecca M., and Disick, Renée S. 1972. *Modern Language Performance Objectives and Individualization: A Handbook*. New York: Harcourt Brace Jovanovich.

Van Ek, J. A. 1975. *The Threshold Level in a European Unit/Credit System for Modern Language Learning for Adults.* Strasbourg: Council of Europe. (Republished 1980 by Pergamon Press as *Threshold Level English.*)

———. 1977. *The Threshold Level for Modern Language Learning in Schools.* London: Longman.

Van Ek, J. A.; Alexander, L. G.; and Fitzpatrick, M. A. 1977. *Waystage.* Strasbourg: Council of Europe. (Republished 1980 by Pergamon Press in an expanded edition as *Waystage English.*)

Vygotsky, L. S. 1962. *Thought and Language.* Trans. E. Hanfmann and G. Vaker. Cambridge, Mass.: MIT Press.

Walsh, Donald D., ed. 1969. *A Handbook for Teachers of Spanish and Portuguese.* Lexington, Mass.: D. C. Heath.

Wardhaugh, Ronald. 1969. *Reading: A Linguistic Perspective.* Harcourt, Brace & World.

———. 1974. *Topics in Applied Linguistics.* Rowley, Mass.: Newbury House.

———. 1976. *The Contexts of Language.* Rowley, Mass.: Newbury House.

Wardhaugh, Ronald, and Brown, H. Douglas, eds. 1976. *A Survey of Applied Linguistics.* Ann Arbor: University of Michigan Press.

West, Michael. 1941. *Learning to Read a Foreign Language and Other Essays on Language-Teaching.* London: Longman.

Whorf, Benjamin Lee. 1956. *Language, Thought, and Reality. Selected Writings of . . . ,* ed. J. B. Carroll. Cambridge, Mass.: MIT Press.

Widdowson, H. G. 1975. *Stylistics and the Teaching of Literature.* London: Longman.

———. 1978. *Teaching Language as Communication.* Oxford: Oxford University Press.

Wilkins, D. A. 1972. *Linguistics in Language Teaching.* Cambridge, Mass.: MIT Press.

———. 1974. *Second Language Learning and Teaching.* London: Edward Arnold.

———. 1976. *Notional Syllabuses.* Oxford: Oxford University Press.

Williams, Frederick, ed. 1970. *Language and Poverty: Perspectives on a Theme.* Chicago: Markham.

Wittich, Walter A., and Schuller, Charles F. 1973. *Instructional Technology: Its Nature and Use.* 5th ed. New York: Harper & Row.

Wylie, Laurence, and Stafford, Rick. 1977. *Beaux Gestes.* Cambridge, Mass.: Undergraduate Press; New York: E. P. Dutton.

Yorio, Carlos A.; Perkins, Kyle; and Schachter, Jacquelyn, eds. 1979. *On TESOL '79: The Learner in Focus.* Washington, D.C.: Teachers of English to Speakers of Other Languages.

Index

Index

Noise, 154–55, 156. *See also* Information theory
Non-native teachers, 130–31, 147–49, 215, 351, 399, 403, 404
Nord, J., 177, 178n
Normal purposes of language, 86, 230–31, 256–57, 469; in communication, 166–67, 245–46, 293, 296. *See also* Tasks in learning and testing
Norms, 352n, 354. *See also* Testing, standardized
Northeast Conference on the Teaching of Foreign Languages (NEC), 528–29
Nostrand, F., 323n
Nostrand, H. L., 323n, 343, 520
Notional-functional approach. *See* Functional-notional approach
Notional syllabuses, 233–35, 257, 258. *See also* Functional-notional approach; Notions or concepts; Wilkins, D. A.
Notions or concepts (functional-notional approach), 233, 235. *See also* Notional syllabuses
Nudelman, J., 330n

Objectives, 1, 6–23, 29–30, 90, 242, 358, 380n, 384, 496; communication, 57, 147, 151, 265; cultural, 314–15, 317, 323–24, 335, 343; linguistic, 8, 10, 15, 17, 19, 20, 392; reading, 35, 38, 57, 260, 263, 286, 288; statements of, 18–21; writing, 308. *See also* Audio-lingual method; Careers, languages for; Case for foreign-language study; Liberal education; Performance objectives; Societal pressures
Objective tests. *See* Testing
O'Brien, M. C., 529
O'Connor, P., 203n
Ogawa, Y., 526
Oller, J. W., 181, 227n, 357n, 378n, 395, 448n, 529

Olson, L. L., 450n
Operant conditioning. *See* Behaviorism
Optimal age for learning a second language, 445–56. *See also* Early language learning; Second-language acquisition
Oral courses. *See* Conversation, courses for
Oral exercises. *See* Exercises; Oral reports; Structural pattern drills
Oral interview. *See* Foreign Service Institute Rating Scales of Absolute Language Proficiency; Testing
Oral introduction to course. *See* Pre-reading period
Oral reports, 45, 105, 206, 229, 244, 250, 285, 294, 306, 337; as test, 244
Oral survival course. *See* Conversation, courses for
Order of skills. *See* Skills, order of learning
Ornstein, J., 520
Orthography. *See* Spelling
Osgood, C., 318–19, 530
Oskarsson, M., 530
Out-of-class use of language. *See* Communication, out of class
Overall language proficiency tests. *See* Testing, integrative

Pace of learning, 278, 349, 355, 403–4, 429–30
Palmer, H. E., 36, 40n, 54, 55, 60, 278n, 530
Palmer, L., 395, 530
Paluszny, M., 451
Panini, 67
Papalia, A., 530
Papo, E., 519
Paralanguage. *See* Body language
Parker, W. R., 530
Parole (Saussure's term), 68–69. *See also* Langue (Saussure's

Index